Tom McNally's Fishermen's Bible

Edited by Tom McNally

Distributed by

SHOOTER'S BIBLE INC.

55 Ruta Court
South Hackensack, New Jersey 07606

FOLLETT PUBLISHING COMPANY
Chicago

About the front cover:

On the cover, you see an unusual shot of two fingerling largemouth bass, photographed in a 30-gallon wall tank in Tom McNally's home in Glenview, Illinois.

Second printing

Library of Congress Catalogue Card Number: 73-99591
International Standard Book Number: 0-695-81096-0

Contents

In the biggest fish story ever, giant coho salmon and happy angler come together on Lake Michigan.

THE COHO STORY:

With the introduction of cohos, Lake Michigan has become the stage for a salmon spectacular

1: How Great Lakes salmon fishing came about

One spring morning in 1968 a perch fisherman sitting on a Lake Michigan breakwater at Chicago had a vicious strike. Line peeled from his reel as the fish he'd hooked raced over the surface of Lake Michigan. The surprised fisherman lurched to his feet, applied pressure, and gradually worked the powerful fish back. With extraordinary good luck he eventually landed a sleek, silver-sided fish that weighed exactly 12 pounds. The perch fisherman was beside himself with joy, for in all the years he'd fished the Chicago lake front never before had he seen such a fish.

And one May afternoon last year two businessmen in Waukegan, Illinois went out for lunch. They went from their office to a delicatessen where they ordered sandwiches and beer to go. They then drove to a nearby marina, boarded a runabout, and soon were trolling lures a half-mile offshore in Lake Michigan. With sandwiches in one hand, rods in the other, they soon caught several chrome-colored fish that ranged 3 to 5½ pounds apiece. In 45 minutes they caught seven, then they quit and hurried back to their office where they resumed the routines of business.

Through most of June, 1968, and again through June, 1969, steel workers in East Chicago and Gary, Indiana could leave the mills, go to the lake front, and frequently catch bright, plump, gamey fish by casting lures around docks and piers where—until recently—no decent fish were known to be.

By August and September, 1968, and through the summer of '69, Michigan anglers from Benton Harbor north to Frankfort were getting giant, lustrous fish averaging 12-13 pounds but many weighed 18 and 20 pounds—and these by fishermen used to catching nothing more from Lake Michigan than a diminutive, 8-inch perch.

In the fall of 1968 tens of thousands of fishermen congregated at various spots around the big lake—fishing from rocky shores, beaches, piers, breakwaters, docks; from small boats in rivers emptying into the lake; and in the lake proper from boats big and small. Many of the fishermen, angling in Lake Michigan for the first time, went wild-eyed over catches of silvery fish weighing 8 to 22 pounds.

The cause of all the furor—and of considerable adventure and misadventure—is a fish new to Lake Michigan, the silver or coho salmon. Following the introduction of cohos a veritable miracle has occurred in Lake Michigan; the salmon have changed the lake from a near icthyological desert into an almost too-good-to-be-true angler's paradise.

Actually, the Lake Michigan coho fishing of 1968 left much to be desired in that many fishermen on many sorties caught few if any salmon. But while that year's fishing compared not at all to the spectacular sport enjoyed by salmon anglers in Autumn, 1967, it nonetheless was exciting enough for fishermen who previously caught nothing from big, open, cold, wind-swept Lake Michigan.

The coho salmon in the Great Lakes are *Oncorhynchus kisutch*, Pacific Ocean cohos and, in fact, came from eggs imported by the Michigan Department of Conservation from the coastal states of Oregon, Washington and Alaska. The Lake Michigan coho is the same as those in the Pacific; they are identical in appearance, although the Lake Michigan variety tends to be larger; they are equally game, and both the Pacific and Lake Michigan cohos are a gourmet's delight, especially when smoked.

The Lake Michigan coho story actually had its beginning in the minds of Doctors Howard Tanner—until recently Michigan's Fish Division Chief—and his successor, Wayne Tody.

But first, a little history: years ago Lake Michigan provided excellent sport and commercial fishing for lake trout, whitefish, yellow perch, chubs and smelt. Then the fishing went to pot. How quickly the lake's fishing deteriorated is shown in commercial catch statistics: in 1946 commercial fishermen marketed 5,500,000 pounds of lake trout; in 1953, merely seven years later, they marketed only 402 pounds. Parasitic, blood-sucking sea lampreys were blamed for destroying lake trout populations, but over-fishing by

Coho fishermen greet dawn at the mouth of Michigan's Platte River.

commercial netters also had much to do with the decline of lake trout, as well as with the decline of many other valuable Lake Michigan food fishes.

A large cooperative program was initiated to reduce the lampreys and it has been highly successful. But hardly had fishery biologists learned to control lampreys than another problem—alewives—came to Lake Michigan. These small 6 to 8-inch fish, members of the herring family, moved inland from the Atlantic via the St. Lawrence seaway. With predatory fish such as lake trout almost non-existent in the lake, the alewives took over and by 1966 comprised 90% of the fish population by weight. Alewives have a three-year life cycle, so millions die each spring and summer. Their carcasses befouled beaches so badly in '67 that Lake Michigan property owners cried for relief, as did the tourist industry in areas around the lake. The summer of 1967 .saw 200,000,000 pounds of rotting alewives on Lake Michigan beaches, and the Michigan tourist industry alone reported a loss of $55,000,000 because people wouldn't visit beaches smelly with alewives.

Members of the Michigan Conservation Department for some time had been studying the Lake Michigan problems. What to do about the dwindling sport and commercial fishery? What to do about the alewives? What might bolster the tourist industry?

It was decided a "dream" fish should be introduced—one that would find Lake Michigan environs ideal, one that would be important as a sport and commercial fish, one that would multiply satisfactorily, and one that would consume alewives. Many species were considered, among them striped bass, *Roccus saxatilis*, but Doctors Tanner and Tody argued that the best would be Pacific salmon.

They felt that anadromous fish (those that live in the sea but migrate up fresh water rivers to spawn) might be best for Lake Michigan, since hopefully, the young would migrate from streams where they were stocked to the "sea" (the Great Lakes), grow fat on alewives, mature, and then return to spawn in the inland rivers. (Their sense of smell directs salmon from open waters to specific rivers. Acute olfactory glands enable them to distinguish the "odors" of rivers and to find their "home" streams. Studies have shown that only about 3% of mature salmon ever become "lost" and stray to streams other than where they were spawned.) Michigan biologists figured a fish of such habits could be readily "managed," and, compared to deep-going lake trout, would be easy for fishermen to catch. Of the various kinds of Pacific salmon available, cohos were selected as a first choice and Chinook or king salmon as a second.

Cohos were believed to be best for the Great Lakes for

several reasons: they adapt readily to fresh water; in the ocean they seldom go deeper than 35 feet, which makes them easy targets for fishermen (deep-going fish are hard to find, hard to catch); they are not especially wary and are reasonably game when hooked.

Moreover, since cohos are anadromous and migratory, it was believed they would provide many sport fishing opportunities. Michigan biologists figured that in spring salmon probably would be caught in the extreme lower part of Lake Michigan. In early summer, they'd likely be off Milwaukee and southern Michigan; still later in the summer they'd probably move along the central Michigan shore, then in early fall go farther up the Michigan coast. (As the biologists had hoped, cohos *do* migrate in Lake Michigan They follow the schools of alewives and also move according to water temperature, preferring a temperature of about 55 degrees.) Also, since cohos move into rivers in fall and winter to spawn and die, Michigan's fishery biologists felt anglers who had no boats or didn't care to fish Lake Michigan could get a crack at the salmon when they arrived in the spawning rivers.

Cohos were favored for other reasons, too. They have a three-year life cycle: they hatch from the egg, grow to maturity, spawn and die in three brief years. They have a rapid growth rate. (Fish that require years to grow to "catchable" sizes, such as lake trout and muskies, cannot usually satisfy the demands of fishermen in areas having heavy fishing pressure.) In addition, it was expected that cohos would be easy to "manage" by prohibiting or allowing commercial netting, by regulating the numbers of salmon spawning each fall, and by increasing or reducing the quantity of salmon eggs handled in hatcheries. The Michigan Conservation Department thereby could readily check the numbers of salmon roaming Lake Michigan. Should there be too many, large scale commercial netting could be permitted. (Michigan is hopeful that the salmon fishery will develop sufficiently so that commercial fishing will be feasible and that the once large Lake Michigan commercial fishing industry will be revived.) Should there be too few salmon the hatchery program could be expanded, and more young salmon released each spring.

If cohos would be right for Lake Michigan, perhaps Chinook salmon would also. Chinook or king salmon, *Oncorhynchus tsawytscha*, grow to giant size—commonly to 40-50 pounds in the Pacific—and they rate highly as table fare. But since Chinooks have a four-year life cycle, Michigan decided to put the emphasis in its early salmon program on the coho, although Chinook, too, would be introduced.

Thus plans were launched to bring Pacific salmon to

Artist portrays three-year life history of coho salmon. Chinooks have four-year cycle.

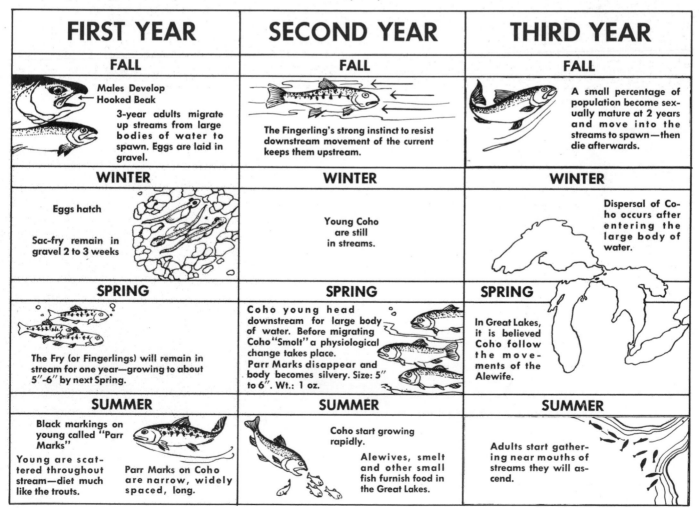

FIRST YEAR	SECOND YEAR	THIRD YEAR
FALL	**FALL**	**FALL**
Males Develop Hooked Beak. 3-year adults migrate up streams from large bodies of water to spawn. Eggs are laid in gravel.	The Fingerling's strong instinct to resist downstream movement of the current keeps them upstream.	A small percentage of population become sexually mature at 2 years and move into the streams to spawn—then die afterwards.
WINTER	**WINTER**	**WINTER**
Eggs hatch. Sac-fry remain in gravel 2 to 3 weeks	Young Coho are still in streams.	Dispersal of Coho occurs after entering the large body of water.
SPRING	**SPRING**	**SPRING**
The Fry (or Fingerlings) will remain in stream for one year—growing to about 5"-6" by next Spring.	Coho young head downstream for large body of water. Before migrating Coho "Smolt" a physiological change takes place. Parr Marks disappear and body becomes silvery. Size: 5" to 6". Wt.: 1 oz.	In Great Lakes, it is believed Coho follow the movements of the Alewife.
SUMMER	**SUMMER**	**SUMMER**
Black markings on young called "Parr Marks". Young are scattered throughout stream—diet much like the trouts. Parr Marks on Coho are narrow, widely spaced, long.	Coho start growing rapidly. Alewives, smelt and other small fish furnish food in the Great Lakes.	Adults start gathering near mouths of streams they will ascend.

Lake Michigan, and with many biologists in the Michigan Conservation Department crossing their fingers, the first shipment of salmon eggs arrived from Oregon in Fall, 1964.

Cohos are highly adaptive to hatchery culture. Of the first 1,000,000 coho eggs provided Michigan gratuitously by the Oregon Conservation Department, 850,000 of them hatched and grew to the parr stage at the Michigan Conservation Department's Platte River Fish Rearing Station. By March, 1966, the fish had reached the "smolt" stage, a period when physiological change takes place and the thyroid gland enlarges and deposits crystals in the scales, giving the fish their bright, silvery color. They then ranged 5 to 6 inches in length. It is at this time, in the wild state, that young cohos begin downstream treks from the spawning grounds out to the open sea. So Michigan's fishery biologists now removed their smolts from the rearing ponds and released them in three clear-water streams thought to be suitable for salmon.

Approximately 264,000 of the smolts were stocked in the upper Platte River; and 395,000 went into Bear Creek, a feeder stream of the Big Manistee River. Both the Platte and the Manistee are in the central part of Michigan's lower peninsula and drain into Lake Michigan. A bit later in the spring of 1966, 192,500 coho smolts were planted in the Big Huron River, on Michigan's upper peninsula where it runs into Lake Superior. (Chinook smolts were stocked in the spring of 1967 in the Little Manistee River, Muskegon River and Big Huron.)

The cohos released in Lake Michigan streams in spring, '66, followed the instincts of young salmon hatched in the wild, and swam downriver into the big lake. Out there they fed well and grew fat. The first coho caught following that initial planting, a mere three months after being released, was a "90 day wonder" that in that time had grown from 4 to 15 inches and achieved a weight of 1¼ pounds.—That was a phenomenal weight gain of roughly 2,000% in about 12 weeks!

Through the summer and fall of 1966 more cohos were taken—all of them unexpectedly and all of them far ahead of schedule so far as Michigan fishery biologists were concerned. They hadn't expected to see any salmon caught until the summer of 1967. Instead, through the summer of 1966, fishermen reported getting cohos at countless spots all around Lake Michigan. Cohos were caught in Michigan off Manistee, Ludington, Grand Traverse Bay, Whitehall, Frankfort and, in Wisconsin, around Green Bay and Two Rivers. The range in weight of the cohos that first season varied considerably but by late fall some weighing 6

Mature cohos that have returned to spawn crowd a holding pool at hatchery facility on upper Platte River.

pounds were reported. These were all "jack" salmon—early maturing or precocious males, and that was 1966—the first "Year of the Coho." It was just the beginning.

In early spring, 1967, an odd coho weighing 5 to 8 pounds was taken in Illinois or Indiana waters by hopeful fishermen who were "just testing to see if there were any of those salmon around." Few were caught, though, because few fishermen were out. But by August of that year the first mature coho was caught by a fisherman casting at the mouth of the Manistee River at Manistee, Michigan. The salmon weighed 12 pounds! That sudden, unexpected, wonderful, beautiful catch out of Lake Michigan made newspapers, radio and television—and set off a mad dash of fishermen for the shores of the big lake. Word quickly went out: *"The cohos are back!" "The cohos have come home!" "The salmon are running!"*

Fishermen began congregating at the hot spots, the mouths of the parent streams where salmon were grouping prior to making their upstream spawning runs. Big hauls of big cohos were made almost daily August through mid-October off the mouths of the Manistee and Platte Rivers, as well as in the rivers proper and in small feeder streams well inland. Hundreds of boats were being launched every day in Lake Michigan, and sport fishermen accounted for thousands of cohos averaging 14 pounds—a full 5 pounds more than the typical three-year-old Pacific Ocean coho. Quite a few were taken that weighed 18 to 20 pounds. The best recorded officially was a 22 pound, 5 ounce silver salmon!

The impact of such remarkable fishing on Midwesterners who, for the most part, formerly were satisfied with catching bluegills and walleyes, was just short of explosive. Fishermen from all over swept into towns such as Manistee, Frankfort, Arcadia and Huron, and what previously had been peaceful communities became sort of a fisherman's Coney Island. It was like a gold rush. Motels were booked weeks in advance. Rental fishing boats were impossible to obtain. Restaurants were mobbed around dawn when fishermen wanted breakfast, and again after dark when they thronged for dinner. Gasoline stations were being pumped dry. Fishing tackle shops were "having a run" and were selling out. One Manistee outboard motor dealer reported selling more motors in August, 1967, than he had in the 10 years previous. Popular coho lures were unattainable, were selling for $10 apiece, or were *being rented* at $5 a day, the fisherman getting his $10 deposit back only when the lure (one normally selling for about $1.35) was safely returned. Quickly outfitted charter boats were hiring for $75 to $125 a day, four anglers, eight hours of fishing—or until each caught two salmon. (In early '67 there were 15 charter fishing boats operating in Michigan. Today there are more than 100 and even charter boat "associations" have been formed.)

Highways leading to the fishing areas were clogged those busy fall days of 1967. Camping areas and trailer parks were filled to capacity, too. Boat launching sites, both public and private, were congested beyond belief with hundreds of autos and boats lined up for launching each day hours before daybreak. One boat-landing reported a coho fishing boat being launched every 30 seconds. The operator of a boating facility at the mouth of the Platte River said that one day more than 4,000 boats used the landing. Coho

Hundreds of swirling salmon froth the water and others leap high as migrating fish moving upriver to spawn and die are trapped in conservation department weirs on Platte River.

Aerial photo shows Platte River delta and portion of Lake Michigan. Thousands of salmon are taken here each fall as mature fish congregate for up-river spawning run.

fishermen spent an estimated $2,000,000 in Manistee County alone. The Manistee County Chamber of Commerce announced tax sales receipts for just September and October, 1967 were $309,000 more than those for the same period of the previous year. Sales tax receipts in other areas in "coho country" increased 50 to 150%. For sure the fishermen had arrived and all had "coho fever"—and little wonder when so many of them were getting yard-long salmon, 15-pounders that tore tackle apart as wave after wave of mature cohos moved inshore and up the rivers to spawn.

Grumbling heard during that first real coho fishing season was never directed at the fishing, only at the shortage of services and accommodations desired by the incoming hordes of anglers. For the most part Midwest fishermen were never happier, but the coho madness reached a zenith on September 23, 1967.

Some 2,000 small boats were plying Lake Michigan waters off Frankfort that day. The day dawned clear and bright and seemed full of promise to the coho fishermen, estimated at 9,000. But by mid-morning the Frankfort Coast Guard station raised its storm warning flag, signalling the fishing boats to leave the then calm lake. Most of the fishermen, some far out, never saw the flag; others who did had no idea what it meant; some few who recognized the warning ignored it. The now historic squall struck with sudden, dark fury and near gale-force winds whipped the treacherous lake. Some 200 fishing craft were destroyed, and 7 fishermen drowned.

The very next day approximately 500 small boats were out again after salmon.

Shortly after that the 1967 "coho season" ended.

The Michigan Conservation Department claimed satisfaction, naturally enough, with the good early return of cohos and of the obvious success of the new salmon program. More than 40,000 cohos were taken that first year by anglers. Commercial fishermen out of Indiana, not then prohibited from netting salmon, took about 21,000 in gill nets. Cohos moved far up the natal streams, Bear Creek and Platte River, and from weirs (traps) in those streams, fishery biologists removed for egg-taking and the hatchery program another 184,348 salmon. Cohos stripped of eggs or milt were sold to commercial fish wholesalers.

That '67 season there was a 35% return, or harvest, of the total number of cohos stocked in Michigan streams. With Pacific Coast rivers getting only an annual return of 4 or 5%, the Michigan return was phenomenal.

Voila! Success!! *Super Success!!!*

With such excellent early results, nothing better could be done but to expand the Great Lakes salmon program. More salmon eggs were imported from Oregon, and from Washington and Alaska, too, for development at the Michigan hatcheries. The conservation department began building additional hatcheries and rearing stations, so that millions of young salmon could be released in various Great Lakes streams annually. Already since the initial stockings Michigan has released young coho or Chinook salmon in many rivers in addition to the Platte, Bear Creek, and Big

Huron. Upper peninsula rivers emptying into Lake Superior which have been stocked are the Ontonagon River at Ontonagon; Falls River at L'Anse; Cherry Creek at Marquette; Anna River at Munising; and the Sucker River at Grand Marais. New rivers emptying into Lake Michigan that have been planted with salmon are the Whitefish River at Escanaba; Thompson Creek, Thompson; Bear Creek, Petoskey; Boyne River, Charlevoix; Boardman River, Traverse City; Little Manistee River, Manistee; Pere Marquette River, Ludington; and the Muskegon River, Muskegon. Lake Huron rivers that have been stocked are the Carp River, St. Martin's Bay; Ocqueoc River, Ocqueoc; Thunder Bay, Alpena; Au-Sable River, Oscoda; and Tawas River, Tawas City. In the spring of 1969 Michigan stocked its salmon rivers with 4,000,000 more cohos as well as with hundreds of thousands of Chinook salmon. (Chinook of 125 pounds have been taken in the Pacific. If Chinook introduced to Lake Michigan thrive as have the cohos, then Midwest fishermen have some interesting years ahead.)

In the spring of 1968 fishermen eagerly awaited the salmon runs, and thousands watched anxiously for opportunities to try for the new miracle fish of Lake Michigan. The earliest angling was along the Indiana shore, where salmon caught averaged 3-5 pounds. Then fish were being taken off Chicago, from breakwaters where hundreds of fishermen gathered every morning through April and May when the fishing there was best. After that the cohos moved northward along the northern Illinois and southern Wisconsin coast, where some caught weighed 8-12 pounds. By late summer the fish crossed the lake and started grouping in schools off the mouths of the natal rivers—the Platte and Manistee, and they then averaged 12 pounds with some going to 18.

With the publicity and acclaim given the cohos during the 1967 season, thousands of fishermen from all over the United States—from as far away as Florida—headed for places like Manistee and Frankfort in August, September, and October, 1968. They came for fish that, heretofore, they would have had to journey all the way to the Pacific Northwest to catch. They came with trailered boats, cartop boats, campers, house-trailers, tents—and they swelled the local economy. As an example of the economic change to some Michigan communities, Bob Miller, a Platte River tackle shop and boat-livery proprietor, said that ordinarily September brought an income of $3,500 to $4,000 in his operation. "But in September, 1968 we grossed nearly $50,000," he said. Like many other businessmen in coho country, Miller expanded his business. He constructed a new marina on the lower Platte, added a fleet of fiberglass rental skiffs, and built a cocktail lounge and restaurant.

A Manistee gas station owner, pumping gas for 26 hours without sleep one very long fall day, yawningly reported his sales were up 600%. Tackle shops nearly sold out. Fishing licenses were not available. New motels were being built, restaurants enlarged. New boat-launching ramps were constructed, as well as camp grounds and trailer parks. And fishermen were ecstatic, once more crazed by "coho fever."

One evening a small boat buzzed up to a landing in Manistee. A fisherman jumped out, gleefully holding high an 18 pound coho for everyone to see. Down the beach

Coho "hot spot" most years is here at mouth of Manistee River.

came his young wife—shouting, smiling, running pell-mell. She leaped into her husband's arms—and wife, fisherman and fish all fell happily backwards into Manistee Lake . . . *kerplunk!!* The fisherman had come all the way from Pennsylvania to catch his salmon, yet he cheerfully reported that the coho was well worth the travel, time, expense, *and* the ducking.

Earlier that same day another fisherman, with a big coho on his line, stumbled about in the Platte River trying desperately to coax the fish into his landing net. Intent on that, he failed to notice that a press photographer in a small helicopter was easing down on top of him. When only a few dozen feet separated the helicopter and the fisherman, the fisherman suddenly looked up, and went almost dumb with shock at seeing the plane so close. The fishing rod went flying as the fisherman dove for shore . . . and missed! While the helicopter circled for more photos, the drenched fisherman scrambled and retrieved his rod, but the salmon was gone. He was so mad that when the helicopter angled down a second time, he threw his landing net at it.

Something happened, though, to the coho fishing in Fall, 1968. There was good fishing off Manistee in August, but after that the fishing became spotty, to say the least. The 1968 coho season was a great disappointment to thousands of anglers who journeyed many hundreds of miles to fish for salmon. Fish were caught, of course, thousands of them —but for most fishermen the fishing wasn't what it should have been and many fishermen returned from many trips without any cohos.

The weather wasn't conducive to good fishing most of the time when the schools were off the Manistee and Platte River mouths. High winds kept fishermen off the lake when the fish were stacked up like cordwood out there. But, according to figures released by the Michigan Conservation

Contented angler used spin-cast gear and small Rapala to catch spring-time coho off Waukegan, Illinois. Cohos taken in spring range 3 to 5 pounds, but may exceed 20 pounds when mature in fall.

First Chinook salmon "jacks"—like this 8-pounder—were caught by Michigan fishermen in Muskegon River.

Department, more than 60,000 cohos averaging 10 pounds were caught by mid-October, 1968, and the total for that season—according to the Conservation Department—exceeded 100,000. A lot of fishermen, however, question those figures.

Perhaps the biggest difference between the '68 coho fishing and that of '67 was that not many salmon showed up off Manistee which, in 1967, was *the* place for cohos. Some fish arrived at Manistee and moved into both the Big and Little Manistee Rivers, but thousands more went to Platte Bay, about 40 miles north of Manistee, and went up the Platte River. There were so many salmon jammed into pools and holes in the Platte that they blacked out the stream bottom. You could stand on the Route 22 bridge spanning the narrow Platte, about two miles from the river's mouth, and watch school after school of salmon passing below on their relentless journey upstream.

Something else notable about the 1968 season was the appearance for the first time of numerous Chinook salmon. The best run of Chinooks was in the Muskegon River, where the fish went upstream as far as Newaygo Dam in the town of Newaygo. That was a run of "jack" Chinooks, and with no mature female Chinooks in the river, the run therefore was a spawning hoax. But fishermen got their licks in, and many a Midwesterner caught his first Chinook or king salmon from the Muskegon that fall. Most of the Chinook jacks weighed 5 to 7 pounds, but some went as high as 12.

Generally speaking, the salmon runs of 1968 simply did not reach expectations and were well under the 35% return of salmon that was realized the year before. The Platte River had an estimated 20-25% return, while Bear Creek had a return of less than 3%. No one knows for sure why fewer salmon came back to the rivers that year, nor does anyone know precisely what happened to the bulk of the fish. There may have been a sizable die-off in Lake

Michigan, or perhaps many cohos that had been released as smolts in Bear Creek returned as adults to the Platte River. Or possibly, smolts released in the headwater streams never survived to reach Lake Michigan.

There was no official opinion from the Michigan Conservation Department as to why there were not as many salmon in 1968. Michigan biologists explained, however, that even on the Pacific Coast there is no big run of salmon every year. The return of fish there varies year to year, and there are good years and bad years. Thus there is no reason, say fishery biologists, why similar good years and bad years shouldn't be expected among Great Lakes salmon.

Currently there is no commercial netting for Lake Michigan salmon. The states involved—Michigan, Wisconsin, Illinois and Indiana—signed an agreement prohibiting any commercial fishing for salmon except limited netting done at the request of and under the supervision of a state conservation department. Some such netting is done at various times to determine the location and depth of salmon schools, and the quantity of fish. Salmon taken under conservation department supervision are sold legally and reach local markets and restaurants.

Realizing that a quality sports fishery is of far more economic value than a commercial fishery, the Great Lakes states are determined that commercial interests will not destroy the current salmon program. While it is hoped that the salmon population can be increased sufficiently to permit some netting and marketing of salmon, the conservation departments involved are pledged not to allow premature, unrestricted commercial fishing to endanger the salmon program.

All has not been joy and jubilation in Michigan's salmon project.

At the peak of the coho runs, fist-fights among fishermen crowding to launch boats were not uncommon. Accidents occurred on congested back roads, and many an

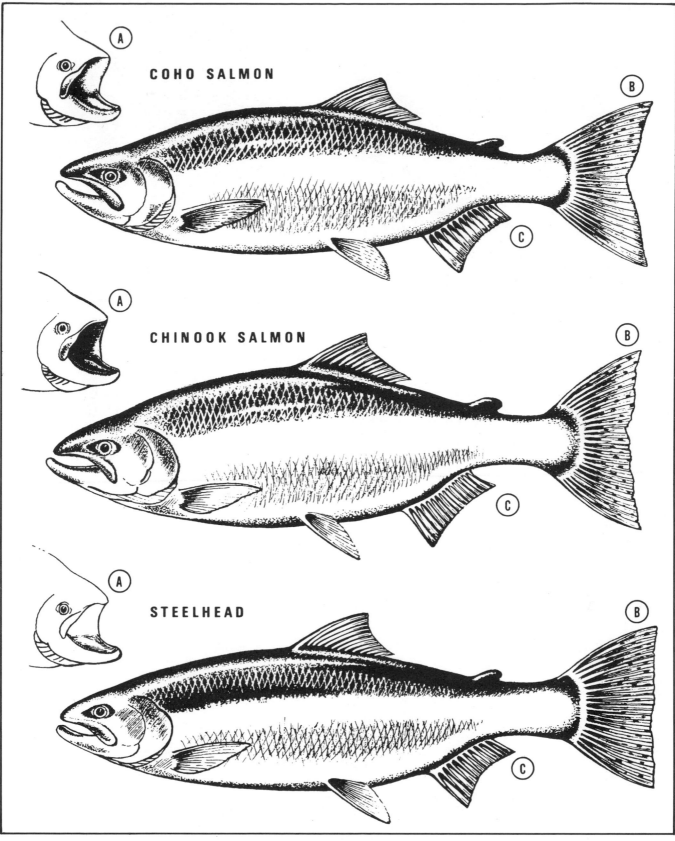

HOW TO IDENTIFY GREAT LAKES TROUT AND SALMON

Coho, Chinook, and steelhead trout look much alike. Best ways to identify them is by mouth coloration, the shape and spotting of caudal fin (tail), and number of rays in anal fin. In sketches "A" coho salmon have white or grayish-white gums; Chinook have a black mouth and gums; and steelhead have a white mouth and gums. In sketches "B" coho have a forked tail with spots on the upper-half only; Chinook have a rather serrated tail with spots on all of the tail; and steelhead have a squared tail covered with spots. In sketches "C" coho have anal fins containing 12 to 15 rays; Chinook have 15 to 19 rays; and, finally, steelhead have 12 or fewer rays in the anal fin.

These coho "jacks"—early-maturing salmon—were caught by a fly fisherman in the Manistee River.

unattended parked auto was damaged by some reckless driver who left no note behind. Fishermen parked illegally in many places and received police summonses. Fights broke out among fishermen when a careless troller crossed and cut someone's line. Salmon left unguarded by fishermen who'd caught them were stolen. Trespass and damage to private property along the salmon streams weren't unusual. Littering prevailed.

The silly season started for sure in the fall of '68 when many fishermen, angered because they couldn't catch salmon by legal methods in Lake Michigan, became really sour when they saw tens of thousands of cohos filling inland streams. (At one time there were so many salmon in Bear Creek that oxygen levels in the water were cut in half, and fishery biologists feared mass suffocation would result.) Despite efforts by dedicated state conservation officers, many people entered "off limits" spawning areas and snagged, speared, netted, kicked and even clubbed salmon to death. A couple of men—they shouldn't be referred to as fishermen—actually went into a conservation department weir and stole egg-filled salmon. They were apprehended and paid fines of $82 each.

Arrests for salmon fishing violations one afternoon on just the Platte River resulted in fines totalling $500. Because of the misconduct of some—frequently mere onlookers who had no interest in fishing but somehow felt entitled to "state" fish—Bear Creek, Little Manistee, and the Platte River were closed to fishing for parts of both the 1967 and 1968 seasons.

All mature salmon entering Michigan streams in the fall die. Their internal organs begin to atrophy as soon as they start their final, upstream journey. They no longer need food, cannot feed, and do not feed. (Non-feeding salmon are caught by fishermen, however, because they strike lures out of anger, agitation, or in defense of spawning areas.) Of the sexually mature salmon taken from Michigan Conservation Department weirs in fall, 1967, none could have resumed "normal" life. The stomachs of all the fish had

shriveled to a fraction of normal size, and their entire intestinal tracts were in such condition that they could not have sustained life any longer.

Anglers are able to catch only a small percentage of the Great Lakes salmon. Thus, when spawning time arrives in the fall, thousands of salmon—doomed to die—ascend the inland streams. They literally choke the smaller waterways such as Platte River and Bear Creek. At one time at a weir on the Platte, cohos were entering the trap at a rate of 30 per minute—and it was taking biologists there three to six minutes to examine, classify, and process each fish. An impossible situation.

Because soon-to-die multitudes of valuable salmon cannot be allowed to spawn unattended in small streams, then to die and to pollute the water with wilted carcasses, the Michigan Conservation Department contracted with a fish-packing firm to remove surplus salmon from too-full weirs. For all practical purposes the fish removed from weirs in the fall of 1968 by Blackport Packing Company of Grand Rapids were dying—were already dead. But seeing Blackport trucks carting salmon off to market infuriated many uninformed bystanders. Near riots broke out at weirs, especially at the Bear Creek weir where wardens suffered verbal and physical abuse and finally state police officers had to be called in to control the unruly crowds.

Some people complained loud and long that the Michigan Conservation Department was "needlessly butchering salmon that belonged to sportsmen" and "sneakily" selling them to the Blackport firm just to reap a big profit.

"Salmon not caught by anglers nor needed for reproduction purposes become surplus and must be utilized or wasted," explains Wayne Tody, Fisheries Chief. "There has been unanimous agreement among Michigan Conservation Department officials that such a high-quality fish as the coho should not be subjected to spearing, snagging or dip-netting. Consequently, surplus salmon are diverted to commercial markets where they can be used as food. But that does not in any way reduce or affect the sport fishing side of the new Great Lakes salmon fishery."

The money paid the Conservation Department, about $312,000, went into the Department's fishery management program and will help pay for new hatcheries.

While the presence of thousands of huge silver and Chinook salmon in Lake Michigan and others of the Great Lakes is the biggest fish story in years, establishing salt water salmon in fresh water is nothing new. More than 30 years ago a number of ichthyologists were convinced cohos could be successfully adapted to a completely fresh water existence. Japanese fishery biologists adapted the Pacific Masu salmon to a complete fresh water cycle. Chinook salmon were planted in Lake Ontario in the years from 1919 to 1925, and some reached weights of 30 pounds. In 1933 Ohio stocked both coho and Chinook salmon in Lake Erie. From 1946 thru 1954, Montana planted coho fingerlings in Georgetown Lake, a completely fresh water lake. British Columbia stocked cohos in Cultus Lake in 1953. Excluding Japan's Masu program, however, most attempts at establishing salmon in fresh water have not enjoyed the fabulous success of the Michigan project. The reason, basically, is that today more is known about cohos and other salmon, and better science is involved along with superior hatchery facilities.

THE COHO STORY:

2: The distribution and migration of salmon in the Great Lakes

The Great Lakes salmon program started in three streams: Bear Creek (a feeder stream of the Manistee River) and the Platte River, on Michigan's Lower Peninsula, and the Big Huron River on Michigan's Upper Peninsula.

Since those initial plantings, however, many dozens of "new" streams have been stocked with both coho and Chinook salmon in Michigan. Moreover, other states—such as Wisconsin and Pennsylvania—have introduced salmon smolts into various streams so that today not just Lake Michigan and Lake Superior are involved in the Great Lakes salmon fishery, but also Lakes Huron and Erie.

But it is Lakes Michigan and Superior, that will be considered in some detail here since these lakes are the "oldest" in the salmon program and therefore will provide the important fishing during the next few years.

Michigan has introduced either coho or Chinook salmon, or both, into at least 14 streams emptying into Lake Michigan. The rivers—and Lake Michigan beyond the river mouths—that will provide substantial fishing include the Platte, Big and Little Manistee, Pere Marquette and Carp Rivers, and Thompson Creek.

Streams feeding Lake Superior that have been planted with cohos and/or Chinook, and which will give good fishing include the Big Huron River, Anna and Sucker Rivers. A total of at least seven Lake Superior rivers have, however, been planted with salmon and, hopefully, will one day provide good fishing.

Chinook salmon are going to be the big news in Michigan in the fall of 1970, and that will be the time of the first really major run of full-size, adult, mature, spawning Chinooks. (Some Chinooks returned to certain Michigan rivers in the fall of 1968-69, but they were precocious or early-maturing "jack" salmon that, for the most part, weighed under 12 pounds.)

On these pages appears a listing of streams and rivers of the Great Lakes that have been stocked by the various conservation departments with coho or Chinook salmon. The list gives the quantity of salmon released in each stream, and the date. Thus it is a suitable guide to where salmon sport fishing will occur.

Michigan, of course, is the leader in developing a Great Lakes salmon fishery, but other Great Lakes states are getting involved—partly due to "pressure" from sport fishermen. Illinois is not shown on the list as being involved with salmon but, in fact, Illinois procured coho smolts and released 10,000 in the harbor of the Great Lakes Naval Station near Waukegan. The fish were released in the spring of 1969 after being held in underwater "pens" for some time so that they would become "acclimated" to the water and, perhaps, develop a "homing" instinct and return to Illinois waters as adults.

Also appearing on these pages is a detailed map showing all areas of the Great Lakes that have been planted with salmon. Areas that were stocked with coho salmon are marked with a black-circled "C," those stocked with Chinooks a white-square "C."

Following the spectacular success of its early salmon plantings—in Bear Creek, the Platte and Huron Rivers—the Michigan Conservation Department has endeavored to "spread out" its salmon fishing. This was desirable not only to provide more fishing for more people, but also to reduce the fantastic angling pressure that had occurred on the Platte River and Bear Creek, and at Manistee. (Bear Creek flows into the Manistee River which winds into Lake Michigan at the town of Manistee.)

Doubtlessly there will be salmon fishing in all the areas indicated on the map, though in varying degrees. And late summer and fall will, of course, be the best times to fish the areas where salmon were stocked because it is in late summer and fall that the salmon "come home" to spawn.

And that brings us to the migrations of Great Lakes salmon.

RIVERS STOCKED WITH COHO-CHINOOK SALMON

COHO

Quantity	Location	Date
MICHIGAN (Lake Superior)		
192,400	Big Huron River, Baraga County	1966
467,000	Big Huron River, Baraga County	1967
32,000	Presque Isle River, Gogebic County	1968
174,990	Anna River, Marquette County	1968
60,000	Falls River, Baraga County	1968
50,000	Ontonagon River, Ontonagon County	1968
40,000	Sucker River, Alger County	1968
25,000	Cherry Creek, Marquette County	1968
MICHIGAN (Lake Michigan)		
264,000	Platte River, Benzie County	1966
394,800	Bear Creek, Manistee County	1966
46,400	Thompson Creek, Schoolcraft County	1967
433,200	Little Manistee River, Manistee County	1967
502,700	Platte River, Benzie County	1967
749,995	Bear Creek, Manistee County	1967
308,400	Platte River, Benzie County	1968
201,869	Brooks Creek, Muskegon County	1968
74,175	Big Manistee River, Manistee County	1968
148,365	Little Manistee River, Mainstee County	1968
100,538	Brewery Creek, Antrim County	1968
100,000	Whitefish, Delta County	1968
98,450	Pere Marquette River, Mason County	1968
52,060	Bear River, Emmet County	1968
25,000	Thompson Creek, Schoolcraft County	1968
50,015	Porter Creek, (Boyne River), Charlevoix County	1968
18,000	Clam River, Muskegon County	1968
MICHIGAN (Lake Huron)		
74,987	Au Sable River, Iosco County	1968
176,790	Cold Creek, Iosco County	1968
100,110	Thunder Bay River, Alpena County	1968
50,000	Carp River, Mackinac County	1968
MINNESOTA (Lake Superior)		
100,000	French River, St. Louis County	Spring 1969
NEW YORK (Lake Erie & Lake Ontario)		
5,100	Cattaraugus Creek, Erie County	January 1968
25,000	Salmon River, Oswego County	March 1968

Quantity	Location	Date
OHIO (Lake Erie)		
30,000	Chagrin River, Lake County	March 1968
100,000	Chagrin River, Lake County	Spring 1969
	Conneaut Creek, Ashtabula County	
	Huron River, Erie County	
200,000		Spring 1970
PENNSYLVANIA (Lake Erie)		
80,000	Walnut & Elk Creek, Godfrey and Trout Runs, Erie County	May 1968
WISCONSIN (Lake Michigan)		
25,000	Lake Michigan	1968
200,000	Algoma, Door County	1969
(planned)	Kewaunee, Kewaunee County	
	Manitowoc, Manitowoc County	
	Sheboygan, Sheboygan County	

CHINOOK

Quantity	Location	Date
MICHIGAN (Lake Superior)		
33,460	Big Huron River, Baraga County	1967
50,000	Cherry Creek, Marquette County	1968
MICHIGAN (Lake Michigan)		
538,650	Little Manistee River, Manistee County	1967
52,180	Little Manistee River, Manistee County	1967
210,560	Muskegon River, Muskegon County	1967
321,912	Little Manistee River, Manistee County	1968
364,780	Muskegon River, Muskegon County	1968
MICHIGAN (Lake Huron)		
200,000	Ocqueoc River, Presque Isle County	1968

The Great Lakes salmon fishery is similar to that of the Pacific. That is, young salmon (smolts) are released into certain rivers and streams feeding the Great Lakes; they migrate into the Lakes—roam the lakes as coastal salmon roam the Pacific—then return as mature salmon to spawn and die in their natal rivers. So Great Lakes salmon, like Pacific salmon, are easy to find when back in or near the rivers, but when in the open lakes they can be as elusive as a pay raise.

Lake Michigan, for example, is 307 miles long, 923 feet deep, with 22,400 square miles of surface, and 1,170 cubic miles of water. In other words, it is no lily pond. Finding salmon schools in *THAT* much water frequently takes

some doing.

Fortunately, however, the salmon already have established specific patterns that aid fishermen in locating them. Some years the pattern varies some, but by and large the Lake Michigan fish winter in the extreme southern end of the lake, distribute themselves more generally through the southern end in early spring, then gradually move northward along both coasts of the lake from late spring until late summer. By very late summer and early fall the salmon schools begin congregating at river mouths preparatory to up-stream spawning runs.

In general when the salmon are in the Great Lakes they go where their food is—alewives and smelt. In Lakes Michi-

MAPS DEPICT SEASONAL MOVEMENTS OF SALMON IN LAKE MICHIGAN

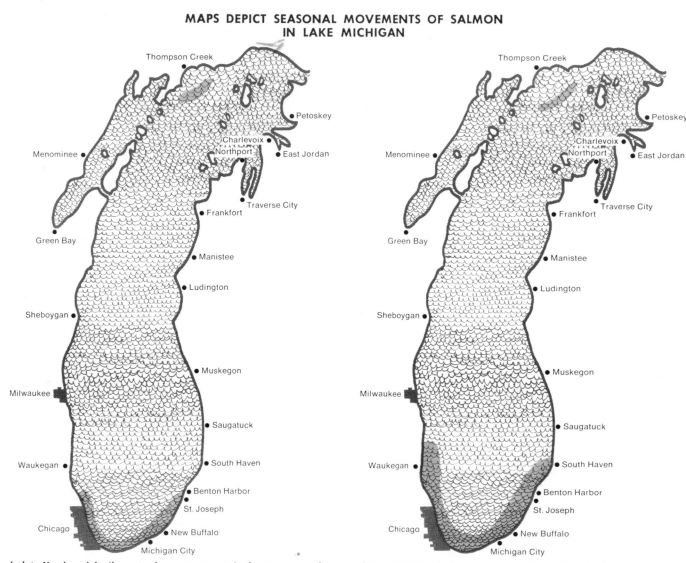

In late March and April, most salmon congregate in the extreme southern part of Lake Michigan. Small numbers of salmon from Thompson Creek plantings remain in the north.

As water warms in May, salmon distribute along both southern shores of the lake.

gan and Huron they feed primarily on alewives; in Lake Superior chiefly on smelt. Alewives prefer water of moderate temperatures (50-60 degrees), and that's where they and the salmon will be in the spring. Early in the season alewives are in the southern portion of Lakes Michigan and Huron, even before the water warms to the 50-degree range. At this time the salmon are found hard on the heels of the alewives, very near shore, and on or near the surface. Throughout April, shortly after the ice is out, salmon stay concentrated in the southern waters. In Lake Michigan, cohos, usually fish ranging from 2 to 4 pounds, are caught in April along the extreme southern Michigan shore, off Indiana shores, and at points along the Illinois lake-front, including from piers, docks, and breakwaters in Chicago.

Ordinarily in April and early May fishing for "spring" cohos is very good around Michigan City, Indiana, and Chicago. The spring of '69, however, was an exception and for some reason the normally good early salmon fishing was not realized. The weather was bad—with prolonged, unseasonable cold and rain—and unusual northwest winds roiled the waters of the lakefront, which may have had something to do with the shortage of salmon.

As the days grow longer and the sun warmer in May, Lake Michigan salmon begin a gradual movement northward out of the southern part of the lake. Fishermen begin getting them off Waukegan, Illinois, Racine and Kenosha, Wisconsin, and near Milwaukee. This is when the schools really begin to move, and to expand northward—again apparently following alewives, as well as seeking the water temperatures they prefer.

All the while the salmon are, of course, increasing in size. Rising temperatures increase rapidity of metabolic changes, and the fish need more food.

By June Lake Michigan's salmon and alewives move out of the extremely shallow southern waters. Some schools are then found north and east of Waukegan, well out in the lake—sometimes in 60 to 90 feet of water. The fish start a sort of drift—out from shore and toward the north. Much

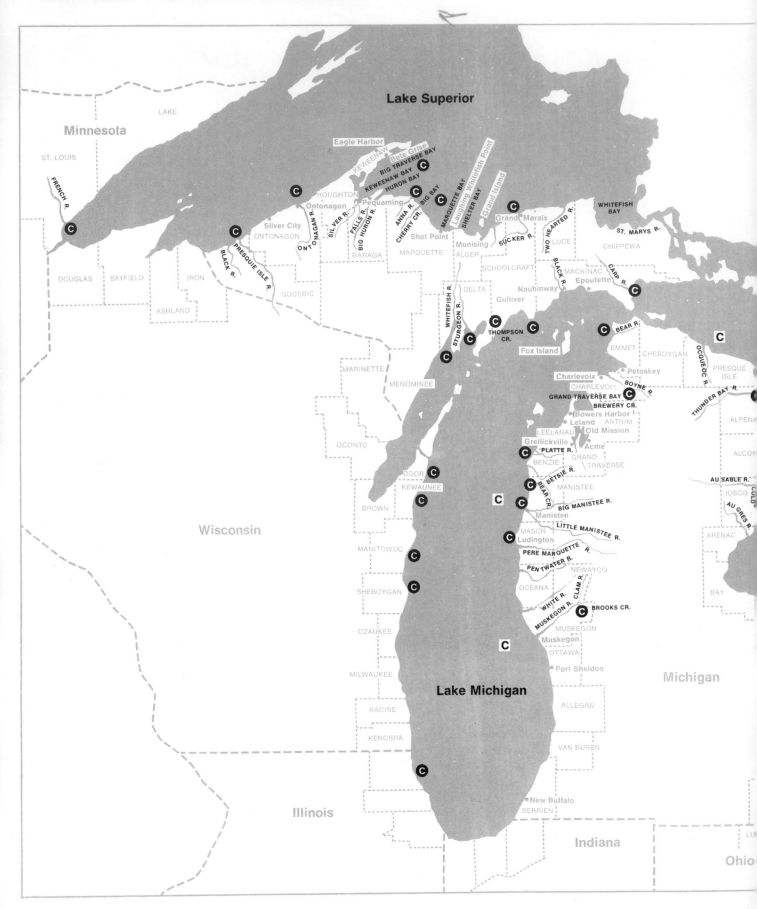

COHO **C**   CHINOOK **C**

DER BAY

Lake Huron

JEFFERSON

HURON

Lake Ontario   **C**   SALMON R.

OSWEGO

LA

SANILAC

ORLEANS   MONROE   WAYNE   CAYUGA

NIAGARA

ST. CLAIR

ERIE   **New York**

MACOMB

C CATTARAUGUS CR.

Lake Erie   **C**   CHAUTAUQUA

ELK CR.

YNE

ASHTABULA

C   LAKE   **Pennsylvania**

OTTAWA   **C**   CHAGRIN R.

ERIE   LORAIN   UYAHOGA

SANDUSKY   HURON R.

depends on general weather and water temperature, but the salmon will move noticeably by the middle of June. Usually they will be in two major schools by June 15—one off Milwaukee, Wisconsin, the other on the Michigan side off Saugatuck.

In Lake Huron, coho schools also will be divided by early summer, moving out from the southern end of the lake upward. In Lake Huron in June, schools should be off Goderich, Ontario, and off Harbor Beach and Huron City, Michigan.

Both coho and Chinook salmon will distribute in July about as they do through June, but come August their movement depends less on their food supply, alewives, and more on the location of their spawning rivers. Salmon spawn and die in the fall, and by August they are becoming "ripe" (developing eggs or milt) and so start moving toward the natal rivers. At this time the fish still feed actively but are not deterred in their urge to start upstream to spawn.

Toward the end of August and into September, mature coho and Chinooks will be concentrated in the big lakes close to the mouths of the spawning rivers. Many thousands

at this time, especially September, will ascend the spawning rivers. It is at this time of year that fishermen have their best luck, being afforded the opportunity of trolling through vast schools of large fish congregated off the mouths of spawning rivers.

By early October the runs will, so far as fishermen are concerned, be terminated. By then the weather usually is sufficiently severe to make any sort of Great Lakes boat fishing impractical.

Intensely cold Lake Superior causes salmon to spread out considerably more than they do in Lakes Michigan and Huron. As a result, movements of salmon in Superior have not been so easily charted. However, it's known that in the early part of the season salmon hang in the southern part of the lake, feeding on smelt, and then expand considerably as the water warms but still remain spread out along the southern shore. Towards fall, they congregate at the mouths of natal rivers.

There are some salmon spawning runs even through the winter in the Great Lakes, but as a rule the runs are terminated, at least in bulk, by mid-October. But the following spring, of course, the cycle begins anew.

Through June and July, salmon break into two large schools in the southern portion of the lake, while Thompson Creek salmon have moved little.

By late August and September, fish begin general movement toward and into spawning rivers. The best fishing ordinarily occurs at this time.

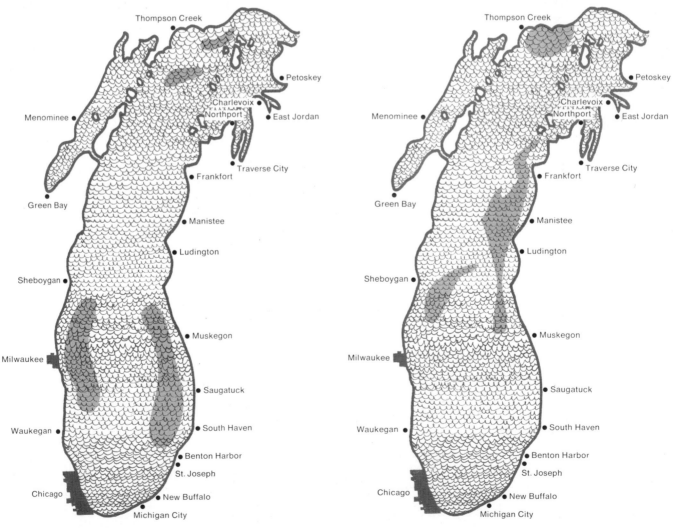

THE COHO STORY:

3: Coho tackle and fishing methods

Fishermen crowd breakwater at Chicago in early spring casting small lures for cohos. Cohos 3½ to 5 pounds lie in foreground.

Trolling with light tackle off Waukegan, Illinois, Ralph Brown (left) watches Bill Cullerton net his spring-time coho. Brown used light Johnson spin-cast outfit and small "Rapala" lure.

When "coho madness" struck Great Lakes fishermen in 1966 and 1967, American fishing tackle manufacturers and tackle retailers were quick to recognize the new and unusual demands for "coho tackle." Not being the type of businessmen to let anything get in the way of a sale, a great deal of tackle suddenly sprouted labels such as "coho reel," "coho rod," "coho line," etc. In actuality most of the tackle was the same old gear; it simply was given the new magical name of "coho."

Some tackle has been newly designed specifically for Great Lakes coho fishing, and much of it is practical, premium merchandise. However, most of the typical fishing tackle owned by the average fresh water fisherman will do for Great Lakes salmon fishing, with perhaps some minor change, such as the addition of heavier and/or more line to reels. Also, any "specialized" tackle that may be desired by a Great Lakes salmon angler has, in fact, been in use in other areas for years. In other words, the fisherman who now wishes to do some surf casting in Lake Michigan needs a surf casting outfit, the same type gear that has been in use by East, Pacific, and Gulf Coast anglers for years. When the fisherman visits a Midwest tackle shop, though, to buy his surf casting outfit he finds it labeled "Coho surf outfit."

There are several ways to fish for Lake Michigan salmon, and the tackle varies according to the fishing method. (Tackle and methods for Lake Michigan apply to all of the Great Lakes).

Starting in very early spring, young salmon (smolts) can be taken in the rivers and streams as they begin down-river migrations. Light tackle should be used for this fishing. Fly and spinning gear is most appropriate. Fly rods of practically any length and weight can be used, although the most sport and possibly the most fish will be had with light rods 6 to 8 feet. Ultra-light spinning tackle is ideal for smolt fishing.

Fly fishermen should use nymphs and small streamer flies, and fish for the smolts as they would for trout. Spin-fishermen also should use trouting techniques, casting tiny jigs, spinners and spoons.

Later in the spring salmon are taken in the lower rivers by fishermen casting spoons, spinners, and small plugs—from piers, jetties, breakwaters, sea-walls, rocky shores, and from boats. Some trolling is done in the lower rivers, beyond the river mouths, and close-in along the lake shores. This early fishing—in March and April—usually is restricted to shore areas because of weather, but the fish

Typical salt water type surf-casting tackle got this fisherman a bright, 14-pound coho.

generally are in shallows then, anyway.

Almost any tackle will do for this fishing. The cohos at this season average under 5 pounds—most weighing between 2 and 3 pounds—so heavy gear isn't needed. A typical bass fishing outfit is perfect, whether it be spinning, spin-casting, or bait casting gear. For spinning the ideal rod is 6½ to 7½ feet long, medium action, with 6 to 10 pound test line. The spin-cast rod should be about 6 feet, medium weight, 8 to 15-pound test line, and the spin-cast reel should be a quality one having reasonably good line capacity (100 yards) and a reliable drag. The bait casting outfit can be a rod 5 to 6½ feet in length, medium action, with a quality level-wind reel holding 10, 12, or 15-pound test line.

In late March, April, and May many thousands of cohos are in the southern portion of Lake Michigan feeding on smelt coming in to spawn along the beaches. At this season many fishermen line breakwaters in Chicago—casting their lures out into the lake and reeling them back—and frequenty they make good hauls of salmon right in the shadows of Chicago skyscrapers. Long casts frequently are desirable in this fishing—because the longer the cast the longer the retrieve, and the longer the retrieve the more

water that is covered . . . and naturally the more water fished the better chances of taking fish. Casts of 150 to 200 or more feet are desirable.

Surf casting tackle is suitable for distance casting from breakwaters, jetties, etc. Spinning gear (open face reels) is the most popular, although some adequate spin-cast outfits can be rigged, and some good casters also can utilize surf-type level-wind reels on big two-handed casting rods. An ideal spinning outfit would consist of a two-handed, medium-heavy, 7½ or 8 foot glass rod, with matching open-face reel loaded with 10 to 15-pound test line.

Small lures are the rule for this shore casting. Popular ones include small jigs (Crawford, Bass-Buster, and Doll-Fly jigs are excellent), spoons such as the Johnson Silver Minnow, Spoon'plug, and Dardevle, and various spinners such as the Mepp's No. 5. Tiny plugs also work well, and thus far the most popular are Heddon's new "Tad-Polly" and "Tiny-Tad," the "Rapalas," and silver "Flatfish." There are, however, many other excellent salmon lures, such as the Creek Chub "Pikie Minnow," Cisco "Kid," 1100, "Big Dig," and "Cut-Plug."

By May and through most of June the small boat fleet is out, and then it is chiefly trolling within a few miles of shore for cohos ranging 3 to 5 pounds, on the average, although some fish 8 to 12 pounds will be taken. Ordinarily the salmon are found on or near the surface—seldom more than 15 feet down—so not much if any lead weight is needed, and light tackle can be used. Bass-type spinning, spin-cast, and bait casting gear is adequate, 8 to 15-pound line, and smallish lures such as those already described put fish in the boat.

Depth-finders are useful in locating fish, and slow trolling is the rule.

For most fishermen, salmon in Lake Michigan and other Great Lakes are hard to find in July and early August because the schools move well offshore into deep water. But normally from mid-August through October, the schools of big, mature fish start moving shoreward and grouping in the vicinity of the spawning rivers. Bays and river mouths swarm with salmon ranging 8 to more than 20 pounds—with the average most seasons being 12 or 13 pounds. Many thousands of salmon move into the rivers, adding to the quantity and variety of the fishing available in the fall. This, then, is when the real salmon fishing begins.

Tom McNally shows 18 pound coho taken by trolling at 15 feet in Lake Michigan off mouth of Manistee River in early September. Tackle included Southern Tackle Company medium-heavy, 6-foot bait casting rod; Ambassaduer 6000 level-wind reel; 12 pound test monofilament line; and series 200 "Spoonplug" lure.

Countless fishermen work the spawning rivers (portions of rivers at times are closed to fishing), fishing with fly, spinning, spin-cast and bait casting tackle. The tackle for this fishing should be sturdy because now one is working for large fish, which, when hooked in the confines of river or stream, literally go wild. They leap into overhanging limbs, foul lines in brush, dive under snags, and dash crazily downstream. Bait casting, spinning and spin-cast rods should be of stiff action, and 15 or 20 pound test line is about right. The fly fisherman needs an 8 to 9½-foot rod, heavy action, and a large capacity, single-action reel loaded with at least 150 yards of 15-pound test squidding line for backing, behind a GBF(WF-8) or GAF(WF-9) fly line. Large streamer flies get the most strikes for fly fishermen, while plugs, spoons, and spinners of the type described earlier work for casters. Bait fishermen also get salmon when in the rivers in the fall, using live minnows or hooks loaded with gobs of nightcrawler worms. It may surprise some Pacific salmon anglers, but nightcrawler worms have accounted for thousands of salmon in Michigan rivers.

Surf fishing also becomes truly important in the late summer through fall as the schools of mature fish begin

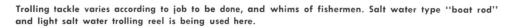

Trolling tackle varies according to job to be done, and whims of fishermen. Salt water type "boat rod" and light salt water trolling reel is being used here.

Fly fisherman casts for cohos in lower Platte River in Michigan . . .

grouping at river mouths and moving upstream. Surf fishing is extremely popular from Lake Michigan beaches near the Platte River mouth, for example, and normally dozens of big salmon will be taken there daily during the fall run. Surf tackle and lures as described before do the job, and no particular technique is involved other than casting out and reeling in.

Most fishermen in fall troll the bays and open waters of the big lakes, in areas not far from the spawning rivers and where the salmon schools are known to be congregated. Wheeling gulls frequently reveal the presence of salmon, but porpoising fish also are seen frequently. There's little trouble at this time of year in finding salmon; where the other boats are is where the salmon are, and on fair-weather days there'll be a zillion boats trolling over the salmon schools.

A variety of lures—most of which have already been named—are suitable for taking the salmon by trolling when the fish are concentrated in Fall. But to repeat, easily the most successful lures are the "Spoonplug," "Rapala," silver "Flatfish," "Tad-Polly," "Dardevle," and "Mepps No. 5" spinner. Ordinarily the fish are taken by slow-trolling, at depths of 10 to 20 feet. At times, however, Great Lakes salmon go extremely deep—something they rarely do in the Pacific—often to depths of 70-100 feet. (The clear water in parts of the Great Lakes, such as Lake Michigan's Platte Bay, may encourage the salmon to go deep.) When salmon are down so far considerably less weight is required to get lures or bait down, and at times some fishermen use as much as a pound or two of lead. A sinker-release mechanism should then be used, so that the heavy sinker drops free on the strike, and some sport is had in playing the fish.

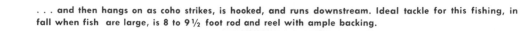

. . . and then hangs on as coho strikes, is hooked, and runs downstream. Ideal tackle for this fishing, in fall when fish are large, is 8 to 9½ foot rod and reel with ample backing.

Cigar smoking angler fishing Michigan's Muskegon River seems non-plussed as Chinook salmon attempts to leap falls at town of Newaygo. Spinning or bait casting tackle is ideal for this fishing.

Great Lakes salmon fishermen have done little natural bait fishing, trolling chiefly with lures, but probably some Pacific Coast bait-fishing systems—such as "mooching"— would also work in the Great Lakes. "Mooching" is a technique of using cut bait (herring) and drifting with the bait fished deep with lead and a sinker-release. "Mooching" doubtlessly would take Great Lakes salmon also, although possibly alewives, smelt, suckers, ciscoes, chubs, and yellow perch would be the best baits.

The tackle used for fall trolling is highly variable— all depending upon the fisherman, and his particular fishing methods. If not fishing deep with much lead, light bait-casting or spinning outfits with ample 10-20 pound test line are fine; if going deep with considerable lead—or with big "flashers" (ultra-large, spoon-like fish attractors) or "cowbell" rigs—then heavier outfits are needed. Light salt water trolling rods known as "boat rods" are ideal for this type of heavy trolling, along with light salt water trolling reels. The line for this sort of heavy, deep trolling should be 20 to 30-pound monofilament; heavier than that is not necessary.

Many Midwest fishermen used to catching nothing much stronger than largemouth bass and bluegills have raved over the "fighting qualities" of coho salmon. Actually, the coho when hooked in open water makes one long, strong run on feeling the hook—and all one need do then is let the fish go and take line off the reel. Most of the time the fish will take well under 100 yards of line. After that, it is a simple matter to pump and reel the salmon in. There is weight there, to be sure, but not really too much resistance.

In close, a hooked coho performs like a lake trout in that he will roll over and over, tangling himself in the line. For that reason "shock" leaders of fairly heavy mono (20 or 30-pound test) are desirable and should be 4 to 6 feet long.

Most important is to "play" a salmon, just as any other good fish should be played. If the angler "horses" a coho or Chinook, applying too much pressure because he's anxious and excited, he'll lose it just as surely as—if he used the same poor technique—he'd lose a sunfish in the local farm pond.

4: The future of salmon fishing in the Great Lakes

Hatchery production of salmon is the key to Great Lakes salmon program. From eggs like these, big salmon grow.

To avoid congested scenes like this (Bear Creek on Michigan's Lower Peninsula), Michigan is expanding its stocking program and introducing salmon to more rivers and streams.

Salmon anglers in boats and wading jam Lake Michigan shore near mouth of Platte River at peak of fall spawning run. Scenes like this attest to popularity of Great Lakes salmon fishing, and the need for enlarging and continuing the program.

So far as fishery biologists are concerned, never has there been a better thing than coho and Chinook salmon in fresh, inland waters.

Always the common bugaboo in the management of any fishery, where biologists are concerned, is control. But the coho and Chinook salmon fishery that has been inaugurated in mid-America's Great Lakes is completely controllable.

To begin, coho salmon have a three-year life cycle; Chinook salmon a four-year cycle. Excluding rare variances, three years or thereabouts pass between the time a coho, or silver salmon, is hatched and dies on a spawning bed; and four years in the case of Chinook or king salmon.

Both coho and Chinook salmon introduced into the Great Lakes are stock coming from eggs imported from the West Coast and hatched in Michigan hatcheries. The salmon fry are reared in hatcheries through the parr stage to the smolt stage, at which time they are released in suitable rivers feeding the Great Lakes. The smolt migrate

downstream into the lakes. In the case of cohos, they average sixteen months of age when moving into the open lakes. They feed heavily and wax fat in the big lakes, grow to maturity, and sixteen months or so later, they return to the "home" inland rivers as adult coho salmon to spawn and die.

It is easy to see from this life-cycle routine how fishery biologists can control or "manage" a Great Lakes salmon fishery. If it is felt there are too few salmon in the lakes, more hatcheries can be built, and more salmon smolts obtained for stocking in the rivers. Commercial fishing can be prohibited. A daily limit can be set on hook-and-line fishermen, and returning salmon can be protected as they ascend spawning streams.

If it is felt there is insufficient distribution of salmon, more rivers in varied areas can be planted with salmon, either cohos or Chinooks or both. Outdated and useless dams constructed years ago on rivers that would be suitable

Back "home" to spawn come two big cohos. These fish are leaping a fish-ladder at a Michigan Conservation Department salmon weir on Bear Creek. Fish are trapped in weirs on way to spawning and eggs removed for use in salmon propagation program. Much of the future of Great Lakes salmon fishing depends on construction of additional salmon hatcheries.

for salmon can be destroyed, and fish introduced to such rivers.

If it is felt that there are too many salmon in the Great Lakes (what a happy thought!), rod-and-reel fishermen can be given great angling liberties, such as being allowed to deliberately snag and foul-hook fish moving into spawning rivers. Commercial fishermen can be permitted to reap many tons of salmon and market them. Moreover, hatchery and stocking programs can be curtailed to naturally reduce the salmon population on an annual basis.

It must be understood that the Great Lakes salmon fishery—unlike that on the Pacific Coast—is artificial and man-made, and therefore is manageable. If Michigan's conservation department, and others, ceased their Great Lakes salmon programs, it is virtually certain there would be no salmon in the inland lakes in a period of five or six years. Rivers feeding the Great Lakes do not provide the

"natural" spawning areas found in parts of the Pacific Coast—much of which is wild and comparatively uninhabited timberland.

Thus fishery biologists—if given authority to set regulations and provided other necessary public cooperation—can absolutely control the Great Lakes salmon program. It is important to understand these possibilities because some commercial interests, as well as a few misinformed sportsmen's groups, have complained over Michigan's coho and Chinook programs. Some commercial fishermen claim a burgeoning salmon population will destroy Great Lakes yellow perch (which are a small part of the salmon's diet), that they will decimate smelt, etc., etc. Some sports fishermen claim salmon populations will clean out trout streams, that the carcasses of dead salmon will pollute rivers, etc., etc. Without explaining in detail that none of those *minus* factors can develop seriously, consider merely the fact that *if*, and *when*, it was determined that salmon were, in fact,

Coho fishermen create traffic jam at boat-launching site on Lake Michigan. With more hatcheries and greater distribution of cohos in the future, and with states other than Michigan cooperating in a Great Lakes salmon stocking program, such congestion will be rare.

destroying smelt populations, polluting rivers or what not —the salmon could be TURNED OFF about as readily as one would close a dripping spigot. It's a thing called CONTROL!

So salmon in the Great Lakes are the best thing that's come along in years. They've rejuvenated fishing in America's heartland, and there's no reason to believe that the future is not bright, indeed, for Great Lakes salmon and Great Lakes salmon fishermen.

Wisconsin has stocked salmon in streams emptying into Green Bay and Lake Michigan. Minnesota has stocked streams with cohos that feed Lake Superior. Ontario is cooperating in prohibiting commercial catches of cohos and also plans stocking of some northshore Lake Superior streams. Ohio has planted the Chagrin River, a tributary to Lake Erie, with 25,000 coho young. Ohio is studying and will select other streams for similiar plants. Pennsylvania released more than 100,000 coho smolts in Pennsylvania streams feeding Lake Erie. (Precocious or early running "jack" cohos were caught in some Pennsylvania Erie streams in the fall of '68.)

"Indiana is definitely considering a coho and Chinook planting program," says Woodrow Fleming, Indiana's Fish Division Chief. If and when Indiana plants coho and/or Chinook, fishermen in southern Lake Michigan could expect almost year-around salmon fishing. Early spring would see the usual initial fishing for young or "developing" salmon that winter in the southern portion of the lake, and then fall would bring a "return" to Indiana waters of mature salmon.

Wayne Tody, Chief of Michigan's Fisheries Division, has said straight out that in the "next 20 years Lake Michigan will be the finest sport fishing area in North America." By the 1980's or sooner, he says, anglers will be catching 1,500,000 or more fish, weighing 5 to 30 pounds each, on hook and line *annually* from Lake Michigan alone. The fish, of course, will be mostly coho and Chinook salmon.

Sea lamprey control in Lakes Michigan and Superior, and an abundant food supply, help guarantee the future of Great Lakes sport fishing. There's an overabundance of alewives to feed salmon (particularly in Lakes Michigan and Huron), along with smelt (abundant in Lake Superior, as well as Michigan and Huron), and lesser forage such as deep-water sculpins and whitefish and chubs.

Michigan also plans a wide expansion of its hatchery facilities, and even as this is being written, new salmon hatcheries are being constructed in key areas in Michigan. Other Great Lakes states are doing the same, though not as extensively as Michigan.

"Our present facilities are capable of producing four to five million salmon a year," Wayne Tody has said. "But on our drafting tables we are laying out plans for five new fish-rearing stations that will cost $10,000,000. Altogether these new hatcheries will be able to produce 30,000,000 fish—mostly salmon smolts—yearly."

The next move for Michigan—and other states interested in providing salmon fishing—is to provide fish passage to spawning and angling areas now blocked by needless dams and, in some instances, natural barriers.

Ultimately, Michigan expects to be planting up to 30,000,000 salmonids—chiefly coho and Chinook salmon —annually.

5: 150 Bass fishing tips from 15 experts

LAMONT ALBERTSON is a professional guide in West Palm Beach, Florida. He fishes all of the central and south Florida rivers and lakes, and has been an enthusiastic bass fisherman since childhood.

Lamont Albertson has been featured in stories in *Field & Stream, True, Argosy, Sports Afield,* the *Chicago Tribune,* and other media. Because of his vast knowledge of bass fishing areas, of the habits of southern bass, and of bass fishing techniques, his services as a guide are in great demand.

ALBERTSON'S TIPS:

1. Concentrate your casts on "fishy" spots, but don't cast right next to stumps or a weed patch where you figure there may be a bass. Cast beyond these likely-looking areas, and then bring your lure past them.
2. If you see bass feeding, try to determine the kind of baitfish they are working on, and then select a lure that is suitable. Fish the lure with an action that simulates the movements of the baitfish.
3. During extreme hot weather, fish early in the morning and late in the evening. In extreme southern areas (Florida and the Gulf states) bass are most active when the water has cooled.
4. In cold weather, fishing is usually best during the brighter, warmer hours of the day. Frequently the very best fishing is from 10 a.m. to 3 p.m.
5. During any period of extreme weather—hot or cold—fish slow and easy, and deliberately. Use both underwater and surface lures.
6. Never cast at random, or with boredom or disinterest. Always pick a target at which to cast—a clump of bushes, a log, rocks, weeds, etc., and always think that the cast you are about to make is the one that's going to get a 10 pound bass.
7. Strive to become an accurate caster. Accuracy is more important than distance, most of the time.
8. Use varying tactics when retrieving a lure. Try a fast retrieve then slow; try loud splashing with a surface lure, then a sharp, jerking, gurgling retrieve. You've got to attract a bass's attention.
9. Fish protected areas. Fish the lee side of a lake or river, in the shelter of a high bank, wooded shore, etc. Keep the wind in your favor. Let the wind drift you over the areas to be fished—that means less commotion with oars and more free time to cast.
10. Always keep your eye on the lure. Keep slack out of your line. Be ready and set for a strike at all times. One instant of carelessness and you might miss the fish of a lifetime.

8. Be "sensitive" in fishing. Be ultra-alert. Often big bass take very lightly, as when they suck in a plastic worm or porkrind eel. At times you will only sense a change in line "action" when a big bass takes.

9. Carry three pre-rigged rods with you in your boat. Have lines of different tests or diameters on each, and start fishing with the heaviest, going down to the lightest. You might also rig one with a surface lure, one with a plastic worm or porkrind eel, and the third a jig, weedless spoon, or whatever.

10. For fishing in weeds, try a floating plastic worm hooked through the nose. Use a safety pin type of snap, No. 5 size, and to get sufficient casting weight, attach a split-shot sinker by clamping it on the shank of the safety pin snap.

BILL BINKELMAN of Milwaukee is in the sporting goods and publishing business. His regularly published *Fishing Facts and Secrets* newspaper has become a sort of bible to many thousands of fishermen who rely upon it for the latest angling news and fishing tips.

Binkelman is schooled in deep water fishing techniques, including "spoonplugging," jigging, and plastic worm fishing. He is the author of *Nightcrawler Secrets,* a booklet that probably contains more useful information on worm fishing than any other book available.

BINKELMAN'S TIPS:

1. If you want big bass, fish deep. That means down to 12 or 20 feet, or more. *Believe* in deep-water schools.

2. Save those "choice" shallow water spots. Every lake has some such places that attract and hold some large fish. Fish such spots only on the tough days such as after a cold front. Don't wear them out.

3. A lake's bottom governs 95% of the movements of bass. For example, an open spot in an otherwise weedy shoreline will pull and hold fish. So will a clump of weeds on an otherwise weed-free, sandy bottom.

4. Bass have an affinity for old concrete. Thoroughly fish old dams, culverts, bridge pilings, etc. Cast very close to such structure, within inches of it. Find the exact spot where the bass are.

5. When fishing a plastic worm, give it a little flash. Add a 2½ inch strip of white porkrind to the hook. Sometimes that little garnish will triple your catch.

6. Tiny split rings attached to the eye of a lure will vastly improve its action. Such rings reduce knot wear, too.

7. Human odor on a bait or lure will shy fish away. Use a few drops of green surgical soap on your hands when starting to fish. The soap is easy to carry.

HURLEY CAMPBELL is a popular outdoor writer based in Baton Rouge, Louisiana. He's the outdoor columnist for the *Baton Rouge Morning Advocate,* and is a staff correspondent for *Outdoor Times.* He also is a frequent contributor to *Western Outdoor News, Field & Stream, Sports Afield* and other national magazines.

He is an officer and "guiding light" in the Outdoor Writers Association of America, and has held top positions in that organization. Widely traveled, Campbell is experienced in bass fishing in all areas—from the wilds of Canada to the hidden bayous of the Gulf Coast.

CAMPBELL'S TIPS:

1. Just had a tussel with a good bass? Then snip about 4 or 5 feet of your line and re-tie the lure. The line could have become frayed and weakened.

2. Having trouble getting your plastic worm to float properly? One good way to cure that problem is to insert a wooden

match stick into the worm, and then break it into small parts. The wood will help float the worm and, being broken, it will not interfere with the worm's action.

3. When casting a spoon among lily pads try to land the lure on a pad. Leave it there, but gently wiggle it so the pad ripples the water. Then when you pull the spoon off there's a good chance a bass will be waiting to hit it.

4. Pin-point accuracy is the trademark of the angler who takes bass consistently, especially in waters where snags are plentiful. Time you spend on the lawn practicing casting will pay off for you.

5. If you're fishing a top-water plug, have another rod rigged with an underwater lure. Often a bass that will only swirl at a top-water lure will slam into an underwater lure if offered just after he has missed the surface plug.

6. When fishing a brushy shore, cast a number of times to the same spot. Often a fish can be "pulled" from back in the brush to hit a plug that has been *splaaatting* into the same spot for a number of times.

7. For the serious bass angler, fast-drying touch-up paint is a "must" for his tackle box. Largemouths (smallmouths, too) can distinguish color, and frequently touch-up paint will transform a failing lure into a successful one.

8. Fish an area thoroughly when trying for big bass. The larger the fish the less likely he is to move any distance to take food or to hit a lure.

9. The schooling bass of many big southern impoundments usually are small. Use a lure that will sink rapidly and work it several feet under the school. Often larger bass are down there waiting for the bait into which the school bass are tearing to drift down to them.

10. Although swivel-snaps make changing lures easy and quick, it is better to tie a line directly to a plug because snaps always reduce some of a lure's natural action.

BOB CARY when not fishing resides near Ely, Minnesota, but most of his time is spent in a canoe or tent some-

where in the borderland wilderness country of Quetico-Superior, on the U.S.-Canadian border. Bob is former Outdoor Editor of the *Chicago Daily News,* and a former resident of Plainfield, Illinois, a town about 60 miles from the midwest metropolis.

Bob wisely gave up both the *Daily News* stint, and his more-or-less urban living, to transfer to the Ely area and undertake a new livelihood and life. Bob now operates a wilderness outfitting organization, and in his spare time (he gets a little in the winter), he does free-lance writing for magazines such as *Outdoor Life, Field & Stream,* etc.

CARY'S TIPS:

1. Bass will often strike surface lures and not get hooked. Remove the front treble hooks on a surface plug, leaving only the rear hooks, for better hooking qualities.

2. Smallmouth bass have smaller mouths and smaller appetites than largemouth bass. Lures in ¼-ounce size, and smaller, and jigs from ⅛ down to 1/16 ounce are best for smallmouths. And smaller streamer flies, as small as size 10, are better on smallmouths than are big, bushy flies.

3. Most large bass strike surface lures that have "rested" motionless for at least a full minute. The big ones rarely bother to hustle after a surface lure that's busily popping along. Work 'em slow and easy.

4. Two deadly combinations for smallmouth bass are: 1) A yellow plastic worm and 3/16 ounce jig. 2) A leadhead jig with half of a fresh nightcrawler impaled on its hook.

5. When fishing a spinner for bass retrieve it just fast enough so that the revolving spinner puts constant tension on the rod tip. Such a slow retrieve not only gets more fish but it also causes the spinner to put less twist in the line.

6. Smallmouth bass in lakes are school fish, with the smaller bass frequently schooled nearer the surface, the larger bass schooled deeper down. The fisherman who consistently works his lures (or bait) deep near the bottom will usually get the larger fish.

7. Fresh-killed frogs are better bait for bass than live frogs because they can be manipulated better and fished deeper. Frogs should be killed quickly, just before using, and their bellies punctured to release air. If the legs are snapped between the bone joints, the frogs will have a sinking, fluttering action in the water that is irresistible to bass.

8. Stream bass are more easily taken by a wading angler fishing upstream rather than down. This is true whether fishing artificials or live bait. Live bait should be fished without a sinker and allowed to drift back downstream with the current, following up-stream casts. Keep slack out of the line to avoid missing strikes and hanging-up on bottom.

9. Smallmouth bass just can't resist striking a fly rod hair frog cast onto a rock and then flicked gently into the water. One reason this casting method works so well is that there is little surface disturbance caused by the fly line falling to the water, and the splatting-down of the bug.

10. Hellgrammites, the larvae of the Dobson fly, are superb smallmouth baits. They're best when the head is cut off and the body threaded onto a hook from the tail forward, which turns the hellgrammite inside-out.

JACK CRAWFORD is a Wisconsin lure manufacturer and bass fisherman, but not necessarily in that order. He is, in fact, first of all a bass fisherman. But of course, his angling experiences range far beyond bass fishing, since Jack also is a skilled walleye, lake trout, and northern pike fisherman.

More than anything else Jack Crawford is a jig fisherman, and he has crafted and manufactures some of the finest and most original lead-head jigs ever made. His latest jigs, for example, have silhouettes similar to the lines of an isosceles triangle. They sit on the bottom with their hooks up at about a 45-degree angle, and it is almost impossible for one of these Crawford jigs to foul.

CRAWFORD'S TIPS:

1. Jig vertically. It can be done either by casting or drifting. Vertical jigging can be done even in weeds and brush, and at some distance from the boat, too. To jig vertically, use a sliding bobber. Cast it out, then pay out line until the jig hangs below the bobber and on bottom. Then all you need do is raise and lower the jig.
2. Weedless jigs are not, contrary to some fishermen, also "fish-less." I've taken thousands of large bass on weedless jigs, and have failed to hook only a few—no more than I'd miss hooking with a non-weedless jig.
3. Black marabou jigs lying motionless (but the marabou "winging" will wave and have action) on the bottom often take cold water smallmouth bass when all else fails. The slightest movement of the water causes marabou to undulate and flutter in a life-like way. Smallmouths will pick them right off the bottom. Set the hook hard. Best size marabou jigs are ⅛ and ¼ ounce.
4. Knots wear out quickly. Put a No. 1 split ring on your

jigs, for better knotting and, even more important, for a freer and better action of the jig.

5. In fishing jigs, vary the retrieve. A good one is a very slow retrieve, merely crawling the jig across the bottom in 18 or 20 inch c-r-a-w-l-s. The short, fast, 1-2-3 jerking retrieve also is good. Still another good way to fish a jig is with several 10 or 12 inch hops, then allowing the jig to rest motionless for nearly a minute. After the long pause, give a big sweep with the rod. Bass usually hit right then! If no fish, continue with some 10-12 inch hops, another long pause, and so on.
6. A jig with plastic worm attached is deadly. Use a floating worm. When the jig is on the bottom the worm's tail will rise and "flirt." Very tempting.
7. A jig fished with a live minnow also is a great lure. Or you can use an ordinary bait hook with minnow attached, and a No. 3 or 5 lead sinker "Gremlin," for casting weight.
8. Custom-made jigs with four inch feather "tails" should be in your tackle box. Certain color combinations and types of feathers such as mallard breast have been proven very effective.
9. Bright-colored ⅛ and ¼ ounce jigs jerked rapidly alongside underwater logs, weeds, brush piles, often will pull out large bass. Work the jig rapidly.
10. Bass will frequently strike in the white-water wake of an outboard motor. Cast into or troll in the wake, fishing at depths of 5 to 10 feet.

MURRAY CROWDER has been a bass fisherman for more than 40 years. As a boy growing up in the Ozarks of Missouri, he learned about stream smallmouths, and in the years since then he has fished for bass in waters from the Atlantic to the Pacific, and from the southern Canada lakes to the bayous of Louisiana and Mississippi. The Ozarks still beckon to him hardest though, and not a season passes that Crowder will not be seen often floating the Buffalo or plugging the shoreline of Bull Shoals Reservoir.

Crowder currently is a fishing and tackle consultant to Sears, Roebuck & Company, as well as a newspaper outdoor columnist and freelance outdoor writer. He is a frequent guest on outdoor radio and TV shows, and is a noted angling instructor and lecturer. He is a past president, Outdoor Writers Association of America, and resides in Spring Valley, Illinois.

CROWDER'S TIPS:

1. Remember that big bass, as a general rule, are found in deeper water than small bass. Fish accordingly.
2. Study bass habits. Learn where to look for them—in particular lakes—during warm, hot, cool and cold weather. Where do the bass go during cold fronts? Do they migrate to special areas in hot weather? The more you know about bass, the more you'll catch them.
3. When fishing with live minnows in a river or stream, hook the minnows through both lips so that they will face naturally into the current. When pond or lake fishing, hook the minnow well back under the dorsal (top) fin, but not through the backbone. Use as little weight as possible so that the bait can swim naturally.
4. When using whole crayfish for bait, hook the crustacean from below the head up through the space between the eyes. Bass swallow crawfish tail-first.
5. If you use a spinner (small ones are best) in front of live bait, have it about 12 or 14 inches ahead of your bait, not right against the bait.
6. Nightcrawlers and other worms should be hooked only through the head. Hooking worms through their "belt" or ring will kill them quickly. And smart bass leave a dead worm alone.
7. Most large bass will grab a live bait, swim a few feet away, then stop. Don't set the hook until the bass starts off again.
8. If fish are ignoring your top-water lure, yet you know the bass are feeding close to the surface, try putting a real or a plastic worm on the rear hooks of your floating plug. A worm—real or otherwise—sometimes makes the difference in getting strikes or no strikes.
9. Weedless spoons and porkchunk are great in weeds and lily pads. To make them more effective try wiggling your rod tip as the spoon or porkchunk starts across a thick weed patch or onto a lily pad.
10. Big bass favor the same areas. It's an old rule, but a good one: if you get a nice bass at a particular spot, fish the place again in a couple of days because another nice bass probably will have moved in.

BILL CULLERTON, of Elmhurst, Illinois, is a tackle company representative, handling Johnson reels, Rapala lures, and other lines. You'll encounter Bill at sports shows around the Midwest, or almost anywhere giving casting demonstrations and fishing lectures. He's the fishing "star" in numerous angling movies, and in TV fishing tackle commercials. He's done countless radio and TV outdoor shows, and is an extremely popular instructor and lecturer on angling.

A superb caster, Cullerton's angling experiences range from taking tiger fish in Africa to giant tarpon in Costa Rica, bonefish in British Honduras, Atlantic salmon in Labrador—and to bluegills in Midwest farm ponds. But more than anything else Cullerton is a bass fisherman's bass fisherman, and he's taken both largemouth and smallmouth bass in waters from Florida to Manitoba—and in countless spots between.

CULLERTON'S TIPS:

1. Easily one of the best bass-catchers ever devised is the black porkrind eel. Fish an eel 4 to 6 inches long with a black bucktail lead-head jig. Fish it right on bottom, snaking it slowly along by merely lifting, then dropping, the rod tip. Bass will hit the eel at its head, taking the jig's hook, so set the hook hard and fast as soon as you feel a strike.
2. A porkrind eel can also be fished alone, using spinning or spin-cast tackle and no lead or, at least, a minimum of lead weight. Cast the eel to likely spots and fish it slowly with short twitches of the rod tip. Now and then bump it along with 3 or 4 quick twitches of the rod tip. When a bass takes, let him have the eel for a bit before setting the hook. Fished this way, a bass will hit an eel broadside and wear it like a mustache for a while before starting to swallow it.

3. **Keep hooks sharp!**
   Always carry a hone or small file and "touch up" all hooks on a lure, or bait hooks, before fishing. Sharpen them periodically while fishing, too. Jig hooks should be checked and sharpened frequently since they dull from bumping rocks, etc.

4. Fly rod popping bugs are killers when bass are in the shallows. As a general rule poppers should be allowed to rest motionless after falling to the water, then popped gently. Sometimes, though, a steady *pop . . . pop . . . pop* retrieve gets more strikes. Also, use bullet-shaped bugs—ones that do not pop—when bass aren't coming to your poppers. You can skip and slide a bullet-like bug across the surface, or pull it under. Frequently bass will take a bullet-type plug just under the surface while refusing to come on top for a popper.

5. Too many fishermen these days have forgotten about, or don't know about, pork chunk. Frog-type pork chunk is a remarkable largemouth lure. It's available in colors these days—pure white, black, green-and-white with "frog" spots, yellow and even purple. All are good, but I prefer pure white, the green-white frog type, and white frog type chunk having a piece of red yarn threaded through the body. Fish pork chunk alone, with a single 5/0 hook, or fish it with a small spinner in front. Pork chunk with a weedless hook eased through lily pads will not fail to get bass if the fish are there.

6. Keep your tackle in tip-top shape. Reels not cleaned and oiled will not function properly and will give casting trouble. If you've got casting problems, you can't concentrate on fishing.

7. A single spinner with a single hook with a single strip of porkrind attached is a "different" and effective bass lure. Cast it into pockets in lily pads and weeds, and let it flutter down. A spinner and small porkstrip can be cast with heavy fly outfits or ultra-light spinning gear.

8. When fishing for bass in shallows strive to keep boat noises at a minimum. Oar locks should be greased or padded. Don't splash with oars or paddle unnecessarily. Bass are spooky and wary fish, hard to fool.

9. Give *action* to lures by stroking with your rod. Seldom is it that the built-in action of any lure cannot be improved by skillful manipulation of the rod by the angler.

10. Learn to "*hunt*" bass. Bass are school fish following the spawning season, and they spend most of their time down deep. Start fishing shallows, but keep working deeper until you locate bass. Move around, continually trying different areas and techniques.

CHARLEY ELLIOTT'S byline is known to millions of American sportsmen. As a field editor of *Outdoor Life* magazine, and a constant contributor of features to that magazine, he has a dedicated and enthusiastic following. At home in Covington, Georgia, Elliott also works as outdoor columnist for the *Atlanta Constitution*.

Elliott has an extensive outdoors background: former District Forester for Georgia; Director of State Parks; Commissioner, State Natural Resources Department; Director, State Game and Fish Commission; Regional Public Relations Director, National Park Service. He is the author of nine books on hunting and fishing.

Moreover, Elliott is a veteran bass fisherman, fully schooled in all techniques from deep water tactics to taking them on top.

ELLIOTT'S TIPS:

1. Bass sometimes strike a lure more quickly when it is moved slowly—and at other times a fast-moving lure gets the best results. Vary the speed of your retrieve, or of trolling, until you find the speed and action the bass want at a particular time.

2. If you catch a bass when trolling across an underwater point, go back as close as possible to the place where the fish struck and fish the area thoroughly. Often you'll find a school of bass lying there, on or close to the bottom.

3. When trolling, keep the tip of your rod well behind you. This permits you to set the hook quickly and firmly when you get a strike.

4. When fishing clear water—even if from a boat—wear dark clothing or clothing of subdued color. A white shirt reflects light that may spook a bass, especially a fish in shallow water.

5. We all like to see a jumping bass, but in the air a bass has more chance of throwing the hook. Sometimes when a bass starts his jump you can pull him down with a tight line and sweep of your rod tip low along the water.

6. It's possible to fish a surface lure too slow, but I've seen few anglers who did not fish one too fast. Let a top-water lure lie until the ripples it caused in the surface disappear, then work the rod tip just enough to barely move the plug. Some top-water lures are designed for a fast retrieve, but most are not.

7. Bass hang around underwater snags and brush. In deep water such cover is more easily fished with a jig or deep-going lure, fishing the lure directly underneath the boat. Fish it with an up-and-down action, a pumping motion. Working a lure this way down deep catches fish and lessens chances of hanging-up.

8. Bump trolling lures along the bottom. This makes for erratic action of a lure and gives it the appearance of a wounded baitfish trying to get away.

9. Streams flowing into a lake bring in fresh water, food, and sometimes cooler or warmer water, depending on the season. Much of the time bass will congregate at or near the mouths of such tributaries.

10. Fish from top to bottom. Try all depths until you locate fish.

HAROLD ENSLEY is the "Sportsman's Friend" of Kansas City, Missouri. He is the host and producer of a weekly TV show carried on nine networks in eight states, covering fishing and hunting and related outdoors activities. In addition, he does a 15-minute radio outdoor program three times weekly.

Harold Ensley is synonymous with bass fishing. He fishes at least three or more times a week, usually at mid-America lakes and rivers, but often in distant spots such as Great Bear Lake in the Arctic. He is an extremely hard-working angler, casting without let-up from the time he gets on the water until time forces him to quit. Fifteen and 20-hour fishing days are not unusual but rather the rule for Ensley. His determinedness when fishing, patience, skill and knowledge of bass has helped him to win many important angling contests.

ENSLEY'S TIPS:

1. Buy good equipment. Your gear doesn't have to be expensive but it should be practical. For example, when fishing thick reeds or other heavy growth a cane pole with line and lure could be effective bass gear, but if casting a Canadian lake for smallmouths you'd probably need a good spinning outfit, or a heavy bait casting outfit if fishing flooded timber areas of a big TVA lake. So try to be sure the tackle you have is the best type for the bass fishing you'll do.

2. Just as important as having good equipment is the ability to use it properly. You must use your gear *effectively* to catch bass. Become an accurate caster. And distance is something you should work on, too, because while accuracy is most important there also are times when you need to make a *long* accurate cast.

3. Learn to "read" water. Water levels, time of year (e.g., spawning time), bottom formation, cover, food conditions —all these govern the location of bass. You can't catch bass if you can't find them, so you must be able to "read" the water.

4. Learn how to select the right lure. Almost any lure will take bass some time or other, but there are situations when certain types of baits are more productive than others. Most bass fishermen have their own pet lures, and they catch more fish on them because they have confidence in those baits and also because they use them most often. The type, color, and size of the lure you use should be determined by the discoloration of the water, depth you need to fish, kind of cover, kind of food, etc. For example, in discolored water I'd select a vibrating lure, such as a "Single Spin" or a "Twin Spin," and I'd use a larger one than normal and in yellow.

5. The way you "work" or fish a lure is very important. Different lures require different techniques. When using vibrating baits or ones that wiggle sharply through the water, I work the lure with the reel crank. With "soft" lures—such as a leadhead jig-and-eel or plastic worm—I work the lure with the rod tip, picking up the loose line with the reel crank.

6. Develop a sense of touch. With experience you'll learn to properly "feel" a lure as you work it, and you'll also be able to feel fish when they merely touch your lure.

7. Knowing how to hook striking bass is one of the marks of the expert. With some lures it's necessary to set the hook the instant a fish touches it. With other lures it's better to let a bass take the lure as you would if fishing a live minnow. With vibrating lures set the hook instantly; with soft lures, let the fish have it for a short time.

8. To put fish in the boat, you must know how to "play"

them, too. Never reel a hooked bass right up to your rod tip. Try never to bring a bass in closer than a rod's length of line away. This gives you some line with which to cushion any quick run the bass may make at the boat.

9. Be a "stubborn" fisherman. By that I mean: keep your patience, keep up your hopes, and never quit. Never slack off in your efforts.

10. Finally, it helps a lot to be "lucky." I don't know quite how to explain what being "lucky," as I mean it, is all about, but it's something all good bass fishermen have. Maybe it's just that little extra bit of confidence that makes the "lucky" fisherman get ten bass when everybody else catches two, and to get two when everybody else gets none.

BEN HARDESTY is a name known to all veteran fishermen. He currently is Vice President of the Shakespeare Tackle Company in Kalamazoo, Michigan, having just moved to that position from the Presidency of the Pflueger Tackle Company, a Shakespeare holding, in Akron, Ohio.

Hardesty is a former long-time world's professional casting champion, and while just a boy was winning casting tournaments one after the other. Possessing extraordinary coordination and timing, Ben remains one of the finest casters in the world today.

His fishing experiences cover about everything—rainbow trout in Chile; brown trout in Argentina; bonefish in the Bahamas; smallmouths in Canada; brook trout in Michigan; largemouths in Bull Shoals, and still more. Ben Hardesty has fished for, and taken bass, in about as many lakes and rivers as anyone.

HARDESTY'S TIPS:

1. Check all knots before fishing. Check points are:
   1) Line tied to reel spool.
   2) Line-to-leader knot.
   3) Knot connecting leader to snap, swivel, or lure.

2. Always carefully adjust the casting drag on your reel according to the weight of the lure being used. A rule-of-thumb is to adjust the drag so the lure barely pulls line from the reel when the lure is allowed to hang loosely at the rod tip.

3. When casting with a bait casting rod, keep the handles turned up. This permits the free wrist action necessary for good casting.

4. Also when bait casting, keep your thumb on the bottom side of the spool flange, at the edge of the spooled line. This allows comfortable and sensitive control of the line to prevent backlashing or over-spin.

5. Always stop the forward motion of a lure in flight just before it hits the water. Do this whether you are bait casting, spinning, or spin-casting. The reasons for halting a lure's flight, just over the target, are many: It reduces the possibility of backlashing with a bait casting reel. It provides better line-control if spinning or spin-casting. It makes for a tight line when the lure hits the water so that you are prepared for any sudden strike. And, finally, halting a lure over the target actually has it slanting back towards you as it enters the water, so the lure actually is "swimming" immediately, and so appears life-like the instant it's in the water.

6. Work surface lures slowly, deliberately. Alternate between hard and soft "pops" or twitches of a top-water lure, fishing the lure with your rod tip.

7. Semi-surface lures can be worked either on the surface, underwater, or both on top and below the surface. I prefer to work such lures both ways. I fish them on top for a while, and if no bass come then I pull them under. If that doesn't work, fish a lure on the surface for a few feet, then pull it under, then go back to the surface, repeating that technique.

8. Underwater lures with built-in action can be worked continually from the end of cast back to the boat, either slow or steady, fast and steady, or a variation of both. Underwater lures, such as lead jigs and plastic worms, can be activated by working or "pumping" the rod, or by letting the lure sink to the bottom, then pumping the rod to make the lure bounce along the bottom.

9. Whenever a fish strikes, hit back at him hard to set the hooks. Many bass are lost because the angler never puts the hooks into them. You *must* set the hooks.

10. When playing a hooked bass keep a tight line and the rod high. Always have the fish fighting the bend of the rod.

BING McCLELLAN is boss-man at the Burke Company in Traverse City, Michigan. And that means nothing to you unless you happen to be a plastic worm fisherman, in which case you'll recognize the Burke name. Burke plastic "Erthworms" have been demolishing bass in many areas for many years.

Bing McClellan is an outstanding angler and bass fishing expert, and his novel and original plastic worms, and special worming "kits," attest to his expertise.

The well-traveled McClellan has fished most of the important bass waters in America, and therefore understands the complexities of bass fishing in all areas.

McCLELLAN'S TIPS:

1. There are fishermen who are good fishermen for the same reason there are good golfers and good bowlers; they learn the basics, practice a lot, use the best equipment, and experiment. By all means have fun when fishing, but *fish seriously.*

2. When fishing a lake new to you, try to get a topographical map of the lake and study it. Note where the deep holes and submerged bars are. Also, ask local fishermen to point out "good" spots to you on the map. When they do that, you have a valuable tip—where *not* to fish.

3. Be equipped so that you can fish from top to bottom. Bass seldom fit their feeding habits to your favorite technique, so learn the various methods of surface, medium depths, and deep-water fishing. And always have a selection of lures suitable for fishing the different depths.

4. Slow your pace when fishing. Nearly every fisherman works lures too fast. Plastic worms are a good example of lures that *must be* fished slowly. Make your phoney worms just c-r-a-w-l over the bottom.

5. Spit on every knot before you tighten it. The spittle acts as a lubricant, helps to draw the knot properly tight, and it prevents a cutting action that creates minute fractures in mono when it is knotted dry.

6. Most big bass are found near heavy cover. When a lunker hits your lure, and he's near rough cover, set the hook hard—try to break the rod when you set—and then get the bass out of there in a hurry. Go ahead, horse him right out of there and put him in the boat.

7. Use sufficiently heavy tackle when bass fishing in weeds or lily pads. Ultra-light gear is sporty but it's useless in rough cover. Many of the guides that fish the bass impoundments of the mid-south use rods 5 or 5½ feet long and of fairly stiff action, casting reels that are free-spool and have star drags, and line testing 17 to 24 pounds.

8. Rig two rods and you'll almost double your fishing efficiency. Rig one with a surface lure, the second with a sinking lure, such as deep-running plug, plastic worm, jig, etc. Having two rods already rigged allows you to fish surface or deep with no lost time. Also, if you are fishing the top-water lure and you miss a strike, quickly chuck the underwater lure back at the fish and he may take it.

9. Color *is* important in bass lures. Which color is best on a particular day depends upon light conditions, mood of the fish, etc. But fish can discern colors, or shades of colors, in fact they can distinguish 24 different shades of the spectrum. So carry lures in a wide assortment of colors, and keep changing lures while fishing until you find the one the bass are hitting best.

10. If you want to eat bass you catch, the best place to keep them until you finish fishing is in a boat's live well. A stringer is okay, too, but be sure to string a bass through both lips since he'll live longer that way.

JOE MEARS is Outdoor Editor of the *Independent* and *Star News* in Pasadena, California. He also is western field correspondent for *Outdoor Life* magazine, and has been a field editor for that magazine for many years.

As a free lance writer and photographer covering all phases of fishing, hunting, camping and nature stories, Joe Mears' byline is known and loved by millions of outdoorsmen. He is a past president of the Outdoor Writers Association of America, and is active in many western and national conservation organizations.

Joe is a dedicated and skilled angler who has fished for bass in many states, as well as in Canada and Mexico.

MEARS' TIPS:

1. If fishing a lake for the first time, try to go out with one of the area's good fishermen or with a guide. They can show you a lot about a lake in a short time.

2. If bass won't take your surface plugs, try bottom-scratching with a plastic worm. When a bass takes your plastic worm don't set the hook too soon. Give him a chance to mouth the worm properly before hooking him.

3. Cynics say lures are designed to catch fishermen, not fish. But I've proved to my own satisfaction, over the years, that a well-stocked tackle box with various colors and sizes of spoons, worms, plugs, spinners, etc. pays off. Again, ask locally which lures are best, and if you don't have any then buy some.

4. Most fishermen know popping bugs will sometimes take big bass when they're in shallow water, but few realize that streamer flies and "Wooly Worms" often are killers. I took my largest bass at Lake Henshaw, California, on a streamer fly while fishing for crappies.

5. Waterdogs or salamanders are probably the very best bait on lakes of the lower Colorado River, on Mead, Mohave, and Havasu Lakes where I do most of my bass fishing. In fishing waterdogs be sure not to use a sinker that is too heavy or the bait will not swim naturally. Often I use no weight at all, and use as light a spinning outfit as possible, or a fly outfit.

6. Good fishermen don't object to getting snagged or fouled occasionally if it means catching bass. So don't hesitate to fish in holes, in weeds, or far back in flooded trees, or around brush piles and sunken logs, rocks and so on.

7. If various plugs don't get bass for you, try spoons in different sizes, colors, and types. Use a good swivel when fishing spoons, so that you will not develop a twist in your line.

8. Weather is a major factor in bass fishing. I've had good fishing when there was a heavy ripple or light chop on the water, and I've also had some fine fishing on rainy days.

9. Although I'm old-fashioned enough to prefer a bait casting outfit, I suggest that beginning fishermen start out with spin-cast or spinning outfits. They're easiest to handle and, in fact, are virtually fool-proof. But I believe a bait casting outfit gives the greatest accuracy. The free-spool bait casting reels are best.

10. Trolling is ridiculed by many veteran bass fishermen, but remember that on a strange lake you can cover a lot of water and find the bass quicker by trolling. Be sure to troll different lures, and at varying depths and speeds.

DON NICHOLS, of LaGrange Park, Illinois, is a jet airliner pilot for United Airlines. As such he works an average of 10 or 12 days, or less, a month—since by law commercial airline pilots may fly only so many hours a month. This is of interest because it means Nichols gets a lot of free time, and—you guessed it—he uses it all bass fishing.

Don Nichols is a "spoonplugging" addict and knows as much about that method of bass fishing as anyone short of "spoonplugging's" originator, Buck Perry. Don is especially expert at deep-trolling and locating bass, and he has thorough knowledge of bass habits. He's a skilled caster, too, not only with bait casting and spinning gear but with the fly rod as well. Moreover, he has fished bass in many scattered areas, and has been a consistent winner in various bass fishing contests.

NICHOLS' TIPS:

1. When casting to a school of bass, get fish you hook out of and away from the school as quickly as possible. A hooked bass fighting near a school will likely spook the other fish.

2. Vary the speed of your retrieve, whether casting or trolling, until you determine what is the best speed. Never stay with one speed for a long period of time unless it is producing fish. Many bass fishermen are reluctant to fish a lure fast, and as a result they find the fishing very tough on days when bass want a fast-moving lure.

3. When a bass strikes, set the hooks hard, especially when into large bass. Excepting the soft cheek areas, a big bass's mouth is hard and difficult to penetrate with hooks. More big bass are lost because the fisherman did not set the hooks hard enough than are lost because hooks were set too hard.

4. When using a porkrind eel or plastic worm as a trailer on a jig or other jump-type lure, try different lengths until you find the best length for the water and weather conditions existing at the time. Trailers 3 to 4 inches long will be effective at times; other times a trailer 10 to 12 inches long will be necessary.

5. When fishing weed beds make a number of casts parallel to and close to the outside edge of the weeds. Bass tend to lie just inside a weed line facing open water. That is especially true if the weeds are thick.

6. When using a feather or bucktail jig experiment with various jig sizes until the best size for the existing water and weather conditions is determined. Sometimes a jig as small as 1/16 ounce will be more effective than larger ones regardless of the size of the bass.

7. To catch large bass consistently, once the spawning season has ended, fish the drop-offs near deep water.

8. When a large bass is caught in deep water, fish the surrounding area thoroughly. A large bass taken in deep water is pretty good evidence that a number of big bass are nearby.

9. Don't neglect the middle of the day when fishing for bass. While early morning and late evening are excellent times to fish, many days the noon hour will be better, and this is especially true when fishing deep water.

10. When fishing deep for bass, keep your lure working right on the bottom, or as close to bottom as possible, at all times.

ELWOOD ("BUCK") PERRY, of Hickory, North Carolina, has been acclaimed nationally for "breaking the bass barrier" by developing the "spoonplug" system of bass fishing. Perry invented the "spoonplug," a weird-looking, push-faced, up-ended spoon that goes down deep and, unlike most other deep-running lures, stays there. But the spoonplugs, when fished the "spoonplugging way," take almost unbelievable numbers of bass, and from lakes many fishermen consider "fished out."

Perry has fished for bass in every major bass fishing area in America. He has made fishing news in every bass fishing area, proving out his bass fishing theories time and again. Stories of Perry and his bassin' techniques and his record-making catches have been documented in hundreds (repeat, hundreds) of newspaper articles, on radio and television, and in magazine articles.

PERRY'S TIPS:

1. Learn proper trolling techniques as well as how to cast. One important item in trolling for bass is to keep lures in proper "position." This means if a lure is designed to be fished at a depth of 6 feet, then troll it in water 6 feet deep; if a lure operates at 10 feet, then troll it in water 10 feet deep.

2. Contrary to the beliefs of many fishermen, clear water is not the best in which to fish for bass. If you have a choice, fish water on the dingy side. Clear water makes fish go deep, and also develops weeds that make lure penetration difficult.

3. The two or three day period following a cold front is about the most difficult time to catch bass because few bass will visit the shallows at this time. The fishermen who know about deep-water "structure" and how to fish it are the ones who will get bass during such difficult periods.

4. The older and the bigger the bass, the tighter they "school" in deep water. At the same time, they become more reluctant to venture into shallow water. Thus the better catches of large bass will be made by fishing deep water.

5. Too many bass fishermen put too much faith in the size, color, and action of a lure. They give no thought to how fast the lure should move, or how deep it should be fished. Fishermen should understand that if they do not put a lure or bait where fish are, and move it at a speed to make them hit, then size, color, and action of a lure will do little in putting fish on a stringer.

6. A lot of fishermen believe bass become sluggish in hot weather. Nothing could be farther from the truth. Fish are cold-blooded, so heat increases their body functions— and that is one reason why a fisherman should increase his retrieve or trolling speed in hot weather.

7. Learn all you can about the form or "make-up" of the bottom of your favorite bass lake. Know where the deep water is. Know where the bars and reefs are. Know where muck bottom, hard sand, shell, or clay bottoms are. Keep a record of shallow areas that produce fish, and learn where the nearby bass-holding bottom "structure" is in those areas.

8. So far as consistently successful bass fishing is concerned, at all times except during the spawning season, the shorelines of a lake are good only for holding water in the lake. In other words, if you want bass, and big ones, ignore the shallows and fish deep.

9. Some fishermen when fishing deep water feel that they can cast anywhere and take bass. This isn't so. Bass can

be, and usually are, schooled on the bottom very tightly in deep water. When you get a bass fishing deep, try to repeat those "winning" casts exactly.

10. Fishermen often ask me: "How do I stay with a school of bass once I've found it?" "And what do I do to catch a lot of bass from such a school, instead of just a few?" The answer to both questions is *speed!* The lure must be fished as fast as possible. And the tackle must be tough enough to get a hooked fish out of the school and into the boat as quickly as possible. If the lure is fished too slowly, or if a hooked bass is played too slowly, the school will be lost . . . and only a few fish . . . instead of many, taken.

VIRGIL WARD lives in Amsterdam, Missouri, which is where he manufactures his famous line of "Bass Buster" jigs. But most of the time Virgil is "tending business" not in Amsterdam but at some bass lake far from the plant turning out his popular jigs; but then a lure manufacturer necessarily gets out and "tests" his products. This "testing," though, is precisely why Ward produces top quality jigs, and it also is the reason he is a top flight bass angler.

In addition to manufacturing jigs, Ward conducts "The Virgil Ward Show," a TV outdoor program carried on five stations in Missouri and Kansas. Ward is a member of the Fishing Hall of Fame; winner of the World Series of Sport Fishing, 1962; winner of the National Championship of Sport Fishing, 1964; and also winner of the Outdoor Writers and Broadcasters National Fishing Tournament, 1964.

WARD'S TIPS:

1. When your buddy is after bass with a noisy, top-water lure, but not getting any, try casting a small marabou jig a few feet beyond his lure. Follow his lure with a slow, steady retrieve. Quite often this technique will be very effective.

2. A single spinner type of lure (with a large blade), such as the "Tarantula," can be deadly when fished with a split-tail porkrind eel attached. Retrieve it swiftly across the surface, especially when fishing impoundments that are new and have flooded woods.

3. Before the water warms in the summer, try fishing the "Single Spin" lure with a 4 inch long split-tail porkrind eel. Work it deep and slow. Use a retrieve so slow that the spinner blade on the "Single Spin" doesn't rotate but merely wobbles back and forth.

4. When fishing a "Single Spin" as described, be alert for a strike. The strike may only be a slight drag on the line, or just a "tap." Set the hook at anything that feels "different."

5. The fisherman who knows where to find an underwater spring in a lake will get bass in the hot summer months. Bass congregate around cool-flowing, underwater springs.

6. When using a jig-and-worm, make the cast, let it settle to the bottom, then allow it to remain motionless for 30 seconds or so. Frequently, when you start to retrieve it you'll find a bass already has the lure in his mouth. But don't set the hook immediately. Instead, wait until the bass moves off 8 or 10 feet and then set the hook hard.

7. A lead-head jig with a fiber hook-guard, making it weedless, with a porkrind "eel" or "spring lizard" attached, is a deadly lure in the hands of a good jig fisherman. In fishing one of these lures, cast to ledgy banks and slowly pull the jig off each succeeding ledge. Be ready for strikes as the jig drops from one ledge to the next.

8. When bass are chasing shad on the surface, a top-water lure is great if you can reach the school of bass before they go down. But don't give up just because the school disappears. Instead, try fishing the same area with a ⅜ ounce "Bass Buster" white marabou jig. Make a cast, let the "Buster" sink a few feet, then begin a slow, pumping retrieve. Set the hook hard at the first sign of a strike.

9. Forage fish such as minnows and shad congregate around bridge supports, so bass will be nearby. Use a ⅛ ounce jig in fishing these areas. Let the jig settle a few feet following your cast, reel up slack and get the rod tip close to the surface of the water, then sweep the rod back quickly with a whip-like action. Repeat that technique until the jig is at the boat. This swift fishing of a jig puts a lot of bass on the stringer.

10. When fishing a river for smallmouths, cast at about a 45-degree angle back of the boat. Then fish your lure with a slow, dragging kind of retrieve, keeping the lure coming in very steadily. You'll snag up here and there and lose some lures, but you'll get bass.

A day's fishing on an ocean-going cruiser can be
expensive. If you want good fishing and
your "money's worth," know what to expect of a
charter captain and what he expects of you.

6: The care and feeding of a charter boat guide

One afternoon last January a charter cruiser eased into its mooring at Miami's Pier 5, and dislodged four long-faced, disgruntled fishermen. Their catch totaled two barracuda and one bar jack. The fishermen tramped off the pier, passing happy groups of other incoming anglers who had large catches of kingfish, dolphin, bonito, and several with mountable Atlantic sailfish.

"What happened to you?" asked one charter captain of the skipper who'd just docked and emptied his cruiser of the four luckless fishermen. "Everybody got fish today except you."

"I wouldn't have put those %$X&°$X% into fish if my life had depended on it," replied the angered captain.

"Why not?" pressed the first captain. "What happened?"

"They rubbed me wrong the minute they got on my boat," said Captain Mad. "And they did a good job of it all the rest of the day."

It turned out the four fishermen were beginners at the charter boat game and, of considerably more importance, lacked any understanding of the fundamental courtesies.

To begin, they arrived at the dock 45 minutes late.

The captain of an offshore charter cruiser usually is aboard his craft and readying it for the day's fishing at least an hour before scheduled departure time. He'll have the engines warming and the boat ready to go when you arrive. The captain himself will never be late, and the least he expects of a party is that they be punctual.

Once aboard Captain Mad's cruiser, and late nearly an hour, one of the four fishermen piped up with: "Well, what are we waiting for? Let's get this tub moving."

Captain Mad gave a short lecture on tardiness, and explained further that his ship was not a "tub" but rather a $65,000 Concorde.

Only one of the four fishermen had worn sneakers. The other three had old street shoes and one wore a pair of loafers having spikes. Captain Mad grimaced when he saw that, knowing what hardheeled shoes, and worst of all, spikes, do to mahogany decking. Experienced fishermen know they should wear regular yachting or "boat" shoes, sneakers or some other comparable footwear—for their own comfort as well as to avoid scraping and scarring of decks.

Once out fishing, The Ugly Four criticized Captain Mad's fishing techniques, with such remarks as: "All the other boats are fishin' down that way"; "This bait isn't fresh enough"; "We're trollin' too slow just to save gas"; "How about takin' us out where the fish are?"; "This tackle looks like it came from the Poor Farm"; and "The other boats are getting fish, why aren't we?"

After a time it rained, and Captain Mad had to provide each of The Ugly Four with rain parkas. They complained about the rain and complained about the parkas, which weren't exactly new.

An offshore charter boat captain generally is obliged to provide suitable tackle, but nothing more. Fishermen are supposed to have proper footwear, clothing that is appropriate and comfortable, lunches (it's polite and expected to bring lunch and pop or beer for the captain and mate), rain gear, caps, sun-tan lotion and any other incidental items that will contribute to their personal comfort and add to their enjoyment of the day.

It's not a charter captain's duty to wet nurse anyone.

One of the Four Ugly Fishermen tore one of Captain Mad's rain parkas, and promptly blurted out—"I ain't payin' for it. It was old and rotten." Well, the $30 parka wasn't that old and it most certainly wasn't "rotten," and Captain Mad wasn't going to ask for its dollar value or a replacement. But a sportsman would have either paid the captain for the parka he ruined or would have later replaced it.

In the course of their fishing Captain Mad attempted to instruct the four fishermen in the niceties of handling deep-sea tackle. But each of the four, striving to impress their equally inexperienced companions, took a negative attitude to everything the captain suggested. One of the fishermen had set his drag much too light, and refused to tighten it at Captain Mad's suggestion. Shortly a good dolphin hit, streaked off, and put an over-run tangle of line on the reel that made the reel look like one giant Brillo pad. The dolphin was 150 yards out when the line snapped.

Thus Captain Mad had one of his best reels put out of service, and suffered the expense of hundreds of yards of "lost" line because most of the line on the reel, hopelessly tangled, had to be cut off.

Deep-sea fishing line is expensive. It is not unusual for it to cost well over $50 to spool-up some big game reels with some lines.

Fishermen going out on charter boats without tackle of their own are merely *loaned* tackle by the skipper. As a rule no extra charge is made by the Captain for providing tackle, but he expects fishermen to use it the way he tells them to, and he also rightly expects replacement or payment for any loss or damage to his gear. Many charter boat skippers, having suffered too much loss of tackle, have an understanding with their parties before going out that payment will be made for any tackle lost or damaged through carelessness by the angler. A few other charter skippers, having been "burned" too many times, rent their tackle instead of loaning it at no charge. The small rental fees collected from each party merely provides a kitty for replacement of rods, reels, lines, etc. destroyed by novice or careless fishermen. Charter-boating is a business, and to be successful and pay the skipper a livable return, it must be run like a business.

Most charterboat guides are not in the business because they expect to get rich. They are offshore charter captains, out there sailing the blue every day because they love fishing, love the sea, and love their independence. But they can't sail and can't fish unless they not only meet expenses but also "make a living."

A lot of inexperienced, blue-water fishermen object to the rates charged by charter guides. It is a little difficult to set a national average for ocean charterboat fishing, but these days it would be difficult to find a skipper who'd take a party of four out for a full day of fishing for less than $85. Not many charge over $135. But whatever the fee, the difference between profit-and-loss each day a charter captain fishes is slight. If line is lost or a reel busted, there go the day's profits. If he has to sail too far for too long on a particular day to find fish, there go that day's profits. And the days that he has no charter because of weather, necessary (or other) cancellations, are days with no pay.

And a charter captain's expenses are great. He has high

Charter boats roar out of Miami docks for start of a day's fishing. How pleasant it will be depends on more than the fish.

insurance costs, boat maintenance, gas and oil, dockage fees, bait and tackle costs, *ad infinitum*.

When Captain Mad saw that dolphin taking off with his line, and the remaining line a tangled mess on the reel, he steered for waters where he knew there'd be no fish. He had *HAD* it with The Ugly Four!

He tuned the radio out so his party wouldn't hear the happy fish-catching reports being traded back and forth by other charter captains trolling only a few miles away. And he made the day as short as possible, getting the four fishermen back at dockside as soon as he could convince them that fishing was hopeless.

Possibly Captain Mad didn't handle the situation exactly right. Perhaps he should have informed the four fishermen of their errors now and then, and warned that if things didn't change he'd cancel the trip, take them ashore, and return their money. Many skippers would have done it that way.

But the point is The Ugly Four were wrong and got about what they deserved. The pity is that this sort of thing happens every day, in deep-sea fishing ports everywhere.

Some fishermen, because four of them get together and pay, say, $25 apiece for a day's fishing, expect too much.

For example, one morning early, four fishermen sauntered up to a charter cruiser at Garrison Bite, Key West. There was a sign hanging over the boat's stern reading: "Open today. Party of 4 or 6." The fishermen stepped up and said to the captain, "Hey! You need a party, huh? Can you guarantee us some fish?"

The captain looked at the man steadily, then said:

"No, I can't guarantee you any fish. I'm just a charter boat captain, not God. Ordinarily I can guarantee the average party a pleasant and wholesome day on the water, and most always some fish. But I not only will not guarantee you guys any fish, but I couldn't guarantee that you'd enjoy fishing. And anyway, I'm not now open for charter."

With that the captain removed the sign, and didn't replace it until he saw the the four would-be fishermen drive off.

You'll get the most for your money from about any charterboat skipper if, when you arrive at the dock at the appointed time, you appear pleasant and eager for a day of gentlemanly fun. Don't call the skipper "Hey, YOU!" or the mate, "Hey, BOY!" The skipper has a name, as does the mate. The captain prefers to be called Captain so-and-so, or just "Cap'n" or "Skipper." Under laws of the sea the captain is the ruling authority when you are aboard his boat, regardless of your station in life or money. So maybe your captain for the day *is* "just a fishin' guide"— but he's entitled to and expects a certain amount of respect, and in turn he respects YOU.

A charter captain's boat is where he works every day. It may also be where he lives. A number of skippers sleep and "housekeep" aboard their boats, for various reasons. That cuts expenses. "Living aboard" can also be very comfortable, convenient, time-saving, and also downright pleasant. So a charter captain's boat may also be his "home," and he'll appreciate it if you conduct yourself accordingly when aboard his "home." That means that one doesn't disrupt the order of things, go where he has no business going, put his feet on the "furniture," and so on. Treat an offshore captain's boat as though it were your own, and you'll be welcome back the next time.

There's nothing wrong with imbibing a bit when on an offshore fishing trip. In fact, it is almost the rule. Hardly anyone goes off for a hot day's fishing without plenty of food and drink. Appetites for both are bound to flourish. You'll be thirsty, as well as hungry, and if you are one who enjoys a drink you'll doubtlessly want beer, gin and tonic, maybe even martinis, bourbon or scotch. Fine. You're there to enjoy yourself. You've come to relax and to have fun. But the rules aboard Captain So-And-So's boat are the same as at home: a gentleman and sportsman imbibes with moderation, a bum and a bore drinks too much and gets plastered. A drunk aboard an offshore fishing cruiser is a drag to everyone. He worries the skipper silly because he might fall overboard. He interferes with the serious fishing, and ruins everybody's good time. Almost surely he'll get sick, which the captain or mate will have to clean—and a skipper and his mate feel a little differently about cleaning up after a drunk as compared to cleaning up after a poor soul legitimately sea-sick.

So take your booze and enjoy it—*moderately*. You won't make "brownie points" with the captain, otherwise.

Don't knock an offshore charter captain for not getting you into fish. Just as in all other kinds of fishing, there are days when one skipper of an offshore cruiser literally kills 'em and other skippers miss by a mile. But the next time out results can be reversed. Luck plays its part. However, there certainly are blue-water skippers who are more experienced and are better fishermen than others, and therefore produce decent catches more frequently. So it will help if you strive to learn who the "good fishermen" are and, if possible, arrange to charter them.

If you have a good day fishing offshore with a captain and mate it is customary to give a tip—but not to the captain, give it to the mate. How much? That depends on many things. How many fishermen involved? How good, or how bad, was the fishing? Regardless of fishing results,

did you have a really good day, a mediocre one, or a downright bad one? Was the boat clean? The equipment good? Did the captain and mate do all they could to show you a good day's fishing? If you feel things were not right, because the captain and mate were not right, no tip is in order. You are under no obligation to tip—no more than you *must* tip a cab driver. But if you feel a tip is in order, as is usual, these days you can hardly tip less than $5. If it's been a good day give $10 or $20, and if it's been really great and you can afford it, then the sky is the limit. Tips of $50 and even $100 are not particularly unusual among the "well-heeled" when they have a big day and get a trophy "sail" or marlin for over the fireplace.

Many fishermen making their first bluewater trips are upset when the skipper turns the boat for port after 5 or 6 hours of fishing. The fishermen think they're being shortchanged. Actually, very few charter skippers give 8 hours of fishing; usually it is less. But some, of course, go right on fishing well past the "regular time," simply because they want to fish and want to get their paying customers into fish.

It's wise to find out, though, what length the "fishing day" is supposed to be before making your charter. If you want an 8-hour fishing day, tell the captain. If his normal rate is for 5 hours, he'll make an adjustment and charge you a little more to fish 8 hours, or he'll simply tell you he fishes 5 hours and no longer.

The thing to understand is that, even when a charter skipper has you out for "only" 5 hours, he'll probably put in a 10 or 12 hour day. He's up with the sparrows, getting the boat ready, bait and so forth, and he goes to bed pretty late after cleaning his cruiser, cleaning fish, re-rigging tackle, etc. It isn't the easy life you may think, and regardless of how short *you* think the captain's day may be, it really is a long one.

The best rule in arranging for a day of offshore fishing with a boat captain new to you is to have a full understanding of what is to be done. Don't hesitate to ask questions: Exactly what time do you want us at the dock? When will we return? How much money for us four, or us five, or six? Will you provide the bait? How much bait and what kind? Where will you take us to fish? How much running-time is involved? What sort of fish are we likely to get? Has the fishing been good lately? If we fish hard the way you recommend, what are we likely to catch? How many? What size? Shall we bring lunches and drinks or will you arrange for them? And so on. There's nothing like having a complete understanding of what things are all about BEFORE you start out.

None of the foregoing is intended to indicate that offshore charter skippers are the world's nicest guys, that all of them are honest, and all are good fishermen. Quite the contrary may be true. There are a lot of "bad apples" running boats for hire, although they assuredly are in a minority.

Nonetheless there are some skippers around who will "take you for a ride," and so you should guard against the "bad guy" captain, the one who wears a black hat rather than a white one. If you check beforehand, and hit him with questions such as outlined, chances are you'll learn in advance which skipper wears a hat black, and which wears a hat white.

To catch trout under the low water conditions
of summer and early fall, the
dedicated fly fisherman must play —

7: The midging game

Tiniest of the tiny, this is a selection of Orvis size 28 Midge dry flies.
They are pictured in comparison to a regular No. 16 dry.

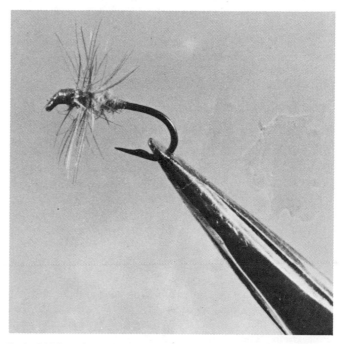

Typical Midge, shown in fly-tying vise, has only short body or thorax
and hackling.

Selection of Orvis size 20 and 22 Midges. They are photographed with a regular No. 12 dry fly.

There is probably no phase of dry fly fishing more perplexing to anglers than fishing over midging trout. The spectacle of trout rising to something unseen can unhinge the most rational of anglers, but those who take the trouble to learn what midge fishing is about find it one of the most fascinating forms of angling.

Midges are minute aquatic insects of the order *Diptera*. They include the *Chironomids*, small mosquito-like flies which don't bite, and countless tiny gnats, including the troublesome "punkies," which do bite. Midges are common to most trout streams and usually are present in great numbers. Despite their small size, midges are valuable trout food and often trout prefer them to larger insects.

Dry flies imitating midges needn't have complicated patterns; generally only a body and hackling are necessary. Of extreme importance is the size of the fly, its form, and the imprint the fly makes on the water's surface film. Real midges do not have tails, so the midge dry should float satisfactorily without a supporting tail. Tails on midge patterns enlarge the fly, and destroy the compact impression they should have (as natural midges make on the surface.)

Authentic size is probably the most important feature of a good midge dry fly. While some of the larger *Chironomids* can be satisfactorily tied on size 18 hooks, most midge dries are best on size 20 to 28 hooks. The selection of midge hackle is critical too, because the fibers should not be longer than twice the gap of the hook. Needless to say, a size 14 hackle tied on a size 20 hook simply makes a size 14 fly. (The exception is the Spider or Variant tie, which does not apply here.)

Female midges lay their eggs on the water then fall spent to the surface, much like Mayfly spinners. Spent midges often are on the water in great numbers, particularly on warm summer evenings, and trout will lie just under the surface in flat water, tipping up rhythmically to take them. The typical rise to a drifting spent midge is quiet and subtle, often belying the size of the taking trout. The trick is to time your cast so that the fly is over the trout at the precise moment of the rise. Accuracy in casting is important too, because the trout will seldom move out of position to take your artificial fly.

The Spent Midge pattern is a favorite of mine, in sizes 20, 22 and 24. The body is made with black tying thread, ribbed with yellow silk. Grizzly hackle is wound criss-cross fashion at the thorax position. Then the Grizzly fibers on top and bottom are trimmed close to the hook, leaving a flat mass of hackle extending out from either side of the fly. Thus the hackle simulates both the spent wings and legs of the natural fly. If the hackle is properly flared the fly will balance well and will float flush on the water.

There is one midge—a small, black-bodied gnat of the genus *Hilara*—which frequently swarms over the water, flying a figure-eight pattern a few inches above the surface. I've seen trout in still water leap out to take these buzzing insects, but it's a difficult fishing situation to cope with since the naturals seem to stay above the water. However, on the South Branch of Michigan's beautiful AuSable River, my wife and I found a clue to this condition that has been helpful. We were fishing above Chase Bridge when the little gnats started buzzing over the surface. The trout were not jumping for them, but periodically a dis-

Chauncy Lively of Pittsburgh developed this "Mating Midge." It is size 22.

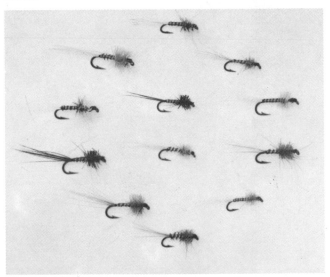

Orvis' new Midge Nymph selection is a non-pupal form of midge fly. Only their small size puts them in Midge category (Nos. 16 and 18 light-wire hooks). During low-water periods of summer, they are excellent on trout too wary to be fooled by larger flies. These are the first commercially-tied Midge Nymphs.

tinct black speck would show on the water, and invariably it was sucked-in by a good trout. Curious about these drifting specks, I picked one up and found it to be a pair of mating gnats. Evidently the erratic flight of the gnats over the surface is their mating flight, with actual mating taking place on the water.

Our solution to the problem was surprisingly simple. Just experimenting, we tied some size 22 dries with dun hackle wound fore-and-aft, and a body of black kapok between. The fly worked like a charm on those tough AuSable browns. We named the new fly pattern "The Mating Midge." I have since substituted grizzly hackle for dun, because grizzly is easier to see on the water. The griz-

Marion Lively casts a Midge on Pennsylvania's well-known Penn's Creek.

zly pattern seems to be equally effective.

Punkies are the tiny gnats Indians and fishermen call "no-see-ums." They have a special affinity for the wading angler, whose best defense is a thick cloud of smoke from a good pipe. But—as miserable as they make life for fishermen—punkies also can bring on a trout rise and thence some mighty fine fishing with the tiniest of dry flies.

The Punkie artificial fly has a yellowish-orange kapok body, and a honey or cream hackle on a size 28 hook. The hackle is positioned further back on the hook than normal to give the fly stability on the water. Because of the shallow bite of the tiny hook, I bend the point out at a slight angle away from the shank. Increasing the bite improves hooking, and is good to do with all hooks smaller than size 22.

Pennsylvania's Penn's Creek is a large limestone stream noted for its Mayfly hatches. It also has a strain of superselective brown trout which sometimes turn up their noses at the emerging Mayflies and, instead, turn their attention to midges on the water. One evening a friend and I were on the "Flies Only" water below Poe Paddy when the trout began midging. But instead of taking with typical, quiet rises, the trout were boiling furiously, often leaping clear of the water. We fished several midge patterns in the conventional way but they received scant attention from the trout. Finally, by putting my face near the water and looking across the stream, I could just discern midges scooting over the surface. Evidently these were ovipositing females, brushing off their eggs by making contact with the water. I started skating a midge dry across the surface and it was nailed immediately by a fine brown that promptly broke off. In the half-hour before dark we hooked trout on nearly every cast by skating midges across-stream, but inevitably as many fish broke off as were landed. The frail tippets needed in midge fishing are simply not built to withstand the shock of a slashing trout, not against a taut leader. But it was fast, exciting angling, and it didn't seem to matter whether our flies were riding on the surface or slightly under, so long as they were moving.

The Skating Midge is the simplest of all midge patterns, having only a small, stiff hackle ahead of a short body. Color doesn't seem to matter much, so I tie my Skating Midges in only two color combinations: cream hackle with natural kapok body, and grizzly hackle with a body of black kapok. Hook sizes are 20 and 22.

The number of genuine midge species is almost infinite, so, an artificial midge of almost any color will be right at one time or another. Kapok is an ideal material for midge bodies because it will not absorb water and it can be readily dyed with common household dyes.

That old saw, "it takes a big lure to catch a big fish," doesn't necessarily hold true on streams where trout are inclined to feed on midges. On the "Catch-and-Release" section of Pennsylvania's Spring Creek there is a good midge hatch nearly every evening from spring until fall,

and the trout are generally receptive to midge flies. Here it is possible to catch trout of better than 3 pounds on a size 22 midge.

Ideally, tackle for midge fishing should be as light as possible. The rod should bend from tip to butt, and it should take a line no heavier than a No. 5 weight, and preferably a No. 4. Leaders should have tippets no heavier than 6X, and sometimes 7X and 8X are necessary for the smallest midges. Threadline monofilament, the sort used for ultralight spinning, is great as tippet material and it can be obtained in the finest diameters. Tippets should be relatively long, two feet or more, since the stretch of the fine monofilament acts as a shock absorber. The best way to strike a fish in midge fishing is not to strike at all. A gentle tightening of the line by gradually raising the rod tip is all that's necessary to send the tiny hook home, provided it's sharp.

Midge fishing, with its refined tackle, is one of the most satisfying forms of fly fishing. A good trout taken on a diminutive fly and hair-like leader is a rich reward. And the angler who is willing to investigate the habits of midging trout—and to learn the techniques of fishing for them—will find that he has unlocked one of the great mysteries of fly fishing for trout.

Chauncy K. Lively

Size 22 Midge fished in surface film of run in background accounted for this mid-summer, low-water brown trout.

8: The best way to bone and fillet fish

There are many ways to bone and to fillet fish. And some methods work as well with one species of fish as with another, while some methods are good only with certain kinds of fish. Probably the most common method of filleting is cutting straight down to the backbone just behind the gill plate, then running the knife along the backbone and cutting all the way to the tail. The meat is then usually cut away from the rib cage and, finally, the fillet is skinned. There's no denying that system of filleting is a good one, but sometimes it leaves bones in the meat, and it *is* time-consuming with some species of fish. The method of filleting and boning depicted here, in pictures and words, was developed by Jessop B. Low, Ph.D., of the Utah Division of Fish and Game. It's a fast, simple method—leading to excellent fillets with no bones—and it works as well on snappers as it does on trout. Try it and see!

1. It's easy to fillet those trout you just caught. All you need is a fillet knife or thin-bladed butcher knife, cutting board, platter, and a special tool for a special trick: a table fork.

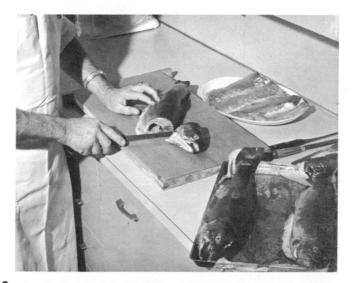

2. After cleaning the fish thoroughly, tackle your filleting job by cutting off the fish's head, tail and dorsal fin on the back. Cutting of the dorsal fin now makes filleting a little easier.

3. Next, turning the fish on its back, cut down through to the backbone that part of the fish from its anal opening to its tail. This divides the fish in half and enables you to spread it apart.

4. Now is the time to bring the table fork into play. Using one tine of the table fork, start at the head end of the fish and working towards the tail end, lift each rib free from the meat.

5. Free all of the ribs on both sides of the fish with your fork. If you do this carefully, you shouldn't leave any bones and the entire backbone and rib cage is removed easily in one piece.

6. Now that the ribs are free from the meat, squeeze down with your fingers on the bones that extend along the fish's back. This frees the rest of the backbone. Then, remove entire rib cage.

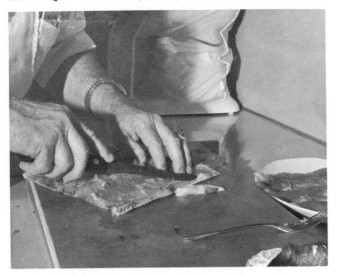

7. The next step is to remove the remaining fins, those called the anal and pectoral fins. Also, now is the time to cut your boneless fish in half. Removing the skin is the final procedure.

8. Holding the fish securely by the tail-end, flesh side up, cut down through the meat to the skin with your knife. Cut just ahead of your fingers, leaving a patch of meat for them to grip.

9. Firmly gripping the tail-end of the fish with your fingers, draw the knife along between the skin and the meat. "Voila," you have a fillet. With a little practice, skinning becomes easy.

10. That's all there is to this quick, easy way to boning and filleting. Prepared in your favorite way, filleted trout or other fish makes a tasty treat without the bothersome bones.

9: Ice fishing for bluegills

Not too many years ago it was something of a chore to catch a mess of bluegills through the ice. But things have changed drastically with new ice fishing methods and equipment.

Today's modern ice fisherman zips along with all his gear in a snowmobile, and ice fishing is so comfortable nowadays that on a nice, winter weekend it's not uncommon to see upwards of 500 men, women and children out ice fishing on one lake. Their prime target usually is the colorful and plentiful bluegill.

Almost every inland lake is stacked with "gills." Some with overpopulation harbor the stunted variety, but many hold the real saucer-sized bluegills that are sought by the modern ice fisherman. These fine little scrappers afford many hours of enjoyment to the winter angler. And, strange as it may seem, this gaily-colored battler can put up quite a fight before he is pulled through the ice hole.

A serious bluegill fisherman is equipped with at least two kinds of bait and two ice rods, plus a multitude of miscellaneous items. The most important part of his equipment is a combination sled and seat, either homemade or commercially produced, used to transport his gear to the fishing site.

Lanterns and catalytic heaters help keep the ice angler warm on cold, wind-swept lakes. A comfortable seat on the sled makes it easy for him to relax, and he'll probably have a new type of ice-auger that can cut through 12 inches of ice in nothing flat.

Those items are the basics for catching bluegills and other fish through the ice. But if you are a real ice fishing addict, you might add a motor-driven auger, a portable shanty, and other non-essential items which make the job a little easier and more comfortable. A welcome addition to ice fishing gear in recent years is battery-operated electric socks. But none of those things are necessary—they're just conveniences.

All that's really needed to catch bluegills is one ice rod, a selection of tiny ice-fishing spoons, a metal or plastic strainer for cleaning out the ice hole, and an auger to cut the hole. Those items can be purchased for about $15.

Finding bluegills is simple. All you need do is drive to a lake and look for the crowd. That's where the bluegills will be. Once at the right spot, cut, chop, or drill a hole through the ice. After the hole is cleaned out, tie an ice spoon to your line, clamp on a test weight or sinker, and lower it to the bottom. When bottom is reached adjust the bobber (provided with pre-rigged ice rods) so the spoon is about 6 inches off bottom. Then the weight is pulled up, bait threaded onto the spoon's hook, and the works then lowered to the pre-adjusted depth.

Bait for bluegills and other panfish usually consists of three popular types: wax worms, corn-borers or mousies. All of these can be purchased at your local bait shop.

To entice bluegills to the bait, use a gentle jigging motion with the rod. After a few jiggles the bait can settle down. Repeat until you have a bite. Constantly watch the bobber to score on these light-biting fish. When the bobber quivers set the hook gently, then haul the fish up hand-over-hand. If need be, add new bait or re-adjust the old one so that it covers the hook completely.

Members of "frostbite brigade" gather at a productive bluegill spot on a Michigan lake.

Bluegill ice fishing isn't always easy. Winter fishing can be just like summer fishing. There are good days and bad days. So, if after a reasonable length of time you don't have any action, it's time to change either the spoon or the depth at which you're fishing. The common practice is to adjust the bobber another 6 inches which will put the bait a foot off bottom. Somewhere, at some depth, the bluegills *will* be found. It's just a question of experimenting with different baits and different depths until you hit the right combination.

If you've given different depths and baits a thorough test, and are still fishless, try a new hole. Often moving as little as six feet can make a big difference. Bluegills run in schools, and usually travel in a definite path. Once you find this route, you'll have a ball catching these little scrappers.

There are many tricks to the bluegill trade. And most of them are learned by practical experience. I believe the most important thing to consistently taking "gills" is the choice of line. Most pre-rigged rods come with 4 to 6 pound monofilament. That's much too heavy for winter bluegill fishing. One or two pound test is heavy enough for these finicky feeders. After all, the heaviest bluegill you can expect to hook will probably weigh well under a pound. In fact, a mess of one-pounders would be something to

Plump bluegills like these are ice angler's reward.

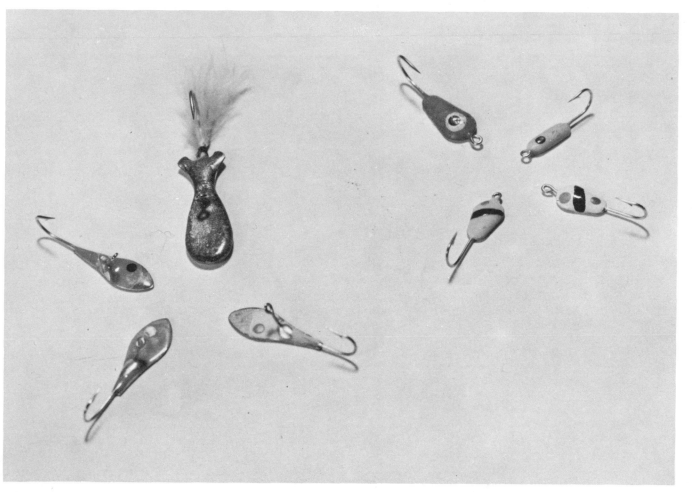

"Swimming spoons" (at left) are new ice fishing lures. When jigged lightly they remain in life-like horizontal position. Older type jigs (right) hang vertically in the water and are pumped up-and-down with rod action.

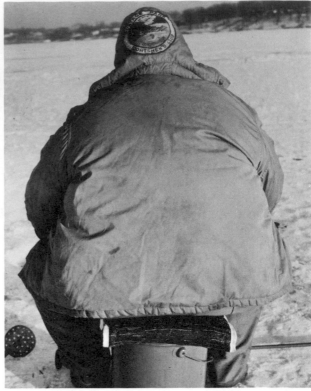

Portable shelters serve as windbreaks. A largemouth bass took this Illinois fisherman's bluegill bait.

A bucket to sit on, warm clothes, and safe, thick ice make it a bluegiller's day.

Some of necessary ice fishing gear includes screw-like ice auger, and ladle to skim ice from hole.

Stubborn bluegill fisherman sticks it out until dark, knowing that early evening can be one of best times for winter bluegills. Electronic "fish-finder" is useful aid.

brag about. Thus everything for fishing winter bluegills should be on the delicate side, including the soft touch you impart to the spoon. At times bluegills will hit a moving bait, but most of the time they wait until it hangs motionless before sucking it in. Either way, the name of the game is slow-and-easy.

There aren't many secrets out on the ice. It's pretty hard to hide the fact when you're catching fish. You'll find ice fishermen the friendliest bunch you've ever run into. They give advice to the beginner, and often they'll show you how to rig and at what depth to fish. After a few trips out on the ice you'll realize that here is fishing well worth the nominal investment required and the few hardships you might encounter.

On many lakes it is possible to drive right out on the ice to the fishing grounds. Although for safety reasons this is not recommended, it nonetheless makes the whole fun-packed sport a lot easier. The rule I use for driving onto the ice is to do it only when lots of others are doing it. Most of the time it adds to your fun if you walk out and get the needed exercise.

One of the best ice fishermen I know has a special system he uses to locate bluegills. He shies away from crowded lakes and favors small, less popular ones. He starts fishing by cutting his first hole in deep water. He then cuts a series of holes going shoreward into shallower water. Bluegills usually move from deep to shallow water in late afternoon. Once the deep water hang-out is found, he follows the fish without having to chop a new hole every time things get slack. This system saves a lot of time when the bluegills start moving.

That same fisherman never uses anything but one-pound test line. He uses small BB split-shot sinkers, and the smallest, most sensitive bobber. On days when the bluegills are hitting lightly, he gets plenty. Yet other fishermen, with heavier equipment, find it hard to detect the light bites.

In recent years a new type of ice spoon has been developed. The old standard tear-drop spoon had the eye at one end; newer models have the eye about a third of the way back from the front end and on top of the spoon. This tying position allows the spoon to hang horizontally in the water instead of vertically. When this new type of ice fishing spoon is moved upwards slowly, it swims much like a live minnow. To make these spoons still more effective, tie them with a loop of line instead of tight to the spoon's eye. This gives them better swimming action.

Despite what some people might think, the new electronic fish-finders can be very helpful in winter ice fishing as well as during summer's open-water fishing. The more sensitive ones, such as the one produced by Lowrance, can be used on top of the ice. A little water will form a conductor for the transducer. It will record the depth and bottom conditions right through the ice regardless of its thickness. Included in my ice fishing gear is a coffee can filled with a mixture of water and anti-freeze. I can scoop out a hole, pour in this mixture, then lower the transducer. It tells me exactly the depth, type of bottom, and whether or not I am over fish.

Placed in a hole next to the one I'm fishing, the machine tells me at what depth fish are running. Then it's just a matter of adjusting my bobber until I get my bait in that magic layer of water. The better depth and fish-finder

Snowmobiles have invaded ice fisherman's world. Because they make it easy to fish many different areas of a lake, snowmobiles are popular with some fishermen. Others, however, dislike snowmobiles and feel their noise causes fish to stop biting.

machines are expensive, but they are as important to fishing as a good rifle or shotgun is to hunting. They'll add fish to the pot—and that's the object of the game. If you're a serious fisherman, one of these electronic wonders should be standard equipment for you.

Fishing an unfamiliar lake for winter bluegills can be hard work. If you decide the ice-fishing crowds aren't for you, then look for new lakes to fish.

When on a strange lake look for a point of land where you're sure there's a shallow bar leading to a drop-off. Start fishing beyond the point in deep water and work toward the shallows. It might take 10 or more holes until you hit pay-dirt, but once the schools of bluegills are found you can have some fantastic fishing.

The usual depth for winter bluegills is 10 to 15 feet. At times you might hit them deeper—say 20 feet, but by and large you'll score most consistently in 10 to 15 feet of water. This is especially true during early morning and late afternoon. The most active time for bluegills seems to be from the time the sun sinks below the trees until dark. This is consistently true during sunny, winter days.

One day last winter a friend and I went by snowmobile to a remote Michigan lake. After two hours of punching holes in different spots, we found the bluegills. We had worked along a sand bar, until we hit the drop-off and found the fish right there on the edge of the deep water. We caught them two at a time. Most were around 10 inches, but a few were 12 and over.

The color of ice fishing spoons can make the difference between a few bluegills and a pail full. I always start with a fluorescent orange spoon. If that doesn't work, I switch to a yellow one or one that is yellow-and-black. As a last resort I try green.

When buying ice spoons be sure to select different colors and sizes. You won't be far wrong getting ones that are yellow, orange, or combinations of those colors.

Finally, remember that to really enjoy ice fishing there are a few items truly worthwhile. A gas lantern or some kind of heater placed under your sled's seat is pure ecstasy when the weather gets rough. If you don't want to bother with electric socks, get a pair of boots with felt liners. There is nothing warmer than felt liners. Rubber insulated boots, on the other hand, just don't stand the gaff in really cold weather.

Hand-warmers are a blessing, especially when your hands get numb from hauling in fish and baiting the hook. A windbreak made of canvas or plywood keeps that cutting cold from getting to you. Many types and sizes of portable shanties are now on the market. One of these, with a lantern inside, makes for real comfort on a blustery, winter day.

I suggest two pair of gloves. One should be large mittens; the second, finger gloves fitted inside the mittens. They'll keep your hands warm, and you can shed the mittens and still do some work with your hands protected.

Another good item is a stocking cap with holes cut in it for your eyes and nose. It will keep you twice as warm as an ordinary cap with ear flaps. The secret to staying warm on the ice is to have warm feet and hands. If they're warm, you won't have any trouble.

Ice fishing has become a family sport. You'll be surprised at the number of family groups you'll see out on the ice. If you can convince your family to give ice fishing that first try, and if you provide them with the right clothing, you'll be heckled all winter to go again.

John Gleason

. . . SOME POINTERS

"Chumming" often brings fish to an ice hole. Chumming can be done by cutting up worms, pieces of fish, minnows, etc. and sprinkling them into the hole. Also good for chumming is oatmeal, crushed egg-shell, canned corn, peas, tiny pieces of silver foil from a cigarette pack, and pieces from crushed Christmas tree bulbs.

Worms, fish-flesh, oatmeal and the like often draw small baitfish which in turn attract larger gamefish such as northern pike and walleyes. Foil, egg-shell, and pieces of Christmas decorations flash and sparkle in the water and will attract fish from some distance.

□

Part of an old toboggan, or a couple of skis the kids have discarded, can be used to make the bed of a fine ice fishing sled. All you need do is nail a suitable wooden box to the toboggan (cut in half to appropriate size) or to the skis, one

on either side of the box (skis also should be cut to suitable lengths).

An ordinary child's sled, with box mounted on it, also makes an ideal ice fishermen's rig. Such outfits are needed for hauling bait, lunches, thermos, rods and other tackle, heaters, etc. to and from the ice fishing spot.

□

Some of the best baits available to the ice angler come from the fish he catches.

The eye of a yellow perch impaled on a small hook will catch you more perch. You can trim a small sliver of wedge-shaped skin with a little flesh attached from the belly of a perch, bluegill, crappie or walleye and use it for bait. Be sure to jiggle the rod slightly when using these fish-flesh "wedges" so the bait will seem alive.

Pieces of fish gills and fins also make good ice fishing baits.

In the dead of winter most fish are somewhat lethargic and do not move around much. Since they probably won't come to you, you'll have to go find them.

Regulations of most states prohibit the number of "rods" or lines the ice angler may employ at a time, but there is not usually a restriction as to the number of holes you can try.

So cut several holes, at varying locations, and try all of them until fish are located.

□

Don't discard old, worn-out fly lines.

While most ice fishermen prefer regular ice "rods" and "reels" with monofilament line, others have found that old fly lines make very serviceable ice fishing lines.

Being thicker than light nylon, fly lines are easier to handle with gloved hands (which may also be a little numb). Of course, a leader must be used with the fly line, but it can be a short one.

□

Ice-creepers are worth having if you do much ice angling. These spiked foot-coverings may fit over only the front half of the foot, or they may cover the entire foot. Either type is useful, and works satisfactorily in helping you to stay on your feet when walking on ice.

Good ice-grippers are inexpensive (far less than a doctor's fee for setting a broken leg or patching a banged knee), and they make hiking over ice less tiring.

□

One of the best ways to catch walleyes and lake trout through the ice when the fish are in deep holes is with live minnows, preferably shiners, golden roaches, and chubs ranging 4 to 8 inches.

Tie a heavy sinker to the end of the line. Four feet up from the sinker tie on a 6 foot length of monofilament, with hook attached. Fasten a minnow to the hook, and lower away through your ice hole.

The sinker will settle to the bottom, but the minnow will be able to swim freely—and attractively—with no hindrance from the sinker's weight.

□

It's desirable when ice fishing to attract fish in every way possible.

You can try "chumming" fish in various ways, or drawing them by lowering spinners or flashy spoons on lines which will sparkle and flash and get the attention of fish.

Many experienced ice fishermen even brighten the surfaces of lead sinkers they use, knowing that every bit of flash helps bring fish to the bait. Split-shot sinkers rubbed around in a handful of steel wool will brighten; a knife scraped over a larger lead sinker will give it a bright surface.

□

With experience at deepwater jigging a fisherman learns to take fish without even feeling bites or nibbles. He sets the hook in a taking fish almost intuitively.

A jig-and-snatch technique is used in working the bait. The bait is jiggled actively for a time, then a sudden upward yank is made which, hopefully, catches a fish at the moment he sucks in the baited hook. Once the angler gets this method down pat it is remarkably effective.

□

The ice angler after panfish such as white bass, bluegills, crappies and perch usually finds fish at the end of points, over bars, around rocky ledges and in deep holes.

However, fishermen who want northern pike or Eastern chain pickerel usually find these fish in weed beds, which means in shallow bays or coves in most lakes.

□

In general it is desirable to set the hook quickly in fish that tend to nibble at bait, fish such as yellow perch, bluegills and crappies.

But northern pike and walleyes, as well as chain pickerel, should be given slack line and time to "fool" with a minnow before the angler sets the hook. Such fish tend to seize the bait broadside and go off with it, with the hook not in their mouths; and they take their time in turning the minnow and swallowing it.

Give these species enough time to "run" with a minnow, to properly "mouth" it, then set the hook hard.

□

Night fishing often is more productive for the ice angler than is daytime fishing.

The most productive hours for ice fishing for any species seem to be shortly after daybreak, around noon, at dusk, and after dark. Why this should be isn't readily explainable, but history proves such times to be best as a rule.

Night fishing often is exceptionally good through the winter season, although many fishermen ignore this fact. In some areas the finest crappie fishing is had late at night by fishermen working with gasoline lanterns set up on the ice. Possibly the light of the lanterns attracts fish to the baits.

□

Whether you fish surf, bay, or
brackish river, here are the special

10: Techniques for
Pacific stripers

Birds wheeling over surf show fishermen Pacific bass are feeding.

Striped bass fishing on the Pacific Coast has been growing in popularity ever since "linesides" were introduced in 1879 to California waters from New Jersey's Navesink River. Pacific anglers have learned many techniques of striper fishing from bass addicts on the East Coast, so today you'll find thousands of "striped bass buffs" along the Pacific.

The Atlantic stripers that were introduced to Pacific coastal waters took to their new environment so well that they spawned successfully in the brackish waters of the river deltas. Interest in fishing this great new western gamefish has risen steadily right along with the increasing population of "stripers," and today the striped bass is considered the top salt water gamefish of the California Coast.

There are three chief reasons why striped bass have prospered so well on the West Coast: they are the delta rivers, the coastal bays, and the Pacific Ocean. The great Pacific, San Francisco and other bays, and the rivers provide ideal feeding and spawning grounds for stripers. Though the rivers, bays, and ocean are all linked together, each offers a specific kind of striped bass fishing. California striper fishermen even classify their bass fishing according to type—either delta, bay or surf.

Different angling techniques, baits, lures and rigs are used depending on the area fished.

FISHING STRIPERS IN PACIFIC SURF—

Mid-June along the Pacific Coast marks the arrival of spawning smelt and anchovies. Migrating northward from the warmer waters of southern California and Mexico, these small fish swarm by the hundreds of thousands along the sandy beaches of central California. It is here that the smelt (or grunion) find beaches with just the right consistency of sand and gravel in which to lay and fertilize their eggs. It is the smelt and anchovies that attract striped bass to California's inshore waters in mid-June.

Large adult stripers, returning from upriver spawning runs, feed heavily on the smelt to restore the fat and vigor lost from spawning. The fish that run the beaches are husky bass; though school fish, they will range from 15 to 25 pounds. Occasionally a 30-pounder will be taken.

Most of the action occurs close to shore, usually as the smelt are spawning in the surf. The stripers push constantly on the baitfish, and thrash the surface in a frenzy. The sight of a full scale "bass bust," as it's called, is something that draws merchants from their stores, causes traffic jams, and in general creates considerable excitement.

Usually the smelt spawn two or three times a day, which means the bass will "bust" two or three times a day. By June 15 the bass runs are usually heavy, and they generally last until mid-August when the baitfish schools have been depleted and scattered. The peak of the surf striper fishing ordinarily is between July 1 and 5.

It is easy to spot bass "busts" far offshore, as well as when close-in, because a bass feeding orgy attracts shearwaters. Shearwaters are black-and-white sea birds similar to seagulls. They feed on baitfish scraps left by the striking bass. During a good bass riot the sky will be black with diving, screeching shearwaters.

There are many party boats that chase surf-feeding bass,

but most anglers fish from the beaches. Surf-casting for these savage "linesides" is extremely productive. And the surf striper fishermen of the West Coast are every bit as professional and dedicated to their sport as are those striper hounds on the Atlantic's Cape Cod.

A Pacific surf caster's tackle consists of a heavy surf rod ranging in length from 10 to 15 feet. Reels (either spinning or casting) are loaded with as much 20 to 40 pound test monofilament or braided nylon as they will hold.

Waders or wet suits are standard clothing, but some surfers brave the 50-degree water bare-legged.

Less than 10% of Pacific surf-casters use bait. Feeding bass occasionally will take a dead baitfish or cut bait, but lures or plugs are the proven baits for these surf-roaming bass. The idea is to hit the beaches during a bait spawn—when you can see the stripers busting all over the surface. Anglers tossing 4 ounce metal lures or large plugs cast beyond the first breakers then retrieve at a moderate pace. If a bass "bust" is on and you place your lure properly, you're sure to pick up a fish. These surf stripers hit hard, and it takes muscle and coordination to manipulate a hooked fish through the heavy surf and onto the beach. Few Pacific surf-casters use nets or gaffs. The accepted way to beach a Pacific striper is to slide him onto the beach with the aid of an incoming wave.

Distance is important in Pacific surf-casting. Since the surf is continually rough, anglers must cast their lures beyond the white water of the rolling breakers. Through necessity many Pacific surf addicts have developed into fine distance casters. Flat, 4 ounce metal lures (usually

Night fishing in California surf accounts for many large stripers.

Husky bass is gaffed after being hooked while trolling outside surf. Boat fishing often is more successful than surf casting.

chrome) are preferred since they can be cast great distances.

Surf-casters who are sure-footed and who like to get away from the elbow-to-elbow beach crowds take to the rocky cliffs for their fishing. Usually after heavy feeding sprees the stripers will abandon the bait schools, if only briefly, to come in close to the rocky cliffs where they can rest in deep, surging pools. It is here that the "rock hounds," using big jointed underwater plugs and attractive surface lures, tease the resting bass into striking. From a spot high above a rocky ledge you can easily see a school of bass in the clear water below. If the fish do not strike readily the rock casters use noisy surface plugs to tease the bass into hitting.

On days when the coastal bass runs are heavy, as many as 400 stripers will be caught in a few hours from beaches less than a mile long.

FISHING STRIPERS IN PACIFIC COASTAL BAYS—

San Francisco Bay annually supports a very heavy run of striped bass. Migrating stripers come in from the Pacific Ocean to spawn, swimming under the Golden Gate Bridge into 'Frisco Bay. They then pass through connecting San Pablo Bay. Here a few stripers migrate to the Napa River, which empties its brackish waters into San Pablo Straits. The majority of the fish, however, push on to the Suisun Bay region, where they have a choice of two main fresh water rivers and a maze of slough areas in which to spawn. Sweet waters from the mighty Sacramento and San Joaquin Rivers, backed up by high tides, fill hundreds of twisted miles of excellent striper spawning sloughs.

Fishing pressure is heaviest in San Pablo and San Francisco Bays. The spring runs of striped bass virtually flood these bays, the stripers fattening on anchovies, smelt and

Ten popular—and productive—metal lures and plugs used by Pacific Coast striped bass anglers.

School bass frequently swarm in Pacific coastal bays. Legal minimum size in California is 16 inches.

Selection of streamer flies that do the job with Pacific stripers.

herring before migrating into the river delta areas.

Bait, lure, plug and fly fishing all are accepted methods of angling for bay bass. In the lower southern end of San Francisco Bay, many anglers prefer the shallow, tidal flats for their fishing. Here school bass in pursuit of baitfish gather on the evening incoming tides, and provide excellent sport for light tackle anglers. Heavy lures are out because of the shallow water on the flats. But, wobbling lures up to ½ ounce can be deadly.

For the fly-rodder, the flats described are about the only place along the entire coast where a fly fisherman can toss a streamer fly with a floating line and really take fish. Other areas call for heavy sinking lines.

From early spring through fall, San Francisco Bay usually is alive with feeding striped bass. In April, May and June, school bass come in to feed and fatten before heading for the spawning areas. By July, and through August and September, the spawned-out bass return to again feed and fatten.

Some bait fishing takes place during the spring, summer and fall months, but the majority of successful bay bass fishermen find wobbling lures, flies and plugs best.

Party boat angling for bass is extremely popular and effective in both San Pablo and San Francisco bays. Live bait, lead jigs, plugs and metal lures are effective.

Trolling for stripers in the bays is also very good. Most popular method is trolling a 1 or 2 ounce lure or plug with a porkrind strip. Best trolling speed is about 4 knots. Trolling is productive because the fishermen can move about the bay until they run across a school of stripers.

There is as much or more shore fishing around the bays as there is boat angling. Though shore anglers are limited

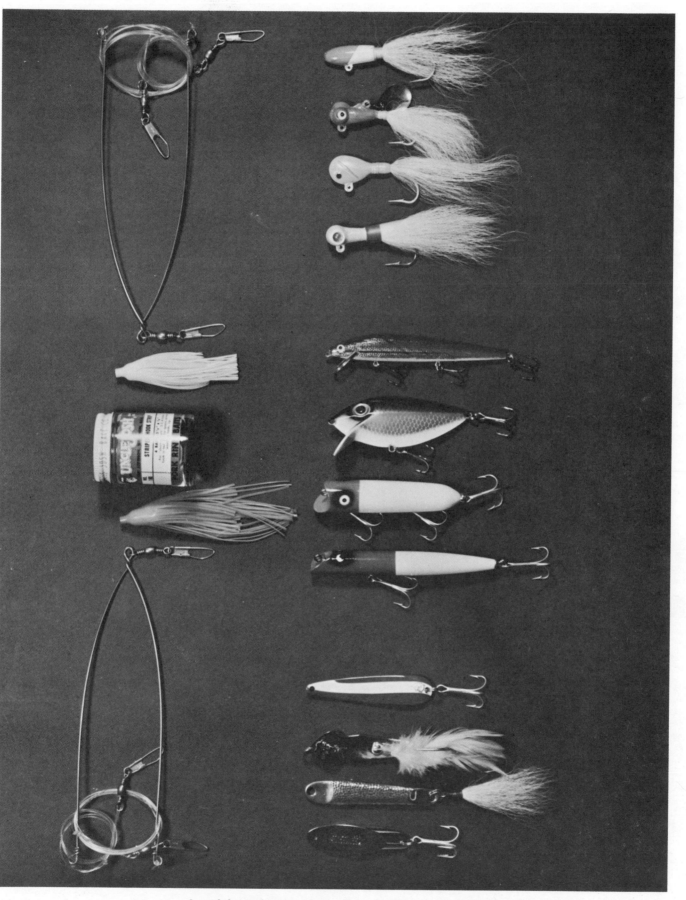

A good choice of spoons, plugs, and jigs for stripers in the Pacific Coastal bays. Some coastal anglers use two lures by rigging with spreaders, shown at left in photo.

Bay anglers cast small (½ ounce) plugs and jigs for stripers and usually do well.

Delta rivers feeding the bays are prime spots to find large spawning stripers.

With three nice bass draped over side of Jeep, bay anglers spot birds working over stripers.

Still fishermen use cut bait to work an upper river area for spawning bass.

Larry Green (left) and companion with bass taken on flies in San Francisco Bay.

in their fishing areas, they do well with stripers on high tides.

Bay bass, whether school fish or big loners, can range in size from 6 inches to 40 pounds. The average is probably between 6 and 15 pounds.

FISHING STRIPERS IN PACIFIC RIVER DELTAS—

The coastal river delta areas with their hundreds of miles of brackish, tide-affected waterways, are the vital nursery of the entire West Coast striped bass fishery. Ninety per cent of the Pacific spawn comes from the delta country. Steelhead, Pacific salmon, and also shad share these remarkable spawning grounds with stripers.

The majority of the big stripers taken in California come from delta waters, as it is there that the huge adult female bass—ripe with spawn—come to nest in late spring. The only reason more anglers do not fish the deltas is because the delta waters are discolored by snow water during the spawning season. The water is so dirty then that using spoons, plugs, or flies is almost useless.

The only really effective way of taking those big stripers (they often exceed 50 pounds) is with cut bait or live bait fished on or near the bottom. The stripers find food pri-

marily through their sense of smell, as they seek locations for spawning. Good cut baits include sardines, anchovies, squid, sand crabs, pile worms and mackerel. Live baits such as bullheads, shiner perch, or fresh water minnows are also productive.

When fishing cut baits most anglers use a sliding sinker type rig, which allows the bass to pick up the bait, run and swallow it, before he feels any resistance. Fishing the sliding sinker rig with either a free-spool reel, or an open bail on a spinning reel, is the best method.

When fishing live baits, a slider-type sinker sometimes is used, but most live bait anglers employ a small float that is adjusted to keep the bait just off bottom. A large 5 to 7 inch bullhead of the salt water variety is the preferred bait for big bass.

Most bait fishermen in the delta areas fish large sloughs stripers swim through to reach smaller sloughs where they spawn. Some trolling from small skiffs and party boats is done in the big, lower sloughs—places such as where the San Joaquin and Sacramento Rivers meet.

Thus, from the rolling breakers of the Pacific Ocean, through the rich bays and into the river deltas, California is now "home" to the Pacific Striper.

Larry Green

11: Fishing underwater structure for bass

My wife, Margie, and I were unloading our boat when a couple of local fishermen came over to admire the limits of largemouth bass we'd caught.

"Boy! Are you people lucky!" one of the surprised fishermen exclaimed. "My partner and I fished all day but we caught only one small bass. What'd you catch *those* on?"

I told them the lure we had used, then went on to say that they should have asked *how* we caught our bass rather than *what* we caught them with. I further explained that, while the lure we had used was a good one, *where* we had used it had been the key to our success. I told those curious fishermen that although Margie and I had never fished that lake before, still we were able to catch a good string of bass because we concentrated on *fishing underwater structure*.

As the two fishermen started away one turned and said: "We'll have to get some of those lures if they're what the bass are hitting."

Margie just looked at me and shrugged. "If they won't listen," she said, "you can't do anything about it." Maybe I gave those fishermen a poor explanation of structure fishing, and perhaps I tried to explain too much too soon. Whatever—I've experienced the same thing many times: try to tell a bass fisherman that it is important *where* he fishes, and still he'll ask you what lure to use.

With so much written that extolls the "killing qualities" of this lure or that one (as in tackle ads), it is not surprising that the average angler thinks the lure is the key to successful bass fishing. He keeps searching for a magic lure, failing to understand that it is not the lure but rather where and how it is fished.

When E. L. "Buck" Perry, the "Spoonplug Man" from Hickory, North Carolina, first proposed his bass migration theory some 20 years ago, and emphasized fishing deep underwater structure, he was ridiculed by most fishermen. However, Perry's theories have withstood the test of time and have proved highly successful for those fishermen with the patience to try something new. Unfortunately, not many fishermen have been exposed to Perry's methods enough to become skillful at fishing underwater structure. Worse, some refuse to believe in Perry's system and so they continue fishing in the same old way—and not catching the same old bass. Something else hard to understand is that fishermen unhesitatingly fish underwater sand bars and reefs for walleyes or lake trout, yet they can't be persuaded to fish those same areas for bass.

Underwater structure can best be defined as a section of lake bottom elevated above the surrounding bottom. Such structure has many forms. It can be a hump of land forming an underwater "island," or it can be a shoreline peninsula, or point, that, running out from shore, continues on underwater. Underwater structure also can be the shoulder of a submerged channel, or the bank of a river or stream flooded via construction of a dam. Underwater sand bars and reefs are additional kinds of structure.

Regardless of type, underwater structure will be important to your fishing success only if it extends to, or is immediately adjacent to, the deepest water in the area. Deep water is necessary because it is the "home" area of mature bass; contrary to popular opinion, bass exceeding 3 pounds spend most of their time in deep water. Except for the spawning period, and for short periods in the fall, adult bass spend little time in the shallows. If you want to catch bass consistently after the spring spawning season, you *must* accept the fact that mature bass are nearly always deep.

Some fishermen will conclude that if bass are deep most of the time, all they need do to catch them is to fish deep. That would be correct except for two things: bass in deep water are tightly schooled and hard to locate, and while down deep they are at least semi-dormant and reluctant to strike.

Fortunately, bass will leave their deep water sanctuaries once or twice a day if conditions are favorable. When they

The day is young, so this "structure" fisherman starts by casting the shallows off a point. He'll probably soon move to deeper water, knowing that's where big bass are most of the time.

do leave their deep water hideouts, they follow definite "paths" or routes to, along, and over the underwater structures mentioned earlier—the structure that is *nearest* the deep water. When moving out of the deep water a school of bass occasionally will migrate all the way to the shallows, but usually they swim only as far as the edge of the underwater structure. After the spawning period the only way you can catch bass consistently is to understand their deep water habits or "patterns," and to fish the underwater structure. Incidentally, fishing the deep, underwater structure can be productive even during the spawning season since all of the bass don't spawn at the same time, and some do not spawn at all. Thus there always are many bass with "deep water patterns" even during the spawning season. However, it is not my intent here to discuss spawning season angling methods, but rather to explain the techniques of fishing for bass deep—which is where they are through most of the angling season.

The bass fisherman must be able to locate, and to recognize, important underwater structure. What is "important" structure?

As explained earlier, "important" or good structure will be near deep water. It also will have an abrupt drop-off or "break" at the deep water end, and it will be fairly flat on top. Structure with a steep grade from the shallows to the deep water, and without a discernible drop-off at the deep water, is not important structure and will produce few bass, if any. The deep end of the structure should be in comparatively deep water, with the water at the break or drop-off greater than eight feet. Many lakes do not have breaks deeper than 6 or 8 feet, so there's no choice but to fish those shallow drop-offs. When there are deeper breaks, however, they are the better ones to fish.

A contour map is useful in locating a lake's important underwater structures. Many state conservation departments, as well as sporting goods stores, have contour maps of area lakes available free or for a slight charge. Deep water areas are shown on such maps, and they are good places to begin looking for important underwater structures. A particular contour map may show contour lines

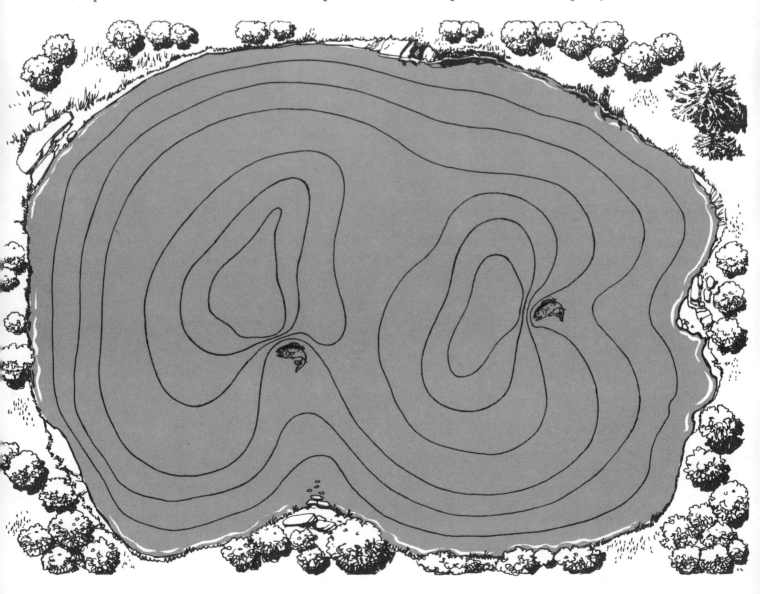

Contour map sketch of a lake—Predictable bass contact points are marked with a fish.

very close together, near deep water, and that indicates a sharp drop-off at that point. If the contour lines then become more separated, from the sharp break shoreward, that indicates a relatively flat area is adjacent to the deep water —so you can bet your sweet bass that you've found, just with a map, an important underwater fishing structure.

The next step, of course, is to go fishing and to take the map along. Cast or troll the structure until you have it outlined, identified, and "pin-pointed" in your mind. An electronic depthfinder will help and, in fact, will locate underwater structure for you even when you do not have the aid of a contour map.

Asking questions of local fishermen also is helpful in locating underwater structure. There's usually someone who can tell you where the deepest water in a lake is, and may volunteer that a certain section of the shore is good when the bass "are biting." You can be certain that that part of the shoreline is not far from important underwater structure and a deep hole used by the bass. Nearly always good underwater structure will be found somewhere between the shore recommended as a good fishing area, and the deep water. If you've fished a lake before, and if at time you've caught fish along a certain shore, apply the same technique and begin working from shore out towards deeper water, continually searching for good underwater structure that you can identify and outline.

When on a lake and fishing, another easy way to find underwater structure is to locate a peninsula, or point of land, extending into the lake. The underwater portion of a point can be checked with an electronic depth-finder, or by casting, to determine if it has the characteristics of important structure. The profile of a peninsula or point of land will *usually* indicate its slope underwater, but not always.

It's simple logic to utilize a point on shore to find underwater structure. Not so logical is to find good underwater structure by using *flat areas* on shore. Lakes that are surrounded by rough, hilly terrain will have points of land that generally result in poor underwater structure as the points continue out into the water. Such points usually are too short, too steep, to be productive of good bass fishing.

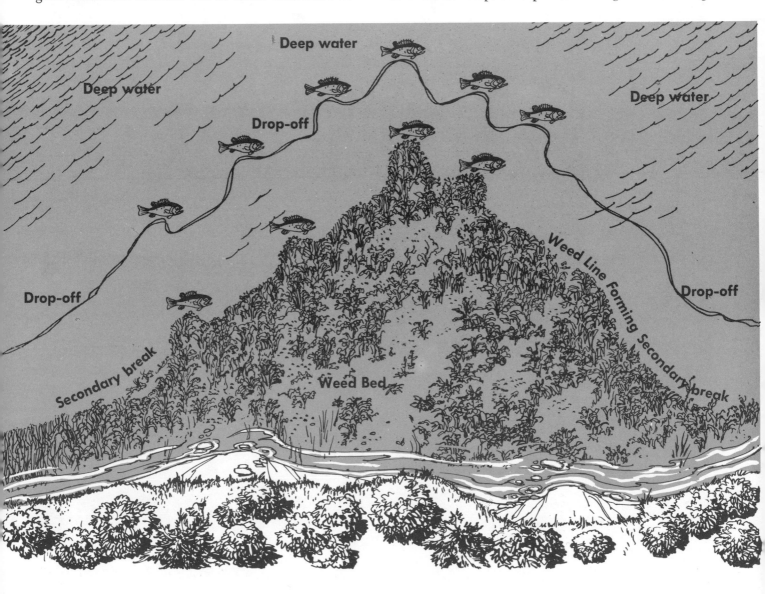

Large underwater structure showing probable bass contact points marked with a fish.

A not unusual catch for "structure" fishermen. Guide Forrest Wood of Flippin, Arkansas holds results of 1 ½ hours of structure fishing at Bull Shoals Reservoir.

On such lakes a break in the normally rough shoreline—such as a small meadow, field or other relatively flat area—nearly always is a sign of good underwater structure nearby. There's usually good structure at such places because the top of the structure will be flat, compared to the structure formed by the steep points of land that extend into the water. Some of the best underwater structures I have fished were in lakes surrounded by rough terrain. I simply ignored the more obvious points or peninsulas, after a cursory check, and concentrated on the structures indicated by the relatively flat areas ashore. Such underwater structures usually are broad, flat areas that extend into a lake some distance, and then break sharply down at deep water.

Another simple method of locating good underwater structure is to check weed beds. Weeds need sunlight to grow, and so can grow only at depths penetrated by sun-light. Thus the clearer the water, the deeper you'll find weeds. Generally speaking in any lake (all other factors suitable) weeds will grow out to the point where the water drops off to a depth where there is insufficient penetration of sunlight at the bottom for weeds to grow.

Weed patches can indicate underwater structure provided the top of the structure is not deeper than weed growth. If the depth of weed growth is not the same as the depth of water at the drop-off, the entire structure will be outlined by weeds. If the deepest part of the structure is deeper than the weed growth, it may still be indicated by the weed patches, especially structure that starts shallow and slowly deepens to the drop-off. The outside edge of the weeds will follow a fixed depth and will outline the shallow part of the structure. By fishing from the edge of the weeds out to the deep water, the outline of the structure at the drop-off can be determined.

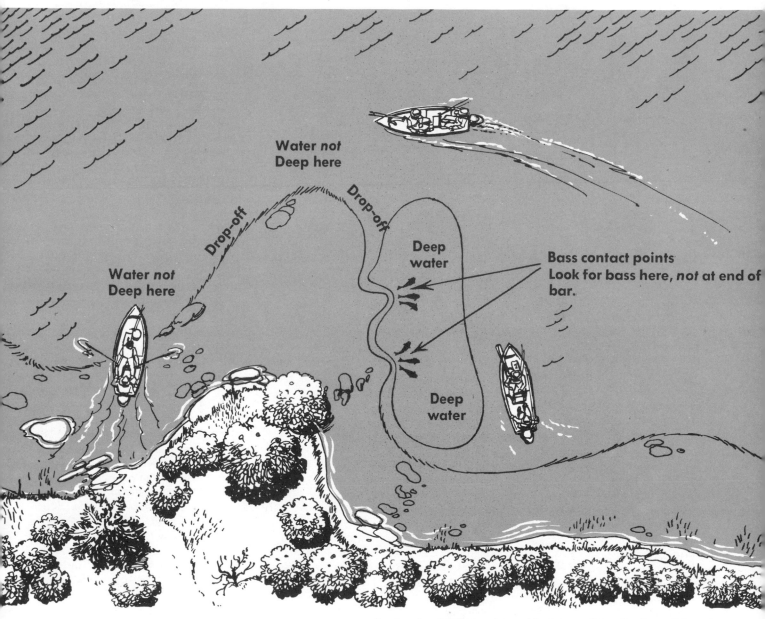

Structure showing deep water on side of narrow bar rather than off its end.

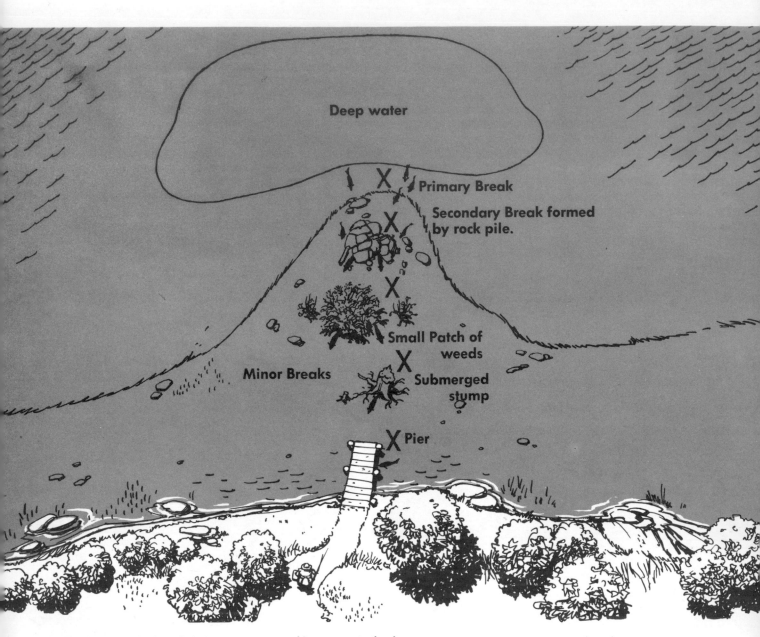

Deep water

X Primary Break

Secondary Break formed
by rock pile.

X Small Patch of
weeds

Minor Breaks X Submerged
stump

X Pier

X—Stopping points for bass during any movement reaching near or to the shore.

Learning *how to locate* underwater structure is of little value unless you also know *how to fish it*. It is especially important to know *where* on a given structure you should concentrate your fishing efforts.

When bass leave deep water they normally move only as far as the drop-off before they halt. They may remain at that break for a time, and then return to the deep water or, if conditions are right, they may continue over the structure to another break. This second break could be anything that alters the relatively flat profile of the general structure. It could be a weed line, a pile of rocks, a sunken tree or log, a sharp rise in the profile of the structure, etc. The migration of bass from deep water toward shore will not necessarily be a continuous move, but rather a series of moves from one break to the next. When bass return to the deep water from any of these breaks, they usually

return in the same way—that is, stopping at each break along the way. When bass are spooked, however, they'll rush back to the deep water without halting at any of the breaks.

When a normal migration of bass occurs and they continue on towards shore and into shallow water (6-8 feet deep), the fish will scatter and individually move to those small "breaks" that are common in shallows—a pier, anchored boat, tree stump, piling, rocks, and so on. When such a strong, inshore migration or movement of bass occurs the angler who fishes the stumps, piers, etc. will have top fishing. Unfortunately, such complete, inshore migrations do not occur often, so the fisherman who does shallow water fishing exclusively will go fish-less most of the time.

Because bass stop and hold at breaks on major underwater structure, concentrate on those breaks when fishing any structure. If the break covers a small area, such as a rock pile or narrow bar, fish the entire area. When a break is formed by the drop-off of a large underwater structure, then a different approach is required. The break line could be a half-mile long if the structure is large, and considerable time could be wasted trying to fish all of it. Fortunately bass don't contact a structure at its drop-off in random fashion when they leave deep water. Instead, they swim out of deep water at only a few places, and those places are determined according to the structural characteristics of the drop-off. These "contact points" do not change from day to day, not even from year to year; they remain contact points indefinitely unless the structure changes. By knowing what structural features to look for you can predict most of the contact points along a given drop-off, and can then concentrate your angling at these points. When contact points are identified a marker buoy can be placed over them, and your fishing can then be guided by the markers.

There are a number of structural characteristics that may determine bass "contact points" along a drop-off, but usually only three are of major importance: 1) structure closest to the deepest water in the area; 2) an abrupt drop-off into the deep water; 3) a projection or bulge at the drop-off. The key is the deepest water in the area, and its location must be determined to know *where* on the structure you should concentrate your fishing. Never assume that the deepest water is off the end of an underwater point or bar. Quite often the deepest water in the area will be to one side of a bar. On such structure the *side* of the bar rather than its end will be the area in which contact is made as bass leave the deep water.

When you are certain of the location of deep water in the vicinity of structure, concentrate your efforts on that part of the structure nearest the deepest water. Look for places where the drop-off is steep, and for bulges in the break line. Any and all such spots could be contact points for bass when they leave the deep water. When a deep hole that bass "use" is quite large, and when the adjacent structure also is large, then you can expect a number of bass contact points. When the deep hole covers only a small area, and when the underwater structure is small, there'll be only a few contact points, and possibly only one. Remember that a contact point can be a small pile of rocks or any other small obstruction or projection on the break line or drop-off. Those are the places to fish.

When in water deeper than 8 feet, bass nearly always are right on the bottom. So your lure should be fished on or very close to the bottom, particularly when fishing a drop-off or any deep break. The exception is when fishing a weed line—then all depths should be fished. If fishing a steep, abrupt drop-off be sure to fish the entire slope from the deep water to the very top of the structure, and to keep your lure on the very bottom all the time. Bass at the drop-off will generally be located about even with, or just below, the top of the structure. But at times, and particularly if the drop is considerable, you'll find the bass well down the drop-off slope.

The length of time bass remain at a break may vary from a few minutes to an hour or more. A lot depends on the clarity of the water and its depth. Bass will visit a break more frequently, and stay for longer periods, if the water is dingy rather than clear. Structure with a deep drop-off, say 15 feet or more, also encourages frequent visits from deep-water bass, and because of the good depth they are likely to stay for comparatively long periods.

In very clear water bass are reluctant to move out of deep water onto structure unless the drop-off is very deep or the light penetration low, as on a cloudy day or in early morning and late evening. Many fishermen prefer to fish clear-water lakes, but good fishing for bass on such lakes is harder to find than on lakes with dark, dingy water. This is not to say, of course, that there is no good bass fishing

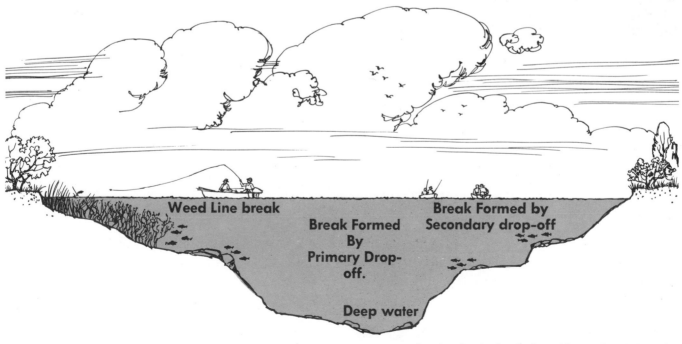

Structure showing breaks formed by weeds and drop-offs.

Fishing structure takes other species in addition to bass—like these big walleyes from Lake Wisconsin, a dammed area on the Wisconsin River in central Wisconsin.

structure will, as a rule, indicate the outline of the structure. A weed line break will have characteristics similar to those found in a break line that is formed by a drop-off. But a weed line will, of course, be in water of a constant depth, the depth depending on water clarity.

When fishing a weed break concentrate on that part of the weed line adjacent to deep water, and give special attention to weed projections nearest the deep water. One difference in fishing a weed line break—as opposed to fishing open-water drop-offs—is that all depths of water along the edge of the weeds should be fished. Also, since bass are more inclined to scatter along the edge of weeds than they are at another type of drop-off, the entire weed line near the deep water should be fished.

The best way to start fishing a weed line is to ease in close to the weeds, quietly as possible, and anchor your boat at a spot right against the weeds. Then cast parallel to, and as close to the weeds, as possible. All depths should be worked, from the top of the weeds to the bottom. And check back into the weeds, using weedless and surface lures. However, if the weeds are unusually thick—a matted wall—then fish the open pockets and the outside weed line, fishing especially carefully any bulges and projections of the outside weed edge.

Sometimes an underwater structure will have a sharp rise, in effect making the structure two-level. The drop-off from the first level to the second may be only a foot or so, or it may be several feet. The deeper the water at a secondary drop-off the more important the break, although even if the water isn't particularly deep bass will stop at this break during any movement towards shore. All the suggestions I've given for fishing a drop-off at deep water apply to fishing a break formed by a secondary drop-off. That is, fish the section nearest the deep water thoroughly, and be on the lookout for projections (rocks, stumps, etc.) on the break and concentrate on fishing around those. Again, all the limitations imposed due to clarity of water, depth, light penetration, etc, apply to fishing secondary drop-offs just as they do to fishing primary drop-offs. Always—the deeper and dingier the water the more frequent bass movements are, and the longer they stay at a particular break.

It's important to remember, of course, that the least important breaks on any underwater structure are tree stumps, logs, rocks, etc. that are located in shallow water. Contrary to what most fishermen believe, such cover in shallow water is not a permanent "home" to mature bass—and they will not be found around such cover in decent numbers once their deep water "patterns" are established following the spawning season.

For a variety of reasons there are bass fishermen who never will learn to fish underwater structures properly. That will be their loss.

With fishing pressure and boating traffic increasing yearly on our "civilized" lakes and rivers, bass fishing will become less rewarding for more and more fishermen. But those bass fishermen who are willing to change their old-time tactics of continuously casting along shore, and who concentrate on finding and fishing the underwater structures, not only will catch more bass in spring and fall but many more through the "dog days" of summer, as well.

Don Nichols

on clear-water lakes; to the contrary, there is superb fishing on many lakes having gin-clear water. But such lakes usually provide the best fishing (excluding spring and fall) if fished on dark, cloudy days, or in the late evening and pre-dawn hours—and if the fishing is done on the deep-water breaks.

As indicated earlier the drop-off is the primary break on an underwater structure, but the other breaks such as weed lines, ridges, etc. can be very productive when a strong bass migration continues beyond the drop-off. Of all the secondary breaks one of the most important to the bass fisherman is the break formed by a weed line.

Much of this was explained previously, but it is important to your successes as a bass fisherman to remember that the outside edge of underwater weeds growing on

12: Glossary of knots

Tarpon fishing is a test of the angler's knot-tying skills.

A friend once wrote that a knot is "a means of fastening together the parts of one or more flexible materials such as rope, line, or leader, or of fastening such material to a stanchion, mast, or cleat. Knots include bends, hitches, and splices."

That is probably as good a definition of a knot as is possible, but it doesn't help the fisherman who wants to learn how to tie one.

The average angler under average fishing conditions need know only a few knots. For example, probably 90% of fishing situations can be taken care of by the fisherman who knows how to tie a "clinch knot," a "barrel knot," a "double surgeon's knot," and a "nail knot." However, there are many dozens of different kinds of knots, and under certain circumstances each is valuable. Thus a skilled fisherman can tie several kinds of knots.

All other factors being normal, the angler's knots are the weakest part of his equipment. More prize fish are lost because knots pull out, slip, or cut themselves than are lost because of a broken line, fractured rod, or jammed reel. In some kinds of fishing—say, still-fishing for bluegills—knot-tying may be relatively unimportant; but in other kinds of fishing, such as tarpon angling, billfishing, taking large northern pike on flies, etc., skillful knot-tying means the difference between boating fish and losing fish.

In learning to tie a new knot it is better to practice it with heavy cord or light rope rather than with monofilament or other fishing line. The heavier material will show more clearly how the knot is shaped and formed, and once the knot is quickly and easily tied with heavy material it then can be readily tied with fishing line.

After a knot is formed it must be slowly and carefully drawn up tight. Almost without exception, knots that are not properly tightened pull out. In some instances it is easier to tighten a knot in heavy monofilament nylon if the line is moistened with saliva prior to forming the knot.

Any knot will reduce the strength of fishing line to some extent, and this includes the so-called "100% Knot." But some knots, such as the "Double Surgeon's Knot," reduce line strength more than others. The average quality knot, however, when properly tied should reduce line strength to no more than 85% and the best knots will give around 95% of the line strength.

SINGLE SHEET BEND **DOUBLE SHEET BEND** **DOUBLE EYE KNOT**

1. Tie a "Single Running" Knot (half-hitch) to end of leader and push thru eye of hook.

2. Pass loop over bend of hook and draw up to hook eye.

3. Take short end of "Single Running" Knot, push under loop, against the shank, and draw tight.

4. Finished knot.

SLIDING OVERHEAD KNOT **ROUND-TURN FISHHOOK TIE**

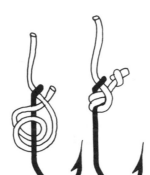

RETURN KNOT

This is used for tying a fly or lure to a leader, and it may also be used for tying the tippet end of your leader to your fly. It is a little more difficult than the Turle or Figure Eight Knots, but it is very strong and especially well adapted for nylon leaders. The easiest way is to tie it directly on the hook, as follows.

Figure 1

Thrust the end of the leader through the eye of the hook. Pass it down behind the hook and up the front, holding the loop open between your thumb and forefinger, as shown in Fig. 1.

Then make a second turn behind the first, holding the loop again open, as shown in Fig. 2.

TURLE KNOT

Figure 2

Next pass the end under both loops, and pull on the standing part of the leader. As the coils draw up, be sure that the loops are pushed over the eye of the hook, as shown in Fig. 3.

DOUBLE TURLE KNOT

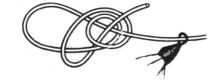

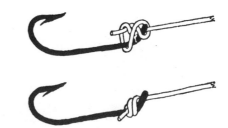

Figures 3 and 4

Finally, pull up the knot tightly and it will appear as in Fig. 4. This is the neatest and probably the most secure of all hook knots.

FIGURE EIGHT KNOT

CLINCH OR "HALF-BLOOD" KNOT

IMPROVED CLINCH OR PANDRE KNOT

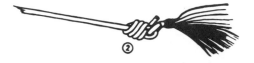

JAM KNOT WITH AN EXTRA TUCK

CLINCH ON SHANK

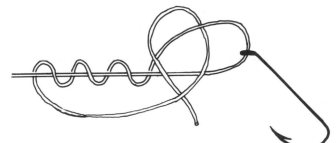

DOUBLE LOOP CLINCH KNOT

LOOP KNOT

JANSIK SPECIAL

HOMER RHODE LOOP

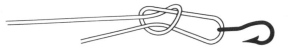

DAVE HAWK'S DROP LOOP KNOT

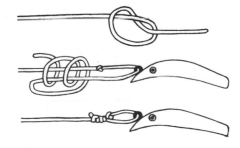

Tie a simple knot in leader about 5 inches from end and draw it tight. Pass end of leader thru eye of lure bringing it back parallel with running leader. Bend terminal down and around, forming a circle below parallel strands. Pass end around and thru circle in leader twice. Draw it tight, slowly. Pull on lure and the jam knot will slide down to the simple knot, leaving lure attached with a loose loop permitting it to vibrate or wiggle freely.

NAIL LOOP

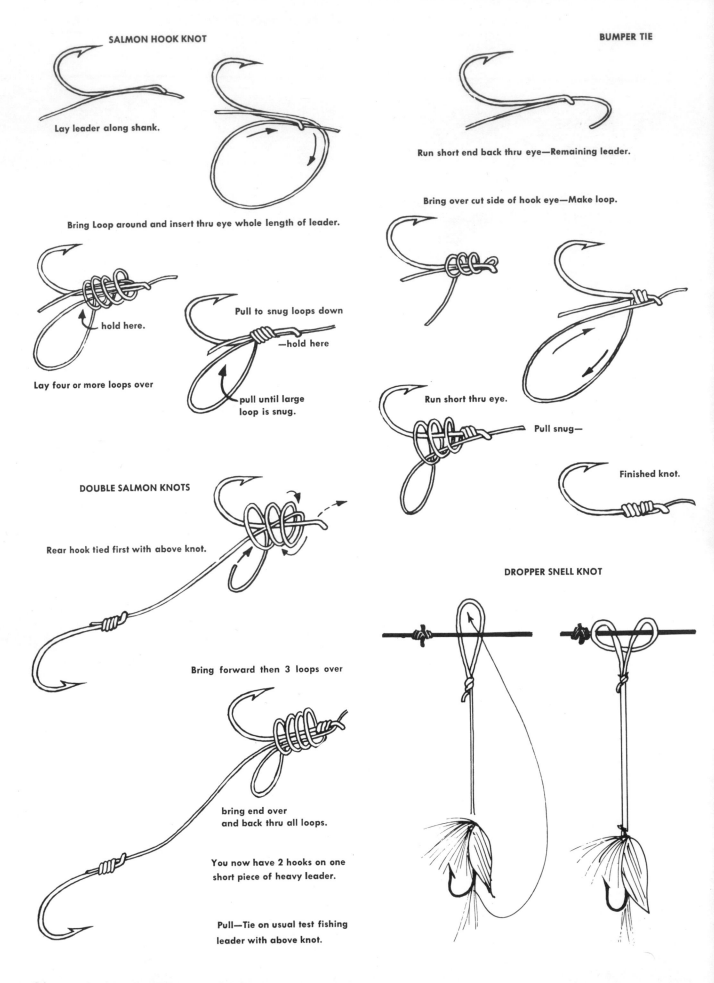

SALMON HOOK KNOT

Lay leader along shank.

Bring Loop around and insert thru eye whole length of leader.

hold here.

Lay four or more loops over

Pull to snug loops down
—hold here

pull until large
loop is snug.

DOUBLE SALMON KNOTS

Rear hook tied first with above knot.

Bring forward then 3 loops over

bring end over
and back thru all loops.

You now have 2 hooks on one
short piece of heavy leader.

Pull—Tie on usual test fishing
leader with above knot.

BUMPER TIE

Run short end back thru eye—Remaining leader.

Bring over cut side of hook eye—Make loop.

Run short thru eye.

Pull snug—

Finished knot.

DROPPER SNELL KNOT

OVERHAND DROPPER TIE

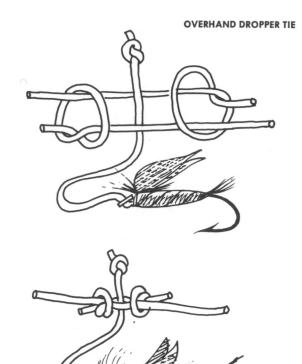

PERFECTION LOOP KNOT

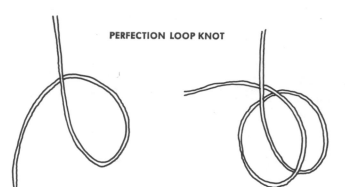

1. The Perfection Loop Knot is tied by first making a single loop (left) and then another loop over it as at right.

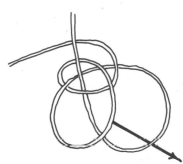

2. Holding the loop bases between a thumb and forefinger, a small wrap is made between the two loops. Then as the arrow shows, the top loop is passed through the lower.

EXTENSION BLOOD KNOT

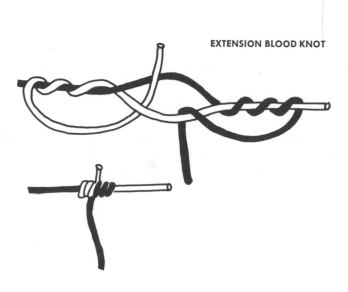

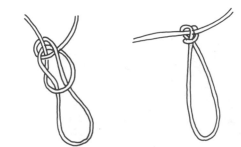

3. The knot is completed by pulling all the slack leader into the dropper loop until the knot becomes hard as at right. The final loop should be 2½ to 3 inches long.

EMERGENCY DROPPER KNOT

This is also used for tying dropper snells to a leader. As shown below this knot is simple and strong, but is recommended only in cases where tying the Extension Blood Knot is impractical.

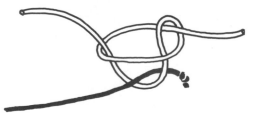

IMPROVED DROPPER LOOP

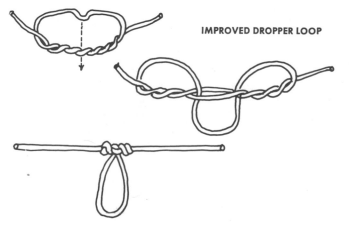

MULTIPLE CLINCH KNOT

This is used for joining a line to a leader. Many bait casters use nylon leaders of 6 or 8 feet in length, and consequently they need a knot which will join the line to leader with little or no bulk so that it will pass from the reel through the guides with a minimum of friction. Such a knot is subject to extreme wear, and for this purpose the Multiple Clinch Knot illustrated below is ideal.

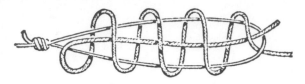

DOUBLE IMPROVED CLINCH KNOT

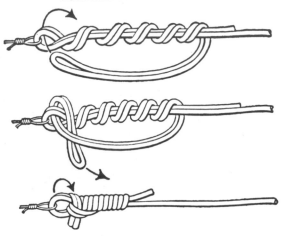

COMPOSITE KNOT

1. Six Turns—Tighten Heavy Knot First

2. Clip ends close

SURGEON'S KNOT

BLOOD KNOT

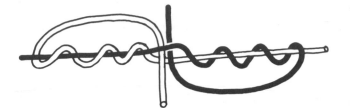

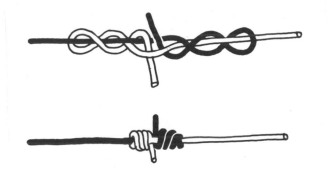

IMPROVED BLOOD KNOT

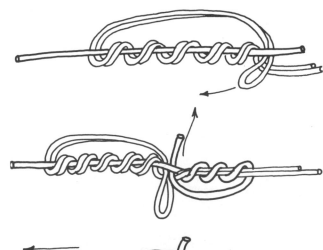

TUCKED SHEET BEND KNOT

For joining a line to leader, this is the safest and easiest knot to tie.
In this knot the end of the line is brought back and "tucked" through
the loop on the end of the leader. The four following illustrations show
the method of tying this knot.

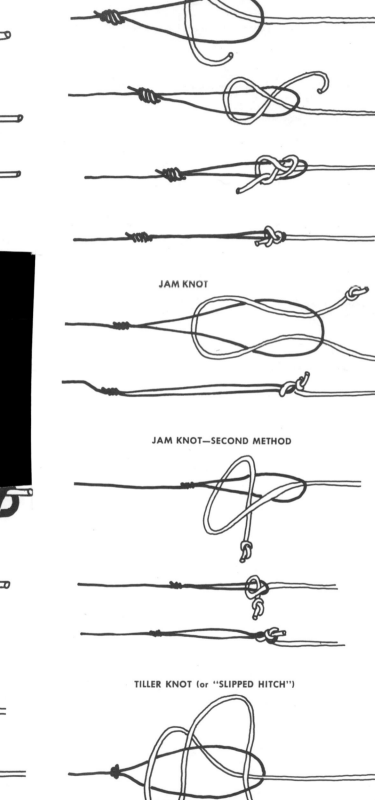

JAM KNOT

JAM KNOT—SECOND METHOD

TILLER KNOT (or "SLIPPED HITCH")

LEADER KNOT
(for tying Nylon to Nylon)

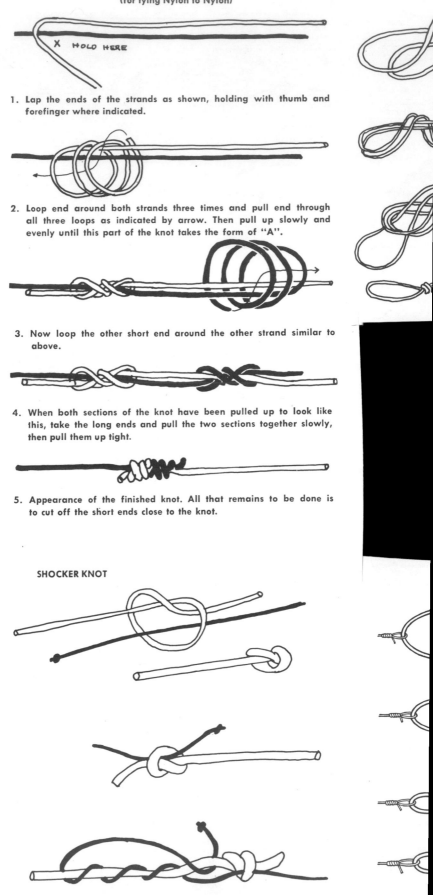

1. Lap the ends of the strands as shown, holding with thumb and forefinger where indicated.

2. Loop end around both strands three times and pull end through all three loops as indicated by arrow. Then pull up slowly and evenly until this part of the knot takes the form of "A".

3. Now loop the other short end around the other strand similar to above.

4. When both sections of the knot have been pulled up to look like this, take the long ends and pull the two sections together slowly, then pull them up tight.

5. Appearance of the finished knot. All that remains to be done is to cut off the short ends close to the knot.

SHOCKER KNOT

NAIL KNOT

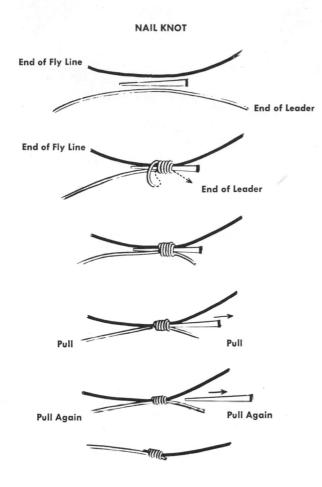

Pull

Pull

Pull Again

Pull Again

NAIL KNOT USING LINE LOOP INSTEAD OF NAIL

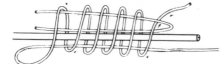

Make approx. 6 turns with end of leader, as illustrated. Bring end of leader out through loop in short section of monofilament.

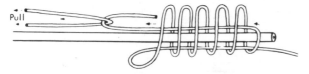

While holding loops together with thumb and forefinger, grasp both ends of short section with other hand, and pull entire piece, along with end of leader, back through 6 loops as shown. Trim section of mono.

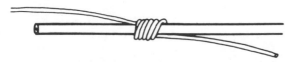

Pull leader from both ends to tighten around body of fly line.

Trim the end of fly line and leader at ⅛." Be sure knot is pulled up tight before trimming.

DOUBLE NAIL KNOT

OFFSET NAIL KNOT

"KEY" KNOT SPLICE OR "KEY LOOP"
(Also called Albright Special)

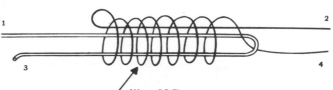

Wrap 12 Times
on Light Monofilament

Hold lines at position B and position A. Retaining position A firmly with thumb and forefinger, pull line 3 tight. Retaining position B, pull line 2. Holding lines 1 and 3, draw knot tight. Trim 3 and 4 close to knot. This knot ties nylon braid to monofilament or monofilament to monofilament. Flows thru guides for spinning, and makes a non-slipping, small splice for tying fly line to leader.

KNOT FOR FASTENING BACKING TO REEL

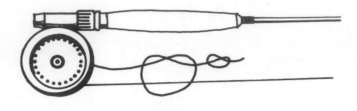

NEEDLE KNOT

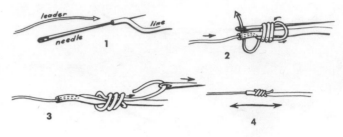

KNOTTING BACKING TO FLY LINE

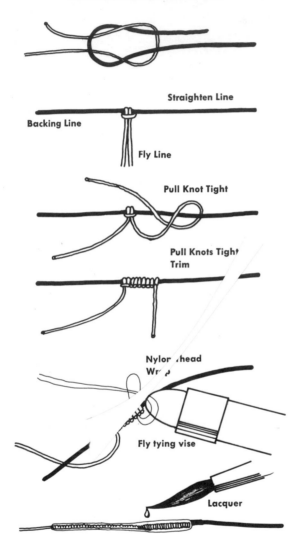

Straighten Line

Backing Line

Fly Line

Pull Knot Tight

Pull Knots Tight
Trim

Nylon Thread
Wrap

Fly tying vise

Lacquer

THE CROTCH SPLICE

← 2¼" → ← 2¼" →

1. Fray out line ends for about an inch. A pin or needle does this job.

2. Spread the frayed ends as shown and push forked fibers together.

3. Wrap splice as shown, cut off protruding fibers.

4. Wrap over thread splice and lacquer.

MAKING A FLY LINE LOOP ← 3" →

1. Dip 3-in. length of line butt in acetone or nail-polish remover and scrape clean.

CUT---

2. Fray end and cut.

3. Fold trimmed end to form loop.

4. Wrap tightly with nylon thread, leaving open loop. Varnish, or lacquer.

QUICK FLY LINE SPLICE

← 1¼" →

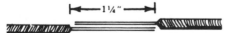

1. Clean 1¼ inch of each line end with acetone or nail-polish remover and place lines side-by-side.

2. Wrap ends together with tight turns of fine nylon thread. Give finished splice two or three coats of varnish.

FORMING FLY LINE LOOP ← 1" →

1. Clean and scrape an inch of the fly line end.

2. Place ends of a piece of bait-casting line to fit as shown above.

3. Wrap with nylon thread and varnish.

Want to be alone? Want to camp under the stars?
Want to catch big pike, smallmouth bass,
walleyes, lake trout? And for not much money?
Then a fly-out, camp-out, fish-back
Canadian wilderness trip is for you.

13: Poor (and rich) man's fly-out fishing trip

Big Twin-Beechcraft can make wilderness flights with two canoes aboard, plus passengers and camping gear, tackle, etc. Fishermen are flown out to wilderness lakes, then camp and paddle back.

The author of this story, Bob Cary, is a former big-city outdoor writer who gave up a metro newspaper job to "take to the woods permanently." He now runs "Bob Cary's Canadian Border Outfitters," at Box 117, Ely, Minnesota, 55731. If you like what he reports on in this article, write him in Ely for details.

You can make a full week's fly-in canoe vacation into some of the north country's finest bass, walleye, northern pike and lake trout fishing waters for less than $85. It's a fact!

The cost includes float plane charter, canoe, tent, sleeping bags—all necessary equipment plus a week's supply of specially-packed trail foods. But these trips are only for the angler who has a yen for adventure in his makeup, who has at least a rudimentary knowledge of camping, and who can read a map. These trips are the north country's newest fishing adventure, and they involve flying into 3,600 square-mile Superior-Quetico Wilderness on the Minnesota-Ontario border, then fishing and camping as you travel back out by canoe.

Where I live, in the heart of wilderness 16 miles northeast of Ely, Minnesota, (only a rifle shot from the Canadian border) canoes are a way of life and float planes are used more than the family car. Nobody knows who originated it, but the fly-out, canoe-back idea was as inevitable as the warm spring winds that roll up from the south each April, banish the snow and open the 1,400 wilderness lakes that lay frozen rockhard all winter under 40 below zero temperatures. Each spring, as soon as the ice cover is off, we start flying.

In the Superior-Quetico area two main flying services are used for canoe trips. Pat Magie's Wilderness Wings Airways is located in Ely and operates Cessna 180's for two men and their equipment, and a Twin Engine Beechcraft for four or more men and gear. And at Atikokan, Ontario, on the new highway linking Fort William with Fort Frances, is Earl Thurier's "Pioneer Airways" which uses float-equipped Cessnas for the small jogs and a big Husky for the heavy loads.

In the Superior-Quetico country there are over 20 good canoe routes where an angler and his partner (or groups of four, six or eight) can fly out and canoe back—but let's just consider two of the best and give details.

A Cessna 180 is used frequently for "fly-out", "canoe-back" trips. Canoes are lashed to pontoons.

Canada Customs station on island in Basswood Lake is a check-in point for border area canoeists.

At Ely, Minnesota, there are ten experienced outfitters who put together canoe camping outfits for about $9 per person per day. That price includes all food and equipment, right down to the cooking kits and matches. Grumman canoes are most commonly used although Aluma-Craft canoes run a close second. In this granite country, experience has shown that aluminum canoes stand the wear better than anything else. Also, the light-weight metal canoe is a distinct advantage both in transporting by plane and also on an angler's shoulders as he portages from one chain of lakes to another.

All equipment is scaled down in weight. Special back-packing tents are used—the kind that weigh only 8 pounds in 7 x 9 size and with over 6 feet of headroom. Sleeping bags are Dacron-filled and vary from as little as 4 pounds to 6 pounds. Air mattresses or foam pads provide a comfortable night's sleep, and the whole outfit for two men, cooking equipment and all, stows in a single No. 3 Duluth pack.

The food goes in a second large Duluth pack, box-reinforced and plastic-lined to prevent damage or watersoaking. Modern trail foods duplicate just about anything the sportsman eats at home, and include such tasty entrees as steaks, chicken, pork chops, ham, beef-and-gravy, etc. The freeze-dried foods also include spuds, rice, and an assortment of other vegetables. You get a full meal by simply adding water and heat.

For the outdoorsman who isn't too sure of his paddling ability, there are lightweight 3 horsepower and 1½ horsepower outboard motors for rent to be used either on a squareback canoe or, with a light aluminum sidebracket, on a double-end canoe. Five gallons of outboard gas will take two anglers over almost any Superior-Quetico route they select.

Personal gear includes the angler's fishing tackle, toilet articles, first-aid kit, insect repellent, clothing, camera and film. All else is furnished by the outfitter. For canoe wear, recommended clothing is tough pants, wool sox with ankle boots (sneakers are also good in the canoe), wool and cotton shirts, extra underwear, and a hat or cap to protect from sunburn.

All the gear described can be assembled in two packsacks, although some fishermen using an outboard and traveling heavier may take three.

Most charter flights out are made from the Wilderness Wings seaplane base at Ely, or from any dock owned by an outlying outfitter. A single canoe is lashed to the floats of a Cessna 180, or two canoes can be transported inside the cargo hold of a Twin Beech. Packsacks and tackle are stowed in the cabin, so now we climb aboard, fasten seat belts, and the trip gets underway.

First stop is at the Canadian Customs station on Ottawa Island on Basswood Lake, just a few minutes by air from Ely. Here we list our equipment with the customs officer, pay a duty of 40¢ per day on our food and pile back into the plane. On the return trip we will check through U.S. Customs at Ely.

We take off again and soon a breathtaking panorama of green forest and blue lakes stretches below us. In places there are bright patches of meadow, with light green wild rice growing beyond the edges of nearby muskeg. Here and there a ribbon of river twists through the forest, in places slow-moving and black, in other places rushing over granite ledges and white with foam. Before long the pilot throttles back, drops the flaps, and the plane touches down. The floats throw thin showers of spray as we taxi to a sand beach where the orange and white flag of Canada flies over a Ranger Station. This is the "jumping off" point where our $8.50 non-resident fishing licenses and $5 camping permits are purchased, and it is also where we glean bits of information on where the fish are hitting and on what.

The canoe is removed from the plane, loaded with our gear, we climb in, certain that we have our map handy in a water-proof plastic case, and then we push off into the

It looks rough, but fisherman in reasonable condition doesn't have much trouble portaging both canoe and motor.

Bob Cary is *where-it-is* and shows *what-its-all-about*. For just a few dollars a day, *YOU* can do a wilderness fly-out, camp-out trip and get smallmouths like this.

wild country. The plane roars once again, skips over the lake's surface, and vanishes in the sky. There is a great silence—made complete when the ranger's cabin disappears behind the first point of land—and now we are at last in a land little changed from that era when Pierre Radisson, Grosseliers, Peter Pond and Alexander MacKenzie crossed these same waters in birchbark craft to explore the fur country to the north and west.

From La Croix there is a portage to McAree Lake, so seldom used muscles complain in the arms and legs as the canoe and our packsacks pull down with unaccustomed weight. On the shore of McAree fishing rods are rigged and underwater lures, spinners, or jigs are tied on. Across from the portage a rocky reef juts out of the water, and the first cast brings a smashing strike from a husky smallmouth bass.

Two more bass follow the first, but all three are released. (The food pack contains thick steaks for our first night's supper).

Farther down the shore is a slick heading into a thunderous rapids where McAree spills down a six foot incline into Brewer Lake. At the top of the rapid, just before it dips into the foam, our jigs pick up four fat walleyes and these, too, are released. The fishing was just an interval to "get the-kinks-out" and to see if the fish were hitting.

Next we canoe southward three miles to Rebecca Falls, a white torrent that drops into McAree in twin chutes of foam from Iron Lake above. Opposite the falls, on a flat shelf carpeted by pine needles and sheltered by a grove of huge Norway pines, we pull in and set up our first camp. The tent is slung under a frame of birch poles, and soon a pot of coffee is steaming at a rock fireplace.

Lunch is a hurried affair because, there before us, is the big pool of Rebecca Falls. It's as full of fish as a man could wish! For several hours in the afternoon sunlight, we hurl an assortment of lures into the swirling waters as the canoe drifts around in the eddies. In spring it is possible at Rebecca Pool to catch lake trout, walleye, northern pike and smallmouth bass on successive casts, but now, in warm weather, the trout are in the depths of the lake . . . but the other three species are filling the pool. (I know four men who once fished Rebecca Falls and in six days caught and released, by actual count, over 700 walleyes. And I've been there when there were no walleyes, but the place crawled with slabsided smallmouth bass).

A trail winds around part of Rebecca Falls. It's a narrow path over slippery rocks, and looks directly down into Rebecca's roaring cauldron. At the end of the trail is another pool where several five pound smallmouth bass are always ready to smash lures. Around more granite ledges, to the east, is yet another, larger torrent—Curtain Falls. Curtain Falls drops 30 feet with such thunder that it is almost impossible to hear someone shouting who is standing right next to you. Five rapids curl and break in a series below the falls where it tumbles into Iron Lake. The lower four of these can be run by canoe, and in each pool below the chute other schools of bass, walleye and northern pike lie waiting.

Fishing fever somewhat abated, we finally head back to our camp at Rebecca Falls and sit before the fire in the long northern twilight while steaks hiss and sizzle on the grill. And later, as night comes on and the stars fall to

After a day of fishing and paddling, walleye fillets, beans and coffee would delight a gourmet.

rest on the pine tips overhead, we step into the tent, zip the mosquito door shut, and crawl into dry, fluffy sleeping bags for a night of unbroken rest.

On succeeding days, we portage past Rebecca and Curtain Falls to aptly-named Crooked Lake, with its 14 miles of meandering channels and dozens of islands. The bays we fish for walleyes and northern pike, while the weedbeds and reefs are loaded with surfacing bass in the evenings. When we feel like it, we gorge on platters of golden-fried walleye fillets. At other times, we play chef with the various packaged foods that make up our slowly-dwindling grub pack.

We spend two days in the rocky chasm of the Basswood River, taking bass after bass from the series of currents, rapids and falls that dot its course all the way to big Basswood Lake. At one point, just upriver from an ancient voyageur's campground at Table Rock, we pause to observe a series of Indian pictographs stained into a rock overhang more than 300 years ago by a Dakota or Ojibwa hunting party.

The last day of our trip the last big portage is negotiated around Upper Basswood Falls and onto broad Basswood Lake. And here, like the Indian canoemen of history, we offer a silent prayer for a good tail wind so that we may push our fragile craft the final 27 miles back to civilization before sundown. For a week we have turned the clock back more than a century . . . and are the better for it.

A second trip, if we are in a mind for a similar adventure another year, can be made from Beaverhouse Lake to Quetico Park Headquarters at French Lake on the north perimeter of the Superior-Quetico wilderness. From Earl Thurier's base on Crystal Lake, we'll fly with our canoe and gear to a Ranger Station on Beaverhouse that once was the site of a trading post for local fur traders. Earl will land the plane and we'd taxi to the Ranger Station. We'd go through the formalities of checking in, procuring licenses and travel permits, and then we'd push off eastward toward the rapids and portage that mark the entrance into long Quetico Lake.

This is trout, walleye and northern pike country, so maybe we'd troll a spoon while cruising down Quetico to a small, un-named lake that leads into big, clear, Jean

Giant pike like this—which Bob Cary says weighed 25 pounds—are fairly common rewards for flying out-canoeing back.

Beautiful, usually nameless spots like this walleye hole are spotted throughout the Quetico-Superior wilderness.

Lake. If lucky, we'd have picked up a couple four pound lake trout while trolling, and these we'd butter and bake in aluminum foil for dinner. But if our luck was poor or it was the warm part of the year and the trout were too deep, we would take a short side trip up a narrow, winding beaver channel cut through the muskeg and push our canoe onto tiny Conk Lake. Conk Lake is teeming with walleyes, black-backed and orange on the belly, and they'd hit our yellow plastic worms and small spinners greedily. We would pick out four of the fattest and head back up the beaver channel to Jean Lake, where we'd make our first main camp.

Probably we'd enjoy several days of top sport with the Jean Lake trout, silvery warriors of 5 to 20 pounds. From Jean Lake we'd portage to Budside, south through Rouge Lake and into Sturgeon Lake. On the east shore of the north arm of Sturgeon, most likely we would pause for a time at a rustic log cabin to swap yarns with rangers from Ontario's Department of Lands and Forests who live there, off-and-on, during the summer months. It could be that a black bear and its cub are "working" the area, and with that warning we'd seek out an island campsite far from shore where the raiding she-bear would not be tempted to invade our camp for the grub pack.

On our last day we'd break camp early and head north to Dore Lake. In French, "dore" means walleyes, so for the last time we'd unlimber our tackle and spend a couple hours hooking these marble-eyed fish. We wouldn't keep any because we'd have long lost the compulsion to "put something on the stringer" unless it was for immediate food. And then we'd cross the Pine Portage to 16-mile-long Pickerel Lake. From Pickerel Lake we'd push into French River, thence over the last 1½ miles of French Lake to the Quetico Park Ranger Station. There we would be met by Earl Thurier, our gear loaded onto his truck, and then we'd be whisked to his lodge on Crystal Lake. At the lodge we'd drown in a piping hot shower, and later fill ourselves on fried chicken.

This then, is how Superior-Quetico fly-out, canoe-back trips are. They are not for everyone, only for the adventurous. There are days on any such trip when it will rain and your boots will be a sodden mess from daylight to dark. And there are mosquitoes, as well as those tiny, pesky blackflies at some periods in early summer. But there is also peace and solitude . . . and some of the finest fishing to be found this side of the Happy Hunting Grounds.

Bob Cary

14: Tying the McNally smelt

Professional fly-tyer Jim Poulos of Wheeling, Illinois at work turning out "McNally Smelt" streamers.

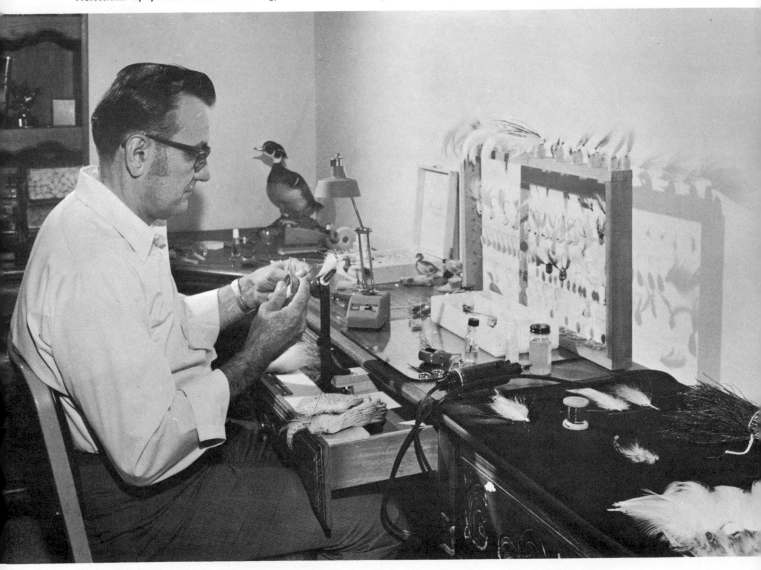

Necessity—thought to be invention's mother—is responsible for the creation of the original smelt streamer fly pattern.

Coho salmon that were introduced to Lake Michigan feeder rivers a few years ago feed primarily on alewives when the salmon are in the big lake, but they also take large numbers of smelt, particularly in the spring when smelt move into the shallows to spawn.

Since there was no realistic fly pattern already established that would adequately represent a 4 to 6-inch long silvery-sided smelt, Tom McNally went to work at his fly-tying vise and, after several weeks of experimenting, developed the "McNally Smelt." The fly is, first of all, *smelt-size*. Secondly, it is *smelt-shaped*. Thirdly, it is *smelt-color*.

The "McNally Smelt" is tied on a regular shank 1/0 salt water hook. (Larger hooks can be used if desired.) Depending upon materials, the fly should be between 4 and 6 inches in length from hook-eye to tip of tail, which is the average size of smelt taken in the spring in the Great Lakes. The basic body materials in the fly are white bucktail, saddle hackles and polar bear hair, and when tied-in in the proper proportions they give the fly exactly the correct silhouette—long and thin, flat-sided, but with smelt-like thickness at the shoulder. Basic color is white, with a silvery sheen, dark edging along the top, and a broad silver stripe running lengthwise through the body. These are the coloring characteristics of smelt—true-to-life right to the silvery stripe along the side.

The "McNally Smelt" is a very easy fly to cast despite its large size. It is not nearly as air-resistant as most large streamers, and being well "balanced" it cuts through the air when cast. It is very effectively trolled, too, particularly for coho and Chinook salmon, and like most flies can be used with spinning and bait-casting tackle when casting weight is added.

Depending upon the gamefish sought, time of year and area fished, various styles of retrieve are effective with the new smelt fly. As a general rule the fly should be twitched along in foot-long hauls, first fast and then slow. Sometimes it is best to retrieve the fly swiftly along close to the surface; other times it is most productive if allowed to sink several feet, then worked back in 3-foot jerks. For coho salmon a slow, almost steady retrieve normally gets the most strikes, but at times—especially in river fishing—it is best to yank the streamer forward a foot, then allow it to "rest" motionless, sinking, for a few seconds; then this is followed by another sharp yank, etc.

The "McNally Smelt" has proven to be an extraordinary coho salmon fly, and has taken large numbers of springtime cohos in the Chicago and Waukegan, Illinois areas, and "fall" salmon in Lake Michigan, and in Michigan's Manistee, Platte, and Pere Marquette Rivers.

In addition to Great Lakes salmon, the smelt fly has proved effective on largemouth black bass, walleyes, northern pike, lake trout, Arctic char, large brown trout in Montana's Missouri River and Argentina's Chimehuin, and a wide assortment of salt water gamefish, notably tarpon and snook.

Only one commercial fly-tyer is now producing the "McNally Smelt." He is Jim Poulos, 24 S. Wheeling Avenue, Wheeling, Illinois.

Smelt fly was originally designed to take cohos like this from Michigan rivers, but streamer has proved effective for other gamefish as well.

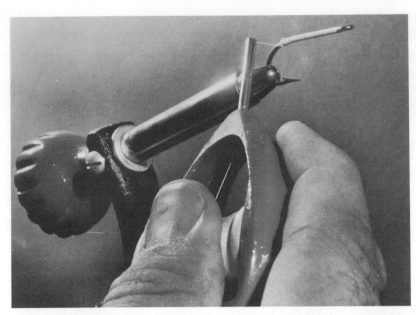

1.
Salt water type, 1/0 hook (flat or "ball" eyed) is wrapped with heavy white nylon thread to start smelt fly. Fly is tied without a body. Materials needed include white bucktail hairs; long, webby saddle hackles of white and grizzly; polar bear hairs; strands of peacock herl; mallard duck breast feathers; broad silver tinsel (or Mylar strips); and pearlescence lacquer.

2.
With hook-shank thread-wrapped (care is taken to see that any opening between hook-eye and shank is closed), generous amount of white bucktail hairs are tied in near bend of hook. Hairs should be about 3 inches long, and care should be taken to see that they are tied in securely to avoid pulling out. A drop of lacquer on bucktail ends helps assure long "wear."

3.
In next step long, webby, soft saddle hackles are secured to hook shank with hackle butts tied in near hook eye. Hackles should be 4 to 6 inches long, and on thin side. At least 4 white hackles are used, and no less than 2 grizzly hackles. Feathers should be tied over and around white bucktail. Hackle butts are trimmed and given a drop of lacquer, then more thread windings made at fly head to smooth the tie.

4.

With grizzly hackles tied in on either side of streamer, next step involves tying-in peacock herl strips and polar bear hair. Peacock is tied in first, at top of fly, with 8 to 10 strands adequate. Herl should be just an inch or so shorter than hackles. Polar bear hairs are tied in to shape "belly" of fly and to add irridescence common to real smelt. Polar hairs should extend well beyond hook and add bulk to fly body.

5.

In final steps 2 strips of silver tinsel or Mylar are tied in to form brilliant silvery stripe along fly's body. Strips must be tied in very tightly and ends should be lacquered to prevent pull-outs. Duck breast feathers (barred) are tied in, one on either side, to form fly's "cheek." Wrapping thread is then tied off with whip-finish knot, and coated with pearlescence lacquer.

6.

Completed fly is bulky when dry (top), but smooths out into realistic smelt shape when wet (bottom). Peacock herl strips on top of fly give it dark coloring there, as occurs on genuine smelt. Silver tinsel strip adds silvery line that is dominant on sides of real smelt. Fly's lacquered head can be as shown here, or broader at base and more tapered.

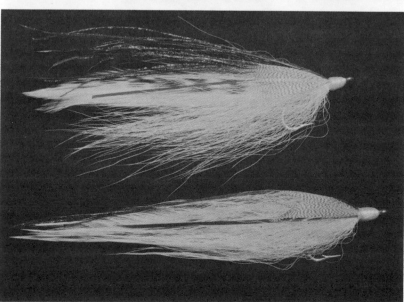

15: The fundamentals of fishing

Of the 50,000,000-odd people who go fishing in America and Canada each year, a large portion are "beginners." To them in particular this special insert—*a book within a book*—is specifically dedicated.

Thousands of excellent books have been published on angling, but heretofore there has been no text available teaching the novice the basics, the *true fundamentals*, of fishing.

Getting started at fishing is difficult, and each angler's first learning is a slow, hard process. But the material that follows in these pages should aid greatly in reducing the time it takes the beginner to bridge the gap from absolute novice to advanced angler stage or even the expert category. (T.McN.).

THE VARIOUS FISHING SYSTEMS

STILLFISHING is probably the simplest kind of angling. It is portrayed on calendars by a barefoot boy or an old man. The boy is sitting on a bank with a long cane pole in his hands, a can of worms at his side, and his faithful dog is hunched on the bank curiously staring at the water. The old man is reclining against a stump, displaying the serenity, patience, and complacency of old age. Either way, this is how most people think of stillfishing—but it's about as accurate as believing the moon is made of cheese or that the world is flat.

Stillfishing—whether from bank, boat, pier or jetty—demands the least amount of knowledge about fish and fishing, yet it accounts for more panfish than all other systems of angling combined. Good strings of game fish also are taken by stillfishing, particularly largemouth black bass.

A stillfishing outfit is the least expensive angling equipment attainable. The barefoot boy always is shown with a hickory pole that he collected along the stream bank, but even a more elaborate outfit consisting of a Calcutta cane or a glass pole, a float, length of line, hook and sinker can be acquired for only pennies. However, stillfishing can be done elaborately and scientifically, using efficient rods

and reels that are more generally used for specific kinds of casting. When only a pole is used, the stillfisherman must yank his fish out of the water and flip it onto the bank behind him or into the boat. If a large fish is hooked it can be lost easily with such tactics unless the pole and line are heavy. Using a reel, the stillfisherman can "play" his big fish by giving and taking in line.

In its fundamentals, stillfishing involves motionless angling. In other words, the fisherman sits in a boat or on a bank and peacefully dunks some type of bait. Casting of no kind is involved, nor is action or movement imparted to the bait. Artificial lures such as plugs, spoons or flies are not used so no cast-and-retrieve technique is employed.

In its advanced forms, stillfishing is done with a casting rod, fly rod, or spinning rod, in conjunction with the appropriate reels. Besides the added advantage of being able to "reel in" fish or give large ones line when necessary, this kind of equipment makes it possible for the fisherman to cast his baited rig some distance from the boat or bank. This is of value when, in bank fishing, it is desirable to fish the deeper water away from shore.

There are a number of methods of rigging a bait for stillfishing, as well as a large variety of baits that can be used. The most common bait is earthworms, particularly the larger ones known as "nightcrawlers." Some stillfishermen use one baited hook, others two or more. A common method is to employ a wire gadget called a "spreader," shaped like an inverted "U," with a baited hook dangling from each end.

Live minnows are used most often for crappies, yellow perch, bass, walleyes, and northern pike. Other good stillfishing baits include crayfish (particularly the soft shell variety), hellgrammites (the aquatic larvae of the dobson fly), nymphs (larvae of small aquatic insects), grasshoppers, cockroaches, meat, or concoctions of flour and meal or the flesh of other fish. Frogs are especially good bait for bass, as well as northern pike and muskellunge. Best bait for

A pole, can of worms, hooks and line are ll a still fisherman (or boy) needs.

muskies are large minnows up to 10 inches in length, such as suckers, chubs, dogfish minnow, or bluegills, perch, and even small bullheads with their fins removed.

BAIT CASTING is a method of fishing wherein the angler casts an artificial lure by swinging the rod, much as you would swing a stick to throw an apple off its end. Bait casting often is erroneously called "plug casting" because the lures generally used are called plugs. The cast lure furnishes propulsive movements to the spool of the reel, pulling line from the reel. At completion of the cast, the angler retrieves his extended line, and the attached lure, by turning the reel handles which revolve the spool. A bait casting reel actually is nothing more than a tiny winch.

Most bait casting rods nowadays are made of glass, which is exceptionally strong, light, and can be properly tapered for superior action. Other materials still used are bamboo and steel.

Glass bait casting rods are ultra-light—even lighter than bamboo rods—and do not require much upkeep. Glass rods are impervious to ordinary heat, cold, fresh or salt water. It is unnecessary to varnish them, or even to dry them before putting them away. The only repairs ever required are perhaps an occasional replacing of guides, and for the average fisherman this may never be necessary.

Glass rods also withstand the ordinary abuses of fishing better than rods of other materials. The normal stresses of casting or playing a fish will never break a good glass rod.

Another important feature of glass rods is that they will not warp or take on a "set" as bamboo rods often do. A "set" is a permanent bend to the rod, usually occurring near the tip.

Generally speaking, two kinds of rod handles are available with modern bait casting rods. One is the "straight handle"; the other, "offset." Most all bait casting rods today come with offset handles. An offset handle has a recession in which the casting reel is seated, while a straight handle does not. Most offset handles have "trigger" grips for the caster's forefinger; some straight handles have "triggers," some do not.

Most experts prefer casting rods having offset handles because the reel is housed very low so that the caster's thumb makes easy contact with the edge of the reel spool. This is important during "thumbing" of the reel which is

A fisherman using bait casting tackle leads a chunky bass to the net.

done to control the cast. With a straight-handled rod it is necessary to reach up with the thumb to contact the reel spool because the reel is mounted on the rod.

Most bait casting reels are quadruple multiplying. This means the spool turns four times when the handle is turned once. They also have level-wind devices which spool line evenly. "Anti-backlash" devices, or "brakes" that slow the revolving spool towards completion of the cast, help prevent snarling of line and are of particular value to beginning casters.

Most bait casters use lines that are too heavy. The line test should be selected not so much on the size of fish you hope to catch, but on the weight of the lures to be used and the kind of water you'll be fishing. If working heavy plugs in snag-filled or weedy lakes, then a heavier line should be used than when fishing small lures in sandy-bottom lakes. Most popular line test for average fresh water bait casting is 15 pounds.

A common mistake of beginning bait casters is to put too little line on the reel. Enough line should go on the reel so that the line is about ¼-inch from the edge of the reel spool. It is, however, unnecessary to fill all of the reel with quality line. A cork arbor can be put on the spool to act as a "filler," or any old line can be put on to half fill the spool. All you'll need for most fresh water fishing is about 50 yards of good line, which can be put on over the arbor or old backing line.

Always use a leader as a connecting link between your line and lure. The leader can be ordinary monofilament nylon. You may want a wire leader in fishing for northern pike, walleyes or muskellunge which have needle-like teeth and can easily sever an ordinary line or leader. Snap swivels or ball bearing swivels can be attached to the leader end to enable quick changing of lures. Be sure snaps and swivels you use are of stainless steel or brass so they'll resist rusting and not weaken. Ball bearing swivels prevent twisted or raveled line.

SPINNING is a term coined in America for bait casting with a stationary spool reel. In other words, nearly the same thing is accomplished in spinning as in bait casting, the only real difference being in the operation of the reel. In bait casting the weight of the lure pulls line from the reel by revolving the spool; in spinning, the weight of the lure under forward momentum pulls line from a stationary spool. Visualize wrapping line around the forward end of a stick, and tying a stone to the line. If you point the stick, then throw the stone, the line will be pulled off the end of the stick. This is the same principle in spinning.

Many American anglers feel spinning is a specialized method of casting ultra-light baits and lures—those "too light for bait casting and too heavy for fly casting." While it's true spinning gear is perfect for handling extra light lures—those too small to be cast well with bait casting tackle—spinning equipment can also be used to handle even the heaviest artificial lures and natural baits. Spinning is an easy method of casting any weight lures or baits, from 1/16-ounce to 5 ounces and heavier. The real advantage of a good spinning outfit is its ability to successfully cast lures weighing from ⅜-ounce all the way down to 1/16-ounce. Lures of such weights often are difficult, if not

Spinning is casting with an open, stationary-spool reel.

impossible, to handle well with the ordinary revolving-spool bait casting reel.

Spinning has a number of important advantages which make it a good, universal system of fishing, and its appeal to fresh water fishermen after panfish, trout, and bass is common knowledge.

The mechanics of making a good cast with spinning gear are the same as those with a bait casting outfit, but the manual handling of the spinning reel and line is different. Just as in bait casting, the flexing and power of the rod shoot the lure out, and the force that is transferred to the lure pulls the line after it.

Spinning is considerably simpler than bait casting because perfect control of the line is unnecessary. A beginner at bait casting may have some trouble with line snarls resulting from the spool revolving too fast or too slow, but none of these problems are present in spinning.

You can't get a "backlash" or an "over-run" in spinning, no matter what weight lure is used. With spinning there is no reel-spool inertia to overcome at the start of the cast, so extremely light baits and lures may be cast great distances with fine diameter line. Even an absolute beginner, someone who never before has handled a fishing rod, can learn to make smooth, efficient casts with spinning tackle in a fraction of the time that is required to master the first steps of bait-casting.

All rod movements used in bait casting are employed in spinning. The big difference is in manipulation of the reel. To start a cast with a spinning reel you must open a "bail," secure the line on the tip of your index finger, and flex the rod back then forward. On the forward movement the line is released from the finger tip and the lure pulls the line off the stationary spool. To slow or halt progress of the lure, you merely drop the tip of your index finger to the edge of the spool, thus contacting the line. With most spinning reels the bail automatically picks up the line to be rewound onto the spool as soon as the reel handle is turned forward. In bait casting the reel always is mounted on the top of the rod, while in spinning the reel is mounted on the botttom of the rod.

In addition to the advantages of being able to use ultra light as well as heavy lures, spin fishermen have the added value of monofilament lines which are nearly invisible in water, and the opportunity to make a cast and then wind the reel handle without having to change the rod from one hand to the other.

SPIN-CASTING is the newest system of fishing to be developed. Actually, spin-casting *is* spinning! The difference is that instead of an open-face stationary spool reel being used, a closed-face stationary spool reel is used. Also, because American fishermen for years had become wedded to the old bait casting rod and reel, where the reel is mounted on top of the rod, manufacturers recognized a big potential for a kind of spinning reel that could be mounted on top of an ordinary bait casting rod. So this is the modern spin-casting reel; a closed-face spinning reel that mounts on top of a specially designed spin-casting rod, or an ordinary bait casting rod.

Spin-casting is really spinning but uses a closed-face reel rather than an open face.

In fly casting, the line carries the leader and fly, and the line is cast rather than a lure.

These fishermen—trolling for salmon in Lake Michigan—are fishing four rods. Two are set in home-made cross-bar rigging.

Spin-casting offers most of the important advantages of spinning, and not all of spinning's disadvantages. In spin-casting, a large variety of lures in different weights can be cast, including ultra-light lures originally meant only for spinning; there's no need for bait casters to discard old casting rods and buy new ones; and no finger manipulation of pickup bails is necessary as with most spinning reels. All considered, spin-casting is probably the least difficult system of casting. For the average fisherman, spin-casting is a quick, efficient way to casting ease—and it will perform satisfactorily under most angling conditions.

FLY CASTING is the most graceful and picturesque form of casting. It is also the most difficult! It takes practice and patience, plus physical and mental coordination, to be a *good* fly caster. What is a good fly caster? A fisherman is a skilled fly-rodder when he can cast a GAF (WF-9) line 100 feet or more and do it effortlessly with no more than two false casts; when he can handle 70 or 80 feet of HCH (DT-7) line on an 8-foot trout rod, and do it gracefully and effortlessly; when he has mastered the "double haul"; when he can shoot line on both the backcast and forward cast; when he can rollcast, throw curves to the left and right, cast a "tight bow," and execute all the other so-called trick casts employed by veteran fly fishermen.

What is fly casting? By way of definition, it is a method of casting whereby the weight of the line furnishes the momentum to carry the lure, or fly. In all other forms of casting—bait casting, spinning, and spin-casting—the weight of the lure pulls the line after it. In fly casting, the lure merely rides along, attached to a nylon leader tied to the end of the line. In fly casting it is the *line* which is cast. The heavy line "works" the rod as the caster moves the rod back and forth. On the backcast the line extends straight behind the caster, bending the rod. When the rod straightens and flexes forward, with an assist from the caster, it furnishes the propulsion that drives the line forward to the target. The fly follows along, and lights on the water.

The fly reel contributes nothing to the cast. It merely furnishes storage space for the weighty fly line which is sized and designed to "work" the rod. A simple back-and-forth motion of the fly rod, with the line moving in cadence in front of and in back of the caster, is enough to throw the line and carry the fly 70 or more feet when timing is correct.

Many casters, in striving for distance, attempt to "power" the cast and thus lose all semblance of timing, muscular coordination, and application of rod power. Failing in developing timing, they attempt to make up for this with strength—little of which is properly transmitted to the rod.

The basic mechanics of fly casting are the application of power from a pivot point, with haltering—yet coordinated—movements. There are pauses; points where power is expended; and drifts; but all are combined into one smooth, graceful motion. Almost all casts begin with "starting" power, then advance to "speed up" power on the forward cast.

Few fly casters recognize the important part played by the left hand during casts. This hand is the line controller, holding the line and keeping it taut at all times to guarantee complete power and delivery.

TROLLING is a system of angling in which the lure, or bait, is trailed behind a slow-moving boat.

There are many kinds of trolling, for many kinds of fish, but generally speaking, trolling is a kind of *deep* fishing. Among its other advantages, trolling makes it possible to work a lure or a bait over much more water than would be possible by casting or stillfishing. Trolling is especially valuable in *locating* fish.

In its essence trolling is letting a lure or bait out behind a boat by "feeding" out line, the boat moving ahead under either oar or motor power. For most fresh water trolling slow progress is desirable, with the boat moving at about 3 miles per hour. When trolling with an outboard, wise fishermen keep varying the speed until they find the rate at which the fish hit best on that particular day. Modern outboards are exceptionally fine trolling power plants, with most now having throttle arrangements on the steering grip so that the fisherman can steer and control speed with one hand while holding his rod in the other. A few states, such as Wisconsin, prohibit trolling with an outboard in certain waters, but where it's legal, motor trolling is productive and time-saving.

Almost any tackle can be used in trolling, but for top sport certain rigs are preferred. In light trolling for bass and panfish, any fairly stiff bait-casting or spinning rod will do provided the fishermen do not wish to work at great depths and small lures or bait are used. Nearly any multiplying reel also will do for such simple trolling.

In working for large lake trout, however, or other species that hang out in exceptionally deep water, more specialized outfits are used. Rods are usually 5 to 5½ feet long and are stout. They may be bait casting rods; ones known in the East as "boat rods," or the manufacturer may have dubbed them "trolling" rods.

Ordinary nylon bait-casting line serves nicely for light trolling, but when it's deep-going lake trout you're after, it is often necessary to revert to a wire or lead-core line that helps keep the lure or bait down deep. Special reels having a large line capacity are needed when metal lines are used. Salt water reels are used by many lake trout fishermen because of their large line capacity and other features that suit them to trolling.

Several different terminal rigs are used in trolling, probably the most important having a heavy lead sinker on a separate line from the one to which the hook and bait, or lure, is attached. The sinker line suspends from the fishing line, and is weaker. Thus if the sinker fouls on bottom, its weaker line breaks and the balance of the rig is saved. Also, this type of rigging tends to keep the lure closer to the bottom.

Pear-shaped sinkers, called "Dipsey" sinkers, are best because they are rounded on the bottom and will slide over many rocks and other obstructions without getting caught. Most common terminal gear arrangement is one known as a "triangle trolling rig." It consists of a three-way swivel, with the main line attached to one end; the weak sinker line to another; and the line going to the baited hook or lure tied to the third end of the swivel. This permits the lines to stand out in different directions without fouling one another. The line the lure is attached to should be longer than the sinker line.

Many different lures and baits are employed in trolling. Most common is a spoon, or a spinner and hook arrangement such as the famous June-Bug spinner. Fluted spoons —many of the double or triple variety—also are popular. Baits for trolling are usually minnows, worms, or small eels.

KINDS OF LURES

A SURFACE LURE is any artificial lure that floats and remains on the surface during the retrieve.

Under certain conditions there is no better way to take largemouth black bass than with surface plugs. The top water lures also score well on smallmouth black bass, muskellunge, northern pike and sometimes trout. Even walleyes will take surface lures occasionally. Best of all, surface lures are fun to use because the fisherman has the extra excitement of seeing and hearing striking fish. Nothing causes a lake to switch ends like a largemouth bass walloping a surface plug. It's like a miniature explosion—and you'll swallow your heart every time a bass hits on top.

Surface lures have one thing in common, in that they all create a commotion or ripple on the water which at-

Surface lure.

tracts fish. Fish usually strike these lures believing they are a wounded minnow struggling across the surface; a swimming frog or mouse; or some kind of large bug that has fallen to the water and is kicking madly toward shore.

Probably the most popular surface lure is a type called "poppers." They have either flat or cupped heads, generally float with the tail slightly below the surface, and give a resounding "pop" when the fisherman jerks the line. These lures have the added fish-getting attraction of top-water sound. Even when a bass can't see one of these surface disturbers, he'll hear its commotion and come to see what kind of critter is paddling around the surface.

Another popular type of surface lure is the "puddling plug." These create surface commotion but do not pop. Some have revolving heads; some, metal extensions that break the water; still others have propellers fixed to the head or tail, or both. One famous top water lure has a large cupped face-plate that causes the plug to wobble from side to side, with a gurgling sound, as it is reeled across the surface.

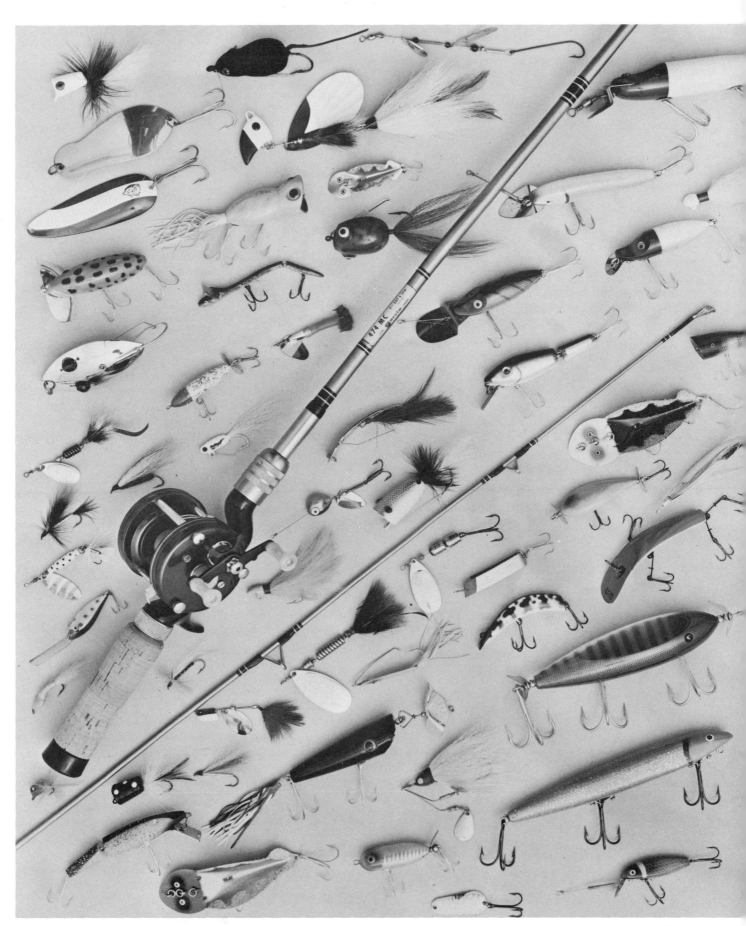

A full assortment of plugs, spoons, spinners and jigs.

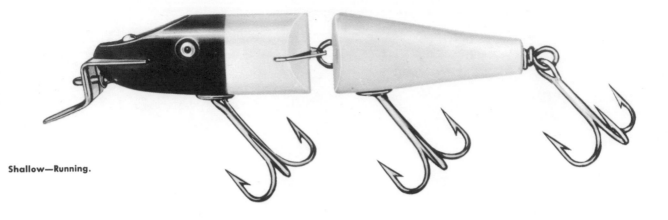

Shallow—Running.

All surface lures are designed to stir up the water and to imitate some tiny creature that is helpless, or swimming slowly along the surface. Either way, a surface lure is a sure way to excite a bass.

FLOATING-DIVING LURES are ones that float as soon as they strike the water but dive as the fisherman begins to reel.

Most are designed to imitate a minnow, and so are shaped like tiny fish. Some floating-diving lures, however, are of the "mouse" variety—perhaps even having fuzzy finishes that simulate a mouse's fur. A few plugs in this class have cut-away fronts, slashed at about a 45-degree angle, which causes them to dive when reeled in. Almost all floating-diving plugs work only a foot or two below the surface. A common way to fish them is to cast to a likely spot, allow the lure to rest motionless for a moment, then twitch it lightly. A few more light twitches and pauses, and the fisherman reels steadily to dive the plug under water. After reeling the plug along a few feet, the fisherman stops reeling and the plug re-surfaces. After a brief pause, the caster again twitches the lure a few times by jerking the rod tip, then resumes the reeling routine.

Floating-diving lures, also called semi-surface plugs, may be of one-piece construction or jointed. Jointed plugs are two-piece and have a lively wiggling action. Most of the famous underwater and deep-diving plugs are also available in floating-diving models.

SHALLOW-RUNNING LURES are any of a large variety that sink slowly after striking the water, then swim along at depths of from 4 to 12 feet.

They're designed, of course, for fishing over weed beds or in lake shallows where there are stumps, submerged logs or rocks that may foul a deep-running lure.

Shallow-running lures are best fished very slowly, or by reeling, stopping, then jerking the rod tip to activate the lure and make it act like a wounded minnow. Sometimes slow reeling followed by fast reeling pays off with lures of this type.

Often fish will feed at particular depths, and the shallow-running lures make it possible for you to work fish carefully when they are not too far down. Several kinds of shallow runners, in different colors and finishes, should be in every fisherman's tackle box.

MEDIUM-RUNNING LURES are those that travel at depths ranging from about 6 to 15 feet. They can be obtained in almost any size or shape, as well as in different weights.

Like all other plugs, the majority of medium-running lures today are made of plastic, though some popular types still are made of wood.

Most medium underwater plugs have a metal lip or "face plate" that gives them action. When the lure is drawn through the water, the resistance of the water on the metal lip causes the plug to move first to one side, then the other—giving it a wobbling or darting motion.

On most medium-running lures that have a metal lip, you can regulate the depth at which the lure operates by altering the angle of the lip. Bending the lip down will cause the plug to swim near the surface; bending the lip up will cause it to dive deeper. There is a limit, however, to the depth at which such baits can be made to operate. Thus special deep-diving plugs still are necessary when you want to fish very deep.

Besides controlling depth of medium runners by bending the lip, it usually is possible to vary the depth somewhat by varying the speed. This causes a lure to operate at a specific depth, since some medium-runners travel shallow when reeled slowly, while others travel deeper the slower they are reeled.

DEEP-RUNNING LURES usually operate at depths greater than 15 feet. Most good deep-runners will work around 25 feet down.

Any sinking lure can be allowed to settle deeply, but most will rise upwards during the retrieve, having a tendency to plane in the water until they reach the depth for which they were designed to operate. Such lures are of little value when a fisherman wants to work really deep, since they'll be well down only during the initial part of the retrieve. After that they begin rising toward the rod tip.

Well-designed deep-runners, however, go down and stay down throughout the retrieve. This way the lure is crawling along the bottom, down deep where you want it, throughout most of the retrieve.

The designers of many deep-running lures forget to build in a tantalizing action as well as "fish appeal" while concentrating on making a lure that will work deep. As a consequence, they end up with a lure that operates well

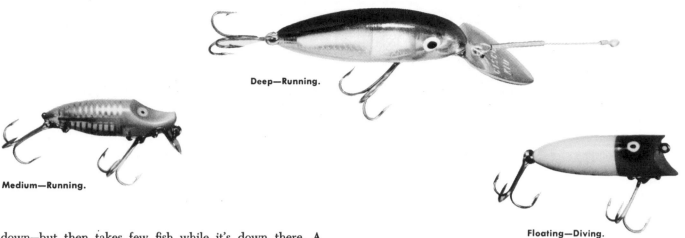

Medium—Running.

Deep—Running.

Floating—Diving.

down—but then takes few fish while it's down there. A quality deep-running lure should not only go down quickly and stay down, but should have a life-like wiggle and colorful finish.

SPOON-LURES usually are long, oval-shaped disks made of metal. They come in a variety of shapes, colors and sizes—but nonetheless always have at least a faint resemblance to a tablespoon.

Popular finishes are plain silver or chrome, pearl, and either spotted or striped with red and white. Some have small "flap" tails or feathers attached near the tail hook to give added action.

Weedless spoons are an absolute must in every tackle box. A well-equipped angler will have not one but several weedless spoons. Bass, northern pike, and muskellunge favor weed beds, and unless you are equipped with some weedless spoons you can't work the weeds where the fish are lying in wait for some easy meal.

A strip of porkrind will improve any spoon. It's placed on the hook so that it trails behind, waving and fluttering, as the spoon is drawn through the water. Because of their special design spoons wobble and dart and reflect light that attracts fish. Fish can spot such a lure from great distances.

Few other lures account for as many fish from as many places, season after season, as does the ordinary spoon. They've been demolishing fish for centuries, and most likely always will. It's interesting to note that spoons are the oldest lures in the world, the first being used around 3000 B.C., yet they still are one of the most important lures of the dozens found in every angler's tackle box.

ARTIFICIAL BAITS once was a term used to identify plugs, spoons, or any type of lure excluding "natural" bait. Natural bait, of course, is real bait such as worms, minnows, bugs, etc. Today, however, with the advent of extremely life-like plastic "baits," fishermen now term these "artificial baits."

Most of these artificial baits are very realistic. Some plastic worms, for example, even *feel* like real worms. They're soft and spongy, have perfectly natural coloring, and do everything but bleed when you impale them on a hook.

The best artificial baits are made of soft, pliable vinyl plastic—and are realistic in every respect, from natural coloring to translucent "feelers" which wiggle and dance in the water.

Johnson spoons in various sizes and finishes.

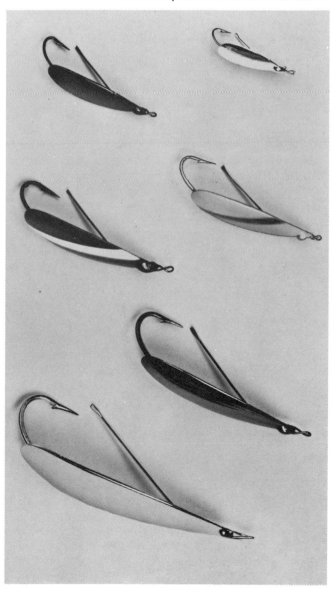

Artificial baits can be used to take a large variety of fish—from pan-fish and perch to large northerns and muskellunge.

FLIES are hooks dressed with wisps of feathers, tinsel, fur, hair, and countless other kinds of materials. Many are tied to represent, as nearly as possible, certain real insects, bugs, nymphs, or minnows. But many do not even remotely imitate any natural insect, minnow, or bug—yet they catch fish.

To have a complete understanding of fly types, the popular "patterns," what the specific artificial flies represent, and how they should be fished, can become a major study and involve years of experience. However, all that isn't necessary for a basic, working knowledge of artificial flies.

Strictly speaking, there are two divisions of artificial flies. One includes *wet* flies, the other *dry* flies. For purposes of definition, a wet fly is any fly fished under the surface of the water, and a dry fly is one fished on the surface, or floating.

Types of flies in the wet fly division are streamer flies, nymphs, and a type known simply as "wet flies." Dry fly types include bivisibles, spent-wings, May flies or "drakes," upright wings, fan wings, parachute flies, midges, spiders, and many more.

An important and broad class of flies is the "terrestrials," which may be either sinking or floating. These flies represent members of the large terrestrial group of insects, which covers insects that are common to the land rather than water. The more common artificial terrestrial flies are ants, grasshoppers, beetles, caterpillars, and spiders.

Streamer flies are tied long and sparse, and are used to imitate minnows on which fish feed. Nymphs are flies made to represent the larvae of aquatic insects. Wet flies are smallish, have "wings" tied back over the hook shank, and usually are not tied to represent any specific real insect. These wet flies can be taken by trout in mistake for a

This large assortment of artificial plastic lures includes sea worms, a squid, snakes (yes, fish do eat snakes), spiders, crickets, hellgrammites, nymphs, grasshoppers, beetles, grubs, caterpillars, frogs, crayfish, dragon flies, crabs and fresh water shrimp.

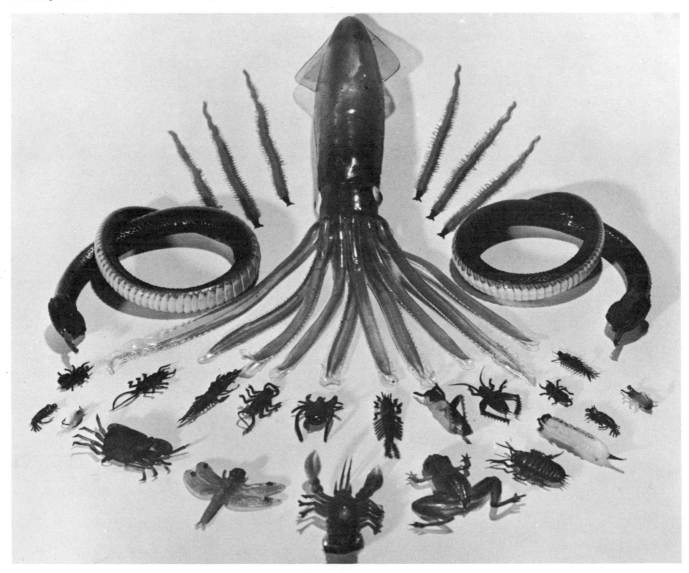

A selection of flies.

A large assortment of fly rod bugs.

drowned natural insect, a nymph, or even a minnow—depending on the size and form of the fly and how it is used.

Bivisible and spider types of dry flies are bushy, well-hackled jobs that float well and can be skittered over the surface. May flies or drakes represent the May fly group of real insects, and these are among the most important artificial flies for trout fishermen everywhere.

All popular flies are tied according to "patterns"—which means specific materials and colors are used. The flies have names, too, such as the Royal Coachman, Mickey Finn, Parmachene Belle, Yellow Sally, Silver Doctor.

Do not be overly concerned with patterns in building up a stock of flies, but try instead to collect a representative assortment of types.

BUGS are tiny floating lures made of wood, cork, balsa, or plastic material, usually dressed with feathers or hair. The hooks of quality bugs never turn in the bodies.

Bugs are designed to be cast with a fly rod or a spinning rod, but best presentation is with fly tackle. Bugs are killers on bass and panfish, but they take all other species of gamefish, too.

Bug sizes range from very small, weighing only a few grains and meant to catch panfish with a fly rod, to large ones of around ¼-ounce for bass and northerns and designed for use with a spinning rod. Bugs imitate frogs, tiny mice, moths, bees, wounded minnows, locusts and such large insects, or anything else in the way of food that fish might expect to see on the surface.

The colors and "dressings" of bugs vary greatly, but the most popular colors are brown, green, orange, yellow, black, red-and-white, or white. Another type of common bug, in addition to ones of the materials named earlier, is the soft-bodied variety. These usually are made of deer hair.

While many fishermen try bass bug fishing then give it up shortly, after failing to master this heavy-duty fly casting quickly, more anglers should strive to perfect bugging technique. There is no surer way of taking largemouth bass when the fish are in the shallows.

PORK LURES are ones made of porkrind, the tough skin of hogs. It comes either in thin, long strips, or in chunks of toughened fat layers with the skin attached.

Porkrind strips are available in different lengths, shapes and colors, as are pork chunks. Most popular pork chunks are cut to the rough shape of a frog. Most popular color is pure white. Both porkrind strips and chunks are packaged in small jars containing solutions of formaldehyde or strong salt mixtures.

Pork chunk is heavy enough to be cast by itself with spinning tackle or light bait-casting outfits, but porkrind strips are very light and must be attached to the hooks of spoons, spinners, or even plugs. A thin strip of porkrind adds a rippling, fluttering action to a lure—and is deadly on bass.

Strips of porkrind that are too large can kill the action of a lure and also cause fish to strike short and miss the hook. For this reason, some porkrind strips are available which have a "tail hook" set well back near the end.

Three types of spinners.

When using porkrind with a spoon, keep it less than 1½ inches long. If too long, it will slow the action of the spoon; loop over the spoon or hook on the cast; or cause short strikes.

SPINNING AND SPIN-CASTING LURES can be almost any kind of spoon, plug, or spinner-fly combination, but there also are large varieties of lures made especially for spinning or spin-casting.

Plugs, spoons, etc. weighing ⅜-ounce or more can be handled easily with spinning and spin-casting tackle, provided line diameter matches the weight of the lure. But since most spinning and spin-casting fishermen use the equipment with fine-diameter lines, most lures made especially for spinning and spin-casting are lightweight, weighing under ⅜-ounce.

Spinning lures have another peculiarity in addition to their generally small size; most are of the "hardware" variety. This undoubtedly is partly due to the foreign influence, but the fact remains that most spinning lures are of the spinner type. They have a cast body to provide weight, and some kind of revolving spinner at the head. Almost all spinning lures have the additions of metal blades, feathers, or "tails." Some spinning and spin-casting lures are shaped like small fish or frogs, and thus fall into the plug category. However, the major attraction provided by most spinning and spin-casting lures is flash. Their revolving spinners, flaps, spoon blades, or tails—brass, copper, chrome, or bead bodies—reflect light and sparkle in the water, thus attracting game fish and drawing strikes.

Spinning and spin-casting lures seem particularly effective in clear water, compared to the larger standard plugs and spoons. These tiny lures are considerably more life-like, and nearer in size to the natural foods fish prey upon. In clear water, fish are less apt to detect the fine monofilament lines used in spinning and spin-casting. Every spinning and spin-cast fisherman should be certain to include spinner-fly combinations in his assortment of lures, as well as some plain spinner-type lures, and several small, wobbling spoons—particularly chrome spoons and ones striped or spotted in red and white.

FISH HABITS

No one can understand fish or be a very successful angler without learning some of the basics that make fish tick.

Fish breathe by means of their gills, which remove oxygen from the water and pass it on to the blood stream. Some fish, because of differences in gill structure, require more oxygen than others. Trout, for example, live only in water having a very high oxygen content, while carp, which need less oxygen, can survive in muddy, polluted, warm water. Fast moving, shallow water—such as the typical trout stream—has a large oxygen content because the water is aerated as it breaks over falls, along rapids and riffles.

Fish in slow moving rivers or ponds get oxygen that is put into the water from surface action caused by wind, but chiefly oxygen derived from aquatic plants. Plants take in carbon dioxide, which is given off by fish, and fish take the oxygen which is given off by plants. It's for this reason that most good fishing lakes have weed beds or lily pads.

Fish propel themselves through the water by their fins and tails. The large fin on a fish's back is called the *dorsal* fin; the tail is the *caudal* fin; the small fin some species have on the back just above the tail is the *adipose* fin; the first paired fins back of the head are the *pectoral* fins; the next paired pair going back along the fish's belly are the *pelvic* fins; and the last single fin on the belly just below the tail is the *anal* fin.

tection, but not all. Catfish, for example, have no scales. Black bass have large, bony scales; trout have very small ones and do not even have to be "scaled" for cooking.

The bodies of nearly all fish are covered with a mucous, protective coating. It helps reduce friction when they move through the water, and also protects them from disease and parasites. When important game fish are to be returned to the water, it's wise to first wet your hands as dry hands can break this slimy coating and fungus may attack and eventually kill the fish.

Fish of most species have a well-developed sense of touch, but they apparently are not particularly sensitive to pain—thus lady anglers need not be squeamish about "hurting" fish when they hook 'em!

WHERE TO FIND FISH is what every successful fisherman learns with experience, but for the novice there are certain characteristics of each fish which, if known, will help him catch fish at the outset.

In general there are two distinct kinds of fresh water fish; the "game" fish or predator types, and the non-game fish or non-predators. A predator fish eats other fish and insects as well as small animals, while non-predators feed chiefly on plankton, various refuse, and occasionally insects.

Largemouth black bass, smallmouth black bass, northern pike, muskellunge, and walleyes are the most important fresh water gamefish. All of them like to hide in cover—places that help conceal them and which give them a vantage point to watch for minnows, frogs, etc. that may swim by. When a careless minnow passes a concealed bass or other gamefish, the gamefish makes a meal of him by rushing out and seizing the hapless minnow.

Largemouth black bass are found in rivers and lakes, and occasionally in slow moving streams. They like quiet, still water—and do not thrive in extremely cold rivers or

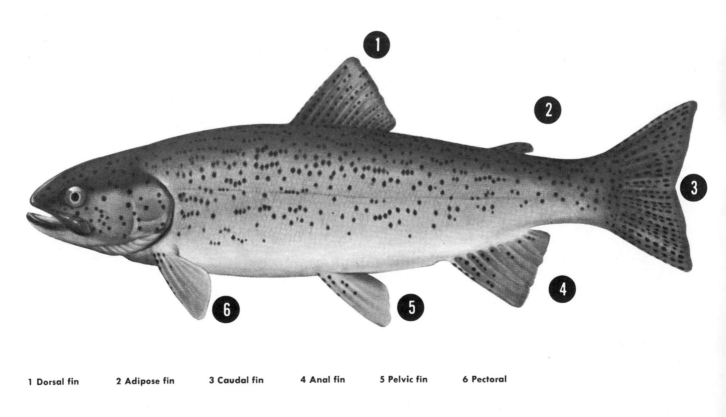

1 Dorsal fin   2 Adipose fin   3 Caudal fin   4 Anal fin   5 Pelvic fin   6 Pectoral

lakes. The largemouth is predominantly a southern fish, but is found in all states.

They hide out around lily pads, around stumps and logs, and under brush piles. Largemouth bass, as well as smallmouth bass, are primarily school fish since they are members of the sunfish family. In old age, however, big bass seem to become solitary. Favored cover spots in lakes, such as beside a weathered old stump, always seem to hold a good bass—even if you consistently catch one there. As soon as one is caught from the spot, another invariably moves in.

Largemouths like weedy, protected bays—and—although they get along well in some sand or gravel-bottomed lakes —the best bass lakes usually are mud-bottomed. Largemouths are widely stocked by most state conservation departments, and if there is a man-made farm pond or two in your area, be sure to try them.

Smallmouth black bass, although they are close cousins to the largemouth, hang out in different places. You'll find smallmouths in many cool, swift rivers and streams, as well as in clear, cold, deep water lakes. They thrive best in the northern states, and very few southern areas provide good smallmouth fishing.

While smallmouths like cover types very similar to those preferred by the largemouth, the nature of the water generally inhabited by smallmouths does not always provide for much good cover. In other words, many fine northern smallmouth lakes are sandy and rocky—free of lilies, stumps, etc., so the smallmouths hang out around submerged bars, rocky points, or in the depths where sunlight penetration is slight.

If you locate smallmouths in a lake full of weeds, stumps, sunken logs, etc., then fish for them around those cover spots—but bear in mind that the water temperature is important. Smallmouths like cool water, and though a lake may have good cover in the shoreline shallows, the bass may not be there but out in deeper water which is cooler.

Northern pike also like to hide, and have a strong preference for weed beds and lily pads. They'll snake slowly through weeds searching for minnows, frogs, and other foods—or lurk motionless, deep in the lily pads. When weeds and lilies aren't available, they'll hide around stumps, beaver houses, logs, and brush. The same is true of muskellunge, but more so. A musky *always* haunts cover, except when the shallow water grows too warm for him to be comfortable. Then muskies move out over gravel bars, and off points, seeking the depth where water temperature is best.

Proper depth according to water temperature is considerably more important to walleyes than is cover. But when the shallows are cool, especially at night, they'll move in and out of deep water to feed. Walleyes are nocturnal feeders, for the most part, so it often is a waste of time to look for them along shore during the daylight hours. An offshore weed bed or the end of a sandy bar in 20 or 30 feet of water is a good place to find walleyes.

Lake trout, also called mackinaw trout or togue, are cold water fish and are found only in the shallows of northern lakes very early in the spring and again in late fall. Otherwise they go deep, often to 70 feet or more, and only very deep fishing takes them. Cover is generally unimportant

In old age large bass tend to become solitary.

Good lakes for northern smallmouths are usually rocky and have sand or gravel bottoms.

Northern pike prefer weed beds and lily pads, and the large ones are products of wilderness waters.

in fishing for lakers, although they frequent sudden drop-offs and long, submerged bars.

Brook, brown, and rainbow trout live in fast-moving, clear, cool, and unpolluted streams, although some clean, cold lakes also give good trout fishing. Trout always try to escape the direct rays of the sun, so you'll find them in good cover spots providing shade and where the current is moving well enough to be properly aerated. Trout *never* inhabit river back eddies or other spots that are *dead* water, water with no current, little or no oxygen, which is perhaps partly stagnated. Look for trout at the edges of current runs, behind rocks and boulders in fast water, under logs and overhanging trees, beneath undercut banks, and in deep holes and pools. Smallmouth bass in rivers like the same kind of places.

White bass, often mistakenly called "stripers" in the Midwest, are difficult to find. They move around in schools, constantly on the go, and may be filling a bay one day then be clean across the lake in open water the next. The best way to find white bass is to troll slowly with tiny lures, and keep constant watch for signs of surfacing fish.

Crappies also are school fish, feeding heavily on small minnows. They like fairly deep water, at around 15 feet late in the spring, and successively deeper as the water warms. Good average depth at which to find crappies is about 20 feet. When you find them, you'll catch not one but dozens.

Deep holes, with perhaps a bottom weed bed or brush pile, are great places to find both black and white crappies.

Lakes that are very shallow and become *too* warm never provide really good crappie fishing. Since they are predominantly lake fish, you'll not often encounter good crappie schools in small rivers.

Sunfish, bluegills and other similar panfish usually are found in shallow water, close to shore, around brush piles, bars, or weeds. Yellow perch are found in much the same places as crappies, but they have a slightly stronger preference for weeds in water 10 to 15 feet deep.

Carp are bottom fish, located in muddy, still lakes—but they have a way of adapting themselves to almost any kind of river, stream, or lake. Best places to find them are in the shallows of silted lakes in early spring, and a bit deeper as water warms. Even in extremely hot weather, however, you'll find carp frequent the shallows where they roil the water and root up the bottom.

Catfish, bullheads, channel catfish and such also are bottom feeders. Channel cats and bullheads prefer fairly cool lakes, while catfish like it warm. Mud bottom lakes are best, and none of these species ever deliberately haunt cover spots. Look for them in open water, at depths of about 10 feet, and keep your bait right on the bottom or a foot or so from bottom. If there's a catfish around, he'll find your bait eventually and take it.

FISH MIGRATIONS occur day and night, spring, summer, fall and winter—but in varying degrees according to the species and season.

It's important for the beginning fisherman to have some

knowledge of fish migrations, approximately when and why they occur, the frequency of movements, and which species of fish migrate sufficiently to affect fishing. Without at least a basic understanding of fish migrations, an angler can spend most, if not all, of his time fishing in unproductive water.

In spring largemouth black bass move into shallows where they spawn, usually when the water temperature reaches about 65 degrees. They remain in the shallows after spawning, but go deeper as the water warms. Early in the season they may stay only 10 or 12 feet down during the day, moving into the very shallow water towards dusk to feed. Often they'll spend the night close in to the bank, not moving out again until the sun is high and hot the following morning.

From mid-summer until early fall, bass will school in the deepest holes, leaving them along set migration routes for the shallows when they feed. Treks to the shoreline to feed usually occur at dusk and at night, but sometimes bass schools leave the deep holes to feed during the hottest, brightest part of the day.

Unlike some other species, bass do not move around a lot, although they migrate often. In other words, in hot weather bass will go deep—sometimes down more than 50 feet—until they find the right kind of bottom water temperature, and oxygen. Occasionally they leave this deep area for the shallows, but they never desert the general area entirely unless some major change occurs in the environment, such as pollution of a particular section of the lake. So if you have good bass fishing in a certain bay one day, you can be sure the bass are nearby the next time you come back. On your first trip to that bay you may have caught bass in the shallows, then perhaps none on the second trip even though you fished hard. Failure on the last trip most

Clean, cold, high-country lakes give good trout fishing, particularly in the early season.

White bass.

likely was due to the bass deserting the shallows and moving very deep—where you couldn't reach them.

In the fall, as the water cools, bass again spend more time in the shallows, but not to the extent most fishermen believe. The time that shoreline water is just right for a bass's comfort is short-lived in the fall, so they move out again to the deeper water which cools much slower than the shallows. About the time the crimson leaves of fall begin dotting your favorite lake, you can figure the bass are deep again. As the water gets really cold they go deeper, and become less active and do almost no feeding.

Smallmouth black bass follow a migration pattern similar to the largemouth's except that they prefer lower temperatures than largemouth bass and so spend a shorter part of each season in the shallows. In many lakes having both largemouth and smallmouth bass, you'll find largemouths hugging the brushy banks while smallmouths at the same time are out in 20 feet of water.

While largemouths living in rivers may migrate little, smallmouths move around a lot. In the spring, as spawning time nears, smallmouth bass begin a seasonal trek into clear, cold tributary streams. Here they fan out circular nests in the gravel, and the female bass lays eggs which are fertilized by the males. After spawning they drop back to the main river, and then migrate only for reasons of comfort. If the main flow becomes too warm, and thus drops in oxygen content, the smallmouths will move upstream or congregate around the mouths of feeder brooks where the water is cooler and contains more oxygen.

Muskies migrate little, and except during the spawning season, April and May, they live nearly solitary lives. Often in the spawning season dozens of muskies will move into one particular area.

Northern pike also are solitary fish, preferring to hunt alone, and making only minor migrations to deeper water in warm weather. Walleyes, however, are school fish and roam lake bottoms almost constantly. Except when resting in deep holes, walleyes are extreme vagrants compared to species such as largemouth bass and muskellunge. In spring, schools of walleyes move out of deep lakes and go up rivers to spawn. Walleyes are especially vulnerable to fishermen during their spawning runs because they are in shallower water and are more easily located than when on the bottom of a deep lake.

White bass have similar habits, except that they travel in even tighter schools than walleyes, and frequently these schools surface, churning the water white—an uncommon occurrence for walleyes.

Among the panfish—which include sunfish, perch, bluegills, and crappies—probably only the crappie migrates to any extent. The major rule to locating crappies is to fish varying depths and places, until a school is found. Usually crappies will hang out in one spot at a depth that is suitable to them for weeks at a time.

Catfish, carp, bullheads, etc. have no migrations of importance to hook-and-line fishermen.

WHAT FISH FEED ON is what is primarily available, and what they are equipped to feed upon. Most fish eat other fish. In an exaggerated chain of events, visualize a tiny minnow gulping down a ¼-inch long sunfish that has just hatched from the egg; a crappie some 4 inches long appears and eats the minnow; next comes a largemouth black bass weighing perhaps a pound, and he eats the little crappie; now comes a muskellunge, who promptly bites the bass in half.

Largemouth bass feed chiefly on small minnows, with the most common size being 2 to 3 inches long. They also eat small sunfish, bluegills, perch, and crappies—but ordinary minnows, such as shiner minnows, make up the bulk of the largemouth's diet. Bass also eat frogs, as well as an occasional snake, small bird, bugs, nymphs, worms, field mice, crayfish, and nearly any other live critter in or on the water that is of suitable size.

Northern pike have about the same tastes. They eat mostly small minnows or fish, but you could take them on

Bottom fishing with chicken livers got these catfish in Fox River, Illinois.

nearly any bait or lure a bass would grab.

Smallmouth bass also eat almost anything a largemouth will, but he consumes larger quantities of nymphs, crayfish (particularly soft-shell crayfish), and hellgrammites. Minnows, frogs, and insects round out the smallmouth's diet.

Muskellunge are one of the greatest predatory fish, and so eat anything that swims, struggles, flops or flies in or on the water. However, they eat mostly other fish, simply because this is what is most often available. Probably the common sucker comprises the larger part of the musky's diet, followed by large shiner minnows, chubs, dace, crappies, walleyes, perch, small bass and pike. In general, an average size musky of about 10 pounds wants a sizable mouthful. A sucker, shiner, etc. of less than 5 inches in length isn't likely to interest him.

Walleyes feed chiefly on minnows—ones about 3 inches long—but like largemouth bass and northerns they'll take a variety of other baits, particularly nightcrawler worms.

Among the panfish, only crappies and perch eat many minnows. Most any minnow will do, but it should be less than 2 inches long. Like all other panfish, crappies and perch take worms greedily, insects, etc.

Carp, catfish, and bullheads are bottom scavengers and best all-round bait for them is worms. Certain doughy mixtures, however, are excellent for carp. Catfish and bullheads bite well on chicken liver or chicken entrails, as well as on small squares of plain white soap. Night fishing is particularly productive for catfish and bullheads.

COLORS FISH PERCEIVE has long been a matter of

heated debate among fishermen, but thanks to scientific tests it is now known with reasonable certainty which colors, or shades of color, are recognizable to fish.

Tests with largemouth black bass were conducted in an aquarium. A colored tube was placed in the water, and when a fish approached, food was forced into the water through the tube. A differently colored tube was placed in the water, and when fish approached it an electrical current was put into the water to give them a mild shock. Subsequently, the fish learned to distinguish between colored tubes that contained food, and ones that were always followed by an electrical jolt. The fish retained the ability to remember the colors and the proper association of either food or shock for periods of up to one month.

Even shades of colors were tried, and results were the same. The fish could distinguish between shades of red, green, yellow, and blue.

A German scientist, Conrad Herter, proved fish also could distinguish *form*. He did this by placing a large letter "R" in an aquarium and feeding the fish. Then he put the letter "L" in the water and did not feed the fish. The fish soon learned to swarm around the letter "R" to be fed, but they'd ignore "L."

While fish can perceive colors in their environment probably almost as well as a human can in his environment, it is important to understand that depth and water clarity have much to do with the way a fish sees color.

If the water is discolored—perhaps yellowish, orange, or brown from siltation, or black like swamp water, or blue or green—then this color will somewhat alter the colors fish see. In cloudy or dirty water, the intensity of color is changed.

There can be no color without white light, which is sunlight. Thus the depth of water is directly related to the intensity of color. Water absorbs light rapidly, so the deeper a fish is, the duller the colors he sees. Thus at certain depths, a fish will be able to distinguish only certain groups of colors.

In order for a red lure to reflect red, some white light must reach it. Otherwise it will be black. At about 25 feet in most lakes, water will filter out nearly all the red of the spectrum—so if someone tells you one day that he could catch walleyes at 35 feet on *only* a red lure, something is wrong. This is because the red lure would have appeared black to the fish, as would a green one, a yellow one, a white one . . . or any other.

For deep fishing the best colors for lures are orange and yellow. These colors need the least white light, and this is why fishermen everywhere have learned that yellow is a good color in lures.

In spring walleyes go up rivers to spawn, or they'll group below impassible falls such as this. Areas of this sort always should be fished.

Smallmouth bass do not grow to as large a size as largemouth bass, but this string from Rainy Lake, Ontario, contains some good-size smallmouths.

Red and orange apparently produce special reactions in fish. They incite them to action. Red may be associated with blood, but there's no hint as to why orange should incite fish to strike.

Fish have remarkably keen eyesight. Trout often strike at tiny leader *knots* of nearly invisible nylon. They do this chiefly when feeding on minute insects known as midges, probably because the size of the knots approximate the size of the midges. Also, light rays hitting the knots create an illusion, and small bubble streaks in the water caused by the moving knots adds to the attraction.

SOUNDS FISH "HEAR" are not sounds but *vibrations*. Fish have an inner ear. Along the center line of the body is a series of minute organs known as the lateral sense line, and it is through this that fish are able to pick up vibrations.

A fish can't "hear" fishermen sitting in a boat and talk-ing, because he isn't equipped to pick up the sound waves of their voices. But if one of the fishermen scuffs his feet on the bottom of the boat, or kicks his tackle box, *vibrations* are put into the water which fish *can* detect.

So fishermen can talk, shout, sing, argue or laugh—and not disturb fish. However, boat noises—including the sounds of rowing and paddling—as well as heavy walking along a bank or scuffling along a stream bed, can be de-tected by fish. The wise angler strives always to move around quietly, particularly when fishing from banks for wily species such as trout.

FACTS ABOUT FRESH WATER SPECIES

LARGEMOUTH BASS usually are greenish black, being darkest along the back and turning lighter towards the belly which is ivory white. A dark green or black mottled stripe runs along a largemouth's side from just behind the

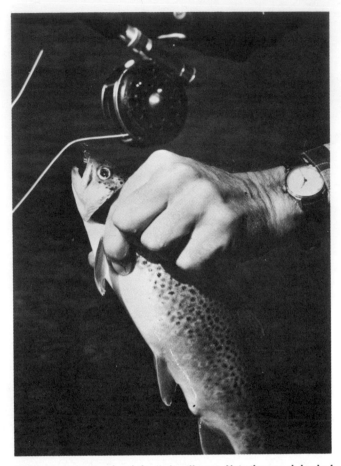

Brown trout are considered the "wisest" trout. Note the nymph hooked in the nose of this brown from Pennsylvania's Slate Run.

eye to the tail. The upper jaw of a largemouth bass extends to beyond the eye.

The largest bass are found in the southern states, where they feed and grow twelve months of the year. Bass grow much slower and attain smaller maximum sizes in the north. For example, an 8-pound bass may be a real prize in certain Minnesota lakes, but wouldn't be considered large in Florida where ones of 15 pounds are taken every year.

SMALLMOUTH BASS are close cousins to the largemouth, both belonging to the sunfish family. Smallmouths, however, never attain the large sizes of largemouths and prefer colder water; they grow faster and larger in clear, northern rivers and lakes.

It's easy to distinguish a smallmouth from a largemouth. A smallmouth bass's mouth *is* considerably smaller than a largemouth's. While the upper jaw of the largemouth extends to beyond the eye, in the smallmouth it extends only *to* the eye.

The general shape of both bass is similar, but their coloration differs. Smallmouths usually are a brassy or bronze color, with a series of blackish-grey stripes running vertically down the sides, and three more stripes running backwards from the eyes.

The smallmouth is one of the gamest fish in fresh water, though they average only about a pound. A 5-pounder is

a big smallmouth anywhere, although some of up to 7 pounds are caught every year in some Kentucky and Tennessee lakes.

TROUT include brook, brown, rainbow and "lakers" or lake trout.

Brook trout commonly are the smallest, being found in the tiniest cold water streams. Requiring more oxygen than any of the other trout, brookies thrive only in the cleanest, coldest water.

The brook trout is colorful, having irregular, wormlike markings on the back, with red and blue dots on the sides, and red, black, and white edgings on the fins. They are extremely belligerent and active, and are the easiest of all trout to catch.

Brown trout are the "wisest," the most difficult to catch consistently. They rise to dry flies better than other trout, but do more night feeding. Browns can live in warmer water than the other trout, so are more generally distributed. Overall color is brownish, blending to yellowish below, with dark brown, black, red, and orange spots.

Rainbow trout are the best fighters, often leaping two or three times their own length out of the water when hooked. They are great migrants, frequently moving out of streams into deep water lakes, and back again.

Most fishermen feel rainbows derive their name from the brilliant red stripe running laterally down their sides, but this is only partly true. A hooked rainbow often leaps out of the water and rolls over, momentarily hanging in a curve, and when the sun is right the fish's stripe looks like a miniature rainbow over the water.

Lake trout average the largest of all trout, but have limited distribution. Best fishing for them is in Canada, although some Wisconsin and Michigan lakes provide fair laker fishing at times—particularly in the fall and winter.

Lakers of 20 or 30 pounds are not uncommon, and 50-pounders are taken in Canadian lakes. Deep trolling is usually the best method, or bait-casting in the shallows just after ice-out.

Lakers have deeply forked tails, and are grayish, with many light-colored spots of orange or pink.

WALLEYES are one of the best food fish. Some fishermen call them "pike perch" or "jack salmon." Average size is about 1½ pounds, but 3- and 4-pounders are common. At least a few 15-pound walleyes are caught each spring from Kentucky's Cumberland River during the annual spawning run.

Walleyes are yellow to brownish green, with an overlay of dusky blotches or mottlings. A bronze or brassy color is common. The eyes, as indicated by the fish's name, appear to be clouded over and become very white soon after being caught.

NORTHERN PIKE are the scourge of every small, living thing in fresh water. True northerns are cold water fish, thriving best in weedy lakes full of suckers or other small fishes for them to prey upon. A "good" northern weighs 5 or 6 pounds, but in some remote Canadian lakes 20 pounds is not uncommon. Northerns are long, thin fish—usually of bluish-green color, with side markings of irregular rows of yellow or gold spots.

This giant lake trout—in the 40-pound class—was taken in Saskatchewan's Black Lake.

Giant northern pike are the "despoilers" of every living thing in fresh water.

MUSKELLUNGE are like over-grown pike, having the same general shape and the same bad disposition. Although muskies are "moodier" than northerns, not hitting with regularity and abandonment, they are one of the most predatory fishes found in fresh water.

Muskellunge are the fresh water angler's big prize, because of their size if nothing else. A "small" muskie weighs 10 pounds, while a good one is about 20 pounds. Some of 40, and sometimes 50 pounds, are caught every year in northern Wisconsin and New York State. The current world's record musky was taken in New York's St. Lawrence River.

Muskies are usually dark green or gray, graduating to olive and brown on the sides, and whitish on the belly. Most have mottled bars or splotchings.

PANFISH are smaller fresh water fish sought by fishermen. They are "game" for their size, take artificial lures, and are often considered a table delicacy. Among the important panfish are black and white crappies, yellow perch, sunfish, and bluegills.

Of these, crappies grow largest, sometimes to 3 pounds or more. All of the panfishes are found in good numbers through most of the country. Lakes are their primary habitats, although they can be numerous in large rivers.

ROUGH FISH. is a biological term meant to include species of fish that generally are detrimental to game fish populations when they become too plentiful. Primary rough fish is the carp, a European import that is credited with destroying many prime bass fishing areas by roiling the water and eating bass spawn. Other fish that could be included in the "rough" category are catfish, suckers, chubs, and bullheads. Bullheads, catfish, and suckers, however, are fine hook-and-line fish and good eating. Bullheads and catfish can be a delicacy any time, but suckers usually are good only in the early spring.

THE EFFECTS OF WEATHER AND WATER CONDITIONS ON FISHING should be thoroughly understood by every fisherman. The weather and condition of the water can affect your sport so much that they can be the difference between a full creel and a complete day spent at nothing more than casting practice.

Weather affects some fish more than others. Many expert bass and musky fishermen will not go fishing if the barometer is low or falling. A low or falling barometer generally foretells a storm or major change in the weather, and such conditions rarely bring about good fishing. Some fishermen, however, feel it matters little if the barometer is low or high, so long as it is steady. They believe a *changing* barometer foretells poor fishing.

A falling barometer usually precedes exceptionally poor bass fishing, but when the barometer switches from low to a rise—there may be a bass waiting at the end of every cast. The best fishing always comes during a period when the barometer is rising steadily but slowly.

It isn't always possible to check a barometer before going fishing. Sometimes you're already on the lake, perhaps camping out or staying at a resort. So you're up in the morning and ready to go—and that's when you take a look around at the weather, not before. If you can see the undersides of the leaves on trees on a summer day, fishing is apt to be poor. The reason for the undersides showing, of course, is that a light breeze is working, which usually precedes a thunder shower.

No one, not even the biologists, knows exactly why a low barometer or other weather conditions should affect fishing, but there are theories. One is that a fish's air bladder is affected by a falling barometer, which drives the fish to deep water where he is able to swim in greater comfort. Proponents of this theory add that this is "nature's way" of protecting fish, since lightning sometimes strikes open water and fish in the shallows or near the surface might, conceivably, be killed. Theories or no, fish go deep when a major storm approaches and the barometer is falling.

A barometer does not always fall drastically from a short rain storm, although it generally does when thunder and lightning are mixed in. A light shower on a hot summer day might actually improve fishing, since it cools the atmosphere, stirs up the fish after a period of lying doggo, and aerates and cools the surface of the water. Some very good bass, trout, and walleye fishing sometimes comes during a rainfall.

Walleyes, in particular, hit well on cloudy, overcast, rainy, windswept days. Walleyes are different and seem to like overcast weather conditions. Muskellunge are much the same, and most musky veterans will tell you their favorite weather condition is a muggy, overcast, threatening day, and if there's a good breeze rippling the lake, so much the better.

However, for bass and trout most fishermen prefer unchanging, clear weather.

It's important to realize, though, that the *season* of the year means a lot. In spring, when water is cool, a bright, warm, summery day often is best for bass, trout and panfish—with best fishing usually from 10 a.m. until 2 p.m., the hottest part of the day. A cold, cloudy day at this time of year has the effect of prolonging winter conditions, and keeping fish inactive. Later, as the water warms under the summer sun, a cloudy day with some rain can momentarily break the "dog day doldrums" that usually hit all fishing in August and early September.

If you should be caught fishing during a severe weather change, and good luck that you'd been having along the shoreline suddenly switches to bad luck, change your tactics and fish the deep water and drop-offs. You can do this by trolling, by casting heavy lures and giving them time to sink to bottom, or by stillfishing with bait just off the bottom. When a shoreline suddenly becomes unproductive in the face of a major weather change, you can bet the reason is that the fish have left the shallows for deep water. Your problem then is to relocate, and find the fish.

In many ways water conditions have even more of an effect on fishing than weather. Always fishermen are heard to complain that the water is "too dirty" or "too clear." It never seems to be just right! What is "just right" depends on the season of the year, the place you're fishing, and the species of fish you're trying for.

Generally speaking, extremely turbid (dirty or muddy) water means poor fishing for the important gamefish species, and particularly so if using artificial lures. Fish

Fishing at the mouth of a cool, incoming stream (left, background) produced a 3-pound brook trout for this spin fisherman.

In spring, a bright, warm day is usually best for bass. This string was taken at Bull Shoals, Arkansas, one sunny day in April.

can't see a lure as well in dirty water as in clear. They can't see bait as well either, but they can smell bait to certain degrees, some kinds of fish being considerably better at smelling than others. The carp, bullhead, and catfish fisherman expects to fish muddy water; it's the nature of the species he's after to live in turbid water. These fish are equipped with special organs to help them smell and find food even when they can't see well.

But when after bass, trout, and northerns, extremely muddy water will hinder your fishing. Best thing to do is to select larger plugs than usual, and to retrieve them very slowly. Also, the lures based on sound for attraction are good under murky water conditions. Spoons, spinners, and such lures that flash and reflect light also are good when the water is muddy. A favorite color in plugs under such conditions is yellow, followed by silver-sparkle, all black, green, and red-and-white. Yellow apparently is the easiest

color for fish to see in muddy water.

Extremely turbid water has a lower oxygen content than does clear water, so fish may be more sluggish, and perhaps lying deeper than usual in muddy water. Sometimes a lake is murky or turbid only for several feet under the surface, while below that it is reasonably clear. If, during muddy water conditions, you fail to connect by fishing on or near the surface, use a flashy lure that sinks fast. Make a cast, and pay out line as long as it rolls from the reel spool. When the line stops moving, the lure has settled on the bottom, and you can begin jigging it up and down.

For trout, bass, and panfish, fly fishermen should use large streamers when the water is muddy from spring rains. Yellow streamers with silver tinsel bodies are best. The sparkle of tinsel attracts fish, and the big flies are easier for them to see.

In extremely clear water, fish can see great distances

and are less apt to be fooled by run-of-the-mill lures. In clear water use a longer and finer leader if fly fishing, and be certain to use a monofilament leader if bait-casting. Spinning and spin-cast fishermen, of course, have continuous leaders, in a sense, since the lines used are monofilament. Under clear shallow water conditions, spinning often is the best way to fish since small, light lures can be handled easily, cast great distances, and the line is less visible to the fish. In very clear water tiny lures are preferred. In clear water fish are much more easily deceived by small lures. If the water is calm, or slightly riffled, top water lures often will out-produce underwater lures.

Water temperature also affects fishing. When water becomes uncomfortably warm, as on hot, sultry days, lake fish will move into deep holes or to the mouths of cool feeder streams. River and stream fish will move out of poorly aerated shallows to hole up under falls and at the base of rapids, where the water is colder and there's more oxygen. Those are the places to fish, skipping all the shallow and "dead" water areas.

Remember that fish are cold-blooded critters, so their comfort is directly related to their environment. Cool water keeps most fish active; hot water tends to make 'em sluggish; and really cold water makes most species inactive and semi-dormant.

At certain "ideal" temperatures, each species of fish is at his active best, feeding with vigor, and so is more apt to strike a lure or take bait. For trout, water temperature of 62 to 68 degrees seems best. Muskellunge are most active when the water temperature is around 52 degrees. Walleyes like water temperatures under 60 degrees; northern pike, about 68; smallmouth bass, around 65; largemouths, about 70; and panfish from 65 to about 80. Don't expect good bass fishing when lake temperature drops below 48 degrees, and whenever the surface water is above 80—fish deep.

When walleye fishing and the temperature in the shallows climbs to more than 65 degrees, start probing the deep holes. Don't expect to find any kind of trout, not even browns, which can withstand warmer water than brooks or rainbows, if the stream remains at a temperature greater than 80 or 85 for any length of time.

FISHING TECHNIQUES

FINDING FISH is a matter of being in the right spot at the right time.

Many fishermen spend too much time trying to find "killer" lures or bait, and they work the same old spots day after day instead of first being sure they are fishing water that has fish.

Trolling is the best way to search for, and to find, fish.

Knowing how to locate fish is the "Ace-in-the-Hole" possessed by the expert angler.

As explained earlier, many kinds of fish are migratory. This doesn't mean that the stump where you hooked a big one last June won't hold another big one next June—but there probably won't be a big fish there in August. Water around that stump might be the right temperature for a bass in June, but it probably will be too hot in August for a bass to be comfortable there. Learn to *hunt* fish.

Every lake, river, and stream has its "hot spots," but they are not all productive all of the time. Besides the time of year and water temperatures, fluctuating water levels cause fish to move about, as does a migrating food supply. In the big TVA lakes, where bass feed heavily on shad minnows, the bass follow the constantly moving schools of shad minnows. In nearly all the major lakes, schools of bait fish play a major part in the movements of gamefish.

As a general rule, start looking for gamefish such as bass, northerns and muskies in the shallows. Begin by casting surface lures right up against the bank. Work them carefully around brush piles, sunken stumps, and trees and over weed beds. If there's no action try a shallow-running lure, casting farther out from shore. Gradually fish deeper, until finally you are scraping the bottom with a deep-running lure.

If you fail to locate fish, leave the area and move to a new place. If you've been working the windward side of a lake, try the lee side. During all your moving around be sure to keep an eye open for signs of fish. You might see one jump clear, spot one as he rolls on the surface and causes a swirl, or you may even see tiny bait fish skipping over the surface as they try frantically to escape feeding gamefish.

Always be sure to fish rocky points; places where there are sudden drop-offs; sheltered bays that have cover; sand and gravel bars; in weed and lily pad beds, along the deep edges of weed beds, and in deep holes. Weed beds some distance from shore and at depths of 15 to 30 feet usually are good.

As a broad guide, you can expect to find bluegills, sunfish, rock bass, and such panfish in the shallows throughout the spring, summer, and early fall. Warm water doesn't seem to bother most of the panfishes. They'll stay in the shallows, up against the shaded banks, even in sultry August weather. The only time these fish move very deep is in late fall, when water temperature drops and they move out into deep water to spend the winter, not going shoreward again until spring.

Carp spend almost all their time in extremely shallow water, and in spring move into quiet, shallow, muddy bays where they spawn in only inches of water. Catfish and bullheads like depths of 10 to 12 feet through most of the spring and summer.

Largemouth black bass, as well as smallmouths, northerns, walleyes, and muskies, stay in shallows only as long as the water is reasonably cool for them—with largemouths taking higher water temperatures than the other species. Smallmouths and walleyes prefer deeper water than other fish. As soon as spring wanes, you can expect to find smallmouths and walleyes in deep water most of the time. Walleyes usually go deeper than smallmouths. On a given day smallmouths may be down about 12 feet, while walleyes are at 20 feet. Muskies rarely go very deep, but they often desert shoreline shallows for weed beds or bars in the middle of bays where the water may be 15 or 30 feet deep.

One of the best ways to locate fish is by trolling. In hot weather gamefish will move into protected shallows to feed along about sundown, possibly stay most of the night, then move out again soon after daybreak. But once the fish have left the shoreline there is more of a problem locating them—and this is where trolling comes in handy.

Most fishermen start by trolling shallow-running lures as close to shore as possible, gradually moving out into deeper water and using deep-running lures. They try the bays, along drop-offs at cliffs; over sand bars and weed beds; and finally in the far out, open water where it seems no sane fish would ever have reason to go.

Trolling is the only way to cover a lot of water, which is what must be done when trying to locate fish. Work into this cove, along that cliff, over that sand bar—until finally you get a strike. Then row or drift to cast lures, or stillfish with bait. By trolling, a lure always is in the water, checking out this area and that. Trolling is an especially productive method of finding fish when working a lake or river for the first time. If you fish the same water much of the time, you soon learn where fish hang out, but on new lakes where all the bays and coves look the same, trolling is the method that will find fish for you the fastest.

Generally speaking, slow trolling is the best technique, but there are times when fast trolling—with the motor almost wide open—gets the most strikes. As you try one spot after another, change the trolling speed and keep varying lures. Often fish will take a particular lure trolled at a particular speed, and refuse everything else offered them.

Fish also can be located by stillfishing: just move around from place to place until you catch fish. Most veteran stillfishermen keep altering the depth at which they fish their bait, knowing that there may not be any fish 10 or 12 feet down, and there may not be any 50 feet down—but a school of crappies could be hanging out at some depth in between.

A good sinker assortment, containing different styles of sinkers as well as different weight sinkers, makes it easy for the stillfisherman to alter the depths he fishes as well as the kind of bait used. "Pinch-on" sinkers are best when fishing fast streams; bell sinkers are good with line-spreaders or when using more than one baited hook; and split-shot sinkers are useful when only slight weight is wanted. Always try to fish bait with as little lead as possible, remembering that live bait acts more natural in the water when little or no lead is on the line.

Different sizes of push-button floats also are useful to

In shallow water tiny surface plugs are deadly on bass.

the stillfisherman in locating fish. These floats make it possible to change the depth at which a bait is fished merely by pressing a button and pulling out the line. With such floats you can accurately measure, in feet or yards, the distance between the float and your bait.

A thermometer also helps in locating fish. As indicated earlier, all fish have temperature preferences, and once you learn the water temperature that the fish you are after like best, it is a simple matter to make temperature readings at different depths to locate the water which is most comfortable to the fish. Temperature and barometric pressure conditions *are* influential upon the habits of fish, particularly fresh water species. At various temperatures fish will be active, inactive, hungry, "off their feed," or even in semi-hibernation.

Fish normally seek water temperatures equal to their body temperatures. In shallow lakes, streams, and rivers it is easy to tell how active fish will be. An ordinary thermo-

A lead-head jig with black pork rind eel bounced tantalizingly over the bottom fooled this Monroe Reservoir (Indiana) bass into striking.

meter lowered to about 3 feet below the surface will give you the temperature of the shallows. However, make deeper readings by lowering the thermometer to various depths with about 10-foot separations.

In foul weather, fish generally go deep, particularly during extremely violent thunderstorms coupled with lightning. In spring or summer when heavy rainfall muddies parts of rivers and lakes, look for fish in the clearer water areas —places away from incoming streams that bring silt and mud. Good places to locate fish almost any time are the mouths of little bays and coves, or the mouths of feeder streams or rivers. In summer, fish will congregate where there are spring heads or cool streams flowing into a lake.

Knowing the bottom formation of a lake is a sure way to locate fish. Thermometer reading will give the temperature of water; soundings will give the depth; but it's also good to know the kind of bottom at the spot you are fishing. Try to learn the high spots, drop-offs, holes, channels, and complete contours of bottoms. The types of bottom—such as sand, mud, or gravel—are closely related to the lives, feeding habits, and movements of fish. Where there are gravel shoals there'll usually be walleyes in the spring, autumn, and on dark, summer nights. As summer's heat warms the water, the walleyes will go out to the deep gravel bars, or stay in cool channel currents—but never over mud bottoms. Largemouth bass, on the other hand, like mud bottoms and shelves, and they prefer rocky, sandy, or gravelly bottoms.

Knowing how to locate fish is the ace in the hole of the expert angler. A habit of veteran fishermen, whenever they are on new water for the first time, is to hire a guide. If this isn't possible, try to get a local fisherman to accompany you. Often dock operators, game wardens, or sporting goods store owners will gladly take the time to show you where to fish or even accompany you. Fish the "hot spots" other people tell you about, but never spend too much time in one place.

If unable to get a guide when visiting a new lake, ask questions before leaving the dock. Find out where fish are caught most often, and on what lures and baits. Find out where the deep water is, the shallow water, and location of weed beds, lily-pad bays,—the spots where fish are likely to be. If necessary, have someone draw a rough map of such places and take it with you when you head out fishing. Do plenty of exploring—and remember that a day or two spent at learning about a lake or river is the big part of locating fish. You can't catch fish until you find them!

TAKING FISH ON THE SURFACE is the sportiest way to catch fish. A largemouth bass taken on a popping bug, for example, will give you a charge like a $4 shotgun. And many times no other fishing system will account for bass the way fly rod popping bugs will!

Almost all of the important fresh water species will hit topwater bugs and plugs. Panfish will take small fly rod bugs. Largemouth and smallmouth bass hit bugs greedily when the fish are in the shallows; white bass will take poppers and small surface lures; and northern pike and muskellunge will chew the paint off plugs and lures fished on the top. The walleye, however, a notorious bottom-scratcher, rarely hits on the surface. In some lakes, walleyes are taken on surface lures but this is the exception rather than the rule.

For most surface fishing, small to medium size lures are best. Remember that big fish will hit small lures, but small fish won't often strike big lures.

Surface popping bugs are absolute "musts" for bass fishermen. A good bug has a sturdy body; is mounted on a long-shank hook extending downward from the bug; is constructed to pop well and "pick up" easily; and there are no unecessary frills attached. Long hooks reduce the number of strikes missed, while too much hair or feathers make a bug difficult to cast. The color of surface lures isn't particularly important, but yellow, white, black, green, orange, and red ones sometimes mean extra fish.

Probably the small size of bugs is what makes them especially appealing to gamefish. Bugs hit the water with a slight life-like "splat," instead of with the loud splash of oversized, heavy plugs. A fly rod bug acts natural on the water, much like a real locust or grasshopper.

More bass are taken on surface plugs than on any other kind of lure. Also the majority of muskies are hooked on topwater lures.

A surface plug or bug is extremely realistic on the water. Each time you twitch or "pop" a surface lure, a stream of bubbles filters down into the water, then curves to the surface again. It is this bubble trail that causes fish to investigate!

In extremely shallow water use small surface plugs or bugs. Put them down lightly by stopping the cast before the lure hits the water, and allow them to "rest" motionless

When weeds are extra thick, retrieve slowly for less chance of fouling the lure.

for some time before beginning the retrieve. Many fishermen allow a topwater lure to sit perfectly still until all the rings caused by its falling to the water have subsided. When the surface again is glass calm, they twitch the lure. Work surface lures lightly and slowly, with frequent pauses between twitches. Sometimes it's good just to tighten the line enough to make a topwater plug nod its head a little . . . repeating this maneuver over and over.

Sometimes, particularly in the fall, a very fast retrieve works well with surface lures. On this kind of retrieve pop the lure along steadily and fast, making the water fly, but don't work the lure too hard. Try several methods on one retrieve, until you find the retrieve the fish like most on a particular day. I cast to a likely spot, let the lure rest motionless for several seconds, then give it a slight "pop." Wait, pop it again, wait again. Then pop the lure along steadily but slowly for three or four feet, then rest it again —this time waiting a long while before "popping" it again. After that work the lure very hard and fast, stopping only occasionally. Once the lure is about half-way back to the boat, work it straight in with steady twitches of the rod tip.

Always be sure when working a surface lure that you have as little slack as possible in the line. If you have slack and a fish hits, chances are you won't hook him. Keep slack out of the line, and when a fish hits raise the rod tip sharply as fast as you can to drive the hooks home. A fast, hard movement of the rod is absolutely necessary to hook a fair percentage of the fish that strike.

FISHING DEEP is what every angler must learn if he is to catch gamefish consistently, because such fish spend most of their time in deep water.

When you arrive at a lake, particularly one that you are not familiar with, rig a short, stiff trolling rod and attach a deep-running lure, such as a "Spoonplug" or "Bomber." Start trolling back and forth, constantly alternating trol-

ling speed from very fast to very slow. (As a general rule, the colder the day the slower the speed; the warmer, the faster. This is because baitfish, on which predatory fish feed, are lethargic and slow-moving when water temperature is low, but are fast-moving when temperatures are high.)

Study shoreline topography when trolling deep. A hill falling off to a point jutting into a lake may indicate a bar, and there could be a hole or sudden drop-off at its end which holds bass. Be sure to work such areas carefully. Throughout your deep trolling search for holes and bars; check the type of bottom; and mentally pigeon hole each weed bed.

Once you've located fish in a deep-down hole by trolling, anchor the boat and begin casting. This is more sport than trolling and is less apt to spook bass. Bass can be caught anywhere from the shallows to their deep-water sanctuaries, but it's the deep holes where they school that are the real "hot" spots. Here the bass are concentrated, and you'll find even small holes that will hold hundreds of bass on hot summer days.

Anytime you are in an area you know gamefish frequent, but you're not catching any, you can figure the fish are deeper than you are working your lures. In this case you might constantly troll over nearby bars, waiting for fish to leave the very deep holes and migrate over a bar toward shore where they'll feed. Or you can rig up with lead-head jigs and bounce them over the bottom in the deepest water, or try live minnows or some other bait fished just off the bottom.

There are other systems you can use for taking fish down deep.

Any sinking lure can be worked over the bottom. The proper technique is to make a long cast, and count slowly as the lure goes down. By counting you'll learn how long it takes for the lure to reach bottom, and you can then begin your retrieve.

When trying to fish a lure deep, do not retrieve it steadily as this will cause most lures to plane in the water and rise. Instead, reel it a few feet, then stop, allowing the lure to settle again. Often merely twitching the rod tip upwards will raise your lure from the bottom in a tantalizing action, then you can again drop the rod tip to lower the lure. Keep this up, jerking the bait upwards, dropping it, until you score. If fish don't come your way, move to another spot.

Another system of fishing lures deep is to work along cliffs and sharply slanting shores, casting your sinking lure right into the shallows. Let it sink to bottom, then twitch it off the shelf, allowing it to settle to the next level—repeating this maneuver so that the lure works its way down the bank as though it were dropping over a series of steps.

CATCHING FISH OUT OF WEED BEDS isn't as difficult as it may seem to the beginning fisherman.

Muskellunge and northern pike favor weed beds. So do walleyes, largemouth bass, even the panfishes. Gamefish like the weeds because they provide superb cover from which to rush out and grab unsuspecting forage fishes such as minnows and small bluegills. And the minnows and bluegills like the weeds because they give them a place to hide too, as well as a bountiful food supply consisting of tiny aquatic animals and insects.

A good lure for weed bed fishing is a chrome-plated spoon equipped with a wire guard that covers the hook and makes it weed-proof. While the lure is effective by itself, it is deadliest when a thin strip of white porkrind is attached to the hook, or a piece of porkchunk. Split the porkrind strip so that it has a frog-like action. Cast deep into the weeds and bring the spoon back in a haltering, jerking motion.

Best technique for fishing surface weeds is to row slowly along the outside edge of the weeds, casting shoreward. Let the spoon settle, then work it back by jerking the rod tip violently, letting it settle, then jerking again. Change the speed of your retrieve frequently, sometimes fast, sometimes slow, sometimes reeling steadily for several feet, then stopping abruptly and allowing the spoon to settle. Both bass and northern pike frequently hit a spoon after following it for some distance, when they see it stop and begin a weak flutter toward the bottom. This action often infuriates hesitant fish into wild strikes. When weeds are extra thick, it may be best to retrieve slowly and allow the spoon to work its way smoothly through them.

Pocket fishing in weed beds is one of the best ways to take fish. Instead of fishing the weeds helter-skelter, row slowly through the weeds or along the outside edge, fishing only the tiny open pockets. Bass, northerns, etc. like to lie in weeds with their heads pointing toward such pockets, where they watch for passing food-fish. In fishing such pockets don't cast a spoon so that it falls directly into the pocket. Rather, cast it a couple of feet beyond, and swim it into the opening where you think there may be a lurking bass. Dropping your lure directly into a pocket may spook a fish, while casting slightly beyond and bringing the lure into the pocket will not.

Use a casting line slightly heavier than you normally would for weed bed fishing. A stronger line is needed because occasionally any lure will foul, if only momentarily, and with a strong line you can jerk it free and continue fishing. When a fish is hooked in heavy weeds he'll dive and try to foul your line, so a good sturdy line is needed to haul him out. Soon as you get a strike in deep weeds, set the hook fast and hard, then raise your rod high over your head and reel fast. This will keep the fish's head up and you'll be able to skitter him across the weeds.

In deep weed beds it often is productive to fish just over the tips of the weeds, instead of through them. Fish that are some distance away can spot a lure moving over weeds easier than they can one that is moving *through* the weeds. Make a cast over such weeds and let the lure sink to bottom, counting slowly as the lure goes down. On the next cast, count one or two less, and see if you are still running through the weeds. If you are, count a little less on the next cast and your lure should be traveling just over the weeds.

If you fish bait, it often is most productive if dangled in the green depths at the *edges* of weed beds rather than in the weeds. Live bait fished right in weeds often will dart down and hide out of sight of cruising game fish, but bait left at the edge of weeds is in open water and in plain sight of every predator fish working along through the weeds.

However, pocket fishing with bait can be very productive. Here the angler eases up to the open holes and dunks his bait in the opening carefully, allowing it to fish for a time, then moving on to the next hole. Sometimes live bait such as minnows or crayfish can be cast to such holes, allowed to settle briefly, then retrieved for another cast to a fresh spot.

NIGHT FISHING can be deadly for many game species at certain times.

Some fish, in fact, are notorious nocturnal feeders. This includes brown trout, walleyes, bullheads and catfish. Black bass, muskellunge and northern pike sometimes confine all their feeding to the dark hours.

Bass will move into the shallows after dark to feed on minnows, frogs, etc. during the hot summer weeks, although there may not be a single bass along the shorelines during the bright part of each day. As a general rule, fish top-water lures more slowly at night than you would in daytime.

It is not true that the best grounds for night fishing are the brushy or weedy areas. Some of the "hottest" spots for night fishing are the sandy or rocky inshore areas, where you can cast without worrying about getting hooked up. During the daylight hours such spots rarely hold any kind of fish, but at night minnows will swarm into them, and behind the minnows come bass, walleyes, northerns, crappies, and muskies.

The popping sound of a surface plug on the water leads fish to it, and for this reason surface lures usually are best, at night. However, on clear nights don't fail to try a shallow-running, dark-colored lure. The black plugs are best for night fishing, since they show up well against the lighter sky.

Night-feeding fish often give away their presence by their splashing or swirls, so direct your casts to such spots.

When it's so dark you can't see such fish signs, make repeated casts in the direction of the sound.

Always carry a good strong light on night fishing trips, and acquaint yourself with the fishing area during the day, memorizing where the stumps, snags, and weed beds are.

SOME TIPS ON STILLFISHING: Regardless of tackle, technique, or bait used, stillfishermen should endeavor to present bait to fish in a natural, life-like way. For example, you'll catch more trout and bass in streams and rivers if you fish a single worm on spinning gear and cast it upstream, allowing it to wash down naturally with the current. You'll take lunkers this way, whereas you'll be lucky to get even small fish if you merely dunk a worm motionless from the bank.

Use as light tackle as possible for the fish you are after. Line or sinkers that are too heavy wear down live bait and keep it from acting naturally in the water.

Use a float or bobber of the right size for your bait and tackle. Don't use a big one if you're after bluegills, or a small one if you're trying for large pike.

When a fish takes the bait, let him run with it for a minute or two. Northern pike, walleyes, bass, and muskellunge will seize a live minnow and swim slowly off, holding it broadside in their mouths. If you try to set the hook then you'll miss your fish. Give him time to turn the bait and to start swallowing it before you set the hook. When you decide to set the hook, do it fast and hard with a sharp, upward sweep of your rod.

The right hooks should be used in stillfishing. Mustad hooks are very good, with needle-sharp points, and they won't snap or bend if you hook a big one. Nylon-covered, stainless steel wire leaders are right for fishing for the toothy species such as northerns and muskies.

Always carry a good variety of hooks when going stillfishing. You may head out intending to fish only for catfish or bullheads, but black bass may begin prowling; or the bluegills might start hitting. Unless you have several of the right size hooks on hand you may miss out on the best fishing of the day.

Many fishermen use hooks that are too big for small fish, and too small for big fish. Select your hook according to the bait you are using and the kind of fish you're after. Small hooks are right for tiny garden worms and bluegills; a little bigger for average size trout and nymph bait; and larger still for northerns and bass that take 2 to 3-inch long minnows.

Never place sinkers too close to bait. Tiny split-shot sinkers should be used when possible, but when fishing in strong current or in very deep water, heavier sinkers may be necessary. Sinkers should be attached a few feet above a bait, between the hook and the float.

A Potomac River smallmouth fisherman starts out at dusk. Night fishing often is best for many species of fish.

16: Trout fisherman's basic gear

MANY AN ANGLER has a bad time, instead of a good time, when trout fishing simply because he is poorly outfitted. Not even an expert angler, for example, will do his best work if, on a given day he's equipped with a midging outfit when, in fact, conditions dictate use of a big rod and large flies. And no one fishes well when he is too cold or too hot, when wet and miserable, or when being chewed by mosquitoes.

There is certain equipment needed by ALL trout fishermen. But the angler who habitually fishes the same areas will not usually need the varied equipment needed by the fisherman who fishes many different streams and rivers. The eastern angler, usually working small streams, may require only hip boots and a light, 6-7½-foot rod; the western trouter, generally fishing large rivers, will need chest-high waders and an 8-8½-foot rod. The well-traveled angler who today fishes Wisconsin's Pine River, tomorrow Montana's Yellowstone, and next winter Argentina's Traful, will require highly varied gear. Most serious trout fishermen do, in fact, fish varying rivers and streams in the course of any season. Yet even the well-traveled angler need not own a "tackle shop" full of gear; all that's really necessary to be properly equipped for any trout fishing situation is three outfits—light, medium, and heavy. The accessories that go with one usually go with the other, and naturally that simplifies the problem of correctly selecting gear.

Let's begin with the trout fisherman's undies.

In the warmer states ordinary cotton underwear may be adequate even in early spring, but in most good trout areas the weather and water are cold enough at the start of the season to make heavy underwear necessary. Ordinarily a light suit of "long john" woolies will do, particularly if you are out of the water more than you are in it. But if you fish big streams, wearing chest-high waders, heavy woolens will be necessary. With many kinds of warm, lightweight, nylon underwear suits of the "thermo" type now available, a lot of fishermen have discarded their "long johns." The new insulated underwear takes little space in a duffel bag, and is comfortable and warm in the coldest weather. Many trout fishermen wear just the insulated underpants (under regular trousers) when fishing, whether wearing hip boots or waders, but then slip matching insulated jackets on over their fishing shirts if it becomes really cold—such as toward evening when the warm, spring sun has dropped below the trees.

A trout fisherman with the wrong footwear is like an elephant hunter out with a BB gun; neither gets far.

Unless it's extremely cold you should be comfortable with a thin pair of nylon or silk dress socks worn under a pair of good woolen socks. The thin socks are extra insulation, but mostly they allow a kind of foot freedom inside the woolen socks. The woolens provide the real warmth and should be about knee-high. Get them a half-size or a size large so your feet won't be tight and poor circulation result. Too many socks or socks that are too heavy make boots fit so tight there's no air space. Air space is necessary in a boot if your feet are to stay warm. If you fish where there's still snow and ice on opening day you may want an insulated rubber or nylon "bootie" or one of the older type of fleece-lined booties inside your boots. The boots will have to be at least a size larger to use booties.

As to the boots, or waders, one of the first considerations is whether to have the "ankle tight" kind or the loose type. Both have advantages and disadvantages. The ankle-fitting type of hip boot or of chest-high wader is most comfortable. They provide support while wading that looser boots do not. However, ankle-fitting boots are difficult to get in and out of. Loose boots are just the opposite; easy to get in and out of, but they offer almost no ankle support.

You'll also have to decide if you want felt soles on your boots, cleats or hobnail strapping, or ordinary soles. Felt soles are best on all streams, and are absolutely necessary

Hip boots of this type (rubber feet, rubberized-canvas uppers) are lightweight and cool. They're suitable for warm-weather, small stream fishing.

on many. It costs $10 to $15 extra for felt-soled boots, but they're worth it. Felts grip the stream floor and provide walking ease and sure footedness unattainable with ordinary boot soles. Felts are particularly important for older men who've lost some of their cat-like sureness. Quality felted boots can spare you many a wicked fall that may result only in a scraped shin but could mean a broken leg.

Hobnails or cleats must be removed from boots when leaving a creek and hiking down a road for any distance, and most trout fishermen think they're noise-makers in the stream. Thus hobnails and cleats, generally speaking, aren't too popular.

Pure gum-rubber boots usually wear best. Some of the ultra-thin, stretchy boots and waders now available—although light and comfortable—tear easily. The same is

Chest-high waders are needed for big-river fishing. Waders are hot and cumbersome, and not made for long hiking, but are necessary to properly fish some streams.

Select jackets not for warmth but utility. Jackets like this have ample and properly-designed pockets and give sufficient warmth under normal circumstances. In extreme cold, angler may wear a "thermo" type of insulated jacket under fishing jacket.

generally true of nylon or plastic boots. Even twigs, branches and briars can puncture them. And a puncture usually develops into a tear. However, such boots and waders normally are inexpensive.

One kind of felt-soled, loose-ankle hip boots is made of heavy, pure rubber from the boot-foot to just below the knee. At that point the material is rubberized canvas. This isn't as durable nor as warm as pure rubber; these boots are good in warm weather, are considerably lighter than all-rubber boots, and fold into a small pack. The latter feature is especially advantageous when a fisherman is flying to his favorite trout water.

Hip boots or waders? Most trout anglers who do much fishing need both; hip boots for small, shallow streams—chest-high waders for big water. If you operate on a really tight budget and must choose between one or the other, your selection should depend on the kind of streams you fish most. Waders are most expensive, so if the bulk of your fishing is on small streams, get hip boots; otherwise buy chest-high waders. In any case, purchase the best you can afford. Trying to save a buck on boots is false economy. Cheap ones won't serve you well and won't last long.

The fishing shirt and trousers are no problem. Early in the season most anglers wear a woolen outdoors shirt and old woolen trousers. Those specially-designed fishing shirts are not really necessary, but if you like you can go for a pair of knit-cuff fishing pants or the kind that fold over and snap at the cuff for an ankle-tight fit. Socks pull over these trousers easily, and they generally are more comfortable under hip boots or waders.

A good jacket and vest are essential; the jacket for cold

This "Dan Bailey" vest has ample pockets of right size for trout fisher-man's gear, as well as a zip-out (for cleaning) fish bag or "creel."

Important accessories: easily-folded rain parka, polaroid glasses, dry fly oil, snakebite kit, mucilin, extra fly line, pliers, repellent, flashlight, split-shot, hook hone, leader material, boot repair kit, and knife.

weather, the vest for warm days. There are dozens of different fishing jackets and vests available, most of which are excellent. The important thing to look for in a jacket or vest is the right number and size of pockets. Some have far too many small pockets. Get ones having a couple large billows-type pockets to take large fly wallets and big plastic boxes of dry flies. And buy only jackets and vests having full-size billows-type pockets on the back. When on the stream for a long day you can put a few sandwiches and a thermos of coffee in the back pocket, as well as a folded rain parka. Never be without the parka.

Be sure, too, that the jacket and vest you buy are of light-weight, water repellent material. If you kill trout now and then you'll want a zip-in type of "creel" in your garment. Be careful, however, to get one with a thoroughly waterproof fish bag or it won't last beyond opening day. Such "creels" or fish pockets should be washed after use, so if the creel is removable so much the better.

Buy a fishing jacket for its utility, not warmth. What you want is something to keep your gear in—all the dozens of small items every trout fisherman needs. For warmth you can slip a sweater on under the jacket, or one of those nylon insulated vests or jackets mentioned earlier.

A light-weight, water repellent hat (sun-tan color) with a visor will shield your eyes from the sun. This is important because a good trout fisherman strives constantly to see *through* the water to locate trout. Without a cap with a visor, the sun and surface glare will prevent you from spotting many fish. Naturally you're going to do a better job of presenting a fly to the fish that you can see.

Something else about a visored cap: if you wear glasses and it should rain, the visor will keep raindrops from your specs. And every trout fisherman should wear polaroid glasses to help him see *through* the water. One bad thing about visored caps is that they do not have a brim all around. Rain can run off them and pour down the back

of your neck. Of course when it rains hard you can pull out your light, rubberized-canvas rain parka and pull it on over your jacket. The parka's hood will cover your head—cap and all.

The small items stowed in a jacket or vest include fly book or wallets for streamers, nymphs and wet flies; plastic boxes for dry flies; "wheels" of assorted tests of nylon monofilament leader material; a leader pouch (optional); dry fly oil; leader sink; packet of split-shot sinkers; pliers; knife; matches; a hook hone; small wader or boot repair kit; extra fly line; insect repellent; snake bite kit; mucilin or line "cleaner"; clippers; plastic tube for tying nail knot (line to leader butt connection); and a flash light. A flash light, even a small one, can be something of a bother to tote around in a vest or jacket pocket all day, but it's worth its trouble when you tramp out from the river after dark. It's particularly important to carry a light when fishing unfamiliar water.

As all fishermen know, modern fly lines float extremely well as compared to the old silk lines. There is still a place for silk lines in trout fishing, however, and many anglers use them frequently. However, quality, long-floating nylon or synthetic lines are generally preferred, and you needn't grease them often to keep them floating—as is necessary with silk lines. Some fly fishermen never grease a synthetic line. Instead, they use a reel of a type that the spool can be snapped out quickly, and replaced with another spool and line. It's best to have three spools (counting one on the reel). Two spools should be mounted with floating lines, the third with a sinking line. When fishing one of the floaters, and it starts to sink after several hours of fishing, it's an easy matter to remove that spool and replace it with the "fresh" floating line. And the sinking line, of course, is ready for use anytime. Extra reel spools, even two of them, are easily carried in vest or jacket pocket.

The flies needed by a trout fisherman are many and

varied. There are tens of thousands of fly patterns, and every trout fisherman accumulates scores of flies as one season follows another. Generally speaking the eastern trout fisherman will build a stock of small flies while the western angler will tend to patterns tied on larger hooks. All trouters, though, should have a good representative selection of streamers, nymphs, and dry flies. Some fishermen will add wet flies, and perhaps tiny midges, and special terrestrials.

Because of regional variations, there'll be no attempt here to suggest a complete stock of fly patterns, but there are some *types* of flies, and some patterns, that are outstanding fish-getters and are useful to trout fishermen everywhere.

You should have a good stock of nymphs, for example, and be sure to include plenty of Gray Nymphs—a pattern that rainbows in particular go hard for. Other important nymph patterns include the Caddis, March Brown, Big Hole Demon, Stonefly, and Hendrickson. Nymphs of the "attractor" type—as opposed to those meant to imitate a specific real nymph—should be included in your kit.

Some streamer *types* needed are marabous, bucktails, and saddle hackle streamers. White, Yellow, and Black Marabou patterns are good fish-finders as well as fish-

getters. Bucktail streamers, such as the Brown Dace pattern, Dark Tiger, Edson Tiger, and Muddler Minnow (often best fished dry), take a lot of trout, and particularly large browns. Saddle-hackle patterns that are popular include the Black Ghost, Gray Ghost, Royal Coachman, and Silver Doctor.

Your dry fly boxes should contain deer hair flies, bivisibles, spent-wings, standard upright-wing patterns, some fanwings and hair wings, spiders, and variants, and tiny midges. Important patterns include Dark Hendrickson, Light and Dark Cahills, Brown and Black Bivisibles, Irresistible, Phillip's Deer Hair, Mosquito, Tups Indispensable, Adams, Quill Gordon and Black Gnat.

Add to all these some ants, such as the Carpenter Ant, grasshopper patterns (Michigan Hopper), and various beetles and Wooly Worms—and you should be prepared for almost any fishing condition, anywhere, anytime.

Three fly fishing outfits—light, medium, and heavy—will cover any normal trout fishing situation. The angler who habitually fishes for small trout on small mountain or meadow streams heavily brushed-in, will do best with a rod 6 to 7½ feet in length, weighing 1 to 3 ounces, and taking a very light single-action reel mounted with a double-tapered HEH(DT-5) line. For fishing intermediate streams—

Well-equipped trout angler needs full assortment of streamers, nymphs, dry flies, wet flies, ants, beetles, etc. Particular patterns depend on area fished.

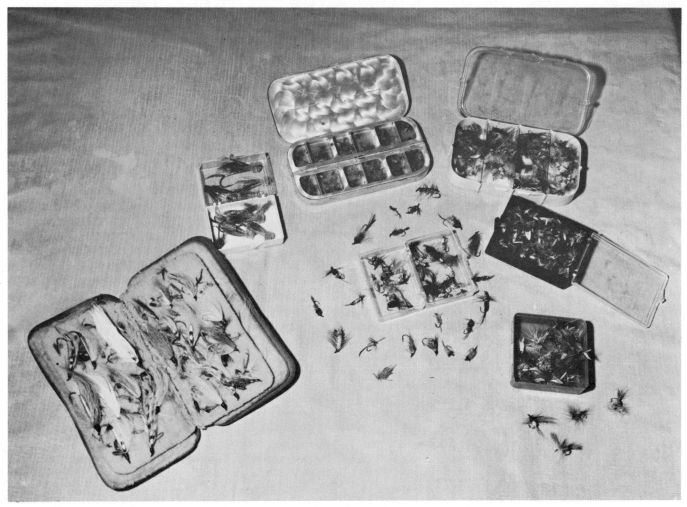

The complete trout fisherman needs only three outfits—(from bottom) light, medium and heavy. Light rod shown weighs 1½ ounces, is 6-feet, and ideal for small-stream fishing. Center rod is medium, 7-feet long, with HDH (DT-6) lines, and just right for medium size trout streams. Top rod is glass, 8-feet, 5-ounces, with GBF (WF-8) line, and well suited to rivers requiring long casts and large, heavy flies.

such as the Au Sable in Michigan, Spring Creek in Montana, or the Tunkhannock in Pennsylvania—a rod 7 to 8 feet long and weighing 3-4 ounces is suitable. Much depends on the rod's action (a 7-foot rod could be stiff enough to require a GBF [WF-8] line), but if it has normal trout action for its length it will take an HDH or HCH line, that is, a DT-6 or DT-7 line.

For big rivers, a comparatively "heavy" outfit is needed. This might be a rod of 8 to 9 feet, weighing 4-5 ounces, with heavy action requiring a GBF (WF-8) line, or a GBG (DT-8) line. Such an outfit, with matching reel, would handle large streamer flies on heavy hooks, and would be right for fishing big water such as Montana's lower Madison, Washington's Quinault, and New York's Delaware.

Whether the rod is bamboo or glass is a matter of personal preference. Many veteran anglers prefer bamboo in the lighter rods, glass in the heavier ones. Reason for this is that glass rods are generally lighter than bamboo, and for the heavier work a glass stick can be less fatiguing.

The all-around trout fisherman—the angler who fishes various streams in widely scattered areas—will do well to equip himself with at least one of each of the type outfits described, because on occasions he'll need light, medium, and heavy gear.

A fair size duffel bag with extra clothing should be taken on all trout fishing trips, if even only a one-day trip. A leather-trimmed, sturdy canvas bag about three feet long and a foot-and-a-half wide will take extra trousers and shirts, your fishing jacket and vest, several pairs of socks, extra cap, loafers or sneakers, and perhaps extra leaders, flies and such. It's a good idea to have extra trousers, shirts, and socks of different weights—some heavy, some light. Quite often the weather will throw you a curve, and if you leave home dressed for cold weather the day is sure to turn into a blister. It won't matter, however, if you can change into light clothing when you hit the stream.

Underwater—in every lake, river and pond—
predatory fish pursue their prey, striking swiftly
out of hunger, anger or boredom. It's
a deadly game and an endless warfare of survival
among those who eat and those who are eaten.

17: Murder in the millpond

With murder in his heart, a musky hovers and awaits his prey.

To ordinary man, a placid millpond may seem like one of the more peaceful corners of the world, and a trickling stream may appear as tranquility itself. But in every submarine world inhabited by fish, there is an endless warfare of survival. In the underwater community of fish, there are enemies and allies. For most fish, daily life is a continuing mortal game of hide-and-seek.

Generally speaking, all fish may be divided into two classes: predators and prey, or those who eat and those who are eaten. The deadly game is waged constantly in all waters holding gamefish (predators) and forage fish (nonpredators).

While many persons, including some anglers, look upon fish as docile and weak creatures, most gamefish in their element are ferocious and skilled exterminators. The black bass, for example, is nothing more than a lip with fins. The northern pike is a needle-nosed gangster. And the muskellunge is a tough-skinned roustabout whose perpetual expression is a sneer.

In many waters the major gamefish will be muskies, northern pike, largemouth and smallmouth black bass, and four species of trout (brook, brown, rainbow, and lake). In those same waters and also in the predaceous class, but considered lesser gamefishes, are black and white crappies, bluegills, and walleyes.

All of the important gamefish are, in fact, fin-propelled mouths that patrol a watery world filled with a squirming abundance of minnows, frogs, crayfish, eels, newts, worms, hellgrammites, and nymphs. In addition to these, a bass, northern pike, or muskie is likely to eat anything live falling on or into the water. This includes small songbirds, ducks, and ducklings, mice, muskrats, snakes, baby raccoons, and other small land animals—and, of course, one another. A bass will eat a bass, and muskellunge are notorious cannibals.

There is the classic case of a 3-pound largemouth bass that choked trying to eat a 3½-pound bass. Somehow, the smaller bass secured the larger one in its mouth head-first,

and got his victim down as far as its dorsal fin. But the hungry bass couldn't get more down, nor could he disgorge the larger bass. Both fish died.

A Pennsylvania fisherman once saw a largemouth bass flopping almost lifeless on the surface. He netted the fish, and discovered the bass had swallowed a shrew that must have fallen into the water. Once in the bass' stomach, the shrew dug thru the fish's stomach wall with its sharp claws and crawled halfway out. The shrew drowned and, naturally, the bass also died.

Years ago while fishing Loch Raven Reservoir near Baltimore, a companion and I found a bass in similar trouble. This one had made the mistake of trying to eat an 8-inch spotted catfish. The bass had taken the catfish stern-first, which is unusual since predatory fish nearly always take large prey head-first. The bass got the catfish down as far as the catfish's pectoral fins, where sharp spines prevented the bass from swallowing more. The bass could not disgorge the catfish, and soon was floundering weakly on the surface.

Swallows and some other birds that sometimes skim low over the water—often dipping their bills into the water either to drink or to pick up floating insects—occasionally become victims of gamefish. Fishermen have reported seeing bass actually leap out of the water and, in effect, "field" low-flying birds the way a baseball player might leap to catch a ball.

Waterfowl conservationists accuse northern pike of destroying thousands of ducklings yearly. A pike will strike a duckling swiftly and gulp it immediately, or might swim cautiously below the duckling, seize a foot, pull the duckling under, and drown it before consuming it.

A major problem at Wisconsin muskie hatcheries is preventing the muskies from eating one another. If a fresh batch of muskellunge fry are put into a holding pond where no other fish are available, in time there probably will be nothing in the pond but one plump muskie. Muskies are so cannibalistic that hatcheries must continually keep them sorted according to size. A 15-inch muskie is not likely to try to eat another 15-inch muskie, but a 15-incher might quickly kill a 13-incher.

A gamefish's digestive system works so rapidly he sometimes can get by with biting off more than he can chew. Once, while skin diving at Grand Bahama Island, I observed a Nassau grouper of about 12 pounds strike a jack crevalle of about 8 pounds. The grouper could hardly get more than the jack's head down, so he merely edged backwards into a coral crevice and relaxed to await gradual digestion.

Often gamefish eat too much. Many kinds of fish, particularly certain salt water species such as bluefish and various kinds of jacks, when on a feeding orgy will devour countless baitfish. But with a lust for blood and a desire to continue their killing melee, they will regurgitate what they've just eaten and go on ripping up baitfish.

Obviously, the gamefish do not always kill forage fish merely to eat them. A predatory fish might strike another fish out of annoyance, for defensive reasons, in anger, out of boredom or curiosity. Scuba diving near Key Largo in 1958, I saw an Atlantic barracuda lash out viciously at a grunt and bite it in half. The 'cuda then hung motionless

Bass at left, one of a group of small largemouths, seizes a hapless golden roach.

Bass in center has his meal but other two must continue their search for food. Most predatory fish will feed at least once daily if able to find and catch smaller fish.

in the water as the grunt halves settled to the bottom.

Most anglers who seek bass, pike, muskies, etc., have experienced catching these gamefish even though their stomachs had been freshly filled. I recall having caught two largemouth black bass that could not possibly have struck out of hunger; the legs of a frog were poking out of the gullet of one, and the tail and lower third of a blue-gill extended from the gullet of the other.

A peculiarity of nature seems to extend from the higher animals to the fish: those who are normally eaten seem to know when those who do the eating are ready to eat, and when they are not. In Africa I have seen wildebeest and impala, common prey of lions, grazing unconcerned within yards of a pride of sunning lions. But when a couple of

lionesses arose, looked at the wildebeests and impalas and began slow circling, the antelopes promptly stampeded. At Lake Geneva in Wisconsin, I once sat on the lake floor with a diving lung and in a rubber cold-water suit and watched largemouth bass, bluegills, and a cloud of shiner minnows sharing an open, rocky pocket in weeds. All was tranquil until, suddenly, a bass bolted toward a small bluegill, which escaped. All the bluegills and minnows immediately evaporated into the weeds.

While gamefish occasionally miss getting their prey, nature has well equipped our predatory fish for piscatorial mayhem. Most of the predators have formidable teeth. Fresh water muskies and northern pike have long, canine teeth, with those on the larger individuals sometimes meas-

Two young bass rest over bottom as they digest minnows taken earlier. Note a minnow tail protruding from jaws of each bass.

A largemouth secures a shiner minnow sideways in his jaws. He may turn it and take it head-first, or merely double the fish before swallowing.

uring half an inch. In addition to these big, snatching-and-holding teeth, muskies and pike have smaller teeth on their tongues and palates. Even the walleye, certainly one of the more sluggish of the predators, has a few long and sharp canine teeth.

However, all of the efficient predators do not have impressive teeth. Largemouth and smallmouth bass have such tiny teeth they are hardly noticeable. But these species have powerful, cartilaginous jaws for seizing and holding.

Teeth or no teeth, all predatory fish have one thing in common—speed. Underwater, I have seen gamefish strike lures with blinding speed, so swiftly the action seemed a blur. At times predatory fish follow their prey, stalking it, then hit like lightning. At other times they rush from places of hiding, taking their quarry by surprise. Rarely does a gamefish bother with a wild, round-the-barn type chase. Rather, when there is successful seizure the pursuit is short-lived—a casual turn, a savage strike, and a forage fish is gulped down.

William P. Braker, Director of Chicago's Shedd Aquarium, says gamefish are much faster than non-gamefish, but they are not as maneuverable. "At close quarters and around cover (rocks, weeds, etc.), a small fish might escape a bass or musky," he said, "but if the smaller fish is unable to hide, it is almost certain to be caught and devoured."

Braker also says some gamefish have special striking habits. "Muskies like to stalk. In open water a musky might go straight for a sucker, but if there is any cover around, he prefers to stalk. He will move up slowly and cautiously toward the sucker, then lunge when just a few feet away."

As a rule, a predatory fish seizes its prey sideways or from the rear. It may then turn its meal around and swallow it head-first. Braker does not believe that muskies or other gamefish scale the fish they catch before swallowing them. I suspect this "scaling" idea is an old wives' tale, and that scaling of a smaller fish in the mouth of a predatory fish is neither possible nor necessary.

However, "muskies like to hold prey in their mouths for a time," says Braker. "They'll hold a fish they've caught and shake it like a dog. Then they flick their heads from side to side, and keep turning the fish around until they can swallow it head-first."

So next time you catch a bass or a musky, don't feel too badly about removing him from the lake. Remember, he may just have committed murder—down there in the deep.

18: Surf fishing tips

1. Many surf fishermen waste time by delivering unnecessarily long casts. Long casts are not always needed. If fish are close inshore, distance casting is time-consuming and a waste of energy. Large fish, such as striped bass of 30-40 pounds, will wander in close to beaches at times.

   When a wave washes onto a beach, it creates a trough or sudden drop-off in which small fish, sand fleas, crabs, etc. are churned up. Often bluefish as well as stripers will hit a lure or bait just as it comes through the wave nearest the dry beach.

2. Some surf fishermen never make decent catches because they spend so much time fighting their tackle. They wrongly strive, at the onset, for a record-breaking cast even though fish may be cruising at their feet. If you try to power the cast a mile, it's not likely to go 50 feet. Take it easy, and let the tackle do the work.

   Make your first cast a short one if only to wet down the line. Put a little more energy into the next one, and the next, but only provided everything goes smoothly on previous casts. Hold your casting distance at the range you can reach without too much effort. This way you will be casting rhythmically, escaping backlashes and other tackle problems, and so will catch more fish because your lure or bait will be in the water longer.

3. When there is no strong tide, little or no wind, and the sea is as flat as a billiard table, long casts may be necessary and more likely to produce fish. As a general rule onshore winds and a high surf will bring small baitfish in close and the gamefish will follow; but in calm water the baitfish stay out, and the gamefish stay with them.

   This doesn't mean that fishing is best, necessarily, when there is a strong onshore wind; but certainly a lot of fish often are caught under such conditions, and when the onshore winds begin to die. Under these conditions the caster who can put out a long line may take the most fish. Three hundred feet or so is considered a long cast.

4. Soft vinyl artificial lures representing sea worms, shrimp, baitfish, squid etc. have become popular with surf casters. But for plastic lures to be most effective, they must be fished right. This is especially true of plastic eels, which probably are the most successful and most popular of the plastic lures designed for salt-water fishing.

   It's important that the plastic eel have a natural swimming motion in the water. Adult eels swim a slow-to-moderate speeds, undulating along in an "S"-shaped path. The best artificial eels have metal lips or "action-heads" that make them wiggle or "swim" in the water. However, the eel must be retrieved at the right speed or it will not have a natural swimming action.

   Regardless of the make of plastic eel you use, test it in clear water to determine the speed at which it "swims" most naturally. Watch how the eel moves when you retrieve it very slowly. Then increase the speed. The best speed is that which gives the eel a slow, steady, side-to-side, "S" type of swimming action.

5. In surf casting the position of the feet is important. A boxer can't deliver a hard blow if his feet aren't planted right, nor can a golfer hit a good tee shot if he isn't standing correctly. Stance is just as important in delivering a good cast.

Assuming you are a right-handed caster (the opposite of what follows will be true for left-handers): your left foot and left shoulder should point at the spot where you want your lure to land. Your right foot should be firmly planted and parallel to the edge of the beach.

Swivel the hips when you cast, and put wrists, arms, shoulders, legs, and the whole of your body from the toes up into the cast. All muscles should be utilized, and end the cast with plenty of "follow-through."

6. Tides are the key to good surf fishing.

Expert guides, charter boat captains, and skilled fishermen all know the importance of tides, yet many novice salt water fishermen pay no heed to tidal conditions. Unless the angler realize how tides can affect his fishing, he may waste precious hours casting when the tide is wrong.

Tides are caused by gravitational forces of the moon and sun. When the tide is rising it is known as the flood tide; when dropping, the ebb tide; and between those times, when the water is neither rising nor falling during the short period of change, it is said to be a "slack" tide.

A moving tide—providing current—is usually more productive than no tide. Fishing in the surf usually is poor during slack tide. The start of the incoming tide is one of the best periods, as is the start of the outgoing tide. Surf fishing around rock jetties, however, frequently is good when the tide is low.

7. Good surf fishermen vary the speed of the retrieve when fishing surface or underwater lures.

As a general rule most salt water fish prefer a swiftly-moving lure, and this is especially true of bluefish, mackerel, etc. Some other species respond best to slowly-moving, tantalizing lures.

Try reeling the lure along as fast as you can, making long sweeps with the rod tip, then slow the retrieve by winding the line in easily and by merely twitching the

rod. Some surf anglers fish out single casts either very fast or very slow, while others prefer to "break up" a retrieve, alternately moving the lure fast then slow.

8. Good natural baits for surf fishing include eels, sea worms, clams, oysters, crabs, baitfish, lobsters and shrimp.

Live baitfish such as herring, sardines and anchovies are excellent and will take gamefish along both the Atlantic and Pacific coasts and the Gulf of Mexico. Baitfish range 3 to 10 inches in length, and two kinds of mullets—striped and white—are consistent fish-takers, as are menhaden and mossbunkers. The oily flesh of most of the baitfish attracts gamefish.

Live eels used whole are a top bait in salt water. Dead eels can be rigged whole and fished as though they were alive, or they can be cut into pieces. Sand eels or lances are good.

Most salt water fish will take sea worms readily, and various sea worms usually are easy to obtain or buy, and also are easy to keep and carry. "Sandworms," "clamworms," "bloodworms," "mussel worms"—all are good. Put two or three on a hook if after big fish, or cast and retrieve a single worm behind a spinner.

9. It's difficult to catch a really big striped bass in the surf. But ones of 30, 40, 50 or more pounds *are* taken every year.

Usually the largest stripers are taken on large lures. A big plug, particularly one of the swimming or popping type surface lures, is hard to beat for bragging-size bass.

Carry a good variety of lures—surface and underwater plugs, jigs, metal squids, heavy spoons and rigged eels. At times the biggest stripers will not hit lures but will take bait. Best baits are whole squid, a glob of several sea worms, or a good-sized live baitfish such as a herring or mackerel.

10. Various rigs are used for bottom fishing with bait in the surf.

The most popular rig makes use of a three-way swivel. The swivel has three loops, or rings. The line is tied to one ring, while a leader with sinker attached is tied to the second ring and, finally, a leader with baited hook is tied to the third ring.

Another commonly-used surfin' rig is the "fish-finder" rig, a handy gadget having a ring on one end and a snap at the other. The snap holds the sinker while the line runs through the ring and is tied to a rawhide thong which is attached to the leader and hook. The "fish-finder" rig was designed to keep the line free from the drag of the sinker when a fish picks up the bait. Because the line moves freely through the ring when the fish moves off with the bait, the fish doesn't feel the weight of the sinker. The angler, however, knows that his line is moving out and that, therefore, a fish has taken his bait.

11. The surf fisherman who moves around has a better chance of catching fish than the man who stays in one place all day.

If fishing bait, make your cast and let the bait lie in one spot for 10 or 15 minutes, then reel it in several feet. Let it lie there for a time, and if no fish picks it up, reel it in a short distance. Repeat this technique until you've practically retrieved the bait. When the cast has been fished out, move several yards up or down the beach, and try a new area. If you have no luck after many tries, move to a new location several hundred yards from where you began fishing.

Generally speaking, the surf angler who uses artificial lures "covers" much more water than the angler using bait. The fisherman using lures is continuously casting and retrieving, and if he moves around just a little his lure will "fish" through many acres of water.

12. Linen lines, braided nylon, or monofilament (single-strand) nylon lines are among the line choices available nowadays to the surf fisherman.

Linen lines require considerable care. They tend to deteriorate rapidly, and unless carefully aired and dried after each use will not last long. Some linen lines may not be continuously true to test, but then that is a possibility with any type of line. Linen lines, and to a lesser degree braided nylon, absorb or "take on" water which creates additional friction and adds to casting problems.

Easily the most popular line among surfers is nylon monofilament. It takes on little water, has a comparatively fine diameter, and with it long, smooth casts are possible. It need not be washed or dried, and requires no care other than occasional use or stretching.

13. Sea gulls are the ocean angler's best friends. They reveal where baitfish are, and where there are baitfish there probably are gamefish.

Gulls congregate over masses of baitfish and will dart down to the surface to pick up shreds and scraps of baitfish left by marauding stripers, bluefish, etc. Sea gulls have very keen eyes, and their sharp vision enables them to detect fish far below the surface.

Most of the time when gulls are seen swarming and diving, that is a good place to fish. On the other hand, feeding gulls aren't always available to show where fish are, so the smart surf fisherman learns also to hunt fish on his own and not to depend entirely on gulls.

14. What is a proper rod for one surf fisherman may not be for another.

One's weight, height, arm length, casting experience, skill and style—all must be considered in selecting a rod. For most surfers a rod that has a tip about a foot longer than their height will serve them best; with such a tip the rod will not be unwieldy, yet it will be long enough to provide casting ease and distance.

The majority of surf rods have butt sections 30 inches long. Those are satisfactory for most fishermen, but anglers of less than average height will do better with rods having butts between 20 and 24 inches in length.

15. Ordinarily the best retrieve with a plastic eel is a steady one, bringing the eel through the water at the speed designed to develop its *prime* action. However, when fish are hard to get there are tricks worth trying with eels.

See if increasing the speed of the lure will get results. Next, try *erratic movement*. Don't do this by jerking the rod and causing the eel to dart, but rather by reeling and stopping, or simply by raising the rod slightly every few seconds while still reeling in steadily. Raising and lowering the rod repeatedly alternately causes an eel to dive and then to swim.

Try bouncing the plastic eel off the bottom, and try also to crawl or "snake" it along over the sand bottom. Not only is bottom-bumping with a plastic eel productive in the surf, but it also takes hard-to-get fish in tidal rips, inlets, and canals.

16. Some of the gear needed by surf fishermen is lightweight rubber or plastic waders, plus a foul-weather hooded rain parka. The parka is handy not just when there's rain but also on those ultra-windy, chilly days. In good weather

the summer-season surf caster may wear bathing trunks or old trousers.

Chains or ice-creepers strapped to booted feet are helpful when fishing rocky areas. Fishermen working from jetties and high rocks, sea walls or piers will find long-handled gaffs useful. A short billy club can be used to subdue a big fish brought to each. Some surfers still use rod sockets (usually leather) of the cup-and-apron type, but today most fishermen merely tuck their long-handled rods between their legs when retrieving or playing fish.

17. An all-around basic surf fishing outfit would be a 9½ to 11 foot hollow glass rod (or a quality bamboo if preferred), with at least three or four guides plus tip-top; a wide-spooled squidding reel with, say, 150 yards of 30 to 45-pound test braided or monofilament nylon line; some stainless steel or heavy mono leaders, and an asssortment of artificial lures and hooks for natural bait.

Spinning is becoming increasing popular among surf fishermen, and for good reason. Long-distance casts are possible with spinning gear, which offers a minimum of trouble to the inexperienced.

A medium-heavy to heavy spinning outfit is desirable for most surfing, which means the line should test 12 to 18-20 pounds. Spinning gear is particularly useful when light lures or baits are needed. Many skilled surf fishermen take both spinning and regular, 'old-time" squidding reel outfits when going fishing.

18. Tide, water conditions, whether clear, turbid or whatever, wind and weather must be considered by the fisherman hunting fish.

When visiting an unfamiliar area take time for reconnaissance before doing any hurried, and perhaps unsuccessful, casting. Surveying a new spot at low tide will reveal sloughs, gullies, channels and holes; as well as bars and points which, when underwater, cause rips at various stages of the tide.

Good places to find fish are rocky points, beach peninsulas, inlets connecting tidal lagoons and the sea, the mouths of bays or the entrances to canals. Baitfish usually get caught up in currents in and near such places, and gamefish usually are around to feed on them. As a rule of thumb, fishing the falling tide around inlet openings and such places is generally more productive than fishing the flood.

19. Knowing fresh water bass fishermen using underwater lures always stop a lure in the air just before it hits the water. They then raise the rod tip and begin reeling so that the lure is active and "swimming" the instant it strikes the water. The reason for doing this is that the angler knows a largemouth bass may be very close to the spot where his lure lands, and unless the lure immediately wiggles along in a life like way, then to the bass it is just another fisherman's plug.

The wise surf caster fishes his lures the same way. Most surf casters agree that the reel should be thrown back into gear, or the spinning reel's bail closed, the instant the lure touches the water. This way the first view of the artificial lure by the fish will be that of a darting, moving—possibly wounded—baitfish or other sea creature.

A fisherman making a cast never knows how close his lure may land to a fish. If a plug, spoon, metal squid, rigged eel or other lure should fall close to a fish and be allowed to momentarily sink with no action whatever, it will probably scare rather than attract a strike from the fish. Without action a lure is merely a block of wood or plastic, or a strip of lead or other metal.

20. When fishing with bait over rocky bottoms it is best to use a round sinker, or a tear-drop sinker. These shapes are least likely to catch in rocks.

When fishing from sandy beaches over a bottom of mud or sand, pyramid sinkers are preferred. Their pointed nose tends to dig them into the sand or mud, and the sharp corners will dig in also so that the tide and wave action do not roll them around unduly.

And be sure not only to use the right *kind* of sinker, but also the right size. Sometimes a little moving or rolling around of cut or other bait may be attractive to fish, other times not. Thus sinkers should be carefully selected for their weight as well as for type.

21. As a general technique in fishing areas where there is no specific hole, basin, slough or trough, cast out as far as you can without taxing your tackle or skill, and then reel up all slack to bring the line tight against the reel. The rod tip should be held as high as comfortable so that as much line as possible is kept out of the water. Keeping unnecessary amounts of line from laying in the water helps reduce the amount of wave action on the line and, subsequently, dragging of the bait.

Incoming waves will gradually wash the bait toward the beach, and this will occur rather quickly if there is a good surf running. Each time the bait is washed shoreward, take up slack so that there is a taut line again. When the sea is flat calm and there is no tidal action to move the bait, then the angler should bring it in a few feet every now and then. Such movement stirs the bottom and sometimes helps draw fish.

22. Fishermen spend lifetimes studying surf fishing conditions and still never know *precisely* when they will and will not catch fish.

Winds can make or break surf angling, and most veteran surf fishermen learn to know which winds are most favorable to the fishing in their bailiwick. Onshore winds certainly make for difficult casting but they roll the water in and sometimes baitfish come with it, and with them come gamefish. Offshore winds make casting easy, but they tend to flatten the surf and often make for bad fishing for many species.

Before and after storms are good times to go surf fishing. However, the water often is turbid following a storm and fishing is not good until it clears.

23. There are many ways to play and land fish while surf fishing.

The reel's drag should be set only tight enough to drive the hooks home when a fish strikes, yet allowing the fish to make a run and to take line under tension. When the fish slows and has a great deal of line out, the reel's drag should be reduced. Yards and yards of line create drag in the water, and if more resistance is added from the reel's drag the line may pop or the hooks pull out. When the fish is finally brought in close, the drag tension may be increased somewhat. When casting, and also when actually playing a hooked fish, check the drag occasionally to be sure the tension is what you want and that the drag hasn't slipped or grabbed.

Most of the time the surf fisherman is working water free of obstructions, so hooked fish should be allowed to run. Seldom is there any need to risk a break-off by trying to hold a fish up tight and to "horse" him in. Take it easy, let the fish "have his head," and when he tires "pump" him in gradually. Always "pump" the fish, that is, bring him toward you by quickly reeling as you lower the rod tip, then raising the rod in a smooth, straight-up sweep as the line is kept tight on the reel. The "pumping" maneuver with the rod is repeated until the fish is landed.

If a hooked fish runs parallel to the shore, follow him. Be especially careful when the fish appears to tire because he may give a sudden spurt. If a fish is caught in the undertow at the time you are ready to beach him, don't fight the force of the undertow. Let the fish go out with the flow, and wait for an incoming wave to help sweep the fish back in.

Many surf anglers are sufficiently skilled at playing and landing fish in breakers that their hooked fish will be washed well up on the beach; other fishermen fare best by using gaffs.

Long-handled gaffs and sometimes nets are used when fishing from sea-walls, jetties, piers, rocks, etc. When fishing around rocks care must be taken to prevent hooked fish from cutting the line or fraying and weakening it. If a hooked fish runs around an obstacle try to move into a position where you can free the line; if that isn't possible, the alternative is to tighten up in an attempt to halt the fish and turn him in another direction.

24. Among the most popular lures for surf fishing are metal squids. They may be of tin, lead, steel or other metals that are chrome-plated.

Metal squids are available in a variety of shapes, weight and sizes, but all are basically elongated, flat and narrow, and designed to imitate a flashing baitfish.

A good way to fish them is with a strip of porkrind attached, with a real or plastic eel on the hook, or with a belly strip of fish-flesh on the hook.

25. Don't look upon your fishing area as merely acre upon acre of blue-green water, a place at which to cast aimlessly. Watch for signs of fish, keeping continuously alert, looking here and there even as you retrieve your lure or bait. Watch for a sudden splash, swirl, or humping wake near your lure which indicates a fish struck and missed or turned away at the last moment. A second quick cast to the same place may result in a hooked fish.

Feeding fish may be seen rushing bait at the surface, or baitfish may be observed scurrying wildly over the top. Frantic activities of small fish are usually a sure sign of feeding gamefish.

At night baitfish flopping on the beach close to the wash may mean predatory fish are feeding nearby. Experienced fishermen are even capable of identifying the slap of a feeding gamefish, sorting that sound from the noise of wind and the crash of breakers.

Too, there are fishermen who claim the ability to detect the presence of certain fish in the surf through their sense of smell. Striped bass reportedly have an odor like thyme; bluefish have the aroma of freshly cut melons, and red drum or channel bass are said to exude a distasteful, acrid scent.

The Gulf waters off the Louisiana coast promise to become one of the hottest big-game fishing grounds in North America. An ecological wonderland developing from the Yucatan current, Mississippi Delta flow, and nearly-bottomless area known as the "DeSota Canyon," draws plankton and, ultimately, hordes of gamefish. Within reach of Louisiana ports are sailfish like this, white and blue marlin, Allison, blackfin and bluefin tuna, and dolphin, broadbill swordfish, oceanic bonito—even Atlantic spearfish.

FEATURE STATES:

Down in "Cajun Country," Both the fishin' 'n livin' are easy

19: Louisiana

Assuming that you enjoy the good things in life—such as fine fishing, superb food, mild weather, excellent scenery —then one of the nice places to be in this world is southern Louisiana. At any time of year south Louisiana's "Cajun Country" offers some of the most unusual and interesting angling to be found anywhere. The area's food is strictly gourmet type, the weather sparklingly sub-tropical, and the scenery is lush greenery almost always flower-studded.

Louisiana offers both fresh water and salt water fishing. In its fresh water lakes, ponds, and rivers are plump bluegills, catfish, and largemouth bass. In the coastal bayou country—where local Cajuns still paddle their tippy pirogues in tending their muskrat traps—fishermen catch a mixture of fresh and salt water species. There are largemouth bass and catfish in these brackish waters, along with seatrout, croaker, flounder, and channel bass. Just beyond the bayou country, in the Gulf of Mexico, there is excellent fishing for pompano, bluefish, red snapper, grouper, red drum, spotted seatrout, sheepshead, Spanish mackerel, and dolphin. Farther out in the Gulf are giant jewfish, snappers and groupers, and—newly discovered—one of the world's great deepwater banks for fabulous marlin, sailfish, and bluefin tuna angling. The open waters of the Gulf also have king mackerel, sharks, cobia, tarpon, and crevalle.

In just the last decade or so, some of the world's most unusual fishing has developed along the Louisiana Gulf Coast. Years ago when one looked out across the broad Gulf all he was likely to see was a flat expanse of blue water, with perhaps a few boats on it and a few gulls wheeling over it. Now, however, look in any direction off the Louisiana coast and you'll see the towering offshore structures of huge oil rigs—hundreds of them—built by oil companies to pump crude oil up from deposits lying far below the bottom of the Gulf of Mexico. Those oil rigs, or offshore platforms, now attract many kinds of fish and provide a very exciting kind of angling. But more about that later.

Let's now go back to inland Louisiana, and point out a few specific spots for some of that good fresh water fishing mentioned earlier. Among the major lakes for largemouth bass are Caddo Lake (partly in Texas), Bayou Bodeau and Gross Lake near Shreveport, and Lake Bistineau near Ringgold.

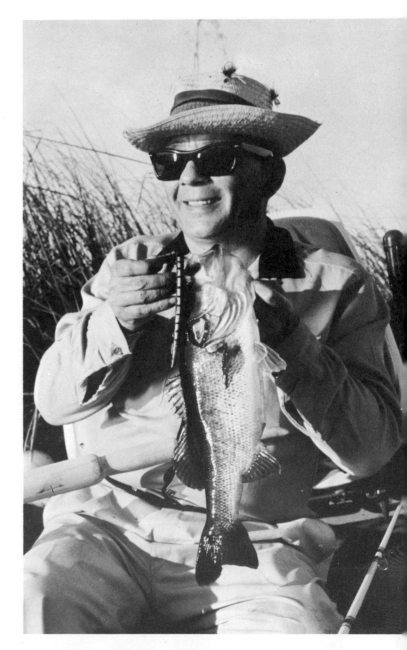

Louisiana's fresh and brackish waters feature largemouth bass, and big catches are common throughout the state.

Offshore oil rigs have created a unique fishery in Louisiana Gulf waters.

Redfish, or channel bass or red drum, are sought avidly by Louisiana fishermen in fall when the "reds" begin inshore runs to spawn in shallow tidal marshlands and channels.

Either this Gulf fisherman has ultra-long legs or the ocean-going vessel has run aground, it would seem. Actually the fisherman (he's working for spring-time channel bass, seatrout) is no deeper than appears while the ship is navigating a deep and well-marked channel. Shallow fishing like this is productive throughout the Gulf Coast country.

Captain Charles Sebastian, skipper of the charter boat "Sea Hawk" out of Grand Isle, plays a bluefish he hooked on a streamer fly while casting at base of oil rig platform.

Victorious skipper shows fly-caught blue.

The Louisiana Wildlife and Fisheries Commission claims that creel surveys have proved Bussey Brake Reservoir to be one of the country's most productive lakes—giving up exceptional catches of largemouth bass, crappies and bream. The 2,200 acre lake is near the town of Bastrop, in the northeastern corner of the state, and was opened to public fishing in 1960. One unusual feature of Bussey Brake is that it is a "fishing lake" devoted strictly to angling and no other water sports. Fishermen long harassed by water skiers and swimmers will appreciate that restriction. Boats, motors, tackle, bait—everything the visiting angler needs—is available at Bussey, which also has a public campground and picnicking area. Hotels, motels, guide service, etc. are available at Bastrop, which also has an airport with lengthy, hard-surface runways.

Toledo Bend Reservoir is America's fifth largest man-made body of water—186,000 acres. The giant reservoir touches three Louisiana counties—DeSoto, Sabine and Vernon, but Logansport is the only Louisiana town on the reservoir banks. There are marinas, motels, etc. catering to fishermen, who fish primarily for largemouth bass.

Black Lake, in northwestern Louisiana, is noted for its extraordinary fishing for "schooling bass"—largemouth packs that drive shad to the surface and then gorge upon them. Accommodations for fishermen at Black Lake are excellent, with some resorts offering full facilities from air-conditioned cabins to first-class guides.

Bass fishing is year-around in the Pelican State—the best of it in the spring—and the daily limit is a generous one of 15 per fisherman.

They call it "sac time" when the crappies are biting in Louisiana, because crappies were called "sac-au-lait" by the French settlers. In late March and early April crappies that inhabit nearly every body of water in the state move into the shallow, brushy edges to spawn, and then fisher-

men enjoy a bonanza, a frenzy of crappie fishing. The Louisiana crappie is a big one, ranging one to three pounds on the average but occasionally even larger. The daily limit is 50.

Certainly much of Louisiana's finest fishing is in its bayou country, the brackish water marsh areas where fresh water mixes with salt and fresh water and salt water fish species intermingle. Near the town of Thibodaux, pronounced "Tib-a-do," is a vast, seemingly endless marshland, and in winter it seems all the ducks in the world stop to visit there. The marsh is alive with largemouth black bass (called "green trout" by the local Cajuns), monster crayfish which are a table delicacy, redwing blackbirds, shore birds of various kinds, muskrats, nutria and yes, cottonmouth moccasins. Several large canals drain the marsh, eventually dumping their water into the Gulf of Mexico. You can get a guide and put a boat into a canal and fish the canal proper, or you can outboard from one canal to another, here and there leaving the canals to fish open marsh "lakes" teeming with bass.

At various times salt water fish move in from the Gulf waters far up canals and sometimes, even out into the brackish marshes. The 600-mile Louisiana Gulf Coast is decidedly discontinuous, broken up into numerous islands and peninsulas, bays and marshes, and here the visiting angler can lose himself from the every-day civilized world —while catching channel bass, sea trout, croakers, flounders, etc.

In this vast salty region, incidentally, are some of America's finest sand beaches. Many are inaccessible except by boat. However, superb sand beaches at Grand Isle, south of New Orleans, and on the Cameron Coast, south of Lake Charles, are easily reached by auto.

No fisherman or other visitor should "do Louisiana" without seeing New Orleans, enjoying the good fishing

Many Gulf party boats bring in 2-300 snappers like this per trip at height of season. Large catches of pompano also are made.

Whoops!! Fisherman tries to swing hooked bluefish aboard but fly pulls out and fish, falling free, drops back into placid Gulf.

right at New Orleans' doorstep as well as the unusual cuisine for which the city is famous. New Orleans is on Lake Pontchartrain, which is connected to the Gulf, and it has good fishing for croaker, sea trout, flounder, tarpon and drum. One of the city's most famous sea food restaurants is built on a long pier extending into the lake, and there (as well as at countless other quality New Orleans restaurants) you can enjoy "boiled" (actually steamed) blue crabs freshly caught from Pontchartrain, or flounder simmered lovingly in rich butter sauce. Be sure, also, to try what probably is Louisiana's most popular and best-known dish—crawfish. These little, fresh water, lobster-like crustaceans are prepared many ways—steamed, boiled, fried, etc. Done any way they are excellent, but perhaps best are French-style "crawfish bisque" and "crawfish étouffée."

New Orleans and the balance of Louisiana's Gulf Coast is the so-called "Cajun Country." This is the state's "deep south," its bayou region—French Louisiana. There French is a byword, the coffee is dark, the people friendly. Though modern communications and technology long ago penetrated this land of romance, old traditions and customs remain. Exiled from Acadia, a parish (county) in Canada in 1755 by the British, the Acadians (commonly called "Cajuns") settled along Louisiana's coast, and they still speak the original "Cajun" French which has been handed down generation to generation. "Cajun" French is French as it was spoken by royalty and the elite of France in the 17th century.

From New Orleans it is a short drive, about 70 miles, to the coastal town of Grand Isle. Here you can arrange a fishing trip far out into the Gulf for big gamesters such as marlin, or fish the oil rigs closer-in for snappers and bluefish, etc. One day a group went to one of the oil rigs aboard Captain Charles Sebastian's cruiser, the "Sea Hawk," and caught red snappers and bluefish one after the other—just as quickly as they cast lures out or lowered baited hooks. The snappers averaged 3 to 6 pounds, and the bluefish weighed about the same.

There always were plenty of fish out in the Gulf beyond Louisiana's shores, but they were scattered until the oil companies built their high "work" platforms and went after the Gulf's oil. The huge structures, some of them in 300 feet of water, attracted minute aquatic life, which attracted small fish, which attracted larger game fish, and, ultimately, sport fishermen.

The fishing in the Gulf is always good and, incidentally, it isn't expensive. Most charter captains charge about $100 a day for oil-rig fishing, but that's for a big party of 8 or 10 people.

More fishermen should discover southern Louisiana, a state that has some of the best angling to be found anywhere—at anytime. Even in the dead of winter Louisiana has top fishing, because spring never really leaves the Gulf Coast.

(For additional information on Louisiana fishing write Louisiana Tourist Commission, P. O. Box 44291, Baton Rouge, La. 70804.)

FEATURE STATES:

From tidewater to the tiniest inland brook,
Maine is one vast fishing hole.

20: Maine

Maine is a river. A freshet. A millpond. A trickle of melting snow. Born in the mountains, it gushes and grows to rushing white water, then falls and wends its way to greet the pounding surf of the sea.

Maine is the ocean, the surf and the tide.

The mist on the lake in the morning.

It is where a forest was put in a trust fund and a law protects the trees.

Maine is where you welcome the sun on your shoulders at noon and the warmth of a blanket at night. It is where ouananiche arch out over dark curling rivers and brilliant brook trout sparkle crimson in swirling waters clear as air.

When the glacier left Maine it created 2,503 lakes and ponds, thousands of streams and brooks that have never been counted or named, and the only Atlantic salmon rivers in the United States.

In Maine there is fishing from ice-out until fall, and through the winter, too, as hardy anglers take 'em through the ice. Maine's lakes are extra-big, like Moosehead, for instance. It is 40 miles long and 20 wide. It's one of the largest bodies of fresh water within one state in the country. The Moosehead-Jackman region alone covers an area nearly as large as Massachusetts. Thousands of anglers can fish here on the same day and never know they are not alone in the world. Fresh water Maine? Black bass—both largemouth and smallmouth but mostly smallmouth. Brown trout. Rainbows. Brookies. Pickerel. Ouananiche, the land-locked salmon. Atlantic salmon. Togue, or lake trout. White perch.

Nature made Maine a paradise for salt water fishermen, too. She wove its rockbound coast for 2,496 miles—around bays, inlets and sandy beaches, and stocked its sea with everything from 1,000-pound bluefin tuna to one-pound mackerel. Striped bass. Tautog. Broadbill swordfish. Salmon. Pollock. Flounder. Codfish. Haddock. They're all there, and fishing them, you breathe the tangy salt sea air and feel the welcoming spray of surf on your face.

Natural populations of many of the most desirable game fishes—such as trout and smallmouths—maintain Maine's reputation as a superb fishing state. A major portion of the state's fishery program is directed towards maintaining natural environment and the good fishing that goes with it. The Pine Tree State is meeting the challenge of increasing fishing pressure by employing well-trained fishery biolo-

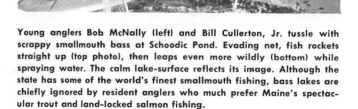

Young anglers Bob McNally (left) and Bill Cullerton, Jr. tussle with scrappy smallmouth bass at Schoodic Pond. Evading net, fish rockets straight up (top photo), then leaps even more wildly (bottom) while spraying water. The calm lake-surface reflects its image. Although the state has some of the world's finest smallmouth fishing, bass lakes are chiefly ignored by resident anglers who much prefer Maine's spectacular trout and land-locked salmon fishing.

Of Maine's salt water species, none is more sought (and found) than the striped bass. Inshore striper fishing starts in May.

Although Atlantic salmon once ranged suitable rivers of the Atlantic seaboard from as far south as Chesapeake Bay, today Maine is the only state in the Union providing angling for *salmo salar*. While Maine's salmon fishing remains limited, major efforts are being made to restore this valued fishery. These anglers are working a "holding" pool on the Narraguagus River, one of the major salmon streams.

gists who practice the latest and best in fish conservation methods. Although wild or "native" fish make up by far the greater portion of fish in the Maine angler's creel, the state conducts an extensive and progressive hatchery program to further insure good fishing.

Maine's Inland Fisheries and Game Department has more than 120 wardens in the field—men who not only enforce the law but who are willing and able to assist sportsmen-anglers in many ways. Too, the state's fisheries division has surveyed well over 1,300 lakes, and anyone fishing one of those lakes will get valuable information from a survey map giving depth and other specific lake features.

Several hundred Atlantic salmon are taken by rod-and-reel in Maine Rivers above tidewater each year. Some of the better rivers for Atlantics are the Sheepscot, in Lincoln County, and the Narraguagus, Pleasant, Machias, East Machias and Dennys in Washington County.

Many thousands of non-resident sportsmen trek to Maine annually in pursuit of one fish—the landlocked salmon. Maine has landlocks in some 200 lakes and rivers, with some of the better-known landlock waters being the West

Branch of the Penobscot River, near the town of Millinockett; Moose River; the upper Kennebec River; Moosehead Lake and its outlets; Millinockett Lake; Sebago Lake; Portage Lake; Chesuncook Lake; the Winthrop-Belgrade Lakes; and Sebec Lake.

Chesuncook Lake is rated one of Maine's most important landlocked salmon waters. It is the state's third largest lake, and is located northeast of big Moosehead Lake and west of Baxter State Park. Baxter Park, incidentally, consists of 201,018 acres of undisturbed forestland. It has been placed "in trust for the people" and is to remain forever in its wild and natural state.

Maine has long been famous for its fly fishing for brook trout, and in Maine some of the most famous trout flies originated (such as the Parmachenee Belle). Brookies are found in hundreds of Maine rivers and streams, brooks, creeks, lakes, ponds and bogs throughout the state. At no point in Maine does one have to go far to find good "speckle" fishing. Some brook trout waters are stocked, but there are many wilderness trout ponds, and going by float plane to back-country brookie spots is common prac-

Trolling offshore, two fishermen and the skipper watch trolled baits as the lookout on the bow scans the sea for prized swordfish.

tice. Canoe float fishing-camping trips are especially popular, particularly on the Allagash River wilderness waterway. Typical Maine brook trout are small, but this depends upon the area fished; tiny brooks, tiny trout; larger rivers and lakes, larger trout. Brookies of ½ to 1 pound are common, but some of 3 to 6 or 7-pounds are also taken.

Notable brook trout waters include the Spencer, Kennebago, Moose, and Penobscot Rivers (to name only a few), and lakes such as the Fish River Lakes, Poushineer Pond, Long, Chamberlain, Chesuncook, Ripogenus, Moosehead, Brassua, the Rangeley Lakes, and Sourdnahunk Lake. Poushineer Pond, in addition to containing good numbers of brook trout, also is one of the few lakes in Maine having the rare blueback trout. Bluebacks are not unlike the Marston trout and Sunapee, and are considered by most ichthyologists to be a landlocked Arctic char.

Rainbow trout are not well distributed in Maine, and perhaps the Wyman dam pool on the Kennebec River at Bingham is the best place to fish for them. Brown trout are more common, are found in hundreds of rivers and lakes, and are rapidly becoming one of the state's most important gamefishes. Anadromous brown trout run from the sea into Alamasook Lake. Big Sebago Lake, though better known for its landlocks, brook trout, and smallmouth bass, periodically gives up some very large brown trout. Androscoggin County has many fine brown trout waters. Not far from the state capital of Augusta is China Lake—almost 4,000 acres of excellent brown trout water. Branch Lake in Hancock County has particularly large browns. Grand Lake, and perhaps especially Grand Lake Stream, in Washington County, are other brown trout waters well worth mentioning.

Not too many years ago smallmouth bass were virtually scorned by Maine natives, and even today many "locals" think of bass as fishermen in less-blessed states consider carp. But many a tourist wants only "bronzebacks" when in Maine, and anglers find them plentiful. In general smallmouths are found in all coastal counties and inland to central Maine. Bass flourish nearly unmolested in scores

Canoeing inland lakes and spinning or fly fishing for brook trout is the prime attraction Maine offers for most "tourist" fishermen.

of Maine lakes and rivers.

Grand Lake and the Schoodic region are prime areas for smallmouth fishing. Big Lake, which empties into Grand Lake (Washington County) is rated by many as one of the best smallmouth waters in the world. Other exceptional smallmouth waters in that area are Junior, Sysladobsis, East and West Musquash Lakes, Little River, Rolfe Brook, Little and Big Walmatogue Streams, Clifford Stream, Scotch Brook, Amazon Stream and Otter Brook. Spednic

Small brooks like this provide fast fishing for small brook trout over most of the "Pine Tree State."

Landlocked salmon is one of the state's top gamefish.

Lake, in the Schoodic Chain, is a 23-mile-long crystalline lake that is literally choked with smallmouth bass. Good, hard-surface roads bisect all of southern and southwest Maine, and top quality fishing camps, resorts, guides, and roadside accommodations are available generally. There are wilderness camps in the northern part of the state, nearly all of them deluxe-type and well managed.

Possibly the greatest prize of all for the bluewater fisherman off Maine's rocky coast is the swordfish. These giants range the entire coast but—as seems to be the case with broadbills everywhere—are not plentiful. The best concentrations of swordfish have been observed 10-12 miles off Cape Elizabeth.

Giant, prized, bluefin tuna also range all of the Maine coast, usually well offshore—big ones weighing over 300 pounds, the school tuna under that. The big bluefins usually are taken by trolling a whole bait with sewed-in hook, while the school tuna seem to favor Japanese feathers trolled at high speed. Drift fishing with mackerel or herring may also be productive, and these baits usually are live-lined at varying depths and buoyed up by a float. The first tuna of each season appear in Maine's offshore waters during the third week of June; fishing is best, however, in July, August, and the first half of September. Later than that, line storms and cooling waters drive the tuna far offshore. Charter craft for tuna angling are available at the ports of Bailey Island, Small Point, Boothbay, and Ogunquit.

Mackerel are generally distributed along the coast, coming close-in in summer. They'll chase baitfish through the bays and into inlets, and can be taken readily on spoons, jigs, wobbling plugs, etc. The first mackerel fishing comes in late May, but seldom is there any decent sport until June. Peak of the mackerel season is July, August, and early September.

The striped bass is Maine's most-sought salt water sport fish. The best fishing is in the coastal rivers, but they also are caught in good numbers in the surf. The river bass usually show an inclination to hit lures and bait in May, while surf bass seldom are active until mid-June or July. Stripers distribute themselves generally over the Maine coast, but a few favored spots include Casco Bay, and Penobscot Bay and River.

Further information on Maine fresh and salt water angling may be obtained by writing Department of Economic Development, Room 211S, State House, Augusta, Maine 04330.

FEATURE STATES:

In the Pacific Northwest,
the King salmon is king.

21: Washington

A reservation Indian sets his nets for migrating coho salmon on a Washington river. Some Indians in the state have special fishing rights.

Certainly in both a commercial and sports vein, the Chinook or King salmon is the most important fish in the Pacific State of Washington. But Washington offers the traveling sportsman far more than giant King salmon; there are coho or silver salmon, sockeye salmon, Kokanee salmon, steelhead, rainbow, cutthroat, golden, brown, brook, lake and Dolly Varden trout, as well as mountain whitefish, largemouth and smallmouth black bass, yellow perch, crappies, bluegills, rock bass, bullheads and catfish.

Thus Washington offers resident and visiting anglers a great variety of important sports fishing, and good fishing of one sort or another is available in the state year-around. It has many hundreds of miles of ocean shoreline teeming with fish (the king or pink salmon being most important), tidal bays and sounds, large roaring rivers, small inland streams and of course, inland lakes both big and small.

Most of Washington's salmon fishing is done at sea or in the sounds because few of the coastal rivers are open to fishing. The Chinook or king salmon fishing generally begins in May—along with the heavy spring rains—and reaches a peak in August. The coho salmon run later, generally peaking in September. The coho fishing offshore, out of ports such as Aberdeen, however, can be excellent in August and good even earlier, in June and July.

Chinook salmon in Washington waters commonly weigh 20 to 30 pounds, but many go 50-60 pounds. The cohos range considerably smaller, although they are no less game, averaging between 8 and 15 pounds. A 20-pound coho is a very large one in Washington waters.

The seacoast town of Westport (on route 105 east out of Aberdeen) is, in addition to Aberdeen, an excellent salmon fishing headquarters. There's a large charter fleet there, and many hundreds of fishermen daily go out from Westport to "mooch" for salmon. "Mooching" is drift-trolling with extra-long, soft-action boat rods, lead sinkers on sinker-release rigs, and usually cut baits of herring or other plentiful baitfish species.

"Mooching" is party-boat fishing, with normally from six to a dozen anglers fishing from one boat. For the most part the Westport fleet is comprised of sea-worthy boats manned by reliable and skilled skippers who know where the fish are day to day and how to get them. It is not unusual for every fisherman on a "mooching" boat to get his daily legal limit of three salmon. The salmon are, of course, delicious table fare and when smoked, are a gourmet's delight. It is possible at Westport, Aberdeen and other Washington ports to have salmon you bring in canned and smoked and shipped to you at your home—complete with labeling printed with the important data of: "Pacific Silver Salmon. Compliments of Joe Walton and caught by him on July 5, 1970 off Westport, Washington. Smoked and Canned by Westport Packing Co."

The Strait of Juan De Fuca, separating Washington's Olympic Peninsula and Vancouver Island, is a veritable salmon fish trap. The towns of Neah Bay, at the entrance to Juan De Fuca, and Sekiu, a few miles farther inland on the strait, are other top salmon fishing charter ports. A great deal of salmon fishing along the coastal bays and protected sounds is done from outboard-powered craft, small cabin cruisers and runabouts, and countless thousands of Washington anglers own and maintain their own "salmon fishing rigs."

"Mooching" while aboard a partyboat out of Aberdeen, Washington, a fisherman hooks into good-size silver salmon and the fish thrashes at the net.

Happy angler lets out a whoop as boat captain swings salmon over the rail. Salmon, steelhead, and trout comprise Washington's "Big Three."

The fisherman who specifically wants to land a giant Chinook could do worse than concentrate his efforts in Puget Sound or more specifically in Skagit Bay. Skagit is renowned for its lunker kings.

Steelhead—the magnificent sea-run rainbow trout—to many fishermen are far more alluring than salmon, and the State of Washington offers considerable opportunity to the steelheader. But steelheading suffers from crowding in Washington, where some 200,000 resident fishermen addicted to steelheads crowd the readily accessible steelhead streams. One way to avoid the steelhead gangs, however, is to boat the rivers—thus reaching and fishing areas not accessible by auto or by easy hiking.

Concentrating on smaller streams rather than the large, publicized, "hot" rivers is another way to avoid angler congestion and to find fish. The small streams contain fewer steelhead but your chances can be better since they also host fewer fishermen

Steelhead fishing is much like deer hunting in that the average fisherman makes a number of trips for each fish he gets. A study by the Washington fish division showed that most fishermen make 9 or 10 trips for steelhead a season, and average two fish total.

When to go for Washington steelhead is rather problematical. So far as winter steelhead fishing is concerned, one Conservation Department investigation showed that December and January were the two best months, with December apparently having the edge, over a period of several years. February, March, and April are the next best months, in the order given. Washington has an energetic steelhead hatchery program, and December catches have been increasing steadily as a result of the Conservation Department's stocking program. Its hatchery-reared fish are re-

leased in the streams as outgoing migrants which mature at sea and return to the rivers to provide targets for anglers.

Steelhead originating in a stream (through natural reproduction or as hatchery transplants) migrate to the ocean where they achieve large size through an abundant food supply. Any time from two years on they return to their parent stream to spawn. When this may be varies considerably from river to river, and the entry of steelhead into a stream from salt water and their progress upstream depends upon water conditions. Low water seems to keep fish downriver and congregated in deep pools; high water keeps them moving upstream to the spawning grounds. The fishing can be very good following a freshet, but usually is poor over periods of low or high water if such conditions persist.

Two "races" of steelhead occur in Washington. Winter-run fish are found in almost all streams west of the Cascade Mountains which empty into salt water. Summer-run fish occur in Columbia River and its tributaries above Bonneville Dam and in about 20% of the major steelhead streams of western Washington. Winter runs move upstream from November to June and spawn in the early spring. Summer-run fish generally travel upstream during June, July, August and September, but may be found as early as February in some streams. Summer runs lay over in deep pools until the following spring, at which time they, too, spawn. Seaward migrants of both races move downstream with the spring runoff.

Among the winter rivers some of the best-known for good catches in December are the Green, Cowlitz, Puyallup, Skykomish, Humptulips, Snohomish, East Fork Lewis, Chehalis, Bogachief, Coweeman, Elochoman, Lyre, Pysht, Naselle and Willapa. Ordinarily the best producers in January are the Nooksack and North Fork Stillaquamish.

Summer and winter Washington's coastal rivers like this one, the Quinault, receive runs of steelhead trout from the sea.

Steelhead fisherman, with Indian guide in attendance, casts from Indian dugout canoe on Quinault River for cutthroat trout which, in certain areas, are an added bonus to steelhead hunters.

Murray Crowder traveled from Illinois to Washington's Quinault River to take this salmon.

Largest producers of summer-run steelhead are the Snake and Columbia Rivers. The Snake is good in early fall, with the lower Columbia River providing its best summer-run angling in July. The Grande Ronde is a top summer-run river, as are the Kalama, Klickitat, Washougal, Lewis, and Wind Rivers.

Washington stocks up to 30,000,000 trout in its lakes and streams annually. Many of these are legal-size trout intended for fishermen to catch shortly after planting, and in many waters exactly that occurs. Easily rainbow trout make up the bulk of the catch, especially in lakes such as Erie, Pass, McMurray, Deer and Hart—all in the northwest corner of the state.

One of the best cutthroat lakes in Washington is Grandy Lake, while smack in the center of Seattle proper is Green Lake, which provides unusually good "metropolitan" rainbow fishing all season. Other good trout producers are Wilderness, Desire and Steel Lakes (near Seattle), and Lear, Summit, Merrill, Merwin, Lawrence, American, and Spirit Lakes.

Washington's finest trout fishing is in its lakes, not its rivers, and there are simply too many good ones to ennumerate here. Almost any part of the state provides fair to excellent lake trout fishing, the most common species taken being rainbow and cutthroat, although Dolly Varden, brown, lake trout and brookies are available.

Regardless of where one is located in Washington, the Conservation Department advises that there should be little trouble locating 2 to 5 pound largemouth bass in various lakes, and good smallmouth fishing in various rivers and streams. "One to three pound smallmouths are readily found in Washington," says the Department.

There's no doubt Washington has considerable "warm water" fishing for species such as the bass, crappie, catfish and so on, but few fishermen, apparently, bother with those when there are salmon and trout to be had. And therein may lie a good tip to the visiting tourist.

Additional information on State of Washington angling may be had by writing State Game Department, 600 North Capitol Way, Olympia, Washington, 98501.

One of the best bass lures today is the
artificial plastic worm. Here
are the secrets of fishing them.

22: Never let a bass
run with a worm

Oh, there's nothing like a worm! A plastic worm, that is. Guide nets a largemouth for plastic-wormer
Bing McClellan.

One of the best bass lures today is the artificial plastic worm. Here are the secrets to fishing them.

Of all the lures developed in recent years, few have enjoyed the popularity and fish-catching success of the plastic worm.

While there's nothing wrong with any natural or real worm, such as a nightcrawler or a red worm, many thousands of fishermen have learned they frequently get excellent results with a phoney plastic worm and, therefore, have no need to fool with a real or "dirty old worm."

Many plastic worms manufactured today are more real looking than a genuine worm. They FEEL like real worms, and some plastic worms are so made that they give off worm-like odors while others have special fish-appealing scents and "flavors" such as licorice or anise. Phoney worms —nearly always made of plastic yet sometimes mistakenly called rubber worms—come in a variety of colors and rigging. Most popular colors—because they are the most productive—are natural brown, black, purple, blue, and red. Yellow worms and pink ones are preferred by some fishermen, and still others like worms that are absurdly spotted or striped with brilliant colors.

According to sales reports given by plastic worm manufacturers, the most popular plastic worm rigging is a three-hook deal, tandem type, with a spinner in front. Too many fishermen utilize only this three-hook, spinner rig. Now there's nothing wrong with the tandem hook and spinner set-up, but there are a lot of other equally good or better ways to fish a plastic worm.

One of the good ways to rig and to fish a plastic worm is to thread a single hook, tied to a one-foot length of monofilament (about 12 pound test), through the body of a plastic worm by running a needle through the worm and pulling the mono and hook after it. This "threaded worm" is cast by adding just enough split-shot sinkers to the line, or leader, to provide casting weight. The split-shot should be about a foot or two ahead of the worm.

This is an ideal plastic worm rig for fishing over weeds, or when fishing snaggy, or weedy shallows. If fishing a shoreline with the *threaded worm*, cast directly shoreward, dropping the worm at the water's edge or close to weeds or lily pads. Let the worm settle to the bottom (slack will come into the line when the worm hits bottom). Lower your rod tip, reel slack out of the line, then give "live" action to the worm by lifting your rod tip with a gentle twitching motion. A bass will usually pick up the worm gently, merely sucking it in, so be alert to any feeling of a "pick-up." Continue moving the worm slowly over the bottom by repeatedly lowering the rod, reeling up slack, lifting the rod lightly to move the worm, and so on. When you feel a fish pick-up the worm give him slack line by quickly lowering the rod tip. Let him chew on the worm for several seconds, then tighten the line and set the hook *hard!* Occasionally a bass will not pick-up a worm fished this way lightly but, instead, will strike violently. On such hits set the hook immediately.

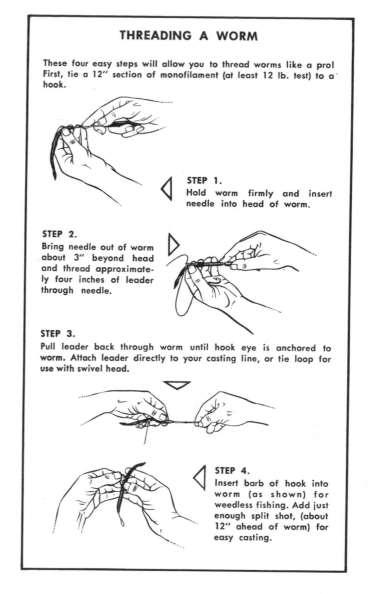

THREADING A WORM

These four easy steps will allow you to thread worms like a pro! First, tie a 12" section of monofilament (at least 12 lb. test) to a hook.

STEP 1.
Hold worm firmly and insert needle into head of worm.

STEP 2.
Bring needle out of worm about 3" beyond head and thread approximately four inches of leader through needle.

STEP 3.
Pull leader back through worm until hook eye is anchored to worm. Attach leader directly to your casting line, or tie loop for use with swivel head.

STEP 4.
Insert barb of hook into worm (as shown) for weedless fishing. Add just enough split shot, (about 12" ahead of worm) for easy casting.

A worm can also be rigged with a *single weedless hook* and—like a *threaded worm* which also is weedless—fished through lily pads and other thick cover. Again, enough split-shot must be added to the line or leader to provide suitable casting weight. The hook should be mounted at the worm's head. Worms rigged this way can be fished right in against the banks and fished through weed, pads, brush and so on in the same manner described for fishing a *threaded worm*. But if you get no hits in close, start casting to deeper water, say 10 or 15 feet out from the bank, letting

SINGLE WEEDLESS WORM—Many fishermen prefer this rigging of worm for shallow fishing in heavy weeds or through snags. To rig a worm this way open weed guard of hook and insert hook's point in head of worm. Thread worm over hook until head of worm is at hook-eye, then bring hook out through side of worm. Engage weed guard. Add split-shot sinkers 12 inches above hook to provide casting weight.

Finished threaded worm is weedless.

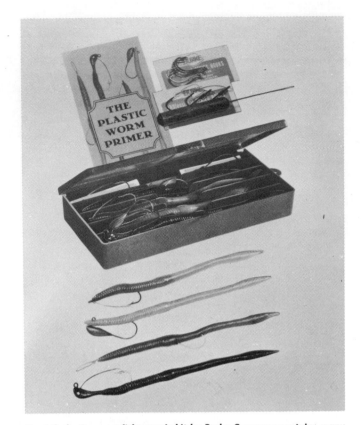

Special plastic worm fisherman's kit by Burke Company contains many vari-colored worms, plus needle-type tool for making special worm-and-hook or lead-head worm rigs. Kit also contains handy booklet describing ways to rig plastic worms. Four different worm rigs are in bottom of photo.

the worm settle gradually to the bottom—be alert when the worm is settling for "pick-ups" by bass. When the line goes slack start a very s-l-o-w retrieve, merely crawling the worm over the bottom. Keep the rod tip low so that you have "striking room" and can drive the hook home *hard* if a bass should hit. Work the worm all the way in, deep as you can, until it comes up right under the boat. Make another cast, to another spot, and keep moving along, fishing that weed-opening there, those lily pads, that rocky point, etc.

An old standby of veteran plastic worm fishermen is the Jig-n-Worm. A worm is attached to a weedless, lead-head jig, and since it will sink at a rate of about one foot per second, it is ideal for deep fishing.

When using a Jig-n-Worm (weedless jigs preferred) you can cast from a boat towards shore, working the jig continually over the bottom, or you can have the boat near the bank and cast out, letting the jig go down, then bringing it slowly back over the bottom. Another way is to anchor or drift in deep water, cast out, let the Jig-n-Worm settle to bottom, then pump it up and down near bottom as you might an ordinary jig.

Sometimes when fishing the fast-sinking Jig-n-Worm it is advisable to pump the worm back in as soon as it hits the water, rather than letting it sink to bottom. Bring it in with a bouncing action. You may fish it this way for the first few casts—just in case some bass are near the surface or shallow—before letting it sink and scratching it across the bottom.

Another way of rigging for deep water fishing with a jig, and when there are snags down there, is to use a special jig having a long hook eye. This jig is called the Self-Weedless Jig-n-Worm and is manufactured by McClellan Industries, Traverse City, Michigan.

SELF-WEEDLESS JIG-N-WORM—This worm and jig rig is popular in TVA lakes and other deep-water impoundments where submerged tree tops are common. Push head of worm down over eye of hook, until hook-eye protrudes through worm's head. Drive hook-point and barb into worm, making hook weed and snag-proof. Jig is heavy enough to provide casting weight.

The worm's head is pushed onto the jig's long hook eye until it protrudes through the plastic, then more of the worm is pushed onto the hook's point and barb, making it weedless and snagless but not bassless. (When you "set" on a taking bass the hook easily drives through the plastic worm and imbeds in the fish's jaw.)

A good way to fish the Self-Weedless Jig-n-Worm is casting from shore, or from a boat close to shore, out to open, deep water. Let the worm sink to bottom, then crawl or "walk" it right up the sloping bank, toward you—feeling it along very s-l-o-w-l-y. Then s-l-o-w-e-r still. Some very large bass are taken this way. You can, of course, reverse this method and fish the bottom going from the bank out by casting in from a boat. Just be sure to allow the Self-Weedless Jig-n-Worm to roll and bounce over the bottom from one shelf or "step" to the next.

JIG-N-WORM—is rigged with weedless hook and looks like this when out of water, but............

............wiggles and wobbles in a life-like manner when in water and fished on bottom through weeds.

Always be alert for bass that may pick up one of your plastic worms and run toward you with it. When this happens you won't feel any tugging on your line; instead you'll experience the odd feeling of having lost contact or "feel" with your lure. Whenever that occurs crank line in as fast as you can, and as soon as you get slack out and feel some resistance, strike to set the hook and do it fast and *hard*. Try to break the rod (you won't) when setting the hook, and you've got a better chance of hooking your fish.

Still another way to fish plastic worms is by trolling. Motor trolling frequently works, particularly if you have sufficient lead to get the worm down, and if you add an attractive flashy spinner a few inches in front of the worm.

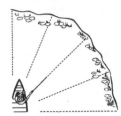

Drift trolling works, too. Let the wind move your boat slowly across the lake or river, while you troll and bounce and drag your worm over the bottom behind the boat. Getting the worm on bottom is just a matter of paying out the right amount of line. Always be sure, though, that you can "feel" the worm nudging bottom.

As already shown, there are several ways of rigging plastic worms to catch bass. It's sometimes argued that fish in one area will hit the worm best if rigged one particular way, while fish in another lake, perhaps a hundred miles distant, prefer the worm rigged by another method. Be that as it may, certainly one of the most effective ways to rig a plastic worm is "Hawk Style."

Dave Hawk is a professional bass fishing guide in Texas, and he's become famous for his plastic worm techniques, some of which are revolutionary. When fishing the worms his way, for example, it is important to *never let a bass run with a worm.*

Rigging a worm "Hawk Style" makes it particularly weedless and snagproof. It is a versatile method, and the worm can be fished at varying depths with ease.

All that are needed to rig a worm Dave Hawk's way is, of course, a plastic worm, 3/0 or 4/0 hook, and an oval-shaped sinker. A pear-shaped sinker will also do if its swivel wire is removed. The sizes of pear-shaped sinkers preferred are No. 9 and 10 (¼ and ⅛ oz.). No. 9 is best for fishing shallow water (under 10 feet), and No. 10 best for deeper fishing.

Regarding these weights, Hawk says "always remember that the lighter the weight used, the softer the worm's action will be and the longer and deeper a bass will take it into his mouth." A heavy head, Hawk adds, causes the worm to "drop off abruptly" after each pull of the line, and this does not catch fish as well as a "soft fall." The drag of the leader or line, however, will cause some drag when deep water fishing that slows the "fall" of the worm, so heavier slip sinkers sometimes can be used very successfully in deep-down angling.

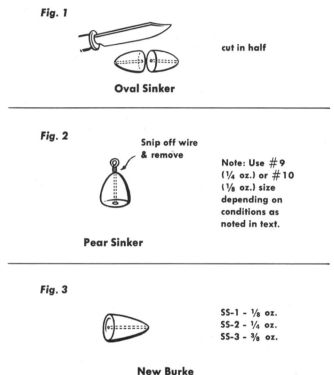

Fig. 1

cut in half

Oval Sinker

Fig. 2

Snip off wire & remove

Note: Use #9 (¼ oz.) or #10 (⅛ oz.) size depending on conditions as noted in text.

Pear Sinker

Fig. 3

SS-1 - ⅛ oz.
SS-2 - ¼ oz.
SS-3 - ⅜ oz.

New Burke Slide Sinker

When fishing a worm "Hawk Style" make a cast and watch the line carefully as the worm sinks, and be sure the reel is engaged and ready for action. Be alert. Ofttimes a bass will pick a worm up as it falls past a limb or log, and by watching the line you will see irregular tugs not caused by the sinking worm. Those tugs you see or feel are caused by the unusual way that a bass hits a worm. A bass usually only swims up to a worm and sucks it in, seldom chasing or smashing at it as they often do plugs, poppers and flies.

While many fishermen prefer letting a bass "mouth" a worm or run with it a few yards, Hawk suggests setting the hook immediately whenever a worm takes.

"Fishing a worm my way you should cast as close to cover as possible," says Hawk. "Let the worm sink, raise the rod gently, then move the lure about a foot. Let it settle back to the bottom, repeat, always raising the lure gently. That's the way to check to see if a fish is on the worm. If a fish is on, you'll feel a throbbing sensation—like a small child pulling on your coat tail for attention. The instant you detect such movement raise the tip of your rod toward the fish so he'll not feel resistance and be warned that something's wrong. Wind up all the slack in the line and strike the bass hard enough to TEAR HIS HEAD OFF! Never let the fish run with the worm! Never wait for the line to tighten! If you felt an original tug, reel up the slack, don't let the bass run, and BREAK HIS BACK!"

Color is important in worm fishing, as in plug, jig, and fly fishing. Red, black, natural, and purple all are very effective, as is a new worm color introduced recently by the Burke worm people. It is an emerald green, and reports on it have been good in all areas. Remember to try all colors, though, because at times one will far outperform the others.

Always fish worms slowly, just over the bottom if possible, and daybreak and dusk fishing frequently is best—but not always: sometimes bass move into shallows to feed during the hottest, brightest part of the day.

The varied techniques to fishing plastic worms are best learned by experience. That is accomplished by rigging a worm, casting it out, and bringing it back in a slow 'n easy crawl. The bass will do the rest.

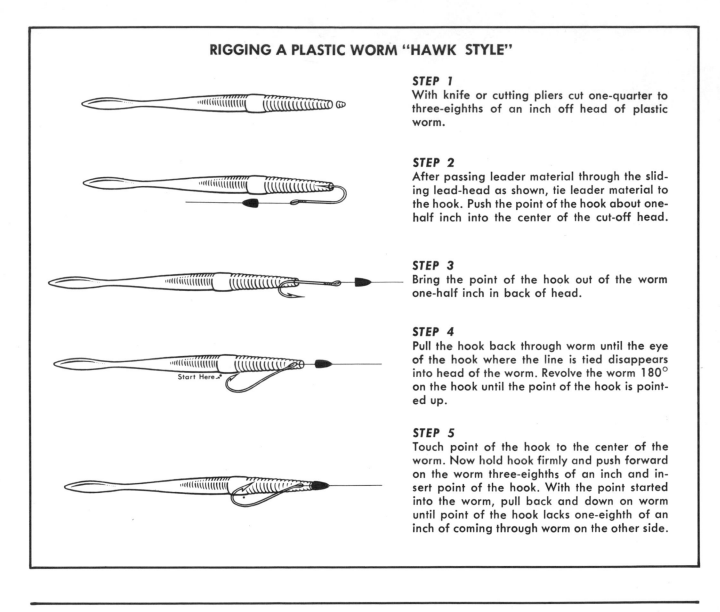

RIGGING A PLASTIC WORM "HAWK STYLE"

STEP 1
With knife or cutting pliers cut one-quarter to three-eighths of an inch off head of plastic worm.

STEP 2
After passing leader material through the sliding lead-head as shown, tie leader material to the hook. Push the point of the hook about one-half inch into the center of the cut-off head.

STEP 3
Bring the point of the hook out of the worm one-half inch in back of head.

STEP 4
Pull the hook back through worm until the eye of the hook where the line is tied disappears into head of the worm. Revolve the worm 180° on the hook until the point of the hook is pointed up.

STEP 5
Touch point of the hook to the center of the worm. Now hold hook firmly and push forward on the worm three-eighths of an inch and insert point of the hook. With the point started into the worm, pull back and down on worm until point of the hook lacks one-eighth of an inch of coming through worm on the other side.

WORMING TIPS

There are hundreds of plastic worms on the market. Are they all the same? Definitely not. Most worms look pretty much like other plastic worms, but some have more durable plastic, some have better action and color, some have lasting color, and some have "natural," worm-like, earthy smell.

Select your brand of worms carefully, trying all or several brands until you find the one that gets you the most fish.

Be sure your hooks are sharp in fishing plastic worms.

File or hone hook points until they are needle-sharp. Hooks must be sharp to drive into a fish's mouth, as well as to punch through a plastic worm when so rigged.

Even after sharpening, check hook points frequently to see if they've been dulled by rocks, gravel, etc.

⊡

The main objective in rigging a worm "Hawk Style" is to achieve a straight worm. Keep the head of the worm pushed up over the hook eye at all times to increase weedlessness.

Also check the point of the hook frequently to see that it has not worked out through the worm.

⊡

Before bringing a worm into your boat, bounce it up and down about 10 times straight below you on the bottom. Bounces or "jerks" should be about 8 inches.

Many fish will trail a moving worm across the bottom, or follow to the boat. "Bouncing" will irritate a lot of followers into hitting.

⊡

Torn or cut plastic worms are repairable.

Two pieces of worm can be heated with a match or cigarette lighter, thus softening the plastic. Push the melted ends together, hold for a few moments until cool, and the parts will re-weld together.

Worms repaired this way are as good as new.

⊡

The soft texture of a worm is the determining factor in how long a bass will hold a worm in his mouth before rejecting it as phoney.

Good worms have a soft texture yet they are tough and durable.

⊡

The Burke Worm Company, Traverse City, Michigan, makes a special sliding sinker for use with plastic worms. The nose of the sinker is tapered so that it will slide more easily through brush, weeds and snags—eliminating some of the chances of hanging up.

One end of the sinker is designed to protect the nose of the worm. Its center hole is very small so when it is threaded on monofilament there is almost no front edge to catch . . . in other words it is pointed and streamlined so that it is difficult for it to foul on snags, as compared to more blunt sinker heads.

Burke makes three sizes: ⅛, ¼, and ⅜ ounce.

⊡

As in most bass fishing, setting the hook in a striking bass when fishing plastic worms is most important.

Try always to keep slack out of your line—without scaring off any bass that picks up your worm. When a bass *does* take, and it's time to set the hook, hit him so hard you'd think you were going to break the rod.

Good fishermen know fish feed partly through their sense of smell, finding and identifying food that way at least to a degree.

Thus the plastic worms that have "scent" added are better fish-takers than those that do not. One company, Burke, adds a chemical to its worms that gives them an "earthy" smell. The chemical makes the plastic worms smell like real worms and, moreover, helps kill any odors on the worms that might repel bass—such as human odor, oil or gasoline odor from outboards, or insect repellent.

⊡

A slip-sinker is best for plastic worm fishing for several reasons.

For one, such a sinker will generally slide up the line— 2 feet or so—when a bass is hooked and fighting. This means the fish can't use the weight of the sinker to help throw the hook. (Fishermen who use lead-head jigs will fully understand the value of this.)

⊡

Whenever you foul your worm on a snag or fork of a tree, pull or twitch the line gently and the worm may bounce free. Don't jerk or pull hard or you may drive the hook through the worm and into the snag past the barb. Sometimes holding a tight, but gently so, line and pointing the rod at the worm, then jiggling the rod tip violently will free a fouled worm.

⊡

Most insect repellents "break down" most plastic worms.

Don't let insect repellent come in contact with your worms, and don't handle worms soon after spraying your hands with repellent.

It's a good idea to wash worms carefully before storing in your tackle box, and don't store worms where repellent might spill on them.

⊡

If your plastic worm with sliding sinker hangs up on a submerged snag, move your boat over the worm then give slack to the line after tightening the line. This will cause the sliding sinker "head" to rise and then drop—possibly dislodging the worm.

Keep a tight line on the worm while moving in with the boat so there will not be any slack line to fall around another snag.

⊡

23: Rigging natural baits: salt water

For the salt water angler who spends most of his waking hours trying to lure the elusive striped bass, a rigged eel should be as much a part of his outfit as waders and a rain parka. When the going gets rough and you want a striped bass more than anything in the world, there's a good chance you can get one if you'll tie on an eel.

Although a rigged eel will account for plenty of striped bass in daylight hours, they are particularly effective after dark. No one really knows how a striper can distinguish a black eel in seemingly black water on a black night, but they do it all the time.

If you're going to join the legions of striped bass fishermen, or if you've never used a rigged eel, add this technique to your bag of tricks. Even though most tackle shops in "striper country" sell eels that are already rigged and ready to fish, it's good insurance to learn how to rig your own.

There are many variations in rigging eels. The method shown is popular and easy to do.

Unless a bluefish takes your eel and chops it up, it can be used over and over.

To preserve an eel store it in a freezer or place it in a jar containing a heavy brine solution. Most veteran fishermen prefer jarring their eels in brine because they can keep the eels with them at all times. A good brine is made by mixing water with coarse grained salt (without iodine). At day's end when finished fishing an eel, simply drop it into the brine jar and it will be ready to fish the next time out. Many striper fishermen prefer an eel that has been preserved in brine to a fresh one. They feel the skin of a brined eel is tougher, yet more limber and works better.

Eels are available in a variety of sizes, from little "shoe-strings" (six inches or less) to big trolling sizes that may exceed fifteen inches in length. Everyone has his own idea of what size eel takes the most and largest fish; and yet, in the final analysis, all sizes work. However, the eels commonly rigged for striped bass measure eight to eleven inches.

There also is a wide variety of block tin squids used in rigging eels. Each is the product of dedicated research and all will catch fish.

Regardless of the size of the eel or the type of tin squid used, the step-by-step procedure for rigging a dead eel is the same.

Mark Sosin

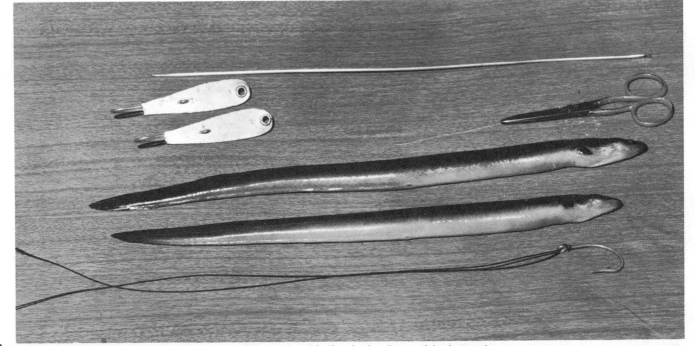

1. Items needed include eels, a long bait-rigging needle, metal squids (for the head), a tail hook rigged with nylon or dacron line, and scissors.

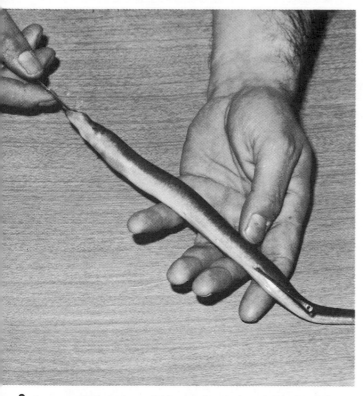

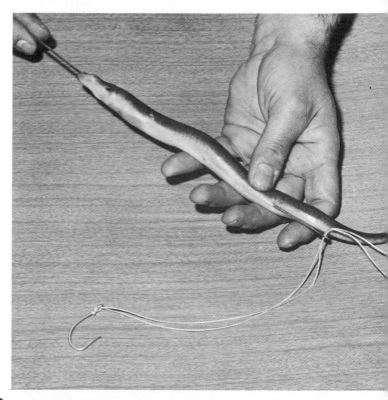

2. Insert needle through mouth of eel and push through the skin of the eel about two-thirds down the body. (This is where the tail hook will seat. Note that this is substantially below the anal opening and is placed here to avoid short strikes.)

3. Slip the tail-hook line through the eye of the needle, and carefully withdraw the needle to pull the line with it.

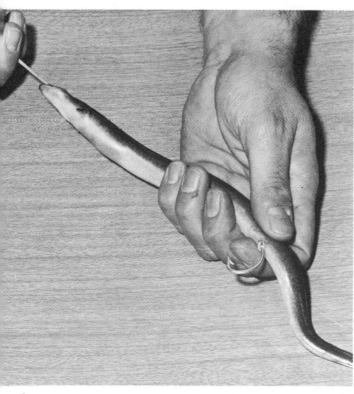

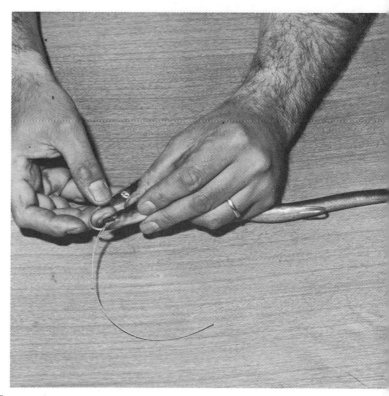

4. Once the needle is extracted, use your finger to pull the line through the eel and to seat the hook. Take time to seat the hook carefully by pulling on the line and working the body of the eel. When the hook is in proper position, the line is tight and only the bend and barb of the hook protrude. The hook shank is concealed inside the eel's body.

5. Insert the hook of the block tin squid through the mouth of the eel, and push it out through the head even with the gill openings. (Most fishermen prefer the tail hook facing down and the head hook turned up.)

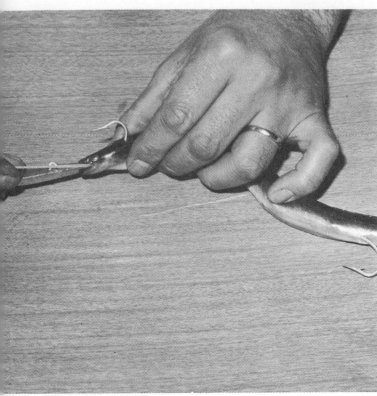

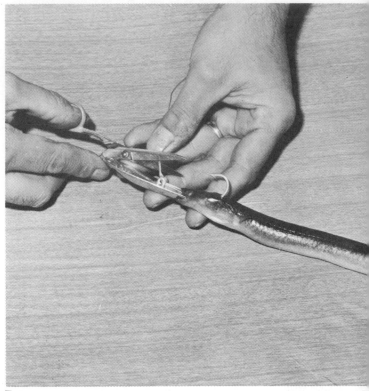

6. When the squid is seated, its hook end will rest snugly in the mouth of the eel. Pull the line from the tail hook tight and insert it in the center eye of the squid.

7. Tie the line securely. If the eel should be ripped loose by a hooked fish, the hooks will be fastened together and still hold the fish. Cut off excess line.

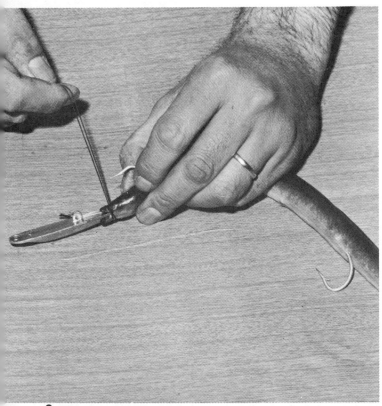

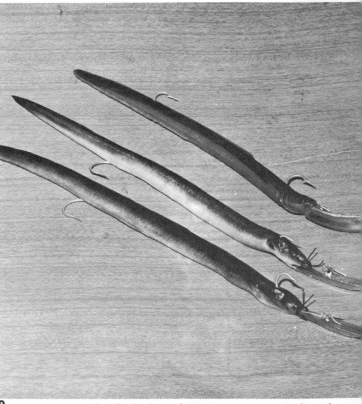

8. Take a short length of light line and tie the mouth of the eel closed around the squid. (This prevents water from ballooning the eel or causing it to act unnaturally during trolling). Trim off excess line.

9. Completed natural but dead eel rigs—bottom two—are neat, sturdy, and effective baits. An artificial plastic eel is at top.

24: Rigging natural baits: fresh water

Fishing with natural (genuine) baits is a deadly art that accounts for some of the largest fish taken in fresh water. Live baits have natural appearance, movement, and odor that attract fish. But to present natural baits to fish properly, one must know how to hook them and the best rigs to use with various baits.

For small and medium-size trout an ordinary garden-worm or earthworm should be used, and the worm should be hooked through its "collar" or "band" (see Fig. 1). The hook can protrude but it should be small, a No. 8 or 6. When possible fish a worm by drifting it naturally with the current, without a sinker. But, when necessary, use the rigs shown in Fig. 2 to get worms into deep holes in swift current.

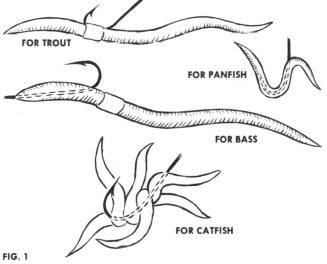

FOR TROUT

FOR PANFISH

FOR BASS

FOR CATFISH

FIG. 1

For panfish such as bluegills use a small worm and hook it through its middle so that the point, barb, and bend of the hook are buried yet both ends of the worm are free to wriggle (Fig. 1).

Large worms, like nightcrawlers, are good for big trout and bass. For bass, hook the worm by running the point

of the hook into the worm's head and out again about an inch or so from the end of the worm's head. When using smaller worms for bass, put two or three on a hook. This

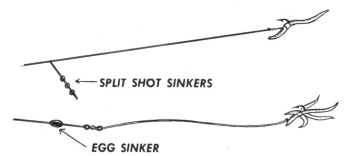

← SPLIT SHOT SINKERS

EGG SINKER

FIG. 2 RIGS FOR WORMING

is also a good way to hook worms when fishing for suckers, carp, bullheads or catfish. For big catfish, of course, it's best to use nightcrawlers or a jumble of several worms (Fig. 1).

Minnows are excellent bait for most fresh water fish—from panfish to large gamefish.

Small minnows (½ to 2 inches long) are best for panfish such as crappies, perch and white bass. Larger minnows (2 to 3 inches) can be used for trout. For black bass, minnows can be from 2½ to 6 or 7 inches long, the ultra-large

FIG. 3 HOOKING MINNOWS FOR STILL FISHING

ones for big Florida largemouths. A minnow 3 inches long is about right for walleyes and chain pickerel. But giant minnows, and suckers 8 or 10 inches long are needed for pike and muskellunge. Most popular bait minnows are creek chubs, fatheads, bluntheads, dace and shiners.

The best way to hook a minnow for stillfishing is through its back just in front of the dorsal fin. To cast a minnow, or to drift or slow-troll it, hook it through both lips (Fig. 3). Minnows also can be sewed to a hook for casting, or for drifting with the current in a stream or river for big trout and bass. Two ways are shown in Fig. 4: the hook at the tail bends the minnow's body so that it wobbles (top drawing) while the second method has the hook protruding from the minnow's mouth (lower drawing).

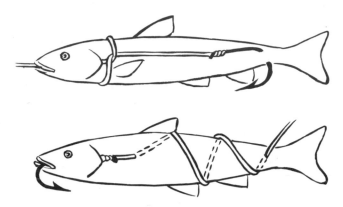

FIG. 4 SEWING DEAD MINNOWS ON HOOKS

Usually minnows are fished on regular monofilament line or leader, and are allowed to swim about naturally. They can also be fished with a float or bobber at varying depths. To get minnows down in a current, add split-shot or rubber-core sinkers a few feet above the bait. To get a minnow down deep yet keep it away from a weed bed on the bottom, use the rig shown in Fig. 5.

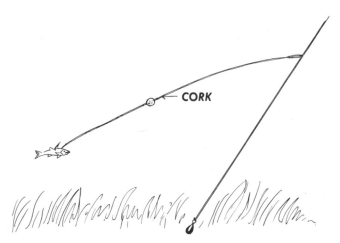

CORK

FIG. 5 DEEP WATER MINNOW RIG

Frogs are excellent bait for black bass, pickerel, pike and catfish. There are several species—such as leopard frogs, pickerel frogs, green frogs and small bullfrogs—that can be used. Frogs are especially good in summer and early fall. Hook a live frog through the lips, cast it out,

and let it swim around naturally. If fishing in lily pads, hyacinths, grass or weeds, use a weedless hook. Another way to hook a frog is in the thick muscle of the leg (Fig. 6). Also, there are many frog harnesses available which can be used to hold frogs yet keep them alive and kicking. Immature frogs (tadpoles or "pollywogs") also can be used for bait. They're best hooked through the lips or tail.

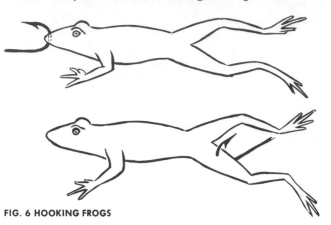

FIG. 6 HOOKING FROGS

One of the top baits for many fresh water fish is crayfish or crawfish—the small, lobster-like crustacean found in most brooks, streams, rivers and lakes. However, crayfish are not always available. At times they can be purchased from bait dealers, but most anglers catch their own by turning over stones in shallow water and grabbing them. Crayfish are easier to find at night when they come out of hiding.

Small crayfish can be used for trout and panfish. Medium-sized ones are good for smallmouth bass and walleyes.

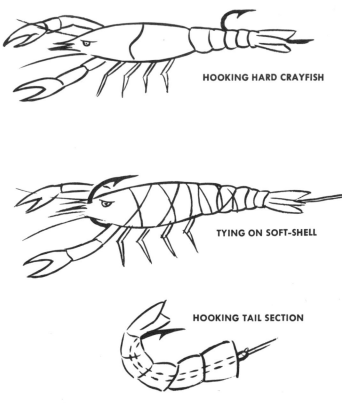

HOOKING HARD CRAYFISH

TYING ON SOFT-SHELL

HOOKING TAIL SECTION

FIG. 7 HOOKING CRAYFISH

Use the meat in crayfish tails as bait for carp and catfish. Soft-shelled crayfish are one of the best kinds of all. But they are fragile and must be tied around a hook with thread or fine nylon monofilament. Hard-shell crayfish can be hooked through the tail (Fig. 7).

Salamanders or newts—called "spring lizards" in many areas—are good baits and can be found in shallow water, or under rocks in moist spots. They are most plentiful in small brooks and around springs. They are active at night, when they leave hiding places under logs, moss and overhanging banks, and can be readily found with flashlights. Salamanders will be taken by trout, bass, large panfish and catfish. They are delicate, so should be hooked lightly through the lips or at the base of the tail (Fig. 8).

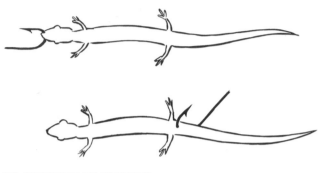

FIG. 8 HOOKING SALAMANDERS

If smallmouth bass are hard to get in a river or stream, try fishing a hellgrammite along the bottom, letting it drift with the current. Few smallmouths will pass up a hellgrammite, which is the larva of the Dobson fly. A mature hellgrammite may measure three inches in length, but most range 1½ to 2½ inches.

Hellgrammites are most plentiful in the fast water of streams and rivers. The best way to catch some is to hold a wire screen or net in the current below rocks. Turn the rocks over, and the flow will sweep the hellgrammites to the screen.

One way to hook a hellgrammite is under the wide collar just behind its head. They stay alive longer this way, so frequently you can catch several fish with one bait. Another way to hook them is through the tail (Fig. 9).

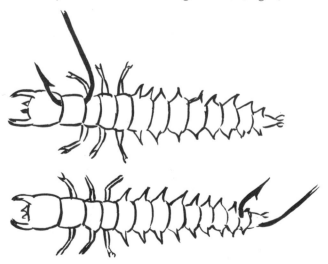

FIG. 9 HOOKING HELLGRAMMITES

If you have trouble with hellgrammites hiding or holding to the bottom, cut off the tiny hooks found at the end of their tails. Besides smallmouth bass, hellgrammites are good for trout, walleyes, sunfish, rock bass and other panfish. Use small hellgrammites for panfish and trout.

Other aquatic insects make good bait.

May fly nymphs are excellent. Some of these nymphs prefer clear, rocky streams where they cling to the stones in riffles; others burrow in the silt and mud of streams and lakes. Many May fly nymphs are too small to use as bait, but large ones make fine baits for trout and panfish. They should be used with tiny No. 12 or 14 hooks and hooked in the "collar" behind the head.

Stone fly nymphs prefer fast streams, where they cling to the undersides of stones. Large stone flies are good bait for trout, whitefish, smallmouth bass, and panfish. Hook them in the collar as you would May fly nymphs (Fig. 10).

Caddis worms build cases around themselves. They are called "stickworms," "caseworms," and "caddis creepers," and they use different material for their cases—such as tiny sticks, stones, sand, or leaves. They crawl around the bottom, or cling to rocks in quiet parts of streams and rivers. They are a favorite food of trout and can be used with their case on a tiny hook, or removed from the case and fished as a grub. Often two, three or four caddis worms on a hook are better than one. In addition to trout, bluegills, perch and other panfish will take caddis worms (Fig. 10).

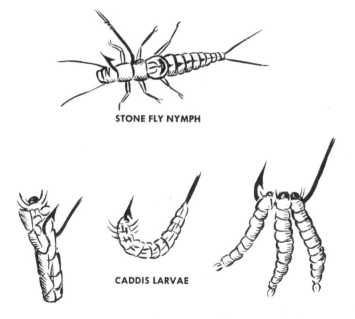

STONE FLY NYMPH

CADDIS LARVAE

FIG. 10 HOOKING WATER INSECTS

Terrestrial insects of various kinds make good baits and usually are easy to obtain and to find in quantity. Grasshoppers become numerous in August and September, and that's the time to use them. Catch 'hoppers in fields, along country roads, on the banks of streams, rivers, lakes. The best time to get grasshoppers is early in the morning when there is dew on the ground and they are slow and easy to catch. Later, when the sun dries the grass, they jump and fly too much.

Grasshoppers will catch big trout and bass, and are best hooked in the neck or through the body. Another way to hook them is to use a small rubber band and wrap it around the 'hopper's body, then insert the hook under the bands (Fig. 11).

Crickets are good bait and can be found where you'll find grasshoppers, but they are most active at night. In daytime look for them under stones, logs, piles of straw or hay. Nowadays you can buy crickets from many bait and tackle dealers. Crickets are rather delicate baits, so use small, fine-wire hooks and hook them in the necks (Fig, 11). Use crickets for trout, bass, bluegills and panfish.

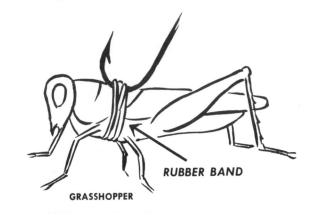

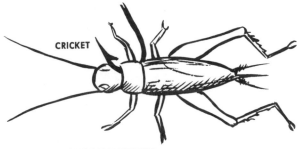

FIG. 11 HOOKING LAND INSECTS

Various beetles (Japanese beetles, May beetles, June bugs, etc.) can be used as bait.

Caterpillars of different kinds also make good baits at times. One of the best is the catalpa worm, which is the larva of the big sphinx or hawk moth. It is found in catalpa trees, hence its name. Catalpas are fine for bluegills, and are best when cut in half or turned inside-out on a hook.

Grubs of Japanese and June bug beetles are good baits. These are the big white grubs found in the ground when digging in the garden for worms. Other beetle grubs live in rotting stumps, logs, or under the bark of trees. To hook grubs insert the hook just under their skin or thread them on the hook.

A bait "grown" just for fishing is the meal worm. This is the yellow and brown larva of a beetle that feeds on grains in mills where wheat, rye or flour is stored. These worms are about an inch long, and they can be hooked through the head or threaded on a hook. They're great for bluegills and other panfish.

"Strip" baits can be cut from the bellies of such fish as yellow perch, sunfish, suckers, chain pickerel and other fish. A strip of fish belly about 3 or 4 inches long, leaving the two pelvic fins on, makes a good bait for pickerel when skittered on top of the water around lily pads and weeds. Another kind of strip can be cut omitting the fins, and thinning by scraping the meat so that it is mostly skin for an inch or so at the tail. This type strip flutters attractively, and it can be cast or trolled with a sinker. Strips take trout, bass, pickerel, walleyes and pike (Fig. 12).

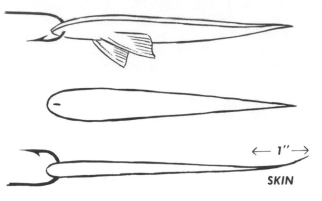

FIG. 12 STRIP BAITS

A good basic rig to use with many baits when you want to cast some distance or to fish on the bottom is shown in Fig. 13. Tie a loop in the line a couple feet above the sinker and attach a leader and hook to the loop. Different size hooks and leader lengths can be used depending on fishing conditions.

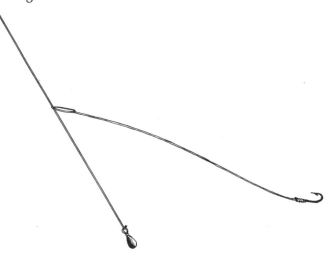

FIG. 13 BASIC BOTTOM RIG

Following are some tips to remember when using natural baits:

Always use fresh bait. A soaked-out worm, feeble minnow, or dead frog catches few fish, but lively ones attract fish.

If you see a fish grab the bait and swallow it, then set the hook immediately. But if you don't see the fish take, wait until the float or bobber goes down, or until the fish moves off, stops, swallows the bait, and starts moving again before you set the hook. Many anglers are impatient and try to set hooks too soon, thus pulling their baits away from the fish.

Vlad Evanoff

25: Trolling rigs: salt water

It is relatively simple to rig, preserve, and use strip baits, and they are effective for offshore trolling anywhere in the world.

Strip baits also have a place in fresh water fishing, and often they are the deciding factor in catching fish. Fresh water enthusiasts generally fashion such baits out of porkrind, but the procedure is the same whether a strip is made of porkrind or of fish flesh.

A strip bait can be made from the flanks or belly section of any fish that swims, but in salt water, strips cut from albacore, bonito, and tuna perform best. Strip baits made of the flesh of these fish are firm and plump, and have a silvery flash that can arouse the killer instinct in any gamefish.

The size of a strip bait depends on the material you have and the type of fishing you will be doing. For most salt water fishing, a ten inch strip broader at the head and tapered toward the tail is ideal. The secret is to remove most of the meat from the strip so that it will undulate easily when trolled behind a moving boat and the action of the water will be less likely to mangle the bait.

Like all bait rigging procedures, there are a number of ways to prepare a trolling bait. The method shown here is popular with anglers on all coasts. Remember that neatness counts and that a bait crafted with care will usually perform better in the water and catch more fish.

Finally, as added insurance, make it a practice to carry a jar of porkrind strips with you when heading for offshore trolling. In the event that natural bait is hard to come by on the ocean, or if you can't find exactly what you want, the pork strip will frequently save the day.

Mark Sosin

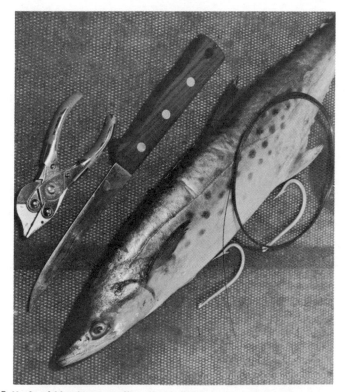

1 Mackerel like this, as well as tuna, albacore, and bonito, make excellent strip baits because of their silvery bellies.

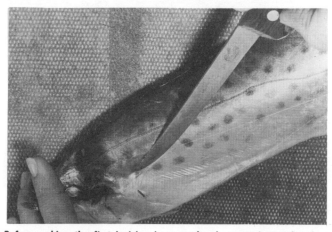

2 Before making the first incision in a mackerel, approximate the size and shape of the strip bait by tracing it with the knife point. The best strips come from the flank or belly area.

3 Using a sharp knife and smooth strokes, cut along the outline of the strip bait. Avoid jagged edges.

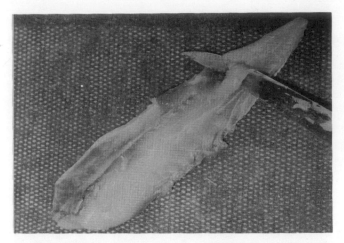

4 Remove the strip bait carefully. A fresh fish is best since the meat will be firm on the skin.

5 Turn the bait so the skin is under and trim the meat so that it is flat in the center and all jagged edges are removed. Taper it toward the tail, leaving just enough meat near the tail to provide body.

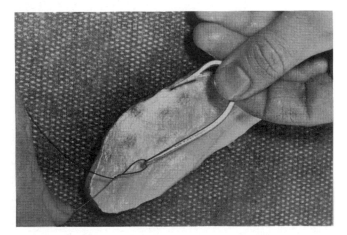

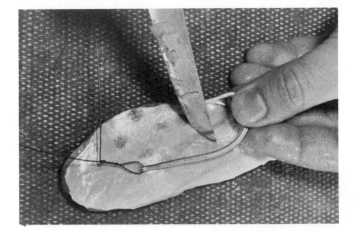

6 A Haywire Twist is used to attach wire leader to the hook. The length of the Haywire Twist is determined by the place where you want the hook to seat. Measure this distance once the Twist is started and when the twist is completed, a six inch tag end of wire should be right near the head of the bait.

7 Use the point of the knife to mark the spot where the hook will protrude. Then double over the strip and slice a hole in the skin with the blade of the knife.

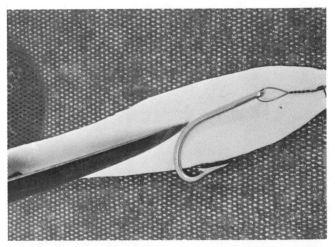

8 For ease of illustration, a porkrind strip, rather than fish flesh, is used in the remaining photos. With a pork bait it is necessary to make an extra hole in the head of the strip for the wire to pass through. This is not necessary with a natural bait because the flesh is sufficiently soft.

9 In marking the spot for the hook to come through a bait, remember to consider the bend of the hook and make the mark above the bend.

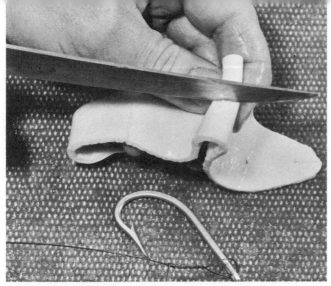

10 Don't try to punch a hole in a bait; instead, slice a neat hole with the knife.

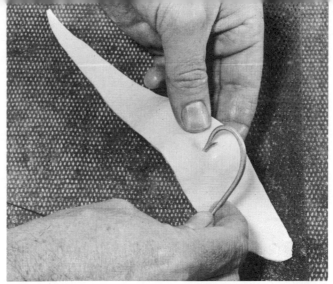

11 Seat the hook in the hole.

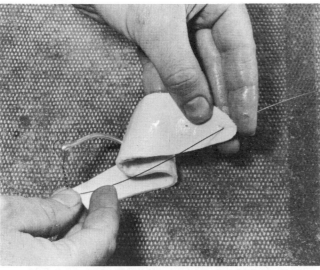

12 The hook should never be placed in a bait more than half-way toward the tail, otherwise its trolling action will be destroyed. The hook may be inserted through either side (meat or skin) depending on preference.

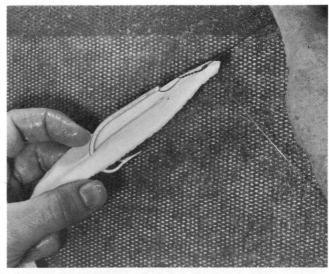

13 Push the short end of the wire through the head of the bait so it comes out the same side as the hook.

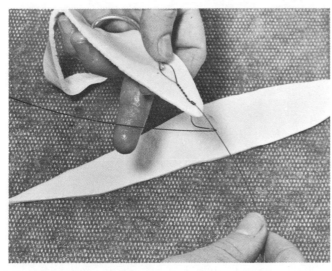

14 A "safety pin" catch eliminates sewing, and is started by putting a curve in the short wire and bending toward the leader. Wire then is bent over the leader sharply so that there is spring tension.

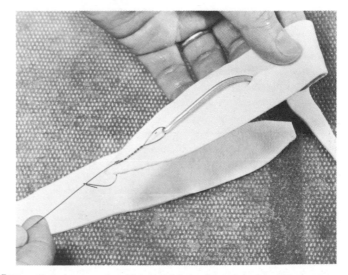

15 Trim off the excess wire. The completed safety pin catch will prevent the bait from riding up on the leader while trolling, or following a strike. Strip bait now is ready to fish.

26: Trolling rigs: fresh water

Trolling in fresh water is one of the most effective methods of taking many kinds of fish, from trout to muskies. It has many advantages over casting or stillfishing, and day in and day out you'll catch more fish if you troll. You cover more territory and various depths by trolling, thus presenting your lure or bait to more fish; the lure or bait is always moving or "working," and it's in the water most of the time. And when trolling one needn't know how to cast or give lures action as when casting—the boat and motor do most of the work.

But while the basic method of trolling is simple, there is much more to trolling than merely letting line out behind a boat and then proceeding to catch fish. You have to know *where* to troll, *when* to troll, *which* baits or lures to use, *how* to get them down to the proper depth and *how* to give them enticing action. Here's where a knowledge of trolling pays off. By using the proper rig for the fish you are after, you'll catch more and bigger fish every time.

The simplest trolling rig—used by nearly every angler and which still catches a lot of fish—is simply attaching a lure or bait to the end of a line, then paying it out behind a boat anywhere from 20 to 150 feet, and running the motor at a slow or moderate speed. Such trolling is often effective in shallow water near shore, along the edges of lily pads or weeds, and over rock and gravel bars. In this trolling the lure or bait usually travels from a few inches to several feet below the surface depending on how much line is out, the speed of the boat, the weight of the lure, and how deep the lure dives or "works." To get a bit deeper a clincher or rubber core sinker should be attached to the leader or line (Fig. 1). Monofilament line is usually best for this type of trolling. Shallow trolling, incidentally, frequently is the best method for catching trout, bass, pickerel, pike, and landlocked salmon.

CLINCHER OR RUBBER CORE SINKER

FIG. 1   SINKER AHEAD OF LURE

Instead of using a single lure or bait, try using two or three when trolling shallow. When fishing for trout, 'for example, it's sometimes effective to troll three different wet fly patterns on a single leader. And when trolling for landlocked salmon it's easy to fish three different streamer flies at the same time; extra flies are tied to 12 or 14 inch long dropper strands of nylon, tied to the base leader. Such multiple fly rigs look like a school of minnows, and often attract more fish than does a single fly (Fig. 2).

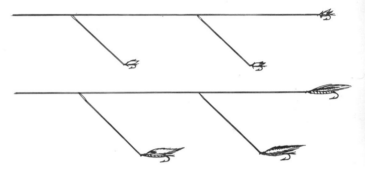

FIG. 2   RIGS FOR TROLLING THREE FLIES

A somewhat similar trolling set-up is the two-minnow rig. It's easy to arrange. Take a length of nylon leader material and tie a loop in it, leaving one strand long and one strand somewhat shorter. Tie a hook to each strand of mono, and impale a small minnow on the top hook and a larger minnow on the bottom hook. This rig can be used with live minnows if drift fishing, and dead minnows if trolling slowly (Fig. 3).

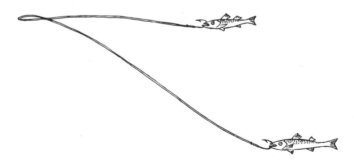

FIG. 3   RIG FOR TROLLING TWO MINNOWS

A lure combination that is especially good when trolling for shad consists of a small spoon tied to the line, a 2-foot leader tied to the spoon's hook, and a small white or yellow jig or "Shad Dart" knotted to the leader (Fig. 4). Although primarily used in trolling, this rig also can be cast. In addition to white and hickory shad, this rig will take white perch, white bass, and also striped bass when the latter are in fresh water.

FIG. 4   SHAD RIG

While trolling shallow water often produces fish—especially in spring and fall, and early morning and late evening—deep-water trolling is usually the most effective.

One novel way to fish a plug near bottom yet avoid fouling is to use a deep-running plug sans hooks, with a three-foot leader tied to it and a floating plug tied to the leader (Fig. 5). The deep-running plug will bump bottom without fouling while the floating plug trailing behind the diver will swim higher and be clear of the bottom.

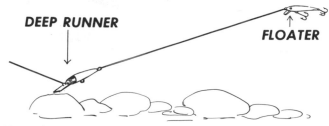

FIG. 5   DEEP-TROLLING COMBO

A similar rig can be used with worms, frogs, minnows or crayfish. Put a large clincher sinker on the leader or line, then add a small cork several inches above the bait. The sinker takes the bait down to the bottom, but the cork float will keep it above any weeds or rocks (Fig. 6). This rig works best when trolling slowly or drifting with a light wind. When you get a bite using this rig, give some slack line so the fish has a chance to swallow the bait.

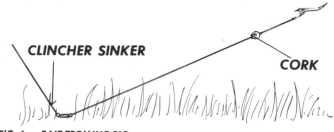

FIG. 6   BAIT TROLLING RIG

There are special trolling sinkers available that help prevent line twist. One is the flat, heart-shaped keel type which, when folded on the line or leader, forms a keel. A somewhat similar keel-type sinker has a bead chain on both ends (Fig. 7).

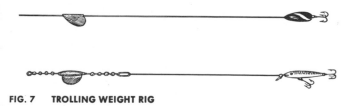

FIG. 7   TROLLING WEIGHT RIG

One fish that is deep most of the time is the walleye. To get them you must usually troll with the sinker dragging bottom.

One good rig for walleyes is a June Bug spinner with baited hooks. The spinner is tied to a 3-foot leader connected to a three-way swivel (Fig. 8). The bait can be a minnow, lamprey eel, or some nightcrawlers. The 18-inch dropper line holding the sinker should be weaker than the other line and leader so that if the sinker fouls it will break off but the rest of the rig is saved.

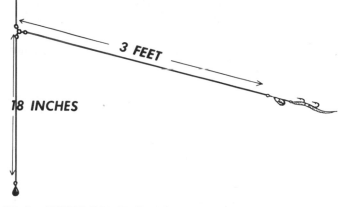

FIG. 8   WALLEYE RIG WITH SPINNER

Another kind of walleye rig consists of a pencil type sinker 12 to 15 inches long. (The lead is usually cast around heavy wire, such as clothes-hanger wire.) The sinker is tied to a three-way swivel by a weak line which will break if the sinker gets snagged. However, the thinness of this sinker makes it more snag-proof than ordinary sinkers. A 3-foot monofilament leader is tied to another eye of the three-way swivel, and the lure is tied to the other end of the leader. This rig produces best when trolled slowly at depths of from 10 to 30 feet, and preferably over rocky bottoms where the long, thin sinker is least likely to snag (Fig. 9).

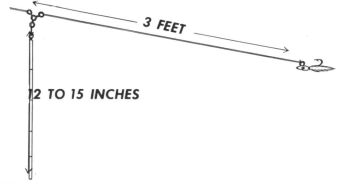

FIG. 9   WALLEYE RIG WITH PENCIL SINKER

Still another rig that is excellent for walleyes combines a three-way swivel, a light plug such as a Flatfish or Rapala, and a bucktail jig on a short, 12-inch dropper line (Fig. 10). The jig provides weight to get the lure down and of course, the rig gives a fish a choice of two lures to strike.

The jig will not get hung up very often because its single hook rides upright in the water. Even so, the jig should

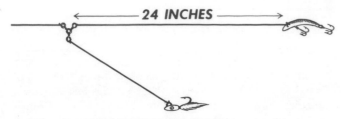

FIG. 10   COMBO RIG FOR WALLEYES AND BASS

be tied on light line that will break if the jig snaps so the rest of the rig is not lost.

On large lakes and rivers with lots of water to cover, and when fish are deep, try the simple arrangement shown in Fig. 11. Use a keel sinker weighing 3 to 6 ounces. The weight of the sinker used depends on how much line is out and how fast you troll. Light sinkers usually are adequate if you troll slowly and pay out considerable line. Heavier ones are needed for fast trolling with a short line.

A 3 or 4-foot wire leader is desirable if fishing for large pike or muskies.

**4 TO 6 OUNCE
KEEL SINKER**

3 TO 4 FOOT WIRE LEADER

FIG. 11   MUSKY TROLLING RIG

When trolling for landlocked salmon and lake trout in deep water during the summer you really have to get down if you want to catch fish. Most anglers use heavy lead sinkers when trolling for salmon and lakers, but best results are had by fishing with lead-core or wire line, heavy fresh water rods or light salt water rods, and salt water reels. (The heavy tackle is needed to take the gaff of deep trolling and fighting large fish up from great depths; and, of course, big salt water reels have the greatest line capacity.)

A good outfit for this extra-deep trolling is Monel wire line testing 20 to 30 pounds attached to about 100 feet of 15 or 20 pound test monofilament line. The lure is tied to the mono. Usually plugs, thin-bladed spinners, and various spoons are the best lures, but bait such as minnows, smelt or alewives can also be used in this deep trolling.

If enough wire line is payed out you can get down pretty deep without any added weight. One advantage of this rig is that the wire line sinks deeper than the mono, and

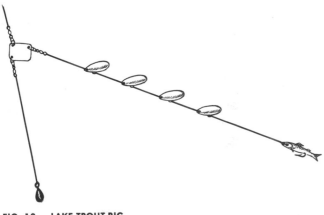

FIG. 12   LAKE TROUT RIG

occasionally it hits a rock, boulder or ridge but the lure will ride high and clear the obstacles.

Lake trout fishermen also frequently use multiple spinners, called "cowbells" or "Christmas trees," rigging them ahead of the lure. A "rudder" is needed to prevent line twist, and a sinker 3 to 8 ounces is used on a dropper line (See Fig. 12). Such trolling rigs can be purchased ready-made from several tackle companies.

Fishing for coho salmon in the Great Lakes has become a big thing, and thousands of anglers head for these mid-America lakes each season in hopes of getting in on the action. Although some cohos are caught by casting from boats and from shore, most are taken by trolling the open waters of the big lakes. Shallow or near-surface trolling often produces cohos, but most of the time you have to go deep to get them.

One of the simple ways to rig when coho aren't too deep is a trolling weight about 4 or 5 feet ahead of the lure (Fig. 13). These weights can be purchased in different sizes, and it pays to have an assortment of sizes from 4 to 12 ounces.

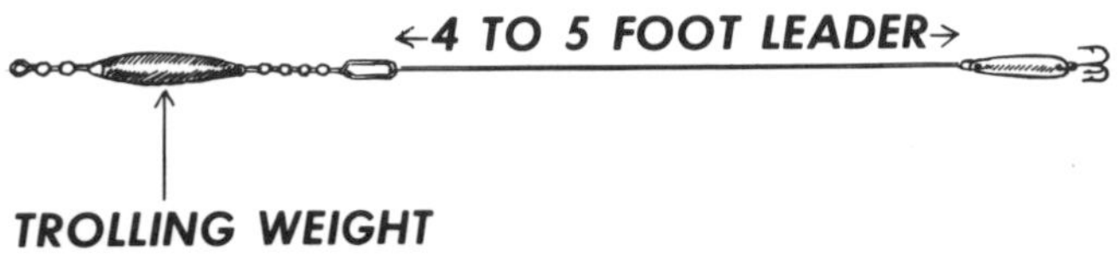

4 TO 5 FOOT LEADER

TROLLING WEIGHT

FIG. 13   COHO SALMON RIG

Anglers fishing for coho also use big "cannonball" sinkers weighing up to 2 or 3 pounds, similar to those used in trolling for striped bass and salmon along the Pacific Coast. Such heavy weights should be used with a "sinker-release" mechanism which releases the weight when a fish is hooked. The sinker is lost but more sport is had fighting the fish.

Metal or plastic planers also are used to take a line and lure down to great depths when trolling. The best have a tripping device which de-activates the planing effect when a fish is hooked. But during the actual trolling these planers put great strain on tackle so usually are used with stiff, heavy, salt water type rods and strong lines.

Coho are also fished with lead-core and wire lines. In fishing moderate depths they can be used without weights, but to get down really deep use a trolling weight between the wire line and the leader.

Incidentally, the most successful coho fishermen use depth-finders. These electronic marvels not only reveal the depth being fished, but also the bottom formation and even salmon and schools of baitfish. Depth-finders and sonar fish-finders are a big help not only in coho fishing but for any kind of trolling on large bodies of water.

Most of the trolling rigs illustrated can be made easily, at home, at a fishing camp, anywhere. It's a good idea to buy several spools of nylon monofilament in different tests, say 10 to 30 pounds, and have them ready. Also get different types and weights of sinkers, special trolling weights, three-way swivels, snaps and barrel-swivels, and, of course, bait hooks. The angler who has a wide assortment of those items is prepared for any fishing situation, and can make up whatever rig is needed for the fishing to be done. It pays, too, to make up several rigs ahead of time before going fishing.

Vlad Evanoff

27: Bag of tricks
for everyday angling

In early summer black bass begin schooling and spend most of their time in deep-water "sanctuaries." Ordinarily these schools "break up" or disperse to the shallows only to feed, and these inshore migrations may occur at any time, not just mornings and evenings.

It's smart to start a day's fishing by working the shallows, but if you don't get bass, move to deeper water. Try deep-down along the edges of drop-offs; beyond points and peninsulas that continue out from shore, and around reefs and bars 30-40 feet down.

⊡

Some fishermen say tadpoles are poor bass bait. Don't believe it!

A friend has seven largemouth bass, 5-6 inches long, in a large home aquarium. Drop a "taddy" in there and even though the bass are well fed (they get live shiner minnows daily) it's like . . . POOWWWW!!! . . . as the little bass strike with blinding speed and the tadpole simply disappears.

Those baby bass are capable of eating a tadpole fully half their size.

⊡

Most fishermen when walking from cars or from one spot to another carry their rods tip-first. If they stumble, the rod tip ofen digs into the ground and . . . "snaaapppp!" Also, a rod carried tip-first tends to catch in limbs and brush, or the line and attached lure will snag.

Best way to carry any rod is butt-first. If you trip and fall forward the rod is safely behind you and *cannot* be broken. Moreover neither the rod, line or lure will foul on leaves, limbs, etc.

Carrying a rod this way—tip first—can result in a smashed rod if the angler stumbles.

Proper way to carry any rod is butt-first. Should the angler stumble the rod is safely behind and cannot be broken.

Don't use large snap swivels or other "hardware" next to a lure unless absolutely necessary. A big snap swivel can frighten away fussy or spooky fish, and a swivel next to a lure can interfere with its action.

When using spoons or spinners, which usually make it necessary to use a barrel swivel or a snap swivel (to prevent line twist), it's best to tie in a small barrel swivel several inches above the lure. This will give a foot or so of separation between the lure and the swivel, will prevent line twist, and yet will not easily scare off fish.

⊡

Do you know about the "strip-cast" method of fishing with a fly rod? It's a super system for fishing delicately with bait, tiny spoons and jigs, or streamer flies.

Any fly rod can be used. The line is ordinary nylon monofilament, 15, 18, or 20 pound test—but the fly reel MUST be one with a tight-fitting spool. If the fly reel's spool is loose-fitting the monofilament can catch between the spool and the reel side-plates, either jamming the spool or cutting the line.

The "strip-casting" outfit is rigged like any fly tackle except mono instead of regular fly line is used.

String line through the guides, attach your bait hook, spoon, or streamer to the end, then pinch onto the line 3 feet up from the hook or lure 5 or 6 lead split-shot sinkers. To cast all you do is strip several yards of line from the reel and let it fall at your feet in loose coils. Now, with the split-shot sinkers hanging down from the rod tip about a foot and the bait or lure dangling beyond, take the rod vertically back to about the two o'clock position, while lightly holding the nylon line in your left hand as you would fly line. Make a quick, flip-like forward cast—shooting for eleven o'clock—and release the line from your left hand. The split-shot sinkers will take off like bullets and pull all that loose line along behind.

You'll be amazed at the ease with which you'll make 90-100 foot casts. Because of the fine nylon line and the split-shot, your bait, fly, or lure will sink quickly. In an instant you can be down 25-35 feet, where the crappies, walleyes, white bass or largemouths are.

If fishing a worm or minnow as bait, merely inch-in the line with your left hand for the retrieve, dropping the line in loose coils at your feet; if fishing a small spoon, streamer fly or other light lure, strip-in line more quickly to give the artificial proper action.

When a fish is hooked it is "played" by stripping line. Not only does "strip-casting" make it possible to fish very light lures, to cast them long distances, and to fish deep—but it provides the extra fun of taking fish on a fly rod.

⊡

Fresh water fishermen know the fish-appeal of porkrind, pork "eels," and porkchunk. But comparatively few salt water anglers use pork. More should, though, because pork is as attractive to salt water species as it is to fresh water gamefish.

Long, broad strips of porkrind can be rigged with hooks and trolled for marlin, sailfish, dolphin, bonito, mackerel, albacore, etc. Smaller porkrind strips can be used with spoons, jigs,

Japanese "feathers," etc. Use "tail-hooks" with big strips of porkrind, and be sure to touch up hooks with a hone.

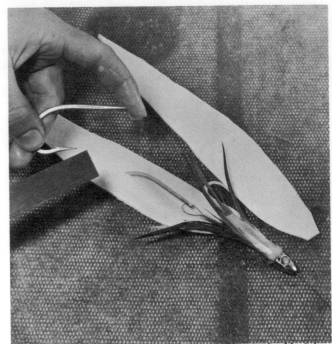

A strip of porkrind on a salt water "feather" adds considerable fish-appeal. Tail hooks should be used and honed to a fine point.

⊡

A new type of bottom fishing—or at least a newly-refined system of bottom fishing—is the "Pop-r-Jig" method.

This remarkably effective technique of deep fishing was devised by Jack Crawford, a jig and lure maker in Milwaukee, Wisconsin.

Crawford's "Pop-r-Jigs" are not true jigs because they float when fished without lead. They are made of wood, are tear-drop shaped, have flat, ball-eye hooks, and tails of bucktail, marabou, saddle-hackles, or combinations of those materials.

"Pop-r-Jig" fishing is done with a special "sliding" sinker, one that has a large hole in it. The sinker is slipped onto the line, then the "Pop-r-Jig" tied to the line. The works are reeled up to the rod tip and a cast made; the sinker provides plenty of casting weight and goes through the air nestled against the jig.

The sinker and lure are allowed to settle to the bottom. Then a few feet of line is payed out. The jig will rise in the water on the slack line, drawing the line easily through the hole in the sinker. The jig will "float" freely, while the sinker remains motionless on bottom. The jig will "float" or "swim" loosely in the water a few feet above the sinker.

When the rod is twitched the lure will dive without moving the sinker, then float upwards again. With repeated twitches of the rod, it is possible to activate a lure at one particular spot on the bottom.

The jig can be made to jump around in a life-like manner—up and down, up and down—rising a few feet or several, and fished in a specific area as long as desirable.

Details on "Pop-r-Jigs" can be had by writing Bill Binkelman, P.O. Box 4169, Milwaukee, Wisconsin 53210.

Two "Pop-r-Jigs": top one has saddle-hackle winging, bottom one has a combination wing of marabou and hackles.

⊡

Fly fishermen frequently reel in their line and leaders completely onto the reel spool. This usually results in the leader burying itself under the line, and the angler later has a hard time finding the leader end. To avoid this problem, drill a small hole in the edge of the fly reel spool and, when finished fishing, stick the leader end through the hole, pushing a few inches of leader through. Now the leader end will be instantly available the next time you go fishing.

To string-up a fly rod with leader and line, instead of trying to thread a thin, hard-to-see leader through the rod's guides, use the fly line. Merely double the end of the fly line over, and push it through the guides; the leader, of course, will follow.

To straighten nylon leaders and to remove all kinks, rub them with a square of soft rubber such as may be cut from an auto tube, or draw the taut leader back and forth against rubber boots, or under the rubber sole of sneakers or shoes.

⊡

When fishing live minnows use lightweight bobbers and *no* sinker.

There is little sense in striving to procure lively, strong, long-living minnows, then harnessing them with big hooks, heavy line, sinkers, and bulky floats.

The livelier the minnow the better chances of catching wily trout, wise bass, and wary walleyes. Use as light line or leader as possible for the conditions, and as small a bobber as will do the job. With no lead, a light line, and a small float, the minnow will be most active and draw the most strikes.

⊡

The successful trout fisherman is the one who doesn't let trout see him.

In shallow, clear trout water, it is easy for brook, brown, or rainbow trout to spot an approaching, careless fisherman. The trout that sees you is a trout you won't catch.

Stay very low when fishing small streams—remembering that the crouch, creep, and crawl system is what puts trout in the pan.

More trout are caught from shallow, clear water by the angler who approaches pools carefully and keeps low while fishing.

If you snag a lure in a tree don't try to pull it loose by yanking with the rod. You could break the rod, or sink the line into the reel spool.

The best way to free a fouled lure is to point the rod directly at the hung-up lure, hold the line in the free hand, and apply a steady pressure. Be sure, when attempting to pull free a hanged lure, that any companion in the boat sees what you are doing; frequently a hung lure will pop free unexpectedly, come flying back, and possibly strike (and hook) an unaware companion.

⊡

Probably more fishing rods are broken in and around autos than anywhere else.

Before going fishing, or when returning from a day on stream or lake, do not lay rods on the ground where they may be stepped on and broken, nor lean them against the car where they may be knocked down and broken, or fall into an open

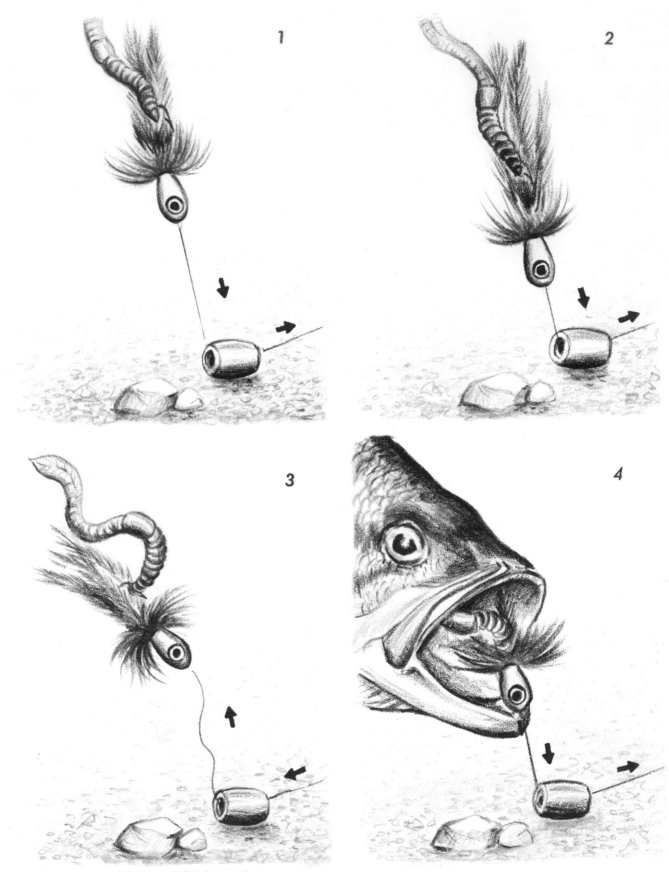

1

2

3

4

"POP-r-JIG" in action:

With floating plastic worm attached, "Pop-r-Jig" and sliding sinker is cast and allowed to settle to bottom. Line is payed out so that jig and worm rise, then rod is twitched so that lure darts toward bottom (Figs. 1, 2). Line is payed out again, and lure rises with slack (Fig. 3). Another twitch with rod (Fig. 4) and nearby bass strikes.

door then crushed when the door is closed. Instead, rest rods carefully in the crotch of a tree or, better still, place them on the roof of the car. They can't be stepped on there, nor caught in the car door.

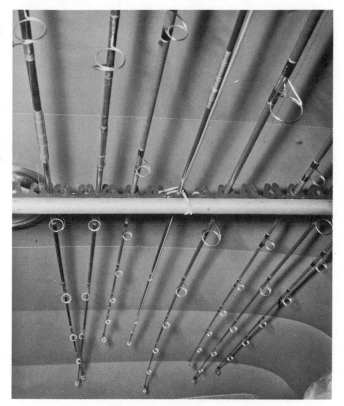

A rod rack like this built into the roof of a station-wagon is good insurance against broken rods. Such a rack, moreover, makes it unnecessary to "take down" tackle when moving from one spot to another or when making long trips.

⊡

Serious fishermen who travel a lot and do considerable fishing are wise to build rod-racks in their station wagons (roof space in coupes and sedans is inadequate for full-size rod racks). Piping can be mounted in a station wagon with rubber rod-holders so that nearly a dozen or so rods can be safely stored, fully assembled. (Many tackle salesmen use such rod-holders in station wagons.)

⊡

Snook, tarpon, striped bass—many different kinds of gamefish—find refuge and food under and around bridges spanning tidal guts, channels and bays. The wise fisherman can find much sport in such areas.

Fish such bridges at night and during a falling tide. On the up-tide side of a bridge fish will be in the shadows cast by bridge lights; on unlit spans fish will lie directly below the edge of the bridge. Cast a lure out at about a 45 degree angle, at least 30 feet in front of your shadow, then retrieve steadily so that the lure swims evenly toward the bridge about a foot under the surface. Let the lure swing under the bridge, hold

it in the current a few seconds—and be prepared to set the hook on a striking fish.

On the down-tide side of a bridge, cast a lure under the bridge so that it hits bottom before coming out below you. Bounce the lure over the bottom. When fish on this down-tide side of a bridge are feeding on the surface, cast parallel to the span so that a steady retrieve swings the lure to the fish in a sweeping arc.

⊡

Does an outboard motor scare fish?

Most of the time, yes . . . but not always. Under certain circumstances and with certain species of fish, an outboard motor acts as an attractor. Northern pike, for example, often are drawn to the bubbly disturbance created by an outboard; and in salt water many species of fish, especially barracuda, will swim in the wake of an outboard.

When fishing in deep water, an outboard often attracts more fish than it spooks. White bass and lake trout are other species that often will swim 10 or 15 feet behind the froth of an outboard.

But don't go outboarding wildly across a bonefish flat, or tearing noisily into a shallow, weedy bay where largemouth bass lurk. *Smart gamefish in shallow water will panic at the sound and disturbance of an outboard motor.*

⊡

What is a "Water-Gator?"

No, it is not a live bait but, rather, a new and sensational lure. Deep-going, it is an especially good walleye lure.

The "Water-Gator" is manufactured by Jack Smithwick, who also produces the famed line of "Devil's Warhorse" baits. The Gator is a bottom bait—so easy to use that anyone who can turn a reel handle can catch fish with it. It has a broad face that makes it a slow swimmer, and the slowest of retrieve speeds doesn't alter its fish-killing action. A Gator can be allowed to sink to the bottom and then worked like a jig by

Close-up of a "Water-Gator."

1. Slow, steady retrieve—seductive, side to side wiggle.

2. Use as you would a jig.

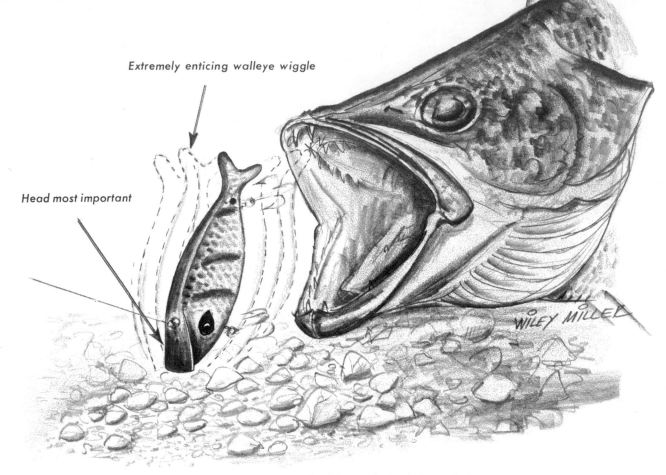

Extremely enticing walleye wiggle

Head most important

A "Water-Gator" can be worked over the bottom like a jig, but the difference is that it has a lively, fish-catching wiggle.

yo-yo-ing. When picked up off the bottom, it wiggles . . . and that is usually when most strikes come.

Further information on the "Water-Gator" can be had from Jack A. Smithwick, c/o Post Office, Shreveport, Louisiana.

⊡

Fish such as walleyes, striped bass, white and yellow bass, largemouth and smallmouth bass, yellow perch, crappies, etc. are school fish. Find one and you find 'em all, so to speak.

It's important, therefore, not to "lose the school" once a fish is hooked. Mark the area where fish are caught by tossing out an inflated balloon tied to a line with a sinker; or use a marker float made of styrofoam, or a float made of an old plastic bottle. Both the styrofoam and plastic bottles should be sprayed with yellow or orange paint for easy spotting, and use them with heavy line and at least 3 ounces of lead weight.

Tape fixed to a fly reel spool and marked with data describing type and weight of fly line, and amount and test of backing line, is helpful angler's guide.

A tip for fly fishermen using various reels and rods, and reels with extra spools and lines, is to mark adhesive tape with the data regarding the kind of line and backing and attach it to each fly reel spool.

For example, a reel spool having a tape attached reading "WF9F, 100-18, Newton," would mean that spool contains a weight-forward, number 9 line, floating type (F), and 100 yards of 18 pound test backing line, and the fly line is a Newton make.

⊡

If your outboard motor's propellor becomes snarled with weeds, usually indicated by cavitation—the prop slips and starts "racing" in the water. It can be easily cleared.

Merely put the motor into reverse for a few moments, and the prop will probably back the weeds off.

When rain or spray puts water into a boat, it usually can be quickly emptied by starting the motor and running the boat with the transom drain plug pulled. Don't forget to replace the plug when all the water is out.

⊡

Speed of retrieve can be a vital factor in taking fish on lures.

Sometimes the slowest possible retrieve is needed to take largemouth bass, other times it is necessary to fish a lure as fast as possible. Too many fishermen believe lures should be fished fast in spring and fall when the water is cool, and slow in summer when the water is warm. They wrongly figure that bass are active when the water is cool, sluggish when it is warm. Actually, the opposite is true.

Bass will more often take a fast-moving lure in summer than they will be in spring or fall, and vice versa. Thera are always exceptions, however, so the smart fisherman tries different retrieve speeds regardless of the time of year or temperature of the water. Keep experimenting with lures, depths, and retrieve speeds until a winning combination is found.

⊡

A simple formula makes it possible to determine the approximate weight of a fish through measurements alone.

This is not always of importance when fish are to be killed since, normally, they then can be weighed. But many anglers release fish they catch, even ones of trophy size.

To figure the weight of a fish accurately to within a few pounds, measure its length and its girth. Length should be determined by measuring from the tip of the lower jaw to the bottom tip of the tail. Girth should be taken at the broadest part of the body.

Apply the measurements taken to this formula: $W = \dfrac{800}{L \times G^2}$

W is the fish's weight in pounds; L its length, and G^2 is the girth squared.

⊡

Old spoons, spinners, etc. can be made nearly new again by cleaning with steel wool and silver polish.

Coating of spoons, etc. with clear nail polish or lacquer adds to life of lure's finish.

A tarnished or rusted spoon or spinner—whether of gold, bronze, brass, copper or chrome finish—can be easily cleaned and restored to nearly-new condition by rubbing with steel wool and silver polish. Use fine steel wool.

The finish of spoons, spinners—even plugs—can be protected and thus will last longer if the lure is coated with clear fingernail polish or clear lacquer. Several dozen lures can be coated in a few minutes.

⊡

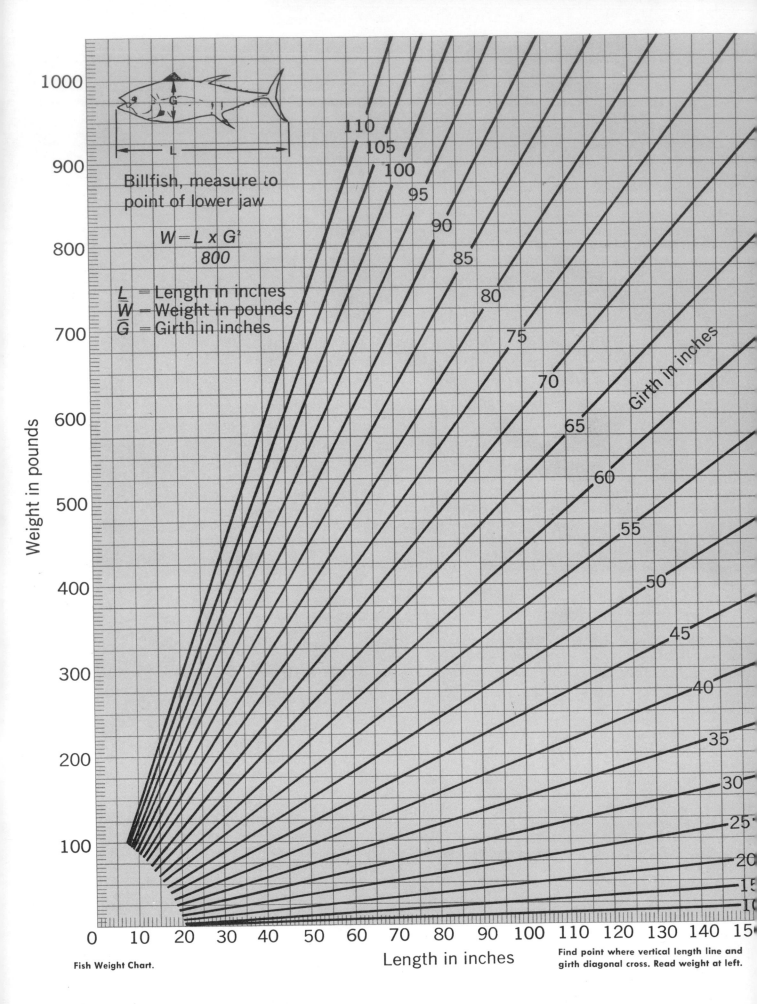

Weight in pounds (y-axis)

1000
900
800
700
600
500
400
300
200
100

Billfish, measure to point of lower jaw

$$W = \frac{L \times G^2}{800}$$

L = Length in inches
W = Weight in pounds
G = Girth in inches

Girth in inches

110
105
100
95
90
85
80
75
70
65
60
55
50
45
40
35
30
25
20
15
10

0   10   20   30   40   50   60   70   80   90   100   110   120   130   140   15

Length in inches

Fish Weight Chart.

Find point where vertical length line and girth diagonal cross. Read weight at left.

Good jig fishermen take time to work their jigs, especially new types, in shallow water near a dock where they can SEE the jig's action. Such close observation builds up in the fisherman's mind an exact picture of what his jig is doing when it's down there in 20 or 30 feet of water. The angler thus creates an intuitive "jig sense," much as skilled trout fishermen develop a "sixth sense" for nymph fishing.

A master at jig fishing can, in his mind's eye, *see* his jig as he makes it quiver, hop, dart, dig, bounce, bump and jiggle over the bottom. He *knows*, always, precisely what his lure looks like down there in the deep.

Fish do not usually *strike* a jig; normally they just halt its forward movement, merely *stopping* it. Strikes, or more correctly "*stops*," most often come just as the jig falls back from a forward and upward jerk.

Such "takes" by fish hitting jigs often are very gentle, almost imperceptible by the novice. The beginner or careless fisherman frequently will jerk a jig right out of a fish's mouth. Strive to get the "feel" of jigging, and always be alert for the lightest touch.

⊡

A sliding sinker, one with a hole through its middle, is useful in bottom fishing with live minnows, plastic worms, or nightcrawler worms.

A Crawford sliding sinker is best, since it has a very large hole and edges are beveled to prevent line-fraying. The line slips through such sinkers readily.

Use a Crawford sliding sinker with a split ring tied to the line a few inches up from the lure. The ring will prevent the hook from entering the hole in the sinker. Rig a hook with a live minnow, a Burke floating "Erthworm" or other suitable floating plastic worm, or with a nightcrawler that has been pumped up with air to make it rise and "float" in the water. A worm can be filled with air by pumping air into it with an empty hypodermic syringe.

Make a cast, allow the sinker to settle to the bottom, then pay out some slack line. The minnow, plastic or real worm will rise in the water, and then can be fished up and down by simply raising and lowering the rod.

One spot on bottom can be fished thoroughly this way, without recasting, by merely dragging the sinker a few feet over the bottom.

⊡

When taking lunch-time breaks from fishing, fly fishermen using floating lines should strip line from the reel and lay it out on rocks or grass to dry. The sun will dry the line quickly, and when fishing is resumed the line will float high.

To grease or "clean" a fly line quickly and evenly, tie the leader tippet to a fence wire or to a tree limb, then walk away with the rod and reel, paying out all of the fly line. Prop the rod against another tree, car, fence or whatever, so that the line is suspended in the air like a clothesline. It is now a simple matter to walk the length of the line applying "cleaner" or a floatant with a cloth or pad.

Wipe excess grease from the line.

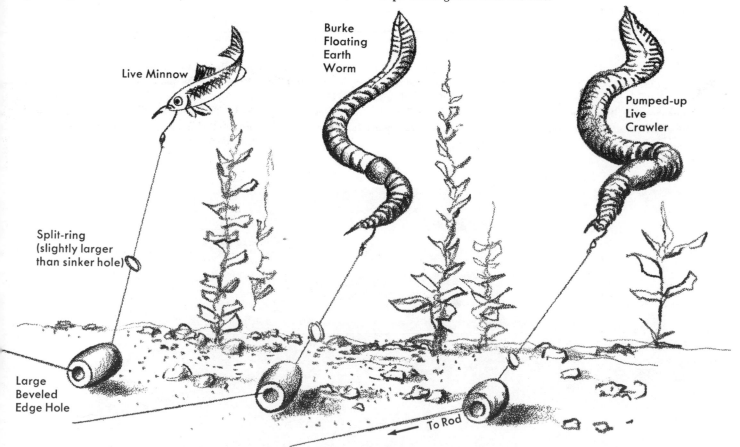

Live Minnow

Burke Floating Earth Worm

Pumped-up Live Crawler

Split-ring (slightly larger than sinker hole)

Large Beveled Edge Hole

← To Rod

A special sliding sinker makes it possible to fish a minnow, phoney plastic worm or genuine night crawler pumped-up with air in one spot with appealing up and down action.

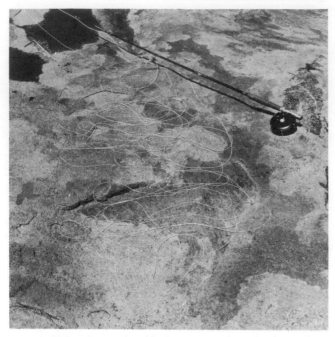

Stripping fly line from reel and laying out on rocks to dry during shore "break" means a high-floating line when fishing is resumed.

⊡

Offshore trolling is not necessarily done far offshore. In many areas, such as at Walker's Cay in the Bahamas, it may be only a 10 minute run from the dock to blue water . . . where the bottom drops away to hundreds of fathoms.

Here in the ocean—as is often the case in fresh water lakes—big gamefish congregate at these drop-offs to feed on smaller fish.

Several members of the tuna clan swarm in Bahamas waters —including little tuna, blackfin tuna, yellowfins and giant bluefin tuna. The bluefins appear in May and June, during their northward migrations, and hundreds of charter boats pursue them as they cruise drop-off edges.

⊡

The northern whitefish, though most readily caught on flies, also can be taken in good numbers by spinning with ultra-light lures.

Tiny spoons such as the Dardevle Spinnie and Dardevle Imp are excellent, as are small spinners (the Mepp's is good), and small jigs. An inch-long jig with white bucktail or impala winging is excellent.

Fish the lure erratically, with quick darts and jerks. Be careful when a whitefish strikes as they have tender mouths.

⊡

"Nodding" is a little-known system of surface bass fishing that requires considerable patience but which pays off in fish.

Nearly any type of surface plug can be used for "nodding." In essence, this is ultra-slow top-water fishing. A cast is made to a likely spot, and the lure allowed to "rest" motionless for a long, long while. Then the lure is merely "nodded," just barely twitched rather than given a sound *pop,* jerk, or twitch.

While any surface lure can be used, the best for this type of fishing is the "Devil's Warhorse," a long thin-bodied floater available in most quality tackle shops. It rests at a 45-degree angle in the water, half-in, half-out. It looks more like a quill-type bobber floating in the water than it does a plug.

For best results the Devil's Horse should be retrieved with short jerks, not pulls, of from 2 to 6 inches. This gives the bait a bobbing or dancing motion. Have at least two-second intervals between jerks—and in true "nodding" technique a much longer pause is desirable. The lure should be jerked up to six different times, then allowed to rest for several seconds . . . even minutes if the angler has the patience for it. This technique should be repeated from point-of-cast to the boat. Always retrieve all the way to the boat, as many fish are lost by not retrieving the lure to the boat. "Nodding" is effective both night and day, with dark nights best.

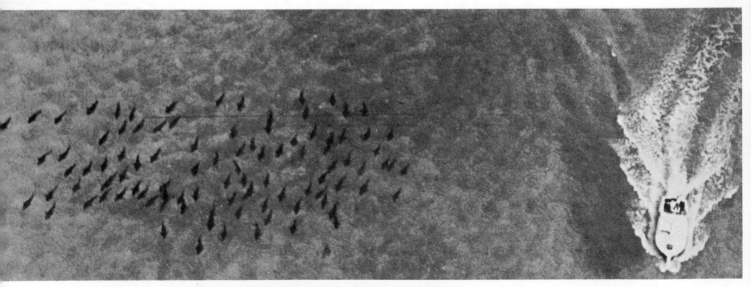

Aerial view of a school of 500-pound bluefin tuna on the banks at Cay Cay, Bahamas.

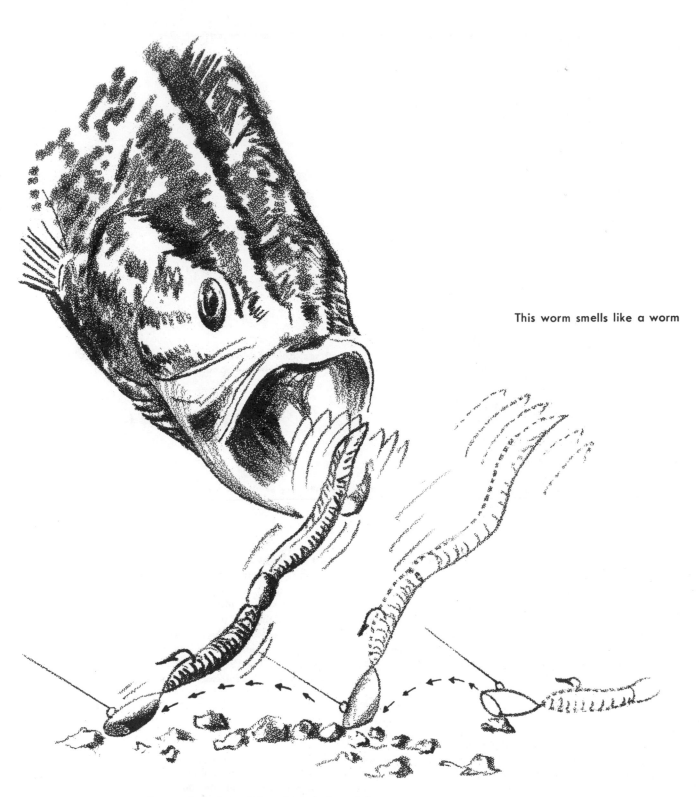

This worm smells like a worm

Tapered design of head tends to catch on bottom and causes enticing wiggle to floating worm.

Flat-faced jig with "floating" plastic worm snakes way over bottom.

It should take you at least—10 full minutes—60 seconds to the minute, to work one cast —don't hurry it. *That big fish will lie right under the lure and watch and watch.*

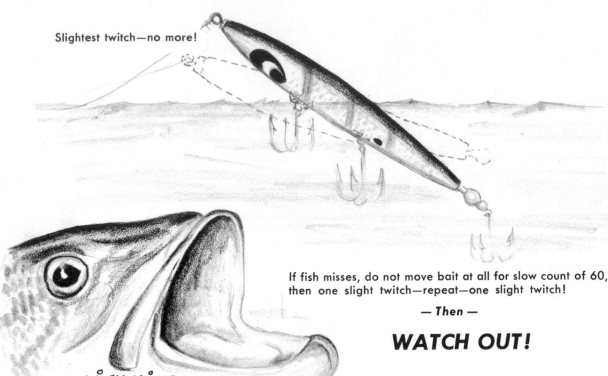

Slightest twitch—no more!

If fish misses, do not move bait at all for slow count of 60, then one slight twitch—repeat—one slight twitch!

— Then —

WATCH OUT!

WILEY MILLER

"Nodding" is a little-known technique of surface fishing with "slim silhouette" plugs of "Devil's Warhorse" type.

⊡

"Devil's Warhorse" lures are available with no spinners, with one stern spinner, or with spinners at bow and stern. The 1000 series of "Warhorse" lures, with *no* spinners, is preferred by a majority of top-water experts. This includes the "professional series"—the A1000, C1000, and E1000. On windy days with riffled water, spinners are desirable, so the best then are the "Warhorse" F100 and F400, both with front and rear propellers, and the F600 with rear propeller.

⊡

Night-time is one of the good times to fish for striped bass. During the spring and fall migrations, daylight activity is common among stripers, but for the major part of the season, night fishing is just about a necessity.

Metal lures are generally not effective in the night tides; but bait-tails and eel-skin jigs often are deadly. Swimming plugs and trolling "tubes" can be excellent, too, and rigged or "Alou" eels are about tops.

Do everything more slowly at night. Jig easily; nurse plugs along; wiggle eels slowly as possible; strip streamers slightly.

All shades of color appear darker at night, so color selection is less critical than in daytime. During new moon or overcast nights use black lures, or grey or purple. If there's a lot of moonlight, try somewhat lighter colors—such as eel-skin blue, amber, chameleon.

Phosphorus sparkling in the water at night like fiery diamonds—"Fire in the water"—is the natural phosphorescence of micro-organisms in the sea. Many fishermen, habitually having poor success under such conditions, refuse to fish. They shouldn't, though, because a slight amount of phosphorus is always present and does no harm to fishing. As the effect gets stronger overcome it by using light monofilament line with no leader. It is the glow of the line, not the lure, which frightens away fish under extreme conditions of "Fire in the water."

⊡

There are countless jigs on the market—jigs with spinners, jigs fished with porkrind eels attached, jigs with plastic worms —and all are good. But don't fail to try the new jig-'n-worm combination that features a jig with a flat face cut at an oblique angle.

The floating plastic worm used with this jig actually smells like a genuine worm, and the jig head makes the worm "flirt" and entice fish. Usually the most effective retrieve for this particular worm is a *12 inch drag*, then *a slight hop*, then *another drag*. As a rule the best speed is *slow*. But if that fails, try a fast 12 to 18-inch jerk, then reel, then jerk again.

The most productive colors in the worm appear to be black, purple, blue, green, and natural.

Save yourself the trouble of digging worms and
the cost of buying them by raising your own

28: The care and keeping of worms

Properly fed and cared for in a "worm bed," nightcrawlers grow long and fat.

Save yourself the trouble of digging worms (or the cost of buying them) by raising your own.

Anyone can raise his own earthworms, either the nightcrawler or angleworm variety, with little expenditure of time or money. And worms can be raised almost anywhere —in the backyard, in the garage, in the basement of a city apartment, or back in the tool shed.

Worms do not require much to grow into big, fat, healthy fish-catchers. All they need is a box or trough with the proper loam, moisture and food in it, and then to be kept in a reasonably dark, cool area.

Nightcrawlers are the large 5 to 8-inch long worms seen on lawns at night after a light rain or sprinkling. They are excellent baits for largemouth and smallmouth bass, yellow perch, trout and the larger panfish such as crappies and white bass. Large brown trout succumb to skilled anglers who fish night crawlers after spring rains by rolling them with split-shot sinkers along the bottom. A favorite method of taking walleyes, also, is to use a nightcrawler or two behind a large spinner and to troll slowly just off bottom.

Angleworms are considerably smaller than nightcrawlers yet they are taken just as eagerly by most fresh water fish. Angleworms are better than nightcrawlers for some fishing, such as for brook trout in small streams, bluegills, rock bass, etc.

A "worm bed," for either nightcrawlers or angleworms, can be made of an old-time washtub, a nail keg, large wooden barrel, a shipping crate or, best of all, you can fashion a special worm box using either new or old lumber. Redwood flower boxes of the window type also make decent worm beds and can be purchased inexpensively,

the cost depending upon the size. The bottom holes in flower boxes must be covered with screening, however, to prevent worms from escaping.

Following are the materials needed for construction of one kind of worm box:

    4 pcs.—2 ft. 4 in. x 6 in. x 1 in. sheeting grade lumber
    1 pc.—2 ft. 4 in. x ½ in. marine plywood
        (for floor of box)
    4 pcs.—¾ in. x ¾ in. x 2 ft. 6 in. strips (for cover frame)
    1 pc.—2 ft. 7 in. x 2 ft. 7 in. window screening
    ½ pound of 2-inch nails
    1 small box of screening tacks

The material listed will cost less than $5 in most areas, and will make a worm box 2 feet, 4 inches square, by 6 inches deep. The box can be assembled in less than two hours, and it will keep up to 400 worms. Such a box is small enough that you'll find storage space for it easily, and you can even take it along in the trunk of the car when going on fishing trips. Instead of purchasing new lumber to construct the worm box you may have suitable scrap lumber on hand. Just be sure not to use any metal plating in the box as it can rust and acid given off by rusting metal will kill worms.

When putting this box together drill about a dozen 1/16th inch holes at random in the plywood bottom so there will be adequate drainage. The four pieces of 2 ft. 4 in. lumber are nailed together to form a square, and the plywood sheet nailed to form the bottom. The ¾ in. stripping is nailed together to make a lid, and the screening tacked to it. The box is finished then, and ready for bedding material and worms.

A better box, in that it is much larger though not readily portable, is 3 ft. high, 3 ft. wide, and 6 ft. long. (See sketch.) It will accommodate 500 or 600 worms. In building this simple box use 2 x 10 inch pine or cypress boards.

Still another kind of worm bed you can make and have as a more-or-less permanent installation is one of cinder construction blocks, glass blocks, or building bricks. Such a worm bed can be constructed under the porch, in an out-of-the-way spot in the backyard, or in the garden. Cinder blocks have holes that would have to be cemented up to prevent worms escaping. But however the "bed" is made, be sure there are some small holes for seepage of water. Worms need water and proper moisture, but too much water will kill them promptly. A worm bed of cinder or glass blocks, or of brick, should be raised slightly above ground level, say with only 75 or 80% of the box below ground level, sunken in the earth. This prevents worms from escaping.

Worm boxes, barrels or what not should be kept in dark or shaded areas, although the box in the illustration is shown with a lid which, of course, keeps the earth in the box shaded and cool.

What goes into your worm box is very important. To thrive worms need suitable soil (or soil substitute), good food, moisture, and proper temperature.

There are many different kinds of material you can use in a worm bed. A combination "bedding" of 1/3 peat moss, 1/3 black loam, and 1/3 manure is preferred by many worm growers. Avoid sandy soil since it can injure the intestinal tracts of worms, and clay is not good either. Some fishermen put a couple inches of soil in the bottom

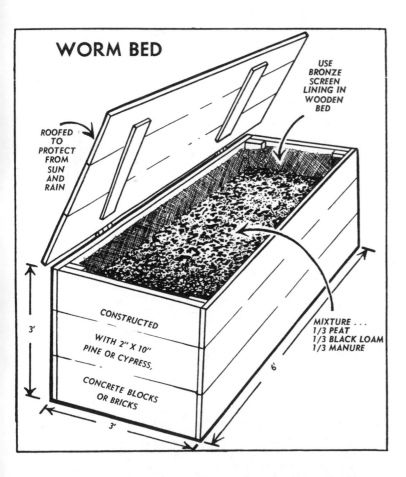

WORM BED

ROOFED TO PROTECT FROM SUN AND RAIN

USE BRONZE SCREEN LINING IN WOODEN BED

CONSTRUCTED WITH 2" X 10" PINE OR CYPRESS,

CONCRETE BLOCKS OR BRICKS

MIXTURE . . . 1/3 PEAT 1/3 BLACK LOAM 1/3 MANURE

3'

3'

6'

of their worm boxes, add four inches of corn husks or leaves or grass, next another layer of soil, and follow that with still other layers of corn husks or soil until the box is filled.

There are worm-keeping experts who feel soil is a bad storage material for worms (even though it is their "natural" environment) and, instead, use dried leaves which are sprinkled lightly with more leaves at least once daily. Some fishermen feel it is too much of a chore, though, to have to sprinkle their worm bed at least once a day. Sphagnum moss is a good material, but like leaves, it must be kept damp.

Most fishermen nowadays prefer a prepared or "commercial" preparation for the worm box. One of the very best of the commercial worm beddings is "Earlybird Worm Bedding," manufactured by the Earlybird Company, P.O. Box 1485, Boise, Idaho, 83701. The Earlybird Company says all you need do with their bedding is "just add worms and water," but the bedding can be improved by mixing with it peat, manure and, of course, food and water.

A very excellent worm bedding can be made by mixing in a 10 quart bucket two 5 pound bags of "Earlybird" bedding and about a quart of water, adding the water gradually and kneading it into the bedding. Next add one-half bucket of Michigan Peat and 2 pounds of sheep manure. Keep adding water until you are able to squeeze it freely from the mixture.

Let this mixture set for a few days before putting worms in. After the worms are in the bed, add water regularly to keep the bed moist. You should always be able to squeeze a little water from the bedding. Adding a handful of one-inch squares of woolen cloth will help the worms too, because it provides a roughage to the bedding which worms seem to love. Spanish moss or burlap bags, kept dampened, can be placed over the top of bedding.

Worms must be kept as cool as possible, with 55 to 60 degrees considered best. Equally important, they need ample moisture. Use a garden-type sprinkler to water your worm bed with one or two quarts of water about every three days. This should be adequate if the worm bedding is of the proper consistency and material.

Always check for dead or dying worms, and remove them. Like "bad apples," they can destroy a worm bed.

Many things can be fed worms. A good food mixture is a half cup of yellow cornmeal and a handful of coffee grounds. Sprinkle this mix over the top of the worm bed, and when it disappears in a day or so, add more. Be careful, though, not to overfeed worms; too much feeding sours the bedding material and will ultimately kill the worms.

Cornmeal with table fat is good worm food. Add a little sugar, if you like, or a bit of syrup, and coffee grounds also are good. Prepared dog and chicken foods are used by some worm farmers.

Worms appear to thrive best on a high fat-protein diet, supplied by such foods as vegetable oil or lard mixed with corn, soybean, or cottonseed meal. For each worm bed that is 6 feet x 3 feet x 3 feet, apply 1½ pounds of shortening or lard mixed with 3 pounds of meal about every two weeks.

Add a little moisture each time worms are fed. You can tell by the location of the worms whether the bedding is too dry, too wet, or "just right." If the bedding is too dry the worms will be at the bottom; if too wet, at the top; but when the moisture is right the worms will be scattered through the top 6 or 8 inches of bedding.

Other food items you can toss onto a worm bed occasionally include crumbled hard-boiled egg, powdered milk, and bread crumbs or crushed cornflakes, along with tiny pieces of lettuce or cabbage leaves.

Getting worms for the worm bed is no real problem.

Start looking for them in areas where there is good black soil, and where the soil is shaded and moist. Both angleworms and nightcrawlers can be collected by spading, but nightcrawlers are best taken at night. They'll emerge partially or completely from their burrows after dark when the grass is moist. Water a lawn a few hours before dark to collect nightcrawlers later. When the crawlers are out they can be stalked and picked quickly off the grass if the worm hunters use a little caution. Nightcrawlers are sensitive to bright light as well as to vibrations in the ground. Walk lightly and slowly as you search for them, and subdue the light from your flashlight by taping red or yellow cellophane over the lens. You can also cut the bright beam of a flashlight by painting the lens with red nailpolish, removing the paint later with nail-polish remover.

Electric shock rods are available on the market for collecting worms, and they work very well as a rule. Still another way to get worms is by "fiddling" for them. Cut two sticks about 1½ feet long, sharpen the end of one, and cut small notches vertically for about half of its length. Shove this stick into the ground and move the other rapidly over the notches. The worms will come scooting out of the ground for about five feet around the partially buried stick. Naturally you've got to do your fiddling where there are worms. If you do it where there are worms they'll come up, though, because apparently they mistake the sounds of your fiddling for the sounds made by a swiftly digging mole—the worm's natural enemy—so they flee to the top of the earth.

Commercially-prepared worm beddings, such as "Early Bird" variety, can be used in worm cribs satisfactorily.

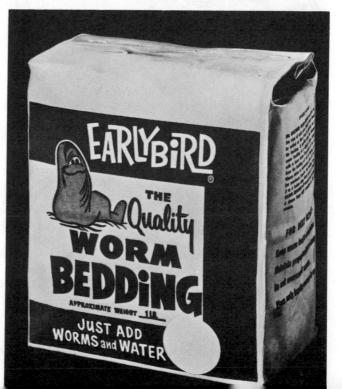

29: Exploded drawings and parts list of two Johnson reels

Among the most popular of all spin-cast reels are those in the Johnson line.

The Dennison-Johnson Company, manufacturers of Johnson spin-cast and magnetic fly reels in Mankato, Minnesota, originated spin-cast reels more than 20 years ago. Millions of the firm's reels have been sold.

The Johnson Company markets its reels under a "lifetime guarantee," and for a few dollars to cover mailing and handling costs, will repair any Johnson reel returned—regardless of the reel's age. Reels sent in for repair or reconditioning also will be filled with new monofilament line—at no cost.

Reels returned to Johnson for servicing should be carefully packaged, and the sender's name and home address should be printed on a card attached to the reel, as well as on the outside of the package. This insures that the reel will be reconditioned, or replaced, and promptly returned to the sender. Packages should be addressed to Service Department Manager, Johnson Reels Company, Johnson Park, Mankato, Minnesota 56001.

Of the Johnson line, two reels are especially popular: the *Century*, a long-time favorite, and the *Sa'Bra*, a newer model that is being very well received. Exploded drawings, parts list and prices are given here.

THE CENTURY Model 100B

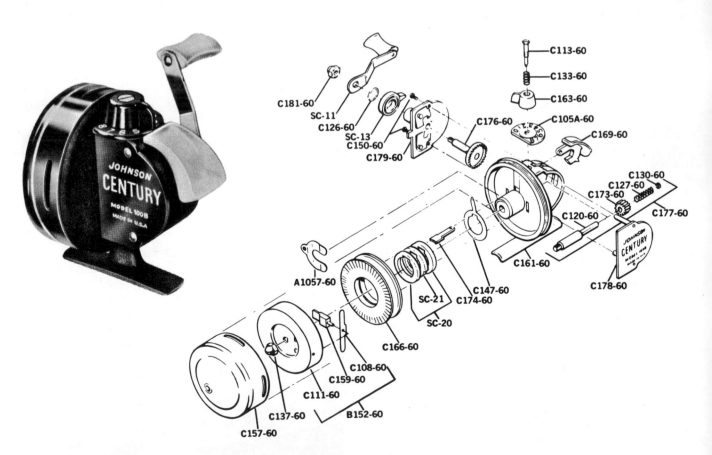

THE SA'BRA Model 130

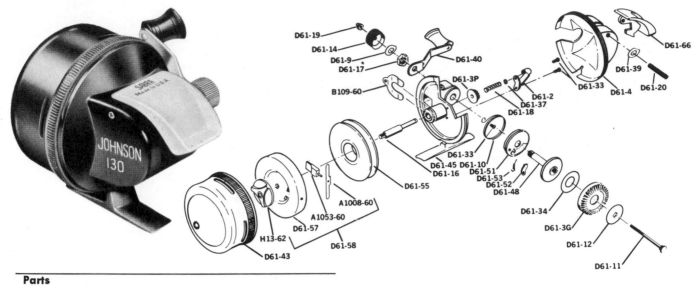

Parts Number	Parts Description	Price
A1006-60	Spool	
A1008-60	Pickup Spring	.20
A1051-60	Crank Handle	.60
A1053-60	Pickup Pin w/slide	1.35
A1054-60	Case Ass'm.	4.95
A1057-60	Spool Clip	
B152-60	Rotor Ass'm.	2.25
C105A-60	Drag Dial	.55
C108-60	Pickup Spring	.10
C109-60AP	Crank Handle (Round Knob)	.35
C111-60	Rotor Only	1.25
C113-60	Drag Adjustment Screw	.30
C120-60	Drive Shaft Only	.80
C121-60	Pinion Gear (See Note "A")	.15
C126-60	Anti-Reverse Snap Ring	.10
C127-60	Drive Shaft Spring	.10
C129A-60	Spool Retaining Ring	.15
C130-60	Drive Shaft Retaining Ring	.05
C131-60	Crank Nut	.15
C133-60	Drag Adjustment Spring	.05
C137-60	Rotor Nut	.20
C147-60	Spool Click	.25
C149-60	Drag Adjustment Bar	.15
C150-60	Side Plate Screw	.05
C157-60	Front Cover Green	1.50
C157-60AP	Front Cover Pink	1.50
C158-60	Drive Shaft Ass'm. Beveled gear	1.10
C159-60	Pick Up Pin Ass'm. w/slide	.90
C161-60	Case Ass'm.	3.80
C163-60	Drag Adjustment Knob	.30
C165-60	Bearing Side Plate w/studs Green	3.00
C166-60	Spool	
C167-60	Name Side Plate w/o studs	1.90
C169-60	Push Button	.30
C170-60	Drag Shoe, Internal 1 piece	.30
C173-60	Pinion Gear	.15
C174-60	Drag Adjustment Bar	.15
C176-60	Crank Shaft Ass'm. Iron gear	.95
C177-60	Drive Shaft Ass'm. Iron gear	1.10
C178-60	Name Side Plate w/studs Green	1.90
C178-60AP	Name Side Plate w/studs Pink	1.90
C179-60	Bearing Side Plate Ass'm. w/o studs Green	3.00
C179-60BF	Bearing Side Plate Ass'm. w/o studs Pink	3.00
C181-60	Crank Nut Jeweled Self Locking	.15

Parts Number	Parts Description	Price
D61-2	Rear Bearing	.75
D61-3G	Large Gear Beveled	.95
D61-3P	Pinion Gear Beveled	.40
D61-4	Back Cover	3.00
D61-4#2	Back Cover Complete w/push Button	4.00
D61-9	Drag Adjustment Spring Washer	.15
D61-10	Anti-Reverse Spring	.35
D61-11	Drag Adjustment Screw	.35
D61-12	Drag Washer, External	.15
D61-14	Drag Adjustment Knob	.75
D61-16	Drive Shaft	
D61-17	Crank Nut	.20
D61-18	Drive Shaft Spring	
D61-19	Drag Lock Nut	.25
D61-20	Push Button Screw	
D61-33	Screw, Rear Bearing	
D61-33	Screw, Anti-Reverse Spring	
D61-34	Drag Washer Internal Teflon	.30
D61-37	Drive Shaft Retaining Ring "E"	.10
D61-39	Push Button Washer	.15
D61-40	Crank Handle	.90
D61-43	Front Cover	2.45
D61-45	Case Ass'm.	5.75
D61-48	Crank Shaft Ass'm.	
D61-51	Anti-Reverse Disc	.75
D61-52	Drive Pawl	.10
D61-53	Click Spring	.25
D61-55	Spool Empty	2.00
D61-55	Spool w/10# Test (130X10)	2.75
D61-55	Spool w/12# Test (130X12)	2.75
D61-55	Spool w/15# Test (130X15)	2.75
D61-55	Spool w/20# Test (130X20)	2.75
D61-57	Rotor only	2.25
D61-58	Rotor Ass'm.	3.80
D61-63	Large Gear	.95
D61-64	Pinion Gear	.40
D61-66	Push Button	.60
H13-62	Rotor Nut	.35
SC-11	Crank Handle (Single Flat Knob)	.60
SC-13	Anti-Reverse Control	.30
SC-20	Drag Shoe External	.10
SC-21	Drag Shoe Internal	.10

30: New flycasting training aid: Pachner's trainer

Two factors generally limit fly casting from becoming easily learned. One is the mis-matching of equipment, mainly rod and line, and the second is lack of instruction, primarily personal, by someone versed in the mechanics of flyrodding.

Assuming the equipment is matched, the individual then must learn either on his own or through assistance by an instructor. Either way, the main hindrance, at this point, in becoming proficient with a fly rod, is to let the rod drop too low on the backcast. This is caused mainly by total wrist action instead of letting the wrist, forearm and elbow work as a unit.

This is a difficult fault to overcome by self-correction or through an instructor. Therefore, "Pachner's Trainer", a fly rod training aid, was designed to put an end to this bugaboo and help make anyone a better caster in a short period of time.

The fly rod training arm is made in two sizes, long and short, to accommodate the variation in individual arm length between men, women and children. The large model is recommended for use with an 8 or 8½ foot rod and the small for use with a 7½ foot fly rod. Additional information, or training arms ($4.95) are available from:

Pro. Sports Pub. Co., 187 S. Schuyler Ave., Kankakee, Ill. 60901.

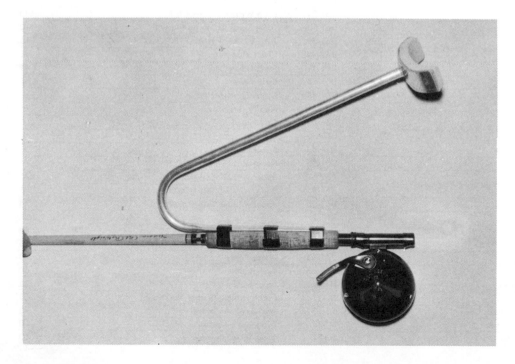

Fly Rod and Training Arm

The training "arm" should be installed as illustrated with vinyl tape. This is sufficient to firmly anchor the arm to the rod grip. Note that the curved arm-bumper on the end of the arm is set at an angle, depending on the model, for either a right or left-handed caster.

9 O'clock Position

This is the starting position for the backcast. To start, raise the rod quickly upwards and carry through to the one o'clock position. The sharp pick-up will cause the line to put a bend in the rod and the bend, wanting to straighten out, will send the line easily rearward. The padded arm bumper will stop the caster's arm from going on beyond the one o'clock position.

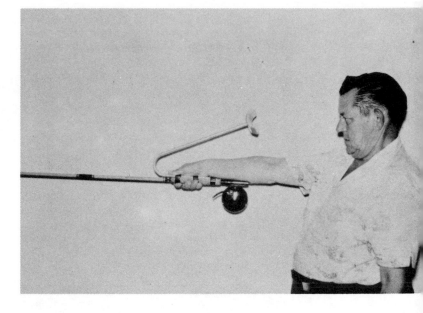

1 O'clock Position

When properly used, the bumper will come to rest on the upper arm approximately midway between the elbow and shoulder. When rod is in this position, caster must hold or "hesitate" long enough for the line to straighten out behind him. This is an important sequence of the fundamentals of fly casting and is unlike spinning and casting where a quick back and forward motion of the rod sends the lure out. The duration of hesitation depends upon the amount of line beyond the rod tip—the longer the line, the longer the wait.

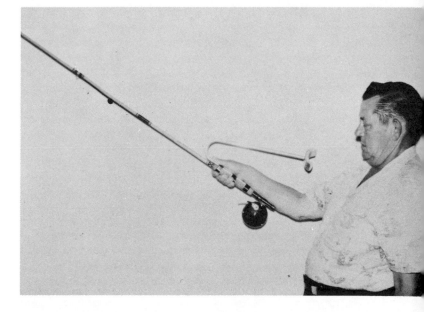

1 O'clock back through 10 O'clock Position

When line has straightened out, start forward cast by powering rod to the 10 o'clock position then relax and let rod float down or "follow-through" to the 9 o'clock position.

31: How to use atom plugs on stripers and blues

Back in the days when I was first stricken with that strange and incurable malady known as "striper fever," the Mecca for New England's striped bass fishermen was Cape Cod Canal. This seven-mile-long, man-made fishing hole was where hundreds of bass fishermen gathered each weekend to try to find ways of conning these great game fish into thinking they were getting something to eat, when all they were really getting were 5/0 hooks in their jaws.

In those days there were two schools of thought on how to fool stripers. One group of fishermen advocated using worms, squid, herring or other natural baits in holes where bass lay while four mile per hour tides raced over their heads. Other fishermen believed that bouncing jigs or eel-skin rigs through those same deep holes at night was the way to get fish. Actually both systems were right because both caught fish.

So we were catching fish at night years ago, but at day-break—when the stripers came to the surface and broke along the entire length of the canal—they stopped hitting and we'd catch nothing. We used to think that the fish were "playing" and just wouldn't hit.

That's what we thought until one guy—smarter or more imaginative than the rest of us—decided that these bass could be taken. He was Bill Walheim, a veteran Canal basser and a man who was something of a loner, often fishing away from the rest of the crowd.

I watched Bill one morning after a night of fishing. I was standing on a high bank near the Canal's Sagamore Bridge, watching him cast and wondering why anyone would be wasting his time fishing in broad daylight. Then, suddenly, right in front of Bill, the canal opened and discharged a pinwheeling striped bass. As soon as Bill landed his fish I scrambled down to see what lure he was using, but the foxy son-of-a-gun had the bass and the lure covered with a large Turkish towel by the time I got there. Of course that was a pretty unneighborly attitude, but it was an effective one, and I had to leave without finding out what he had used for a lure.

However, a secret like that could not be kept forever.

Somebody watched him one morning through binoculars, and soon the secret was out. *Bill Walheim fished a blue swimming plug*! Shortly after that you could not find a blue plug in a tackle store anywhere within driving distance of Cape Cod Canal.

One morning I was lucky though, and found one of Bill's plugs washed ashore. I tied it on, and soon caught my first striped bass on a plug! That old plug still adorns my workbench just to remind me that success is as often good luck as it is good management.

Before long I started making my own plugs. Eventually this plug-making went beyond the hobby stage, the demand for my heavier salt water plugs grew, and the Atom Mfg. Co. was born.

A great deal of care goes into the making of any plug, yet a plug is still just a piece of wood or plastic formed in the general shape of a fish, and it is not going to fool a striped bass or bluefish unless the angler does something to make it *act* like a fish. We manufacturers can only give a plug fish-catching potential. It is up to the fishermen to bring it out.

I've spent many long hours experimenting with plugs, developing new fishing techniques, and testing theories and lures under actual fishing conditions. I've still much to learn, but there are tips I can pass along to aid not only the beginner but also some experienced anglers.

Basically, there are three types of plugs: the semi-surface swimmer, surface poppers, and teasers.

The swimming plugs came first, and probably are the most versatile. The basic action of a swimming plug is either a weaving, side-to-side swimming motion (as in our standard Atom Plugs), or a wobble (as in our new Mackerel Plugs).

Fishing conditions on the Atlantic Coast are such that we are seldom able to actually see our swimming plugs at

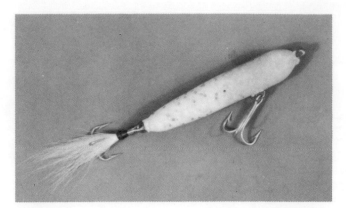

1. Teaser.

2. Spin.

3. Atom Popper.

4. Atom Bucktail.

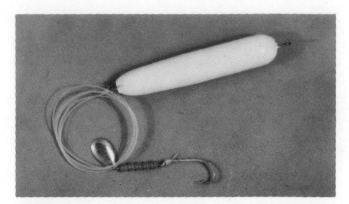

5. Drifting Rig.

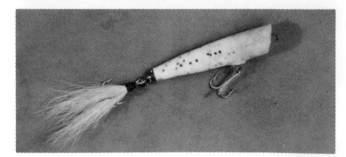

6. Striper Swiper.

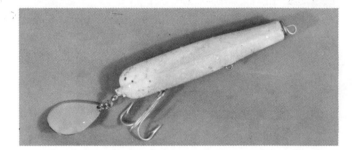

7. Flap Tail.

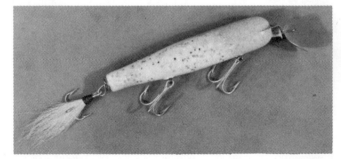

8. Atom Junior.

9. Atom Reactor.

work. Much of the time we are fishing at night and must depend on "feel." "Feel" is accomplished by holding the reel handle sensitively with your finger tips, concentrating on the light resistance of the lure as it is drawn through the water. This touch is developed in quiet water in daylight when the action of the plug can be observed as it swims and the feel of resistance can be sensed by the finger tips. In night fishing, it is accepted practice to fish a swimming plug as slowly as possible yet still give it action. For daytime fishing with swimming plugs a faster, more erratic—but not quick—retrieve is most effective.

When I first started experimenting with Bill Walheim's original striper plug, I found that it had a built-in instability that made it a good bass lure. When a sharp pull was applied the plug would turn on its back and create considerable commotion in the water. When the pressure was released the plug would drop back and resume its normal swimming position and motion. The commotion the plug made in the water was the type of splash a tail-slapping bass would make. What bass found when they raced to the sound of the splashing plug was a *simulated injured baitfish*. That was all any bass needed to be convinced that dinner was on the table. This built-in instability is still used in present-day Atom surface-swimming plugs. On our deeper swimming Mackerel plugs, where the pressure of the water makes the plug twirl, a more stable action has been created.

Striped bass fishing, and bluefishing as well, are done under widely varying conditions, and because of this adjustments must be made not only in the way a plug is fished but in the plug itself.

The key to adjusting the Atom Swimming Plug is in the wire loop to which the line is attached. This is a fine adjustment and must be done carefully and gradually. Bending the wire loop upward slightly will stabilize the plug and cause it to swim deep, while a downward bend will make it less stable and more of a surface lure.

An example of when these adjustments can be used is a boat fisherman working a tide rip. When the tide is flat he wants a less stable plug, one that he can work along top to imitate an injured baitfish, while the boat slowly sags the rip. Then, as the tide begins to flow, he needs more stability in a plug to compensate for the swifter flow of water, so he turns the loop upward. As the speed of the tide increases towards its maximum, the fisherman takes another plug, one identical to the first except that it has heavier hooks and perhaps its eye is bent even farther upward. Finally, with the tide racing at full force, he might adorn his plug with an eel skin and attach still heavier hooks. Thus he maintains the stability of the plugs in order to keep them acting properly under a full range of tidal conditions. No matter what the speed of the tide, our fisherman can give his plugs the necessary degree of stability to impart the desired, "sick baitfish" action.

In river and bay fishing the tide governs the movement of fish and the speed of the rips, but the rate-of-retrieve governs the action of a plug. In surf fishing combing waves tumble a slow-moving, swimming plug, making it a difficult lure to "feel." So in white-water surf fishing, a fast-moving popping plug is the answer to the problem of how to keep ahead of the waves.

To fish ocean shoreline with a swimming plug, find a

Bob Pond, originator of Atom plugs, spins a tidal flat for stripers. Note comfortable positioning of rod butt under elbow.

sheltered cove, or pick a time when the surf is breaking on shore. In surf fishing many casts should be made parallel to the beach or rocks, since stripers and blues often feed in the wash or just beyond shoreline rocks. On a sandy beach the water often washes in over the bars and runs out through the sloughs, creating a rip that should be fished the same as you would fish a tidal river.

There are other ways to fish a swimming plug. I mentioned that an eel skin can be attached to a plug, and that makes a plug one of the deadliest bass lures possible. To attach an eel skin remove the plug's hooks (I use open-eye hooks that are easily removed) and slide the skin on over the tail end of the plug. Tie the skin behind the plug's face plate, replace the hooks, and the job is done. Fish eel-skin plugs slowly, and hang on tight. Big bass love 'em!

A method I have used successfully for bluefish—which are daytime feeders and which often lie offshore in relatively deep water—is to turn up the line-attaching loop just enough to keep a plug under control during a violent retrieve. I then fuss the water by reeling quickly and jerking the rod tip. Then I slow the retrieve, bringing the plug to the surface, and bounce it around a bit. This technique has brought bluefish up from the deep on many occasions. By then giving the plug an injured baitfish action, it's easy to entice them to strike.

Users of Atom plugs once found they could catch fish by reversing a swimming plug. The result was the "Re-

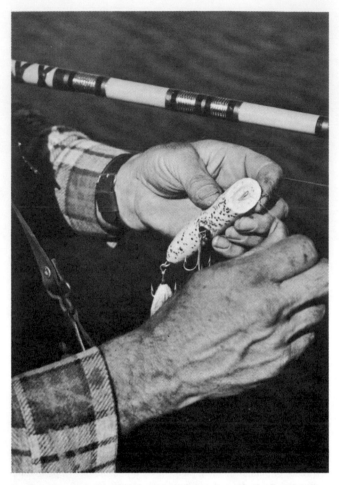

Pond prefers to tie line directly to eye of popping plug for better action.

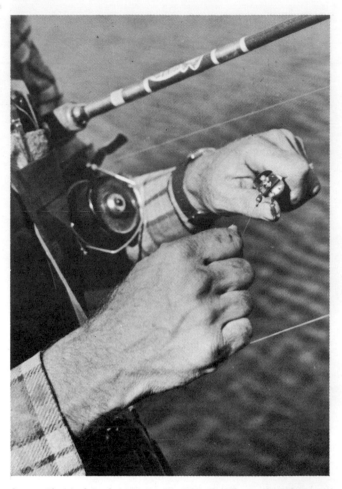

Snap-and-swivel is okay on "swimming" plug that runs underwater. Snap will not interfere with lure's action.

verse Atom," a lure that has had considerable success wherever bass feed on squid.

The first fishermen to try this method improvised with their own plugs, finally turning out a plug specifically designed to imitate squid. They used a standard plug body, amber colored, and rigged it with the front loop underneath rather than directly in front. That made the lure stay on the surface. A couple of holes were drilled in the lure's translucent body to allow water to enter and thus make for better casting weight. These lures were brought to my attention, so soon the Atom Company was producing them.

Surface popping plugs are primarily daytime lures. They are designed to simulate frightened baitfish, skipping across the surface of the water as they flee from predatory stripers or blues. They are heavy-bodied lures that sink slowly when at rest, but dash to the surface when jerked. Their cup-shaped heads are designed to throw up spray as they splash along. Unlike fresh water surface lures, which are designed for a slow stop-and-go type of retrieve, striper poppers should, generally, be fished rapidly. I say generally because there are times when a slow, deliberate retrieve seems to work best.

The fisherman who is most successful with surface poppers is the fisherman who is flexible enough to experiment. The standard retrieve is a splash, followed by a struggling

motion of the plug as it rises to the surface. To create this sort of action some fishermen prefer a long, sweeping jerk of the rod, while others use a short flick of the rod tip to make the plug spurt only briefly. Still other fishermen employ a technique somewhere in between.

The best retrieve is the one that happens to be working on a given day. If you know fish are there, and if they're not hitting, try a slower, or faster retrieve. Try reeling steadily. This produces an underwater "struggle" in the Atom lure as its heavy body tries to sink and the pull of the line, coupled with the sharply slanted face of the plug, tends to bring it back to the surface.

Some things to remember when using Atom or other surface poppers: don't use a snap or swivel; tie the surface plug directly to the line or leader.

Use a rod with stiff action. You will get a quicker, and more effective response, from the lure. A soft, or slow, rod tip produces a lag between the jerk of the tip and the action of the plug.

Put the poppers away at night. They are daytime lures. Rarely, if ever, are they effective after dark, and then usually only when the plug's struggling swimming motion is used.

And for plug fishing for stripers and blues in general, here are some more things to remember: color and size

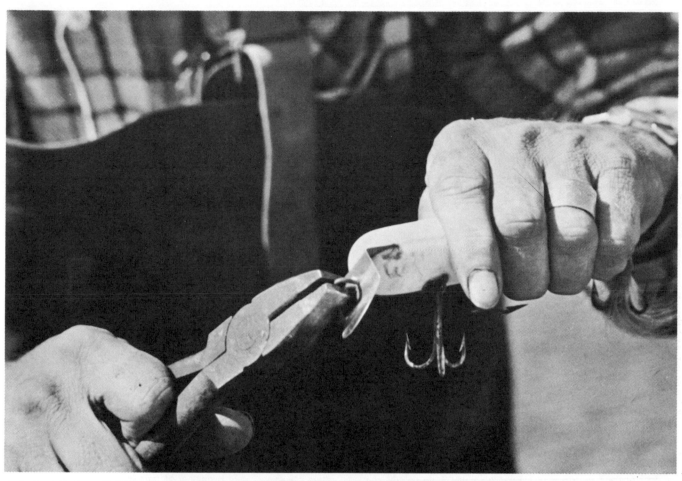

Action and depth at which lure runs can be changed by altering line loop with pliers.

Covering a striper plug with genuine eel skin adds to its fish-getting qualities. A variety of hooks can be attached to plug after it gets eel skin "dressing."

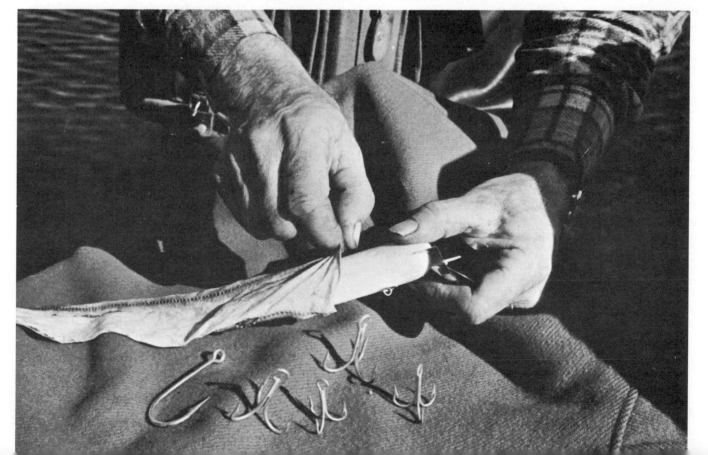

"Casting Squid" represents bait taken commonly by both striped bass and bluefish. Made of tough plastic, double-hooked lure is nearly indestructible.

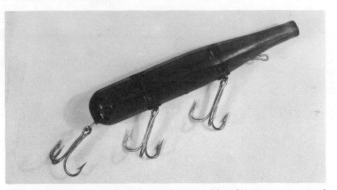

"Reverse" plug, with line-eye beneath tapered head, is transparent and life-like in the water.

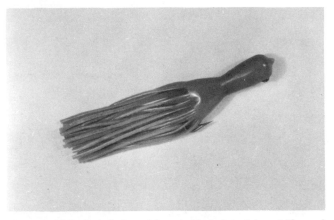

Atom "Squid Jig," six-inch model, casts like bullet, sinks quickly, and has good action. A similar "Squid Jig," 12-inches long, is productive when large squids are present.

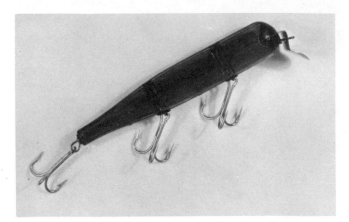

Atom "Swimmer" plug is another of transparent plastic but comes in tinted blue, medium red, and "squid" colors.

of a plug are important. In trout fishing the word is "match the hatch." In a sense, this also applies to striped bass and bluefish angling.

The translucent amber color we use in making the Reverse Atom, for instance, resembles the coloring of a squid. This see-through type of finish is excellent for daytime surface lures. For morning and evening fishing use a lure that matches the color of the bait present. For night fishing use a color that silhouettes well against the night sky.

In the beginning I felt we could take stripers on plugs whether the bass were feeding or not, but experience has shown that it is worth while to seek out feeding fish rather than to plug for those that are sulking on bottom.

Fish are like lazy husbands. They like to have their snacks brought to them. They hang in the rips where food will be washed to them, in the backwash behind rocks, in holes out of the current, or in eddies.

Plug fishing is a hunter's sport. The experienced plugger seldom makes many casts to the same spot unless it contains a school of feeding fish he can see.

When an experienced plugger approaches water he checks its possibilities—noting the rips, eddies, rocks and bars. He chooses his plug with an eye to the size of bait the fish are probably feeding upon. In spring the bait is generally small, perhaps three inches long, while in fall it will be twice that size. He chooses his plug accordingly.

If it is daylight the skilled plug-caster will tie on an appropriate popping or teasing lure, and try to raise a fish in the rip. If unsuccessful after a few casts, he'll move a few feet and try another likely spot.

If fishing a rip his casts will be directly across the rip, his plug swinging in the current into the back eddy. If fishing flat water his casts will be in a fan pattern, as he covers *all* the water. Only after testing all of the promising water will the experienced angler change to a plug of another size and color—just in case the fish are there but are being selective. If it is night he will explore the water with a swimming plug, moving it slowly, working it across, up and down the tide—making the plug come alive with his skillful rod manipulation.

Each fishing trip is as new as today's crossword puzzle; each trip is a new challenge to the angler's ingenuity. What tempted the stripers or blues yesterday may, or may not, tempt them today.

There have been trips when I worked for hours before finding the combination of lure color, size and action the fish wanted. The following day that same combination failed. The fish wanted something else.

So when you go plugging for bass or blues, go prepared to experiment. Don't depend on yesterday's successful techniques. Today is another day.

Bob Pond

At last, here is what every
bass fisherman has been looking for

32: How to fish the Rapalas
by Lauri Rapala

It was more than 35 years ago that I made my first fishing plug. Life was very rough in those days in Finland—where I still live, and work, and fish. Big catches of fish were hard to come by. Even food for the table was scarce at times. I was so poor in those days that I could not afford a fishing net, nor even the twine with which to make one.

Because there was no work, and because we needed fish to eat, I went fishing nearly every day. Real fish bait was expensive and hard to get, so I began making my own artificial lures. I used to tie them to the fishing line, wrap the line around each hand, and trail two lines and two lures behind my boat as I rowed and drifted through the fiords. Many days I'd row 20 miles or more searching for fish. My method made it possible for me to row and to fish at the same time, even though I had no rods. I could tell when a fish struck at any time, and I also had constant contact with my lures and so developed a good "feel" for the way my lures were behaving. I kept improving the lures, which I hand-carved out of pine bark and covered with celluloid. Finally I had lures that looked and "swam" just like herring and shiner minnows, and it is these lures that so many American fishermen use today.

Of course any plug, which is what you Americans call a wooden or plastic lure, is at its best when fished properly. It is certainly possible to get many bass, walleyes, northern pike and other fish on a Rapala or any other lure merely by casting out blindly and reeling it back. But many more fish will be caught with any lure when it is used in the various ways for which it was designed.

My Rapala lures are, first of all, very fish-like in appearance. They are not short and squatty as are so many American-made plugs. Rapalas are long and thin, and are properly tapered to represent the general form of many thousands of different kinds of bait fish that are found in both fresh and salt water. In other words a Rapala looks like a fresh water dace, but it also closely resembles a salt water smelt or grunion.

Lauri Rapala—originator of the world-famous Rapala lure—still hand-carves many Rapala lures for his own use and for his fishing friends. The secrets of his lure design are still closely held, and the Rapala lures are manufactured by skilled hand-craftsmen in Finland. The Rapala has become a "standard" lure in America and elsewhere around the world, and like a few other plugs it doubtlessly will "live forever." Here, in detail, the lure's inventor explains killing techniques for fishing his Rapalas.

Original floating model Rapala—minnow-like in shape and size.

Minneapolis sportsman Ray Ostrom nets a fine 6 pound brown trout that struck his "Micro-Mini" Rapala, a midget model popular with trout fishermen.

Rapalas have the right kind of finish, too, with scales and realistic eyes, and real-looking silvery-white belly strips. These appearances of Rapalas are one of the things that make them good to catch fish.

My plugs also are very light, and this too is important. A real minnow scooting in the water is fast and light; he is not chunky and heavy and clumsy . . . like the American lures. When a Rapala is cast it strikes the water with a light, fishy "splaat!"—not with a loud, fish-scaring "pluunk!"

Maybe more important than anything, though, is the action of a Rapala. A Rapala has a quick-like movement in the water. It wiggles very fast, the way real baitfish do, and it seems to almost come alive as you watch it swim along through the water. And sometimes a Rapala will turn, just a little bit, on its side as it wiggles along, and that drives gamefish wild with hunger because they think the lure is an injured fish.

These are the special new things that make Rapalas good fish baits. Now I will tell you some of the ways you should fish my lures.

Rapala lures are now available in many different models. The original floating model is very versatile and can be fished with numerous techniques and variations. The light-weight, balanced construction of this floating model makes it possible to fish the lure at any rate of retrieve, from the very slowest drift fishing to the very rapid retrieve or trolling speed.

In Finland—when I fished for a living with lines just wrapped around my hands—I needed a lure that would be very active in the water at slow speeds. I could only row, or drift with tide or wind, and for that reason I needed a lure that would respond to not much of a line pull. So this lure is very good when fished slowly, and when you can fish it just as slow as possible, it will have a good wobbling action.

A very good way to fish this lure—and I hope you will try the method—is to sit in the middle of your boat but to one side. Make the boat broad-side to the wind. By sitting at one side of the boat, on the side away from the wind, the other side of the boat will be a little out of water. The wind will catch under it and move you nicely across the lake. Now tie on a floating model Rapala and cast out. Keep the lure out there and just troll it as the wind moves your boat along. You will cover a lot of water this way and catch fish.

In Scandinavia fishermen use mostly spinning tackle, and with it there is no trouble casting the lightweight, floating Rapalas. With 6 or 8 pound test monofilament, cast the Rapala close to the bank, against logs, rocks, stumps, reeds and weeds. At first do not move the plug but let it rest still. Be alert for a strike, because often a fish will bite the lure even as it floats motionless on the surface because it looks in its outline so much like a real live small fish. If a big fish does not come yank your rod gently to make the Rapala hop a few inches. Do that a few times. If still there is no fish, then reel the lure in steadily for about 6 feet. Now stop. Now, after a wait, give the rod another yank to make the Rapala hop. If still there is no fish then reel the lure all the way in, first going slow and then going fast. Keep fishing this way along good cover by shore, changing the Rapalas now and then to try different sizes and colors. If after a while you do not get any fish along the shore or by islands and peninsulas, then go fish the deeper water.

Another good way to fish the floating Rapala along shore is called the "surface popping method." To do this make your cast and allow the lure to rest for about 15 seconds. Then twitch it lightly to simulate a struggling, crippled minnow. Give a second or two more of rest. Retrieve the Rapala along with a slight twitching or pumping motion so that it floats to the surface and then dives, like a little fish that is hurt and is struggling to swim.

This surface popping allows many variations of retrieve, but usually a very slow retrieve is best. Sometimes, though, a very fast pumping retrieve gets result. Yes, it is possible to keep the lure on the surface, darting and struggling along, even with a fast, pumping retrieve. Hold your rod very high when you fish this way. This surface popping method is good for night fishing, and it works very well on bass, snook, sea trout and small tarpon when they are surface feeding.

The way most fishermen fish the floating model Rapalas is with some split-shot sinkers or other lead sinkers attached to the line for additional casting weight and also to take the lure deeper down. A No. 4 or 5 size of split-shot sinker is good to use, if you put it on your line about 6 inches up

from the Rapala. If you will be trolling the Rapala, then you can place the lead on the leader or line about 18 or 36 inches up from the lure. It is best to have the sinker as far from the lure as practical, as sinkers may frighten some fish from striking and, also, a lure does not always shimmy well if it is too close to a heavy sinker.

The farther the weight is from a lure, the deeper running action you will get. Sometimes it is necessary to go very deep for fish like bass. Vary your retrieve or trolling speed until the Rapala has the proper swimming action. It should have a rapid, minnow-like movement. This way of fishing my lures works equally well in daytime or at night.

You can also fish the floating model Rapalas by what I call the deep-water-jigged or slow-trolled method.

To fish them this way use whatever size or weight lead sinker is necessary to get the lure down to the depth you want it. Make your cast, let the sinker go down and allow it to rest fully on the bottom. Pick up all the slack in your line, and then "jig" the Rapala by snapping your rod tip with a sweeping motion 15 or 18 inches. After that let the lead weight settle back to the bottom and then snap your rod up again. Keep repeating this system. What you are doing, in effect, is repeatedly fishing the Rapala in

Proof how good Rapalas are—from the Old Master, himself—is this superb 40 pound Lake-of-the-Woods (Ontario) muskellunge taken by Lauri Rapala while visiting this country and Canada. The musky took a salt water type Rapala, which hangs from its jaw.

one area. The lure will be activated time after time right on the bottom. The floating Rapala will stay clear of the bottom at all times. You needn't worry about snagging. Possibly your sinker will occasionally get fouled but not your Rapala. As in most other fishing with my lures, I recommend that you attach the Rapala to the lightest possible monofilament that the fishing conditions will allow.

The slow-trolled method is the same as the deep-jigged-method except that you work from a slowly moving boat. In some ways this is a better system, because you get your lure fishing in more places and you are more likely to find some fish. If you are after walleyes or black bass when they are deep please be sure to fish my Rapalas either by the deep-water-jigging or the slow-trolled method. You will get fish, I know.

The deep-water-trolled method is yet another way to fish the original Lauri Rapala floating model lure.

This is the best way to fish for lake trout, rainbow trout, salmon, walleyes and bass during bright, warm weather—and for many salt water species. Use a very heavy sinker and attach it to the line about 36 inches ahead of the Rapala. Vary the speed of your trolling until you get exactly the action desired. The leader between the Rapala and the sinker should be the very lightest that the particular day's fishing conditions will allow. I must stress using a light leader of monofilament, because very heavy or stiff monofilament or other line tends to destroy the very delicate and life-like action of my Rapalas. You will not get many fish if you do not permit my lures to work in the water in the manner they were designed to.

After trolling at a slow speed, then vary your speeds from slow to fast and back to slow. A rule-of-thumb is that the warmer the weather, the faster the speed. Contrary to what many Americans believe, it has been proven by scientists that fish are much more active in warm weather than they are in cold. It is in cold water that fish are sluggish, while in warmer water they are lively and brisk. They swim fast and quick in warm water.

I do not mean to be as you Americans say, "commercial," in this letter, but I want you to catch many fish on my Rapalas. Therefore I must tell you that the floating model, the very first I ever make, is in six sizes and you should use all six sizes. The sizes are for special reasons. The new "Micro-Mini" floating model, for instance, is especial for American lakes having small minnows on which bass and walleyes feed. Some ultra-light spinning fishermen use the "Micro-Mini" lure for trout in both American lakes and rivers. They are very good on brown trout in the big Western rivers.

The largest size floating model Rapala is 7 inches long with No. 3 treble hooks. The "Micro-Mini" is only 2 inches long. So you see that between the "Micro-Mini" and the 7-inch Rapala are four other models, each of a different length. So you should always select the one that is the best size for the fishing you are doing. In other words, if you are fishing for smallmouth bass in a small river, and most of the bass weigh under 2 pounds, you probably would want a small size Rapala, from maybe the "Micro-Mini" (2 inches), to the No. 7 Rapala (2¾ inches). If you are fishing for big northern pike, fish that will weigh 10 pounds or more, probably you would not want to fish a Rapala smaller than the No. 11, which is 4⅜ inches long.

The "Countdown" Rapala is a comparatively new type designed for deep fishing.

The "Countdown" model Rapala I designed especially for the new count-down method of fishing. When fishing over deep weed beds or in deep water with numerous rocky snags on the bottom, or over submerged tree-tops, use a "Countdown" Rapala and method of fishing.

The "Countdown" Rapala is weighted and no sinker is necessary. Make a long cast with one. When the lure lands onto the water, reel slack out of your line. Start counting slowly, making one count to each second. When the "Countdown" strikes the bottom or touches the weeds, the line will go slack. Stop counting. But remember what the count was. On your next cast, if you reduce the count by one or two, the "Countdown" Rapala will be just above the bottom or tops of the weeds. By this method you will be able to control exactly the depth at which you fish, and you will be able to avoid snags and weeds but still catch many fish.

Whenever you catch a fish with a "Countdown" Rapala, using the method I've just described, be sure to repeat the same count on subsequent casts because there may be a school of fish feeding at the level where you caught the first one. This is especially true of walleyes, crappies, yellow perch, white bass, striped bass, and largemouth and smallmouth bass as well—all of which are normally schooling fish.

In using one of the "Countdown" models, a steady retrieve is usually the best, but not always. Experiment. Sometimes a stop and go, jigging and pumping retrieve is most effective. Hold your rod tip low to the water on the retrieve. This prevents the lure from swimming to the surface as rapidly as it would with a high rod tip. Also, with your rod tip low to the water, you will be in a better position to strike and set the hooks hard as soon as a fish hits the lure.

The "Countdown" Rapala, incidentally, can also be used in regular casting and trolling. Just determine the best rate of retrieve, or speed of trolling for the best swimming action and fish accordingly. The "Countdown" model casts very well because of its special weighting, and for this reason it is popular with many fishermen especially on days when windy conditions exist. Wind will not interfere much with your casting of a "Countdown." It will just slice through the wind.

There is one Rapala made for what we in Finland call "vertical" fishing. We discovered many years ago in Scandinavia that a lure lying horizontal in the water but pulled

THREE WAYS TO ATTACH RAPALA TO LINE:

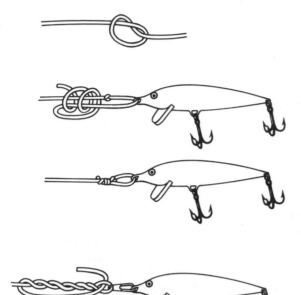

1. "Drop Loop" knot allows lure to swing freely and to have proper action on retrieve. Start this knot by tying a simple overhand or slip knot in the monofilament line about 5 inches from the end. Draw the overhand knot tight. Pass the end of the line through the eye of the Rapala, bringing it parallel with the line. Now bend the line end down and around, forming a double circle around the parallel strands. Draw slowly tight. Pull on the lure so that the jam knot slides down to the overhand knot, leaving the Rapala swinging freely on a loose loop.

2. "Clinch" knot (improved version) is a well-known knot and a good one for connecting line to small snap swivel. Knot is started by inserting loose end of line through snap opening, then bringing line back on itself and wrapping around at least five turns. Pass end of line through first coil, then through large loop, and draw snugly tight.

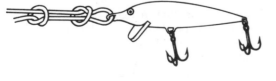

3. "Double 'O' Loop" knot is another good one allowing lure to swing freely. It is a good knot to use for tying line to wire eyes of all Rapala models. Begin by tying a loose single knot in the line 3 inches from its end, then run the end of the line through the lure's eye. Now double the end back against the standing line, passing the line end through the loose single or overhand knot. Next, take the end of the line and tie another overhand knot, this time around the standing line. Draw the knots tight and slowly draw them together so that they jam against each other.

Angler using "Countdown" Rapala counts slowly while weighted Rapala sinks. Lure sinks about one foot per second. If on initial casts fisherman's lure contacts bottom or weeds at count of 7, then subsequent casts count of 6 is made, or even 5, then retrieve is begun.

up and down was most effective on gamefish. Especially ice fishing, and when necessary to fish straight down in very deep holes.

The "Jigging-and-Ice-Fishing" model Rapala (now called "Jigging" model in America), is naturally a fast-sinking lure. It is specially weighted and balanced for vertical fishing. The ring for attaching the line is located at a balance point in the center of the back of the lure. This lure is used, as I said, for vertical fishing, such as in very deep holes, at steep drop-offs as along bluffs and cliff faces, and any place where conventional methods will not work, as in ice fishing.

To fish the "Jigging" Rapala attach monofilament line to the lure directly, or if you prefer attach a very small locking snap. Jig the lure in two or three rhythmical movements, soft motions. Do this with action of your wrist. Do not use your whole arm or shoulder. The secret of this method is to entice the fish to the lure, and after allowing the lure to rest for several seconds, to make the Rapala

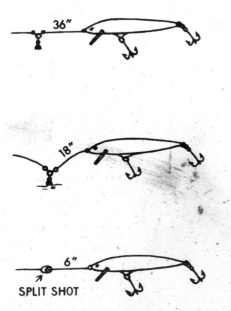

Ways of fishing floating model Rapalas with split-shot lead sinkers, or three-way swivels and sinkers.

quiver ever so lightly so that the lure imitates a minnow that has become frightened. You can do this by tapping the rod with your finger and avoiding any sudden "angry" movements which may scare away the fish. Most fish strike just as the lure comes to rest or as it starts to quiver. Start fishing this lure close to the bottom. That's the best place. But after fishing it for several minutes near the bottom, shorten your line and try the same technique at other depths.

The "Salt Water" model Rapalas for the most part can be fished in any of the previous methods I've recommended. The No. 18 Salt Water model is a floating lure that is slightly weighted to give casting weight. The No. 13 Salt Water model is a sinker, and is good for fishing by the count-down method I talked about earlier.

The important thing to remember in fishing most salt water species is that you should retrieve my Rapalas just as fast as possible. This is especially true for fish like bluefish, dolphin, tuna, barracuda, and so on. An exception, of course, is tarpon which generally like a slow retrieve, as well as sea trout when night fishing.

There are some very special knots you should use when fishing the Rapalas. It must be understood that a bad, heavy knot too close to a lure's eye can interrupt the action of the lure, as can a wire snap or swivel. For best results with the Rapalas, tie the lure directly to the line, or use a very light locking type of snap. Do not use a heavy leader or line since its weight will impair the natural, "free" action of the plug. A light snap, not a snap swivel, is a good way of attaching lure to line but if the snap is poorly made or is too large it can impair the action of the Rapala.

I recommend three knots for use with my Rapalas. These are the well-known "Clinch" knot, the improved type, the "Double 'O' Loop" knot, and the "Drop Loop" knot. Study the accompanying illustrations to learn how to tie them.

I say with modesty that the Rapala is a good lure.

But I say also that it is better—and it will catch more fish for you—if you fish the various models in the ways I've described here.

Good fishing, my friend!

33: The Perfect Bass Boat

Every successful black bass fisherman will tell you the secret to filling a stringer is keeping your lure in the water. With this end in mind, the idea of what to look for in an ideal fishing boat has changed.

The notion that all a fisherman needs to get to the fishing hole is a three-horse kicker and a $2.50-a-day rent boat is outdated. This is the era of the "Super Bass Boats."

Speed has entered the picture. A serious bass fisherman doesn't want to spend his time boat-riding. He wants a boat that is fast and maneuverable, but at the same time able to cover the roughest water of big reservoirs in strong winds without pounding his britches off or getting him soaked.

The "ideal boat" must be able to carry two fishermen, a big ice chest, an assortment of rods and reels, at least two large tackle boxes, a trolling motor, two oversize batteries, gas tanks, an anchor and line, plug knocker, water jug and a few other assorted items, and all without being cluttered.

Such a boat was rigged by the Coolie Marine Company of Tulsa for the Oklahoma Sport, Boat and Travel Show. It may be as near the super bass boat as you can come. It didn't show, but the boat must even have a kitchen sink. —For a $3,262 price tag for a "fishing boat," it must be there someplace!

"There's not a thing on the boat a serious bass fisherman wouldn't want or can't use to improve his chances for catching fish," said Harold Langton, a salesman with 17 years experience in the marine field.

On a 15-foot "Bayou Boat" by Tide Craft, Coolie mounted an electric-starting 65 horsepower Mercury outboard with power trim. You can hardly change baits between fishing spots. The boat runs 46 miles per hour with three 200-pound men aboard.

The power-trim adds $200, but this is a nice luxury. The boat can go where the bass go.

"You don't even have to move out of your seat to lift

This "Super Bass Boat," as it's called by some anglers, is rigged for action. All controls and operation of the boat is done from the bow seat.

New Lowrance Depth Sounder and Fish Locator (center left) is important item of boat's equipment. The two units in one is ideal for high speed bass boats, giving accurate bottom readings and depths at speeds in excess of 20 m.p.h.

the motor," said Langton, pressing a button on the dashboard. "You can pull the prop up and run in shallow water 2 to 2½ feet deep."

The power-trim levels the boat when running full bore. "If you have a 175-pound man in the bow, a lighter fisherman in the middle and a hefty 200 pounder in the stern, just tuck the motor under a little by adjusting the power-trim and the boat levels out," explained Langton.

The 65 horsepower is the smallest outboard Mercury makes with the power-trim accessory—that's why a smaller engine wasn't mounted. That may seem like a lot of motor for a 15-foot boat, but Langton said it handles it nicely and "you can get to where they're hitting in a hurry."

The man in the front is the skipper. All the controls are mounted for operation from the bow pedestal seat. You can sit there and run the big engine via a Jim Stick steering system, a straight-handle that operates the outboard on a push-pull system.

From the same seat, the skipper can maneuver the boat with a foot-controlled trolling motor (mounted on the bow) and not miss a cast; check his Depth Sounder/Fish Locator mounted on the floor near his left foot to spot any fish activity or read the water depth, glance up to check the weather conditions on his barometer, push in the cigarette lighter to smoke, or double-check his direction on his compass.

There are covered night lights on the gunwales near each seat for any nocturnal angling. The sonar device is the new Lowrance Depth Sounder and Fish Locator (two units in one) that has its transducer mounted flush with

the bottom of the boat and can be used at cruising speed day or night.

The boat comes equipped with plastic swivel seats that are mounted on pedestals that double up as dry storage space. The soft seats were padded with heavy vinyl in Collie's shop.

A fisherman can swivel around and keep up with the action without wearing the seat out of his fishing pants. The center seat can be removed by loosening four bolts—if only two fishermen are in the party. With no cross seats the boat is roomy, open and you can easily move about.

The Jim Stick steering has been around for sometime, but there's a new twist in the "ideal bass boat." Vernon Fowlkes of Fo-Mac Manufacturing Company of Tulsa has come up with a "fine-tuned" steering stick. By a simple adjustment, the fisherman can change the control of the stick for steering the motor quickly in tight stump-filled holes. Or when running full bore on a lake, the stick can be adjusted to handle the boat more easily and safely.

Two 12-volt batteries and two 6½-gallon gasoline tanks with outside fuel caps are mounted in the stern. The motor has an alternator and recharges the batteries when running. The inside of the boat is covered with "Astro-Turff." It softens noise, is non-slip, and provides insulation in the winter.

"About the only thing this boat doesn't have on it is a bat-o-meter," said Langston. (That's a meter that tells a fisherman how much juice he has left in his batteries.)

How much would that add to the cost?

"It's a bargain at $7.95," he said.

34: Own your own pond

There are enough new small lakes throughout the United States today to count them in the millions—three and one-half million, to be exact. Wonder where they all come from? They were all man-made. Most are privately owned, and were constructed for recreational purposes—to provide their owners with countless hours of fishing, swimming, hunting and other outdoors pleasures.

Some were built for other reasons too: such as commercial ventures in fish-raising, fee-fishing, improving camping areas, flood control, watering stock and, in some cases, for irrigation. Regardless of pond usage, the fact remains that millions have been built and if you desire, you probably can have your own lake, too. That is, if you qualify.

These tiny lakes often are called ponds and normally are referred to as "farm ponds." Although you don't have to be a farmer to build or to own one, it is necessary to have title to the land under a potential pond site if you desire federal aid in building one. This is the most important factor. From that point on plenty of help is available to see that you wind up with a good pond.

The assistance you can get in building your own bass pond is technical and financial aid from the Federal Government. Two agencies are involved, each in the United States Department of Agriculture. The Soil Conservation Service (SCS) will provide any technical help you may need, while the Agricultural Stabilization and Conservation Service (ASCS) will provide the money, which, incidentally, is paid against the construction costs of a pond on a cost-sharing basis.

Depending upon the area and your qualifications, this cost-sharing between owner and agency will vary from a low of 10% to as much as 50% of the total expenditure involved. Usually the only requirement in getting some real federal aid is that a portion of the land has been farmed at one time or another, and that a portion of the land is being removed from crop productivity. The 10% figure is

the exception rather than the rule, as most cost-share percentages are closer to 40-50%. Considering the average cost of constructing a one-acre pond at approximately $2000, the owner probably will have to pay about half that figure.

To get an idea of the boom in building these little lakes, consider a few figures from the Soil Conservation Service. In 1969 *Farm Pond Harvest*, a magazine that deals with the proper management of these small bodies of water, queried the SCS for a breakdown of the total ponds built in the United States during the previous five years with SCS assistance. SCS reported the total was 274,243, or an average of slightly less than 55,000 new ponds built per year. This constitutes almost 1,100 ponds *per state per year*. These figures take in only those ponds constructed through a federal agency, but many have been built by "going-it-alone," so the overall total of new ponds is really anybody's guess.

The Midwest is noted as being the "heart" of pond country, and surprisingly many of the states in this region list pond-caught fish on their state record charts. These records range through largemouth bass, bluegills and crappies down to bullheads and channel catfish.

Illinois has more than 65,000 "Farm" ponds; Indiana—43,000; Ohio—52,000; Iowa—33,000; Nebraska—30,000; Kansas—83,000, and Oklahoma an impressive 200,000. Even Wisconsin, with all its natural waters, has almost 15,000 small, man-made impoundments. No state, in fact, is without its ponds—New York has 40,000; Tennessee 76,000, and California more than 115,000.

The majority of "farm" ponds today are in private hands, but more and more are being constructed as community projects or by sportsmen clubs and small groups of individuals wanting to get away from the "maddening crowd." By forming clubs or miniature corporations of a half-dozen or so members, buying power is created to purchase the land required for that secluded area—which is another way

Privately owned farm ponds . . . like this one near Richland Center, Wisconsin . . . usually cost around $2,000 to build. The Federal Government, however, will often defer a large part of the cost.

of getting your own private lake.

All projects have to begin somewhere, and once you have the ball rolling contact the local SCS agent for help in checking out tentative pond sites. The factors involved here are: lay of the land, condition and size of the surrounding watershed, and type of soil. They all have a bearing on determining a good pond site. Most important is that the ground holds the water furnished by the watershed, and that the watershed be of sufficient size to keep the pond full or nearly full at all seasons.

Consideration must be given also to construction costs. The surface structure of a proposed pond area should be of a nature that will permit the pond to be built economically and still provide enough water depth so that the pond can be easily managed. SCS technicians can find the answers to the above, and preliminary tests of a pond site always should be made before any land is purchased. If you already own land you're considering for a pond site, then get the technicians out there and you'll soon know whether you have the makings for a pond or not.

Once the pond site is approved, the SCS will notify the ASCS of your plans to build, plus the qualifications of the pond-to-be. At this point, you will learn how much will come out of your pocketbook and how much the government (all us other tax-payers) is going to pay toward the construction of your private lake. As mentioned earlier, cost-sharing can run up to 50%.

In most instances a warm water pond must be at least one acre in size to sustain good bluegill and bass reproduction and provide overall ease of management. Actually, a two-acre pond is better yet and, of course, the larger the body of water the fewer problems likely to arise. This is not to say that all problems are eliminated with a large body of water; actually each lake is a world of its own,

and subject to situations that may require special management techniques. But basically large ponds keep in "balance" better, and respond to "management" more readily than do small ponds.

Trout ponds, which are classified as cold-water ponds, fall into a special category. Because trout will not reproduce in a pond, they must be restocked periodically and usually fed regularly to encourage rapid growth. Under a situation such as this a pond can be as small as one-quarter acre and still produce enough sport and table fare to please the owner. With both types of ponds—warm water and cold water—the investment is governed by the size of the pond.

Once a pond is built and sufficient water has been impounded, it should be stocked with the species of fish desired. Fingerlings are available from the U.S. Fish & Wildlife Service, state conservation department hatcheries, or from private hatcheries. By providing limited public access and turning your project into a semi-private area, the state or federal agencies will provide the fish at no charge. If the pond is to remain private, as in most instances, the fish usually will have to be purchased from a commercial hatchery.

Does the idea of owning your own fishing lake sound good or far-fetched? Well, it's not far-fetched by any means. The "build-your-own-lake" idea is being pursued daily in the manner described, and with satisfying results. Ask any pond owner who's felt the coolness of evening settle in after a hot summer's day, or who has hefted a good stringer of fish as part of the fruits of his planning.

The Soil Conservation Service has offices in just about every county in the United States. That's where you should start if you want to own your own lake.

Wayne Ligler

Tom McNally designs

35: A Revolutionary new fly and bug box

For Fly Fishermen Only

One afternoon a year ago Bill Cullerton and I stepped into a skiff to fish for tarpon at Costa Rica's Parismina River. I'd rigged a fly rod, and now dug into my salmon angler's kit bag for a big streamer fly.

"*Damn!*" I said to Bill. "Look at that!"

My flies and bugs were scattered all through the salmon bag. It was a mess. The bugs and flies had been in a large plastic box, the type that spools of bait casting line are packaged in. But the box had been smashed sometime during transit, probably by the airline's baggage-handling crews, most of whom are not noted for their gentleness in handling traveler's gear. It wasn't the first time I'd had a make-shift fly box smashed.

"I wish to heck some tackle manufacturer would design and produce a decent fly and bug box for fly fishermen," I said angrily, "one that would hold everything a fly fisherman needs and that couldn't be easily broken."

"Why don't you design one?" Bill said. "We'll make it."

Cullerton is a fishing tackle manufacturers' representative, and one of the firms he works for is Plano Molding Company of Plano, Illinois. Plano is the leading manufacturer of plastic tackle boxes.

I jumped at the opportunity to design a fly-bug box for the fly rod angler. There always have been small fly "wallets," pouches, metal and even wood boxes for flies and bugs on the market, but there's never been a box made of the type I had in mind.

First of all, I figured, a good box for the fly fisherman should be *large*. It ought to have ample space for many dozens of popping bugs in various shapes and sizes; space for hundreds of different kinds of flies, both small, large, and ultra-large; there should be room for a dozen "wheels" of nylon monofilament leader material; special compartments for clippers, hook hone, and small file; another compartment for a spare fly reel spool with line, or for a second fly reel; and still another compartment for more flies and bugs, or for

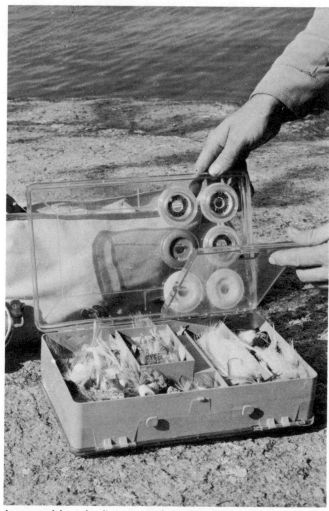

An unusual box, the first ever styled solely for the fly fisherman, it has special compartments in lids for leader material.

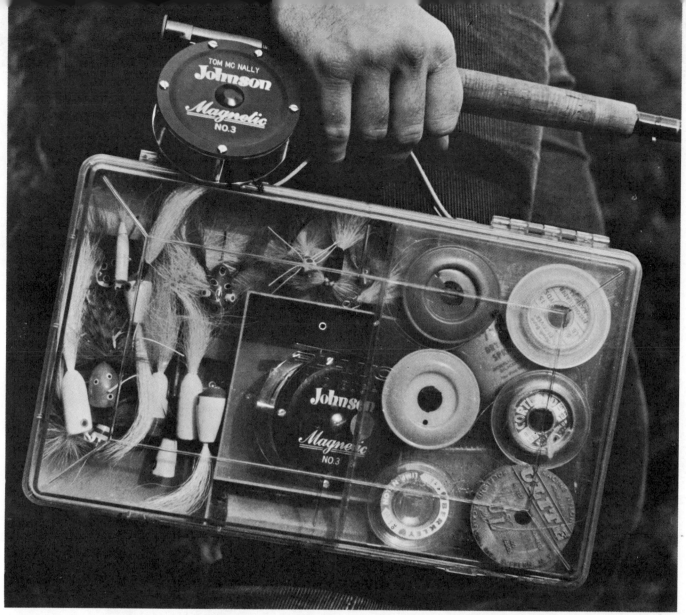

Using new fly angler's box, the fisherman needs only his rod and reel to be completely equipped for a day's angling.

storage of special accessories such as made-up leaders, dry fly oil, insect repellent, knife, leader sink, reel oil or grease, fly line cleaner, and so on.

Every fly fisherman who uses make-shift boxes—such as discarded plastic line boxes of the kind I described earlier, or even one of the large compartmented plastic boxes on the market—knows the problem of finding a specific fly or bug when it is wanted. Flies and poppers usually are all mixed up, and a lot of time can be wasted trying to locate a particular streamer, dry fly, or popper. The same is true of trying to find somewhere in your kit bag, a particular test of nylon leader material. In the past I used to carry all my leader wheels in one compartment of my salmon angler's canvas bag, and when I wanted, say, the six-pound mono, I'd have to take out half the leader wheels or more, before I'd locate the six-pound mono.

So I figured the ideal fly fisherman's box ought to be made of clear "see-through" material, and there should be very special compartments for *all* of the fisherman's gear so that *any* item could be readily located. The ideal fly-rodder's box

would make it unnecessary to grope for a hook hone, a special popping bug, or a particular wheel of leader material.

Also, since many thousands of fly fishermen around the world use one of the various types of "salmon angler's" canvas bags that are on the market, to carry reels, lines, mono, bugs and flies, leader pouches, etc., it seemed essential that the ideal box fit snugly into the so-called "salmon angler's" bags. Finally, the box *had* to be made of unbreakable materials.

I started working on the design of a special fly fisherman's box during our tarpon fishing in Costa Rica. Frequently I'd lay down my rod and scribble notes. Later, at home, I'd often lie awake thinking of the features that would be needed in the *ideal* fly fisherman's box. I wanted to leave nothing out.

Months passed. In that time I made countless fishing trips, always noting any ideas regarding the box that crossed my mind. I noted more carefully than ever the way other fly fishermen carried their necessary gear, and realized again the need for a good fly-bug box. I met periodically with Cullerton, with Jim Henning, President of Plano Molding Com-

With lid closed, one side of box looks like this. Note how flies, reel, etc. show up clearly through "see-through" plastic lid.

Opposite side of box, lid closed, contains monofilament wheels, flies, bugs, etc.

A REVOLUTIONARY NEW FLY AND BUG BOX

pany, and with various plant technicians to exchange ideas and discuss special manufacturing problems.

At last my plans were approved, and Henning put the "Tom McNally Fly and Bug Pak" into production. The box is now on tackle counters all over the country, and already thousands of them have been sold.

The box has all of the features and more that I mentioned earlier as being not only desirable but *necessary* in a good fly-bug box.

First of all, the box is made of rugged, unbreakable Cyco-lac and super-tough Acrylite plastic materials. It cannot be broken or in any other way damaged through rough handling. A 200-pound man can stand on the box and not break it.

The overall size of the box is 12¾ x 8⅛ x 3½ inches. It fits perfectly into the large compartment of any "salmon angler's" bag, and it also fits into a number of large metal and plastic tackle boxes.

Because the box holds *all* of the fly fisherman's needs, the angler going out for an afternoon of bluegill fishing, or bass fishing, or for tarpon or bonefish—or anything else—need take only his fly rod, fly reel, and "McNally Fly And Bug Pak." He'll then have all the gear he'll need, yet not have a lot of stuff to carry.

A major feature of this new tackle box is that it is two-sided. Having clear "see-through" hinged lids, the box opens from either side. Each side of the box has special compartments for the storage of particular items—each of

Here's how one side of two-sided box looks when empty, with bugs, extra reel, and accessories around it.

which always is in its proper place. Let's say, for example, that you've been fishing for bass with a white "Bullet Bug," but now you want to try a yellow "Gerbubble Bug." You'll have no trouble finding the "Gerbubble." Without even opening the box, you look through the lid of one side of the box and see that the "Gerbubble" isn't there; so you turn the box over and, sure enough, through the clear lid you spot the yellow "Gerbubble" in the upper right corner of the bug compartment. You open that side of the box, remove the "Gerbubble," pull the "Bullet Bug" off your leader and put it into the box, then tie on the "Gerbubble." Now you need the clippers to snip off the excess leader. Is there any groping around trying to find clippers? No! With both sides of the box closed—lids closed means wind can't blow

away any item that may be loose in the box, such as a dry fly—you can see the clippers in their own compartment, as well as the hook hone. So you open the box, remove the clippers, snip off the excess leader material at the knot you've just tied, and replace the clippers. Next you take out the hook hone, sharpen the hook of the "Gerbubble," then replace the hone to its special place. In mere seconds you've changed bugs and are back fishing!

Each of the box's lids has a specially-designed compartment for wheels of leader material. Each lid accommodates six wheels, which are kept in place by setting them over plastic pegs and by a clear plastic, hinged lid. The fisherman can put whatever tests of leader material he likes on the 12 pegs, but it is recommended that on one lid the

Side of box shown empty on page 225 looks like this when packed.

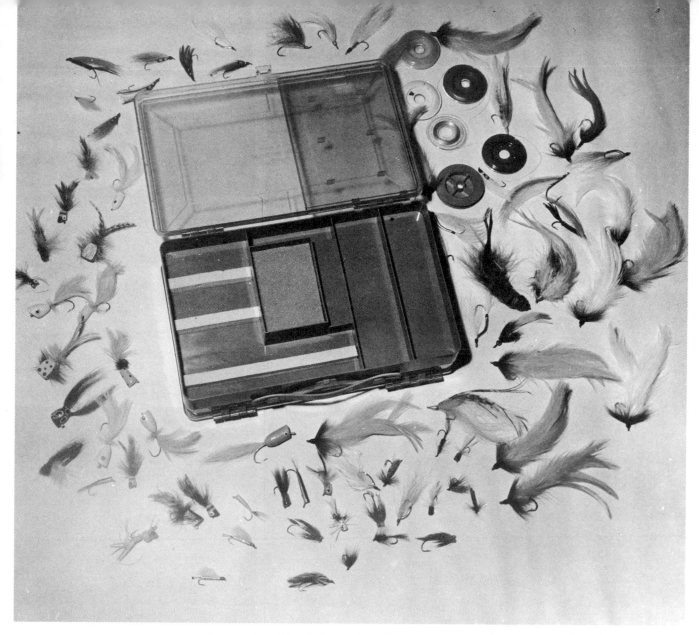

Opposite side of box looks like this when empty. Storage compartments on this side of box will accommodate all of items shown.

angler put wheels of leader material testing 3, 4, 6, 8, 10 and 12 pounds, and on the other lid material testing 15, 20, 25, 30, 40, and 50 pounds. The tests recommended make it possible for the angler to make up any type of fresh or salt water leader.

The value of this leader-material "filing" system may best be explained by a couple of hypothetical angling situations. Let's say you're fishing poppers for bass. You've got a 12-pound tippet on. You spot some bluegill nests, and decide to take some bluegills by twitching nymphs through their nests. You quickly spy a nymph through the see-through cover of your box, as well as the 3-pound test leader material you want to replace the 12-pound bass tippet. That quick! ! !—You've made the change and now you're busily catching bluegills.

Think of salt water fly fishing: a similar situation might occur on a bonefish flat. You're fishing for bones with an 8 or 10-pound tippet and small bonefish fly; then, suddenly, a school of 100-pound tarpon are sweeping over the flat. Very quickly you've got to change from the bonefish

tippet and fly to an 80 or 100-pound test nylon tippet, and a big salt water streamer fly or popper. Because the flies, bugs, leader material, etc. are all immediately available in your bug and fly pak, no time is wasted in getting a lure out there in front of those tarpon.

I'd like to emphasize here that a really valuable feature of the box I've designed is that you can see into any compartment of the box without opening it. This saves time, prevents spillage, and makes groping to find a particular fly or bug, mono material, hone or whatever, unnecessary.

One side of the box is designed with six purposes in mind. A large compartment on one side of the box is for accessories—things like made-up leaders (your own or commercially-made leaders), a rubber square for straightening leaders, insect repellent, dry fly oil, line grease (cleaner), knife, plier, cigarettes, matches, pocket fly box or wallet, any small item of use to the fly fisherman.

Another special compartment on this side of the box is for a spare fly reel, or for a second fly reel spool with line. This compartment will accept nearly any fly reel on

With flies, bugs, leader material wheels, etc. placed in proper compartments, fly fisherman has no trouble finding a specific bug or fly.

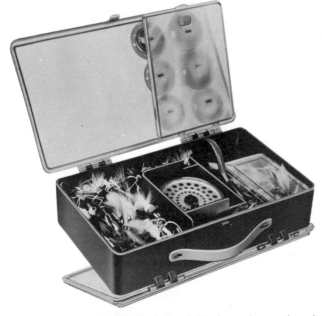

This view of "Tom McNally's Fly & Bug Pak" shows the see-through lids on either side of the two-sided box.

the market today, it's that big. The reasons for having a second fly reel along are fairly obvious, as is the reason for a spare fly reel spool with line. If, for example, you're dry fly fishing or bass bugging one day, you want your line to float high and dry. When it starts to sink, you can switch to another reel with a fresh, dry line and use it, or take the spool out of the reel you're using and replace with the spare spool and fresh, dry line. The fisherman who doesn't care about carrying a spare reel or second spool can use the compartment for other items, such as leader pacs, spinners, split-shot sinkers—anything.

About half the room on this side of the new fly fisherman's box is for flies and bugs. Hooks of flies, bugs, streamers and so on are stuck into tough Polyfoam strips so the lures are stored in orderly fashion—row upon row, one bug or fly after the other.

Also on this side of the "Fly and Bug Pak" is a special file rack. A small file for honing heavy hooks on salt water flies or bugs goes here.

Another compartment takes the fisherman's clippers, his

McNally shows one side of opened bug and fly "pak."

hook hone (for sharpening hooks of fresh water size flies and bugs), or any other small item.

Finally, part of the lid on this side of the box takes six leader wheels—the lighter tests of material could go on this side, heavy tests on the lid compartment on the opposite side of the box.

This brings us, then, to the other side—or side two—of the "Tom McNally Fly and Bug Pak."

This side has five compartments. One is for six additional leader material wheels. Another compartment, divided, is ultra-large and meant to accommodate the fisherman's very large flies—the 5 to 6-inch long streamers used by northern pike, lake trout and bass fishermen, as well as by salt water anglers out for billfish, tarpon, snook, dolphin, etc.

A third compartment on this side of the box is just right for split-shot sinker packets, clippers, hone, waterproof matches—any small item. In the center of this side of the box is a "small fly compartment"—a spot having a Polyfoam

mat where hooks of wet and dry flies, nymphs, streamers or small poppers may be fixed. This is just the place to store your panfish or trout flies and bugs.

The last compartment on this side is for more bugs and flies—all having their hooks stuck into the tough Polyfoam strips, which, of course, keeps the flies and bugs from being shifted around or falling loose.

That about covers this new fly fisherman's box, except for two things.

One, a handy booklet is included with each box, explaining in detail its special features and uses, and giving tips on how to make your own leaders, with diagrams of leader designs, followed with information and diagrams on how to tie knots of special value to fly fishermen.

Secondly, there's the price: the box sells for less than $7.95. If you're unable to find one in the area where you live, then write Jim Henning, President, Plano Molding Company, Plano, Illinois 60545.

Bill Cullerton of Elmhurst, Illinois lowers rod as the big tarpon he hooked in Costa Rica's Colorado River falls back after vain attempt to throw the plug on a high leap.

Two new camps in this Central American country
now make available to almost anyone
some remarkable tarpon and snook fishing.

36: Fishing Frontiers: Costa Rica

Two new camps in this Central American country now make available to almost anyone some remarkable tarpon and snook fishing.

Until recently fishing anywhere in Costa Rica for a non-resident was a problem. The little Central American republic has always had excellent fishing, to be sure, but accommodations at the fishing site, suitable boats and guides and other necessities were seriously lacking. Today, however, two new fishing facilities have opened up some of Costa Rica's finest east coast angling waters.

Señor Carlos Barrantes of San Jose has constructed two new camps on two rivers emptying into the Caribbean—one is

on the wild, jungle-lined Colorado River, the second is on the just as wild Parismina River. Both rivers are about one hundred miles north of the city of Limon. To reach either the camp on the Colorado or the one on the Parismina, it is necessary to fly from San Jose via small charter plane and then land in cow pastures at the camps.

Barrantes, incidentally, was educated in and resided in Chicago for many years, and thus speaks faultless English. He hired two American couples to manage his fishing camps. Host and hostess at the Colorado camp are Lloyd and Eva Boyes of Colusa, California; the couple running the Parismina camp are Dick and Elaine Broberg, also from Colusa.

Fish leaps again, closer to boat and . . .

. . . seconds later, leaps again and this time comes into anglers' boat. This is probably the only photo ever made of a hooked tarpon enroute into a fisherman's boat. No damage was done and the tarpon later was successfully landed.

Tarpon like this 90-pounder, churning the water and starting into a leap, are common at both the Colorado and Parismina Rivers.

Both the Parismina and Colorado Rivers offer some re-markable tarpon fishing. You can go out any afternoon and jump a half-dozen or more tarpon in the 100-pound class. And if you tire of that—which is likely since tussling with giant tarpon is hard work for most people—you can move farther inland and catch hard-pulling *quapote,* high-jumping *muchacha,* or trophy-size snook.

In addition, at either of the camps (only about fifty miles separates the two rivers, with the Colorado most northerly) you'll enjoy spring-like weather, sparkling sun and tropic breezes, exquisite food, comfortable and modern accommo-dations, nearly constant bird-song, the roaring of howler monkeys, and air scented with the fragrance of wild orchids, flame-of-the-forest trees, and a zillion other tropical flowers and plants. Both of the camps are the sort of places where you'd expect Dorothy Lamour, sarong and all, to step from behind a coconut palm at any moment.

But it's the tarpon fishing that will draw anglers from all over the world to the Colorado and Parismina. One day a guest at the Colorado River camp (called *Casa Mar,* meaning "House by the Sea") made a single cast into a lagoon with a big Cheek Chub "Wiggle-Diver" plug. A tarpon of more than 100 pounds struck, bit the plug in half, and took half of it away with him. Another tarpon, same size, immediately struck the remaining half of the plug still tied to the fisher-man's line, and broke it off. The fisherman was pretty upset because he'd made only one cast with his big "Wiggle-Diver," and he'd paid $4.50 for it.

Costa Rica's tarpon can be dangerous, too: in one eight-day period six leaping tarpon plopped into fishermen's boats —and a big, lively tarpon kicking around in a skiff is a serious matter, up with which one can hardly put.

One week, in fact, the Colorado camp was short one native guide into whose boat a tarpon had jumped. The hooked tarpon, 100 pounds or more, went high into the air beside the boat, came down into the skiff, hit the guide and the out-board motor, but luckily missed the angler. The fish damaged the outboard, smashed rods and a tackle box, and hit the

In this remarkable three-photo sequence, Bill Cullerton had beaten a 100-pound class tarpon, and the guide had gaffed it and was holding it at boatside for picture-taking. The tarpon, however, shook free of the gaff just as the cameraman got this photo.

Cullerton then jumped to the stern to play the fish again, and the cameraman got this photo as the big tarpon came out in a half-leap. Arrow points to fish partially hidden by Cullerton.

Last-minute tussle did the tarpon no good, however, and soon the guide again had his gaff in the tarpon's jaw. Native in dugout canoe paddled back and forth to enjoy all the action.

guide so hard in the small of his back that the guide's kidney was injured and he had to be put in bed and placed under a doctor's care.

Tarpon in the 100-pound class are seldom a sure thing when hooked and, as pointed out, can mean trouble even to the most skilled fisherman.

One afternoon Bill Cullerton, a tackle salesman living in Elmhurst, Illinois, the writer, and our native guide left the dock at Casa Mar lodge and outboarded to a nearby lagoon. A few dozen 100-pound tarpon were rolling there, so we began casting big plugs to them with fresh water type bait casting tackle. Soon Cullerton had a smashing strike, a mere fifteen feet from the bow of our fiberglass skiff. I dropped my rod and, with two cameras ready and hanging from straps around my neck, I photographed the tarpon's first wild leap just ten feet from the boat. The tarpon fell back, but came out again in another leap that brought him still closer to the boat—only five feet from the bow. The fish went under the boat and thrashed for a moment on the surface on the other side of the skiff as I aimed a camera while standing on a rear boat seat.

Suddenly the "green" tarpon lurched powerfully upward, and as most of his six-foot length came out of the water, I clicked the camera's shutter release. The fish continued straight up into the air, and when level with my head fell back and dropped smack into the center of the boat. I was too startled and had too little time to transport film and to shoot *that* picture.

The fish momentarily lay in the skiff between Cullerton and me. His head was inches behind Cullerton's feet—Bill was standing in the bow—and the tarpon's tail was only inches from my feet. In disbelief we stood staring at the fish, then

Giant snook also haunt Costa Rica's rivers. Carlos Barrantes, founder of camps on the Colorado and Parismina Rivers, shows a 23-pound snook he took fishing out of Casa Mar lodge on the Colorado.

Muchacha look like shad, fight like baby tarpon, and take flies and other lures greedily. They occur in good numbers in the upper rivers.

the tarpon shook heavily, kicked himself a couple of feet into the air, and fell back into the boat. This time he landed along the left side of the skiff, smack on top of eight rods! I shuddered, feeling sure several rods were smashed. Then the fish lurched upwards again and this time flipped himself over the side.

Somehow neither Cullerton's rod nor line broke. The leader held too, as did the plug's hooks. The fish was still on, and while all of us *whooped* and laughed, Cullerton continued playing the 105-pound tarpon. Eventually we gaffed and boated the fish. It was all very funny but it could have been otherwise. Many a tarpon angler has been knocked out of a skiff by an incoming tarpon, others have had big hooks

jammed into them, and still others have had legs broken by giant tarpon thrashing about in their boats. Miraculously no damage was done when Cullerton's tarpon leaped into our boat. Not a rod was broken, not a tackle box smashed, not a hook driven into any hide, not a man overboard. It was sweet victory all the way, pure triumph with no tragedy.

The Colorado and Parismina are flat, dark rivers meandering through dense, green jungle. Each eventually shapes a broad lagoon, then empties with outgoing tide into the placid Caribbean Sea. In fishing the rivers you hear only the dip-dip of the paddle, the plop of your lures, the tweetling of jungle birds, and the occasional eerie screaming of distant howler or Congo monkeys.

Quapote are hard fighters, and haunt up-river areas along with muchacha. Quapote, muchacha, and snook fishing add variation to a Costa Rican tarpon trip.

The Casa Mar camp is located on the lower lagoon of the Colorado, which is called *Laguna Aqua Dulce,* "Sweet Water Lagoon," and at times you can catch tarpon from it by casting from the dock in front of the main lodge. Most of the time, though, fishermen outboard in about five minutes to another lagoon nearby that normally is alive with tarpon.

The bulk of the fish are 80 to 100 pounds, but some both larger and smaller are usually present. Most fishermen troll with giant plugs in fishing either the Parismina or the Colorado, but trolling isn't necessary. Casting with bait casting gear is more productive, in fact, as well as more sporting. Spinning tackle also may be used effectively, as may fly tackle of proper specifications. Fly fishing is not at its best here, however, since the fish are usually hooked in or very near to deep water, from 60 to 70 feet, or by tidal cuts infested with sharks.

As mentioned previously, there's other good fishing available, too. At either the Casa Mar camp, or at El Tarpon Rancho, the name of the Parismina camp, there is excellent up-river fishing for snook, quapote, and muchacha.

Quapote (pronounced qua-po-tay) weigh a couple of pounds on the average, with 4-pounders not uncommon. They have weird, extensile lips, and small canine teeth that are widely spaced and two-color. The bottom half of a quapote's needle-like tooth is brown; the upper half white.

Quapote are dark green with darker greenish-black stripes, and their fins are much like those of the angelfish family. They are strong fighters, a pleasure to scrap with on light tackle although they rarely leap, and they are fine table fish.

The muchacha (pronounced moo-cha-ka) looks something like a common lake whitefish, or like an American (white) shad. It has large, soft scales, and is silvery-brown, with a deep anal fin and forked tail. Most interesting about the muchacha is that he has an adipose fin, the small fin between the dorsal and caudal fins that is a peculiarity among trout.

Unlike the quapote, the muchacha is a leaper—like a baby tarpon—spending most of the time in the air when hooked.

Fishermen walk from docks on Parismina to the El Tarpon Rancho guest house there.

The muchacha has a small mouth and no damaging teeth, and Costa Ricans say he's not much on the table.

For either quapote or muchacha, light tackle of the sort you'd use for fresh water bass fishing is ideal. Both species take any small lure, including small streamer flies (bonefish bucktails on 1/0 hooks are good) and popping bugs.

On calm days—usually in the early spring—and when tide and wind are right, small boats out of either of the camps can go through the inlets to fish the open sea. Fishermen cast or troll for tarpon, king mackerel, dolphin, wahoo, crevalle, even white marlin and Atlantic sailfish.

Accommodations at both Casa Mar and El Tarpon Rancho are deluxe. At Casa Mar on the Colorado there's a dining room and lounge, and four guest cottages accommodating 16 persons. At Tarpon Rancho on the Parismina, one large building serves as guest quarters, lounge and dining area. The Parismina camp can comfortably house 12 fishermen.

Modern fiberglass skiffs and outboard motors, plus excellent native guides, most of whom speak English, are pro-

vided each fisherman. Tackle is available for those who do not have their own. Trips normally are for one week, though shorter or longer stays are possible. An ideal set-up is to plan three days of fishing on the Colorado River, and three days on the Parismina. The rate is $50 per day per person when two fishermen share a boat and guide; $65 per day for one fisherman.

Most fishermen fly via LACSA Airlines jet from Miami to San Jose, in about 2 hours and 15 minutes, for less than $160 for tourist class, round trip. A charter flight, usually in a Cessna 180, from San Jose to either of the camps, takes around 45 minutes. The best fishing usually is in April and May, but the tarpon angling is superb anytime through the winter months.

Full details, along with colorful brochures, can be had by writing Carlos Barrantes, P.O. Box 2816, San Jose, Costa Rica, C.A. The American agent is Jim Chapralis, Safari Outfitters, 8 S. Michigan Avenue, Chicago, Illinois (Tel: AC 312, 346-9631).

Looking out over a lagoon on the lower Colorado River, on Costa Rica's east coast, is the main lounge and dining room of Casa Mar fishing camp. Fishermen live in four comfortable cottages nearby.

By following the instructions and plans given here, you can have a fine

37: Build-it-yourself ice shanty

Some ice fishermen build deluxe, complicated little "homes" for their ice fishing, but very serviceable and portable ice shanties can be made with a minimum of cost and effort.

For about $40 and around four hours of your time, you can build an excellent portable ice fishing house. All that's needed is some light lumber, sheets of ½-inch fiberboard, and nails. The fiberboard is the same material used in insulating homes.

The 6 x 4 x 6 shanty is highly portable because of prefabrication of sides and roof, with double-headed nails used for final erection at your favorite lake. The panels should be cut and assembled in a garage or some other sheltered spot. Then you can load the panels onto a car-top carrier or into a station wagon, and haul them off to the lake.

The panels are fastened together with double-headed nails so they can be easily removed for dismantling.

The fiberboard sheeting used is wind and rain-proof, but can be painted if desired. The shanty's sloping roof prevents accumulation of snow. You can even put a window in one of these ice fishing huts, using some of the strong, transparent plastic material that's available today.

It takes only six 4 x 8 pieces of fiberboard sheeting to make a shanty large enough for three or four fishermen. Special roll roofing material is used on the top to help weatherproof the shack.

After the ice fishing season, one of these shanties could be used as a storage shed in the yard. And in the fall, when duck hunting rolls around, it could be set up in a favorite marsh and used as a duck blind.

Roof and sides of portable ice fishing shanty are prebuilt, can then be easily moved to erection site.

1 Pre-built walls are fitted together . . .

2 . . . and nailed. Shanty can be slid across ice on its 2 x 6 skids.

3 Except for mounting of roof, on ground, shanty is finished. (Set up this way (less roof) in a marsh, and brushed-in, shanty would make ideal duck blind).

4 With roof on, shanty now gets roofing material to prevent water leakage. Complete plans for the shanty appear on opposite page.

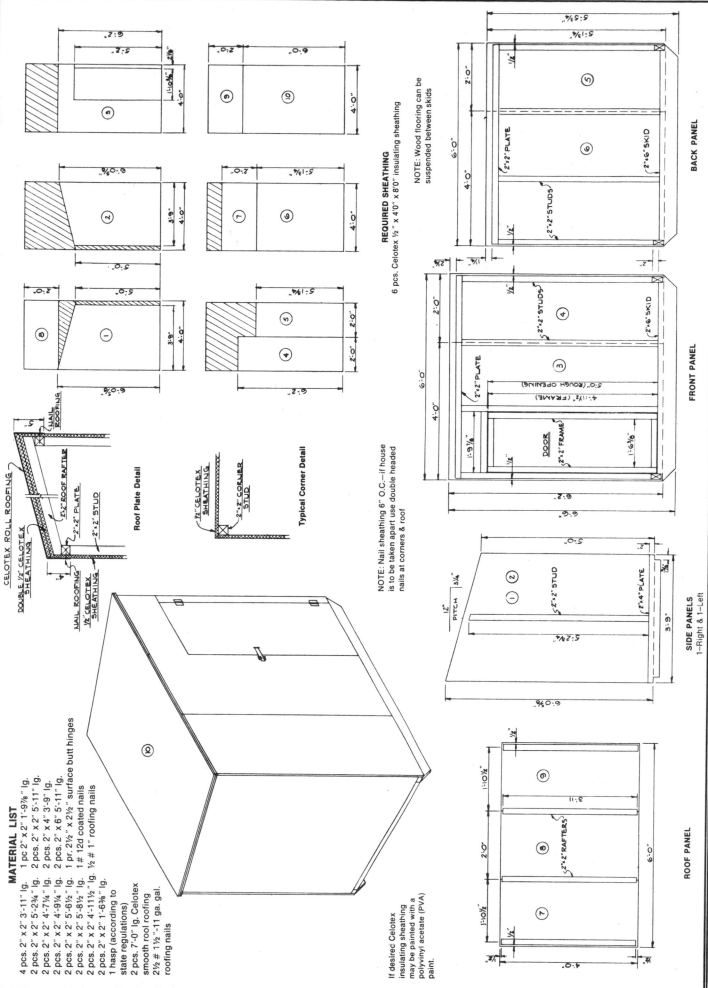

MATERIAL LIST

4 pcs. 2" x 2" 3'-11" lg. 1 pc 2" x 2" 1'-9⅞" lg.
2 pcs. 2" x 2" 5'-2¾" lg.
2 pcs. 2" x 2" 5'-11" lg.
2 pcs. 2" x 2" 4'-7¼" lg.
2 pcs. 2" x 4" 3'-9" lg.
2 pcs. 2" x 2" 4'-9¼" lg.
2 pcs. 2" x 6" 5'-11" lg.
2 pcs. 2" x 2" 5'-6½" lg. 1 pr. 2½" x 2½" surface butt hinges
2 pcs. 2" x 2" 5'-8½" lg. 1 # 12d coated nails
2 pcs. 2" x 2" 4'-11½" lg. ½ # 1" roofing nails
2 pcs. 2" x 2" 1'-6⅜" lg.
1 hasp (according to
  state regulations)
Celotex 7'-0" lg. Celotex
smooth roll roofing
2½ # 1½"-11 ga. gal.
roofing nails

If desired Celotex
insulating sheathing
may be painted with a
polyvinyl acetate (PVA)
paint.

REQUIRED SHEATHING

6 pcs. Celotex ½" x 4'0" x 8'0" insulating sheathing

NOTE: Wood flooring can be
suspended between skids

NOTE: Nail sheathing 6" O.C.—if house
is to be taken apart use double headed
nails at corners & roof

Roof Plate Detail

CELOTEX ROLL ROOFING
DOUBLE ½" CELOTEX SHEATHING
NAIL ROOFING
2½" ROOF RAFTER
2" x 2" PLATE
2" x 2" STUD
NAIL ROOFING
½" CELOTEX SHEATHING

Typical Corner Detail

½" CELOTEX SHEATHING
2" x 2" CORNER STUD

BACK PANEL

2" x 2" PLATE
2" x 2" STUDS
2" x 6" SKID

FRONT PANEL

2" x 2" STUDS
2" x 6" SKID
2" x 2" PLATE
4'-11½" (FRAME)
5'-0" (ROUGH OPENING)
DOOR
2" x 2" FRAME

SIDE PANELS
1-Right & 1-Left

2" x 2" STUD
2" x 4" PLATE
PITCH 3¾
12

ROOF PANEL

2" x 2" RAFTERS

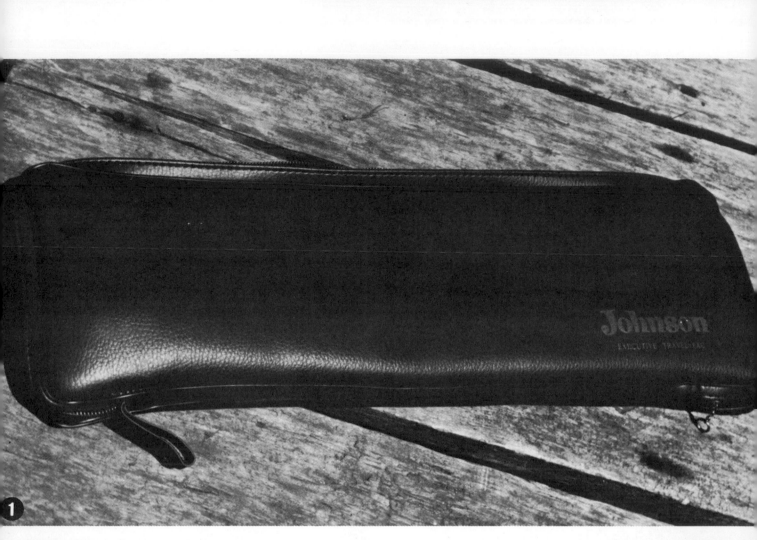

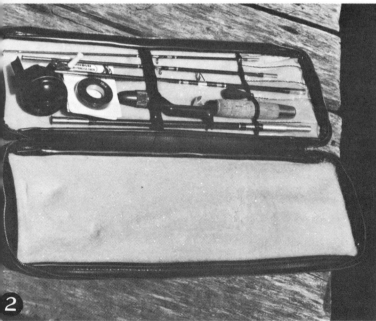

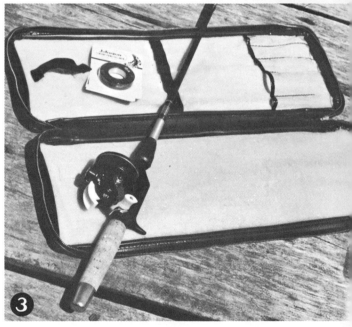

THE JOHNSON REEL Company of Mankato, Minnesota, is making special fishing kits for the traveling businessman. One of the kits contains a glass fly rod, fly reel, and fly line; the other kit a complete spin-cast outfit.

The "Executive Travel-Pac" spin-casting outfit consists of a quality-action, 5-piece glass rod; a Johnson "Century" reel; spool of extra 10 pound test monofilament line; and a plastic practice casting weight. The tackle comes in a leather-finished vinyl, nylon-fleece lined, "Travel-Pac" case. The complete outfit packed in its case fits easily into any ordinary travel bag or suitcase. Photo 1 shows the "Travel-Pac" in case; Photo 2, with case opened; and Photo 3, with rod and reel assembled and ready for fishing.

38: Angler's showcase

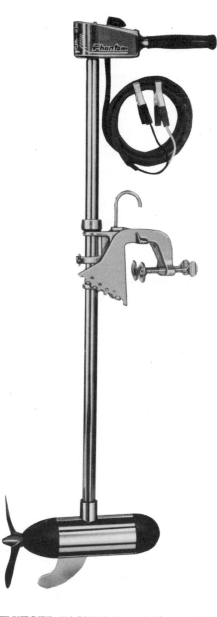

4. THE GARCIA CORP. of Teaneck, New Jersey, has developed an "angler's aid" to benefit fishermen having the use of only one hand and arm. With this unique rod-holder and harness any person minus a hand and/or arm still can fish.

The angler casts with his good arm, places the rod handle in its holder, then retrieves his lure or fishes his bait. A hooked fish can easily be played and brought to net.

Persons interested in this unusual fishing item should write Sal Muley of Garcia.

5. THE PFLUEGER TACKLE Co. of Akron, Ohio is one of many tackle firms now marketing electric motors for fishermen. One of the company's newest is the M-25 "permanent magnet" motor.

The motor provides constant speeds, with 500 pound loads, from a little over 1 m.p.h. to just under 3 m.p.h. It has full 360 degree steering and will lock in position for constant curve courses. Seven position angle adjustment and 30-inch shaft are standard. The M-25 draws 6 amps and develops a thrust of 2 pounds at low speeds, 9 amps and a 4 pound thrust at medium speeds, and 16 amps and over 8 pounds of thrust at high speeds.

Motor operates from either 6 or 12 volt batteries, with 12 recommended.

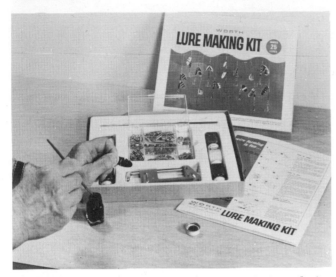

6. THE WORTH Co. of Stevens Point, Wisconsin, is producing an original lure making kit, complete with a wire-forming tool, and all the "fixins" to make 25 or more lures.

With this unique kit fishermen can fashion their own lures, either creating originals or duplicating famous patterns. Called the "LM-1", the kit has all components for French and Reflex type spinning lures, Indiana, Colorado and June-Bug spinners, various jig-spinners, and wire leaders.

Lure making with this kit is simple enough that any beginner, including youngsters, can easily make various lures. Complete, illustrated instructions are included, as well as necessary lure making materials such as spinner blades, beads, lure bodies, hooks, split rings, snaps, swivels, wire shafts, etc. Refills are available. The kit sells for less than $11.

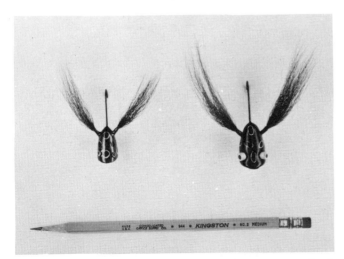

7. HOLIDAY TACKLE Co. of 24 S. Wheeling Avenue, Wheeling, Illinois, is currently producing cork-bodied frogs designed many years ago by Tom McNally. These fly rod poppers are of standard or regular size, and of small size. The smaller bug, intended primarily for smallmouth—although equally effective for largemouths—is called the "McNally Mini Frog."

The "Mini Frog" overall is about 2 inches long and is tied on a size 4, 3X-long hook. Because of its smaller size it casts better than the larger frog, yet when teased across the surface it stirs up big bass.

8. WOODSTREAM Corp., Lititz, Pennsylvania, is offering an "Old Pal" rod satchel that nestles rods in soft, thick plastic "foam" which surrounds the rods when the case is closed. Rod ferrules and guides can't be damaged, no matter how rough the transportation.

Two foam-lined compartments provide space for 14 rods and hold rod sections up to 51-inches in safety. The company states that its Model RS525 Rod Satchel II is ideal for both hunting and fishing—since one side of the case will take guns, the other rods.

The case is light but rugged, and designed to meet airline luggage specifications. Made of rugged ABS plastic, it has an ebony black leather-grain finish. Measuremnts are 52 x 6¾ x 9½ inches, and weight is 11 pounds.

9. ASHAWAY LINE & TWINE MANUFACTURING Co., Ashaway, Rhode Island, is packaging fly lines on factory-wound plastic winders, which are useful for handy storage of the lines and for quick transfer to reels. The line and winder are put up in "see-through" plastic containers, suitable for holding angling accessories.

In addition, the firm's deluxe grade floating and sinking lines come with free angler's clips. The lines are available in double and three-diameter tapers, and in levels.

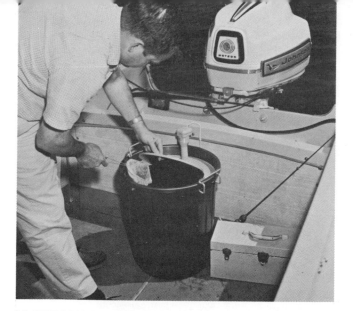

10. THE MARINE METAL PRODUCTS Co., Clearwater, Florida, is helping solve the bait fisherman's problem of keeping minnows alive. The company is making the "Bait Saver," a corrosion-proof aerator for use in plastic portable wells (as shown in photo) or in integral bait wells or tanks.

The "Bait Saver" comes in 6 or 12 volt models and gets its power from a boat's battery. It creates bubble aeration that is ideal for both salt and fresh water baitfish.

11. NORMARK Corp. of Minneapolis, Minnesota has scaled down the regular size model of its world famous "Rapala Fish 'n Fillet" knife and is making a "trout and panfish" model only 9½ inches long overall.

Ideal for cleaning the smaller gamefishes, this new "mini knife" fits easily into most regular-size tackle boxes—something the larger size Rapala knife will not do handily. Blade length of the small Rapala is 4 inches, and it is "progressively double tapered" to resist dulling. The handle of the knife is hand-finished, grained birch, with a German silver ferrule. Retail price is $3.95.

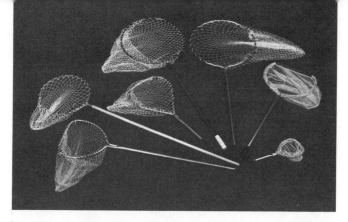

12. THE UMCO Corporation of Cape Girardeau, Missouri is best known for its excellent line of tackle boxes, but the company now is marketing a fine line of landing nets.

Umco has designed seven different nets in hopes of supplying a landing net "to meet the needs of any fisherman." There's typical Umco quality in all of the nets. They have aluminum and wood handles, strong metal frames, bags of cotton, nylon, polyethelen or PVC plastic, and plastic butt caps and grips.

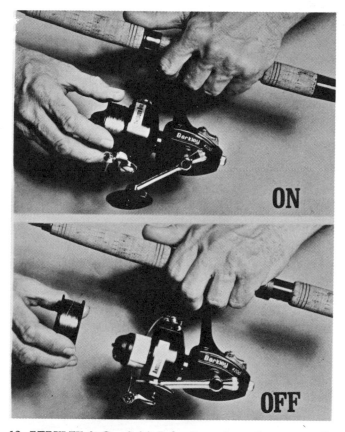

13. BERKLEY & Co., Spirit Lake, Iowa, is putting out an all-purpose spinning reel spool which, when fitted over a special adapter, will readily snap on or off most open-face fresh water spinning reels—including, of course, Berkley spinning reels.

The interchangeable spool is pre-wound with Berkley Trilene monofilament line, in a choice of tests from 2 to 14 pounds. According to Berkley the spool "serves not only as a means of containing the line for shipment from the factory, but also becomes the spool for the reel itself."

A fisherman has to remove the existing spool and drag control knob from his reel, insert the appropriate adapter with its drag control knob from his present reel, and slide the new spool with Trilene line over the adapter.

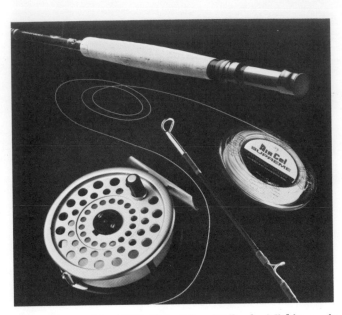

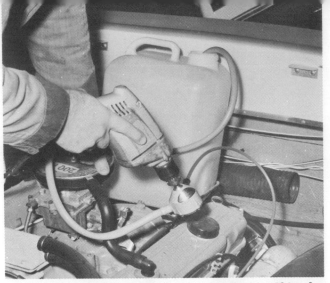

16. HUMBER INDUSTRIES, INC., Cincinnati, Ohio, has come up with a pump which, when connected to an ordinary hand power drill, will bait a boat at the rate of six gallons per minute. Called the "Pump Kit," the rig is a simple but ingenious device small enough to carry in a tool box. To use it the pump's stainless steel shaft is chucked into a ¼-inch or larger portable electric drill. One opening on the pump is the intake, the other the discharge, to which a 5 foot flexible discharge hose is attached.

The rest of the kit includes a spring clip to hold the discharge hose to the receptacle, a discharge tube adapter, and four suction tubes of various lengths and diameters. Price is $14.95.

14. SCIENTIFIC ANGLERS CO., Midland, Michigan, is known internationally for its quality fly casting lines. The company is now also marketing high quality glass fly rods and fly reels.

To help prevent the old problem, found especially among beginners, of mismatching lines and rods, Scientific is packaging complete fly fishing outfits composed of a Scientific rod, reel and line—all matching and "balanced," and selected to do a particular type of fly fishing. The unique outfits are called "System 6," "System 8," "System 9," and so on, depending upon the jobs each is supposed to do.

A "System 9" outfit, for example, is a fairly heavy one suitable for bass bug fishing, steelheads, etc. A "System 6" is perfect for casting a 6-weight fly line and ideal for fishing medium size streams and sheltered lakes for trout, bass and panfish.

Scientific's new fiberglass fly rods have high quality fittings, superb action, finish deep mahogany, and workmanship. The reels are custom-crafted by Hardy in England.

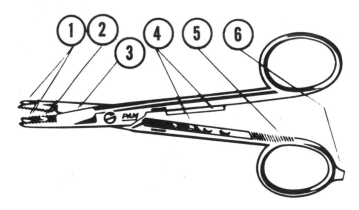

15. PAM PRODUCTS of Buffalo, New York is taking care of a basic fisherman's need with its "PAM Fishing Pliers." A combination of pliers and scissors, this handy tool consists of (1), a fishhook disgorger and hook remover, (2) pliers, (3) a line and leader cutter, (4) a knife edge and four holes for opening split-shot sinkers, (5) a hook file, (6) and a screwdriver.

PAM fishing pliers are available in three finishes: nickel ($3.95), chrome ($4.95), and stainless steel ($5.95).

17. THE JOHNSON REEL Co., Mankato, Minnesota, says its "Citation" Model 110B spin-cast reel is really just the company's famous and popular "Century" reel but with greater line capacity. The "Citation" will take up to 15 pound test monofilament line, and will accommodate 510 ft. of 10 pound line.

The "Citation" features a diachrome rotor, flash-hardened stainless steel guide, high-strength aluminum alloy frame, oil-impregnated bronze bearings, and an attractive green, black and white finish.

18. SHORELINE PRODUCTS, Northport, New York, offers a fisherman's bag they call the "Salt Water Surf Bag." Designed originally for the surfer, the bag also is of considerable use to fresh water anglers, particularly those after coho and Chinook salmon.

The "Surf Bag" is roomy enough to take several large lures, and has a 10-compartment divider as well as a six-compartment front pocket for lures either big or small. An extra compartment on the inside of the bag takes special tools, knife, leaders, snaps, swivels, etc.

A full flap covers all of the bag when closed, and it has a brass twist lock fastener. The bag is made of heavy (No. 6) O.D. canvas, double-stitched for strength. Adjustable shoulder strap and belt loops are sewn in. Divider is aluminum to prevent corrosion. Dimensions: 10 x 4 x 8 inches. Price, $11.95. Also available in five compartment model (9 x 2 x 7 inches) for $8.95.

19. HEDDON TACKLE Co., Dowagiac, Michigan, has introduced a great new angling aid called "Gang O' Shiners."

The "Gang" is an arrangement of six bright aluminum strips mounted on swivels and a long wire leader of about 20 inches. The "Gang" is meant to be used when trolling to attract fish to lures. It is put over on heavy nylon or cord and trolled somewhere near the lures or baits. The three-inch long aluminum strips wobble and flash, reflecting considerable sunlight, and, in effect, represent a school of small, silvery baitfish flashing along.

The "Gang O' Shiners" is used chiefly by salmon trollers in the Great Lakes, but they would be equally effective in many different kinds of trolling, including salt water trolling. Inexpensive.

20. BRITISH SEAGULL MOTORS Co., in Venice, California, is turning out a new Seagull outboard motor called the "Silver Century."

This newest of the Seagull line is 5 h.p. and is meant to be an all-purpose engine. It is light, economical, and easy to operate. Design is ultra-simple and rugged. The power head is geared-down to drive a 5-blade propeller. The manufacturer claims that "Seagull" engines are made for people who "have no knowledge of mechanics." "The native in Argentina, Tahiti, Uganda or Iran can keep a Seagull engine running with ease," says B.S.M. Co. Neglect that would leave most outboard motors inoperable in short order doesn't seem to phase Seagulls, states the maker.

The "Century" is water cooled, has instant-starting magnition, and is made of corrosion-resistant alloys with all-bronze bearings. The water pump is valveless and its case-hardened, nickel steel gears run in oil for longer life. The fuel tank is solid brass. Retail price is $230, with $10 additional for the long-shaft model.

---

21. KING INDUSTRIES, North Muskegon, Michigan, has designed a new device for taking lures down, and keeping them there, during deep trolling.

Called the "Control-O-Plane," it is a combination deep-planing device and hook-release mechanism. The maker recommends its use chiefly for Great Lakes coho salmon, and advises it is also effective in fishing deep for lake trout or steelheads. However, the "Control-O-Plane" can be used successfully in many varied deep water trolling situations.

The "plane" puts the fisherman's lure down where he wants it, with no weight or strain on the rod. The plane travels directly under the boat. Trolling at any speed or depth is possible. The angler knows where his lure is at all times when using this plane, and with it it is even possible to troll deep-down with a fly rod. The manufacturer also advises that the "Control-O-Plane" has a bright finish that helps attract fish. List price, $19.50.

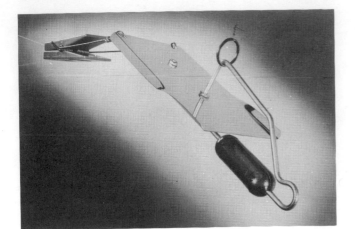

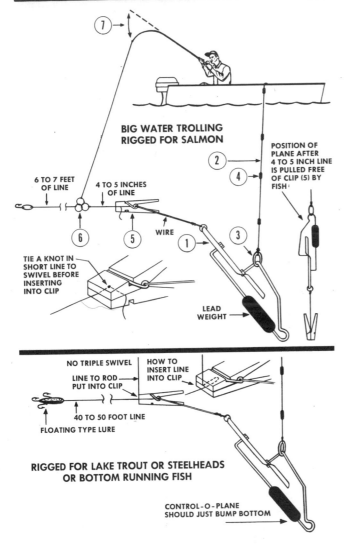

BIG WATER TROLLING
RIGGED FOR SALMON

6 TO 7 FEET OF LINE

4 TO 5 INCHES OF LINE

POSITION OF PLANE AFTER 4 TO 5 INCH LINE IS PULLED FREE OF CLIP (5) BY FISH

TIE A KNOT IN SHORT LINE TO SWIVEL BEFORE INSERTING INTO CLIP

WIRE

LEAD WEIGHT

NO TRIPLE SWIVEL

LINE TO ROD PUT INTO CLIP

HOW TO INSERT LINE INTO CLIP

40 TO 50 FOOT LINE

FLOATING TYPE LURE

RIGGED FOR LAKE TROUT OR STEELHEADS
OR BOTTOM RUNNING FISH

CONTROL - O - PLANE
SHOULD JUST BUMP BOTTOM

Position of CONTROL-O-PLANE in water (1). Lower your rod line and plane line together.
Metal or Monel line, (2) 50 lb. or Nylon line, 80 lb. recommended. Attach one end of line to cam ring (3) on plane. Secure other end to boat.
Fasten barrel swivels (4) every ten feet, or any other method to mark line for depth.

Attach 4 to 5 inches of line to clip (5) and triple swivel (6). Tie a knot in part of line inserted into clip.

Attach line from rod (7) to triple swivel (6), then attach 6 to 7 feet of line from triple swivel to lure.

When fish strikes and hook is set, rod will straighten out and signal your set. The 4 or 5 inch line is released from clip (5) leaving you free to play your fish with no drag or extra weight from plane, which has been released.

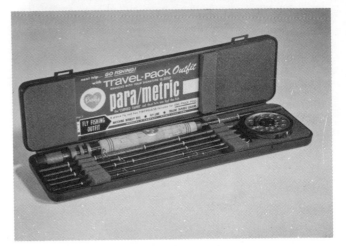

22. BERKLEY & Co., of Spirit Lake, Iowa, is selling a 6-piece fishing rod with "one piece feel" and it's conveniently packed in a Berkley Travel-Pack. The rod has fiber-glass ferrules which "flex with the rod," which Berkley claims gives one-piece feel even with a rod having multiple ferrules.

The Travel-Pack case is something new, too—being made of one-piece polypropylene, a light but tough material. The case has a wood-textured finish and "molded-in" color. Available in the new Berkley Travel-Packs are fly rods, spinning rods, spin-cast rods, and combination spinning-fly rods. The complete fly outfits include matching rods, reels, line, even tapered leaders and flies.

23. GALLASCH FLY BAITS Co. of Richmond, Virginia, is making an excellent line of salt water popping bugs for fly fishermen, as well as fresh water bugs.

Among the fresh water bugs being made by professional fly-tier Bill Gallasch are the hard-to-get but famous "Gerbubble" bugs for bass, developed by Tom Loving of Pasadena, Maryland. Gallasch also is making some "skipping" bugs, and most unusual—a "Sailfish Bug."

The "Skipping Bug" is a typical large-size popper with bucktail winging, but the "Sailfish Bug" is an ultra-large· popper (balsa body) with multiple saddle hackle winging, big salt water hook, and wire leader. It is designed, of course, for taking Atlantic and Pacific sailfish, as well as the various marlins.

For prices and other details write: Gallasch Fly Baits, 8705 Weldon Drive, Richmond, Virginia, 23229.

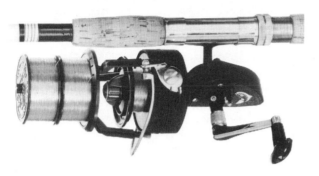

24. THE JOHN S. HADDOCK CO., Inc., Tulsa, Oklahoma,
has produced a spinning reel linewinder that is guaranteed to spool line onto any conventional spinning or spin-cast reel directly—without removing the reel spool—and with no line twist.

The manufacturer says the winder always spools line level and correctly, and when using it there is no way to spool line with a twist. The winder is useful in spooling fresh line on spinning reels ranging from tiny ultra-light reels to salt water surf jobs. The winder will accommodate 100 yard, dual 100 yard, or ¼-pound line spools. List, $2.95.

25. SHAKESPEARE TACKLE CO., Kalamazoo, Michigan,
is making a camouflage fly line. Called the "7000 line," it is said to "camouflage" itself in the water while still providing high visibility to the fisherman. The line has a tough, smooth finish that provides extra wear and "shooting" qualities through the

rod guides. "Millions" of tiny "bulkheads" or air pockets, sealed one from the other, give the line extra good flotation. The line is carefully controlled, weight-wise, to conform to all American Fishing Tackle Manufacturer's Association size-weight formulas.

The new "7000" camouflage, multi-colored line is available in level, double taper, and weight forward tapers.

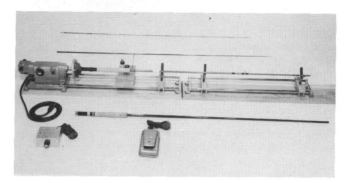

26. HECK FLY & ROD Co., San Francisco, California, has
produced a rod wrapper designed by professional rodmakers that operates electrically to give speed and precision in wrapping rods.

The "wrapper" is complete with a saber saw attachment for cutting rod blanks, high r.p.m.'s for corking, and slow speed turns for trimming a rod blank and wrapping on guides and ferrules.

The machine is ideal for rod repairing, as the chuck will adjust from 3/16 to 1⅝-inches. A variable speed foot pedal comes with the unit and an electronic speed control is available as an accessory.

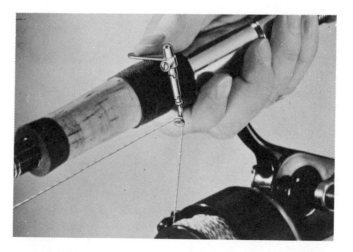

27. GUDEBROD FISHING LINE Co., Philadelphia, Penn-
sylvania, is introducing a "Spin-Trigger" device which is meant to aid the spin-fisherman in holding the line prior to executing a cast.

The "Spin-Trigger" device is attached to a spinning rod handle with tape. It then in effect replaces the angler's index finger in holding the line for casting. The unit makes "casting easier," and "adds distance and accuracy to every cast," according to the manufacturer, The "Spin-Trigger" also makes it possible to release a cast with "natural" thumb action. List price is $3.

28. THE WORTH Co., in Stevens Point, Wisconsin, is distributing a fine anchoring rig named the "Anchormate." It is an inexpensive piece of equipment for small boats, consisting of a free-spooling reel with line and a bow fixture that holds the anchor away from the boat to protect the boat's finish. The position of the anchor also has it ready to drop at any time. A turn of the reel's release button drops the anchor when it hits bottom. To reel in the anchor, crank the handle. If one's hand slips while cranking, the reel action stops automatically, which prevents the anchor from falling away. Retail price, $21.50.

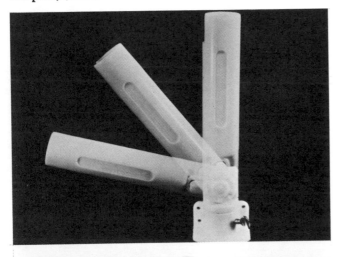

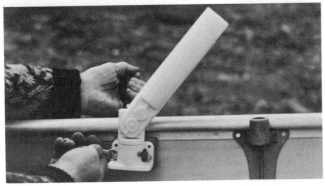

29. TEMPO PRODUCTS Co. of Cleveland, Ohio is marketing a "Tempo Rod Holder," ideal for trolling. The holder consists of a tubular section to hold the rod, plus a base that anchors the unit to the boat. Both pieces are made of Implex, a high-impact plastic that can't corrode.

The holder rotates at 360 degrees and locks in any position. In addition, a push-button adjustment allows the rod to be positioned at low, medium, or upright angles. Inside diameter of the holder is 1⅜ inches, inside depth is 6¼ inches, and overall length is 10½ inches. Price, $5.95.

30. BERKLEY & Co., Spirit Lake, Iowa, in addition to other special fishing "Packs" is making a unique "8-Rods-In-One" fishing outfit. The kit contains a multi-piece Berkley "Para/metric" rod with choice of handles, and matching reels and line so the angler can easily assemble any one of eight different fishing outfits: 4 spinning, 2 fly fishing, and 2 spin-casting. Rod sections include extra butt and tip units so length of rod can vary from 5 feet, 10 inches to 8 feet.

All of the equipment is compactly fitted into a tough but light weight plastic case. Companion items in the kit are a spinning reel, single-action fly reel, and a spin-cast reel, along with matching lines.

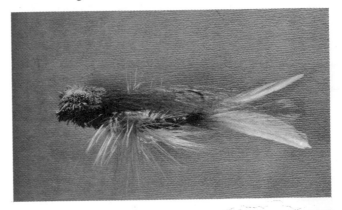

31. BING McCLELLAN, manufacturer of plastic worms and new "Keel flies" [ones totally weedless] at Traverse City, Mich., has now come up with an unusual new kind of fly rod bug.

Called the "Keel Bug," McClellan's lure is made without cork or plastic. It has a deer hair body, clipped deer hair for a head, long deer hair for "winging" and to help make the bug foul-proof, heavy hackling along the shoulder and body, and short saddle hackles for a tail.

The lure is really something between a fly and a bug, but what counts is that it is effective.

Like the "Keel Fly," the Keel Bug is on an inverted hook (point and barb above instead of below) and the hook's shank is bent near the bug's head in such a way that the bug tends to slide over snags and weeds.

The Keel Bug is the first real innovation to come along in fly fishing lures in years.

The hairy little bugs cast very well and are so weedless and snag-proof that you can toss one into a tree without hanging up. They get bass, too.

DEPARTMENTS:

- Rods • Spin-Cast Reels • Spinning Reels • Fly Reels
- Tackle Boxes

39: Reviewing new tackle

Rods

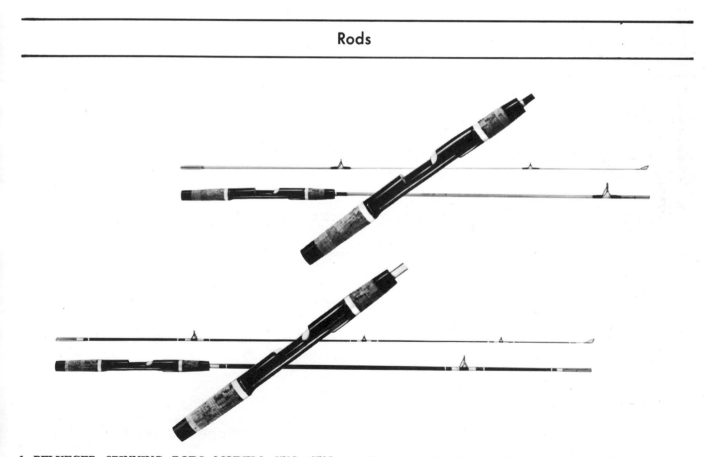

1. PFLUEGER SPINNING RODS MODELS 670S, 671S: Fiberglass rods have unique "plunger" snap-lock reel seats that eliminate locking rings and make reel-seating a one-motion operation. The 670S (at left in photo) is a solid glass rod; the 671S a hollow fibreglass rod. Both rods handle lures ¼ to ⅝ ounces. Ferrules are nickel-plated brass. Guides and tip-top are nickel-plated steel. The 670S model is standard action, and 6½-foot; the 671S is available in 6½ and 7-foot lengths, standard action.

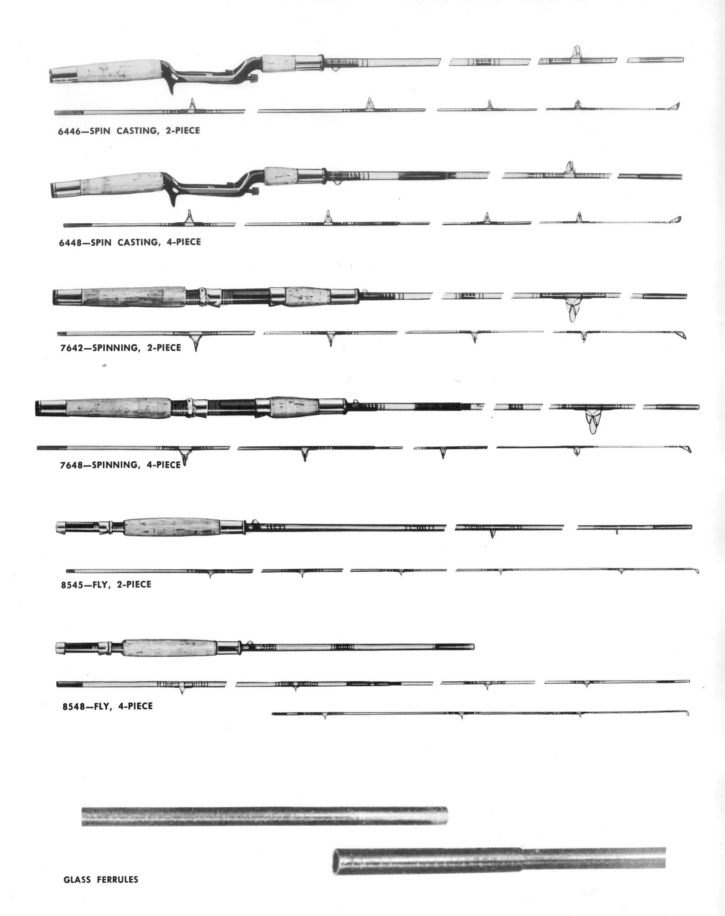

6446—SPIN CASTING, 2-PIECE

6448—SPIN CASTING, 4-PIECE

7642—SPINNING, 2-PIECE

7648—SPINNING, 4-PIECE

8545—FLY, 2-PIECE

8548—FLY, 4-PIECE

GLASS FERRULES

2. HEDDON "MARK GOLDEN 50" RODS: These are two and four piece rods with "one-piece action." Designed as a "traveler's" rod, the 50 series all have Heddon's new "positive, sure-fit" glass ferrules. According to the manufacturer, these rods are non-breakable and non-splintering. Tip-tops are carboloy. Reel seats of aluminum.

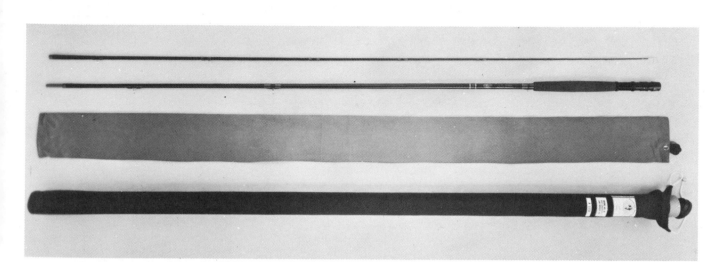

3. SCIENTIFIC ANGLERS "SYSTEMS" RODS: These are custom-crafted rods with precision taper actions. They are of superb quality, and of hollow glass having a deep, rich mahogany finish. Reel seats are anodized aluminum. Bronze nylon thread windings over guides having hollow ground footings. Stripping guides are carboloy. Rods are available in lengths from 7-feet, 2-inches, to 9-feet, 3-inches. Ferrules are "double strength" and twist-off, and lifetime registration numbers on male and female ferrules align the guides. Snake guides are hard chrome. Each rod is supplied with a tailored cloth bag with leather tabs and snap, and a "stronger-than-metal" rod case with fitted fabric cover.

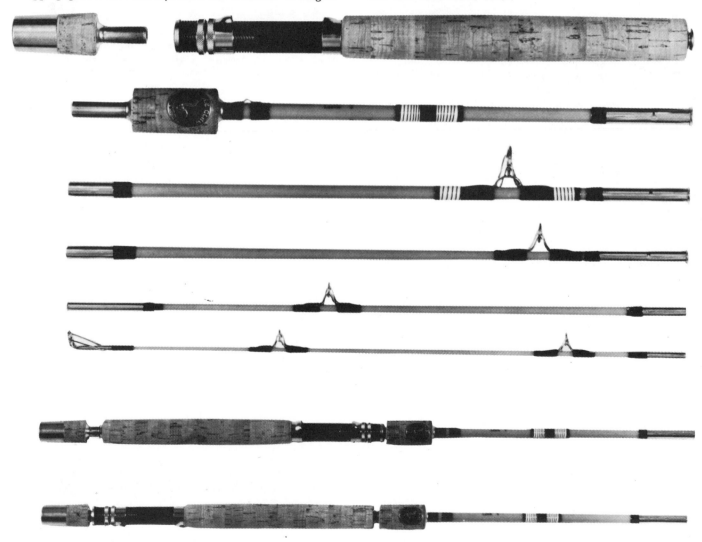

4. EAGLE CLAW "TRAILMASTER" ROD: This is a six piece, combination "universal" spin-fly rod, called the Model 6TMU-6'9" rod. It can be rigged as a fly rod or as· a spinning rod, depending upon where the reel seat is mounted.

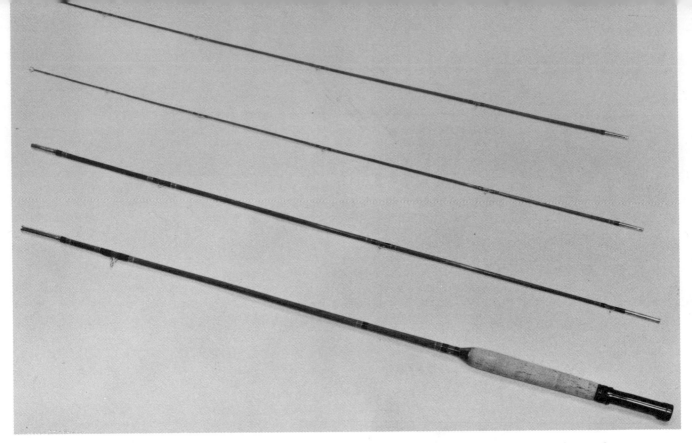

5. HECK BAMBOO RODS: This new line of rods is made of split butt-cut Tonkin cane, finished with hand-rubbing technique. Specie cork grips. Carboloy stripping guides and tip-top, chromed, stainless steel snake guides. Reel seats are anodized aluminum locking or cork. Ferrules are hard-drawn, 18% nickel-silver.

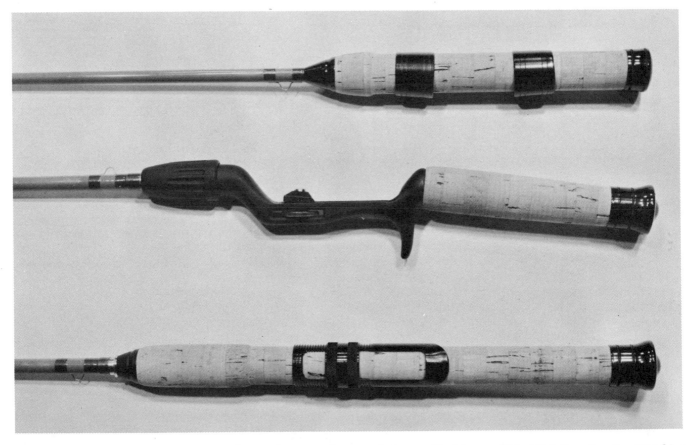

6. HECK "BRONZE" SERIES RODS: These spinning and spin-cast rods are made of phenolic resin blanks, elk-tan finish. Wrappings are red satin. Stainless steel chrome-plated guides and tip-top. Hard-drawn, 18% nickel-silver ferrules. Matching anodized sliding reel-lock, or fixed reel seat. Come packed in cloth bag and polished aluminum cases.

1. GARCIA ABU-MATIC 280: Powerful. Features positive-drive retrieve. Rapid line take-up. Ball-bearing disc drag. With 120 yards, 15-pound Bonnyl line.

2. ZEBCO 800: For fresh or salt water. Corrosion resistant throughout. Dependable. Wide range, smooth drag. Immediate line-pickup. Stationary, self-lubricating gears. Extra, interchangeable spools available with 6, 8, 10, 12, and 15-pound line.

3. ZEBCO 600: Corrosion resistant. Stronger gears. Contoured thumb control. Anodized aluminum cover. Quick, convenient

take-down, and spool change. With 105 yards, 8-pound line. Extra spools available with 4, 6, 10 and 12-pound line.

4. JOHNSON COMMANDER 150: Features revolutionary "Accu-Cast" control, with line "feathering" in exact proportion to thumb pressure. Variable drag. Permalloy gears. Tungsten-carbide pickup. Positive anti-reverse. Up to 15-pound test line. With 280 feet, 12-pound line. Salt water resistant.

5. JOHNSON SABRA 130A: Features "Power Play" action—from full power retrieve to variable multiple-disc drag automatically. Oscillating spool cross-winds line. Permalloy gears. Tungsten-carbide pickup. Stainless steel line guide. Impregnated bronze bearings. Strong, aluminum alloy frame. With 400 feet, 15-pound line.

6. JOHNSON "98": Large line capacity—510 feet, 10 pound line. Inexpensive, ideal "family" reel. Simple, trouble-free construction and operation. No-backlash casting. Instantly adjustable star-drag. Permalloy gears. New, 12-point pickup system. For fresh or salt water.

7. JOHNSON FISKAR I: From full-power retrieve to variable multiple-disc drag automatically. "Trigger" type line release on bottom of reel. "Under-the-rod" design. Permalloy gears. Stainless steel crankshaft and driveshaft. Hi-impact Acrylic gear case. Up to 12-pound line. With 340-feet, 8-pound line. All parts salt water resistant.

8. SHAKESPEARE 1700: Strong, four-unit construction. Comfortable, well-designed push-button. Easy to adjust star-drag control on crank. Eight-point pickup distributes wear. With 12-pound line.

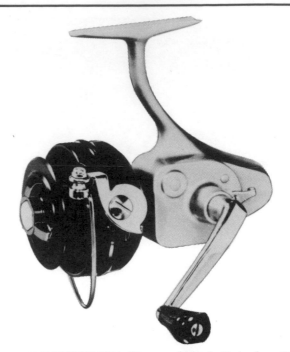

9. SHAKESPEARE 2000: Honey-gold and olive colors. Stainless steel roller and bail. Smooth, two-disc drag. Four-unit construction. One-piece molded spool with 10-pound line.

10. OLD PAL REEL CAT 30: Popularly-priced. Corrosion resistant, epoxy enamel finish. Free-spinning line roller. Ball-bearing drive. Cam-operated bail arm. Convertible right or left-hand wind. Retrieve ration 3.13 to 1. Weighs 10 ounces. Takes 260-yards, 6-pound monofilament, 140 yards, 10-pound.

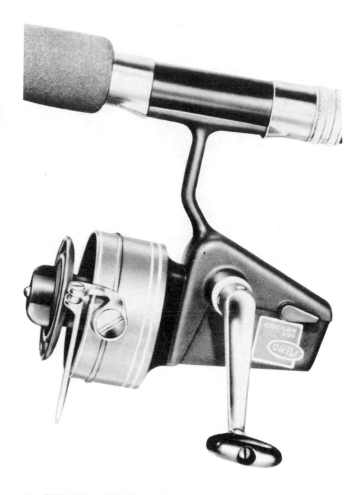

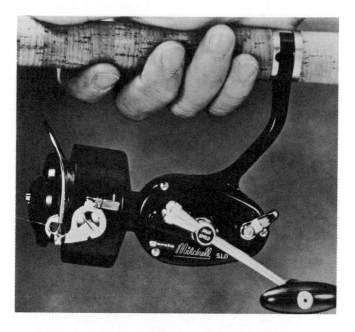

13. GARCIA MITCHELL 510: Unusual new-design reel attaches through special locking mechanism to handles of four matching Conolon rods. Swept-back reel stem eliminates stem-between-the-fingers mounting on rod, gives better balance, control and comfort. Retrieve ratio is 5 to 1. Takes 200 yards, 4-pound mono.

11. OLD PAL COUGAR 600: Improved drag, with 9-disc design. Drag will not vibrate off light settings. For both fresh and salt water fishing. Retrieve ration 3.66 to 1. Weighs 13 ounces. Ball-bearing drive on mainshaft. Stainless steel spool-shaft. Full bail and line roller.

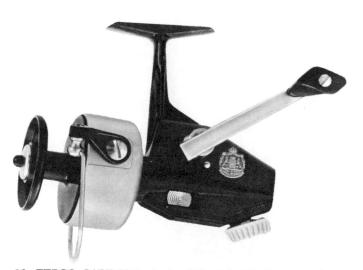

12. ZEBCO CARDINAL 4: Swedish-made. Fresh water size. Stern-mounted, easy-to-get-at drag. Drag knob has 10 calibrated click stops. Ball bearings. Gear ratio of 5 to 1. One revolution of handle spools two feet of line. Slip-proof anti-reverse button. Quick-change spool is one-piece Delrin. Corrosion-proof. Takes 200 yards, 8-pound mono, and up to 18-pound line. Comes with extra spool, take-down tool and lubricant.

14. GARCIA MITCHELL 486: Salt water model is made of stainless materials. Rust and corrosion proof. New anti-inertia brake prevents bail from closing accidentally during casts. Improved "Teflonized" drag.

15. GARCIA MITCHELL 754: Lightweight, single-action. Frame is of aluminum alloy, spool of high-strength light metals. Adjustable drag with large knob. Push-button spool release. Takes 30-yard HCH line with 50 yards of backing. Two other models (752-standard) (756-wide spool) also available.

17. PFLUEGER SUPREME AUTOMATIC: Model 579 reel is of lightweight aluminum. Mounts vertically on rod. Quick take-apart, 3-piece construction. Disassembles at push of a button. Spring lock prevents accidental tripping of retrieve lever. Spring tension can be released by button on spring cap without spool turning. Has 2⅞-inch wide spool with ⅞-inch diameter. Takes fly lines up to size GAF(WF-9).

16. NORIS SHAKESPEARE LTD. "BATTENKILL": New "geared recovery" reel has features which, according to British manufacturer, have never before been combined in a fly reel. Reel features a geared retrieve of 2.5 to 1, a slipping clutch with 8 fixed settings, and a broad rim for "finger-tip" control. Of ultra-light magnesium alloy. Clutch is set according to "type of rod and strength of leader," and may be set lightly to "do all the work of playing the fish," or may be set to slip when fish is being played primarily by finger pressure on spool flange.

18. EAGLE CLAW MODEL ECB: Vertical, automatic. Adjustable "slip-clutch." Side-mounted tension release allows quick line control. Brass-steel gearing. Stainless steel wear ring. Free stripping. Trigger release lever folds flush when not in use. Aluminum spool flange. Takes 26-yards size D(DT-5) line. Weight, 9⅛ ounces.

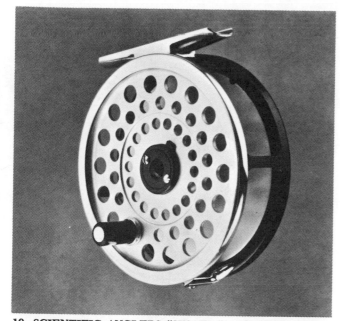

19. SCIENTIFIC ANGLERS "SYSTEM" reels: Eight sizes to match firm's "system" rods-reels-lines. Quality, hand-crafted reels are made by Hardy Brothers, Ltd. in England. Reel's spool can be readily "feathered" by hand. Spool fits flange to precision tolerances . . . no line or leader pinching. Has adjustable click drag, with wide range of settings. Extra spools available, and reel spool can be quickly changed with spring-latch spool release. Unique line-notch cut in spool makes it possible to remove spool without pinching line. Spool is one-piece aluminum, and frame is machined in one piece. Reel is strong, durable, lightweight, with no screws or rivets to work loose from frame.

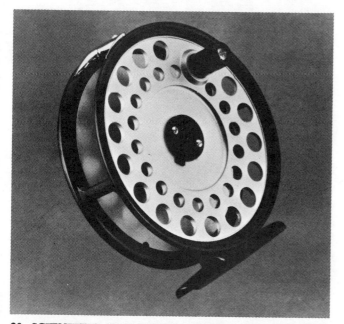

20. SCIENTIFIC ANGLERS "100 SERIES" reels: Available in three sizes. Single-action. Quality made. One-piece frame. One-piece spool. Pressure die castings of high strength aluminum alloy. Reel foot is cast integrally with the frame. Spool handle pivot and cup are cast integrally with the spool. Extra spools available.

Tackle Boxes

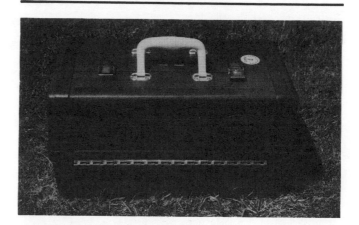

1. HAWTHORNE BOX: A Montgomery Ward product, this is a large heavy-duty plastic box, with seven large capacity trays. Dual handles lock when box is closed. Excellent hinging. Black leather-grain finish.

2. OLD PAL ROYAL COACHMAN (PF6500): Designed with the fly fisherman in mind, this box has a foam-lined compartment under the lid meant to accommodate an Old Pal "Tackle Boxrod." Box has numerous storage compartments for flies, reels, etc. Made of ABS plastic, leather-grain finish. Non-spill safety latch. Watertight. Marine stainless hardware. Weight, 4 pounds. Size 15¼" x 8" x 6½".

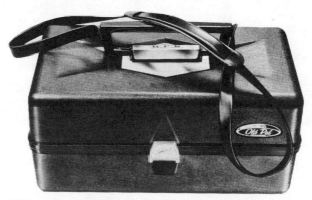

3. OLD PAL "PERFECT BALANCE" HANDLE: A new luggage-style carrying handle is being used on many Old Pal boxes. These "perfect-balance" handles are larger than ordinary tackle box handles, and are shaped for comfort. Handles are available with or without special leather carrying straps that can be attached to small buttons on either end of the handle, for carrying over the shoulder.

4. OLD PAL "TARPON": Features separate compartment for extra large reels, and three trays for various size lures. Made of ABS plastic, with black leather-grain finish. Watertight, with marine stainless hardware. Box is 14" x 7" x 7½" and weighs 3 pounds.

6. THE "ORINOCO" BOX: Named after a Venezuelan river, this box by Vlcheck Plastics Company of Middlefield, Ohio, is designed to accommodate a large assortment of lures in various sizes. Impervious to soft plastic lures, box can't be damaged by oil, gas, bug sprays or salt water. Weight, 4 pounds. Dimensions, 14⅜" x 7⅝" x 7".

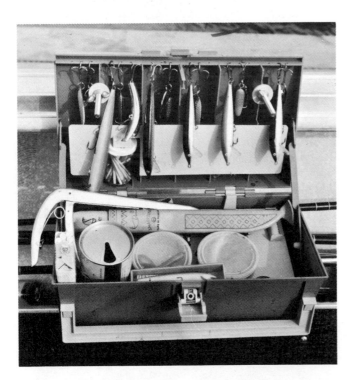

5. PLANO BOAT-TOTE: Made of tough ABS plastic, this box is designed to be attached to the side of a boat gunwale, and thus to be out of the way. Spring-loaded clamps tightened with wing-nuts hold box to gunwale. Holes in top of box take lure hooks. Special compartments handle porkrind and other jars; sinkers; hooks; cigarettes; beverages; snaps; swivels. Length is 13 3/16"; width 5⅜"; and height, 8¼".

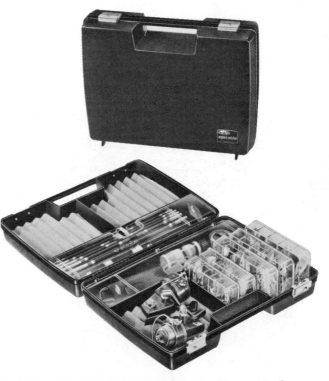

7. THE ANGLER'S SATCHEL: Looking like an attache case, this unusual tackle box by Old Pal is of black leather-grain plastic, and features two foam-lined trays, portions of which have clear plastic covers for "see-through" convenience. Ample space for lures, flies, "break-down" rods, reels and accessories. Removable plastic dividers. Comes with five plastic lure boxes.

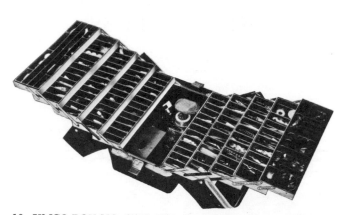

10. UMCO BOX NO. 3500: Ultra-large box is biggest of Umco make. Has 10 full-length trays, 124 lure compartments, and deep bottom area for reels, etc. Available in green, walnut, or blond wood grain finishes.

8. THE ADVENTURER 2000: This totally new tackle box, by Vlchek Plastic Co., Middlefield, Ohio, has nine individual boxes in a handy, removable, tote tray. Under tray is ample space for reels, tools, accessories. Designed specifically for experienced fishermen who use a variety of tackle, its 9 box "library" can be arranged to meet every need. Nine boxes in "library" are 8⅜″ x 4½″ x 1¹¹⁄₁₆″. Overall box size is 19″ x 10¾″ x 10⅛″.

11. UMCO "POSSUM BELLY" BOXES: Unique and original "Possum" attachment adds over 1,000 cubic inches of storage space to box. "Belly" area is held in place tightly by vinyl "lip" and special safety locks. "Belly holds large objects such as reels, spare spools, porkrind jars, etc., and is apart from main box.

9. EAGLE CLAW "TRAVEL MASTER": This Samsonite attache case takes six-piece combination fly and spinning rod, as well as Eagle Claw spinning and fly reels. Spaces for spinning and fly lines, lures, flies, sinkers, etc. Folio file in case will take rain jacket, maps. etc.

12. "MINNI-ALUMINUM" BOX: This box, by Umco Corporation, Cape Girardeau, Missouri, is one of many new minni boxes by Umco. This model B-11 has special "Lur-gard" tray liners—one on each side of box. One side is for casting plugs, other for spinning lures. Box can be clipped to angler's belt or stored in regulation, full-size tackle box. Size is 10¾″ x 5″ x 2½″.

DEPARTMENTS:

40: World fishing records

Compiled by Field & Stream

FRESH-WATER FISH

Field & Stream annual fishing contest entry blanks may be obtained by writing Mike Ball, Fishing Contest Editor, Field & Stream, 383 Madison Ave., New York, N. Y. 10017.

| SPECIES | | CAUGHT BY ROD AND REEL | | | | | CAUGHT BY ANY METHOD | | |
Common Name	Scientific Name	Wt.	Length	Girth	Where	When	Angler	Lb. Oz.	Where
BASS, Largemouth	Micropterus salmoides	22 lbs. 4 oz.	32½"	28½"	Montgomery Lake, Ga.	June 2 1932	George W. Perry	Same	
BASS, Redeye	Micropterus coosae	6½ lbs.	20½"	15⅘"	Hallawakee Cr., Ala.	Mar. 24 1967	Thomas L. Sharpe	Same	
BASS, Smallmouth	Micropterus dolomieui	11 lbs. 15 oz.	27"	21⅔"	Dale Hollow Lake, Ky.	July 9 1955	David L. Hayes	Same	
BASS, Spotted	Micropterus punctulatus spp	8 lbs. 8 oz.	25"	17¾"	Smith Lake, Ala.	May 23 1968	Wreford James	Same	
BASS, White	Roccus chrysops	5 lbs. 4 oz.	17"		Toronto, Kans.	May 4, 1966	Henry A. Baker	Same	
BLUEGILL	Lepomis macrochirus	4 lbs. 12 oz.	15"	18¼"	Ketona Lake, Ala.	Apr. 9 1950	T. S. Hudson	Same	
BULLHEAD, Black	Ictalurus melas	8 lbs.	24"	17¾"	Lake Waccabuc, N.Y.	Aug. 1 1951	Kani Evans	Same	
CARP	Cyprinus carpio	55 lbs. 5 oz.	42"	31"	Clearwater Lake, Minn.	July 10 1952	Frank J. Ledwein	83-8	Pretoria, So. Africa
CATFISH, Blue	Ictalurus furcatus	97 lbs.	57"	37"	Missouri River, S.D.	Sept. 16 1959	Edward B. Elliott	Same	
CATFISH, Channel	Ictalurus punctatus	58 lbs.	47¼"	29⅛"	Santee-Cooper Res., S.C.	July 7 1964	W. Whaley		
CHAR, Arctic	Salvelinus alpinus	27 lbs. 4 oz.	40¼"	26¼"	Tree River, N.W.T.	Sept. 2 1963	W. Murphy	Same	
CRAPPIE, Black	Pomoxis nigromaculatus	5 lbs.	19¼"	18⅝"	Santee-Cooper Res., S.C.	Mar. 15 1957	Paul E. Foust	Same	
CRAPPIE, White	Pomoxis annularis	5 lbs. 3 oz.	21"	19"	Enid Dam, Miss.	July 31 1957	Fred L. Bright	Same	
DOLLY, VARDEN	Salvelinus malma	32 lbs.	40½"	29¾"	L. Pend Oreille, Idaho	Oct. 27 1949	N. L. Higgins	Same	
GAR, Alligator	Lepisosteus spatula	279 lbs.	93"		Rio Grande, Texas	Dec. 2 1951	Bill Valverde	Same	
GAR, Longnose	Lepisosteus osseus	50 lbs. 5 oz.	72¼"	22¼"	Trinity River, Texas	July 30 1954	Townsend Miller	Same	
GRAYLING, Arctic	Thymallus arcticus	5 lbs. 15 oz.	29⅞"	15⅛"	Katseyedie R., N.W.T.	Aug. 16 1967	Jeanne P. Branson	Same	
MUSKELLUNGE	Esox masquinongy	69 lbs. 15 oz.	64½"	31¾"	St. Lawrence R., N.Y.	Sept. 22 1957	Arthur Lawton	102	Minocqua Lake, Wisconsin
PERCH, White	Roccus americanus	4 lbs. 12 oz.	19½"	13"	Messalonskee Lake, Me.	June 4 1949	Mrs. Earl Small	Same	
PERCH, Yellow	Perca flavescens	4 lbs. 3½ oz.			Bordentown, N.J.	May 1865	Dr. C. C. Abbot	Same	

SPECIES		CAUGHT BY ROD AND REEL						CAUGHT BY ANY METHOD	
Common Name	Scientific Name	Wt.	Length	Girth	Where	When	Angler	Lb. Oz.	Where
PICKEREL, Chain	Esox niger	9 lbs. 6 oz.	31"	14"	Homerville, Ga.	Feb. 17 1961	Baxley McQuaig, Jr.	Same	
PIKE, Northern	Esox lucius	46 lbs. 2 oz.	52½"	25"	Sacandaga Res., N.Y.	Sept. 15 1940	Peter Dubuc	Same	
SALMON, Atlantic	Salmo salar	79 lbs. 2 oz.			Tana River, Norway	1928	Henrik Henriksen	103-2	River Devon, Scotland
SALMON, Chinook	Oncorhynchus tshawytscha	92 lbs.	58½"	36"	Skeena River, B.C.	July 19 1959	Heinz Wichmann	126-3	Petersburg, Alaska
SALMON, Landlocked	Salmo salar	22 lbs. 8 oz.	36"		Sebago Lake, Maine	Aug. 1 1907	Edward Blakely	35	Crooked River, Maine
SALMON, Coho or Silver	Oncorhynchus kisutch	31 lbs.			Cowichan Bay, B.C.	Oct. 11 1947	Mrs. Lee Hallberg	Same	
SAUGER	Stizostedion canadense	8 lbs. 5 oz.	28"		Niobara, Nebr.	Oct. 22 1961	Mrs. Betty Tepner	Same	
STURGEON, White	Acipenser transmontanus	360 lbs.	111"	86"	Snake River, Idaho	Apr. 24 1956	Willard Cravens	Same	
SUNFISH, Redear	Lepomis microlophus	2 lbs. 15 oz.	14"	15¾"	Ponte Vedra Beach, Fla.	Mar. 6 1965	Ronald D. Gray, Jr.	4-4	Gordon, Alabama
TROUT, Brook	Salvelinus fontinalis	14 lbs. 8 oz.	31½"	11½"	Nipigon River, Ontario	July 1916	Dr. W. J. Cook	Same	
TROUT, Brown	Salmo trutta	39 lbs. 8 oz.			Loch Awe, Scotland	1866	W. Muir	40	Great Lake, Tasmania
TROUT, Cutthroat	Salmo clarki	41 lbs.	39"		Pyramid Lake, Nev.	Dec. 1925	John Skimmerhorn	Same	
TROUT, Golden	Salmo aguabonita	11 lbs.	28"	16"	Cook's Lake, Wyo.	Aug. 5 1948	Chas. S. Reed	Same	
TROUT, Lake	Salvelinus namaycush	63 lbs. 2 oz.	51½"	32¾"	Lake Superior	May 25 1952	Hubert Hammers	102	Lake Athabaska, Sask.
TROUT, Rainbow, Stlhd. or Kamloops	Salmo gairdneri	37 lbs.	40½"	28"	L. Pend Oreille, Idaho	Nov. 25 1947	Wes Hamlet	42	Corbett, Oreg.
TROUT, Sunapee	Salvelinus alpinus	11 lbs. 8 oz.	33"	17¼"	Lake Sunapee, N.H.	Aug. 1 1954	Ernest Theoharis	Same	
WALLEYE	Stizostedion vitreum	25 lbs.	41"	29"	Old Hickory L., Tenn.	Aug. 1 1960	Mabry Harper	Same	
WARMOUTH	Chaenobryttus gulosus	1 lb. 2 oz.	10"	10"	Cooper River, S.C.	May 18 1968	Robert L. Joyner	Same	
WHITEFISH, Mountain	Prosopium williamsoni	5 lbs.	19"	14"	Athabasca R., Alberta	June 3 1963	Orville Welch	Same	

International Game Fish Association

(to July 1, 1969)

MARINE FISHES

ALL TACKLE RECORDS FOR BOTH MEN AND WOMEN

International Game Fish Association, world record entry forms may be obtained by writing: I.G.F.A., 2190 S.E. 17th St., Ft. Lauderdale, Fla., 33316.

FISH	Scientific Name	Weight	Length	Girth	Place	Date	Angler	Line lbs.
ALBACORE	Thunnus germo	69 lbs. 1 oz.	4' ½"	33¼"	Hudson Canyon, N.J.	Oct. 8 1961	Walter C. Timm	50
		69 lbs.	3' 6"	32½"	St. Helena, Atlantic Ocean	Apr. 7 1956	P. Allen	130
AMBERJACK	Seriola lalandi	120 lbs. 8 oz.	5' 2"	40"	Kona, Hawaii	Oct. 25 1955	C. W. McAlpin	130

FISH	Scientific Name	Weight	Length	Girth	Place	Date	Angler	Line lbs.
BARRACUDA	Sphyraena barracuda	103 lbs. 4 oz.	5' 6"	31¼"	West End, Bahamas	1932	C. E. Benet*	80
BASS, Calif. Black Sea	Stereolepis gigas	557 lbs. 3 oz.	7' 4¼"	78"	Catalina Island, California	July 1 1962	Richard M. Lane	50
BASS, Calif. White Sea	Cynoscion nobilis	83 lbs. 12 oz.	5' 5½"	34"	San Felipe, Mexico	Mar. 31 1953	L. C. Baumgardner	30
BASS, Channel	Sciaenops ocellatus	83 lbs.	4' 4"	29"	Cape Charles, Va.	Aug. 5 1949	Zack Waters, Jr.	50
BASS, Giant Sea	Promicrops itaiara	680 lbs.	7' 1½"	66"	Fernandina Beach, Fla.	May 20 1961	Lynn Joyner	80
BASS, Sea	Centropristes striatus	8 lbs.	1' 10"	19"	Nantucket Sound, Mass.	May 13 1951	H. R. Rider	50
BASS, Striped	Roccus saxatilis	73 lbs.	5'	30½"	Vineyard Sound, Mass.	Aug. 17 1913	C. B. Church*	50
BLACKFISH or TAUTOG	Tautoga onitis	21 lbs. 6 oz.	2' 7½"	23½"	Cape May, N.J.	June 12 1954	R. N. Sheafer	30
BLUEFISH	Pomatomus saltatrix	24 lbs. 3 oz	3' 5"	22"	San Miguel, Azores	Aug. 27 1953	M. A. da Silva Veloso	12
BONEFISH	Albula vulpes	19 lbs.	3' 3⅝"	17"	Zululand, South Africa	May 26 1962	Brian W. Batchelor	30
BONITO, Oceanic	Katsuwonus pelamis	39 lbs. 15 oz.	3' 3"	28"	Walker Cay, Bahamas	Jan. 21 1952	F. Drowley	50
COBIA	Rachycentron canadus	102 lbs.	5' 10"	34"	Cape Charles, Virginia	July 3 1938	J. E. Stansbury*	130
COD	Gadus callarias	74 lbs. 4 oz.	5' 6"	43"	Boothbay Harbor, Maine	June 2 1960	James J. Duggan	50
DOLPHIN	Coryphaena hippurus	76 lbs. 12 oz.	5' 10½"	35"	Bimini, Bahamas	May 28 1964	Charles J. Costello	50
DRUM, Black	Pogonias cromis	94 lbs. 4 oz.	4' 3½"	42"	Cape Charles, Virginia	Apr. 28 1957	James Lee Johnson	50
FLOUNDER	Paralichthys	21 lbs. 4 oz.	3' ½"	35"	Maitencillo, Chile	Dec. 8 1959	Daniel Varas Serrano	50
KINGFISH or TANGUIGUE	S. Cavalla C. Commersonii	81 lbs.	5' 11½"	29¼"	Karachi, Pakistan	Aug. 27 1960	George E. Rusinak	80
MARLIN, Black	Name being revised	1560 lbs.	14' 6"	81"	Cabo Blanco, Peru	Aug. 4 1953	Alfred C. Glassell, Jr.	130
MARLIN, Blue	Makaira ampla	814 lbs.	13' 8"	69"	St. Thomas, Virgin Islands	July 26 1964	John Battles	80
MARLIN, Pacific Blue	Name being revised	1095 lbs.	13' 10"	81"	Kona, Hawaii	May 30 1964	Jack Whaling	130
*MARLIN, Striped	Makaira mitsukurii	465 lbs.	10' 6"	65"	Major Island, New Zealand	Feb. 27 1948	James C. Black	130
MARLIN, White	Makaira albida	161 lbs.	8' 8"	33"	Miami Beach, Fla.	Mar. 20 1938	L. F. Hooper	80
PERMIT	Trachinotus goodei	50 lbs.	3' 7"	34½"	Miami, Florida	Mar. 27 1965	Robert F. Miller	12
POLLACK	Pollachius virens	43 lbs.	4'	29"	Brielle, New Jersey	Oct. 21 1964	Philip Barlow	50
RUNNER, Rainbow	Elagatis bipinnulatus	30 lbs. 15 oz.	3' 11"	22"	Hauai, Hawaii	Apr. 27 1963	Holbrook Goodale	130
ROOSTERFISH	Nematistius pectoralis	114 lbs.	5' 4"	33"	La Paz, Mexico	June 1 1960	Abe Sackheim	30
SAILFISH, Atlantic	Istiophorus americanus	141 lbs. 1 oz.	8' 5"		Ivory Coast, Africa	Jan. 26 1961	Tony Burnand	130
SAILFISH, Pacific	Istiophorus greyi	221 lbs.	10' 9"		Santa Cruz, Is., Galapagos Is.	Feb. 12 1947	C. W. Stewart	130
SAWFISH	Pristis pectinatus	890 lbs. 8 oz.	16' 1"	92"	Fort Amador, Canal Zone	May 26 1960	Jack Wagner	80
SHARK, Blue	Prionace glauca	410 lbs.	11' 6"	52"	Rockport, Mass.	Sept. 1 1960	Richard C. Webster	80
SHARK, Mako	Isurus oxyrhynchus I. glaucus	1,000 lbs.	12		Mayor Island, New Zealand	Mar. 14 1943	B. D. H. Ross*	130
SHARK, Man-Eater or White	Carcharodon carcharias	2664 lbs.	16' 10"	9' 6"	Ceduna, So. Australia	Apr. 21 1959	Alfred Dean	130
SHARK, Porbeagle	Lamna nasus	400 lbs. 8 oz.	7' 9½"	57½"	Fire Island, New York	May 16 1965	James T. Kirkup	80
SHARK, Thresher	Alopias vulpinus	922 lbs.			Bay of Islands, New Zealand	Mar. 21 1937	W. W. Dowding*	130

*Replaces A. Hamann catch weighing 692 lbs. which was determined not to be a Striped Marlin.   *Line not tested.

FISH	Scientific Name	Weight	Length	Girth	Place	Date	Angler	Line lbs.
SHARK, Tiger	Galeocerdo cuvier	1780 lbs.	13' 10½"	103"	Cherry Grove, South Carolina	June 14 1964	Walter Maxwell	130
SNOOK or ROBALO	Centropomus undecimalis	52 lbs. 6 oz.	4' 1½"	26"	La Paz, Mexico	Jan. 9 1963	Jose Haywood	30
SWORDFISH	Xiphias gladius	1182 lbs.	14' 11¼"	78"	Iquique, Chile	May 7 1953	L. Marron	130
TARPON	Tarpon atlanticus	283 lbs.	7' 2 3/5"		Lake Maracaibo, Venezuela	Mar. 19 1956	M. Salazar	30
TUNA, Allison or Yellowfin	Thunnus albacares	269 lbs. 8 oz.	6' 9"	53"	Hanalei, Hawaii	May 30 1962	Henry Nishikawa	180
TUNA, Atlantic Big-Eyed	Thunnus obesus	295 lbs.	6' 6½"	40"	San Miguel, Azores, Portugal	July 8 1960	Dr. Arsenio Cordeiro	130
TUNA, Pacific Big-Eyed	Parathunnus sibi	435 lbs.	7' 9"	63½"	Cabo Blanco, Peru	Apr. 17 1957	Dr. Russel V. A. Lee	130
TUNA, Blackfin	Thunnus atlanticus	36 lbs.	3' ¼"	27⅞"	Bermuda	July 14 1963	Joseph E. Baptiste, Jr.	50
TUNA, Bluefin	Thunnus thynnus	977 lbs.	9' 8"	94½"	St. Ann Bay, Nova Scotia	Sept. 4 1950	D. Mcl. Hodgson	130
WAHOO	Acanthocybium solandri	149 lbs.	6' 7¾"	37½"	Cat Cay, Bahamas	June 15 1962	John Pirovano	130
WEAKFISH	Cynoscion regalis	19 lbs. 8 oz.	3' 1"	23¾"	Trinidad, West Indies	Apr. 13 1962	Dennis B. Hall	80
WEAKFISH, Spotted	Cynoscion nebulosus	15 lbs. 3 oz.	2' 10½"	20½"	Ft. Pierce, Fla.	Jan. 13 1949	C. W. Hubbard	50
YELLOWTAIL	Seriola dorsalis or S. grandis	111 lbs.	5' 2"	38"	Bay of Islands, New Zealand	June 11 1961	A. F. Plim	50

International Game Fish Association

RECORD CATCHES FOR BOTH MEN AND WOMEN

130 LB. LINE TEST RECORDS (over 80 lbs., up to and including 130 lbs.)

FISH	Scientific Name	Weight	Length	Girth	Place	Date	Angler
ALBACORE	Thunnus germo	69 lbs.	3' 6"	32½"	St. Helena, Atlantic Ocean	April 7 1956	P. Allen
AMBERJACK	Seriola lalandi	120 lbs. 8 oz.	5' 2"	40"	Kona, Hawaii	Oct. 1955	C. W. McAlpin
BARRACUDA	Sphyraena barracuda						
BASS, Calif. Black Sea (Tie)	Stereolepis gigas	514 lbs.	7' 2"	82"	San Clemente, Calif.	Aug. 29 1955	J. Patterson
		514 lbs.	7' 6"	80"	Box Canyon California	Nov. 15 1961	Joe M. Arve
BASS, Calif. White Sea	Cynoscion nobilis						
BASS, Channel	Sciaenops ocellatus						
BASS, Giant Sea	Promicrops itaiara	389 lbs.	7'	73"	Marathon, Fla.	May 8 1955	R. H. Martin
BASS, Sea	Centropristes striatus						
BASS, Striped	Roccus saxatilis						

FISH	Scientific Name	Weight	Length	Girth	Place	Date	Angler
BLACKFISH or TAUTOG	Tautoga onitis						
BLUEFISH	Pomatomus salatrix						
BONEFISH	Albula vulpes						
BONITO, Oceanic	Katsuwonus pelamis	38 lbs.			Black River, Mauritius	March 15 1961	Frank Masson
COBIA	Rachycentron canadus	102 lbs.	5' 10"	34"	Cape Charles, Va.	July 3 1938	J. E. Stansbury*
COD	Gadus callarias						
DOLPHIN	Coryphaena hippurus	72 lbs. 8 oz.	4' 10½"	35¼"	Honolulu, Hawaii	March 13 1956	G. Perry
DRUM, Black	Pogonias cromis						
FLOUNDER	Paralichthys						
KINGFISH or TANGUIGUE	S. Cavalla C. Commersonii	76 lbs. 8 oz.	5' 3"	31"	Bimini, Bahamas	May 22 1952	R. E. Maytag
MARLIN, Black	Name being revised	1560 lbs.	14' 6"	81"	Cabo Blanco, Peru	August 4 1953	Alfred C. Glassell, Jr.
MARLIN, Blue	Makaira ampla	810 lbs.	13' 1"	68"	Hatteras, N. Carolina	June 11 1962	Gary Stukes
MARLIN, Pacific Blue	Name being revised	1095 lbs.	13' 10"	81"	Kona, Hawaii	May 30 1964	Jack Whaling
MARLIN, Striped	Makaira mitsukurii	465 lbs.	10' 6"	65"	Mayor Island, New Zealand	Feb. 27 1948	James C. Black
MARLIN, White	Makaira albida	152 lbs.	8' 3"	40"	Bimini, Bahamas	March 14 1936	Mrs. M. B. Stevens*
PERMIT	Trachinotus goodei	38 lbs. 8 oz.	3' 4½"	31¼"	Boca Grande, Fla.	Sept. 9 1953	R. H. Martin
POLLACK	Pollachius virens						
RUNNER, Rainbow	Elagatis bipinnulatus	30 lbs. 15 oz.	3' 11"	22"	Kanai, Hawaii	April 27 1963	Holbrook Goodale
ROOSTERFISH	Nematistius pectoralis	100 lbs.	4' 6"	32"	Cabo Blanco, Peru	Jan. 12 1954	Miguel Barrenechea
SAILFISH, Atlantic	Istiophorus americanus	141 lbs. 1 oz.	8'5"		Ivory Coast, Africa	Jan. 26 1961	Tony Burnand
SAILFISH, Pacific	Istiophorus greyi	221 lbs	10' 9"		Santa Cruz Is., Galapagos Is.	Feb. 12 1947	C. W. Stewart
SAWFISH	Pristis pectinatus	736 lbs.	14' 7"		Galveston, Texas	Sept. 4 1938	Mr. G. Pangarakis
SHARK, Blue	Prionace glauca	258 lbs.	10' 1"	39½"	Block Island, R. I.	Aug. 8 1959	Theodore Belling
SHARK, Mako	Isurus oxyrhynchus I. glaucus	1000 lbs.	12'		Mayor Island, New Zealand	March 14 1943	B. D. H. Ross*
SHARK, Man-Eater or White	Carcharodon carcharias	2664 lbs.	16' 10"	9' 6"	Ceduna, S. Australia	April 21 1959	Alfred Dean
SHARK, Porbeagle	Lamna nasus	271 lbs.	8' 2"	49"	Looe, England	Aug. 18 1957	Mrs. Hetty Eathorne
SHARK, Thresher	Alopias vulpinus	922 lbs.			Bay of Islands, New Zealand	March 21 1937	W. W. Wowding*
SHARK, Tiger	Galeocerdo cuvier	1780 lbs.	13' 10½"	103"	Cherry Grove, South Carolina	June 1964	Walter Maxwell
SNOOK or ROBALO	Centropomus undecimalis	50 lbs. 8 oz.	4' 7"		Gatun Spillway, Panama	Jan. 2 1944	J. W. Anderson*
SWORDFISH	Xiphias gladius	1182 lbs.	14' 11¼"	78"	Iquique, Chile	May 7 1953	L. Marron
TARPON	Tarpon atlanticus	247 lbs.	7' 5½"		Panuco River, Mexico	March 24 1938	H. Sedgwick*
TUNA, Allison or Yellowfin	Thunnus albacares	266 lbs. 8 oz.	6' 10½"	49½"	Kona, Hawaii	June 22 1959	Brooks Kelley
TUNA, Atlantic Big-Eyed	Thunnus obesus	295 lbs.	6' 6½"	40"	San Miguel, Azores, Portugal	July 8 1960	Dr. Arsenio Cordeiro

*Line not tested.

FISH	Scientific Name	Weight	Length	Girth	Place	Date	Angler
TUNA, Pacific Big-Eyed	Parathunnus sibi	435 lbs.	7' 9"	63½"	Cabo Blanco, Peru	April 17 1957	Dr. Russel V. A. Lee
TUNA, Blackfin	Thunnus atlanticus	Open for record. G. B. Mercorio record for a 44-lb. 8 oz. catch has been withdrawn from the chart as it was determined not to be a Blackfin Tuna.					
TUNA, Bluefin	Thunnus thynnus	977 lbs.	9' 8"	94½"	St. Ann Bay, Nova Scotia	Sept. 4 1950	D. McI. Hodgson
WAHOO	Acanthocybium solandri	149 lbs.	6' 7¾"	37½"	Cat Cay, Bahamas	June 15 1962	John Pirovano
WEAKFISH	Cynoscion regalis						
WEAKFISH, Spotted	Cynoscion nebulosus						
YELLOWTAIL	Seriola dorsalis or S. grandis	79 lbs.	4' 9"	33½"	Cape Brett, New Zealand	May 7 1960	M. F. Hieatt

International Game Fish Association

RECORD CATCHES FOR BOTH MEN AND WOMEN

80 LB. LINE TEST RECORDS (over 50 lbs., up to and including 80 lbs.))

FISH	Scientific Name	Weight	Length	Girth	Place	Date	Angler
ALBACORE	Thunnus germo	48 lbs. 8 oz.	3' 7"	30"	St. Helena, Atlantic Ocean	April 21 1960	Donald J. Taylor
AMBERJACK	Seriola lalandi	119 lbs. 8 oz.	5' 3½"	46½"	Rio de Janeiro, Brazil	Jan. 13 1952	C. de Mello e Cunha
BARRACUDA	Sphyraena barracuda	103 lbs. 4 oz.	5' 6"	31¼"	West End, Bahamas	Aug. 11 1932	C. E. Benet*
BASS, Calif. Black Sea	Stereolepis gigas	496 lbs.	7' ½"	69"	S. Coronado Is., California	June 1 1960	Robert L. Parsons
BASS, Calif. White Sea	Cynoscion nobilis	53 lbs. 8 oz.	4' 3"	29½"	East End, Catalina Island	June 16 1962	Richard W. Cresswell
BASS, Channel	Sciaenops ocellatus						
BASS, Giant Sea	Promicrops itaiara	680 lbs.	7' 1½"	66"	Fernandina Beach, Fla.	May 20 1961	Lynn Joyner
BASS, Sea	Centropristes striatus						
BASS, Striped	Roccus saxatilis	56 lbs.	4' 5½"	33½"	Sandy Hook, N. J.	June 7 1955	Mrs. H. J. Sarnoski
BLACKFISH or TAUTOG	Tautoga onitis						
BLUEFISH	Pomatomus saltatrix	15 lbs. 8 oz.	2' 10½"	19"	Cape Cod, Mass.	Sept. 29 1957	Mrs. Jean Drury
BONEFISH	Albula vulpes	18 lbs. 2 oz.	3' 5½"	17¹⁵⁄₁₆"	Mana, Kauai, Hawaii	Oct. 14 1954	Wm. Badua
BONITO, Oceanic	Katsuwonus pelamis	38 lbs. 8 oz.	2' 10½"	29"	Waianae, Hawaii	June 13 1964	Sneo Okimoto
COBIA	Rachycentron canadus	97 lbs.	5' 6½"	33"	Oregon Inlet, N. C.	June 4 1952	Mary W. Black
COD	Gadus callarias						
DOLPHIN	Coryphaena hippurus	75 lbs. 8 oz.	4' 2"		Mafia Channel, East Africa	Dec. 10 1950	A. Conan-Doyle
DRUM, Black	Pogonias cromis						

*Line not tested.

FISH	Scientific Name	Weight	Length	Girth	Place	Date	Angler
FLOUNDER	*Paralichthys*						
KINGFISH or TANGUIGUE	S. Cavalla C. Commersonii	81 lbs.	5' 11½"	29¼"	Karachi, Pakistan	Aug. 27 1960	George E. Rusinak
MARLIN, Black	Name being revised	834 lbs.	13'6"	71"	Cabo Blanco Peru	Aug. 19 1954	B. E. Devere
MARLIN, Blue	*Makaira ampla*	814 lbs.	13' 8"	69"	St. Thomas, Virgin Is.	July 26 1964	John Battles
MARLIN, Pacific Blue	Name being revised	652 lbs.	10' 3½"	64"	Bay of Islands, New Zealand	Jan. 30 1965	George Wooller
MARLIN, Striped	*Makaira mitsukurii*	430 lbs.	10' 8½"	54½"	Mayor Island, New Zealand	Apr. 9 1955	Mrs. H. J. Carkeek
MARLIN, White	*Makaira albida*	161 lbs.	8' 8"	33"	Miami Beach, Fla.	March 20 1938	L. F. Hooper
PERMIT	*Trachinotus goodei*	34 lbs. 8 oz.	3' ¼"	28"	Naples, Fla.	Feb. 1 1951	R. R. Channel
POLLACK	*Pollachius virens*						
RUNNER, Rainbow	*Elagatis bipinnulatus*	19 lbs. 10 oz.	3' 3"	21¼"	Kona, Hawaii	Feb. 23 1963	Kid McCoy
ROOSTERFISH	*Nematistius pectoralis*	90 lbs.	4' 11½"	32"	Loreto, California	Dec. 22 1960	Clement Caditz
SAILFISH, Atlantic	*Istiophorus americanus*	106 lbs.			Miami Beach, Fla.	1929	W. Bonnell*
SAILFISH, Pacific	*Istiophorus greyi*	198 lbs.	10' 6"	33"	Mazatian, Mexico	Nov. 10 1954	G. N. Anglen
SAWFISH	*Pristis pectinatus*	890 lbs. 8 oz.	16' 1"	92"	Ft. Amador, Canal Zone	May 26 1960	Jack D. Wagner
SHARK, Blue	*Prionace glauca*	410 lbs.	11' 6"	52"	Rockport, Mass.	Sept. 1 1960	Richard C. Webster
SHARK, Mako	*Isurus oxyrhynchus I. glaucus*	880 lbs.	10' 11"	75¾"	Bimini, Bahamas	Aug. 3 1964	Florence Lotierzo
SHARK, Man-Eater or White	*Carcharodon carcharias*	2344 lbs.	15' 1"	108"	Streaky Bay, Australia	Nov. 6 1960	Alfred Dean
SHARK, Porbeagle	*Lamna nasus*	400 lbs. 8 oz.	7' 9½"	57½"	Fire Island, New York	May 16 1965	James T. Kirkup
SHARK, Thresher	*Alopias vulpinus*	413 lbs.	15'	49½"	Bay of Islands, New Zealand	June 28 1960	Mrs. E. R. Simmons
SHARK, Tiger	*Galeocerdo cuvier*	1305 lbs.	13' 7½"	86½"	Coogee Wide, Sydney, Aust.	May 17 1959	Samuel Jamieson
SNOOK or ROBALO	*Centropomus undecimalis*	37 lbs.	3' 9½"	26"	Lake Worth, Fla.	July 28 1959	James P. Nora
SWORDFISH	*Xiphias gladius*	772 lbs.	12' 10"	70"	Iquique, Chile	June 7 1954	Mrs. L. Marron
TARPON	*Tarpon atlanticus*	214 lbs. 12 oz.	7' 4½"	44"	Lagos, Nigeria	Jan. 26 1953	J. N. Zarpas
TUNA, Allison or Yellowfin	*Thunnus albacares*	265 lbs.	6' 1"	53"	Makua, Hawaii	July 31 1937	J. W. Harvey
TUNA, Atlantic Big-Eyed	*Thunnus obesus*	198 lbs.	5' 7"	51"	St. Helena, Atlantic Ocean	April 13 1960	Donald J. Taylor
TUNA, Pacific Big-Eyed	*Parathunnus sibi*	335 lbs.	7' 1"	59½"	Cabo Blanco, Peru	March 25 1953	Mrs. Wendell Anderson, Jr.
TUNA, Blackfin	*Thunnus atlanticus*	37 lbs.	3' 4"	26½"	Capetown, South Africa	Jan. 27 1957	F. D. Derman
TUNA, Bluefin	*Thunnus thynnus*	880 lbs.	9' 1"	81"	Wedgeport, Nova Scotia	Sept. 14 1941	J. Carpenter*
WAHOO	*Acanthocybium solandri*	139 lbs.	6' 9"	33¾"	Marathon, Fla.	May 18 1960	George Von Hoffman
WEAKFISH	*Cynoscion regalis*	19 lbs. 8 oz.	3' 1"	23¾"	Trinidad, West Indies	April 13 1962	Dennis B. Hall
WEAKFISH, Spotted	*Cynoscion nebulosus*						
YELLOWTAIL	*Seriola dorsalis or S. grandis*	108 lbs.			Cape Brett, New Zealand	Jan. 15 1962	Robin O'Connor

*Line not tested.

International Game Fish Association

RECORD CATCHES FOR BOTH MEN AND WOMEN

50 LB. LINE TEST RECORDS (over 30 lbs., up to and including 50 lbs.)

FISH	Scientific Name	Weight	Length	Girth	Place	Date	Angler
ALBACORE	*Thunnus germo*	69 lbs. 1 oz.	4' ¼"	33¼"	Hudson Canyon, N. J.	Oct. 8 1961	Walter C. Timm
AMBERJACK	*Seriola lalandi*	132 lbs.	5' 3"	39¼"	La Paz, Mexico	July 21 1964	Howard H. Hahn
BARRACUDA	*Sphyraena barracuda*	83 lbs.	6' ¼"	29"	Lagos, Nigeria	Jan. 13 1952	K. J. W. Hackett
BASS, Calif. Black Sea	*Stereolepis gigas*	557 lbs. 3 oz.	7' 4¼"	78"	Catalina Island, Calif.	July 1 1962	Richard M. Lane
BASS, Calif. White Sea	*Cynoscion nobilis*	77 lbs. 4 oz.	5' 1"	33"	San Diego, Calif.	April 8 1950	H. P. Bledsoe
BASS, Channel	*Sciaenops ocellatus*	83 lbs.	4' 4"	29"	Cape Charles, Va.	Aug. 5 1949	Zack Waters, Jr.
BASS, Giant Sea	*Promicrops itaiara*	369 lbs.	6' 5"	65"	Marathon, Fla.	April 25 1956	C. F. Mann
BASS, Sea	*Centropristes striatus*	8 lbs.	1' 10	19"	Nantucket Sound, Mass.	May 13 1951	H. R. Rider
BASS, Striped	*Roccus saxatilis*	73 lbs.	5'	30½"	Vineyard Sound, Mass.	Aug. 17 1913	C. B. Church*
BLACKFISH or TAUTOG	*Tautoga onitis*	20 lbs. 14 oz.	2' 8"	30"	Newport, R. I.	Oct. 20 1955	W. R. Peckham
BLUEFISH	*Pomatomus salatrix*	19 lbs.	3'	21"	Nantucket, Mass.	Sept. 25 1958	S. W. Smith
BONEFISH	*Albula vulpes*	17 lbs. 8 oz.	3' 4"	18"	Oahu, Hawaii	Aug. 23 1952	Jack Yoshida
BONITO, Oceanic	*Katsuwonus pelamis*	39 lbs. 15 oz.	3' 3"	28"	Walker Cay, Bahamas	Jan. 21 1952	F. Drowley
COBIA	*Rachycentron canadus*	99 lbs.	5' 3¾"	32¼"	Chesapeake Bay, Va.	July 24 1948	R. B. Frost, Jr.*
COD	*Gadus callarias*	74 lbs. 4 oz.	5' 6"	43"	Boothbay Harbor, Maine	June 2 1960	James J. Duggan
DOLPHIN	*Coryphaena hippurus*	76 lbs. 12 oz.	5' 10½"	35"	Bimini, Bahamas	May 28 1964	Charles J. Costello
DRUM, Black	*Pogonias cromis*	94 lbs. 4 oz.	4' 3½"	42"	Cape Charles, Virginia	April 28 1957	James Lee Johnson
FLOUNDER	*Paralichthys*	21 lbs. 4 oz.	3' ½"	35"	Maitencillo, Chile	Dec. 8 1959	Daniel Veras Serano
KINGFISH or TANGUIGUE	*S. Cavalla C. Commersonii*	78 lbs.	5' 6½"	28½"	Guaryavilla, Puerto Rico	May 25 1963	Ruth M. Coon
MARLIN, Black	Name being revised	584 lbs. 8 oz.	12' 6"	68"	Pinas Bay, Panama	Jan. 14 1962	Helen Robinson
MARLIN, Blue	*Makaira ampla*	620 lbs.	13' 8"	66"	Atlantic City, New Jersey	Aug. 5 1964	Joseph A. Teti, Jr.
MARLIN, Pacific Blue	Name being revised	234 lbs. 8 oz.	9' 2"	44½"	Kona, Hawaii	Aug. 23 1960	Sally B. Perry
MARLIN, Striped	*Makaira mitsukurii*	402 lbs.	10' 9"	52½"	Tocopilla, Chile	Oct. 13 1940	W. E. S. Tuker*
MARLIN, White	*Makaira albida*	159 lbs. 8 oz.	9'	36"	Pompano Beach, Fla.	April 25 1953	W. E. Johnson
PERMIT	*Trachinotus goodei*	47 lbs. 12 oz.	3' 9"	32"	Boca Grande Pass, Fla.	May 5 1960	Frank G. Burke, Jr.
POLLACK	*Pollachius virens*	43 lbs.	4'	29"	Brielle, New Jersey	Oct. 21 1964	Philip Barlow
RUNNER, Rainbow	*Elagatis bipinnulatus*	23 lbs.	3' 6"	19½"	Oahu, Hawaii	May 9 1961	Lila M. Neuenfelt
ROOSTERFISH	*Nematistius pectoralis*	85 lbs. 2 oz.	4' 6"	36"	La Paz, Mexico	Nov. 24 1956	Mrs. Esther Carle

*Line not tested.

FISH	Scientific Name	Weight	Length	Girth	Place	Date	Angler
SAILFISH, Atlantic	Istiophorus americanus	123 lbs.	10' 4"	32¾"	Walker Cay, Bahamas	April 25 1950	H. Teetor
SAILFISH, Pacific (Tie)	Istiophorus greyi	192 lbs.	10' 5"	40½"	La Paz, Mexico	Sept. 6 1950	Gay Thomas
		192 lbs. 7 oz.	10' 3"	42"	Acapulco, Mexico	Oct. 4 1961	W. W. Rowland
SAWFISH	Pristis pectinatus	721 lbs.	15' 5"	71"	Fort Amador, Canal Zone	Feb. 6 1960	Jack D. Wagner
SHARK, Blue	Prionace glauca	334 lbs.	10' 9"	43"	Montauk, N. Y.	Aug. 27 1958	Julius Duciewicz
SHARK, Mako	Isurus oxyrhynchus I. glaucus	683 lbs. 12 oz.	11' 9"	4' 9"	Montauk, L. I., N. Y.	Aug. 10 1956	R. P. Alex
SHARK, Man-Eater or White	Carcharodon carcharias	1876 lbs.	15' 6"	101½"	Cape Moreton, Australia	Aug. 6 1955	Bob Dyer
SHARK, Porbeagle	Lamna nasus	388 lbs.	8' 5½"	62"	Montauk Point, N. Y.	Oct. 28 1961	John S. Walton
SHARK, Thresher	Alopias vulpinus	338 lbs.	12' 8"		Port Stephens Australia	March 2 1957	G. Partridge
SHARK, Tiger	Galeocerdo cuvier	1018 lbs.	13' 3"	68"	Cape Moreton, Australia	June 12 1957	Bob Dyer
SNOOK or ROBALO	Centropomus undecimalis	49 lbs. 8 oz.			Marco, Fla.	June 13 1926	L. S. Caine*
SWORDFISH	Xiphias gladius	492 lbs. 4 oz.	11' 9"	54"	Montauk, Pt., N. Y.	July 4 1959	Dorothea Cassullo
TARPON	Tarpon atlanticus	242 lbs. 4 oz.	7' 4⅖"	43⅖"	Cienaga Ayapel, Colombia	Jan. 7 1955	A. Salazar
TUNA, Allison or Yellowfin	Thunnus albacares	207 lbs.	6' 3"	48"	Kona, Hawaii	July 20 1960	Roger W. Martin
TUNA, Atlantic Big-Eyed	Thunnus obesus	167 lbs.	6' 3"	47"	Miami Beach, Fla.	Jan. 18 1957	Jerry Mills
TUNA, Pacific Big-Eyed	Parathunnus sibi	60 lbs.	3' 11"	32"	Cabo Blanco, Peru	July 29 1962	David H. Fawcett
TUNA, Blackfin	Thunnus atlanticus	36 lbs.	3' ¼"	28⅞"	Bermuda	July 14 1963	Joseph Baptiste, Jr.
TUNA, Bluefin	Thunnus thynnus	518 lbs.	9' 1"	69"	Bimini, Bahamas	May 13 1950	Mrs. G. A. Bass
WAHOO	Acanthocybium solandri	118 lbs. 8 oz.	6' 5"	33"	Vatulele Is., Fiji	July 12 1964	Noel T. Langham
WEAKFISH	Cynoscion regalis	17 lbs. 8 oz.	3' 10"	19"	Mullica River, N. J.	Sept. 30 1944	A. Weisbecker Jr.*
WEAKFISH, Spotted	Cynoscion nebulosus	15 lbs. 3 oz.	2' 10½"	20½"	Ft. Pierce, Fla.	Jan. 13 1949	C. W. Hubbard
YELLOWTAIL	Seriola dorsalis or S. grandis	111 lbs.	5' 2"	38"	Bay of Islands, New Zealand	June 11 1961	A. F. Plim

*Line not tested.

International Game Fish Association

RECORD CATCHES FOR BOTH MEN AND WOMEN

30 LB. LINE TEST RECORDS (over 20 lbs., up to and including 30 lbs.)

FISH	Scientific Name	Weight	Length	Girth	Place	Date	Angler
ALBACORE	Thunnus germo	66 lbs. 4 oz.			Catalina, Calif.	1912	F. Kelly*
AMBERJACK	Seriola lalandi	112 lbs. 8 oz.	5' 7"	40"	Palm Beach, Fla.	Feb. 29 1960	Syl Di Stasio

*Line not tested.

FISH	Scientific Name	Weight	Length	Girth	Place	Date	Angler
BARRACUDA	*Sphyraena barracuda*	44 lbs. 12 oz.	5′ 3″	22¼″	Lagos, Nigeria	Jan. 18 1951	J. N. Zarpas
BASS, Calif. Black Sea	*Stereolepis gigas*	388 lbs. 8 oz.	6′ 6″	72″	Catalina Island, Calif.	Sept. 29 1962	John W. Scott, Jr.
BASS, Calif. White Sea	*Cynoscion nobilis*	83 lbs. 12 oz.	5′ 5½″	34″	San Felipe, Mexico	March 31 1953	L. C. Baumgardner
BASS, Channel	*Sciaenops ocellatus*	69 lbs. 8 oz.	4′ 3½″	33¼″	Cape Hatteras, N. C.	Nov. 16 1958	Jean Browning
BASS, Giant Sea	*Promicrops itaiara*	277 lbs.	6′	66″	Perlas Islands, Panama	March 1 1957	Edward W. Gorham
BASS, Sea (Tie)	*Centropristes striatus*	3 lbs. 9 oz.	1′ 7½″ 1′ 7¼″	13¾″ 12″	Panama City Beach, Fla. Cape Canaveral, Fla.	June 10, 1954 July 5, 1958	R. H. Martin J. B. Johnson, Jr.
BASS, Striped	*Roccus saxatilis*	64 lbs. 8 oz.	4′ 6″	30″	North Truro, Mass.	Aug. 14 1960	Rosa O. Webb
BLACKFISH or TAUTOG	*Tautoga onitis*	21 lbs. 6 oz.	2′ 7½″	23½″	Cape May, N. J.	June 12 1954	R. N. Sheafer
BLUEFISH	*Pomatomus saltatrix*	21 lbs.			Woods Hole, Mass.	Oct. 22 1957	Roland W. Scannell
BONEFISH	*Albula vulpes*	19 lbs.	3′ 3⅝″	17″	Zululand South Africa	May 26 1962	Brian W. Batchelor
BONITO, Oceanic	*Katsuwonus pelamis*	32 lbs. 4 oz.	2′ 11″	25″	San Juan, Puerto Rico	Aug. 13 1961	Antonio Montalvo-Nazario
COBIA	*Rachycentron canadus*	100 lbs.	5′ 11½″	36″	Point Lookout, Queensland	Oct. 4 1962	Peter R. Bristow
COD	*Gadus callarias*	40 lbs. 12 oz.	3′ 9½″	28½″	Ambrose Light, N. J.	March 12 1960	Martin C. Haines
DOLPHIN	*Coryphaenna hippurus*	73 lbs. 11 oz.	4′ 11½″	43½″	Baja Calif., Mexico	July 12 1962	Barbara Kibbee Jayne
DRUM, Black	*Pogonias cromis*	92 lbs.	4′ 3½″		Cambridge, Maryland	Aug. 27 1955	James Aaron
FLOUNDER	*Paralichthys*	20 lbs. 2 oz.	2′ 10″	29¾″	Montauk, L. I. N. Y.	Sept. 20 1958	G. F. Schwinzer
KINGFISH or TANGUIGUE	S. Cavalla C. Commersonii	71 lbs. 8 oz.	5′ 2½″	30″	West End, Bahamas	March 14 1962	George E. Mole
MARLIN, Black	Name being revised	552 lbs.	12′ 3″	62″	La Plata Is., Ecuador	July 3 1953	Mrs. W. G. Krieger
MARLIN, Blue	*Makaira ampla*	480 lbs.	11′ 11″	54″	Bimini, Bahamas	July 23 1949	G. A. Lyon, Sr.
MARLIN, Pacific Blue	Name being revised	185 lbs.	9′ 6″	43″	Baja Calif., Mexico	June 15 1963	Mrs. Robert Brookes
MARLIN, Striped	*Makaira mitsukurii*	425 lbs.	11′ 7″	51½″	Tocopilla, Chile	May 8 1941	S. K. Farrington, Jr.*
MARLIN, White	*Makaira albida*	130 lbs. 4 oz.	8′ 3″	33″	Bimini, Bahamas	April 18 1959	Leonard Hendrix
PERMIT	*Trachinotus goodei*	41 lbs. 2 oz.	3′ 8″	31¼″	Key West, Fla.	April 11 1963	Webster Robinson
POLLACK	*Pollachius virens*	36 lbs.	3′ 10½″	26″	Montauk, N. Y.	May 28 1957	William E. Davis
RUNNER, Rainbow	*Elagatis bipinnulatus*	24 lbs. 4 oz.	3′ 8″	21″	Bermuda	June 20 1963	John Corrado
ROOSTERFISH	*Nematistius pectoralis*	114 lbs.	5′ 4″	33″	La Paz, Mexico	June 1 1960	Abe Sackheim
SAILFISH, Atlantic	*Istiophorus americanus*	97 lbs.	8′ 1″	32″	Puerto Cabello, Venezuela	Feb. 13 1960	Antonio J. Osorio
SAILFISH, Pacific	*Istiophorus greyi*	198 lbs.	11′ 2″	41″	La Paz, Mexico	Aug. 23 1957	Charles Kelly
SAWFISH	*Pristis pectinatus*	664 lbs.	14′ 1½″	61½″	Panama Bay, Panama	Feb. 2 1961	Jack D. Wagner
SHARK, Blue	*Prionace glauca*	350 lbs.	11′ 5″	43″	Sydney Heads, Australia	Oct. 29 1961	John C. Kellion
SHARK, Mako	*Isurus oxyrhynchus I. glaucus*	322 lbs.	9′ 1″	42″	Elberon, N. J.	Aug. 25 1952	W. J. Mahan
SHARK, Man-Eater or White	*Carcharodon carcharias*	1053 lbs.	12′ 8″	68″	Cape Moreton, Australia	June 13 1957	Bob Dyer

*Line not tested.

FISH	Scientific Name	Weight	Length	Girth	Place	Date	Angler
SHARK, Porbeagle	Lamna nasus	191 lbs.	6' 4"	42"	Montauk, N. Y.	May 28 1964	Carl Monaco
SHARK, Thresher	Alopias vulpinus	145 lbs.	10'	40"	Simonstown, S. Africa	April 6 1953	R. C. Wack
SHARK, Tiger	Galeocerdo cuvier	362 lbs.	11' 2"	52½"	Cape Moreton, Australia	July 6 1957	Bob Dyer
SNOOK or ROBALO	Centropomus undecimalis	52 lbs. 6 oz.	4' 1½"	26"	La Paz, Mexico	Jan. 9 1963	Jane Haywood
SWORDFISH	Xiphias gladius	365 lbs.			Catalina, Calif.	1928	J. W. Jump*
TARPON	Tarpon atlanticus	283 lbs.	7' 2⅗"		Lake Maracaibo, Venezuela	March 19 1956	M. Salazar
TUNA, Allison or Yellowfin	Thunnus albacares	185 lbs.	6' 3"	47"	Ft. Lauderdale Fla.	Nov. 29 1957	Frank R. King
TUNA, Atlantic Big-Eyed	Thunnus obesus						
TUNA, Pacific Big-Eyed	Parathunnus sibi	74 lbs.	4' 6"	36"	Ensenada, Baja California	Aug. 11 1968	Edward Weitz
TUNA, Blackfin	Thunnus atlanticus	32 lbs. 6 oz.	3' 1⅛"	26⅔"	Bermuda	July 11 1963	Kenneth C. Smith
TUNA, Bluefin	Thunnus thynnus	172 lbs.	5' 5"	45"	Cape Pillar, Tasmania	May 8 1959	C. I. Cutler
WAHOO	Acanthocybium solandri	107 lbs. 4 oz.	6' ½"	33"	Bahamas	Apr. 4 1965	Mrs. S. F. Briggs
WEAKFISH	Cynoscion regalis	10 lbs. 10 oz.	3'		Fire Is. Light, N. Y.	Sept. 20 1951	J. E. Bailey
WEAKFISH, Spotted	Cynoscion nebulosus	14 lbs.	2' 9½"	18"	Lake Worth, Fla.	Feb. 9 1946	R. N. Rose*
YELLOWTAIL	Seriola dorsalis or S. grandis	88 lbs.	4' 7"	33"	Cape Brett, New Zealand	June 25 1963	J. R. Chibrall

*Line not tested.

International Game Fish Association

RECORD CATCHES FOR BOTH MEN AND WOMEN

20 LB. LINE TEST RECORDS (over 12 lbs., up to and including 20 lbs.)

FISH	Scientific Name	Weight	Length	Girth	Place	Date	Angler
ALBACORE	Thunnus germo	55 lbs. 8 oz.			Catalina, Calif.	1927	W. C. De Mille*
AMBERJACK	Seriola lalandi	101 lbs. 8 oz.	5' 1"	39"	Palm Beach, Florida	Feb. 26 1964	Robert R. Boomhower
BARRACUDA	Sphyraena barracuda	60 lbs. 10 oz.	5' 4½"	26½"	Cairns, Australia	Nov. 5 1968	Desmond R. Schumann
BASS, Calif. Black Sea	Stereolepis gigas	425 lbs.	7' 1"	76"	Point Mugu, California	Oct. 1 1960	C. C. Joiner
BASS, Calif. White Sea	Cynoscion nobilis	72 lbs.	4' 11¾"	30½"	Catalina, Calif.	Aug. 13 1958	Dr. Charles Dorshkind
BASS, Channel	Sciaenops ocellatus	42 lbs.	4' 4"	30½"	Cape Hatteras, N. C.	Nov. 3 1958	John Twachtman
BASS, Giant Sea	Promicrops itaiara	200 lbs. 9 oz.	6' 2¾"	4' 8¼"	Key West, Fla.	June 19 1960	James A. Sumpter
BASS, Sea	Centropristes striatus	6 lbs. 1 oz.	2' ⅛"	17"	Seabright, N. J.	July 13 1958	William Young
BASS, Striped	Roccus saxatilis	67 lbs.	4' 7"	29½"	Block Island, R. I.	May 31 1963	Jack Ryan

*Line not tested.

FISH	Scientific Name	Weight	Length	Girth	Place	Date	Angler
BLACKFISH or TAUTOG	Tautoga onitis	21 lbs.	2' 6"		Jamestown Island, R. I.	Nov. 6 1954	C. W. Sundquist
BLUEFISH	Pomatomus saltatrix	18 lbs. 10 oz.	3' 1¼"	20"	Barnegat Light, N. J.	May 30 1960	Edward E. Schlitz
BONEFISH	Albula vulpes	14 lbs. 13 lbs. 12 oz.	2' 10¼" 2' 6¾"	17½" 17½"	Bermuda Exuma, Bahamas	Dec. 29, 1950 Jan. 3, 1956	Dr. H. R. Becker Mrs. B. A. Garson
BONITO, Oceanic	Katsuwonus pelamis	32 lbs. 8 oz.	3' 0"	26"	San Juan, P. R.	May 23 1959	Juan Casellas, Jr.
COBIA	Rachycentron canadus	91 lbs.	4' 8"	30"	Crystal Beach, Fla.	April 25 1962	Roy English
COD	Gadus callarias	56 lbs.	4' 7"	32"	Stellwagon Banks, Mass.	Aug. 29 1961	James E. Griffin
DOLPHIN	Coryphaena hippurus	57 lbs.	5' 7"	32"	Acapulco, Mexico	Mar. 16 1963	Gregory E. Flynn
DRUM, Black	Pogon as cromis	70 lbs.	4' 7"	37"	Great Egg Harbor, N. J.	Aug. 23 1952	P. Bessor
FLOUNDER	Paralichthys	20 lbs.	3' 1"	32"	Long Island N. Y.	Sept. 7 1948	F. H. Kessel
KINGFISH or TANGUIGUE	S. Cavalla C. Commersonii	77 lbs.	5' 5"	29"	Bimini, Bahamas	May 12 1957	Clinton Olney Potts
MARLIN, Black	Name being revised	290 lbs.	9' 2"	50"	Pinas Bay Reef, Panama	May 6 1962	Frank J. Violette
MARLIN, Blue	Makaira ampla	401 lbs.	8' 4"	38"	Bimini, Bahamas	June 9 1959	P. J. Serrales, Jr.
MARLIN, Pacific Blue	Name being revised						
MARLIN, Striped	Makaira mitsukurii	338 lbs.	10' 5"	47½"	Sydney, Australia	Oct. 20 1968	H. John McIntyre
MARLIN, White	Makaira albida	129 lbs. 4 oz.	8' 7"	33½"	Bimini, Bahamas	April 11 1963	Mrs. J. W. Walters
PERMIT	Trachinotus goodei	41 lbs.	3' 4½"	33"	Islamorada, Fla.	April 18 1951	E. J. Arnold
POLLACK	Pollachius virens	27 lbs.	3' 2½"	23½"	Blanche, N. S.	Aug. 25 1954	Cecil Griffith
RUNNER, Rainbow	Elagatis bipinnulatus	25 lbs.	4'	23"	Pinas Bay, Panama	May 9 1965	Donald J. S. Merten
ROOSTERFISH	Nematistius pectoralis	78 lbs. 8 oz.	4' 11"	31"	La Paz, Maxico	Nov. 10 1961	Harrison Reno
SAILFISH, Atlantic	Istiophorus americanus	108 lbs. 8 oz.	8'	34"	Miami, Florida	Apr. 17 1969	James L. Clayman
SAILFISH, Pacific	Istiophorus greyi	158 lbs.	9' 1"	35½"	Santa Cruz Island, Galapagos	Mar. 4 1954	A. Hall
SAWFISH	Pristis pectinatus	134 lbs.	8' 10"	32"	Long Key, Fla.	Mar. 27 1963	Olive M. Senn
SHARK, Blue	Prionace glauca	293 lbs.	10' 6½"	44"	Montauk, New York	July 21 1963	Lucette Rinfret
SHARK, Mako	Isurus oxyrhynchus I. glaucus	316 lbs.	8' 2½"	48½"	Bimini, Bahamas	May 25 1961	Dorothea L. Dean
SHARK, Man-Eater or White	Carcharodon carcharias	1068 lbs.	12' 6"	77"	Cape Moreton, Australia	June 18 1957	Bob Dyer
SHARK, Porbeagle	Lamna nasus	180 lbs.	8' 7½"	37"	Block Island, R. I.	Aug. 9 1960	Frank K. Smith
SHARK, Thresher	Alopias vulpinus	81 lbs. 8 oz.	6' 7"	30"	Santa Cruz, Calif.	Aug. 2 1958	E. G. Volpe
SHARK, Tiger	Galeocerdo cuvier	341 lbs.	10'	55½"	Cape Moreton, Australia	July 6 1957	Bob Dyer
SNOOK or ROBALO (Tie)	Centropomus undecimalis	36 lbs. 14 oz. 37 lbs.	3' 7"	25"	St. Lucie Inet, Fla. Palm Beach Fla.	July 2, 1939 Apr. 28, 1958	G. Van Wickle* J. J. McDonald
SWORDFISH	Xiphias gladius	180 lbs.	9' 9¾"	40½"	Punta Gorda Baja California	Mar. 20 1969	Stephen Zuckerman
TARPON	Tarpon atlanticus	158 lbs. 8 oz.	6' 8½"	39¼"	New Orleans, La.	Aug. 23 1958	J. J. Lincoln
TUNA, Allison or Yellowfin	Thunnus albacares	145 lbs.	5' 3"	3' 7"	Sydney, Australia	Apr. 4 1959	Bob Dyer

*Line not tested

FISH	Scientific Name	Weight	Length	Girth	Place	Date	Angler
TUNA, Atlantic Big-Eyed	Thunnus obesus	46 lbs.	3' 7"	31"	N. Key Largo, Fla.	Jan. 17 1959	Dorothea Dean
TUNA, Pacific Big-Eyed	Parathunnus sibi	31 lbs.	3' 3"	25"	Cabo Blanco, Peru	May 24 1965	Donald J. S. Merten
TUNA, Blackfin	Thunnus atlanticus	32 lbs. 2 oz.	3' 2"	26¾"	Bermuda	Oct. 23 1968	Mrs. Herbert N. Arnold
TUNA, Bluefin	Thunnus thynnus	114 lbs. 8 oz.	5' 1"	42"	Montauk, New York	July 25 1959	Mundy I. Peale
WAHOO	Acanthocybium solandri	115 lbs.	6' 3½"	32"	Bermuda	July 2 1961	Leo Barboza
WEAKFISH	Cynoscion regalis	8 lbs. 12 oz.	2' 6½"	16"	Ocean City, Md.	June 2 1951	P. V. Mumford
WEAKFISH, Spotted	Cyoscion nebulosus	13 lbs. 12 oz.	3'	19"	Vero Beach, Fla.	Mar. 11 1957	W. Miller Shaw, Jr.
YELLOWTAIL	Seriola dorsalis or Sr. grandis	68 lbs. 5 oz.	4' 6"	30½"	Auckland, New Zealand	Jan. 31 1964	Langman Jos. Henley

International Game Fish Association

RECORD CATCHES FOR BOTH MEN AND WOMEN

12 LB. LINE TEST RECORDS (up to and including 12 lbs.)

FISH	Scientific Name	Weight	Length	Girth	Place	Date	Angler
ALBACORE	Thunnus germo	39 lbs. 8 oz.	3' 7½"	32½"	Balboa, Calif.	July 23 1958	Dr. R. S. Rubaum
AMBERJACK	Seriola lalandi	78 lbs. 4 oz.	5' ¼"	34½"	Key Largo, Florida	Mar. 23 1969	Pamela J. Habicht
BARRACUDA	Sphyraena barracuda	49 lbs. 4 oz	4' 8"	21½"	Margarita, Venezuela	Jan. 9 1960	Gerardo Sanson
BASS, Calif. Black Sea	Stereolepis gigas	112 lbs. 8 oz.	4' 9"	44"	San Francisco Is., Mexico	June 12 1957	D. B. Rosenthal
BASS, Calif. White Sea	Cynoscion nobilis	65 lbs.	4' 10"	28"	Ensenada, Mexico	July 8 1955	C. J. Aronis
BASS, Channel	Sciaenops ocellatus	60 lbs. 8 oz.	4' 2¾"	29¾"	Kill Devil Hills, N. C.	Oct. 24 1954	A. Clark Jr.
BASS, Giant Sea	Promicrops itaiara	242 lbs. 4 oz.	6' 1"	53"	Florida Bay, Miami, Fla.	Mar. 30 1969	Norman Jansik
BASS, Sea	Centropristes striatus	3 lbs. 8 oz.	1' 6½"	13¼"	Panama City Beach, Fla.	Aug. 4 1960	Roy H. Martin
BASS, Striped	Roccus saxatilis	61 lbs. 10 oz.	4' 5"	30"	Block Island, R. I.	July 5 1956	L. A. Garceau
BLACKFISH or TAUTOG	Tautoga onitis	12 lbs.	2' 1½"	20½"	Block Island, R. I.	Oct. 18 1952	D. V. Marshall
BLUEFISH	Pomatomus saltatrix	24 lbs. 3 oz.	3' 5"	22"	San Miguel, Azores	Aug. 27 1953	M. A. da Silva Veloso
BONEFISH (5-Way Tie)	Albula vulpes	15 lbs.	2' 10¼"	18¾"	Islamorada, Fla.	Feb. 28, 1961	Nat Carlin
		15 lbs.	2' 8½"	18½"	Bimini, Bahamas	Mar. 20, 1961	Andrea Tose
		15 lbs.	2' 8"	23"	Bimini, Bahamas	Feb. 7, 1953	Sam Snead
		14 lbs. 12 oz.	2' 8¾"	22½"		Apr. 14, 1954	H. Braman, Jr.
		15 lbs.	2' 7½"	19"	Biscayne Bay, Florida	Apr. 8 1969	William W. Travis
BONITO, Oceanic	Katsuwonus pelamis	24 lbs. 6 oz.	2' 6½"	21"	Walker Cay, Bahamas	Mar. 26 1965	Patricia E. Church

FISH	Scientific Name	Weight	Length	Girth	Place	Date	Angler
COBIA	Rachycentron canadus	70 lbs.	5'	31½"	Gulf of Mexico, Texas	May 13 1955	H. A. Norris, Jr.
COD	Gadus callarias	55 lbs.	5' 6"	38"	Plum Island, Mass.	July 6 1958	W. C. Dunn
DOLPHIN (Tie)	Coryphaena hippurus	53 lbs. 4 oz.	5' 2"	29½"	Acapulco, Mexico	Dec. 18, 1958	Albert H. Allen
		52 lbs. 13 oz.	5' 5"	29½"	La Paz, Mexico	May 31, 1956	Mrs. W. G. Kreiger
DRUM, Black	Pogonias cromis	68 lbs.	4'	36"	Canova Beach, Fla.	March 28 1958	G. Miller
FLOUNDER	Paralichthys	16 lbs.	2' 10¾"	17¼"	Beavertail, R. I.	Aug. 14 1958	C. Martorelli
KINGFISH or TANGUIGUE	S. Cavalla C. Commersonii	52 lbs. 4 oz.	5' 2"	29½"	Hayman Islands, Australia	July 27 1968	Clive H. Michael
MARLIN, Black	Name being revised	186 lbs. 8 oz.	8' 9"	42¾"	Pinas Bay, Panama	Jan. 19 1963	Ray Smith
MARLIN, Blue	Makaira ampla	224 lbs. 8 oz.	9' 2½"	42"	Bimini, Bahamas	April 16 1960	Harry W. Barton
MARLIN, Pacific Blue	Name being revised						
MARLIN, Striped	Makaira mitsukurii	250 lbs.	10' 1"	46"	Palmilla, Baja Calif.	Apr. 16 1965	R. M. Anderson
MARLIN, White	Makaira albida	122 lbs.	8' 3"	44"	Bimini, Bahamas	Mar. 30 1953	Dorothy A. Curtice
PERMIT	Trachinotus goodei	50 lbs.	3' 7"	34½"	Miami, Florida	Mar. 27 1965	Robert F. Miller
POLLACK	Pollachius virens	29 lbs. 12 oz.	3' 7"	24½"	Montauk, New York	May 10 1962	Donald F. Leydon
RUNNER, Rainbow	Elagatis bipinnulatus	18 lbs. 12 oz.	3' 2⅞"	20½"	Las Cruces, Baja California	May 31 1961	Bing Crosby
ROOSTERFISH	Nematistius pectoralis	50 lbs. 11 oz.	4' 8"	32"	Guerro, Mexico	Jan. 15 1961	Joseph Krieger, Jr.
SAILFISH, Atlantic	Istiophorus americanus	85 lbs.	7' ½"	31"	Carayaca, Venezuela	July 15 1962	Guillermo Yanes Pares
SAILFISH, Pacific	Istiophorus greyi	159 lbs.	9' 11"	36"	Pinas Bay, Panama	July 23 1957	J. Frank Baxter
SAWFISH	Pristis pectinatus	102 lbs. 12 oz.	8' 6"	29"	Grassy Key, Florida	June 23 1961	Marjorie M. McClellan
SHARK, Blue	Prionace glauca	181 lbs.	8' 4"	41"	Montauk Point, New York	Sept. 30 1962	John S. Walton
SHARK, Mako	Isurus oxyrhynchus I. glaucus	261 lbs. 11 oz.	7' 4"	44½"	Montauk, N. Y.	Oct. 1 1953	C. R. Meyer
SHARK, Man-Eater or White	Carcharodon carcharias	96 lbs. 10 oz.	5' 7"	27½"	Mazatlan, Mexico	April 30 1964	Ray O. Acord
SHARK, Porbeagle	Lamna nasus	66 lbs.	4' 10"	30"	Montauk, N. Y.	June 8 1958	M. H. Merrill
SHARK, Thresher	Alopias vulpinus	92 lbs. 8 oz.	4' 9"	31"	Long Beach, Calif.	Dec. 12 1959	D. F. Marsh
SHARK, Tiger	Galeocerdo cuvier						
SNOOK or ROBALO	Centropomus undecimalis	37 lbs.	3' 11"	24½"	Boynton Beach, Fla.	June 18 1959	Durling Drake
SWORDFISH	Xiphias gladius						
TARPON	Tarpon atlanticus	170 lbs. 8 oz.	7'	40"	Big Pine Key, Fla.	Mar. 10 1963	Russell C. Ball
TUNA, Allison or Yellowfin	Thunnus albacares	94 lbs. 8 oz.	4' 7¼"	36¼"	The Peak, NSW Australia	May 2 1965	Phillip W. Bensted
TUNA, Atlantic Big-Eyed	Thunnus obesus						
TUNA, Pacific Big-Eyed	Parathunnus sibi	13 lbs. 8 oz.	2' 6½"	18⅞"	Cabo Blanco, Peru	Apr. 23 1963	Stanley W. Good, Jr.
TUNA, Blackfin	Thunnus atlanticus	19 lbs. 6 oz.	2' 8"	21¾"	South Shore, Bermuda	May 17 1956	Frank C. Gamble
TUNA, Bluefin	Thunnus thynnus	56 lbs.	3' 11½"	32"	S. Neptune Is., Australia	Apr. 12 1965	Eldred H. V. Riggs
WAHOO	Acanthocybium solandri	66 lbs.	5' 8"	25"	St. Thomas, Virgin Islands	Feb. 27 1969	Gloria J. Applegate

FISH	Scientific Name	Weight	Length	Girth	Place	Date	Angler
WEAKFISH	Cynoscion regalis	9 lbs. 2 oz.	2′ 11½″	17″	Tuckerton, New Jersey	May 15 1963	Melvin Parker
WEAKFISH, Spotted (Tie)	Cynoscion nebulosus	13 lbs. 13 lbs. 4 oz.	2′ 10½″ 2′ 9″	18″ 18½″	Jupiter, Fla. Cocoa, Fla.	July 19, 1956 Mar. 13, 1957	L. B. Dukes R. L. Fink
YELLOWTAIL	Seriola dorsalis or S. grandis	50 lbs. 4 oz.	4′ 7″	27½″	Bay of Islands, New Zealand	Mar. 24 1969	R. E. E. Blomfield

International Game Fish Association

MARINE FISHES

ALL TACKLE RECORDS FOR WOMEN

International Game Fish Association, world record entry forms may be
obtained by writing: I.G.F.A., 2190 S.E. 17th St., Ft. Lauderdale, Fla., 33316.

FISH	Scientific Name	Weight	Length	Girth	Place	Date	Angler	Line lbs.
ALBACORE	Thunnus germo	55 lbs. 4 oz.			Catalina, Calif.	Sept. 1927	Mrs. L. M. Doxie*	30
AMBERJACK	Seriola lalandi	106 lbs. 8 oz.	5′ 5″	39″	Pinas Bay Panama	July 9 1960	Helen Robinson	80
BARRACUDA	Sphyraena barracuda	66 lbs. 4 oz.	5′ 10″	25-1/5″	Cape Lopez, Gabon, Africa	July 17 1955	Mme. M. Halley	80
BASS, Calif. Black Sea	Stereolepis gigas	452 lbs.	7′ 2¼″	64¼″	Coronado Is., California	Oct. 8 1960	Lorene Wheeler	80
BASS, Calif. White Sea	Cynoscion nobilis	62 lbs.	4′ 9″	28″	Malibu, Calif.	Dec. 6 1951	Mrs. D. W. Jackson	20
BASS, Channel	Sciaenops ocellatus	69 lbs. 8 oz. (30-lb. record for men & women)	4′ 3½″	33¼″	Cape Hatteras, N. C.	Nov. 16 1958	Jean Browning	30
BASS, Giant Sea	Promicrops itaiara	204 lbs.	5′ 11″	51″	Bahia Honda, Fla.	Mar. 1 1958	Mrs. Phyllis Carson	80
BASS, Sea	Centropristes striatus	5 lbs. 1 oz.	1′ 8½″	16″	Panama City Beach, Fla.	July 21 1956	Mrs. R. H. Martin	50
BASS, Striped	Roccus saxatilis	64 lbs. 8 oz. (30-lb. record for men & women)	4′ 6″	30″	North Truo, Mass.	Aug. 14 1960	Rosa O. Webb	30
BLACKFISH or TAUTOG	Tautoga onitis	16 lbs. 8 oz.	2′ 6″	22″	Seventeen Fathoms, N. Y.	Nov. 1 1953	Edna De Fina	50
BLUEFISH	Pomatomus saltatrix	19 lbs. 4 oz.			Long Island Sound, N. Y.	Oct. 19 1958	Elanor Plasko	30
BONEFISH	Albula vulpes	15 lbs.	2′ 8½″	18½″	Bimini, Bahamas	Mar. 20 1961	Andrea Tose	12
BONITO, Oceanic (Tie)	Katsuwonus pelamis	31 lbs. 31 lbs. 31 lbs.	2′ 11″ 2′ 10½″ 2′ 11″	24″ 24½″ 24¾″	Kona, Hawaii San Juan, P. Rico Nassau, Bahamas	June 16, 1963 Dec. 26, 1954 Jan. 25, 1956	Anne H. Bosworth Gloria G. de Marques Mrs. Barbara Wallach	130 50 80
COBIA	Rachycentron canadus	97 lbs. (80-lb. record for men & women)	5′ 6½″	33″	Oregon Inlet, N. C.	June 4 1952	Mary W. Black	80
COD	Gadus callarias	71 lbs. 8 oz. (20-lb. record for men & women)	4′ 10″	31″	Cape Cod, Massachusetts	Aug. 2 1964	Muriel Betts	20
DOLPHIN	Coryphaena hippurus	73 lbs. 11 oz. (30-lb. record for men & women)	4′ 11½″	43½″	Baja Calif., Mexico	July 12 1962	Barbara Kibbee Jayne	30
DRUM, Black	Pogonias cromis	93 lbs.	4′ 2½″	42″	Fernandina Beach, Fla.	Mar. 28 1957	Mrs. Stella Moore	50
FLOUNDER	Paralichthys	20 lbs. 7 oz.	3′ 1″	29½″	Long Island, N. Y.	July 8 1957	Mrs. M. Fredriksen	50

*Line not tested.

FISH	Scientific Name	Weight	Length	Girth	Place	Date	Angler	Line lbs.
KINGFISH or TANGUIGUE	C. Commersonii S. Cavalla	78 lbs. (50-lb. record for men & women)	5' 6½"	28½"	Guayanilla, Puerto Rico	May 25 1963	Ruth M. Coon	50
MARLIN, Black	Name being revised	1,525 lbs.	14' 4"	80"	Cabo Blanco, Peru	Apr. 22 1954	Kimberley Wiss	130
MARLIN, Blue	Makaira ampla	730 lbs.		60¾"	Cat Cay, Bahamas	June 6 1939	Mrs. Henry Sears*	80
MARLIN, Pacific Blue	Name being revised	583 lbs. 8 oz.	12' 3"	60"	Kailua Kona, Hawaii	Jan. 26 1969	Sally H. Rice	130
MARLIN, Striped	Makaira mitsukurii	430 lbs.	10' 8½"	54½"	Mayor Island, New Zealand	Apr. 9 1955	Mrs. H. J. Carkeek	80
MARLIN, White	Makaira albida	152 lbs. (130-lb. record for men & women)	8' 3"	40"	Bimini, Bahamas	Mar. 14 1936	Mrs. Marion Stevens*	130
PERMIT (Tie)	Trachinotus goodei	38 lbs. / 38 lbs. / 38 lbs.	3' 7" / 3' 7" / 3' 4"	31" / 33" / 30½"	Key West, Fla. / Islamorada, Fla. / Islamorada, Fla.	Apr. 9, 1963 / June 11, 1961 / Mar. 21, 1954	Helen Robinson / L. Meulenberg / Mrs. W. Edmunds	30 / 20 / 20
POLLACK	Pollachius virens	29 lbs.	3' 6"	24¼"	Manasquan, N. J.	Nov. 3 1958	Ann Durik	50
RUNNER, Rainbow	Elagatis bipinnulatus	23 lbs. (50-lb. record for men & women)	3' 6"	19½"	Oahu, Hawaii	May 9 1961	Lila M. Neuenfelt	50
ROOSTERFISH	Nematistius pectoralis	85 lbs. 2 oz. (50-lb. record for men & women)	4' 6"	36"	La Paz, Mexico	Nov. 24 1956	Mrs. Esther Carle	50
SAILFISH, Atlantic	Istiophorus americanus	104 lbs. 8 oz.	7' 11"	31"	Miami Beach, Fla.	Mar. 22 1939	Ruth Edmands Pope*	80
SAILFISH, Pacific	Istiophorus greyi	196 lbs.	10' 7"	40"	Acapulco, Mexico	Feb. 9 1951	Mrs. F. Bart	80
SAWFISH	Pristis pectinatus	134 lbs. (120-lb. record for men & women)	8' 10"	32"	Long Key Florida	Mar. 27 1963	Olive M. Senn	20
SHARK, Blue	Prionace glauca	334 lbs. (130-lb. record for men & women)	10' 8"	47½"	Rockport, Massachusetts	Sept. 4 1964	Cassandra Webster	130
SHARK, Mako	Isurus oxyrhynchus I. glaucus	911 lbs. 12 oz.	11' 2"	70"	Palm Beaches, Florida	April 9 1962	Audrey Cohen	130
SHARK, Man-Eater or White	Carcharodon carcharias	1,052 lbs.	13' 10"	72½"	Cape Moreton, Australia	June 27 1954	Mrs. Bob Dyer	130
SHARK, Porbeagle	Lamna nasus	271 lbs. (130-lb. record for men & women)	8' 2"	49"	Looe, Cornwall, England	Aug. 18 1957	Mrs. Hetty Eathorne	130
SHARK, Thresher	Alopias vulpinus	729 lbs.	8' 5"	61"	Mayor Is., New Zealand	June 3 1959	Mrs. V. Brown	130
SHARK, Tiger	Galeocerdo cuvier	1,314 lbs.	13' 9"	89"	Cape Moreton, Australia	July 27 1953	Mrs. Bob Dyer	130
SNOOK or ROBALO	Centropomus undecimalis	52 lbs. 6 oz. (30-lb. record for men & women)	4' 1½"	26"	La Paz, Mexico	Jan. 9 1963	Jane Haywood	30
SWORDFISH	Xiphias gladius	772 lbs. (80-lb. record for men & women)	12' 10"	70"	Iquique, Chile	June 7 1954	Mrs. L. Marron	80
TARPON	Tarpon atlanticus	203 lbs.	7' 11"	44"	Marathon Florida	May 19 1961	June Jordan	80
TUNA, Allison or Yellowfin	Thunnus albacares	254 lbs.	6' 3"	52"	Kona, Hawaii	Aug. 19 1954	Jane Carlisle	130
TUNA, Atlantic Big-Eyed	Thunnus obesus	182 lbs.	5' 8"	56"	Cat Cay, Bahamas	June 2 1958	Mrs. Pablo Bardin	130
TUNA, Pacific Big-Eyed	Parathunnus sibi	336 lbs.	7' 3"	56½"	Cabo Blanco, Peru	Jan. 16 1957	Mrs. Seymour Knox III	130
TUNA, Blackfin	Thunnus atlanticus	32 lbs. 2 oz. (20-lb. record for men & women)	3' 2"	26¾"	Bermuda	Oct. 23 1968	Mrs. Herbert N. Arnold	20
TUNA, Bluefin	Thunnus thynnus	882 lbs.	9' 2"	83½"	Wedgeport, N. S.	Sept. 6 1947	Mrs. A. D. Crowninnshield*	130
WAHOO (Tie)	Acanthocybium solandri	110 lbs. / 110 lbs.	6' 1½" / 6'	36½" / 29"	Port Eades, Louisiana / Walker Cay, Bahamas	June 22 1964 / Apr. 1 1941	Mrs. Homer J. Moore, Jr. / Mrs. A. D. Crowninshield*	130 / 130
WEAKFISH	Cynoscion regalis	11 lbs. 12 oz.	2'7¾"	18"	Newport R., N. C.	Oct. 29 1950	Mrs. L. A. Denning	50
WEAKFISH, Spotted (Tie)	Cynoscion nebulosus	10 lbs. 9 oz. / 10 lbs. 4 oz.	2' 7½" / 2' 6½"	15" / 16"	Jupiter, Florida / Jupiter, Florida	May 30, 1964 / June 1, 1958	Jane H. Cole / Nancy Dukes	30 / 12
YELLOWTAIL	Seriola dorsalis or S. grandis	81 lbs.	4' 9½"	32½"	Cape Brett, New Zealand	May 18 1960	Kura Beale	80

*Line not tested.

International Game Fish Association

12 LB. LINE TEST RECORDS (up to and including 12 lbs.)

RECORD CATCHES FOR WOMEN

FISH	Scientific Name	Weight	Length	Girth	Place	Date	Angler
ALBACORE	*Thunnus germo*	29 lbs. 8 oz.	3' 1"	24½"	San Diego, California	Oct. 5 1963	Jane Holland
AMBERJACK	*Seriola lalandi*	78 lbs. 4 oz.	5' ¼"	34½" (12-lb. record for men & women)	Key Largo, Fla.	Mar. 23 1969	Pamela J. Habicht
BARRACUDA	*Sphyraena barracuda*	39 lbs.	4' 9"	21"	No. Key Largo, Fla.	Jan. 29 1959	Mrs. Walter Bell
BASS, Calif. Black Sea	*Stereolepis gigas*						
BASS, Calif. White Sea	*Cynoscion nobilis*	52 lbs. 6 oz.	4' 6"	27¾"	Newport Harbor, Calif.	June 3 1959	Ruth Jayred
BASS, Channel	*Sciaenops ocellatus*	51 lbs. 8 oz.	4' 2¼"	29"	Cape Hatteras, N. C.	Nov. 19 1958	Joan S. Dull
BASS, Giant Sea	*Promicrops itaiara*	110 lbs.	4' 10½"	39½" (12-lb. record for men & women)	Islamorada, Florida	Aug. 2 1961	Mrs. Gar Wood, Jr.
BASS, Sea	*Centropristes striatus*	2 lbs. 8 oz.	1' 5½"	12½"	Block Island, R. I.	July 12 1957	Mrs. C. Shanks
BASS, Striped	*Roccus saxatilis*	47 lbs.	4' 1½"		Umpqua R., Oregon	Aug. 21 1958	Mrs. Margaret Hulen
BLACKFISH or TAUTOG	*Tautoga onitis*						
BLUEFISH	*Pomatomus saltatrix*	16 lbs. 10 oz.	3'	19"	Montauk, L. I., N. Y.	June 24 1961	Gloria Better
BONEFISH	*Albula vulpes*	15 lbs.	2' 8½"	18½" (12-lb. record for men & women)	Bimini, Bahamas	Mar. 20 1961	Andrea Tose
BONITO, Oceanic	*Katsuwonus pelamis*	22 lbs.	2' 7¼"	22"	Nassau, Bahamas	Aug. 7 1955	Mrs. A. B. Dinwiddie
COBIA	*Rachycentron canadus*	37 lbs.	3' 10"	22½"	Panama City Beach, Fla.	April 20 1960	Mrs. Curtis G. Bane
COD	*Gadus callarias*	14 lbs. 7½ oz.	2' 11"	17½"	Nova Scotia, Canada	July 9 1963	Janet D. Wallach
DOLPHIN	*Coryphaena hippurus*	55 lbs. 2 oz.	4' 11¾"	32½" (12-lb. record for men & women)	Mazatlan, Mexico	Oct. 18 1964	Marguerite H. Barry
DRUM, Black	*Pogonias cromis*	58 lbs. 12 oz.	3' 9⅜"	36"	Atlantic Beach, N. C.	May 8 1959	Juel W. Duke
FLOUNDER	*Paralichthys*	12 lbs. 2 oz.	2' 7¼"	25¼"	Avalon, N. J.	Sept. 8 1957	Mrs. Alfred J. Bernstein
KINGFISH or TANGUIGUE	S. *Cavalla* C. *Commersonii*	41 lbs. 8 oz.	4' 6"	23"	Pompano Beach, Fla.	Jan. 15 1961	Margaret A. Paine
MARLIN, Black	Name being revised						
MARLIN, Blue	*Makaira ampla*	223 lbs. 1 oz.	10' 2½"	42"	Bimini, Bahamas	April 9 1960	Suzanne H. Higgs
MARLIN, Pacific Blue	Name being revised						
MARLIN, Striped	*Makaira mitsukurii*	210 lbs.	9' 6"	40"	Las Cruces, Mexico	June 20 1959	Lynn F. Lee
MARLIN, White	*Makaira albida*	122 lbs.	8' 3"	44" (12-lb. record for men & women)	Bimini, Bahamas	Mar. 30 1953	Dorothy A. Curtice
PERMIT	*Trachinotus goodei*	36 lbs.	3' 6"	29"	Content Key, Florida	Mar. 16 1964	Lynette G. Siman
POLLACK	*Pollachius virens*	15 lbs. 7 oz.	2' 9¾"	19"	Nova Scotia, Canada	July 9 1963	Janet D. Wallach
RUNNER, Rainbow	*Elagatis bipinnulatus*						
ROOSTERFISH	*Nematistius pectoralis*	45 lbs.	4' 4½"	30"	San Jose, del Cabo, Mex.	June 11 1951	Mrs. W. G. Krieger

FISH	Scientific Name	Weight	Length	Girth	Place	Date	Angler
SAILFISH, Atlantic	*Istiophorus americanus*	77 lbs.	8' 2"	28"	Bimini, Bahamas	May 3 1950	Mrs. G. A. Bass
SAILFISH, Pacific	*Istiophorus greyi*	146 lbs. 8 oz.	9' ½"	35½"	Palmilla, Mexico	Nov. 14 1962	Evelyn M. Anderson
SAWFISH	*Pristis pectinatus*	102 lbs. 12 oz.	8' 6"	29"	Grassy Key, Florida	June 23 1961	Marjorie M. McClellan
			(12-lb. record for men & women)				
SHARK, Blue	*Prionace glauca*	150 lbs.	8' 0"	32"	Montauk, New York	July 22 1962	Dorothea L. Dean
SHARK, Mako	*Isurus oxyrhynchus I. glaucus*	52 lbs. 5 oz.	4' 6½"	27¼"	Montauk, L. I., N. Y.	Sept. 11 1953	Anne Bowditch
SHARK, Man-Eater or White	*Carcharodon carcharias*						
SHARK, Porbeagle	*Lamna nasus*						
SHARK, Thresher	*Alopias vulpinus*						
SHARK, Tiger	*Galeocerdo cuvier*						
SNOOK or ROBALO	*Centropomus undecimalis*	32 lbs. 8 oz.	3' 9"	24"	Jupiter, Fla.	Aug. 2 1957	Mrs. Nancy Neville
SWORDFISH	*Xiphias gladius*						
TARPON	*Tarpon atlanticus*	103 lbs. 8 oz.	6' 6"	34"	Islamorada, Fla.	June 16 1958	Mrs. H. M. Roach
TUNA, Allison or Yellowfin	*Thunnus albacares*	46 lbs.	3' 11½"	28"	Greenwell Point, NSW Australia	Feb. 5 1961	Mrs. Signa Patton
TUNA, Atlantic Big-Eyed	*Thunnus obesus*						
TUNA, Pacific Big-Eyed	*Parathunnus sibi*						
TUNA, Blackfin	*Thunnus atlanticus*	26 lbs. 12 oz.	2' 11"	23½"	Bermuda	Oct. 18 1957	Mrs. L. Edna Perinchief
TUNA, Bluefin	*Thunnus thynnus*	39 lbs. 8 oz.	3' 8½"	28"	Tasmania, Australia	May 27 1963	Mrs. Bob Dyer
WAHOO	*Acanthocybium solandri*	66 lbs.	5' 8"	25"	St. Thomas, Virgin Islands	Feb. 27 1969	Gloria J. Applegate
		(Tie 12-lb. record for men & women)					
WEAKFISH	*Cynoscion regalis*	8 lbs. 14 oz.	2' 8"	15"	Fire Island, N. Y.	June 19 1954	Mrs. M. S. Hirsch
		(Tie 12-lb. record for men & women)					
WEAKFISH, Spotted	*Cynoscion nebulosus*	10 lbs. 4 oz.	2' 6½"	16"	Jupiter, Fla.	June 1 1958	Nancy Dukes
		(12-lb. record for men & women)					
YELLOWTAIL	*Seriola dorsalis or S. grandis*	32 lbs.	3' 11"	23"	Ponto Inlet, Northland, N. Z.	Jan. 18 1959	Particia Low

International Game Fish Association

20 LB. LINE TEST RECORDS (over 12 lbs., up to and including 20 lbs.)

RECORD CATCHES FOR WOMEN

FISH	Scientific Name	Weight	Length	Girth	Place	Date	Angler
ALBACORE	*Thunnus germo*	39 lbs. 2 oz.	3' 2¼"	26½"	San Diego, California	Aug. 15 1962	Karen Ann Bateman
AMBERJACK	*Seriola lalandi*	75 lbs.	4' 6½"	30"	Grand Bahama, Bahamas	Mar. 13 1957	Mrs. Charlotte E. Blum
BARRACUDA	*Sphyraena barracuda*	39 lbs.	4' 3"	23"	Palm Beach, Fla.	Feb. 11 1957	Mrs. Gustave Schirmer

FISH	Scientific Name	Weight	Length	Girth	Place	Date	Angler	
BASS, Calif. Black Sea	Stereolepis gigas	125 lbs.	4' 5"	43"	Pinas Bay, Panama	Apr. 30 1969	Mrs. Carl Dann, III	
BASS, Calif. White Sea	Cynoscion nobilis	62 lbs.	4' 9"	28"	Malibu, Calif.	Dec. 6 1951	Mrs. D. W. Jackson	
BASS, Channel	Sciaenops ocellatus	41 lbs. 8 oz.	3' 10½"	27"	Ocracoke, N. C.	Oct. 29 1958	Mrs. Wanda Love	
BASS, Giant Sea	Promicrops itaiara	39 lbs.	3' 5"	30"	Islamorada, Florida	June 30 1961	Mrs. Gar Wood, Jr.	
BASS, Sea	Centropristes striatus	3 lbs. 4 oz.	1' 8"	14"	Block Island, R. I.	July 9 1958	Mrs. Caree Shanks	
BASS, Striped	Roccus saxatilis	57 lbs. 8 oz.	4' 2"	30"	Block Is. Sound, N. Y.	Aug. 28 1959	Mary R. Aubry	
BLACKFISH or TAUTOG	Tautoga onitis	10 lbs. 12 oz.	2' ⅝"	18¾"	Asharoken Beach, Long Island	May 7 1962	Trudy H. King	
BLUEFISH	Pomatomus saltatrix	14 lbs. 10 oz.	2' 10½"	19"	Cape Cod, Mass.	Oct. 11 1957	Jeanne M. Brauneis	
BONEFISH	Albula vulpes	13 lbs. 12 oz.	2' 6¾"	17½"	Exuma, Bahamas	Jan. 3 1956	Mrs. B. A. Garson	
BONITO, Oceanic	Katsuwonus pelamis	23 lbs. 8 oz.	2' 10"	21"	San Juan, P. R.	Aug. 28 1953	Mrs. Maria Palerm de Chapel	
COBIA	Rachycentron canadus	54 lbs. 8 oz.	4' 8"	25¼"	Port Aransas, Texas	July 14 1961	Elizabeth H. Urschel	
COD	Gadus callarias	71 lbs. 8 oz. (20-lb. record for men & women)	4' 10"	31"	Cape Cod, Massachusetts	Aug. 2 1964	Muriel Betts	
DOLPHIN	Coryphaena hippurus	50 lbs.	4' 4"	32"	Cat Cay, Bahamas	April 14 1960	Mrs. Barton G. Gobelmann	
DRUM, Black	Pogonias cromis	62 lbs. 8 oz.	4' 1¾"	35¼"	Cape Hatteras N. Carolina	May 12 1962	Delphin W. Peyton	
FLOUNDER	Paralichthys							
KINGFISH or TANGUIGUE	S. Cavalla C. Commersonii	52 lbs. 8 oz.	5'	24¼"	Boynton Beach, Fla.	June 18 1963	Mildred Schirmer	
MARLIN, Black	Name being revised	225 lbs.	9' 2"	41¾"	Pinas Bay, Panama	Jan. 7 1964	Jeanette Alford	
MARLIN, Blue	Makaira ampla	167 lbs. 8 oz.	9' 2"	39½"	Bimini, Bahamas	April 10 1964	Carole C. Lake	
MARLIN, Pacific Blue	Name being revised							
MARLIN, Striped	Makaira mitsukurii	321 lbs.	10' 7¼"	47"	Iquique, Chile	June 8 1954	Mrs. L. Marron	
MARLIN, White	Makaira albida	129 lbs. 4 oz. (Tie 20-lb. record for men & women)	8' 7"	33½"	Bimini, Bahamas	April 11 1963	Mrs. J. M. Watters	
PERMIT	Trachinotus goodei	38 lbs. 38 lbs.	3' 7" 3' 4"	33" 30½"	Islamorada, Florida Islamorada, Florida	June 11 1961 March 21 1954	Louise Meulenberg Mrs. W. K. Edmunds	Tie
POLLACK	Pollachius virens	18 lbs. 8 oz.	2' 11¼"	22"	Wedgeport, Nova Scotia	July 31 1962	Mrs. Alfred Bridgford, Jr.	
RUNNER, Rainbow	Elagatis bipinnulatus							
ROOSTERFISH	Nematistius pectoralis	50 lbs. 9 oz.	4' 6½"	30"	Baja Calif., Mexico	Nov. 20 1959	Lily Call	
SAILFISH, Atlantic	Istiophorus americanus	78 lbs.	7' 7"		Guanta, Venezuela	Oct. 23 1949	Mrs. F. J. Woodsmall	
SAILFISH, Pacific	Istiophorus greyi	157 lbs.	10' 2"	37"	La Plata Is., Ecuador	Sept. 14 1961	Jeannette Alford	
SAWFISH	Pristis pectinatus	134 lbs. (20-lb. record for men & women)	8' 10"	32"	Long Key, Fla.	March 27 1963	Olive M. Senn	
SHARK, Blue	Prionace glauca	293 lbs. (20-lb. record for men & women)	10' 6½"	44"	Montauk, New York	July 21 1963	Lucette Rinfret	
SHARK, Mako	Isurus oxyrhynchus I. glaucus	316 lbs. (20-lb. record for men & women)	8' 2½"	48½"	Bimini, Bahamas	May 25 1961	Dorothea L. Dean	
SHARK, Man-Eater or White	Carcharodon carcharias	369 lbs.	9' 3"	57"	Cape Moreton, Australia	July 6 1957	Mrs. Bob Dyer	

FISH	Scientific Name	Weight	Length	Girth	Place	Date	Angler
SHARK, Porbeagle	Lamna nasus						
SHARK, Thresher	Alopias vulpinus						
SHARK, Tiger	Galeocerdo cuvier						
SNOOK or ROBALO	Centropomus undecimalis	35 lbs.	3' 7"	25½"	Fort Myers, Florida	Feb. 16 1962	Mrs. Wade Miller
SWORDFISH	Xiphias gladius						
TARPON	Tarpon atlanticus	145 lbs.	6' 6"	39½"	Marathon, Fla.	May 24 1959	Florence G. Clady
TUNA, Allison or Yellowfin	Thunnus albacares	94 lbs. 8 oz.	4' 8½"	36⅞"	Challenger Bank, Bermuda	Sept. 2 1963	Lillian Theresa Howard
TUNA, Atlantic Big-Eyed	Thunnus obesus	46 lbs. (20-lb. record for men & women)	3' 7"	2' 7"	No. Key Largo, Fla.	Jan. 17 1959	Dorothea L. Dean
TUNA, Pacific Big-Eyed	Parathunnus sibi	27 lbs. (20-lb. record for men & women)	2' 10"	24"	Cabo Blanco, Peru	Aug. 13 1955	Mrs. O. Owings
TUNA, Blackfin	Thunnus atlanticus	32 lbs. (20-lb. record for men & women)	3' 2"	26¾"	Bermuda	Oct. 23 1968	Mrs. Herbert N. Arnold
TUNA, Bluefin	Thunnus thynnus	93 lbs.	4' 5⅛"	37½"	Provincetown, Mass.	Sept. 14 1958	Willia H. Mather
WAHOO	Acanthocybium solandri	60 lbs.	5' ¾"	25"	Cat Cay, Bahamas	April 2 1960	Harriet Stadler
WEAKFISH	Cynoscion regalis						
WEAKFISH, Spotted	Cynoscion nebulosus	10 lbs.	2' 6"	18"	Pellicer Creek, Fla.	Feb. 25 1950	Mrs. Bertram Lee
YELLOWTAIL	Seriola dorsalis or S. grandis	54 lbs.	4' 2½"	28½"	Cape Brett, New Zealand	May 23 1963	Elizabeth Vernon

International Game Fish Association

RECORD CATCHES FOR WOMEN

30 LB. LINE TEST RECORDS (over 20 lbs., up to and including 30 lbs.)

FISH	Scientific Name	Weight	Length	Girth	Place	Date	Angler
ALBACORE	Thunnus germo	55 lbs. 4 oz.			Catalina, Calif.	Sept. 1927	Mrs. L. M. Doxie*
AMBERJACK	Seriola lalandi	77 lbs. 8 oz.	4' 8"	33¼"	Palm Beach, Fla.	Mar. 2 1952	Mrs. R. O. Coate
BARRACUDA	Sphyraena barracuda	43 lbs.	5'	26"	Key Largo, Fla.	Dec. 9 1956	Mrs. Robert M. Scully
BASS, Calif. Black Sea	Stereolepis gigas	108 lbs. 8 oz.	4' 7"	42½"	San Pablo, Mexico	Dec. 29 1963	Frances Enfinger
BASS, Calif. White Sea	Cynoscion nobilis	57 lbs.	4' 3½"	28⅜"	Newport Harbor, Calif.	May 1 1952	Mrs. Vera Fellers
BASS, Channel	Sciaenops ocellatus	69 lbs. 8 oz.	4' 3½". (30-lb. record for men & women)	33¼"	Cape Hatteras, N. C.	Nov. 16 1958	Jean Browning
BASS, Giant Sea	Promicrops itaiara	104 lbs.	5' 2"	40"	Marathon, Fla.	Apr. 21 1959	Thelma C. Atwood
BASS, Sea	Centropristes striatus						
BASS, Striped	Roccus saxatilis	64 lbs. 8 oz.	4' 6" (30-lb. record for men & women)	30"	North Truo, Mass.	Aug. 14 1960	Rosa O. Webb

*Line not tested.

FISH	Scientific Name	Weight	Length	Girth	Place	Date	Angler	
BLACKFISH or TAUTOG	Tautoga onitis	8 lbs. 4 oz.	1' 10"	18"	Greenport, L. I., N. Y.	Oct. 22 1968	Bea Harry	
BLUEFISH	Pomatomus saltatrix	19 lbs. 4 oz.			Long Island Sound, N. Y.	Oct. 19 1958	Eleanor Plasko	
BONEFISH	Albula vulpes	12 lbs. 6 oz.	2' 6"	17¾"	Bimini, Bahamas	Feb. 2 1946	Mrs. C. O. Hohn*	
BONITO, Oceanic	Katsuwonus pelamis	28 lbs. 8 oz.	2' 8¼"	23"	Waianae, Hawaii	June 8 1954	Mrs. C. T. Nottage	
COBIA	Rachycentron canadus	53 lbs.	4' 9½"	29¼"	Morehead City, N. C.	May 29 1961	Dorothy Amos	
COD	Gadus callarias	26 lbs.	3' 5"	25"	Wedgeport, Nova Scotia	July 19 1964	Catherine Bauer	
DOLPHIN	Coryphaena hippurus	73 lbs. 11 oz.	4' 11½"	43½"	Baja Calif., Mexico	July 12 1962	Barbara Kibbee Jayne	
		(30-lb. record for men & women)						
DRUM, Black	Pogonias cromis	74 lbs.	3' 11½"	37"	Island Beach, N. J.	July 12 1956	Mrs. E. H. Conlon	
FLOUNDER	Paralichthys	13 lbs. 11 oz.	2' 9"	27½"	Long Branch, N. J.	Aug. 20 1953	Mrs. Leslie H. Taylor	
KINGFISH or TANGUIGUE	S. Cavalla C. Commersonii	62 lbs. 12 oz.	5' 5"	26"	Cairns, Australia	Sept. 29 1968	Helen H. Brown	
MARLIN, Black	Name being revised	552 lbs.	12' 3"	62"	La Plata Is., Ecuador	July 3 1953	Mrs. W. G. Krieger	
		(30-lb. record for men & women)						
MARLIN, Blue	Makaira ampla	317 lbs. 8 oz.	11' 1½"	43½"	Chub Cay, Bahamas	May 6 1963	Almeta Schafer	
MARLIN, Pacific Blue	Name being revised	185 lbs.	9' 6"	43"	Baja Calif., Mexico	June 15 1963	Mrs. Robert J. Brookes	
		(30-lb. record for men & women)						
MARLIN, Striped	Makaira mitsukurii	289 lbs.	10' 1"	45"	Iquique, Chile	May 18 1954	Mrs. L. Marron	
MARLIN, White	Makaira albida	120 lbs. 10 oz.	7' 5¾"	32¼"	Bimini, Bahamas	Mar. 29 1956	Mrs. M. Meyer, Jr.	
PERMIT	Trachinotus goodei	38 lbs.	3' 7"	31"	Key West, Fla.	Apr. 9 1963	Helen Robinson	
POLLACK	Pollachius virens	20 lbs. 4 oz.	3' 1"	22½"	Wedgeport, Nova Scotia	Aug. 5 1962	Cathy Roth	
RUNNER, Rainbow	Elagatis bipinnulatus	12 lbs. 2 oz.	3' 4"	16¼"	Guerro, Mexico	Jan. 21 1963	Mrs. Joseph Krieger, Jr.	
ROOSTERFISH	Nematistius pectoralis	99 lbs.	4' 11½"	34½"	La Paz, Mexico	Nov. 30 1964	Lily Call	
SAILFISH, Atlantic	Istiophorus americanus	83 lbs. 3 oz.	8' 4¾"	30"	Palm Beach, Florida	Nov. 9 1964	Rose Mary Emmert	
SAILFISH, Pacific	Istiophorus greyi	178 lbs.	9' 11½"	37"	Santa Cruz Is., Galapagos Is.	Feb. 27 1955	Mrs. A. Hall	
SAWFISH	Pristis pectinatus							
SHARK, Blue	Prionace glauca	284 lbs. 8 oz.	10' 8"	42"	Montauk, N. Y.	Aug. 11 1959	Jacqueline Mittleman	
SHARK, Mako	Isurus oxyrhynchus I. glaucus	191 lbs.	7' 3"	40"	Montauk, N. Y.	Aug. 31 1958	Mrs. Lee Reichenberg	
SHARK, Man-Eater or White	Carcharodon carcharias	803 lbs.	12' 5"	70"	Cape Moreton, Australia	July 5 1957	Mrs. Bob Dyer	
SHARK, Porbeagle	Lamna nasus							
SHARK, Thresher	Alopias vulpinus							
SHARK, Tiger	Galeocerdo cuvier							
SNOOK or ROBALO	Centropomus undecimalis	52 lbs. 6 oz.	4' 1½"	26"	La Paz, Mexico	Jan. 9 1963	Jane Haywood	
		(30-lb. record for men & women)						
SWORDFISH	Xiphias gladius	246 lbs. 8 oz.	10' 2¾"	46½"	Louisburg, N. S.	July 13 1941	Mrs. Marion Hasler*	
TARPON		143 lbs. 8 oz.	7' 0"	38½"	Marathon, Fla.	May 2 1959	Joyce Mann	
	Tarpon atlanticus	142 lbs. 14 oz.	6' 4½"	39"	Port Aransas, Texas	Aug. 8 1957	Miss Dale Fleming	Triple Tie
					Miami,	Feb. 24	Helen	
		143 lbs.	6' 5"	39"	Fla.	1960	Miller	

*Line not tested.

FISH	Scientific Name	Weight	Length	Girth	Place	Date	Angler
TUNA, Allison or Yellowfin	Thunnus albacares	102 lbs.	5' 3"	38¼"	Challenger Bank, Bermuda	June 9 1963	Thelma D. Hunter
TUNA, Atlantic Big-Eyed	Thunnus obesus						
TUNA, Pacific Big-Eyed	Parathunnus sibi	13 lbs. 13 lbs.	2' 5" 2' 5½"	18" 18½"	Cabo Blanco, Peru	Jan. 24, 1959 Jan. 21, 1959	Mrs. Thos. Sherwood Tie Beulah Laidlaw
TUNA, Blackfin	Thunnus atlanticus	31 lbs. 4 oz.	3' 1⅞"	26¼"	Bermuda	June 23 1963	Mary Anne Eve
TUNA, Bluefin	Thunnus thynnus	117 lbs. 8 oz.	5' 1³⁄₁₆"	42"	San Diego, California	Sept. 10 1968	Gladys A. Chambers
WAHOO	Acanthocybium solandri	94 lbs. (30-lb. record for men & women)	6' 5½"	30"	Jacksonville Beach, Fla.	July 15 1962	Mrs. Jean Schnabel
WEAKFISH	Cynoscion regalis						
WEAKFISH, Spotted	Cynoscion nebulosus	10 lbs. 8 oz.	2' 7½"	15"	Jupiter, Florida	May 30 1964	Jane H. Cole
YELLOWTAIL	Seriola dorsalis or S. grandis	68 lbs.	4' 6½"	32"	Mayor Island, New Zealand	Apr. 17 1969	Mrs. Marjorie West

International Game Fish Association

RECORD CATCHES FOR WOMEN

50 LB. LINE TEST RECORDS (over 30 lbs., up to and including 50 lbs.)

FISH	Scientific Name	Weight	Length	Girth	Place	Date	Angler
ALBACORE	Thunnus germo	26 lbs. 12 oz.	3' 2½"	23½"	San Diego, California	Aug. 26 1961	Theresa Bullard
AMBERJACK	Seriola lalandi	105 lbs.	5' 3"	37"	Islamorada, Fla.	Jan. 16 1963	Sarah Hull Nuckols
BARRACUDA	Sphyraena barracuda	59 lbs. 8 oz.	4' 11"	25½"	Key Largo, Fla.	Sept. 6 1948	Charlotte Sibole
BASS, Calif. Black Sea	Stereolepis gigas	419 lbs. (50-lb. record for men & women)	7' 3¾"	63½"	Coronado Is., California	Oct. 8 1960	Bettie Sears
BASS, Calif. White Sea	Cynoscion nobilis						
BASS, Channel	Sciaenops ocellatus	54 lbs. 8 oz.	4' 3½"	29"	Oregon Inlet, North Carolina	Oct. 19 1953	Mrs. Robert O. Brownell
BASS, Giant Sea	Promicrops itaiara	183 lbs.	5' 7"	50"	Boca Grande, Florida	May 30 1962	Patricia N. Miller
BASS, Sea	Centropristes striatus	5 lbs. 1 oz.	1' 8½"	16"	Panama City Beach, Fla.	July 21 1956	Mrs. R. H. Martin
BASS, Striped	Roccus saxatilis	58 lbs. 8 oz.	4' 5"	28"	Block Island, R. I.	June 28 1962	Elaine M. Brady
BLACKFISH or TAUTOG	Tautoga onitis	16 lbs. 8 oz.	2' 6"	22"	Seventeen Fathoms, N. Y.	Nov. 1 1953	Edna De Fina
BLUEFISH	Pomatomus saltatrix	14 lbs. 12 oz.	2' 9½"	20"	Cape Cod, Mass.	Sept. 27 1957	Sandra Rosen
BONEFISH	Albula vulpes						
BONITO, Oceanic	Katsuwonus pelamis	31 lbs.	2' 10½"	24½"	San Juan, P. R.	Dec. 26 1954	Gloria G. de Marques
COBIA	Rachycentron canadus	85 lbs.	5' 7"	30½"	Queensland, Australia	Aug. 15 1964	Margaret Keid
COD	Gadus callarias	31 lbs. 4 oz.	4' 1"	30"	Damariscove Is., Maine	Aug. 9 1957	Mrs. Julia Silvia

FISH	Scientific Name	Weight	Length	Girth	Place	Date	Angler
DOLPHIN	Coryphaena hippurus	62 lbs.	4' 8½"	31"	Pompano Beach, Fla.	April 17 1959	Mrs. Fred Galloway
DRUM, Black	Pogonias cromis	93 lbs.	4' 2½"	42"	Fernandina Beach, Fla.	March 28 1957	Mrs. Stella Moore
FLOUNDER	Paralichthys	20 lbs. 7 oz.	3' 1"	29½"	Long Island, N. Y.	July 8 1957	Mrs. M. Fredriksen
KINGFISH or TANGUIGUE	S. Cavalla C. Commersonii	78 lbs. (50-lb. record for men & women)	5' 6½"	28½"	Guayanilla, Puerto Rico	May 25 1963	Ruth M. Coon
MARLIN, Black	Name being revised	584 lbs. 8 oz. (50-lb. record for men & women)	12' 6"	68"	Pinas Bay, Panama	Jan. 14 1962	Helen Robinson
MARLIN, Blue	Makaira ampla	420 lbs.	12' 4"	55"	Chub Cay, Bahamas	Sept. 18 1963	Cynthia Phipps
MARLIN, Pacific Blue	Name being revised	234 lbs. 8 oz. (50-lb. record for men & women)	9' 2"	44½"	Kona, Hawaii	Aug. 23 1960	Sally B. Perry
MARLIN, Striped	Makaira mitsukurii	332 lbs.	10' 4"	48"	Catalina Is., Calif.	Aug. 12 1961	Ruth De Lamar
MARLIN, White	Makaira albida	130 lbs.	7' 11"	34"	Montauk, L. I., N. Y.	Aug. 13 1951	Mrs. P. Dater
PERMIT	Trachinotus goodei	36 lbs.	3' 3"	28½"	Ft. Lauderdale, Fla.	Apr. 19 1951	Helen Jacobsen
POLLACK	Pollachius virens	29 lbs.	3' 6"	24¼"	Manasquan, N. J.	Nov. 3 1958	Ann Durik
RUNNER, Rainbow	Elagatis bipinnulatus	23 lbs. (50-lb. record for men & women)	3' 6"	19½"	Oahu, Hawaii	May 9 1961	Lila M. Neuenfelt
ROOSTERFISH	Nematistius pectoralis	85 lbs. 2 oz. (50-lb. record for men & women)	4' 6"	36"	La Paz, Mexico	Nov. 24 1956	Mrs. Esther Carle
SAILFISH, Atlantic	Istiophorus americanus	95 lbs.	8' 4½"	31½"	Pompano Beach, Fla.	Mar. 16 1952	Mrs. E. C. Minas, Jr.
SAILFISH, Pacific	Istiophorus greyi	192 lbs. (50-lb. record for men & women)	10' 5"	40½"	La Paz, Mexico	Sept. 6 1950	Gay Thomas
SAWFISH	Pristis pectinatus						
SHARK, Blue	Prionace glauca	298 lbs.	11' 6"	40"	Montauk, N. Y.	Oct. 5 1959	Valerie Wuestefeld
SHARK, Mako	Isurus oxyrhynchus I. glaucus	478 lbs.	11'	46"	Broughton Island, Australia	May 17 1957	Mrs. Ron Duncan
SHARK, Man-Eater or White	Carcharodon carcharias	801 lbs.	11' 3"	75"	Cape Moreton, Australia	June 11 1957	Mrs. Bob Dyer
SHARK, Porbeagle	Lamna nasus						
SHARK, Thresher	Alopias vulphinus	248 lbs.	12' 1"	40"	Broughton Island, Australia	Aug. 16 1956	Mrs. Ron Duncan
SHARK, Tiger	Galeocerdo cuvier	458 lbs.	10' 7"	57"	Cape Moreton, Australia	July 3 1957	Mrs. Bob Dyer
SNOOK or ROBALO	Centropomus undecimalis	31 lbs. 8 oz.	3' 5½"	23"	Stuart, Fla.	July 17 1951	Mrs. B. N. Fox
SWORDFISH	Xiphias gladius	492 lbs. (50-lb. record for men & women)	11' 9"	54"	Montauk, Pt., N. Y.	July 4 1959	Dorothea Cassullo
TARPON	Tarpon atlanticus	184 lbs. 8 oz.	7' 2"	40½"	Boca Grande, Florida	June 3 1962	Frances A. Ingram
TUNA, Allison or Yellowfin	Thunnus albacares	154 lbs.	5' 11"	42½"	Pt. Stephens New South Wales	Oct. 17 1963	Mrs. Ron Duncan
TUNA, Atlantic Big-Eyed	Thunnus obesus						
TUNA, Pacific Big-Eyed	Parathunnus sibi	240 lbs.	6' 3¼"	52¾"	Salinas, Ecuador	Jan. 11 1969	Helen C. King
TUNA, Blackfin	Thunnus atlanticus						
TUNA, Bluefin	Thunnus thynnus	518 lbs. (50-lb. record for men & women)	9' 1"	69"	Bimini, Bahamas	May 13 1950	Mrs. G. A. Bass
WAHOO	Acanthocybium solandri	75 lbs.	5' 10½"	29"	Exuma Cay, Bahamas	May 2 1957	Mrs. Eugene A. Yates, Jr.
WEAKFISH	Cynoscion regalis	11 lbs. 12 oz.	2' 7¾"	18"	Newport R., N. C.	Oct. 29 1950	Mrs. L. A. Denning

FISH	Scientific Name	Weight	Length	Girth	Place	Date	Angler
WEAKFISH, Spotted	Cynoscion nebulosus						
YELLOWTAIL	Seriola dorsalis or S. grandis	72 lbs.	4' 2½"	32"	Cape Brett, New Zealand	May 22 1964	Kura Beale

International Game Fish Association

80 LB. LINE TEST RECORDS (over 50 lbs., up to and including 80 lbs.)

RECORD CATCHES FOR WOMEN

FISH	Scientific Name	Weight	Length	Girth	Place	Date	Angler	
ALBACORE	Thunnus germo	22 lbs. 15 oz. 22 lbs. 8 oz.	2' 8¼" 2' 10"	23" 22¼"	San Diego, California San Clemente Is., California	Sept. 29 1964 Aug. 10 1960	Roxanne C. Muise June Pollard	Tie
AMBERJACK	Seriola lalandi	106 lbs. 8 oz.	5' 5"	39"	Pinas Bay, Panama	July 9 1960	Helen Robinson	
BARRACUDA	Sphyraena barracuda	66 lbs. 4 oz.	5' 10"	25-1/5"	Cape Lopez, Gabon, Africa	July 17 1955	Mme. M. Halley	
BASS, Calif. Black Sea	Stereolepis gigas	452 lbs.	7' 2¼"	64¼"	Coronado Is., Calif.	Oct. 8 1960	Lorene Wheeler	
BASS, Calif. White Sea	Cynoscion nobilis							
BASS, Channel	Sciaenops ocellatus							
BASS, Giant Sea	Promicrops itaiara	204 lbs.	5' 11"	51"	Bahia Honda, Fla.	March 1 1958	Mrs. Phyllis Carson	
BASS, Sea	Centropristes striatus							
BASS, Striped	Roccus saxatilis	56 lbs. (80 lb. record for men & women)	4' 5½"	33½"	Sandy Hook, N. J.	June 7 1955	Mrs. H. J. Sarnoski	
BLACKFISH or TAUTOG	Tautoga onitis							
BLUEFISH	Pomatomus saltatrix	15 lbs. (80-lb. record for men & women)	2' 10½"	19"	Cape Cod, Mass.	Sept. 29 1957	Jean Drury	
BONEFISH	Albula vulpes							
BONITO, Oceanic	Katsuwonus pelamis	31 lbs.	2' 11"	24¾"	Nassau, Bahamas	Jan. 25 1956	Mrs. Barbara Wallach	
COBIA	Rachycentron canadus	97 lbs. (80-lb. record for men & women)	5' 6½"	33"	Oregon Inlet, N. C.	June 4 1952	Mary W. Black	
COD	Gadus callarias							
DOLPHIN	Coryphaena hippurus	58 lbs.	5' 5"	32"	Pinas Bay, Panama	Jan. 1 1964	Norma Joyce Kimsey	
DRUM, Black	Pogonias cromis							
FLOUNDER	Paralichthys							
KINGFISH or TANGUIGUE	S. Cavalla C. Commersonii	73 lbs.	5' 7"	26"	Frazers Hog Cay, Bahamas	Feb. 2 1964	Helen Tennenbaum	
MARLIN, Black	Name being revised	796 lbs.	13' 1"	71"	Pinas Bay, Panama	Aug. 16 1961	Helen Robinson	
MARLIN, Blue	Makaira ampla	730 lbs.		60¾"	Cat Cay, Bahamas	June 6 1939	Mrs. Henry Sears*	
MARLIN, Pacific Blue	Name being revised	555 lbs.	11' 11"	58½"	Kailua-Kona, Hawaii	Aug. 9 1964	Mrs. R. H. Baldwin	

*Line not tested.

FISH	Scientific Name	Weight	Length	Girth	Place	Date	Angler
MARLIN, Striped	Makaira mitsukurii	430 lbs.	10' 8½"	54½"	Mayor Island, New Zealand	Apr. 9 1955	Mrs. H. J. Carkeek
MARLIN, White	Makaira albida	142 lbs.	8' 2"	34"	Ft. Lauderdale, Fla.	Mar. 14 1959	Marie Beneventi
PERMIT	Trachinotus goodei						
POLLACK	Pollachius virens						
RUNNER, Rainbow	Elagatis bipinnulatus						
ROOSTERFISH	Nematistius pectoralis	66 lbs.	4' 8"	29½"	La Paz, Mexico	Dec. 1 1964	Lily Call
SAILFISH, Atlantic	Istiophorus americanus	104 lbs. 8 oz.	7' 11"	31"	Miami Beach, Fla.	Mar. 22 1939	Ruth Edmands Pope*
SAILFISH, Pacific	Istiophorus greyi	196 lbs.	10' 7"	40"	Acapulco, Mexico	Feb. 9 1951	Mrs. F. Bart
SAWFISH	Pristis pectinatus						
SHARK, Blue	Prionace glauca	286 lbs.	9' 6"	40½"	Montauk, Point, N. Y.	Sept. 23 1961	Evelyn E. Henry
SHARK, Mako	Isurus oxyrhynchus I. glaucus	880 lbs. (80-lb. record for men & women)	10' 11"	75¾"	Bimini, Bahamas	Aug. 3 1964	Florence Lotierzo
SHARK, Man-Eater or White	Carcharodon carcharias	912 lbs.	11' 11"	71½"	Cape Moreton, Australia	Aug. 29 1954	Mrs. Bob Dyer
SHARK, Porbeagle	Lamna nasus						
SHARK, Thresher	Alopias vulpinus	413 lbs. (80-lb. record for men & women)	15'	49½"	Bay of Islands, New Zealand	June 28 1960	Mrs. E. R. Simons
SHARK, Tiger	Galeocerdo cuvier	1,173 lbs.	12' 4"	84"	Cronulla, N. S. W.	Mar. 24 1963	June Irene Butcher
SNOOK or ROBALO	Centropomus undecimalis						
SWORDFISH	Xiphias gladius	772 lbs. (80-lb. record for men & women)	12' 10"	70"	Iquique, Chile	June 7 1954	Mrs. L. Marron
TARPON	Tarpon atlanticus	203 lbs.	7' 11"	44"	Marathon, Florida	May 19 1961	June Jordan
TUNA, Allison or Yellowfin	Thunnus albacares	193 lbs. 12 oz.	5' 10"	48"	Pompano Beach, Florida	Nov. 7 1957	Mrs. D. W. Miller
TUNA, Atlantic Big-Eyed	Thunnus obesus	62 lbs.	3' 7"	31"	St. Helena, Atlantic Ocean	Oct. 30 1957	Mrs. Brenda Dunlop
TUNA, Pacific Big-Eyed	Parathunnus sibi	335 lbs. (80-lb. record for men & women)	7' 1"	59½"	Cabo Blanco, Peru	Mar. 25 1953	Mrs. Wendell Anderson, Jr.
TUNA, Blackfin	Thunnus atlanticus						
TUNA, Bluefin	Thunnus thynnus	674 lbs.	9' 2"	76"	Watch Hill, R. I.	Aug. 14 1950	Mrs. S. K. Farrington, Jr.
WAHOO	Acanthocybium solandri	96 lbs. 8 oz.	5' 9"	30"	Walker Cay, Bahamas	Apr. 23 1962	Carol K. Pforzheimer
WEAKFISH	Cynoscion regalis						
WEAKFISH, Spotted	Cynoscion nebulosus						
YELLOWTAIL	Seriola dorsalis or S. grandis	81 lbs.	4' 9½"	32½"	Cape Brett, New Zealand	May 18 1960	Kura Beale

*Line not tested

International Game Fish Association

130 LB. LINE TEST RECORDS (over 80 lbs., up to and including 130 lbs.)

RECORD CATCHES FOR WOMEN

RECORD CATCHES FOR WOMEN

FISH	Scientific Name	Weight	Length	Girth	Place	Date	Angler
ALBACORE	*Thunnus germo*						
AMBERJACK	*Seriola lalandi*	81 lbs.	5' 2"	31"	Pinas Bay, Panama	Feb. 13 1960	Mildred Warden
BARRACUDA	*Sphyraena barracuda*						
BASS, Calif. Black Sea	*Stereolepis gigas*						
BASS, Calif. White Sea	*Cynoscion nobilis*						
BASS, Channel	*Sciaenops ocellatus*						
BASS, Giant Sea	*Promicrops itaiara*	161 lbs.	5' 4½"	44"	Marathon, Fla.	Feb. 20 1957	Mrs. Patricia Demaret
BASS, Sea	*Centropristes striatus*						
BASS, Striped	*Roccus saxatilis*						
BLACKFISH or TAUTOG	*Tautoga onitis*						
BLUEFISH	*Pomatomus saltatrix*						
BONEFISH	*Albula vulpes*						
BONITO, Oceanic	*Katsuwonus pelamis*	31 lbs.	2' 11"	24"	Kona, Hawaii	June 16 1963	Anne H. Bosworth
COBIA	*Rachycentron canadus*						
COD	*Gadus callarias*						
DOLPHIN	*Coryphaena hippurus*						
DRUM, Black	*Pogonias cromis*						
FLOUNDER	*Paralichthys*						
KINGFISH or TANGUIGUE	*S. Cavalla C. Commersonii*						
MARLIN, Black	Name being revised	1,525 lbs.	14' 4"	80"	Cabo Blanco, Peru	Apr. 22 1954	Kimberley Wiss
MARLIN, Blue	*Makaira ampla*	606 lbs.	12' 2¾"	63"	Bimini, Bahamas	July 29 1949	Mrs. Harley Earl
MARLIN, Pacific Blue	Name being revised	583 lbs. 8 oz.	12' 3"	60"	Kailua Kona, Hawaii	Jan. 26 1969	Sally H. Rice
MARLIN, Striped	*Makaira mitsukurii*	403 lbs.	10'	52¼"	Tocopilla, Chile	June 21 1940	Mrs. Michael Lerner
MARLIN, White	*Makaira albida*	152 lbs. (130-lb. record for men & women)	8' 3"	40"	Bimini, Bahamas	Mar. 14 1936	Mrs. Marion Stevens*
PERMIT	*Trachinotus goodei*						
POLLACK	*Pollachius virens*						

*Line not tested.

FISH	Scientific Name	Weight	Length	Girth	Place	Date	Angler
RUNNER, Rainbow	*Elagatis bipinnulatus*						
ROOSTERFISH	*Nematistius pectoralis*						
SAILFISH, Atlantic	*Istiophorus americanus*						
SAILFISH, Pacific	*Istiophorus greyi*	163 lbs.	10'	44"	Pinas Bay, Panama	Aug. 14 1964	Nancy Smith
SAWFISH	*Pristis Pectinatus*						
SHARK, Blue	*Prionace , glauca*	334 lbs. (130-lb. record for men & women)	10' 8"	47½"	Rockport, Massachusetts	Sept. 4 1964	Cassandra Webster
SHARK, Mako	*Isurus oxyrhynchus I. glaucus*	911 lbs. 12 oz.	11' 2"	70"	Palm Beach, Florida	Apr. 9 1962	Audrey Cohen
SHARK, Man-Eater or White	*Carcharodon carcharias*	1,052 lbs.	13' 10"	72½"	Cape Moreton, Australia	June 27 1954	Mrs. Bob Dyer
SHARK, Porbeagle	*Lamna nasus*	271 lbs. (130-lb. record for men & women)	8' 2"	49"	Looe, Cornwall, England	Aug. 18 1957	Mrs. Hetty Eathorne
SHARK, Thresher	*Alopias vulpinus*	729 lbs.	8' 5"	61"	Mayor Is., New Zealand	June 3 1959	Mrs. V. Brown
SHARK, Tiger	*Galeocerdo cuvier*	1,314 lbs.	13' 9"	89"	Cape Moreton, Australia	July 27 1953	Mrs. Bob Dyer
SNOOK or ROBALO	*Centropomus undecimalis*						
SWORDFISH	*Xiphias gladius*	759 lbs.	13' 11"	73"	Iquique, Chile	June 30 1952	Mrs. D. A. Allison
TARPON	*Tarpon atlanticus*						
TUNA, Allison or Yellowfin	*Thunnus albacares*	254 lbs.	6' 3"	52"	Kona, Hawaii	Aug. 19 1954	Jean Carlisle
TUNA, Atlantic Big-Eyed	*Thunnus obesus*	182 lbs.	5' 8"	56"	Cat Cay, Bahamas	June 2 1958	Mrs. Pablo Bardin
TUNA, Pacific Big-Eyed	*Parathunnus sibi*	336 lbs.	7' 3"	56½"	Cabo Blanco, Peru	Jan. 16 1957	Mrs. Seymour Knox III
TUNA, Blackfin	*Thunnus atlanticus*						
TUNA, Bluefin	*Thunnus thynnus*	882 lbs.	9' 2"	83½"	Wedgeport, N. S.	Sept. 6 1947	Mrs. A. D. Crowninshield*
WAHOO	*Acanthocybium solandri*	110 lbs.	6' 1½"	36½"	Port Eades, Louisiana	June 22 1964	Mrs. Homer J. Moore, Jr.
		110 lbs.	6'	29"	Walker Cay, Bahamas	April 1 1941	Mrs. A. D. Crowninshield* Tie
WEAKFISH	*Cynoscion regalis*						
WEAKFISH, Spotted	*Cynoscion nebulosus*						
YELLOWTAIL	*Seriola dorsalis or S. grandis*	73 lbs.	4' 9"	31"	Mayor Is., New Zealand	Jan. 5 1959	Marie C. Wilson

*Line not tested

International Spin Fishing Association

Following are the spin fishing world records certified by the International Spin Fishing Association through 1969.

FRESH WATER RECORDS

International Spin Fishing Association, world record entry forms may be obtained by writing: I.S.F.A., P.O. Box 81, Downey, California, 90241.

Line Test	Weight	Date Caught	Angler	Waters Caught
BASS (Largemouth)				
2 lb.	9 lbs. 1 oz.	Jan. 1 1961	Leonard Hartman, Florida	Lake Okeechobee, Florida
4 lb.	9 lbs. 0 oz.	Feb. 10 1961	Keith Grover, California	Lake Mead, Arizona
6 lb.	12 lbs. 12 oz.	Feb. 21 1960	Charles D. Jacobs, Florida	Lake Tarpon, Florida
8 lb.	19 lbs. 0 oz.	June 26 1961	W. A. Witt, Florida	Lake Tarpon, Florida
10 lb.	14 lbs. 13 oz.	Nov. 27 1960	Mrs. Walter Wall, Florida	Lake Tsala Apopka, Florida
12 lb.	10 lbs. 4 oz.	May 3 1968	Wm. Sapauling, Sr., Massachusetts	Quitticas Pond, Massachusetts
BASS (Smallmouth)				
2 lb.	5 lbs. 3 oz.		N. F. Rosen, Pennsylvania	Minnitaki Lake, Ontario, Canada
4 lb.	6 lbs. 1 oz.	Sept. 30 1955	G. M. Schwietering, Wisconsin	Lac Du Flambeau, Wisconsin
6 lb.	5 lbs. 12 oz.	Dec. 21 1968	A. D. Yelton, Tennessee	S. Holston Lake, Tennessee
8 lb.	5 lbs. 8 oz.	Dec. 14 1968	A. Douglas Yelton, Tennessee	Watauga Lake, Tennessee
10 lb.	6 lbs. 4 oz.	Feb. 5 1968	Wm. Kinch, Tennessee	Wautauga Lake, Tennessee
12 lb.	4 lbs. 7 oz.	April 21 1968	John Quimby, Massachusetts	Cochichewick Reservoir, Massachusetts
CRAPPIE				
2 lb.	2 lbs. 9 oz.	Aug. 3 1963	Gene Newman, California	Lake Mead, Arizona
4 lb.	3 lbs. 4 oz.	Feb. 26 1963	Floyd Randolph, California	Puddingston Res., California
6 lb.	2 lbs. 4 oz.	July 27 1963	Ray Caliman, Pennsylvania	Alloway, New Jersey
8 lb.	1 lb. 4 oz.	July 21 1967	Neil Krey, Illinois	Castle Rock Flow, Wisconsin
GRAYLING (Arctic)				
2 lb.	4 lbs. 9 oz.	June 28 1968	John Case, Illinois	Great Slave Lake, Canada
4 lb.	3 lbs. 8 oz.	July 10 1968	Craig Nelsen, Kansas	Great Slave Lake, Canada
6 lb.	4 lbs. 0 oz.		Dale Slocum, Arizona	
8 lb.	3 lbs. 0 oz.	July 24 1962	Mrs. R. B. Brown, Illinois	Camsell River, N. W. T. Canada
10 lb.	2 lbs. 4 oz.	July 10 1967	Richard Renz, California	Great Bear Lake, Canada
12 lb.	OPEN			
MUSKELLUNGE				
2 lb.	18 lbs. 7 oz.	July 15 1959	Leonard Hartman, New York	St. Lawrence River, New York
4 lb.	42 lbs. 3 oz.	Sept. 7 1963	Leonard Hartman, New York	St. Lawrence River, New York
6 lb.	47 lbs. 1 oz.	Sept. 2 1962	Leonard Hartman, New York	St. Lawrence River, New York
8 lb.	59 lbs. 13 oz.	Aug. 6 1960	Leonard Hartman, New York	St. Lawrence River, New York
10 lb.	67 lbs. 15 oz.	Aug. 10 1961	Leonard Hartman, New York	St. Lawrence River, New York
12 lb.	61 lbs. 0 oz.	Nov. 8 1964	Leonard Hartman, New York	St. Lawrence River, New York
PICKEREL (Chain)				
2 lb.	7 lbs. 1 oz.	July 18 1968	Wm. Spaulding, Sr., Massachusetts	Assawamsett Pond, Massachusetts
4 lb.	6 lbs. 14 oz.	May 1 1968	Wm. Spaulding, Sr. Massachusetts	Pocksha Pond, Massachusetts
6 lb.	6 lbs. 15 oz.	July 15 1968	Wm. Spaulding, Sr., Massachusetts	Pocksha Pond, Massachusetts
8 lb.	6 lbs. 0 oz.	April 19 1965	Ralph Campitello, New Jersey	Upper Erskin Lake, New Jersey
10 lb.	7 lbs. 4 oz.	July 28 1968	Wm. Spaulding, Sr., Massachusetts	Pocksha Pond, Massachusetts
12 lb.	7 lbs. 0 oz.	July 18 1968	Wm. Spaulding, Sr., Massachusetts	Assawampsett Pond, Massachusetts
PIKE (Northern)				
2 lb.	17 lbs. 5 oz.	May 8 1961	Leonard Hartman, New York	St. Lawrence River, New York
4 lb.	18 lbs. 14 oz.	June 7 1962	Leonard Hartman, New York	St. Lawrence River, New York
6 lb.	30 lbs. 9 oz.	Aug. 15 1963	Ed Zaleski, Canada	Lake Abitibi, Canada
8 lb.	31 lbs. 0 oz.	Nov. 12 1955	Capt. R. J. Oostdyke, USAF	Nortdeich, Wolfersheim, Germany
10 lb.	16 lbs. 12 oz.	July 21 1955	Wilda Sullivan, California	Lac la Ronge, Canada
12 lb.	OPEN			
WALLEYE				
2 lb.	8 lbs. 11 oz.	Aug. 31 1960	Leonard Hartman, New York	St. Lawrence River, New York
4 lb.	13 lbs. 3 oz.	June 5 1962	Leonard Hartman, New York	St. Lawrence River, New York
6 lb.	13 lbs. 2 oz.	July 5 1963	Floyd Randolph, California	Curren River, Missouri
8 lb.	14 lbs. 8 oz.	Oct. 19 1966	Fred Golden, Michigan	Otter Lake, Michigan
10 lb.	12 lbs. 2 oz.	June 1 1961	Leonard Hartman, New York	St. Lawrence River, New York
12 lb.	9 lbs. 2 oz.	Oct. 19 1962	Leonard Hartman, New York	St. Lawrence River, New York

SHAD (American)

Line Test	Weight	Date Caught	Angler	Waters Caught
2 lb.	3 lbs. 15 oz.	May 23 1964	Henry Drew, Massachusetts	Conn. River, Massachusetts
4 lb.	6 lbs. 8 oz.	May 9 1968	Wm. Spaulding, Sr., Massachusetts	Indian River, Massachusetts
6 lb.	5 lbs. 10 oz.	May 31 1968	R. N. Schliesmayer	Feather River, California
8 lb.	6 lbs. 4 oz.	May 9 1968	Wm. Spaulding, Sr., Massachusetts	Indian River, Massachusetts
10 lb.	5 lbs. 3 oz.	June 6 1967	Henry Drew, Massachusetts	Connecticut River, Massachusetts
12 lb.	7 lbs. 10 oz.	May 17 1968	Wm. Spaulding, Sr., Massachusetts	Indian River, Massachusetts

SHEE

Line Test	Weight	Date Caught	Angler	Waters Caught
2 lb.	OPEN			
4 lb.	22 lbs. 12 oz.	June 28 1957	Mrs. Lily Call, California	Kobuk R., Alaska
6 lb.	14 lbs. 4 oz.	June 28 1957	Mrs. Lily Call, California	Kobuk R., Alaska
8 lb.	13 lbs. 4 oz.	June 28 1957	Mrs. Lily Call, California	Kobuk R., Alaska
10 lb.	17 lbs. 8 oz.	June 28 1957	Raymond F. Call, California	Kobuk R., Alaska
12 lb.	21 lbs. 8 oz.	June 29 1957	Raymond F. Call, California	Kobuk R., Alaska

TROUT (Brook)

Line Test	Weight	Date Caught	Angler	Waters Caught
2 lb.	4 lbs. 2 oz.	July 4 1965	Edwin D. Kennedy, New Jersey	Kepimits River, Canada
4 lb.	4 lbs. 0 oz.	Aug. 29 1953	Morris S. Loyd, California	Humphreys Basin, California
6 lb.	8 lbs. 8 oz.	June 25 1954	Donnell Culpepper, California	Canada
8 lb.	OPEN			
10 lb.	OPEN			
12 lb.	OPEN			

TROUT (Cutthroat)

Line Test	Weight	Date Caught	Angler	Waters Caught
2 lb.	4 lbs. 8 oz.	April 26 1960	Irene Umberham, California	Topaz Lake, Nevada
4 lb.	8 lbs. 15 oz.	April 27 1955	Lee Baun, California	Walker Lake, Nevada
6 lb.	12 lbs. 0 oz.	Mar. 4 1957	Clem DeRocco, California	Walker Lake, Nevada
8 lb.	14 lbs. 7 oz.	Mar. 18 1956	Leonard Hyduke, California	Walker Lake, Nevada
10 lb.	8 lbs. 5 oz.	April 6 1956	Alan C. Zeller, California	Walker Lake, Nevada
12 lb.	7 lbs. 7 oz.	Mar. 14 1958	Ed Baun, California	Walker Lake, Nevada

TROUT (Dolly Varden)

Line Test	Weight	Date Caught	Angler	Waters Caught
2 lb.	5 lbs. 0 oz.	July 30 1960	Art Hamill, Oregon	Metolius River, Oregon
4 lb.	17 lbs. 0 oz.	Nov. 27 1961	Yvonne Donaldson, Washington	Lake Pend Oreille, Idaho
6 lb.	18 lbs. 8 oz.	June 8 1962	Y. Donaldson, Washington	Lake Pend Oreille, Idaho
8 lb.	20 lbs. 0 oz.	May 8 1963	Yvonne Donaldson, Nevada	Lake Pend Oreille, Idaho
10 lb.	OPEN			
12 lb.	OPEN			

TROUT (Brown)

Line Test	Weight	Date Caught	Angler	Waters Caught
2 lb.	9 lbs. 0 oz.	Oct. 16 1959	Ralph Munsen, Oregon	Wickiup Res., Oregon
4 lb.	11 lbs. 1 oz.	Aug. 13 1956	Harold C. Reger, California	Walker R., Topaz, Nevada
6 lb.	18 lbs. 1 oz.	July 9 1967	Julie Stedman, California	Fallen Leaf Lake, California
8 lb.	23 lbs. 0 oz.	May 30 1968	Daniel Mathews, Arkansas	White River, Arkansas
10 lb.	6 lbs. 8 oz.	May 13 1967	Kim MacDonald, California	Birchum Canyon, California
12 lb.	13 lbs. 10 oz.	Oct. 16 1959	Phil Smith, Oregon	Wickiup Res., Oregon

TROUT (Kamloops)

Line Test	Weight	Date Caught	Angler	Waters Caught
2 lb.	24 lbs. 14 oz.	Oct. 17 1962	Ralph Munsen, Oregon	Lake Pend Oreille, Idaho
4 lb.	25 lbs. 13 oz.	May 19 1962	Yvonne Donaldson, Washington	Lake Pend Oreille, Idaho
6 lb.	29 lbs. 12 oz.	Nov. 24 1961	Jim Parsons, Idaho	Lake Pend Oreille, Idaho
8 lb.	25 lbs. 4 oz.	Nov. 17 1960	Lester H. Lundblad, Oregon	Lake Pend Oreille, Idaho
10 lb.	23 lbs. 0 oz.	Oct. 27 1953	Frank P. Natta, Washington	Lake Pend Oreille, Idaho
12 lb.	OPEN			

TROUT (Lake or Mackinaw)

Line Test	Weight	Date Caught	Angler	Waters Caught
2 lb.	19 lbs. 0 oz.	July 27 1965	Edwin D. Kennedy, New Jersey	Great Slave Lake, Canada
4 lb.	37 lbs. 12 oz.	July 26 1966	James Thurston, Canada	Tazin Lake, Canada
6 lb.	28 lbs. 2 oz.	Aug. 16 1964	Dale Slocum, Arizona	Great Bear Lake, Canada
8 lb.	37 lbs. 8 oz.	June 21 1959	Richard Newland, South Dakota	Lac La Ronge, Canada
10 lb.	36 lbs. 0 oz.	July 5 1968	Bob Aurand, California	Great Bear Lake, Canada
12 lb.	46 lbs. 4 oz.	July 16 1968	Dale L. Slocum, Arizona	Great Bear Lake, Canada

TROUT (Rainbow)

Line Test	Weight	Date Caught	Angler	Waters Caught
2 lb.	11 lbs. 0 oz.	May 28 1967	A. C. Andreson, N. Z.	Lake Tarawera, N. Z.
4 lb.	8 lbs. 7 oz.	May 8 1964	John Miner, Florida	Antisana, Ecuador S. A.
6 lb.	17 lbs. 2 oz.	June 29 1958	Keith Davidson, Washington	Pend Oreille R., Washington
8 lb.	25 lbs. 1 oz.	Nov. 5 1954	Jim Parsons, Idaho	Lake Pend Oreille, Idaho
10 lb.	4 lbs. 13 oz.	Feb. 1 1967	Bob Aurand, California	Lago Tra Ful, Argentina
12 lb.	4 lbs. 3 oz.	Oct. 5 1966	A. C. Andreson, N. Z.	Lake Rotorua, N. Z.

TROUT (Steelhead)

Line Test	Weight	Date Caught	Angler	Waters Caught
2 lb.	12 lbs. 1 oz.	May 2 1954	Frank Natta, Washington	Washougal R., Washington
4 lb.	22 lbs. 0 oz.	Feb. 22 1959	Carlyle Brown, Washington	E. Fk. Lewis R., Washington
6 lb.	23 lbs. 10 oz.	Oct. 20 1955	Norman LaFleur, Washington	E. Fk. Lewis R., Washington
8 lb.	24 lbs. 6 oz.	Feb. 21 1959	W. H. Winseman, Jr., Washington	Skykomish R., Washington
10 lb.	28 lbs. 11 oz.	July 5 1952	Rex S. York, California	Klamath R., California
12 lb.	23 lbs. 6 oz.	Oct. 15 1968	Riley Compton	Kispox River, B. C.

TROUT (Golden)

Line Test	Weight	Date Caught	Angler	Waters Caught
2 lb.	4 lbs. 4 oz.	Oct. 14 1961	Michael Mansfield, California	Horton Lake #3, California
4 lb.	3 lbs. 5 oz.	July 12 1960	Dick More, Colorado	Valentine Lake, Wyoming
6 lb.	2 lbs. 2 oz.	July 22 1959	E. L. Sharp, California	Cook Lake, Wyoming
8 lb.	OPEN			
10 lb.	OPEN			
12 lb.	OPEN			

SALT WATER RECORDS

Line Test	Weight	Date Caught	Angler	Waters Caught
ALBACORE				
2 lb.	OPEN			
4 lb.	25 lbs. 10 oz.	Aug. 10 1960	Wm. Hill, Jr., California	Catalina Channel, California
6 lb.	25 lbs. 2 oz.	Aug. 25 1960	H. S. Bonner, California	Catalina Channel, California
8 lb.	25 lbs. 11 oz.	July 31 1957	Dr. E. Z. Hershman, California	Coronados Isl., California
10 lb.	28 lbs. 8 oz.	Aug. 11 1954	H. E. Levitt, California	San Clemente Isl., California
12 lb.	39 lbs. 8 oz.	July 23 1958	Dr. R. S. Rubaum, California	San Clemente Isl., California
AMBERJACK				
2 lb.	6 lbs. 2 oz.	May 29 1961	Roy H. Martin, Florida	Gulf of Mexico, Florida
4 lb.	9 lbs. 6 oz.	May 19 1963	Louis Tesar, Florida	Gulf of Mexico, Florida
6 lb.	14 lbs. 12 oz.	May 6 1962	Louis Tesar, Florida	Gulf of Mexico, Florida
8 lb.	56 lbs. 0 oz.	June 12 1966	Mrs. Carl Dann, III, Florida	Vero Beach, Florida
10 lb.	42 lbs. 0 oz.	Oct. 13 1960	Karl Osborne, Florida	Vero Beach, Florida
12 lb.	50 lbs. 12 oz.	July 29 1964	Mrs. Carl L. Dann III, Florida	Vero Beach, Florida
BARRACUDA (Great)				
2 lb.	15 lbs. 4 oz.	Sept. 11 1963	Dr. Hehenberger, Florida	Gulf of Mexico, Florida
4 lb.	30 lbs. 0 oz.	Mar. 3 1969	Ray Acord, California	Palau Island
6 lb.	25 lbs. 0 oz.	June 18 1966	Skip Mackey, Florida	Big Pine Key, Florida
8 lb.	37 lbs. 4 oz.	June 7 1960	Al Zapanta, California	St. George Cay, Br. Honduras
10 lb.	13 lbs. 14 oz.	April 15 1969	N. J. Brown, Jr., Illinois	Islamorada, Florida
12 lb.	42 lbs. 10 oz.	Oct. 19 1959	Bill Moeser, Florida	Key Largo, Florida
BARRACUDA (Pacific)				
2 lb.	10 lbs. 9 oz.	Aug. 13 1958	Dr. E. A. Hershman, California	Off San Diego, California
4 lb.	10 lbs. 9 oz.	April 17 1960	Bob Dragoo, California	Off Paradise Cove, California
6 lb.	12 lbs. 4 oz.	May 18 1953	H. W. Craine, California	Catalina Island, California
8 lb.	11 lbs. 3 oz.	July 1 1957	Raymond Arblaster, California	Ensenada, BC, Mexico
10 lb.	12 lbs. 9 oz.	Sept. 21 1968	Alfredo Bequillard, Jr.	San Juan del Sor, Nicaragua
12 lb.	12 lbs. 7 oz.	May 20 1960	Ernest Blumenthal, California	Redondo Beach, California
BASS (Black sea)				
2 lb.	OPEN			
4 lb.	OPEN			
6 lb.	8 lbs. 1 oz.	Feb. 24 1963	James Haun, California	Seal Beach, California
8 lb.	23 lbs. 4 oz.	Aug. 24 1958	Geo. Al Teachout, California	Dana Point, California
10 lb.	112 lbs. 8 oz.	June 12 1957	David B. Rosenthal, California	San Francisco Isl., BC, Mexico
12 lb.	83 lbs. 4 oz.	Feb. 23 1958	M/Sgt. J. N. Berto-lino, California	Box Canyon Kelp, Balboa, Calif.

Line Test	Weight	Date Caught	Angler	Waters Caught
BASS (Channel)				
2 lb.	9 lbs. 0 oz.	Jan. 18 1960	James G. Mastry, Florida	St. Petersburg, Florida
4 lb.	37 lbs. 4 oz.	July 6 1961	W. H. Watters, N. Carolina	North Inlet, S. Carolina
6 lb.	53 lbs. 8 oz.	July 24 1960	C. M. Vellines, N. Carolina	Portsmouth Island, N. Carolina
8 lb.	44 lbs. 4 oz.	April 18 1968	Dave Elliott	Cape Hatteras
10 lb.	44 lbs. 4 oz.	Jan. 22 1961	R. E. Robinson, Texas	Galveston, Texas
12 lb.	60 lbs. 8 oz.	Oct. 24 1954	Arthur Clark, Jr., Pennsylvania	Nags Head, N. Carolina
BASS (Kelp)				
2 lb.	8 lbs. 3 oz.	May 17 1961	William Hill, Jr., California	San Diego, California
4 lb.	10 lbs. 7 oz.	July 17 1954	Art Parra, California	Horseshoe Kelp off Long Beach, Calif.
6 lb.	8 lbs. 12 oz.	June 2 1955	Jack L. Rous, California	San Clemente Isl., California
8 lb.	9 lbs. 12 oz.	Oct. 7 1955	Fred Anderson, California	Santa Barbara, California
10 lb.	9 lbs. 8 oz.	June 12 1967	Jack O. Hinshaw, California	Oceanside, California
12 lb.	10 lbs. 2 oz.	June 29 1959	Bob Dragoo, California	Malibu, California
BASS (Sand)				
2 lb.	5 lbs. 2 oz.	June 27 1960	Willis C. Carr, California	Horseshoe Kelp, California
4 lb.	5 lbs. 0 oz.	June 9 1963	Bob Dragoo, California	Newport Bay, California
6 lb.	8 lbs. 4 oz.	Jan. 26 1965	Bob Bennett, California	Newport Bay, California
8 lb.	8 lbs. 14 oz.	May 10 1958	Maj. E. T. Nobles, USMC	Box Canyon, California
10 lb.	7 lbs. 4 oz.	May 14 1964	Roland R. Boyer, California	Newport Bay, California
12 lb.	4 lbs. 15 oz.	June 30 1963	Carlton Bishop, California	San Onofre, California
BASS (Striped)				
2 lb.	9 lbs. 12 oz.	Aug. 24 1968	Mrs. Frances Pasche, Massachusetts	Plum Isle, Massachusetts
4 lb.	21 lbs. 2 oz.	June 1 1967	Newton Homan, New York	West Hampton, New York
6 lb.	48 lbs. 0 oz.	April 20 1961	John Froehlich, Maryland	Susquehanna R. Maryland
8 lb.	46 lbs. 8 oz.	July 22 1958	Ira Sturdivant, Oregon	Coos River, Oregon
10 lb.	57 lbs. 1 oz.	July 8 1963	Jon Kodwyck, New Hampshire	Plum Island, Massachusetts
12 lb.	53 lbs. 8 oz.	May 2 1962	Jack Stewart, Oregon	Coos River, Oregon
BLUEFISH				
2 lb.	2 lbs. 11 oz.	June 26 1962	Ken Hark, Pennsylvania	Pt. Pleasant, New Jersey
4 lb.	10 lbs. 8 oz.	Aug. 26 1968	John Fernandez, New York	Long Island, New York
6 lb.	14 lbs. 12 oz.	July 29 1953	R. B. Rothschild, Pennsylvania	Barnegat, New Jersey
8 lb.	16 lbs. 4 oz.	May 21 1960	Charles H. Johnson, New York	Atlantic Beach, New York
10 lb.	15 lbs. 1 oz.	Feb. 2 1959	W. E. Green, Illinois	N. Lake Worth, Florida
12 lb.	12 lbs. 2 oz.	July 31 1968	Alfred Fayal, Connecticut	Race Rock, New York

Line Test	Weight	Date Caught	Angler	Waters Caught
BONEFISH				
2 lb.	7 lbs. 10 oz.	Mar. 17 1968	Fred Johnson, Alabama	Bahia Honda Key, Florida
4 lb.	11 lbs. 0 oz.	Mar. 29 1968	J. Hilton Parsons, Jr., S. Carolina	Islamorada, Florida
6 lb.	14 lbs. 8 oz.	April 18 1963	Patricia Ross, Wisconsin	Bahama Islands
8 lb.	14 lbs. 2 oz.	Oct. 6 1956	Jack Yamanaka, Hawaii	Honolulu, Hawaii
10 lb.	13 lbs. 3 oz.	Sept. 29 1955	Toru Nakayama, Hawaii	Oahu, Hawaii
12 lb.	15 lbs. 0 oz.	Feb. 28 1961	Nat Carlin, L. I., New York	Islamorada, Florida
BONITO (Atlantic)				
2 lb.	2 lbs. 7 oz.	Nov. 15 1960	G. O. Thorne, Florida	Panama City Beach, Florida
4 lb.	11 lbs. 5 oz.	June 23 1967	John Holcomb, Jr., Florida	Marathon, Florida
6 lb.	7 lbs. 0 oz.	Aug. 19 1968	Jeanette Alford	Haulover Beach, Florida
8 lb.	15 lbs. 12 oz.	May 20 1964	Skip Driggers, Florida	Madiera Beach, Florida
10 lb.	10 lbs. 5 oz.	June 23 1967	John Holbomb III, Florida	Marathon, Florida
12 lb.	12 lbs. 4 oz.	June 23 1967	Wm. Selman, Alabama	Marathon, Florida
BONITO (Oceanic)				
2 lb.	OPEN			
4 lb.	6 lbs. 2 oz.	April 8 1960	Dr. E. A. Hershman, California	Bay of Palms, BC, Mexico
6 lb.	12 lbs. 8 oz.	June 15 1966	John Irvin, Florida	Vero Beach, Florida
8 lb.	9 lbs. 10 oz.	July 26 1963	Wm. S. Rosenthal, Pennsylvania	Barnegat, New Jersey
10 lb.	23 lbs. 7 oz.	Aug. 10 1958	Raymond Kagihara, Hawaii	Oahu, Hawaii
12 lb.	17 lbs. 8 oz.	May 24 1963	Alton Rowland, Florida	Boynton Beach, Florida
BONITO (Pacific)				
2 lb.	8 lbs. 10 oz.	Jan. 12 1961	Wm. Hill, Jr., California	San Diego, California
4 lb.	11 lbs. 2 oz.	Aug. 24 1959	Bob Dragoo, California	Ensenada, BC, Mexico
6 lb.	13 lbs. 8 oz.	Aug. 8 1963	John Miner III, Chile	Antofagasta, Chile
8 lb.	14 lbs. 6 oz.	June 24 1959	George Ramsey, California	Bahia de Palmas, BC, Mexico
10 lb.	12 lbs. 2 oz.	June 26 1959	Clifford Getz, California	Bahia de Palmas, BC, Mexico
12 lb.	17 lbs. 1 oz.	April 3 1953	Dan Alan Felger, California	Coronodos Isl., California
CABRILLA				
2 lb.	OPEN			
4 lb.	OPEN			
6 lb.	16 lbs. 0 oz.	Jan. 14 1966	Bernard Zwilling, California	Rancho Bueno Vista, Mexico
8 lb.	28 lbs. 0 oz.	Nov. 8 1960	Russel Anderson, California	San Jose del Cabo, Baja, California
10 lb.	13 lbs. 0 oz.	Feb. 27 1959	Paul Braslow, California	Bahia de Napola, BC, Mexico
12 lb.	OPEN			
COBIA				
2 lb.	3 lbs. 9 oz.	Aug. 24 1961	John D. Miner III, Florida	Destin, Florida
4 lb.	28 lbs. 0 oz.	Sept. 2 1961	Phil Francis, Florida	Pine Isl. Sound, Florida
6 lb.	47 lbs. 0 oz.	June 18 1966	Mrs. Carl Dann, III, Florida	Vero Beach, Florida
8 lb.	52 lbs. 8 oz.	April 17 1968	James Masters	St. Petersburg, Florida
10 lb.	50 lbs. 0 oz.	Sept. 28 1961	Richard Delvalle, Florida	Tampa Bay, Florida
12 lb.	64 lbs. 8 oz.	April 3 1965	Tommy Norred, Florida	Destin, Florida
CORBINA				
2 lb.	4 lbs. 7 oz.	April 17 1966	Milton S. Miller, California	Laguna Beach, California
4 lb.	7 lbs. 4 oz.	June 18 1967	Tom W. Miller, California	Ventura, California
6 lb.	7 lbs. 6 oz.	July 10 1967	Butch McCullough, California	Newport Bay, California
TIE 6 lb.	5 lbs. 8 oz.	May 29 1959	Curt Fetters, California	San Clemente, California
8 lb.	5 lbs. 3 oz.	Sept. 9 1962	Geo. Stickler, California	Newport Bay, California
10 lb.	12 lbs. 0 oz.	July 12 1963	Jack Smith, Florida	Peralas Islands
12 lb.	47 lbs. 6 oz.	April 15 1962	Jay Walton, Florida	Crystal Beach Pier, Florida
CORVINA				
2 lb.	11 lbs. 4 oz.	Oct. 5 1961	Willis Carr, California	Salton Sea, California
4 lb.	8 lbs. 0 oz.	Aug. 9 1963	Billy Harmon, California	Salton Sea, California
6 lb.	12 lbs. 4 oz.	May 2 1962	Ira Shoemaker, California	Salton Sea, California
TIE 6 lb.	12 lbs. 4 oz.	May 16 1964	H. J. Ray, California	Salton Sea, California
8 lb.	34 lbs. 0 oz.	May 25 1961	Mrs. Maurine Cloe, California	San Felipe, Baja, California
10 lb.	25 lbs. 8 oz.	May 15 1962	Willis Carr, California	Salton Sea, California
12 lb.	23 lbs. 4 oz.	April 7 1968	Ed Hammerschmidt, California	Salton Sea, California
CROAKER (Spotfin)				
2 lb.	8 lbs. 2 oz.	Feb. 3 1963	Milton Miller, California	Newport Bay, California
4 lb.	8 lbs. 0 oz.	Mar. 12 1961	Ben D. Martin, California	Newport Bay, California
6 lb.	11 lbs. 13 oz.	July 9 1963	Robert Austin, California	Agua Hedionda Lag., California
8 lb.	10 lbs. 9 oz.	Aug. 1 1964	Monte Anderson, California	Newport Bay, California
10 lb.	7 lbs. 12 oz.	Mar. 25 1959	Jim Cunningham, California	Newport Bay, California
12 lb.	9 lbs. 8 oz.	April 24 1962	Richard Harrison, California	Newport Bay, California
CROAKER, YELLOWFIN				
2 lb.	2 lbs. 3 oz.	April 2 1961	Ronald Buhr, California	Newport Bay, California
4 lb.	1 lb. 2 oz.	June 16 1963	W. R. Sides, California	Newport Bay, California
6 lb.	1 lb. 10 oz.	June 16 1963	James Haun, California	Newport Bay, California
8 lb.	OPEN			
10 lb.	OPEN			
12 lb.	OPEN			
DOLPHIN				
2 lb.	3 lbs. 2 oz.	June 25 1966	Fred Johnson, Alabama	Marathon, Florida
4 lb.	18 lbs. 9 oz.	May 24 1967	John C. Fernandez, New York	Bahia Honda Key, Florida
6 lb.	31 lbs. 0 oz.	Aug. 5 1952	Myron J. Glauber, California	Las Cruces, Mexico

Line Test	Weight	Date Caught	Angler	Waters Caught
8 lb.	36 lbs. 4 oz.	July 17 1965	Mrs. Carl Dann, III, Florida	Pinos Bay, Panama, C. Z.
10 lb.	35 lbs. 3 oz.	May 24 1957	Robert Bruchez, California	Rancho Buena Vista BC, Mexico
12 lb.	33 lbs. 0 oz.	April 5 1953	Myron J. Glauber, California	Mazatlan, Mexico

DRUM (Black)

Line Test	Weight	Date Caught	Angler	Waters Caught
2 lb.	1 lb. 14 oz.	Dec. 3 1960	G. O. Thorne, Florida	Panama City Beach, Florida
4 lb.	30 lbs. 8 oz.	Jan. 25 1969	James Masters, Florida	St. Petersburg, Florida
6 lb.	45 lbs. 0 oz.	Jan. 14 1958	Gus Getner, Texas	S. Padre Island, Texas
8 lb.	64 lbs. 0 oz.	July 20 1960	Joseph Bucciarelli, New Jersey	Manahawkin, New Jersey
10 lb.	53 lbs. 0 oz.	May 20 1966	Joseph D. Dove, Maryland	Cape Charles, Virginia
12 lb.	46 lbs. 8 oz.	May 18 1968	Joseph D. Dove, Maryland	Cape Charles, Virginia

HALIBUT

Line Test	Weight	Date Caught	Angler	Waters Caught
2 lb.	13 lbs. 0 oz.	Sept. 7 1963	Henry Riecke, California	Balboa, California
4 lb.	32 lbs. 0 oz.	May 20 1962	Joseph Mraz, California	L. B. Breakwall, California
6 lb.	38 lbs. 8 oz.	July 4 1965	Eugene L. Duke, California	Newport Bay, California
8 lb.	57 lbs. 2 oz.	June 1 1958	Merlin Wilson, Oregon	Coos Bay Bar, Oregon
10 lb.	74 lbs. 1 oz.	June 3 1957	Paul McDonald, Oregon	Coos Bay, Oregon
12 lb.	35 lbs. 8 oz.	Sept. 6 1964	Al Binder, California	Santa Barbara Isl., California

JACK CREVALLE

Line Test	Weight	Date Caught	Angler	Waters Caught
2 lb.	7 lbs. 4 oz.	Dec. 6 1966	Ted C. Eggers, Florida	Lake Worth, Florida
4 lb.	17 lbs. 8 oz.	Jan. 3 1966	G. S. Braden, Florida	Dry Tortugas, Gulf of Mexico
6 lb.	14 lbs. 8 oz.	Mar. 18 1955	Dr. Earl Hershman, California	Mazatlan, Mexico
8 lb.	25 lbs. 8 oz.	April 19 1957	Harry Y. Okamura, Hawaii	Oahu, Hawaii
10 lb.	39 lbs. 8 oz.	June 16 1961	Bill Lund, Florida	Hobe Sound, Florida
12 lb.	32 lbs. 2 oz.	Aug. 1 1965	Mrs. Carl Dann, Florida	Vero Beach, Florida

LADYFISH

Line Test	Weight	Date Caught	Angler	Waters Caught
2 lb.	3 lbs. 0 oz.	Dec. 22 1960	Allen Dix, New York	Lake Worth, Florida
4 lb.	6 lbs. 0 oz.	June 28 1959	Jackson Morisawa, Hawaii	Pearl Harbor, Hawaii
6 lb.	5 lbs. 9 oz.	Mar. 26 1954	Dr. Alexis A. Burso, Hawaii	Oahu, Hawaii
8 lb.	12 lbs. 5 oz.	Jan. 26 1956	Dr. Alexis A. Burso, Hawaii	Pearl Harbor, Hawaii
10 lb.	8 lbs. 0 oz.	Mar. 3 1957	Ralph Ohtani, Hawaii	Oahu, Hawaii
12 lb.	4 lbs. 1 oz.	Oct. 6 1960	Wm. L. Smith, Florida	Panama City Beach, Florida

LING COD

Line Test	Weight	Date Caught	Angler	Waters Caught
2 lb.	OPEN			
4 lb.	OPEN			
6 lb.	OPEN			
8 lb.	32 lbs. 8 oz.	May 31 1959	Geo. M. Badalick, Washington	Puget Sound, Washington
10 lb.	19 lbs. 0 oz.	May 15 1955	Wm. C. Espe, Washington	April Point BC, Canada
12 lb.	17 lbs. 9 oz.	July 21 1956	Frances Ford, Washington	Neah Bay, Washington

MACKEREL (King)

Line Test	Weight	Date Caught	Angler	Waters Caught
2 lb.	12 lbs. 0 oz.	June 17 1962	Douglas Carl, Florida	Gulf of Mexico, Florida
4 lb.	12 lbs. 12 oz.	April 29 1962	Nancy Tobias, Florida	Gulf of Mexico, Florida
6 lb.	40 lbs. 0 oz.	April 19 1964	James L. Gerling, Florida	Anna Maria Island, Florida
8 lb.	36 lbs. 6 oz.	May 30 1966	John H. Irvin, Florida	Vero Beach, Florida
10 lb.	43 lbs. 1 oz.	April 28 1959	Eugene Wilhite, Florida	St. Petersburg, Florida
12 lb.	44 lbs. 0 oz.	May 20 1963	Clyde Fore, Florida	Anna Marie, Florida

MACKEREL (Spanish)

Line Test	Weight	Date Caught	Angler	Waters Caught
2 lb.	8 lbs. 0 oz.	Feb. 15 1964	Dr. Hehenberger, Florida	Miami, Florida
4 lb.	9 lbs. 3 oz.	April 8 1960	Dr. Earl Hershman, California	Bahia de Palmas, Mexico
6 lb.	7 lbs. 0 oz.	April 6 1960	Dr. Earl Hershman, California	Bahia de Palmas, Mexico
8 lb.	7 lbs. 10 oz.	July 8 1961	Gene Levin, Florida	Ft. Walton Beach, Florida
10 lb.	8 lbs. 8 oz.	Nov. 2 1958	Richard Gregory, Florida	Palm Beach Pier, Florida
12 lb.	13 lbs. 0 oz.	March 8 1958	Lily Call, California	Loreto, BC, Mexico

MARLIN (Black)

Line Test	Weight	Date Caught	Angler	Waters Caught
2 lb.	OPEN			
4 lb.	OPEN			
6 lb.	OPEN			
8 lb.	176 lbs. 6 oz.	Aug. 2 1962	B. Zwilling, California	Rancho Buena Vista, B. C. Mexico
10 lb.	247 lbs. 0 oz.	Jan. 2 1967	Dr. Carl Dann, III, Florida	Pinas Bay, Panama
12 lb.	312 lbs. 3 oz.	July 17 1958	Robert Gaxiola, California	Guaymas, Mexico

MARLIN (Striped)

Line Test	Weight	Date Caught	Angler	Waters Caught
2 lb.	OPEN			
4 lb.	129 lbs. 0 oz.	June 8 1962	Dr. R. Rubaum, California	Palmilla, B. C. Mexico
6 lb.	OPEN			
8 lb.	126 lbs. 7 oz.	Mar. 14 1958	Al Zapanta, California	Mazatlan, Mexico
10 lb.	183 lbs. 7 oz.	July 15 1958	Robert Gaxiola, California	Guaymas, Mexico
12 lb.	165 lbs. 0 oz.	Mar. 15 1955	Harry V. Goza, Jr., California	Mazatlan, Mexico

MILK FISH

Line Test	Weight	Date Caught	Angler	Waters Caught
2 lb.	OPEN			
4 lb.	12 lbs. 13 oz.	Dec. 9 1956	Thomas Shintani, Hawaii	Pearl Harbor, Hawaii
6 lb.	11 lbs. 6 oz.	Aug. 20 1955	James Nakai, Hawaii	Hilo, Hawaii
8 lb.	17 lbs. 9 oz.	Aug. 30 1964	Curtis Ohama, Hawaii	Hawaii
10 lb.	18 lbs. 2 oz.	Aug. 20 1958	Hank Uechi, Hawaii	Oahu, Hawaii
12 lb.	21 lbs. 3 oz.	Dec. 4 1957	Robert E. Becht, Hawaii	Honolulu, Hawaii

OPALEYE

Line Test	Weight	Date Caught	Angler	Waters Caught
2 lb.	4 lbs. 3 oz.	Mar. 17 1962	Jim Phelan, California	Laguna Beach, California
4 lb.	4 lbs. 0 oz.	Oct. 27 1968	Roger J. Lawrence, California	Long Beach, California
6 lb.	5 lbs. 8 oz.	June 4 1967	Roger J. Lawrence, California	Long Beach, California

Line Test	Weight	Date Caught	Angler	Waters Caught
8 lb. TIE	4 lbs. 8 oz.	April 28 1957	Wallace Crook, California	Long Beach, California
8 lb.	4 lbs. 8 oz.	Sept. 8 1968	Charles Brain, California	Laguna Beach, California
10 lb.	4 lbs. 10 oz.	Mar. 6 1966	Jessie Harmon, California	Laguna Beach, California
12 lb.	4 lbs. 5 oz.	Oct. 3 1958	Carl N. Wood, California	Laguna, California

PALOMETA

Line Test	Weight	Date Caught	Angler	Waters Caught
2 lb.	OPEN			
4 lb.	OPEN			
6 lb.	OPEN			
8 lb.	OPEN			
10 lb.	11 lbs. 0 oz.	May 24 1957	Wm. J. Caldwell, California	Rancho Buena Vista, BC, Mexico
12 lb.	OPEN			

PERCH (Salt water)

Line Test	Weight	Date Caught	Angler	Waters Caught
2 lb.	3 lbs. 7 oz.	Mar. 18 1962	Al Teachout, California	Oxnard Beach, California
4 lb.	4 lbs. 10 oz.	May 16 1966	John Smart, Washington	Dungeness, Washington
6 lb.	5 lbs. 3 oz.	June 4 1967	Roger J. Lawrence, California	Long Beach, California
8 lb.	3 lbs. 10 oz.	Mar. 31 1956	Tom Payne, California	Baja California, Mexico
10 lb.	4 lbs. 1 oz.	April 12 1957	P. T. Peterson, California	Santa Monica, California
12 lb.	3 lbs. 12 oz.	April 7 1956	J. F. Johnson, California	Hermosa Beach, California

PERMIT

Line Test	Weight	Date Caught	Angler	Waters Caught
2 lb.	18 lbs. 12 oz.	Oct. 11 1962	B. A. Knauth, Florida	Big Pine Key, Florida
4 lb.	24 lbs. 0 oz.	Sept. 23 1968	Stanley Fried, Florida	Biscayne Bay, Florida
6 lb.	28 lbs. 8 oz.	July 27 1959	Mrs. Frances E. Fitts, Florida	Grand Cay, Bahamas
8 lb.	32 lbs. 4 oz.	Sept. 3 1963	Rex Cole, Florida	Boca Grande, Florida
10 lb.	41 lbs. 4 oz.	Mar. 19 1968	Walt Reed, New York	Marathon, Florida
12 lb.	40 lbs. 8 oz.	May 18 1967	A. Martin Mondl, Florida	Bahia Honda Key, Florida

POMPANO

Line Test	Weight	Date Caught	Angler	Waters Caught
2 lb.	2 lbs. 13 oz.	May 28 1961	G. O. Thorne, Florida	Gulf of Mexico, Florida
4 lb.	5 lbs. 3 oz.	June 4 1963	Roy Martin, Florida	Gulf of Mexico, Florida
6 lb.	5 lbs. 2 oz.	June 24 1967	Thomas J. Fisher, Florida	Choctawhatchee Bay, Florida
8 lb.	6 lbs. 3 oz.	Feb. 2 1959	Mrs. Myrtis Shrives, Florida	Vero Beach, Florida
10 lb.	12 lbs. 8 oz.	June 14 1960	Harry Gearhart, Jr., Florida	Guantanamo Bay, Cuba
12 lb.	5 lbs. 12 oz.	Dec. 13 1958	Mrs. Myrtis Shrives, Florida	Vero Beach, Florida

POMPANO (African)

Line Test	Weight	Date Caught	Angler	Waters Caught
2 lb.	OPEN			
4 lb.	7 lbs. 12 oz.	Mar. 6 1969	Ray Acord, California	Palau Island
6 lb.	27 lbs. 8 oz.	July 15 1967	Bernard Zwilling, California	Baja, California
8 lb.	24 lbs. 8 oz.	Feb. 1 1969	Bob Kilgore, Florida	Triumph Reef, Florida
10 lb.	11 lbs. 0 oz.	June 15 1964	Joyce Perkins, California	
12 lb.	17 lbs. 8 oz.	Aug. 11 1963	Charles Loften, California	Rancho Bueno Vista, B. C. Mexico

ROOSTERFISH

Line Test	Weight	Date Caught	Angler	Waters Caught
2 lb.	10 lbs. 2 oz.	April 4 1960	Dr. Earl Hershman, California	Bahai de Palmas, BC, Mexico
4 lb.	OPEN			
6 lb.	27 lbs. 8 oz.	July 15 1967	Bernard Zwilling, California	Baja, California
8 lb.	24 lbs. 9 oz.	July 17 1958	John G. Lowe, California	Guaymas, Mexico
10 lb.	50 lbs. 0 oz.	Sept. 6 1954	Maurice Levy, Jr., California	Loreto, BC, Mexico
12 lb.	50 lbs. 11 oz.	July 15 1967	Ron Zollinger, California	Rancho Bueno Vista, Baja California, Mexico

SAILFISH (Atlantic)

Line Test	Weight	Date Caught	Angler	Waters Caught
2 lb.	OPEN			
4 lb.	OPEN			
6 lb.	34 lbs. 8 oz.	Feb. 8 1968	Stu Apte, Florida	Stuart, Florida
8 lb.	57 lbs. 8 oz.	Nov. 24 1968	Stu Apte, Florida	Marathon, Florida
10 lb.	56 lbs. 0 oz.	Feb. 8 1968	Stu Apte, Florida	Stuart, Florida
12 lb.	63 lbs. 0 oz.	Nov. 21 1959	Earl Bowers, Jr., Florida	Marathon, Florida

SAILFISH (Pacific)

Line Test	Weight	Date Caught	Angler	Waters Caught
2 lb.	OPEN			
4 lb.	95 lbs. 0 oz.	April 10 1968	Stu Apte, Florida	Pinas Bay, Panama
6 lb.	123 lbs. 1 oz.	April 24 1959	Ben Rodkin, California	Mazatlan, Mexico
8 lb.	128 lbs. 0 oz.	May 24 1960	Evelyn Fuller, California	Mazatlan, Mexico
10 lb.	132 lbs. 0 oz.	Dec. 11 1958	George Ramsey, California	Mazatlan, Mexico
12 lb.	145 lbs. 0 oz.	Mar. 14 1955	Dr. Earl Hershman, California	Mazatlan, Mexico

SALMON (Chinook)

Line Test	Weight	Date Caught	Angler	Waters Caught
2 lb.	25 lbs. 8 oz.	Sept. 2 1966	John Smart, Washington	Double Bluff, Washington
4 lb.	43 lbs. 8 oz.	Aug. 22 1968	Gordon Prentice, California	Campbell River, Canada
6 lb.	53 lbs. 6 oz.	July 30 1955	Buzz Fiorini, Washington	Rivers Inlet, BC, Canada
8 lb.	55 lbs. 4 oz.	Sept. 21 1963	J. A. Bell, Brit. Columbia, Can.	Alberni Inlet, Brit. Columbia, Can.
10 lb.	42 lbs. 8 oz.	July 10 1955	Herman Hudson, Oregon	Coos Bay Bar, Oregon
12 lb.	56 lbs. 0 oz.	Oct. 16 1955	Al Weismeyer, California	Smith River, Oregon

SALMON (Silver)

Line Test	Weight	Date Caught	Angler	Waters Caught
2 lb.	18 lbs. 5 oz.	Oct. 29 1966	John Smart, Washington	Whidbey Island, Washington
4 lb.	22 lbs. 12 oz.	Oct. 27 1968	John Smart, Washington	Whidbey Island, Washington
6 lb.	23 lbs. 10 oz.	Sept. 25 1966	John Smart, Washington	Quillayuter, Washington
8 lb.	19 lbs. 15 oz.	Sept. 27 1964	John W. Smart, Washington	Whidbey Isl., Washington
10 lb.	20 lbs. 0 oz.	July 25 1967	Oscar Hagen, California	Shelter Cove, California
12 lb.	22 lbs. 8 oz.	July 27 1953	Henry B. Helmuth, California	Trinidad, California

SALMON (Sockeye)

Line Test	Weight	Date Caught	Angler	Waters Caught
2 lb.	OPEN			
4 lb.	OPEN			
6 lb.	OPEN			
8 lb.	5 lbs. 0 oz.	July 10 1957	Mrs. Lily Call, California	Brooks Falls, Alaska

Line Test	Weight	Date Caught	Angler	Waters Caught
10 lb.	6 lbs. 12 oz.	July 10 1957	Mrs. Lily Call, California	Brooks Falls, Alaska
12 lb.	OPEN			

SHARK (Bonito)

Line Test	Weight	Date Caught	Angler	Waters Caught
2 lb.	OPEN			
4 lb.	OPEN			
6 lb.	31 lbs. 4 oz.	Aug. 29 1960	Bob Dragoo, California	Paradise Cove, California
8 lb.	OPEN			
10 lb.	OPEN			
12 lb.	63 lbs. 3 oz.	Aug. 22 1956	Fred Mihaylo, California	Catalina Island, California

SHARK (Mako)

Line Test	Weight	Date Caught	Angler	Waters Caught
2 lb.	21 lbs. 12 oz.	Feb. 7 1967	A. C. Andreson, N. Z.	TI Point N. I., N. Z.
4 lb.	OPEN			
6 lb.	31 lbs. 4 oz.	Aug. 29 1960	Bob Dragoo, California	Paradise Cove, California
8 lb.	OPEN			
10 lb.	OPEN			
12 lb.	261 lbs. 11 oz.	Oct. 1 1953	Chuck Meyer, New York	Montauk Pt., L. I., New York

SHARK (Thresher)

Line Test	Weight	Date Caught	Angler	Waters Caught
2 lb.	OPEN			
4 lb.	20 lbs. 1 oz.	June 19 1960	Clifford Garver, California	Catalina Channel, California
6 lb.	OPEN			
8 lb.	OPEN			
10 lb.	OPEN			
12 lb.	OPEN			

SNAPPER (Gray)

Line Test	Weight	Date Caught	Angler	Waters Caught
2 lb.	OPEN			
4 lb.	OPEN			
6 lb.	OPEN			
8 lb.	OPEN			
10 lb.	5 lbs. 10 oz.	May 19 1963	Curtis Bane, Florida	Gulf of Mexico, Florida
12 lb.	OPEN			

SNAPPER (Mutton)

Line Test	Weight	Date Caught	Angler	Waters Caught
2 lb.	OPEN			
4 lb.	6 lbs. 9 oz.	Mar. 21 1967	Fred Johnson, Alabama	Big Pine Key, Florida
6 lb.	8 lbs. 10 oz.	June 11 1961	Eugene Heiman, Florida	Little Torch Key, Florida
8 lb.	14 lbs. 9 oz.	April 30 1968	Dave Chambers, Jr., Florida	Biscayne Bay, Florida
10 lb.	16 lbs. 12 oz.	Mar. 26 1961	John W. Shiel, Florida	Boynton Beach, Florida
12 lb.	9 lbs. 13 oz.	Mar. 21 1967	Fred Johnson, Alabama	Big Pine Key, Florida

SNAPPER (Yellowtail)

Line Test	Weight	Date Caught	Angler	Waters Caught
2 lb.	OPEN			
4 lb.	2 lbs. 2 oz.	Oct. 27 1967	Fred Johnson, Alabama	Marathon, Florida
6 lb.	OPEN			
8 lb.	4 lbs. 12 oz.	Jan. 5 1963	John W. Shiel, Florida	Bonyton Beach, Florida
10 lb.	2 lbs. 6 oz.	Oct. 28 1967	Fred Johnson, Alabama	Marathon, Florida
12 lb.	1 lb. 4 oz.	Mar. 21 1967	Nancy Johnson, Alabama	Big Pine Key, Florida

SNOOK

Line Test	Weight	Date Caught	Angler	Waters Caught
2 lb.	11 lbs. 9 oz.	Feb. 11 1961	Leonard Hartman, Florida	Caloosachatchee River, Florida

Line Test	Weight	Date Caught	Angler	Waters Caught
4 lb.	25 lbs. 8 oz.	July 12 1963	T. C. Eggers, Florida	Lake Worth, Florida
6 lb.	26 lbs. 12 oz.	June 6 1964	Theodore C. Eggers, Florida	Lake Worth, Florida
8 lb. TIE	32 lbs. 8 oz.	Mar. 2 1959	Roy S. Patten, Florida	Boca Raton Lake, Florida
8 lb.	32 lbs. 8 oz.	July 9 1960	J. H. Klinck, Florida	Palm Beach Canal, Florida
10 lb.	30 lbs. 0 oz.	July 29 1959	Chas. H. Warwick, III	Lake Worth, Florida
12 lb.	31 lbs. 8 oz.	May 3 1959	F. Dwight Foster, Florida	Loxahatchee River, Florida

TARPON

Line Test	Weight	Date Caught	Angler	Waters Caught
2 lb.	17 lbs. 5 oz.	Mar. 14 1966	Fred Johnson, Alabama	Bahia Honda Key, Florida
4 lb.	18 lbs. 12 oz.	Mar. 12 1966	Fred Johnson, Alabama	Bahia Honda Key, Florida
6 lb.	88 lbs. 0 oz.	May 17 1955	Chuck Meyer, New York	Summerland Key, Florida
8 lb.	53 lbs. 4 oz.	June 9 1960	Al Zapanta, California	Belize, Br. Honduras
10 lb.	115 lbs. 0 oz.	Aug. 18 1958	Gus Getner, Texas	Port Isabel, Texas
12 lb.	95 lbs. 8 oz.	April 12 1963	Stuart Apte, Florida	Big Pine Key, Florida

TOTUAVA

Line Test	Weight	Date Caught	Angler	Waters Caught
2 lb.	OPEN			
4 lb.	OPEN			
6 lb.	OPEN			
8 lb.	OPEN			
10 lb.	20 lbs. 6 oz.	Mar. 11 1958	Harold Lane, California	San Felipe, BC, Mexico
12 lb.	28 lbs. 14 oz.	Feb. 24 1962	Bob Dragoo, California	Gulf of California, Baja, California

TRIPLETAIL

Line Test	Weight	Date Caught	Angler	Waters Caught
2 lb.	7 lbs. 2 oz.	June 25 1966	Gerald Braden, Florida	St. James, Florida
4 lb.	14 lbs. 0 oz.	Oct. 1 1965	Gerald Braden, Florida	San Carlos Bay, Florida
6 lb.	24 lbs. 4 oz.	May 20 1965	Gerald S. Braden, Florida	Caloosahatchee R., Florida
8 lb.	20 lbs. 14 oz.	Aug. 9 1967	Brownie Hayes, Florida	Pine Island, Florida
10 lb.	18 lbs. 8 oz.	July 1 1968	Loretta Rollins	Pine Island, Florida
12 lb.	32 lbs. 0 oz.	Sept. 28 1960	Clarence Wieder-echt, Louisiana	Venice, Louisiana

TUNA (Bluefin)

Line Test	Weight	Date Caught	Angler	Waters Caught
2 lb.	OPEN			
4 lb.	16 lbs. 0 oz.	Sept. 20 1953	Dr. A. E. Moore, California	Guadalupe Isl., Mexico
6 lb.	15 lbs. 6 oz.	Aug. 26 1962	Harry Vickers, California	San Diego, California
8 lb.	8 lbs. 8 oz.	July 23 1966	Wm. Rosenthal, Pennsylvania	Barneget Bay, New Jersey
10 lb.	28 lbs. 0 oz.	July 17 1957	Ralph Chevalier, California	Long Beach, California
12 lb.	30 lbs. 4 oz.	Oct. 7 1956	Glenn R. Bracken, California	Catalina Isl., California

TUNA (Little)

Line Test	Weight	Date Caught	Angler	Waters Caught
2 lb.	5 lbs. 7 oz.	Nov. 5 1960	G. O. Thorne, Florida	Panama City Beach, Florida
4 lb.	13 lbs. 6 oz.	June 25 1960	G. O. Thorne, Florida	Panama City Beach, Florida
6 lb.	15 lbs. 2 oz.	Sept. 18 1965	Wm. Rosenthal, Pennsylvania	Barneget, New Jersey
8 lb.	19 lbs. 0 oz.	May 27 1960	Dick Craik, Florida	Panama City, Florida

Line Test	Weight	Date Caught	Angler	Waters Caught
10 lb.	18 lbs. 9 oz.	July 18 1959	Robert G. Ryder, Florida	Palm Beach, Florida
12 lb.	19 lbs. 0 oz.	Feb. 8 1959	William Yamashita, Hawaii	Oahu, Hawaii

TUNA (Yellowfin)

Line Test	Weight	Date Caught	Angler	Waters Caught
2 lb.	OPEN			
4 lb.	OPEN			
6 lb.	23 lbs. 11 oz.	July 16 1967	Bernard Zwilling, California	Rancho Bueno Vista, Baja California, Mexico
8 lb.	18 lbs. 3 oz.	Sept. 25 1960	Chet Umberham, California	Newport, California
10 lb.	26 lbs. 6 oz.	Dec. 21 1960	N. R. Rehm, California	Cabo San Lucas, Baja, California
12 lb.	27 lbs. 3 oz.	July 16 1967	Ron Zollinger, California	Rancho Bueno Vista, Baja California, Mexico

WAHOO

Line Test	Weight	Date Caught	Angler	Waters Caught
2 lb.	OPEN			
4 lb.	OPEN			
6 lb.	OPEN			
8 lb.	OPEN			
10 lb.	37 lbs. 9 oz.	Sept. 30 1968	Harold Alford, Florida	Haulover Beach, Florida
12 lb.	50 lbs. 0 oz.	Mar. 24 1969	L. J. Spire, MD, New York	Virgin Islands, Territory of U.S.

WEAKFISH

Line Test	Weight	Date Caught	Angler	Waters Caught
2 lb.	8 lbs. 5 oz.	April 30 1959	S. F. Still, Florida	Banana Riv., Florida
4 lb.	10 lbs. 7 oz.	April 6 1969	J. C. Yokel, Florida	Port Canaveral, Florida
6 lb. TIE	9 lbs. 12 oz.	Feb. 17 1962	John Zeman, Florida	Cocoa Beach, Florida
6 lb.	9 lbs. 12 oz.	Feb. 8 1969	David Brown, Florida	Port Canaveral, Florida
8 lb. TIE	11 lbs. 1 oz.	Mar. 19 1957	Gus Getner, Texas	Arroyo Colorado, Texas
8 lb.	11 lbs. 1 oz.	Jan. 25 1959	Harry Evans, Florida	Sebastian Inlet, Florida

Line Test	Weight	Date Caught	Angler	Waters Caught
10 lb.	10 lbs. 4 oz.	April 2 1966	Jack Smith, Florida	Jensen, Florida
12 lb.	12 lbs. 9 oz.	May 11 1957	Gus Getner, Texas	Arroyo Colorado, Texas

WHITEFISH

Line Test	Weight	Date Caught	Angler	Waters Caught
2 lb.	1 lb. 4 oz.	April 18 1959	B. W. Sapulski, California	Redondo Beach, California
4 lb.	OPEN			
6 lb.	8 lbs. 5 oz.	June 10 1956	Lenny York, California	Santa Monica, California
8 lb.	OPEN			
10 lb.	OPEN			
12 lb.	OPEN			

WHITE SEA BASS

Line Test	Weight	Date Caught	Angler	Waters Caught
2 lb.	3 lbs. 12 oz.	April 14 1957	Robert Salamon, California	Dana Pt., California
4 lb.	12 lbs. 5 oz.	Aug. 20 1958	Dr. Earl Hershman, California	San Onofre, California
6 lb.	38 lbs. 14 oz.	May 20 1952	Rex S. York, California	Coronodos Isls., California
8 lb.	35 lbs. 8 oz.	July 19 1953	Wilfred Sargent, California	San Clemente, California
10 lb.	45 lbs. 8 oz.	July 15 1959	John Mullen, California	Pt. Hueneme, California
12 lb.	65 lbs. 0 oz.	July 8 1955	C. J. Aronis, California	Ensenada, BC, Mexico

YELLOWTAIL

Line Test	Weight	Date Caught	Angler	Waters Caught
2 lb.	12 lbs. 6 oz.	Aug. 23 1959	Bob Dragoo, California	Ensenada, BC, Mexico
4 lb.	26 lbs. 4 oz.	April 27 1957	Floyd Randolph, California	Torrey Pines, California
6 lb.	26 lbs. 6 oz.	Oct. 11 1962	Willis Carr, California	La Jolla, California
8 lb.	22 lbs. 8 oz.	Feb. 25 1958	Dr. Earl Hershman, California	Rancho Buena Vista, BC, Mexico
10 lb.	42 lbs. 0 oz.	April 7 1955	Albert M. Zapanta, California	Rancho Buena Vista, BC, Mexico
12 lb.	36 lbs. 13 oz.	April 4 1951	D. Tomlinson	Coronado Isle, California

DEPARTMENTS:

41: State fishing records

The state fishing records listed here are based on information provided by the various state conservation departments. There are considerable differences in record-keeping by the various states: some states do not maintain big-fish records, some states having both fresh and salt water fishing list records for only fresh water species, some states list only certain species of fish in their records, and some states recognize for record purposes large fish taken from private waters, while some other states do not.

ALABAMA

Species	Wt.	Where	When	Angler
BASS, Rock	6 lbs. 1/2 oz.	Hallawakee Creek	Mar. 24 1967	Thomas L. Sharpe
BASS, Smallmouth	10 lbs. 8 oz.	Tennessee River	Oct. 8 1950	Owen F. Smith
BASS, Spotted	8 lbs.	Lewis Smith Lake	Mar. 8 1966	Bob Hamilton
BLUEGILL	4 lbs. 12 oz.	Ketona Lake	Apr. 9 1950	T. S. Hudson
SUNFISH, Redear	4 lbs. 4 oz.	Chattahoochee State Park	May 5 1962	Jeff Lashley

ALASKA

FRESHWATER Species	Wt.	Where	When	Angler
BURBOT	22 lbs. 8 oz.	Lake Louise	May 3 1968	Robert Bronson
CHAR, Arctic	17 lbs. 8 oz.	Wulik River	Sept. 26 1968	Peter Winslow
GRAYLING, Arctic	4 lbs.	Ugashik Lake	July 30 1967	Joseph Carlone
PIKE, Northern	20 lbs. 8 oz.	East Twin Lake	Mar. 24 1968	Frank Scott
SHEEFISH	39 lbs. 8 oz.	Kobuk River	Sept. 19 1966	Roger Alt
TROUT, Lake	28 lbs. 2 oz.	Crosswind Lake	Aug. 23 1968	Marguerite Ryfkogel
TROUT, Rainbow	18 lbs.	Anchor River	Sept. 5 1968	Delvin Lynds
WHITEFISH	4 lbs. 12 oz.	Lake Creek	Aug. 3 1968	Curtis Duhon

SALTWATER Species	Wt.	Where	When	Angler
HALIBUT	249 lbs.	Tenakee	July 24 1966	Richard Zinn
SALMON, King	66 lbs. 6 oz.	Craig	June 12 1966	Wayne Jones
SALMON, Pink	7 lbs. 1 oz.	Lake Creek	Aug. 4 1968	H. M. Hershberger
SALMON, Silver	21 lbs. 8 oz.	Young Point	Aug. 18 1968	Thomas Kelly

ARIZONA

Species	Wt.	Where	When	Angler
BASS, Largemouth	14 lbs. 10 oz.	Roosevelt Lake	1966	Unknown
BASS, Smallmouth	3 lbs.	Apache Lake	Mar. 1969	Edward Goodhart
BASS, Striped	28 lbs. 14 oz.	Colorado River	Mar. 1969	Tom Ryan
BASS, White	4 lbs. 10 oz.	Upper Lake Pleasant	1967	Unknown
BLUEGILL	3 lbs. 5 oz.	San Carlos Reservation	1965	Ernest Garcia
CATFISH, Channel	35 lbs. 4 oz.	Topock Swamp	1952	Unknown
CATFISH, Flathead	65 lbs.	San Carlos Lake	1951	Pat Coleman
CRAPPIE, Black	4 lbs. 10 oz.	San Carlos Lake	1959	John Shadrick
PIKE, Northern	8 lbs. 14 oz.	Lower Lake Mary	1967	Fred Wong
TILAPIA	2 lbs. 6 oz.	Salinity Canal	1968	Naomi Walker
TROUT, Brook	8 lbs. 3 oz.	Big Lake	1943	Unknown
TROUT, Brown	12 lbs. 2 oz.	Little Colorado River	1948	Unknown
TROUT, Cutthroat	6 lbs. 9 oz.	Big Lake	1943	Unknown
TROUT, Grayling	1 lb. 7 oz.	Big Lake	1942	Unknown
TROUT, Rainbow	21 lbs. 5 oz.	Colorado River	1966	John Reid
WALLEYE	4 lbs. 2 oz.	Canyon Lake	Mar. 1969	Freddie Watson

ARKANSAS

Species	Wt.	Where	When	Angler
BASS, Largemouth	12 lbs. 1 oz.	Lake Norfork	May 20 1961	Edwin Stout
BASS, Rock	1 lb. 6 oz.	Lake Norfork	May 5 1963	Randy Screws

Species	Wt.	Where	When	Angler
BASS, Smallmouth	7 lbs. 5 oz.	Bull Shoals Reservoir	Apr. 1 1969	Acie Dickerson
BASS, Spotted	5 lbs. 15 oz.	Lake Bull Shoals	Sept. 15 1967	Clarence Clark
BASS, Striped	9 lbs. 4 oz.	Arkansas River	Mar. 15 1968	Donald Rice
BASS, Warmouth	1 lb. 7 oz.	Spring River	Sept. 25 1965	Jay Kaffka
BASS, White	4 lbs. 9 oz.	Lake Greers Ferry	Mar. 15 1967	Jimmy West
BLUEGILL	1 lb. 14 oz.	Lake Overcup	July 17 1966	Forrest Fields
CATFISH, Blue	44 lbs.	Arkansas River	Nov. 6 1966	Amos Howrey
CATFISH, Channel	18 lbs.	Lake Fayetteville	Mar. 27 1963	Elmer Powers
CATFISH, Flathead	33 lbs. 8 oz.	Little Red River	May 12 1966	Grover Hawkins
CRAPPIE, Black	3 lbs. 14 oz.	Private Reservoir	Mar. 16 1966	Junior Berryman
CRAPPIE, White	4 lbs.	Private Pond	Mar. 24 1968	Charles White
GAR, Alligator	215 lbs.	Arkansas River	June 31 1964	Alvin Bonds
PICKEREL, Chain	4 lbs. 12 oz.	White River	Mar. 7 1962	Bob Sweet
SAUGER	3 lbs. 15 oz.	Lake Norfork	Mar. 23 1967	Lucille Cantwell
SUNFISH, Green	1 lb. 6 oz.	Farm Pond	Apr. 25 1966	Bill Jones
SUNFISH, Longear	4 oz.	Saline River	July 3 1965	Charlie Thompson
SUNFISH, Redear	2 lbs. 8 oz.	Lake Boswell	Oct. 30 1961	Charlie Henderson
TROUT, Brown	25 lbs.	Upper White River	Sept. 8 1963	Tom Gulley
TROUT, Rainbow	15 lbs. 8 oz.	Little Red River	Mar. 1 1968	David Kitchens
WALLEYE	19 lbs. 12 oz.	White River	Feb. 12 1963	Mrs. L. E. Garrison

CALIFORNIA

Freshwater Species	Wt.	Where	When	Angler
BASS, Largemouth	14 lbs.	Round Valley Lake	May 30 1948	C. E. Schreiner
BASS, Smallmouth	7 lbs. 11 oz.	Trapper's Slough	Nov. 16 1951	C. H. Richey
CATFISH, Channel	35 lbs.	Topoc Swamp	Oct. 1952	W. L. Tull
CATFISH, White	15 lbs. 1 oz.	Snodgrass Slouth	June 1 1951	O. J. McArdle
CRAPPIE, Black	4 lbs.	Mendota Pool	Mar. 16 1956	Alex Berg
CRAPPIE, White	4 lbs.	Irvine Lake	May 17 1952	D. B. Gaddas
SHAD, American	6 lbs. 2 oz.	Yuba River	June 4 1967	Hal W. Janssen
STURGEON	277 lbs. 8 oz.	Snag Island	Oct. 30 1954	C. Diangson
TROUT, Brook fly-casting	9 lbs. 12 oz.	Silver Lake	Sept. 9 1932	Texas Hanes
TROUT, Brown open	24 lbs.	Regulator Lake	July 14 1945	Dave Hanny
TROUT, Cutthroat	13 lbs.	Independence Lake	July 1967	L. A. Johnson
TROUT, Lake	32 lbs. 12 oz.	Lake Tahoe	Winter 1926	John E. Pomin

Species	Wt.	Where	When	Angler
TROUT, Rainbow	21 lbs. 3 oz.	Feather River	Sept. 26 1926	Leslie Korth
TROUT, Steelhead	21 lbs. 6 oz.	Smith River	Nov. 15 1948	Howard Dunlap

Saltwater Species	Wt.	Where	When	Angler
BASS, Striped	65 lbs.	San Joaquin River	May 1951	Werdell Olson
BASS, White Sea Calif.	74 lbs. 4 oz.	Playa del Rey	Mar. 8 1941	William Hartness
CORVINA	27 lbs. 8 oz.	Salton Sea	May 26 1968	Leonard Johnson
MARLIN, Blue	402 lbs.	Catalina	Aug. 12 1934	Lula O. Carson
MARLIN, Striped	372 lbs.	Catalina	Aug. 15 1948	Dr. R. W. Post
SAILFISH, Pacific	140 lbs.	Las Cruces	Apr. 9 1954	Dr. P. C. Samson
SALMON, Chinook	67 lbs. 9 oz.	San Francisco Bay	Aug. 26 1947	K. M. Jacobsen
SALMON, Silver	18 lbs. 5 oz.	Humboldt Bay	Sept. 11 1950	T. W. Nelson, Jr.
YELLOWTAIL, Pacific	30 lbs. 3 oz.	San Diego	June 12 1954	C. W. McGranahan

COLORADO

Species	Wt.	Where	When	Angler
BASS, Largemouth	9 lbs.	Boyd Lake	1964	Ernest Werkmeister
BASS, White	4 lbs. 7 oz.	Adobe Creek Reservoir	1968	Pedro Martinez
CATFISH, Channel	25 lbs. 9 oz.	Smith Lake	1968	Ron Pasley
PIKE, Northern	22 lbs.	Bonny Reservoir	1965	Mrs. George Shutte
SALMON, Kokanee	3 lbs.	Rawah Lake #3	1963	Wesley Nelson
TROUT, Brook	7 lbs. 10 oz.		1940's	George A. Knorr
TROUT, Brown	23 lbs.	Animas River	1961	Jesse Brown
TROUT, Cutthroat	16 lbs.	Twin Lakes	1964	George Hranchek
TROUT, Lake	36 lbs.	Deep Lake	1949	R. H. Wisley
TROUT, Splake	6 lbs. 12 oz.	Island Lake	1967	Paul Patton

CONNECTICUT

Species	Wt.	Where	When	Angler
BASS, Largemouth	12 lbs. 14 oz.	Mashapaug Lake	1961	Frank Domurat
BASS, Smallmouth	7 lbs. 10 oz.	Mashapaug Lake	1954	Frnak Domurat
BULLHEAD, Brown	2 lbs. 14 oz.	Pritchard Pond	1968	Albert E. Podzunes, Jr.
CATFISH, White	8 lbs. 8 oz.	Candlewood Lake	1958	Thomas Molloy
CRAPPIE	3 lbs. 13 oz.	Lake Saltonstall	1955	Raymond Stopka
PERCH, White	2 lbs. 8 oz.	Connecticut River	1961	Barney Walden
PERCH, Yellow	2 lbs. 2 oz.	Amos Lake	1967	Stanley Warykas

Species	Wt.	Where	When	Angler
PICKEREL, Chain	7 lbs. 11 oz.	Compensating Reservoir	1967	Sebastian Urso
PIKE, Northern	16 lbs. 11 oz.	Connecticut River	1960	Frank Domurat
SHAD	8 lbs. 9 oz.	Connecticut River	1968	Donald Thompson
TROUT, Brook	4 lbs. 6 oz.	Housatonic River	1950	Fred Mazzafemo
TROUT, Brown	16 lbs. 4 oz.	Mashapaug Lake	1968	Albert Jarish
TROUT, Lake	29 lbs. 13 oz.	Wononscopomuc Lake	1918	Dr. Thompson
TROUT, Rainbow	9 lbs. 7 oz.	Saugatuck Reservoir	1962	Ed Mayo
WALLEYE	14 lbs. 8 oz.	Candlewood Lake	1941	George Britto

DELAWARE

Freshwater Species	Wt.	Where	When	Angler
BASS, Largemouth	8 lbs. 10 oz.	Lums Pond	May 23 1966	Ted Derrick, Jr.
BLUEGILL	1 lb.	Griffiths Pond	May 12 1966	Walter Rybicki
CRAPPIE	3 lbs. 3 oz.	Noxontown Pond	May 13 1967	Harry Nicholson III
PERCH, White	1 lb. 1 oz.	Augustine Beach	May 6 1967	Jack B. Denson
PERCH, Yellow	1 lb. 8 oz.	Voshell Pond	Sept. 30 1967	Jessie B. Ring
PICKEREL, Chain (tie)	5 lbs. 4 oz.	Noxontown Pond	May 16 1967	Michael Bienicewicz
	5 lbs. 4 oz.	Lake Como	July 19 1967	Ronald Ruehle

Saltwater Species	Wt.	Where	When	Angler
ALBACORE	13 lbs. 4 oz.	Delaware Lightship	Aug. 30 1967	Gerald Steele
BASS, Channel	52 lbs.	Surf-Indian River Inlet	June 4 1966	Robert Padgett
BASS, Sea	3 lbs.	"B" Buoy	July 7 1967	Dr. Oscar W. Eady
BASS, Striped	30 lbs.	Indian River Inlet	July 29 1966	Hency C. Couchman
BLUEFISH	13 lbs. 6 oz.	Delaware Lightship	June 17 1967	Peter F. Straaten
DOLPHIN	31 lbs. 8 oz.	N. E. Delaware Lightship	Aug. 9 1967	Elmer Z. Delp
DRUM, Black	60 lbs. 8 oz.	Delaware Bay	May 6 1967	Charles A. Tigue
FLOUNDER	16 lbs. 10 oz.	Masseys Landing	Sept. 14 1967	Delbert Carty
KINGFISH	1 lb. 9 oz.	Surf-Lewes	Oct. 10 1967	Barnard C. Muir
MARLIN, White	79 lbs.	S. E. Delaware Lightship	July 17 1967	John A. Cummings
SHARK	390 lbs.	Bowers Beach	July 29 1967	Richard Muschamp
TAUTOG	9 lbs.	2nd Breakwater Lewes	June 3 1967	Richard M. Morris
TUNA	45 lbs.	S. E. "A" Buoy	Sept. 10 1966	Charles J. Lewis
WEAKFISH	3 lbs. 12 oz.	Indian River Inlet	July 20 1967	Frank Prekup, Jr.

FLORIDA
(No Records Maintained)

GEORGIA

Freshwater Species	Wt.	Where	When	Angler
BASS, Largemouth (World's Record)	22 lbs. 4 oz.	Montgomery Lake	June 2 1932	George Perry
BASS, Rock	2 lbs. 10 oz.	Jacks River	July 4 1967	John R. Cockburn, Jr.
BASS, Smallmouth	6 lbs. 2 oz.	Lake Chatuge	July 2 1968	Robert Parson
BASS, Spotted	6 lbs.	Lake Allatoona	Feb. 11 1967	Elton Elrod
BASS, White (tie)	4 lbs. 14 oz.	Lake Lanier	Jan. 11 1966	Albert Pittman
	4 lbs. 14 oz.	Lake Lanier	Mar. 26 1968	Clyde Vaughan
BLUEGILL	2 lbs. 8 oz.	Altamaha River	Sept. 29 1965	Lee Berry
BOWFIN	14 lbs.	Okefenokee Swamp	May 5 1968	Randall Lee Brown
CARP	35 lbs. 6 oz.	Sweetwater Creek	Apr. 17 1967	Albert B. Hicks, Sr.
CATFISH, Flathead	29 lbs.	Lake Blue Ridge	May 21 1968	James Chastain
CRAPPIE, Black	4 lbs. 3 oz.	Lake Jodeco	Apr. 30 1967	Kenneth Kirkland
CRAPPIE, White	4 lbs. 4 oz.	Lake Hartwell	Apr. 27 1968	Charles McCullough
MUSKELLUNGE	38 lbs.	Blue Ridge Lake	June 1957	Rube Golden
PICKEREL, Chain (World's Record)	9 lbs. 6 oz.	Homerville Georgia	Feb. 1961	Baxley McQuaig, Jr.
SUNFISH, Redear	2 lbs. 12 oz.	Private Pond	May 2 1967	C. E. Morris
TROUT, Brook	2 lbs. 1 oz.	Toccoa River	Apr. 1 1967	Jay Tipton
TROUT, Brown	18 lbs. 3 oz.	Rock Creek	May 6 1967	William M. Lowery
TROUT, Rainbow	12 lbs. 4 oz.	Coosawattee River	May 31 1966	John Whitaker
WALLEYE	11 lbs.	Lake Burton	Apr. 13 1963	Steven Kenny

Saltwater Species	Wt.	Where	When	Angler
BASS, Striped	63 lbs.	Oconee River	May 30 1967	Kelly A. Ward

HAWAII
(No Records Maintained)

IDAHO

Species	Wt.	Where	When	Angler
BASS, Largemouth	10 lbs. 15 oz.	Anderson Lake		Mrs. M. W. Taylor
BASS, Smallmouth	5 lbs. 14 oz.	Snake River	May 1962	B. B. Bacharach
BLUEGILL	3 lbs. 8 oz.	C. J. Strike Reservoir	May 1966	Darrell Grim
BULLHEAD	2 lbs. 3 oz.	Lake Coeur d'Alene	1954	
CATFISH, Channel	20 lbs. 9 oz.	Snake River	1963	Cecil R. Beckman
CRAPPIE	2 lbs. 8 oz.	Shepherd Lake	1954	Mrs. Carl Tifft
LING	14 lbs.	Kootenai River	1954	P. A. Dayton

Species	Wt.	Where	When	Angler
PERCH	2 lbs. 8 oz.	Murtaugh Reservoir		Dewey Julian
SALMON, Chinook	45 lbs.	Salmon River	Sept. 5 1964	Hurbert Staggie
SALMON, Kokanee	3 lbs. 10 oz.	Moose Creek	Sept. 1958	Ted Miller
SALMON, Sockeye	4 lbs.	Redfish Lake	1957	Marc Wride
STURGEON	394 lbs.	Snake River	1956	Glen Howard
TROUT, Brook	6 lbs. 10 oz.	Deep Creek Reservoir	1958	Donald Kotschevar
TROUT, Brown	25 lbs. 12 oz.	Palisades Reservoir	Mar. 1969	Jim McMurtrey
TROUT, Cutthroat	18 lbs. 6 oz.	Upper Island Park Reservoir	1944	
TROUT, Cutthroat—Rainbow (Hybrid)	23 lbs. 4 oz.	Blackfoot Reservoir	1957	Phil Adderly
TROUT, Dolly Varden	32 lbs.	Pend Oreille Lake	1949	Nelson Higgins
TROUT, Golden	5 lbs. 2 oz.	White Sands Lake	1958	George Wolverton
TROUT, Kamloops	37 lbs.	Pend Oreille Lake	1947	Wes Hamlet
TROUT, Lake	54 lbs. 5 oz.	Priest Lake	Apr. 1964	Russ Herman
TROUT, Rainbow	19 lbs.	Hayden Lake	Nov. 1947	R. M. Williams
TROUT, Steelhead	28 lbs. 10 oz.	Clearwater River	Feb. 1964	Mrs. Emery Wilson
WHITEFISH, Mountain	5 lbs. 4 oz.	South Fork Payette River	1941	

ILLINOIS

Species	Wt.	Where	When	Angler
BASS, Largemouth	10 lbs. 10 oz.	Farm Pond	1964	James N. Chamblin
BASS, Rock	1 lb. 7 oz.	Lake Michigan	1964	Laddie Vavrin
BASS, Smallmouth	5 lbs. 10 oz.	Braidwood Recreation Club Lake	1964	Alfred Kuriger
BASS, White	3 lbs. 4 oz.	Mississippi River	1959	Mrs. Marjorie Davis
BLUEGILL	2 lbs. 10 oz.	Strip Mine	1963	Rip Sullivan
BUFFALO	48 lbs.	Mississippi River	1936	C. B. Merritt
BULLHEAD, Black	3 lbs. 4 oz.	Farm Pond	1966	Greg Aubrey
BULLHEAD, Yellow	5 lbs. 4 oz.	Fox River	1955	Bill Snow
CARP	42 lbs.	Kankakee River	1928	Clarence Heinze
CATFISH, Blue (tie)	65 lbs.	Alton Lake	1956	Ernest Webb
	65 lbs.	Alton Lake	1956	Andrew Coats, Jr.
CATFISH, Channel	20 lbs.	Strip Mine	1963	Tom Giles
CATFISH, Flathead	51 lbs.	Hennepin Canal	1950	Les Beyer
CRAPPIE, Black	4 lbs. 4 oz.	Craig Lake	1967	Gilbert Parker
CRAPPIE, White	4 lbs. 5 oz.	Farm Pond	1967	Alice Edwards
GAR	157 lbs.	Mississippi River	1944	Clarence Cousins
PADDLEFISH	30 lbs.	Mississippi River	1959	Harold Ehler
PERCH, Yellow	2 lbs. 5 oz.	Strip Mine Lake	1951	William Hodgson
PIKE, Northern	20 lbs. 2 oz.	Strip Mine Lake	1952	Raymond Kindlespire
SAUGER	5 lbs. 12½ oz.	Mississippi River	1967	Bill Rolando
SHEEPSHEAD	35 lbs.	DuQuoin City Lake	1960	Joe Rinella
STURGEON, Lake	47 lbs.	Mississippi River	1958	Ernest Falica
SUNFISH, Redear	1 lb. 11 oz.	Farm Pond	1966	Larry L. Smith
TROUT, Brook	4 lbs.		1960	Shirl Laughlin
TROUT, Brown	7 lbs. 1 oz.	Rock River	1967	Dr. Edward Krivacek
TROUT, Rainbow	3 lbs.	Gravel Pit	1954	Bruce Muench
WALLEYE	14 lbs.	Kankakee River	1961	Fred Goselin

INDIANA

Species	Wt.	Where	When	Angler
BASS, Largemouth	11 lbs. 11 oz.	Ferdinand Reservoir	1968	Curt Reynolds
BASS, Rock	1 lb. 8 oz.	Farm Pond	1964	Earl J. Heick
BASS, Smallmouth	6 lbs. 3 oz.	Cataract Lake	1963	Art Gundlach
BASS, Spotted	1 lb. 12 oz.	Muscatatuck River	1968	Bill Gahl
BASS, White	4 lbs. 3 oz.	Lake Freeman	1965	James Wagner
BLUEGILL	2 lbs. 12 oz.	Farm Pond	1965	Freeman Miller
BOWFIN	10 lbs. 13 oz.	Wabash River	1967	Peter Jack Walters
BULLHEAD	3 lbs. 9 oz.	Strip Pit	1966	Roy Curtright
CARP	38 lbs. 1 oz.		1967	Frank J. Drost
CATFISH, Blue	15 lbs. 4 oz.	Farm Pond	1967	Ed Nash
CATFISH, Channel	20 lbs.	Tippecanoe River	1964	Lurton Sharp
CATFISH, Flathead	79 lbs. 8 oz.	White River	1966	Glen T. Simpson
CRAPPIE	4 lbs. 7 oz.	Farm Pond	1965	Mary Ann Leigh
MUSKELLUNGE	12 lbs.	Little Blue River	1965	Jim Vinyard
PERCH, Yellow	1 lb. 11 oz.	Farm Pond	1966	Jim Harper
PIKE, Northern	20 lbs. 12 oz.	Bass Lake	1964	George L. Byer
SALMON, Coho	14 lbs. 5 oz.	Lake Michigan	1968	Toby Bocanegra
SAUGER	5 lbs.	Wabash River	1964	N. L. Merrifield
SHEEPSHEAD	30 lbs.	White River	1963	Garland Fellers
SUNFISH, Redear	2 lbs. 11 oz.	Farm Pond	1964	Joan Janeway
TROUT, Brook	1 lb. 13 oz.	Beaver Dam	1966	Tim Arney
TROUT, Brown	10 lbs. 9 oz.		1968	Frank Coussens, Jr.

Species	Wt.	Where	When	Angler
TROUT, Rainbow	8 lbs. 5 oz.	Pretty Lake	1963	Francis Layson
TROUT, Steelhead	14 lbs. 10 oz.	Lake Michigan	1968	Chester Janik
WALLEYE	11 lbs. 12 oz.	White River	1963	Walter Williams

IOWA

Species	Wt.	Where	When	Angler
BASS, Largemouth	9 lbs. 15¼ oz.	Cold Springs	May 1 1968	Richard A. Milner, Sr.
BASS, Smallmouth	6 lbs. 3 oz.	West Okoboji	June 1966	Marvin Singer
BASS, White	3 lbs.	Black Hawk Lake	Sept. 1967	Donald Cole
BLUEGILL	2 lbs. 1 oz.	Farm Pond	June 1966	Chet Ryan
BULLHEAD	4 lbs. 8 oz.	Farm Pond	Apr. 1966	Dennie Karas
CARP	47 lbs.	Gravel Pit	Mar. 1967	Raynard James
CATFISH, Channel	25 lbs. 3 oz.	Rock Creek	June 1964	Lawrence Carpe
CATFISH, Flathead	62 lbs.	Iowa River	July 1965	Roger Fairchild
CRAPPIE	4 lbs.	Lake Darling	May 1964	Harold Conrad
PADDLEFISH	58 lbs. 13 oz.	Missouri River	Oct. 1965	Grace Holtzmann
PERCH, Yellow	1 lb. 13 oz.	Mississippi River	Sept. 1963	Neal Palmer
PIKE, Northern	21 lbs. 14 oz.	Gravel Pit	Aug. 11 1968	Lyle Hetrick
SAUGER	5 lbs. 2 oz.	Mississippi River	Nov. 1963	Art Hurlburt
SHEEPSHEAD	46 lbs.	Spirit Lake	Oct. 1962	R. L. Farran
TROUT, Brown	12 lbs. 14½ oz.	Elk Creek	Nov. 1966	Billy Lee
TROUT, Rainbow	13 lbs. 8 oz.	Richmond Springs	Nov. 13 1968	C. Melvin Vaughn
WALLEYE	14 lbs. 2 oz.	Spirit Lake	Oct. 7 1968	Herbert Aldridge

KANSAS

Species	Wt.	Where	When	Angler
BASS, Largemouth Black	11 lbs. 3 oz.	Private Lake	Jan. 6 1965	Charles Prewett
BASS, Spotted (Kentucky)	3 lbs. 12½ oz.	Marion County Lake	Apr. 5 1964	John I. Waner
BASS, White	5 lbs. 4 oz.	Toronto Reservoir	May 4 1966	Henry A. Baker
BLUEGILL	2 lbs. 5 oz.	Farm Pond	May 26 1962	Robert Jefferies
BUFFALO	29 lbs. 14 oz.	Kanopolis Reservoir	Oct. 1 1965	E. V. Harrelson
BULLHEAD	4 lbs. 3½ oz.	Farm Pond	June 18 1961	Frank Miller
CARP	27 lbs. 8 oz.	Lake Miola	May 18 1968	Milford Whitney
CATFISH, Channel	32 lbs.	Gardner City Lake	Aug. 14 1962	Edward S. Dailey
CATFISH, Flathead	86 lbs. 3 oz.	Neosho River	Aug. 24 1966	Ray Wiechert
CRAPPIE, Black	4 lbs. 10 oz.	Woodson Cty. State Lake	Oct. 21 1957	Hazel Fey
CRAPPIE, White	4 lbs. ¼ oz.	Farm Pond	Mar. 30 1964	Frank Miller
GAR	28 lbs.	Neosho River	June 17 1966	Mike Carter
PADDLEFISH	26 lbs.	Kaw River	Sept. 19 1962	John C. Huston
PIKE, Northern	17 lbs. 15 oz.	Council Grove Reservoir	Mar. 4	Clarence F. Nelson
SHEEPSHEAD	27 lbs.	Howard City Lake	June 27 1953	Louis Hebb
STURGEON	4 lbs.	Kaw River	Nov. 17 1962	J. W. Keeton
SUNFISH, Green	2 lbs. 2 oz.	Strip Pit	May 28 1961	Louis Ferlo
WALLEYE	10 lbs. 9 oz.	Lovewell Reservoir	June 1 1968	Floyd Stone

KENTUCKY

Species	Wt.	Where	When	Angler
BASS, Kentucky	5 lbs. 12 oz.	Dale Hollow Lake	May 25 1957	Robert G. Raque
BASS, Largemouth	13 lbs. 8 oz.	Greenbo Lake	Aug. 3 1966	Delbert Grizzle
BASS, Smallmouth (World's Record)	11 lbs. 15 oz.	Dale Hollow Lake	July 11 1955	David L. Hayes
BASS, Striped	34 lbs. 8 oz.	Lake Cumberland	Nov. 3 1964	Benny Polston
BASS, White (tie)	5 lbs.	Kentucky Lake	July 11 1943	Lorne Eli
	5 lbs.	Lake Herrington	June 5 1957	B. B. Hardin
BLUEGILL	3 lbs. 6 oz.	Buchanon Pond	May 30 1955	William S. Wooley
BUFFALO	24 lbs. 12 oz.	Rolling Fork River	Aug. 14 1952	T. W. Wade
CARP	35 lbs. 4 oz.	Barren River	Sept. 12 1952	Thomas F. Disman
CATFISH, Blue	60 lbs.	Tennessee River	July 8 1956	Normal Beth
CATFISH, Flathead	97 lbs.	Green River	June 6 1956	
CRAPPIE	4 lbs.	Harrods Creek	June 19 1951	Darrell Whitmer
GAR	40 lbs.	Ohio River	Aug. 8 1956	Kelsie Travis, Jr.
MUSKELLUNGE	39 lbs. 14 oz.	Green River	Jan. 1969	Willard Parnell
SHEEPSHEAD	31 lbs.	Kentucky Lake	June 2 1956	Jack Rowe
SPOONBILL	72 lbs.	Lake Cumberland	Mar. 6 1957	Ralph Pierce
STURGEON	36 lbs. 8 oz.	Lake Cumberland	Oct. 3 1954	Barnev Frazier
SUNFISH, Redear	2 lbs. 5 oz.		May 30 1964	R. C. Masters
TROUT, Rainbow	11 lbs. 3 oz.	Cumberland River	Jan. 31 1963	Ervin Moffett
WALLEYE	21 lbs. 8 oz.	Lake Cumberland	Oct. 1 1958	Abe Black

LOUISIANA

Freshwater Species	Wt.	Where	When	Angler
BASS, Largemouth	11 lbs. 11 oz.		Nov. 1958	Elwin Husser
BASS, Spotted (Kentucky)	4 lbs. 3 oz.			Carroll Perkins

Species	Wt.	Where	When	Angler
BREAM	2 lbs. 8 oz.		1959	Grant M. Kelly
CATFISH	46 lbs.		June 1966	E. F. Whitteborg
CRAPPIE	4 lbs. 4 oz.		April 1950	Welzie Garrett

Saltwater Species	Wt.	Where	When	Angler
AMBERJACK	83 lbs.		July 1959	George Tucker
BARRACUDA	40 lbs.		Sept. 1966	J. J. Jones
BLUEFISH	10 lbs. 6 oz.		July 1968	Ken Rushing
BONITO	24 lbs. 9 oz.		July 1949	Stirling Couch
COBIA	149 lbs. 12 oz.		May 1965	Garnett L. Caudell
CROAKER, Atlantic	4 lbs. 14 oz.		1966	Joseph D. Toups, Jr.
DOLPHIN	56 lbs. 12 oz.		June 1968	Wayne Plaisance
FLOUNDER	11 lbs. 1 oz.		Nov. 1967	Clarence Craig
JACK CREVALLE	40 lbs.		July 1953	Edwin F. Stacy, Jr.
MACKEREL, King	58½ lbs.		Aug. 1968	Ray Cox
MACKEREL, Spanish	6 lbs. 8 oz.		Oct. 1959	Al Hoeke
MARLIN, Blue	565 lbs.		Aug. 1966	Al R. Childress, Jr.
MARLIN, White	134 lbs.		July 1967	Dennis L. Good
POMPANO	6 lbs. 3 oz.		Mar. 1967	Louis U. Thornton
REDFISH	56 lbs. 8 oz.		Sept. 1963	O. L. Comish
SAILFISH	96 lbs.		Oct. 1953	John Lauricella
SHARK, Mako	280 lbs.		Aug. 1967	Leander H. Perez, Jr.
SHEEPSHEAD	11 lbs. 8 oz.		1955	Mrs. Aubrey Bares
SNAPPER	74 lbs.		Oct. 1963	Jim Meriweather
SPADEFISH	8 lbs. 3 oz.		Aug. 1963	Charles Sebastian
TARPON	198 lbs. 8 oz.		Sept. 1951	Oswald Frey
TRIPLETAIL	39 lbs. 8 oz.		July 1959	Mrs. Jimmy Toups
TROUT, Sea	12 lbs. 6 oz.		May 1950	Leon Mattes
TUNE, Blackfin	18 lbs.		Aug. 1966	Franklin C. Fisher, Jr.
TUNA, Bluefin	440 lbs.		May 1963	Jim Meriweather
TUNA, Yellowfin	196 lbs. 8 oz.		May 1966	Guy C. Billups, Jr.
WAHOO	110 lbs.		1964	Mrs. Bud Moore

MAINE

Species	Wt.	Where	When	Angler
BASS, Black	11 lbs. 10 oz.	Moose Pond	1968	R. Kamp

Species	Wt.	Where	When	Angler
PERCH, White	4 lbs. 10 oz.	Messalonskee Lake	1949	Mrs. E. Small
PICKEREL, Chain	6 lbs. 4 oz.	Pemaquid Pond	1968	L. Daigle
SALMON, Atlantic	26 lbs. 2 oz.	Narraguagus River	1959	H. Smith
SALMON, Landlocked	22 lbs. 8 oz.	Sebago Lake	1907	E. Blakeley
TROUT, Brook	8 lbs. 5 oz.	Pierce Pond	1958	D. Griffin
TROUT, Brown	19 lbs. 7 oz.	Sebago Lake	1958	N. Stacy
TROUT, Lake	31 lbs. 8 oz.	Beech Hill Pond	1958	H. Grindle

MARYLAND

Freshwater Species	Wt.	Where	When	Angler
BASS, Largemouth	10 lbs. 1 oz.	Loch Raven Reservoir	May 1966	Jerry Sauter
BASS, Smallmouth	7 lbs. 10 oz.	Liberty Reservoir	July 1967	Charles Marshall
BLUEGILL	1 lb. 8 oz.	Farm Pond	Aug. 1966	Warren W. Priestly
CARP	32 lbs. 9 oz.	Potomac River	June 1966	Lawrence Pearl
CATFISH	24 lbs.	Potomac River	Oct. 1964	James E. Turner
CRAPPIE	4 lbs. 3 oz.	Loch Raven	May 1962	Edward Glover
MUSKELLUNGE	31 lbs. 8 oz.	Susquehanna River	June 1966	Dan Wise
PICKEREL, Chain	7 lbs.	Port Tobacco Creek	May 1965	Donald W. Williams
PIKE, Northern	18 lbs. 12 oz.	Susquehanna River	Apr. 1967	Warren J. Myers
TROUT, Brown	8 lbs. 5 oz.	Deep Creek Lake	May 1958	W. Richards
WALLEYE	8 lbs.	Susquehanna River	May 1964	Henry A. Lau

Saltwater Species	Wt.	Where	When	Angler
ALBACORE	16 lbs.	Great Gull Bank	Sept. 8 1966	Walter R. Gillette
BASS, Channel	62 lbs.	South Marsh Island	June 17 1966	Mickey Moore
BASS, Sea	6 lbs. 8 oz.	Fenwick Shoal	June 23 1965	A. C. Morris
BASS, Striped	50 lbs. 1 oz.	Dumping Grounds	July 22 1965	Carol Rothwell
BLUEFISH	18 lbs. 8 oz.	E. of Ocean City	Nov. 1 1968	Lester J. Smack
COBIA	90 lbs. 8 oz.	S. W. Middlegrounds	July 27 1965	Levin W. Willey
CROAKER (tie)	4 lbs.	Buoy 16AA	Sept. 26 1964	Doris H. Gray
	4 lbs.	Buoy 16AA	Oct. 8 1964	Willie McNair
DOLPHIN	39 lbs.	Jackspot	Sept. 9 1967	Glenn Allmon
DRUM, Black	81 lbs.	Island Rock	May 28 1967	John H. DeMott
FLOUNDER	15 lbs.	Sinepuxent Bay	Sept. 4 1965	Floyd Flinchbaugh
KINGFISH	2 lbs.	Assateague Island	Oct. 16 1966	James M. Volk

Species	Wt.	Where	When	Angler
MARLIN, White	114 lbs. 8 oz.	Jackspot	July 18 1965	Joseph Pessagno
PERCH, White	2 lbs. 8 oz.	Devil's Hole	Nov. 26 1967	Robert L. Hughes
PERCH, Yellow	2 lbs.	City Yacht Basin	May 17 1965	Thomas Estvanik
PICKEREL, Chain	6 lbs. 8 oz.	Susquehanna River	May 19 1965	James N. Grant
PORGY	6 lbs. 3 oz.	Fenwick Shoal	July 4 1966	Pearl L. Hopple
SHAD, Hickory	3 lbs. 14 oz.	Pocomoke River	Apr. 8 1968	Louis G. Rever
SHAD, White	7 lbs. 8 oz.	Patuxent River	Apr. 18 1968	Robert L. Harris
SHARK	279 lbs.	Sinepuxent Bay	Aug. 28 1965	John Brice Long
SHARK, Mako	119 lbs. 8 oz.	40 Fathom Line	Aug. 17 1967	Edward Bretschneider
SPOT	1 lb. 4 oz.	Snake Reef	June 28 1967	Annette Krichinsky
TAUTOG	14 lbs. 4 oz.	Fenwick Shoal	July 10 1966	Charles Gross
TROUT, Sea	7 lbs. 2 oz.	Holland Island	Oct. 2 1967	Leven A. Anderson, Jr.
TUNA	55 lbs. 8 oz.	East of Ocean City	Sept. 3 1966	Leonard Goddard
WAHOO	67 lbs.	Jackspot	Sept. 8 1968	E. R. Bounds
WEAKFISH	6 lbs. 2 oz.	Inlet	Aug. 10 1967	Joseph G. Sukle, Jr.

MICHIGAN

Species	Wt.	Where	When	Angler
BASS, Largemouth	11 lbs. 15 oz.	Big Pine Island Lake	June 25 1934	William J. Maloney
BASS, Smallmouth	9 lbs. 4 oz.	Long Lake	1906	W. F. Shoemaker
BASS, Rock	3 lbs. 10 oz.	Lenawee Cty. Lake	June 26 1965	Edward Arnold
BLUEGILL	2 lbs. 10 oz.	Silver Lake	Aug. 5 1945	F. M. Broock
CATFISH, Channel	47 lbs. 8 oz.	Maple River	Aug. 6 1937	Elmer Rayner
CRAPPIE, Black	4 lbs. 2 oz.	Lincoln Lake	June 1947	E. Frank Lee
MUSKELLUNGE	62 lbs. 8 oz.	Lake St. Clair	June 23 1940	Percy Haver
PERCH, Yellow	2 lbs. 10 oz.	Lake Huron	June 28 1951	Priscilla Schott
SHEEPSHEAD	17 lbs. 4 oz.	Muskegon	June 26 1954	Mike Thomas
TROUT, Brook	9 lbs. 12 oz.	Au Sable River	1909	Jack Trasher
TROUT, Brown	21 lbs. 8 oz.	Crystal Lake	June 14 1969	Arthur Huls
TROUT, Lake	88 lbs.	Lake Michigan	1864	G. B. Goode
TROUT, Rainbow	21 lbs. 10 oz.	Manistee River	Oct. 2 1967	Mrs. Joseph Purgiel
WALLEYE	17 lbs. 3 oz.	Pine River	Nov. 8 1951	Ray Fadely

MASSACHUSETTS

Species	Wt.	Where	When	Angler
BASS, Largemouth	12 lbs. 1 oz.	Palmer River	May 9 1963	George Pastick
BASS, Smallmouth	6 lbs. 12 oz.	Pleasant Lake	May 14 1967	Thomas Paradise
BLUEGILL	1 lb.	Bog Pond	Oct. 17 1965	Robert Barrett
BULLHEAD	5 lbs. 9 oz.	Conn. River	June 8 1963	Mrs. Erna Storie
CATFISH, Channel	13 lbs. 8 oz.	Conn. River	July 18 1964	Robert Thibodo
CRAPPIE	2 lbs. 9½ lbs.	Merrimack	June 8 1965	George Olsson
PERCH, White	2 lbs. 4 oz.	Halfway Pond	June 9 1965	Richard Rock
PERCH, Yellow	2 lbs.	Grt. Herring	May 9 1966	Anthony Scolaro
PICKEREL, Chain	9 lbs. 5 oz.	Pontoosuc Lake	1954	Mrs. James Martin
PIKE, Northern	24 lbs. 8 oz.	Onota Lake	Jan. 13 1967	Kris Ginthwain
SHAD	7 lbs. 10 oz.	Indian Head	May 1968	William Spaulding
TROUT, Brook	6 lbs. 4 oz.	Otis Reservoir	June 24 1968	Thomas Laptew
TROUT, Brown	19 lbs. 10 oz.	Wachusett Reservoir	May 19 1966	Dana DeBlois
TROUT, Lake	13 lbs. 1 oz.	Quabbin Reservoir	Sept. 13 1963	LeeRoy DeHoff
TROUT, Rainbow	8 lbs. 4 oz.	Deep Pond	Oct. 15 1966	Roger Walker
WALLEYE (tie)	8 lbs. 8 oz.	Quabbin Reservoir	July 15 1965	Joseph Schwartz
	8 lbs. 8 oz.	Conn. River	June 7 1964	Peter Yeskie

MINNESOTA

Species	Wt.	Where	When	Angler
BASS, Largemouth	10 lbs. 2 oz.	Prairie Lake	1961	Harold Lehn
BASS, Smallmouth	8 lbs.	West Battle Lake	1948	John A. Creighton
BLUEGILL	2 lbs. 13 oz.	Lake Alice	1948	Bob Parker
CARP	86 lbs.	Minnesota River	1906	C. A. Cameron
CATFISH, Channel	37 lbs.	White Bear Lake	1962	Larry Peterson
CATFISH, Mud	60 lbs.	St. Croix River	1960	Al Stoll
CRAPPIE	5 lbs.	Vermillion River	1940	Tom Christenson
DOGFISH	10 lbs.	Lake Minnetonka	1941	Roger Lehman
MOONEYE	1 lb. 8 oz.	St. Croix River	1948	Frank Bradac
MUSKELLUNGE	56 lbs. 8 oz.	Lake-of-the-Woods	July 24 1931	J. W. Collins
PERCH, Yellow	3 lbs. 4 oz.	Lake Plantaganette	1945	Merle Johnson
PIKE, Northern	45 lbs. 12 oz.	Basswood Lake	May 16 1929	J. V. Schanken
SAUGER	4 lbs. 3 oz.	St. Croix River	1963	John Most
SHEEPSHEAD	26 lbs. 12 oz.	Blackduck Lake	1968	
STURGEON, Lake	236 lbs.	Lake-of-the-Woods	1911	
TROUT, Brook	9 lbs. 7 oz.	Ash River	1958	Frank Hause
TROUT, Brown	16 lbs. 8 oz.	Grindstone Lake	1961	M. Lovgren
TROUT, Lake	43 lbs. 8 oz.	Lake Superior	May 30 1955	G. H. Nelson

Species	Wt.	Where	When	Angler
TROUT, Rainbow	14 lbs. 8 oz.	Arrowhead River	Aug. 1 1933	E. O. Culbertson
WALLEYE (tie)	16 lbs. 8 oz.	Sturgeon Lake	1949	John E. Norkeli
	16 lbs. 8 oz.	Lake-of-the-Woods	1959	Mitch Rebarcheck

MISSISSIPPI

Species	Wt.	Where	When	Angler
BASS, Largemouth	13 lbs. 2 oz.	Theo Costas Lake	May 2 1963	Noel L. Mills
BASS, White	5 lbs. 2 oz.	Grenada Spillway	July 9 1969	Eddy Vaughn
BLUEGILL	2 lbs. 5 oz.	Mississippi River	May 20 1963	Leonard Busby
BOWFIN	16 lbs. 4 oz.	Ross Barnett Reservoir	Nov. 25 1967	Don R. Bush
CARP	74 lbs.	Pelahatchie Lake	June 13 1963	Curtis Wade
CRAPPIE, White	5 lbs. 3 oz.	Enid Reservoir	July 31 1957	Fred Bright
PADDLEFISH	23 lbs. 12 oz.	Ross Barnett Reservoir	Dec. 19 1968	Bob G. Ponds
PICKEREL, Chain	4 lbs. 4 oz.	Ross Barnett Reservoir	Apr. 25 1966	Mrs. Robert W. King
SUNFISH, Redear	2 lbs. 2 oz.	Lake Tiak O'Khata	July 2 1963	Ben Smythe

MISSOURI

Species	Wt.	Where	When	Angler
BASS, Largemouth	13 lbs. 14 oz.	Bull Shoals Lake	Apr. 1961	Marvin Bushong
BASS, Smallmouth	6 lbs. 7 oz.	Valley Dolomite Pond	1952	Burl Koester
BASS, Kentucky	7 lbs. 8 oz.	Table Rock	Apr. 6 1966	Gene Arnaud
BASS, Rock	2 lbs. 12 oz.	Big Piney River	June 15 1968	William J. Rod
BASS, White (tie)	4 lbs. 8 oz.	Lake Norfolk	1952	Robert Ketchum
	4 lbs. 8 oz.	Bull Shoals Lake	Oct. 27 1962	Mrs. A. G. Morris
BLUEGILL	3 lbs.	Pond at Bevier		Mike Giovanni
BOWFIN	19 lbs.	Duck Creek	Mar. 1963	Clois Coomer
BUFFALO	35 lbs.	Osage at Osceola	May 1964	Bill Bradley
CARP	36 lbs. 8 oz.	Farm Pond	June 1968	Clifford McGinnis
CATFISH, Blue	117 lbs.	Osage River	July 25 1964	Anzel Goans
CATFISH, Channel	28 lbs. 6 oz.	Lake Jacomo	Aug. 12 1968	Earl Selsor
CATFISH, Flathead	74 lbs.	Osage below Bagnell Dam	May 30 1964	Emmett Stampleton
CRAPPIE, Black	4 lbs. 8 oz.	Fish Pond	May 28 1967	Ray Babcock
CRAPPIE, White	3 lbs. 12 oz.	Sugar Creek Lake	May 1964	Dee Embree
PADDLEFISH	110 lbs.	Lake of the Ozarks	Apr. 17 1966	Jim Ruth
STURGEON	53 lbs.	Missouri River	1950	
SUNFISH, Longear	1½ lbs.	Kenney Pond	June 30 1966	Tom Nelson
TROUT, Rainbow	13 lbs. 12 oz.	Bennett Spring	1960	H. N. Branson

Species	Wt.	Where	When	Angler
TROUT, Brown	6 lbs. 8 oz.	Montauk State Park	June 28 1968	John McCulley
WALLEYE	20 lbs.	St. Francis River	1961	John T. Vacholek

MONTANA
(No Records Maintained)

NEBRASKA

Species	Wt.	Where	When	Angler
BASS, Kentucky Spotted	3 lbs. 11 oz.	Sand Pit	Mar. 24 1968	Tom Pappas
BASS, Largemouth	10 lbs. 11 oz.	Sand Pit	Oct. 2 1965	Paul Abegglen, Sr.
BASS, Rock	2 lbs.	Frenchman River	May 28 1966	Violet Kelly
BASS, Smallmouth (tie)	3 lbs. 15 oz.	Lake McConaughy	May 12 1962	George Ford
	3 lbs. 15 oz.	Red Willow Reservoir	Mar. 26 1968	Leonard Dicke
BASS, Striped	2 lbs.	Lake McConaughy	Aug. 4 1968	Emmett Mostek
BASS, White	4 lbs. 15 oz.	Sand Pit	1962	Frederick Baldwin
BLUEGILL	2 lbs. 8 oz.	Farm Pond	Aug. 27 1968	Charles Randolph
BUFFALO	33 lbs. 8 oz.	Seirs Lake	Sept. 4 1966	Mrs. Lyle Clemens
BULLHEAD	3 lbs. 8 oz.	Smith Lake	July 28 1963	Alfred E. Porter
CARP	28 lbs. 2 oz.	Hall County Lake	May 18 1967	Harry Lassen
CATFISH, Blue	81 lbs.	Gavins Point Dam	Nov. 16 1967	Louis Psotta
CATFISH, Channel	31 lbs. 12 oz.	Ericson	1944	Bob Nuquist
CATFISH, Flathead	59 lbs.	Missouri River	Nov. 30 1961	Ralph Adair
CRAPPIE	3 lbs. 15 oz.	Lake McConaughy	Apr. 29 1962	Delmer Butler
MUSKELLUNGE	13 lbs. 6 oz.	Merritt Reservoir	June 14 1967	Richard Anderson
PADDLEFISH	72 lbs.	Gavins Point Dam	July 6 1961	Lyle Sawatzke
PERCH, Sacramento	1 lb. 13 oz.	Clear Lake	Feb. 25 1968	Calvin Thornton
PERCH, Yellow	2 lbs.	Conway Lake	Jan. 16 1966	Joe Adams
PIKE, Northern	27 lbs. 8 oz.	Lake McConaughy	July 14 1962	Cletus Jacobsen
SAUGER	8 lbs. 5 oz.	Missouri River	Oct. 22 1961	Mrs. Betty Tepner
SHEEPSHEAD	23 lbs.	Carter Lake	June 10 1963	Robert D. Bennett
SUCKER	4 lbs.	Lake Minatare	Apr. 29 1968	Jack Keller
SUNFISH, Green	1 lb. 1¼ oz.	Farm Pond	May 23 1968	William Fattig
SUNFISH, Redear	1 lb.	Fremont Lake	May 30 1968	Buss Schneider
STURGEON	26 lbs. 14 oz.	Lewis and Clark Lake	Apr. 9 1967	Steve Brik
TROUT, Brook	5 lbs. 1 oz.	Pawnee Springs	Nov. 3 1965	Joe Gray
TROUT, Brown	11 lbs. 4 oz.	Lake McConaughy	1950	L. B. Eby

Species	Wt.	Where	When	Angler
TROUT, Rainbow	12 lbs. 8 oz.	Lake McConaughy	Aug. 4 1968	Wayne Rath
WALLEYE	16 lbs. 1 oz.	Lake McConaughy	June 13 1959	Don Hein

NEVADA
(No Records Maintained)

NEW HAMPSHIRE

Species	Wt.	Where	When	Angler
BASS, Largemouth	10 lbs. 5 oz.	Lake Potanipo	May 1967	G. Bullpitt
BASS, Smallmouth	6 lbs.	Pleasant Lake	1968	Mrs. Dudley Dean
PERCH, White	3 lbs.	Winnipesaukee Lake	May 1965	A. Santos
PERCH, Yellow	2 lbs. 4 oz.	Heads Pond	Mar. 1969	R. Hebert
PICKEREL, Chain	8 lbs.	Plummer Pond	Apr. 26 1966	C. R. Akerly
PIKE, Northern	16 lbs. 1 oz.	Spofford Lake	May 1967	D. Graves
SALMON, Land-locked	18 lbs. 5 oz.	Pleasant Lake	Aug. 31 1942	Mrs. E. D. Clark
SPLAKE	8 lbs. 5 oz.	White Lake	May 9 1963	R. Walker
TROUT, Brook	9 lbs.	Pleasant Lake	1911	A. V. Woodruff
TROUT, Brown	15 lbs. 4 oz.	Connecticut River	May 30 1953	Calvin Hall
TROUT, Lake	28 lbs. 5 oz.	Newfound Lake	Apr. 24 1958	Albert Staples
TROUT, Rainbow	13 lbs.	Dublin Lake	1953	
TROUT, Sunapee	11 lbs. 5 oz.	Sunapee Lake	Aug. 1 1954	E. Theoharris
WALLEYE	8 lbs. 7 oz.	Connecticut River	Apr. 1968	F. Fradeau

NEW JERSEY

FRESHWATER Species	Wt.	Where	When	Angler
BASS, Largemouth	10 lbs. 12 oz.	Mt. Kimble Lake	1960	Logan Whitesell
BASS, Rock	1 lb. 2 oz.	Lake Hopatcong	1968	Harold Webb
BASS, Smallmouth	6 lbs. 4 oz.	Delaware River	1957	Earl Trumpore
BASS, Striped (landlocked)	23 lbs. 8 oz.	Union Lake	1952	Mrs. Albert Beebe
BLUEGILL	2 lbs.	Farm Pond	1956	Silas Matthews, Jr.
BULLHEAD, Brown	22 lbs. 15 oz.	Spring Lake	1966	Robert Dorf
CATFISH, Channel	28 lbs.	Greenwood Lake	1918	William Otten
CRAPPIE	3 lbs. 5 oz.	Alloway Lake	1961	William Hanna
PERCH, White	2 lbs. 8 oz.	Lake Hopatcong	1950	Robert Huber
PERCH, Yellow	4 lbs. 3 oz.	Bordentown	1865	C. C. Abbot
PICKEREL, Chain	9 lbs. 3 oz.	Lower Aetna Lake	1957	Frank McGovern

Species	Wt.	Where	When	Angler
PIKE, Northern	18 lbs. 13 oz.	Shepherd Lake	1967	Richard Vezirian
SALMON, Land-locked	8 lbs.	New Wawayanda Lake	1951	John Mount
TROUT, Brook	6 lbs. 8 oz.	Lake Hopatcong	1956	George Hornung
TROUT, Brown	16 lbs. 11 oz.	Greenwood Lake	1964	Howard Devore
TROUT, Rainbow	8 lbs. 5 oz.	Greenwood Lake	1964	Fritz Benzavitch
WALLEYE	12 lbs. 12 oz.	Delaware River	1934	Stanley Norman

Saltwater Species	Wt.	Where	When	Angler
ALBACORE	69 lbs. 1 oz.	Hudson Canyon	1961	Walter Citimm
BASS, Channel	46 lbs.	Sandy Hook	* 1953	R. D. Alexander
BASS, Sea	6 lbs. 2 oz.		1958	Nick Ferrante
BASS, Striped	64 lbs. 8 oz.	Great Egg Harbor River	1968	L. Albertson
BLACKFISH	21 lbs. 6 oz.	Cape May	1954	R. Sheafer
BLUEFISH	22 lbs. 11 oz.	17 Fathom	1968	Sigmund Cruszkowski
BONITO	13 lbs. 8 oz.	Sandy Hook	1945	Frank Lykes, Jr.
COD	81 lbs.	Brielle	1967	Joseph Chesla
DOLPHIN	45 lbs.	Cape May	1963	Frank Notaro
DRUM, Black	92 lbs.	Delaware Bay	1944	Herschel Layton
FLOUNDER, Winter	3 lbs. 2 oz.	Great Egg Harbor River	1968	Frank Coleman
FLUKE	19 lbs. 12 oz.	Cape May	1953	Walter Lubin
MARLIN, Blue	620 lbs.	Atlantic City	1964	Joseph Teti, Jr.
MARLIN, White	123 lbs.	Ambrose Light	1968	Merrill Arden
POLLACK	43 lbs.	Brielle	1964	Philip Barlow
SHARK, Mako	322 lbs.	Elberon	1952	W. Mahan
SWORDFISH, Broadbill	530 lbs.	Wilmington Canyon	1964	Edmund Levitt
TUNA	787 lbs.	Brielle	1950	Ray Fromm
WAHOO	90 lbs.	Beach Haven	1965	Edward McFadden
WEAKFISH	17 lbs. 8 oz.	Mullica River	1952	A. Weisbecker, Jr.

NEW MEXICO
(No Records Maintained)

NEW YORK

Species	Wt.	Where	When	Angler
BASS, Largemouth	10 lbs. 6 oz.			
BASS, Smallmouth	9 lbs.	Friends Lake Outlet	1925	George Tennyson

Species	Wt.	Where	When	Angler
MUSKELLUNGE	69 lbs. 15 oz.	St. Lawrence River	1957	Arthur Lawton
PIKE, Northern	46 lbs. 2 oz.	Sacandaga Reservoir	1940	Peter Dubuc
SALMON	16 lbs. 14 oz.	Lake George	1958	Neil Hughes
TROUT, Brook	8 lbs. 8 oz.	Punchbowl Pond	1908	William Keener
TROUT, Brown	21 lbs. 5 oz.	Owasco Lake	1954	Thomas Klink
TROUT, Lake	31 lbs.	Follensby Pond	1922	Malcolm Hain
TROUT, Rainbow	21 lbs.	Keuka Lake	1946	Earl G. Crane
WALLEYE	15 lbs. 3 oz.	Chemung River	1952	Blanche Baker

NORTH CAROLINA

Freshwater Species	Wt.	Where	When	Angler
BASS, Largemouth	14 lbs. 15 oz.	Santeetlah Reservoir	Apr. 26 1963	Leonard Williams
BASS, Smallmouth	10 lbs. 2 oz.	Hiwassee Reservoir	June 1953	Archie Lampkin
BASS, Striped (landlocked)	33 lbs. 8 oz.	Mt. Island Reservoir	Jan. 16 1967	A. E. Taunt
BASS, White	4 lbs. 15 oz.	Fontana Reservoir	July 27 1966	Leonard Williams
BLUEGILL	4 lbs. 5 oz.	Edneyville Pond	July 27 1967	Danny Case
CRAPPIE	4 lbs. 8 oz.	Tillery Lake	1960	Henry Griffin
PICKEREL, Chain	8 lbs.	Gaston Reservoir	Feb. 13 1968	John H. Leonard
SHAD	5 lbs. 4 oz.	Cape Fear River	Apr. 6 1968	Randall H. Neal
SHELLCRACKER	4 lbs. 4 oz.	Lee County Pond	Feb. 3 1968	Bill Arnold
TROUT, Brook	2 lbs. 8 oz.	Garden Creek	Apr. 2 1966	Harper L. McMillian
TROUT, Brown	12 lbs.	Nantahala River		Jim Gaddy
TROUT, Rainbow	14 lbs. 1 oz.	Glenville Reservoir	Mar. 6 1949	Max Q. Rogers
WALLEYE	13 lbs. 4 oz.	Santeetlah Reservoir	May 1966	Leonard Williams

Saltwater Species	Wt.	Where	When	Angler
ALBACORE	22¼ lbs.	Morehead City	1965	Mike Bach
AMBERJACK	120 lbs.	Wrightsville Beach	Dec. 1964	Merrill Lockfaw
BARRACUDA	44 lbs. 1 oz.	Southport	Aug. 19 1957	Ralph Taylor
BASS, Channel	75½ lbs.	Hatteras	Nov. 29 1941	Capt. Bernice Ballance
BASS, Striped	53 lbs.	Hatteras Island	Dec. 3 1965	Raymond Basnett
BLUEFISH	21½ lbs.	Kitty Hawk	Nov. 7 1967	Joseph J. Menzaco
BONITO	21 lbs.	Wrightsville Beach	July 19 1957	Swift M. Boatwright
COBIA	97 lbs.	Oregon Inlet	June 4 1952	Mary W. Black

Species	Wt.	Where	When	Angler
CROAKER	2 lbs. 1 oz.	Surf City	May 2 1958	William Moye
DOLPHIN	63 lbs.	Cape Hatteras	1934	Tom Eaton
DRUM, Black	82¼ lbs.	Surf City	Apr. 23 1955	C. E. Workman
FLOUNDER	14½ lbs.	Carolina Beach	Nov. 14 1961	Dan Holt
MACKEREL, King	57 lbs.	Cape Lookout	Oct. 1966	Russel Dement
MACKEREL, Spanish	9¾ lbs.	Carolina Beach	Sept. 20 1963	C. R. Pfaff
MARLIN, Blue	810 lbs.	Cape Hatteras	June 11 1962	Gary Stukes
MARLIN, White	106¾ lbs.	Wrightsville Beach	June 6 1964	L. T. Davis
POMPANO (tie)	5 lbs. 9 oz.	Fort Fisher	Oct. 19 1957	Dorothy Lipman
	5 lbs. 9 oz.	Kure Beach	June 18 1965	Alice B. Nelson
SAILFISH	75 lbs.	Hatteras	Aug. 25 1953	Atlas B. Windham
SHEEPSHEAD	12 lbs. 1 oz.	Southport	Aug. 20 1959	J. Hunter Barden
SPOT	1 lb. 2 oz.	Carolina Beach	Sept. 27 1955	Landis Lee
TARPON	152 lbs.	Wrightsville Beach	June 1 1961	Bobby Kentrolis
TUNA, Blackfin	21 lbs.		Sept. 25 1968	Evelyn Colbert
TUNA, Bluefin	491 lbs.	Cape Hatteras	May 29 1963	Dick Derbyshire
TUNA, Atlantic Big-Eyed	195½ lbs.	Oregon Inlet	June 28 1958	Earl C. Bigger
TUNA, Yellowfin	188 lbs.	Oregon Inlet	1960	J. R. Tribby
WAHOO	80¾ lbs.	Morehead City	May 28 1968	Ed Johnston
WEAKFISH	12¼ lbs.	Wrightsville Beach	Dec. 29 1961	John Kenyon, Jr.
WEAKFISH, Spotted	9¼ lbs.	Topsail Beach	Oct. 25 1955	W. H. Goodman
WHITING (tie)	3 lbs. 1 oz.	Carolina Beach	Oct. 24 1955	Milton Warwick
	3 lbs. 1 oz.	Topsail Beach	Nov. 21 1959	William T. Gulledge

NORTH DAKOTA

Species	Wt.	Where	When	Angler
BASS, Largemouth	7 lbs. 12 oz.	Welk Dam	1951	George Marquardt
BASS, White	4 lbs.	Oahe Reservoir	1968	Edwin Shlenker
BLUEGILL	2 lbs. 12 oz.	Strawberry Lake	1963	Bud Hystad
CARP	21 lbs. 12 oz.	Red River	1958	Don J. Pasco
CATFISH, Channel	26½ lbs.	Lake Sakakawea	1968	Clyde Coe
CRAPPIE	3 lbs.	James River	1958	John Kinney
PERCH, Yellow	2 lbs. 2 oz.	Lake Audubon	1966	Norman Hanson
PIKE, Northern	37½ lbs.	Lake Sakakawea	1968	Melvin Slind

Species	Wt.	Where	When	Angler
SAUGER	8 lbs. 3 oz.	Garrison Tailrace	1957	Henry Anderson
SHEEPSHEAD	8 lbs. 8 oz.	Sheyenne River	1964	Elliam Kuchera
TROUT, Brown	5 lbs. 14 oz.	Hiawatha Reservoir	1968	Dr. W. C. Voglewede
TROUT, Rainbow	9 lbs. 11 oz.	Garrison Tailrace	1960	Michael Stoick
WALLEYE	15 lbs. 12 oz.	Wood Lake	1959	Blair Chapman

OHIO

Species	Wt.	Where	When	Angler
BASS, Largemouth	9 lbs. 8 oz.	Choppers Lake	May 26 1966	Ed Hutchins
BASS, Rock	1 lb. 15½ oz.	Deer Creek	Sept. 3 1962	George A. Keller
BASS, Smallmouth	7½ lbs.	Mad River	June 17 1941	James Bayless
BASS, Spotted	5 lbs. 4 oz.	Lake White	May 2 1967	Roger Trainer
BASS, White	3 lbs. 6 oz.	Lake Erie	Aug. 24 1954	Julia Morrison
BOWFIN	3 lbs. 12 oz.	Lake Hope	Apr. 27 1968	Marvin A. Kuhens
BULLHEAD	3 lbs. 14¾ oz.	Glandorf Lake	May 9 1966	Roy Kuhlman
CARP	50 lbs.	Paint Creek	May 24 1967	Judson Holton
CATFISH, Channel	25 lbs.	Piedmont Lake	May 10 1964	Charles J. McGrath
CATFISH, Flathead (tie)	65 lbs.	Clendening Lake	May 25 1962	Almer Affolter
	65 lbs.	Muskingum River	July 5 1968	H. M. Schmelzenbach
CRAPPIE, Black	3½ lbs.	Scioto Lakes	Apr. 10 1968	M. W. Grover
CRAPPIE, White	3 lbs. 3 oz.	Muzzy Lake	July 27 1968	Christy Buckeye
GAR	25 lbs.	Ohio River	Aug. 31 1966	Flora Irvin
MUSKELLUNGE	39¼ lbs.	Leesville Lake	Apr. 27 1968	Harold Miller
PERCH, Yellow	2 lbs. 8 oz.	Lake Erie	Nov. 14 1954	J. H. Olasky
PICKEREL, Chain	6 lbs. 4 oz.	Long Lake	Mar. 25 1961	Ronald Kotch
PIKE, Northern	14 lbs. 6 oz.	Lake Erie	Mar. 18 1961	Gary Beatty
SHEEPSHEAD	18 lbs.	Maumee River	June 18 1957	Ralph Degrange
SUCKER	9 lbs. 10¾ oz.	Rocky River	Apr. 10 1954	Milan Kutner
SUNFISH	2 lbs. 1 oz.	Farm Pond	Apr. 27 1968	Gary L. Manring
TROUT, Brook	2 lbs. 11 oz.	East Branch Chagrin River	June 30 1955	S. Graboshek
TROUT, Brown	13 lbs. 8 oz.	Cold Creek	Sept. 10 1942	J. S. Harris
TROUT, Rainbow	10 lbs. 8 oz.	Pickerel Creek	July 5 1951	John Fedlam
WALLEYE	15 lbs.	Pymatuning Reservoir	Nov. 13 1951	William Heathman

OKLAHOMA
(No Records Maintained)

OREGON
(No Records Maintained)

PENNSYLVANIA

Species	Wt.	Where	When	Angler
BASS, Largemouth	8 lbs. 8 oz.	Stillwater Lake	1936	Stanley Pastula
BASS, Rock	3 lbs.	Swatara Creek	1966	John H. Rhodes
BASS, Smallmouth	6 lbs. 2 oz.	Conodoguinet Creek	1937	Ed Meadows
BLUEGILL		Hills Creek Lake	1965	Donald W. Correll, Jr.
BULLHEAD	11 lbs. 8 oz.	Allegheny River	1966	John Moore, Jr.
CARP	52 lbs.	Juniata River	1962	George Brown
CATFISH, Channel	18 lbs.	York Haven Dam	1964	Thomas J. Booth
CRAPPIE	3 lbs. 8 oz.	Lake Ontelaunee	1967	Allen L. Roen
MUSKELLUNGE	54 lbs.	Conneaut Lake	1924	Luke Walker, Jr.
PERCH		Oneida Dam	1936	Herman Rausch
PICKEREL, Chain	8 lbs.	Shohola Falls	1937	Frank Streznetcky
PIKE, Northern	19 lbs.	Somerset Lake	1962	Mahlon Waley
SHAD, American White	7 lbs. 4 oz.	Delaware River	1965	Vincent Graziano
SHEEPSHEAD	14 lbs.	Virgin Run Lake	1964	Gregory Parella
SUCKER	9 lbs. 12 oz.	French Creek	1938	George Kemper
TROUT, Brook	4 lbs. 4 oz.	Swago Lake	1966	Beth Ann Riker
TROUT, Brown	24 lbs.	Lake Wallenpaupack	1967	Frank Kociolek
TROUT, Lake	24 lbs.	Crystal Lake	1952	Mrs. Arthur Cramer
TROUT, Rainbow	9 lbs. 8 oz.	Logan Branch	1961	Paul Roberts
WALLEYE	12 lbs.	Allegheny River	1951	Firman Shoff

RHODE ISLAND
(No Records Maintained)

SOUTH CAROLINA

Species	Wt.	Where	When	Angler
BASS, Largemouth Black	16 lbs. 2 oz.	Santee-Cooper	1949	
BASS, Striped	55 lbs.	Lake Moultrie	Jan. 29 1963	Tiny Lund
CATFISH, Channel	58 lbs.	Lake Moultrie	July 7 1964	W. H. Whaley
CRAPPIE, Black	5 lbs.	Lake Moultrie	1957	

Species	Wt.	Where	When	Angler
CRAPPIE, White	5 lbs. 1 oz.	Lake Murray	Mar. 6 1949	Mrs. H. F. Owen
PICKEREL, Chain	6 lbs.	Lake Marion	Jan. 10 1962	H. F. Avinger
TROUT, Brown	13 lbs. 4 oz.	Chauga River	July 27 1961	Julian Addis
WARMOUTH	1 lb. 2 oz.	Cooper River	May 18 1968	Robert L. Joyner

SOUTH DAKOTA

Species	Wt.	Where	When	Angler
BASS, Largemouth	8 lbs. 12 oz.	Hayes Lake	1957	Verne Page
BASS, Rock	1 lb. 3 oz.	Pickerel Lake	1966	Ronald Schulz
BASS, Smallmouth	1 lb. 4 oz.	Orman Dam	1968	Mrs. Warren Ower
BASS, White	3 lbs. 14 oz.	Enemy Swim Lake	1964	John Yunker
BLUEGILL	2 lbs. 1 oz.	Roy Lake	1965	John Smith
BUFFALO, Bigmouth	34 lbs.	Lake Mitchell	1965	Harry Durst
BUFFALO, Smallmouth	7 lbs. 6 oz.	James River	1966	Bill Lynch
BULLHEAD, Black	2 lbs. 14 oz.	Stock Dam	1968	Paul Schumacher
BULLHEAD, Brown	2 lbs. 7 oz.	Crystal Lake	1963	Norman Clark
BURBOT	10 lbs. 2 oz.	Oahe Reservoir	1968	Edmund K. Arndt
CATFISH, Blue	100 lbs. 8 oz.	Missouri River	1964	Bob Millage
CATFISH, Channel	55 lbs.	James River	1949	Roy Groves
CATFISH, Flathead	35 lbs. 4 oz.	James River	1966	Daniel Leair
CRAPPIE, Black	3 lbs. 2 oz.	Fort Randall Reservoir	1964	Richard Hermanek
CRAPPIE, White	2 lbs. 11 oz.	Oahe Reservoir	1967	Al Pfeifle
GAR, Longnose	13 lbs. 9½ oz.	Missouri River	1965	Terry Coulson
GAR, Shortnose	15 oz.	Hipple Lake	1965	Ned Fogle
PADDLEFISH	92 lbs. 8 oz.	Big Bend Tailwaters	1969	Harvey J. Jansen
PERCH, Yellow	1 lb. 15 oz.	Potts Dam	1968	Paul Herichs
PIKE, Northern	33 lbs. 8 oz.	Enemy Swim Lake	1939	Leroy Nelson
SAUGER	7 lbs. 7 oz.	Oahe Tailwaters	1960	Harvey Holzworth
SHEEPSHEAD	12 lbs. 9 oz.	Lake Mitchell	1966	Harry Durst
STURGEON, Lake	25 lbs.	Missouri River	1968	Delbert Henn
STURGEON, Shovelnose	13 oz.	Oahe Tailwaters	1963	C. E. Titus
SUCKER	11 lbs. 11 oz.	James River	1967	Vernon A. Sarha
SUNFISH, Green	13 oz.	Hayes Lake	1964	Ned Fogle
TROUT, Brook	5 lbs. 6 oz.	Deerfield Reservoir	1966	Tom Sawyer
TROUT, Brown	18 lbs. 3 oz.	Rapid Creek	1928	Jess Wickersham

Species	Wt.	Where	When	Angler
TROUT, Rainbow	11 lbs. 8 oz.	Pactola Reservoir	1967	Fred Wolfe
WALLEYE	15 lbs.	Lake Kampeska	1960	Carl Wiese

TENNESSEE

Species	Wt.	Where	When	Angler
BASS, Largemouth	14 lbs. 8 oz.	Sugar Creek	Oct. 17 1954	Louge Barnett
BASS, Rock	2 lbs. 8 oz.	Stones River	1958	Bill Sanford
BASS, Smallmouth	11 lbs. 15 oz.	Dale Hollow Reservoir	July 13 1955	D. L. Hayes
BASS, Spotted	3 lbs. 8 oz.	Kentucky Lake	Aug. 15 1965	Ted Heathcott
BASS, Striped	17 lbs. 12 oz.	Watts Bar Reservoir	Oct. 11 1968	William Sullivan
BASS, White	4 lbs. 10 oz.	Pickwick Tailwaters	1949	Jack Allen
BASS, White (Striped Bass Hybrid)	14½ lbs.	Kentucky Lake	Mar. 1967	Robert Woffard
BLUEGILL	2 lbs. 8 oz.	Linger Lake	Sept. 13 1956	Forest Kidwell
BOWFIN	10 lbs.	Kentucky Reservoir	Sept. 10 1967	Lela Chaffee
BUFFALO	23 lbs.	French Broad River	May 20 1957	Bill Archer
BULLHEAD, Brown	1 lb. 15 oz.	Forked Deer River	Aug. 6 1968	Jerald Ledbetter
CARP	42 lbs. 8 oz.	Boone Lake	Aug. 12 1956	Al Moore
CATFISH, Blue	102 lbs.	Tennessee River	June 28 1955	Paul Walker
CATFISH, Channel	24 lbs.	Laurel Hill Lake	Aug. 26 1967	Carl Spencer
CRAPPIE, Black	1 lb. 11 oz.	Brown's Creek	Apr. 17 1968	William Cantrell
CRAPPIE, White	5 lbs. 1 oz.	Garner Brown's Pond	Apr. 20 1968	Bill Allen
GAR, Longnose	23 lbs.	Pickwick Tailwaters	1963	Jimmy Gauvitts
MUSKELLUNGE	28 lbs.	Dale Hollow Reservoir	Apr. 12 1967	Will Speck
PICKEREL, Chain	5 lbs. 12 oz.	Kentucky Lake	1951	Donald Orgain
SAUGER	6 lbs. 10 oz.	Old Hickory Lake	Dec. 4 1965	Jack Goodman
SHEEPSHEAD	47 lbs.	Watts Bar Reservoir	Jan. 2 1955	Grover Parriman
SUNFISH, Redear	1 lb. 12 oz.	City Lake		F. Goforth
TROUT, Brook	4 lbs.	Roaring Branch	Aug. 4 1968	Randy Wiggs
TROUT, Brown	26 lbs. 2 oz.	Dale Hollow Tailwater	May 1958	George Langston
TROUT, Rainbow	12 lbs. 10 oz.	Doe Creek	Apr. 1958	Jack Wilson
WALLEYE	25 lbs.	Old Hickory Lake	Aug. 3 1960	Mabry Harper

TEXAS

Species	Wt.	Where	When	Angler
BASS, Largemouth	13 lbs. 8 oz.	Medina Lake	1943	H. R. Magee

Species	Wt.	Where	When	Angler
BASS, Spotted	4 lbs. 4 oz.	Lake Texoma	Apr. 1951	Townsend Miller
BASS, White	5 lbs. 4 oz.	Colorado River	Mar. 1968	Raymond Rivers
CATFISH, Blue	70 lbs.	Marsh Lake	1965	Tolbert Crowder, Jr.
CATFISH, Channel	36 lbs. 8 oz.	Pedernales River	1965	Mrs. Joe L. Cockrell
CATFISH, Flathead	104 lbs.	Lake McQueeney	1956	C. B. Boyett
CRAPPIE	4 lbs. 8 oz.	Sam Rayburn Lake	1967	Mrs. Hank Roberson
GAR, Alligator	279 lbs.	Rio Grande River	1951	Bill Valverde
GAR, Longnosed	50 lbs. 5 oz.	Trinity River	1954	Townsend Miller
REDFISH	5 lbs.	San Antonio River	Nov. 1968	Randy Walton
SHEEPSHEAD	55 lbs.	White Rock Lake	1924	Asa Short
TROUT, Rainbow	4 lbs. 12 oz.	Guadalupe River	1968	Ron Sharp

UTAH

Species	Wt.	Where	When	Angler
BASS, Largemouth	8 lbs.	Lake Powell	1967	Dale Brown
CARP	30 lbs.	Great Salt Lake Marshes	1960	Ralph Merrill
GAR	20 lbs.	Green River	1958	Lois Walker
SALMON, Kokanee	4 lbs.	Utah Lake	1967	Park Leo
SQUAW FISH	14¾ lbs.	Green River	1961	Phil Dotson
TROUT, Brook	6¼ lbs.	Uintahs	1944	George Walkup
TROUT, Brown	25 lbs. 5¼ oz.	Logan Reservoir	1924	Wilford W. Smart
TROUT, Cutthroat	26¾ lbs.	Strawberry Reservoir	1930	Mrs. E. Smith
TROUT, Lake	36 lbs.	Fish Lake	1960	Katherine White
TROUT, Rainbow	21½ lbs.	Mill Creek Reservoir	1947	LaMar Westra
WALLEYE	10 lbs.	Provo River	1967	P. J. Keller

VERMONT
(No Records Maintained)

VIRGINIA

Species	Wt.	Where	When	Angler
BASS, Largemouth	12 lbs. 12 oz.			
BASS, Rock	2 lbs. 2 oz.			
BASS, Smallmouth	8 lbs.			
BASS, Striped (landlocked)	29 lbs. 12 oz.			
BASS, White	2 lbs. 12 oz.			

Species	Wt.	Where	When	Angler
BOWFIN	17 lbs. 8 oz.			
CATFISH, Channel	26 lbs. 8 oz.			
CATFISH, Flathead	45 lbs.			
CRAPPIE	4 lbs. 13½ oz.			
GAR, Longnose	18 lbs. ½ oz.			
MUSKELLUNGE	20 lbs. 8 oz.			
PICKEREL, Chain	7 lbs. 4 oz.			
SUNFISH	4 lbs. 3 oz.			
TROUT, Brook	3 lbs. 2 oz.			
TROUT, Brown	11 lbs.			
TROUT, Lake	5 lbs. 6 oz.			
TROUT, Rainbow	9 lbs. 14 oz.			
WALLEYE	17 lbs.			

WASHINGTON

Species	Wt.	Where	When	Angler
BASS, Largemouth	11½ lbs.	Newman Lake	July 1966	Don Milleten
BASS, Smallmouth	8¾ lbs.	Snake River	Apr. 1967	Ray Wanacutt
CATFISH, Channel	12½ lbs.	Snake River		
CRAPPIE, Black	4½ lbs.	Lake Washington		John W. Smart
TROUT, Brook	7 lbs.	Lake Cavanaugh		Vincent Fox
TROUT, Brown	22 lbs.	Sullivan Lake	May 1965	R. L. Henry
TROUT, Cutthroat	8¾ lbs.	Coffee Pot Lake	1956	Al Thomas
TROUT, Cutthroat (sea-run)	4 lbs.	Tahuya River	Apr. 1963	S. Thorniley
TROUT, Dolly Varden	22½ lbs.	Tieton River	Apr. 1961	Louis Schott
TROUT, Lake	30¼ lbs.	Loon Lake	June 1966	Ken Janke
TROUT, Rainbow	22½ lbs.	Waitts Lake	1957	Bill Dittner
TROUT, Steelhead	33 lbs.	Snake River	Jan. 1962	Homer Scott
WALLEYE	10 lbs.	Banks Lake		Oscar Carlson

WEST VIRGINIA

Species	Wt.	Where	When	Angler
BASS, Largemouth	9 lbs. 2 oz.	Bull Creek	1966	Allen Quimby
BASS, Rock	1 lb. 12 oz.	Big Sandy Creek	1964	Warren Ryan
BASS, Smallmouth	8 lbs.	New River	1963	Estill Basham
BASS, Spotted	2 lbs. 5 oz.	Bluestone Spillway	1964	Myrle Shelor

Species	Wt.	Where	When	Angler
BASS, White	4 lbs.	Kanawha Falls	1964	Robert Peyton
BLUEGILL	2 lbs. 4 oz.	Farm Pond	1964	Dennis Criss
CARP	36 lbs.	West Fork	1964	
CATFISH, Bullhead	3 lbs.	Ohio River	1964	Robert McCord
CATFISH, Channel	19 lbs.	Coal River	1963	Donald Forman
CRAPPIE	3 lbs. 4 oz.	New River	1963	Violet Cole
GAR	17 lbs.	Little Kanawha	1952	A. J. Keith
MUSKELLUNGE	43 lbs.	Elk River	1955	Lester Hayes
PADDLEFISH	70 lbs.	Little Kanawha	1965	Charles Morgan
PERCH, Yellow	12 oz.	New River	1964	Dwight Kidd
PICKEREL, Chain	3 lbs. 5 oz.	Little Capon	1963	Clarence Llewellyn
SHEEPSHEAD	25 lbs.	Kanawha Station	1954	Bill Dawkins
STURGEON	12 lbs. 5 oz.	Ohio River	1949	Emett Wheeler
TROUT, Brook	3 lbs. 5 oz.	Mill Creek	1968	Robby George
TROUT, Brown	16 lbs.	South Branch River	1968	Paul Barker
TROUT, Golden	2 lbs. 15 oz.	Spruce Knob Lake	1968	Ted Thomas, Jr.
TROUT, Rainbow	10 lbs.	Spruce Knob Lake	1956	John Manley
WALLEYE	15 lbs. 14 oz.	Greenbrier	1946	Dale Adkinson

Species	Wt.	Where	When	Angler
BLUEGILL	1 lb. 12 oz.	Bass Lake	Aug. 12 1968	Walter Skriver
CARP	57 lbs. 2 oz.	Lake Wisconsin	Aug. 28 1966	Mike Prorok
CATFISH, Channel	44 lbs.	Wisconsin River	1962	Larry Volenec
CATFISH, Flathead	61 lbs.	Fox River	June 28 1966	Mike Tanner
CRAPPIE	4 lbs. 8 oz.	Gile Flowage	Aug. 12 1967	Allen A. Dollar
MUSKELLUNGE	69 lbs. 11 oz.	Chippewa Flowage	Oct. 20 1949	Louis Spray
PERCH, Yellow	3 lbs. 4 oz.	Lake Winnebago	1954	Mike Lamont
PIKE, Northern	38 lbs.	Lake Puckaway	Aug. 6 1952	J. A. Rahn
SALMON, Coho	19 lbs. 9 oz.	Lake Michigan	July 2 1969	Lyle Budnick
SAUGER	1 lb. 3 oz.	Lake Winnebago	May 20 1968	Lawson A. Bauer
SHEEPSHEAD	22 lbs. 4 oz.	Lake Wisconsin	July 3 1966	Mike Kreevich
SPLAKE	14 lbs. 4 oz.	Ada Lake	June 7 1967	Bill Keeler
SUNFISH, Green	1 lb. 9 oz.	Wind Lake	Aug. 23 1967	Thomas Tart
TROUT, Brook	9 lbs. 15 oz.	Prairie River	Sept. 2 1944	John Mixis
TROUT, Brown	18 lbs. 12 oz.	Brule River	Aug. 30 1940	Steve Weyandt
TROUT, Lake	47 lbs.	Lake Superior	Sept. 9 1946	Waino Roose
TROUT, Rainbow	16 lbs. 10 oz.	Lake Michigan	Oct. 12 1967	Charles Cromer
WALLEYE	18 lbs.	High Lake	Sept. 26 1933	Tony Brothers

WISCONSIN

Species	Wt.	Where	When	Angler
BASS, Largemouth	11 lbs. 3 oz.	Lake Ripley	Oct. 12 1940	Robert Milkowski
BASS, Smallmouth	9 lbs. 1 oz.	Indian Lake	June 21 1950	Leon Stefoneck
BASS, White	3 lbs. 9 oz.	Wisconsin River	1962	J. L. Griffith

WYOMING
(No Records Maintained)

DISTRICT of COLUMBIA
(No Records Maintained)

DEPARTMENTS:

42: State conservation departments

ALABAMA
Department of Conservation, Administrative Building, Montgomery, Ala.

ALASKA
Department of Fish and Game, 229 Alaska Office Building, Juneau, Alaska

ARIZONA
State Game and Fish Commission, Arizona State Building, Phoenix, Ariz.

ARKANSAS
State Game and Fish Commission, Game and Fish Building, State Capitol Grounds, Little Rock, Ark.

CALIFORNIA
Department of Fish and Game, 722 Capitol Ave., Sacramento, Calif.

COLORADO
State Game and Fish Department, 1530 Sherman St., Denver 2, Colo.

CONNECTICUT
State Board of Fisheries and Game, State Office Bldg., Hartford 14, Conn.

DELAWARE
Board of Game and Fish Commissioners, Dover, Del.

FLORIDA
Game and Fresh Water Fish Commission, 646 W. Tennessee, Tallahassee, Florida

GEORGIA
State Game and Fish Commission, 401 State Capitol, Atlanta 3, Ga.

HAWAII
Division of Fish and Game, Box 5425, Pawaa Substation, Honolulu 1, Hawaii

IDAHO
Department of Fish and Game, 518 Front St., Boise, Ida.

ILLINOIS
Department of Conservation, State Office Bldg., Springfield, Ill.

INDIANA
Department of Conservation, Division of Fish and Game, 311 W. Washington St., Indianapolis 9, Ind.

IOWA
State Conservation Commission, E. 7th & Court Ave., Des Moines 9, Ia.

KANSAS
Forestry, Fish and Game Commission, Box 591, Pratt, Kansas

KENTUCKY
Department of Fish and Wildlife Resources, State Office Bldg. Annex, Frankfort, Ky.

LOUISIANA
Wildlife and Fisheries Commission, 126 Civil Courts Bldg., New Orleans 16, La.

MAINE
Department of Inland Fisheries and Game, State House, Augusta, Me.

MARYLAND
Maryland Game and Inland Fish Commission, State Office Bldg., Annapolis, Md.

MASSACHUSETTS
Department of Natural Resources, Division of Fisheries and Game, 73 Tremont St., Boston 8, Mass.

MICHIGAN
Department of Conservation, Lansing 26, Mich.

MINNESOTA
Department of Conservation, State Office Bldg., St. Paul 1, Minn.

MISSISSIPPI
State Game and Fish Commission, Woolfolk State Office Bldg., Jackson, Miss.

MISSOURI
State Conservation Commission, Farm Bureau Bldg., Jefferson City, Mo.

MONTANA
State Fish and Game Commission, Helena, Mont.

NEBRASKA
Game, Forestation and Parks Commission, State Capitol Bldg., Lincoln 9, Neb.

NEVADA
State Fish and Game Commission, Box 678, Reno, Nev.

NEW HAMPSHIRE
State Fish and Game Department, 34 Bridge St., Concord, N.H.

NEW JERSEY
Department of Conservation and Economic Development, Division of Fish and Game, 230 West State St., Trenton, N.J.

NEW MEXICO
State Department of Game and Fish, Santa Fe, N.M.

NEW YORK
State Conservation Department, Albany, N.Y.

NORTH CAROLINA
Wildlife Resources Commission, Box 2919, Raleigh, N.C.

NORTH DAKOTA
State Game and Fish Department, Bismarck, N.D.

OHIO
Department of Natural Resources, Wildlife Division, Ohio Departments Bldg., Columbus 15, Ohio

OKLAHOMA
Department of Wildlife Conservation, Room 118, State Capitol Bldg., Oklahoma City 5, Okla.

OREGON
State Fish Commission, 307 State Office Bldg., Portland 1, Ore.

PENNSYLVANIA
State Fish Commission, Harrisburg, Pa.

PUERTO RICO
Department of Agriculture and Commerce, San Juan, P.R.

RHODE ISLAND
Department of Agriculture and Conservation, Veterans Memorial Bldg., 83 Park St., Providence 2, R.I.

SOUTH CAROLINA
State Wildlife Resources Dept., 1015 Main St., Box 360, Columbia, S.C.

SOUTH DAKOTA
State Department of Game, Fish and Parks, State Office Bldg., Pierre, S.D.

TENNESSEE
State Game and Fish Commission, Cordell Hull Bldg., Nashville, Tenn.

TEXAS
State Game and Fish Commission, Austin, Tex.

UTAH
State Department of Fish & Game, 1596 W. N. Temple, Salt Lake City, Utah

VERMONT
State Fish and Game Commission, Montpelier, Vt.

VIRGINIA
Commission of Game and Inland Fisheries, 7 N. 2nd St., Box 1642, Richmond 13, Va.

WASHINGTON
Department of Game, 600 N. Capitol Way, Olympia, Wash.

WEST VIRGINIA
State Conservation Commission, State Office Bldg. No. 3, Charleston, W.Va.

WISCONSIN
State Conservation Department, State Office Bldg., Madison 1, Wis.

WYOMING
State Game and Fish Commission, Box 378, Cheyenne, Wyo.

United States Fish & Wildlife Service
Dept. Of The Interior, Washington 25, D.C.

DEPARTMENTS:

43: Canada and the Bahamas fishing information departments

ALBERTA
Department of Lands and Forests, Edmonton, Alta.

BRITISH COLUMBIA
Fish and Game Branch, Department of Recreation and Conservation, 567 Burrard St., Vancouver 1, B.C.

MANITOBA
Department of Mines and Natural Resources, Winnipeg, Man.

NEWFOUNDLAND
Department of Mines and Resources, St. John's, Newfoundland

NORTHWEST TERRITORIES
Northern Administration Branch, Department of Northern Affairs and National Resources, Ottawa, Ontario, Canada

NOVA SCOTIA
Department of Lands and Forests, Halifax, N.S.

ONTARIO
Department of Lands and Forests, Parliament Bldgs., Toronto, Ontario

PRINCE EDWARD ISLAND
Department of Industry and Natural Resources, Charlottetown, P.E.I.

QUEBEC
Department of Game and Fisheries, Quebec, Que.

SASKATCHEWAN
Department of Natural Resources, Government Administration Bldg., Regina, Sask.

YUKON TERRITORY
Game Department, Yukon Territorial Government, Box 2029, Whitehorse, Y.T., Canada

Bahamas Fishing Information Bureau
The Development Board, Nassau, The Bahamas

DEPARTMENTS:

44: Conservation, professional and sportsmen's organizations

AMERICAN CASTING ASSOCIATION: P.O. Box 51, Nashville 2, Tenn.

AMERICAN FISHING TACKLE MANUFACTURER'S ASSOCIATION: 20 North Wacker Drive, Chicago, Illinois 60606

AMERICAN INSTITUTE OF BIOLOGICAL SCIENCES: Box 9173, Roslyn Station, Arlington 9, Virginia

AMERICAN FISHERIES SOCIETY: 1404 New York Ave., N.W., Washington 5, D.C.

AMERICAN LITTORAL SOCIETY: Sandy Hook Marine Laboratory, Box 117, Highlands, New Jersey

ATLANTIC SEA RUN SALMON COMMISSION: University of Maine, Orono, Maine

ATLANTIC STATES MARINE FISHERIES COMMISSION: 336 E. College Ave., Tallahassee, Florida

FRIENDS OF THE WILDERNESS: 3515 E. 4th Street, Duluth 4, Minnesota

GULF AND CARIBBEAN FISHERIES INSTITUTE: Institute of Marine Science, University of Miami, 1 Rickenbacker Causeway, Virginia Key, Miami 49, Florida

GULF STATES MARINE FISHERIES COMMISSION: 312 Audubon Bldg., New Orleans 16, Louisiana

GREAT LAKES FISHERY COMMISSION: 106 Natural Resources Bldg., University of Michigan, Ann Arbor, Michigan

INTERNATIONAL ASSOCIATION OF GAME, FISH AND CONSERVATION COMM.: 16413 Canterbury Drive, Hopkins, Minnesota

INTERNATIONAL CASTING FEDERATION: 1400 South Peters Street, New Orleans 13, Louisiana

INTERNATIONAL COMM. FOR THE NORTHWEST ATLANTIC FISHERIES: Education Bldg., Dalhousie University, Halifax, North Carolina

INTERNATIONAL GAME FISH ASSOCIATION: Alfred 1, DuPont Bldg., Miami 32, Florida

INTERNATIONAL OCEANOGRAPHIC FOUNDATION: 1 Rickenbacker Causeway, Virginia Key, Miami 49, Florida

INTERNATIONAL PACIFIC SALMON FISHERIES COMM.: Box 30, New Westminster, B.C., Canada

INTERNATIONAL SPIN FISHING ASSOCIATION: P.O. Box 81, Downey, California

IZAAK WALTON LEAGUE OF AMERICA: Glenview, Illinois

NATIONAL ASSOCIATION OF MARINE ANGLER'S CLUBS: Box 117, Highlands, New Jersey

NATIONAL FISHERIES INSTITUTE, INC.: 1614 20th St., N.W., Washington 9, D.C.

NATIONAL PARTY BOAT OWNER'S ASSOCIATION: Box 117, Highlands, New Jersey

NATIONAL WILDLIFE FEDERATION: 1412 16th St., N.W., Washington, D.C.

NEW ENGLAND ADVISORY BOARD FOR FISH & GAME PROBLEMS: 319 Linwood St., West Lynn, Mass.

NEW ENGLAND OUTDOOR WRITER'S ASSOCIATION: 1003 N. Westfield St., Feeding Hills, Mass.

OUTBOARD BOATING CLUB OF AMERICA: 307 N. Michigan Blvd., Chicago, Ill.

OUTDOOR RECREATION INSTITUTE: 5003 Wapakoneta, Washington 16, D.C.

OUTDOOR WRITER'S ASSOCIATION OF AMERICA: 105 Guitar Bldg., Columbia, Missouri

PACIFIC MARINE FISHERIES COMM.: 741 State Office Bldg., 1400 S. W. Fifth Ave., Portland 1, Oregon

SPORT FISHERY RESEARCH FOUNDATION: 1404 New York Avenue, Washington 5, D.C.

SPORT FISHING INSTITUTE: Bond Bldg., Washington 5, D.C.

THE BROTHERHOOD OF THE JUNGLE COCK: 10 E. Fayette St., Baltimore, Md.

THE CAMP FIRE CLUB OF AMERICA: 19 Rector Street, New York 6, New York

TROUT, UNLIMITED: 900 Lapeer Avenue, Saginaw, Michigan

U.S. FOREST SERVICE, U.S. SOIL CONSERVATION SERVICE, U.S. BUREAU OF OUTDOOR RECREATION, U.S. FISH AND WILDLIFE SERVICE, U.S. NATIONAL PARK SERVICE: Washington 25, D.C.

U.S. TROUT FARMERS ASSOCIATION: 110 Social Hall Avenue, Salt Lake City 11, Utah

WILDLIFE MANAGEMENT INSTITUTE: 709 Wire Bldg., Washington 5, D.C.

DEPARTMENTS:

45: Directory of fishing tackle manufacturers and importers

Acme Tackle Company, 350 Dexter St., Providence, Rhode Island (Lures)

Actionrod, Inc., 912 W. State St., Hastings, Michigan (Rods)

Airlite Plastics Co., 2915 N. 16th St., Omaha, Neb. (Bobbers, Decoys, Minnow Buckets)

Aladdin Laboratories, Inc., 620 S. 8th St., Minneapolis, Minn. (Perrine Fly Reels)

Allan Manufacturing Co., 325 Duffy Ave., Hicksville, N.Y. (Fishing Rod Hardware)

Alliance Manufacturing, 3121 Milwaukee Ave., Chicago 18, Ill. (Landing Nets, Fish Bags, Tackle)

Al's Goldfish Lure Co., 516 Main St., Indian Orchard, Mass. (Lures)

American Foreign Ind., 640 Sacramento St., San Francisco, Cal. (Importers)

The American Pad and Textile Co., 6230 Bienvenue St., New Orleans 17, La. (Fishing Clothing, Life Vests, Cushions)

Anglers' Mfg. Corp., 1345 W. Thorndale Ave., Chicago, Ill. (Fishing tool)

Fred Arbogast Co., Inc., 313 W. North St., Akron, Ohio (Lures)

Arndt & Sons, Inc., 1000 Fairview Ave., Hamilton, Ohio (Baits)

The Arnold Tackle Corp., Box 87, Paw Paw, Mich. (Ice Fishing Tackle)

Art Wire and Stamping Co., 227 High St., Newark 2, N.J. (Tackle)

Atlantic Lures, Inc., 85 South St., Providence, R.I. (Lures, Terminal Tackle)

Bait Boy Products, 708 60th St. NW, Bradenton, Fla. (Bait Bucket Aerator)

Baker Mfg. Co., Box 60, Columbia, Pa. (Hookout)

Bay De Noc Lure Co., Box 71-2, Gladstone, Mich. (Swedish Pimple Lure)

The Bead Chain Mfg. Co., 110 Mountain Grove St., Bridgeport, Conn.

Berkley & Co., Inc., Highway 71 & 9, Spirit Lake, Iowa ("Trilene" Line leaders)

Betts Manufacturing Company, Park Falls, Wisconsin (Rods)

Black Panther Tool Co., 4051 S. Iowa Ave., Milwaukee, Wis. (Bob-er-Lite)

Bomber Bait Co., Gainesville, Texas

Boone Bait Co., Inc., Forsyth Road, Winter Park, Florida (Lures)

Bornemann Products Co., 2117 Rockwell Rd., Aurora, Ill. (Depth O Plug)

Bradlow, Inc., 3923 W. Jefferson, Los Angeles 16, Cal. (Quick Finessa Reel)

Brainerd Bait Co., 1564 Englewood Ave., St. Paul 45, Minn. (Dr. Spoon)

Bronson Reel Co., Bronson, Mich. (Fishing Reels, Rods)

Vernon Brown Co., 20 N. Wacker Dr., Chicago 6, Ill. (Spot Marker)

Browning-Silaflex Co., 1706 Washington Ave., St. Louis 3, Mo. (Rods)

L. Brust Mfg. Co., 1301 N. 14th Ave., Melrose Pk., Ill. (Saf-t-Grip)

Buckeye Bait Corp., 120 Liberty St., Council Grove, Kansas (Fishing Floats)

H.C. Buicke & Sons, 3431 Falls Blvd., N. Tonawanda, N.Y. (Fish Hook Holder)

Paul Bunyan Co., 1030 Marshall St. NE, Minneapolis, Minn. (Lures)

Burke Flexo-Products Co., 3249 Barlow Rd., Traverse City, Mich. (Lures)

Tony Burmek, 4173 N. 17th St., Milwaukee, Wis. (Burmek's Secret Bait)

Buss Mfg. Co., E. Lanark Ave., Lanark, Ill. (Buss Bedding)

Carron Net Company, 1623 17th St., Two Rivers, Wisconsin

Central Molding & Mfg. Co., 1509 Central Ave., Kansas City, Mo. (Tackle Boxes)

Champion Products Co., 2525 Park Ave., Muskegon Hts., Mich. (Handle Rod)

John Chatillon & Sons, 85 Cliff St., New York 38, N.Y. (Fish Scales)

Cisco Kid Tackle Co., Boca Raton, Fla. (Cisco Kid Lures & Rods)

Conolon Corp. (Garcia), 636 W. 17th St., Costa Mesa, Cal. (Rods)

Continental Arms Corp., 697 Fifth Ave., New York, N.Y. (Micron and Alcedo Reels)

Cortland Industries, Inc., Fishing Line Division, 67 E. Court St., Cortland, New York (Fishing Lines)

Cosom Corp., 6030 Wayzata Blvd., Minneapolis, Minn. (Bait Bucket)

Cover Guard Mfg. Co., 1414 S. Michigan, Chicago 5, Ill. (Rods & Reel Cases)

Creme Lure Co., Post Office Box 87, Tyler, Texas (Plastic Lures)

Ed Cumings, Inc., 2305 Branch Rd., Flint, Mich. (Nets, Rod Cases)

Davis Mills, Inc., Lake City, Tennessee (Nets)

Day Bait Co., 1824 Howard St., Pt. Huron, Mich. (Preserved Baits)

Dayton Bait & Marine Prod., Inc., 2701 S. Dixie Dr., Dayton 9, Ohio (Floats, Rod Holders)

De Long Lures, 18118 Syracuse Ave., Cleveland 10, Ohio (Plastic Lures)

Detty's Fish Gripper, 132 Atkins Ave., Lancaster, Pa. (Fish Gripper)

De Witt Plastics, 26 Aurelius Ave., Auburn, N.Y. (Boxes, Stringers, Buckets)

Dura-Pak Corp., 611 Pearl St., Sioux City, Iowa (Terminal Tackle)

Dynamic Sales, Inc., (Roddy Recreation Products, Inc.), 1526 W. 166th St., P.O. Box 431, Gardena, Cal. (Rods, Reels, Line)

Enterprise Mfg. Co., (Pflueger), 110 N. Union St., Akron, Ohio (Reels, rods)

Lou J. Eppinger Mfg. Co., 6340 Schaefer Highway, Dearborn, Mich. (Dardevle Lures)

Ero Mfg. Co., 714 W. Monroe St., Chicago, Ill. (Life Vest and Boat Cushions)

Glen L. Evans, Inc., Caldwell, Texas (Lures)

Ever-Wear Seal Co., 850 Main St., Lake Geneva, Wis. (Worm Lure)

Fabrico Mfg. Corp., 1300 W. Exchange Ave., Chicago 9, Ill. (Stocking Foot Wader, Parkas)

Falls Bait Co., Chippewa Falls, Wisconsin (Lures)

Famous Keystone Kits Corp., 1344 W. 37th St., Chicago 9, Ill. (Fishing Kits)

Feurer Bros. Inc., 77 Lafayette Ave., North White Plains, N.Y. (Reels)

The Fish Net and Twine Co., Menominee, Michigan

Florida Fish Tackle Mfg. Co., 2100 First Ave. S., St. Petersburg, Fla. (Lures)

Frabill Mfg. Co., 234 W. Florida St., Milwaukee, Wis. (Minnow Buckets, Boat Seats)

Isaac Franklin & Son, 1218 Warner St., Baltimore 30, Md. (Nets, Crab Traps)

Gapen Fly Co., Onoka, Minnesota

The Garcia Corp., 329 Alfred Ave., Teaneck, N.J. (Rods, reels, line and lures)

B.F. Gladding & Co., Inc., South Otselic, N.Y. (Line, Tackle Boxes)

Gliebe Co., 1154 Myrtle Ave., Brooklyn 21, N.Y. (Terminal Tackle)

B.F. Goodrich Footwear Co., 36 Nichols Ave., Watertown 72, Mass. (Fishing Footwear)

Great Lakes Products, Inc., 312 Huron Blvd., Marysville, Mich. (Rods, Reels)

Gudebrod Bros. Silk Co., Inc., 12 S. 12th St., Philadelphia, Pa. (Line)

The Hamilton-Skotch Corp., 295 Fifth Ave., New York 16, N.Y. (Tackle Boxes)

Harben Mfg. Co., 2328 Olive St., Racine, Wis. (Fish Scaler)

Harnell, Inc., 4094 Glencoe Ave., Venice, Cal. (Fishing Rods)

Harrison Industries, Inc., 250 Passaic St., Newark, N.J. (Centaure & Cargem Reels, Lures)

James Heddon's Sons, Dowagiac, Mich. (Rods, reels, line, lures)

Helin Tackle Co., 4099 Beaufait, Detroit 7, Mich. (Flatfish Lures)

Hettrick Mfg. Co., Taylorsville Rd., Statesville, N.C. (Fishing Clothing)

Hodgman Rubber Co., Tripp St., Framingham, Mass. (Waders, Fishing Clothing)

The Hofschneider Corp., 848 Jay St., Rochester 11, N.Y. ("Red Eye" Lures)

Holliday Reel Co., 1025 N. Main St., Akron 10, Ohio

Horrocks-Ibbotson Co., 20 Whitesboro St., Utica 2, N.Y. (Rods, reels, lures)

Hurricane Import Co., 70 Tenth St., San Francisco, Cal.

Ideal Fishing Float Co., Inc., 20th & Franklin St., Richmond 3, Va.

International Seaway Trading Corp., 1387 W. 9 St., Cleveland 13, Ohio

Irving Raincoat Co., 657 Broadway, New York 12, N.Y.

Jamison Tackle Co., 3654 Montrose, Chicago 8, Ill. (Lures)

Jet Aer Corp., 165 Third Ave., Paterson, N.J. (Insect Repellent)

Albert J. John Mfg. Co., 118 W. 69th St., Chicago, Ill. (Lead Sinkers)

Louis Johnson Co., 1547 Old Deerfield Rd., Highland Park, Ill. (Johnson Lures)

Johnson Reels, Inc., Johnson Park, Mankota, Minnesota

Kar-Gard Co., 2201 Grand Ave., Kansas City, Mo. (Lure Retriever)

Kennedy Mfg. Co., P.O. Box 151, Van Wert, Ohio (Tackle Boxes)

Kinfolks Inc., Main St., Perry, N.Y. (Hunting Knives)

Klamerus & Co., 4557 W. 59th St., Chicago 29, Ill. (Rod Holders)

Kolpin Bros. Inc., 119 S. Pearl, Berlin, Wis. (Fishing Accessories)

L & S Bait Co., Inc., 148 S. Vasseur Ave., Bradley, Ill. (L & S Mirrolures)

Land-O-Tackle, Inc., 4650 N. Ronald St., Chicago, Ill. (Lure Bodies, Components)

Lazy Ike Corp., 512 Central Ave., Fort Dodge, Iowa

Lectromatic Sports, Inc., 11405 E. 7th Ave., Aurora 8, Colo. (Battery Powered Reel, Rods)

Leisure Lures, 7315 Atoll Ave. (Box 353 Station 1) North Hollywood, Cal. (Plastic Lures)

Le Trappeur, Inc., Southwest Industrial Park, Westwood, Mass. (Luxor Reels)

Liberty Mfg. Co., 4026 N. 20th St., St. Louis 21, Mo. (Terminal Tackle)

Liberty Steel Chest Corp., 16 Dowling Place, Rochester 5, N.Y.

Lisk Fly Mfg. Co., 659 S. Spring St., Greensboro, N.C. (Lures, Rods)

Little Atom Lures, 1415 N. California, Chicago, Ill. (Orig. Pinkie Lures)

Longfellow Corp., 31795 Groesbeck Highway, Fraser, Mich. (Rods)

Lutz Pork Bait Co., 1234 Jefferson, Kansas City 5, Mo. (Pork Baits)

Magic Snell Tackle Co., Inc., 45 Niagara St., Canandaigua, N.Y.

Marathon Bait Co., Box 298, Wausau, Wisconsin

Martin Reel Co., Martin St., Mohawk, N.Y.

Mason Tackle, Otisville, Michigan (Line)

Maybrun Mfg. Co., 2250 Clybourn Ave., Chicago, Ill. (Pinchers, Pliers, Knives)

Meinzinger & Rade Co., 19000 Doris, Livonia, Mich. (Hooks, Scalers)

W. W. Mildrum Jewel Co., 230 Berlin St., East Berlin, Conn. (Rod Guides & Ferrules)

Mile Hi Tackle Co., P. O. Box 7022, Capitol Hill Station, Denver 6, Colo. (Snelled Hooks, Swivels)

Mill Run Products Co., 1360 W. Ninth St., Cleveland, Ohio (Lures, Stringers)

Mills Products Co., Mills Industrial Pk., Safety Harbor, Fla. (Lures)

Millsite Tackle Co., Howell, Michigan (Box/Stringers)

Minneapolis-Honeywell Co., 2753 4th Ave. S., Minneapolis, Minn. (Fish-o-therm)

Mit-Shel Co., 209 N. Third, Quincy, Ill. (Minnow Buckets)

Molded Carry-Lite Products, 3000 W. Clarke St., Milwaukee 45, Wis. (Bait Buckets)

National Expert Bait Co., Inc., 2928 Stevens Ave., Minneapolis 8, Minn. (Lures)

Nature Faker Lures, Inc., Windsor, Missouri

Newton Line Co., Inc., So. Main St., Homer N.Y. (Line)

O.A. Norlund Co., Div. Mann Edge Tool Co., Lewiston, Pa. (Gaffs)

Norton Mfg. Corp., 2700 N. Pulaski Rd., Chicago, Ill. (Bamboo Fishing Poles)

Oberlin Canteen Co., 212 Summer St., P. O. Box 208, Oberlin, Ohio

Old Pal, Inc., Lititz, Pa. (Minnow Buckets, Tackle Boxes)

Lee E. Olsen Knife Co., 7-11 Joy St., Howard City, Mich. (Filet Knives)

Charles F. Orvis Co., Manchester, Vermont (Orvis Reels, etc.)

Padre Island Co., Inc., 616 S. Staples St., Corpus Christi, Texas (Lures)

Palsa Sales, Box 55, Hales Corners, Wis. (Palsa Lure)

Paw Paw Bait Co., 400 S. Kalamazoo St., Paw Paw, Mich. (Lures)

Penn Fishing Tackle Mfg. Co., 3028 W. Hunting Park Ave., Philadelphia 32, Pa. (Reels)

Perfection Tip Co., 3020 E. 43rd Ave., Denver 16, Colo.

Phantom Products, Inc., 1800 Central, Kansas City, Mo. (Rods, Reels)

Phillips Fly & Tackle Co., Alexandria, Pa.

Plano Molding Co., 113 S. Center Ave., Plano, Ill. (Plastic Tackle Boxes)

Plas-Steel Products, Inc., Walkerton, Indiana (Rods)

J.R. Plasters Co., 111 N. Denver Ave., Kansas City 23, Mo. (Trot Lines, Floats, Leaders)

Plastics Research Corp., 3601 Jenny Lind, Fort Smith, Arkansas (Lures)

Plastilite Corp., P.O. Box 35, Ames Station, Omaha, Neb. (Floats, Minnow Buckets)

Prescott Spinner Co., P.O. Box 239, Mankato, Minnesota

Rapala, P.O. Box 5027, Minneapolis 6, Minn.

Rettinger Importing Co., 380 Lafayette St., N.Y. 3, N.Y. (Fishing Rainwear)

C. C. Roberts Bait Co., Mosinee, Wis. (Mud Puppy Lures)

St. Croix Sales Corp., Park Falls, Wis. (Fishing Tackle)

Scientific Anglers, Inc., 1012 Jefferson, Midland, Mich. (Fly Lines)

Seneca Tackle Co., Inc., 56 Cooper Square, N.Y. 3, N.Y. (Lures)

The Servus Rubber Co., 1100 Block Second St., Rock Island, Ill. (Fishing Footwear)

Sevenstrand Tackle Mfg. Co., 1207 Euclid Ave., Long Beach, Cal. (Leaders & Rods)

Shakespeare Co., 241 E. Kalamazoo Ave., Kalamazoo, Mich. (Rods, reels, line)

Sheldons, Inc., Hwy. 45 N, Antigo, Wis. (Mepps Spinners, etc.)

Shurkatch Fishing Tackle Co., Inc., S. Elm St., Richfield Springs, N.Y. (Gaffs, Floats, Terminal Tackle)

Simonsen Industries Inc., 1414 S. Michigan Ave., Chicago 5, Ill. (Tackle Boxes)

Skirt Minnow Seine Mfg. Co., P.O. Box 144, East Liverpool, Ohio

Snagproof Mfg. Co., 4153 E. Galbraith, Cincinnati 36, Ohio (Lures)

South Bend Tackle Co., Inc., Miami, Fla.

Sportsmen, Inc., 131 Saw Mill River Rd., Yonkers, N.Y. (Rods)

Staz-On Bait Co., Inc., Golden Pond, Kentucky

Steppe Importing Co., P.O. Box 32, RR #6, Guelph, Ontario (Fish Baskets)

Stratton & Terstegge Co., 1520 Rowan St., Louisville, Ky. (Tackle Boxes, Minnow Buckets)

Style-Cast Tackle Corp., 29866 John R., Madison Hts., Mich. (Rods)

Suick Lure Mfg. Co., Antigo, Wis. (Lures)

Sunset Line & Twine Co., Petaluma, Cal., Florence, Ala.

Sutton Co., Naples, New York (Lures)

Tack-L-Tyers, 939 Chicago Ave., Evanston, Ill. (Fly Tying Kits)

Taylor Instrument Co., Rochester 1, N.Y. (Fishermans Barometer)

Thompson Fishing Tackle Co., P.O. Box 275, Knoxville, Tenn. (Lures)

Townsend Engineering Co., P.O. Box 1433, Des Moines 5, Iowa (Fish Skinners)

True Life Minnow Harness, 29251 Grandview, Mount Clements, Mich.

True Temper Corp., 1623 Euclid Ave., Cleveland 15, Ohio

Tycoon/Fin-Nor Corp., 4027 N.W. 24th St., Miami 48, Florida

Umco Corp., Spring Park, Minnesota (Tackle Boxes)

Uncle Josh Bait Co., 524 Clarence St., P.O. Box 386, Fort Atkinson, Wis.

Union Steel Chest Corp., 54 Church St., LeRoy, N.Y.

U.S. Rubber Co., 1230 Ave. of Americas, N.Y. 20, N.Y. (Fishing Footwear)

Vlchek Plastic Co., P.O. Box 97, Valplast Rd., Middlefield, Ohio (Tackle Boxes)

Walker International, 2101 W. Lafayette, Detroit 16, Mich. (Tackle Importers)

Water Gremlin Co., 4370 Otter Lake Rd., White Bear Lake, Minn. (Lead Sinkers)

Water King Sales, P.O. Box 10, Pearl Beach, Michigan (Rods)

Weber Dot Line Mfg. Co., 4601 W. 47th St., Chicago 32, Ill. (Nets, Fish Bags, Rod Cases)

Weber Tackle Co., 133 W. Ellis St., Stevens Point, Wisconsin

West Indies Ocean Products Corp., Port Everglades (P.O. Box 13114 Sta.), Ft. Lauderdale, Florida (Shrimp Bait)

H.A. Whittemore & Co., Inc., 32 Kearney Rd., Needham Hts., Mass. (Lures)

Whopper-Stopper, Inc., P.O. Box 793, Sherman, Texas (Lures)

Williams Gold Refining Co., Inc., 2978 Main St., Buffalo 14, N.Y. (Lures)

Woodstock Line Co., 83 Canal St., Putnam, Conn. (Line)

World Famous Sales, Inc., 1601 S. Michigan Ave., Chicago 16, Ill. (Rain Suits, Tackle)

The Worth Co., P.O. Box 88, Stevens Point, Wis. (Terminal Tackle)

Wright & McGill Co., 1400 Yosemite, Denver 8, Colo.

York-Eger Mfg. Co., Inc., P.O. Box 1210, Sanford, Fla. (Nets, Lures)

Zebco Corp., 1131 E. Easton, Tulsa, Oklahoma

DEPARTMENTS:

46: Professional fly tyers

DAN BAILEY, Dan's Fly & Tackle Shop, Livingston, Mont.

PAT BARNES, Barnes' Fly Shop, West Yellowstone, Mont.

WAYNE BUSZEK, Visalia, Calif.

GEORGE CORNISH, Driftwood Marina, Box 296, Avalon, N.J. 08202.

RUBE CROSS, 606 Public St., Providence, R.I.

HARRY DARBEE, Livingston Manor, N.Y.

JIM DEREN, Angler's Roost, Chrysler Bldg., New York 17, N.Y.

ART FLICK, Westkill, N.Y.

BILL GALLASCH, 8705 Weldon Drive, Richmond, Va. 23229.

DON GAPEN, Gapen Fly Co., Anoka 8, Minn.

H. J. GREB, 2188 N.W. 24th Ave., Miami, Fla.

BILL KEANE, Box 371, Bronxville, N.Y. 10708.

ED KOCH, Koch's Tackle Shop, 936 Franklin St., Carlisle, Pa.

EDDIE LACHMANN, Amherst, Wis.

MERTON PARKS, Parks' Fly Shop, Gardiner, Mont.

PHIL PATTERSON, Phillip's Fly & Tackle Co., Alexandria, Pa.

JIM POULOS, 24 S. Wheeling Ave., Wheeling, Ill.

HANK ROBERTS, 1033 Walnut St., Boulder, Colo.

HELEN SHAW, 246 E. 46th St., New York 17, N.Y.

NORM THOMPSON, Angler's Guide, 1805 N.W. Thurman, Portland 9, Ore.

DICK RIDEOUT, 78 Katahdin Ave., Millinocket, Me.

*Professional fly tyers not named here and wishing to be included in the fly tyers listing, 1971 Tom McNally's Fishermen's Bible, are urged to write Tom McNally, c/o Follett Publishing Co., 201 N. Wells St., Chicago, Ill. 60606.

DEPARTMENTS:

47: Fly tying materials supply houses

Each firm listed does not carry complete lines of fly tying materials. Write for catalogs or merchandise sheets.

ALL-LURE TACKLE CO., 47-10 48th St., Woodside 77, N.Y.

ANDY'S QUALITY FLY TYING MATERIALS, P.O. Box 269, Peabody, Mass.

BILL CATHERWOOD, 399 Marshall St., Tewksbury, Mass.

R. S. CHASE CO., P.O. Box 208, South Duxbury, Mass.

DANIELSON FLY MFG. CO., P.O. Box 94, Mercer Island, Wash.

DERSH FEATHER AND TRADING CORP., 494 Broadway, N.Y. 12, N.Y.

F & S PRODUCTS CO., R-250, W. Sixth St., Mansfield, Ohio.

FINNY SPORTS (DD), Toledo 14, Ohio

GENE'S TACKLE SHOP, Box 162, Newark, N.Y.

HACKLE HOUSE, P.O. Box 1001, San Mateo, Calif.

D. E. HECHT, 80 University Place, New York 3, N.Y.

HERTER'S CO., Waseca, Minn.

E. HILLE ANGLER'S SUPPLY HOUSE, P.O. Box 269, Williamsport, Pa.

M. J. HOFFMAN CO., 989 Gates Ave., Brooklyn 21, N.Y.

J. J. KLEIN, LTD., 2077 E. Gouin Blvd., Montreal 12, Quebec, Canada

MANGROVE FEATHER CO., 42 West 38th St., New York 18, N.Y.

MARTIN TACKLE & MFG. CO., 431 Eastlake Ave. E., Seattle 9, Wash.

NETCRAFT CO., Box 5510, Toledo 13, Ohio

PASSLOFF, INC., 19 West 36th St., New York 18, N.Y.

PRIEST RIVER TACKLE CO., Landfall, Coolin, Idaho

REED TACKLE CO., Box 390, Caldwell, N.J.

HANK ROBERTS, INC., 1033-37 Walnut, Boulder, Colo.

M. SCHWARTZ & SONS, INC., 321 E. 3rd St., New York 9, N.Y.

SHOFF FISHING TACKLE CO., 407 W. Gowe St., Kent, Wash.

SONNIES, P.O. Box 126, Wilmot, Wis.

TACK-L-TYERS, 939 Chicago Ave., Evanston, Ill.

D. H. THOMPSON, 335 Walnut Ave., Elgin, Ill.

THOMPSON FISHING TACKLE CO., 2308 N. Broadway, Knoxville, Tenn.

UNIVERSAL VISE CO., P.O. Box 335, Holyoke, Mass.

E. VENIARD, LTD., 138 Northwood Road, Thorton Heath, Surrey, England

WOODSLORE PRODUCTS, Box 821, Costa Mesa, Calif.

WORTH CO., P.O. Box 88, Stevens Point, Wis.

PAUL H. YOUNG CO., 23800 W. Eight Mile Road, Southfield, Michigan

DEPARTMENTS:

48: Rod building kits and supplies

DUNTON & SON, INC., 4 Fiske Ave., Greenfield, Mass.

FINNY SPORTS, 462 Sports Bldg., Toledo 14, Ohio.

GLIEBE CO., 1154 Myrtle Ave., Brooklyn 21, N.Y.

HERTER'S CO., Waseca, Minn.

E. HILLE ANGLER'S SUPPLY HOUSE, P.O. Box 269, Williamsport, Pa.

IOWA ROYAL RODS, Perry, Iowa.

MAKIT FISHING ROD MFG. CO., 113 Adolph St., Fort Worth 7, Texas.

E. MILTENBERG, INC., 43 Great Jones St., New York 12, N.Y.

NETCRAFT CO., Toledo 13, Ohio.

CHARLES F. ORVIS CO., INC., Manchester, Vermont.

PASTOR & CO., 11423 Vanowen St., North Hollywood 3, Calif.

PRIEST RIVER TACKLE CO., Landfall, Coolin, Idaho.

REED TACKLE CO., Box 390, Caldwell, N.J.

REEDER MFG. CO., Box 346, Vancouver, Wash.

SHOFF FISHING TACKLE CO., 407 W. Gowe St., Kent, Wash.

PAUL H. YOUNG CO., 23800 W. Eight Mile Road, Southfield, Mich.

DEPARTMENTS:

49: Roster of American casting association

CALIFORNIA

DOUGLAS SM ROD & GUN CLUB: Lloyd Van Shaw, Sec., 1609 Bentley, Los Angeles 25, Calif.

GASCO ROD & GUN CLUB: Frank Messersmith, 1440 Emory Drive, Whittier, Calif.

GOLDEN GATE ANGLING & CASTING CLUB: C. W. Bird, Sec., 111 Sutter St., San Francisco, Calif.

LONG BEACH CASTING CLUB: Don McGavin, Sec., P. O. Box 4063, Long Beach, Calif. 90804

OAKLAND CASTING CLUB: Sam Neely, Sec., 1100 Jefferson St., Oakland 7, Calif.

PASADENA CASTING CLUB: Earl E. Martin, Sec., 1440 Casa Grande, Pasadena, Calif.

RANCHO ROD & GUN CLUB: Henry Webster, Sec., 354 McCadden Place, Los Angeles 5, Calif.

CONNECTICUT

HARTFORD COUNTY CASTING CLUB: Miss Elsie Seiffert, Sec., 97 Roxbury St., Hartford 6, Conn.

FLORIDA

LUTZ CASTING CLUB: Dr. Karl K. Eychaner, Sec., Box 306, Lutz, Florida

ST. PETERSBURG ROD & GUN CLUB: Mrs. May V. Hunt, Sec., 770 32nd Ave. South, St. Petersburg, Florida

ILLINOIS

CATERPILLAR ROD CLUB: W. Les Matthey, Sec., 1712 N. Eighth St., Pekin, Ill.

JACKSON PARK CASTING CLUB: John Crewdson, Sec., 5756 Blackstone Ave., Chicago 37, Illinois

LINCOLN PARK CASTING CLUB: Herbert Schulz, Sec., 4550 N. Ashland Ave., Chicago 40, Illinois

ROXANA FLY & BAIT CASTING CLUB: Arthur H. Mikkelson, Sec., 403 N. Maple, Roxana, Illinois

INDIANA

GARY ANGLERS CLUB: Bill Chadwick, Sec., 1221 Garfield St., Hobart, Indiana

HAMMOND CASTING CLUB: Mrs. Rosemary Rainford, Sec., 7039 Monroe St., Hammond, Indiana

KENTUCKY

BLUE GRASS ANGLERS: Jack Perry, Sec., 625 Cecil Way, Lexington, Ky.

LOUISVILLE CASTING CLUB: Robert Budd, Sec., 1216 Akers Ave., Jeffersonville, Indiana

LOUISIANA

CRESCENT CITY CASTING CLUB: Ben Fontaine, Sec., P.O. Box 50638, New Orleans, La.

MICHIGAN

DETROIT BAIT & FLY CASTING CLUB: C. W. Wilcox, Sec., 16210 Roselawn, Detroit 21, Michigan

MINNESOTA

IWLA CASTING CLUB: Mrs. Lee Cumberland, Sec., 6629 Park Ave. So., Minneapolis 23, Minn.

MISSOURI

CARONDELET FLY & BAIT CASTING CLUB: Louis Meyer, Sec., 5454 Finkman St., St. Louis 9, Missouri

FERGUSON CASTING CLUB: Mrs. Mildred Deck, Sec., 401 Warfield Ave., Ferguson 35, Missouri

KANSAS CITY BAIT & FLY CASTING CLUB: Fritz R. White, Sec., 5609 Virginia, Kansas City 10, Missouri

NORTHEAST CASTING CLUB: Floyd W. Dessenberger, Sec., 107 N. Lawndale, Kansas City 23, Missouri

ST. LOUIS FLY & BAIT CASTING CLUB: Ed R. Lanser, Sec., 214 Hernan Drive, St. Louis 23, Missouri

NEW HAMPSHIRE

MANCHESTER FLY & BAIT CASTING CLUB: Michael Lang, Sec., 193 Ste. Marie St., Manchester, New Hampshire

NEW JERSEY

PATERSON CASTING CLUB: Frances Caillie, Sec., 212 Gordon Ave., Totowa Boro 2, New Jersey

NEW YORK STATE

BUFFALO ANGLER'S CLUB: Alfred W. Holland, Sec., 17 Briggs St., Buffalo 7, New York

BUFFALO BAIT & FLY CASTING CLUB: Mrs. Edna M. Templin, Sec., 78 Briggs Ave., Buffalo 7, New York

CAMPFIRE CLUB OF AMERICA INC.: Dr. R. A. Clinchy Jr., Sec., 19 Rector St., New York 6, New York

ONONDAGA CASTING CLUB: Mrs. Edna Stafford, Sec., Tully, New York

OHIO

BARBERTON CASTING CLUB: Joseph D. Mullins, Sec., 33 West Long St., Akron, Ohio

CINCINNATI CASTING CLUB: Ray Abrams, Sec., 994 North Bend Road, Cincinnati 24, Ohio

CLINTONVILLE CASTING CLUB: Arthur S. Kiefer, Sec., 86 Erie Road, Columbus 14, Ohio

COLUMBUS CASTING CLUB: Dr. W. T. Behnen, Sec., 148 E. State St., Columbus, Ohio

DAYTON CASTING ASSOCIATION: Herman Stauffer, Sec., 2591 Crestwell Place, Dayton 20, Ohio

DAYTON GYM CASTING CLUB: Mrs. Alma Kettering, Sec., 229 Cushing Ave., Dayton 29, Ohio

DELCO PRODUCTS CASTING CLUB: Joe Dalrymple, Sec., 3609 Fairbanks Ave., Dayton 7, Ohio

E. CLEVELAND ROD & GUN CLUB: Richard J. Siciliana, Sec., 1150 Worton Blvd., Cleveland 24, Ohio

SPRINGFIELD CASTING CLUB: Mrs. William Keener, Sec., 637 S. Clairmont Ave., Springfield, Ohio

TOLEDO CASTING CLUB: Elston Hubbard, Sec., 2305 Scottswood, Toledo 10, Ohio

WHETSTONE CASTING CLUB: Mrs. Barbara Weaver, Sec., 582 Melrose Ave., Columbus 2, Ohio

OKLAHOMA

TULSA ANGLERS CLUB: Tom DeVore, Sec., 1113 South Guthrie, Tulsa 19, Oklahoma

PENNSYLVANIA

LOWER MERION ROD & GUN CLUB: Mrs. Theresa A. LaRue, 606 Georges Lane, Ardmore, Pennsylvania

PHILADELPHIA CASTING CLUB: Sam Weitz, Sec., 517 Spruce St., Philadelphia, Penna.

PITTSBURGH CASTING CLUB: Dorothy Whitesell, Sec., 4609 Butler St., Pittsburgh 1, Penna.

SUBURBAN PHILADELPHIA CONSV. CLUB: Mrs. Ellen A. Dietrich, Sec., 1141 Roosevelt Drive, Upper Darby, Penna.

TENNESSEE

MEMPHIS ANGLERS CLUB: Albert Brandi, Sec., 191 Madison Ave., Memphis 3, Tenn.

NASHVILLE FLY & BAIT CASTING CLUB: John C. Adkins, Sec., 299 Wallace Road, Nashville, Tenn.

TEXAS

COWTOWN CASTING CLUB: Mrs. Irene Tuck, Sec., 5108 Barbara Road, Fort Worth, Texas

DALLAS FLY & BAIT CASTING CLUB: Juanita Leatherman, Sec., 1451 Autumn Leaves Trail, Dallas 16, Texas

HOUSTON ANGLERS CLUB: F. L. Gilbert, Sec., 3123 Plumb St., Houston 5, Texas

LUBBOCK CASTING CLUB: Sam Sayers, Sec., 3211—30th St., Lubbock, Texas

VIRGINIA & WASHINGTON, D.C.

NATIONAL CAPITAL CASTING CLUB: Fred A. Brady Sr., Sec., 5105 Tyburn St. S.E., Washington 22, D.C.

TIDEWATERS ANGLERS CLUB: Marion E. Hutson, Sec., 6785 Norlina Ave., Norfolk, Virginia

WISCONSIN

MILWAUKEE CASTING CLUB: Robert A. Brockman, Sec., 4817 West Villard Ave., Milwaukee 18, Wisconsin

PABST CASTING CLUB: Otto Johnson, Sec., 2139 N. 29th St., Milwaukee 8, Wisconsin

WAUKESHA CASTING CLUB: Clarence Anthes, Sec., 707 N. Moreland Blvd., Waukesha, Wisconsin

CANADA

TORONTO ANGLERS' & HUNTERS ASSN.: R. J. Mitchele, Sec., 85 King St. East, Toronto 1, Ontario

EDUCATIONAL INSTITUTIONS

UNIVERSITY OF ILLINOIS: Thomas Krizan, 201 Men's Old Gym, University of Illinois, Urbana, Ill.

UNIVERSITY OF NEW HAMPSHIRE: Miss Evelyn Browne, Dept. Phys. Ed for Women, Durham, New Hampshire

LADIES CLUBS

CARONDELET WOMEN'S CASTING CLUB: Mrs. Vera Ousley, Sec., 6730 Scanlan Ave., St. Louis 39, Missouri

HEART OF AMERICA ROD & REEL CLUB: Veronica A. Miller, Sec., 2750 Charlotte St., Kansas City 9, Missouri

KANSAS CITY WOMEN'S B & F CASTING CLUB: Mrs. Zelma Stevenson, Sec., 4123 Walnut St., Kansas City, Mo.

LONG BEACH WOMEN'S CASTING CLUB: Oletha Ward, Sec., 4718 Adenmoor Ave., Lakewood, Calif.

WRENTHAM SOCIETY OF SPORTSWOMEN: Mrs Marion E. Cafferky, Sec., 349 East St., Wrentham, Massachusetts

STATE & DISTRICT ASSOCIATIONS

DIXIE AMATEUR FLY & BAIT CASTING ASSN.: H. M. Weenick, Sec., P.O. Box 1347, St. Petersburg, Florida

EASTERN ASSN. OF AMATEUR CASTING CLUBS: Miss Elsie Seiffert, Sec., 97 Roxbury St., Hartford 6, Conn.

GREATLAKES AMATEUR CASTING ASSN.: Mrs. Mollie Schneider, Sec., RR 19—76 Willow Drive, Jeffersonville, Indiana

ILLINOIS AMATEUR CASTING ASSN.: Herbert Schulz, Sec., 4550 N. Ashland, Chicago, Illinois

MICHIGAN AMATEUR CASTING ASSN.: Charles W. Wilcox, Sec., 16210 Roselawn, Detroit 21, Michigan

MIDDLE ATLANTIC ASSN. OF CASTING CLUBS: Mrs. Ellen Deitrich, Sec., 1141 Roosevelt Drive, Upper Darby, Pennsylvania

MISSOURI VALLEY AMATEUR CASTING ASSN.: Mrs. Mildred Deck, Sec., 401 Warfield Drive, Ferguson 35, Missouri

OHIO STATE CASTING ASSN.: Zack Wilson Sr., Sec., 414 E. Beechwold, Columbus, Ohio

SOUTHWESTERN AMATEUR CASTING ASSN.: Mrs. Rilla Hickerson, Sec., 915 South Canton, Tulsa 12, Oklahoma

WESTERN ASSN. ANGLING & CASTING CLUBS: Mrs. Leslie Guggenheim, Sec., 1340 Lombard St., San Francisco, Calif.

(*) AMERICAN CASTING ASSOCIATION: P.O. Box 51, Nashville, Tenn., Phone Cypress 2-9427
Ben Fontaine, Pres., P.O. Box 50638, New Orleans, La.
Paul N. Jones, Exec. Secretary, P.O. Box 50638, Nashville, Tenn.

Valley of the Big Hole. The cut in the distant buttes is site of proposed Reichle Dam which Corps of Engineers would construct to impound many miles of famed Montana trout stream.

(continued from inside front cover)

needed habitat for thousands of moose, bears, wolves, small game, and even the spawning grounds of anadromous salmon.

The move to construct the Rampart Dam was motivated largely by a wish to bolster the state's economy through Federal spending—the usual real reason behind most of the Engineer's dam(n) projects—and many economists said the dam would have served its purpose if blown up the day completed.

Fortunately, nation-wide conservationists, ordinary taxpayers and other interested citizens so severely opposed the Yukon and Colorado River projects that they have been at least temporarily abandoned by the Engineers. So have many other dam projects they've proposed. Sportsmen's opposition to damming has saved Maine's Allagash, Wisconsin's St. Croix, Montana's Yellowstone—if only temporarily. But the Corps of Engineers—pushed, backed and supported by politicians and greedy "businessmen"—still is chipping away at *your* free-flowing rivers, still defiling and destroying rivers that can never be replaced.

No sensible sportsman or conservationist opposes the construction of *necessary* dams. Sportsmen and others do not object if public wildlife land and recreational waters are destroyed because a dam is vital. But much so-called "progress" (profits-taking?) involving the destruction of valued rivers via dam building has proved completely unnecessary. In many cases dams are built because landowners or construction companies will make money, because workers flocking to the area will "bolster the local economy," and because dam building is what builders of dams do.

—Our rivers are about to die, and the public be damned!

One of the loveliest rivers I know is the Big Hole in southwest Montana. It comes up in the Bitteroot Mountains, and flows for well over 100 miles to a junction with the Beaverhead and Jefferson Rivers near the town of Twin Bridges. In its upper reaches it has Montana grayling, one of the rarest fishes in North America, as well as large, brilliantly-colored brook trout. Farther down, as the river quickens and widens, is some of the finest rainbow trout fishing to be found anywhere, and still farther along—all the way to the Jefferson—is classic brown trout water.

The Big Hole flows clean and cool through quiet ranchlands, now rushing through a rocky gorge, now winding through sweet grass meadows, now singing over ripples that wash the banks beneath giant cottonwood stands. To the serious angler it offers all varieties of trout water—long, slick pools for dry flies; deep, curling runs for nymphs; heavy, deep water for big streamers; and lively, sparkling rapids for the wet-fly addict. There is almost no posted land, and I doubt if there